I0831717

From Creation to Consummation

From Creation to Consummation

Volume III

Gerard Van Groningen

Dordt College Press
Sioux Center, Iowa

Printed in the United States of America

Dordt College Press
498 Fourth Avenue, NE
Sioux Center, Iowa 51250

ISBN: 0-932914-59-4

Contents

I

33

Introduction to Biblical Wisdom Literature

I. Introductory Comments

II. Definition of Wisdom Literature

III. Sources of Wisdom Literature

IV. The Revelatory Character of Biblical Wisdom Literature

V. Wisdom Literature and Theology

VI. The Golden Cable in Biblical Wisdom Literature

VII. Conclusion

33

Introduction to Biblical Wisdom Literature

Introductory Comments

Wisdom literature in the Old Testament has been and is correctly distinguished from legal, historical, and prophetic literature.[1] It has unique characteristics; these will be highlighted as this biblical theological study proceeds.

Before an in-depth study of wisdom literature is initiated, a number of relevant factors pertaining to it should be mentioned.

First, only two Old Testament books can be correctly referred to as predominantly wisdom literature, Proverbs and Ecclesiastes. The book of Job, however, is considered to belong to the wisdom literature genre. As will be shown in Part II of this study, the book includes historical and theological doctrinal materials. The Book of Psalms is correctly considered to consist of poetic materials; some of it, however, definitely reveals wisdom characteristics. Song of Songs likewise can be said to include aspects of wisdom literature, as do the Lamentations of Jeremiah. Various scholars have indicated that portions of historical, legal, and prophetic literature should be considered wisdom literature.[2]

Second, any student who endeavors to study wisdom literature should be aware of the wide variety of scholarly interpretations and applications that have been published.[3] One should not be surprised to discover that there is no unanimity concerning origins, authors, historical contexts, purpose, and characteristics of biblical wisdom literature.

Third, the question concerning the literary character and the reliability of the biblical texts of wisdom literature has occupied some scholars. Since a study of the individual texts from a literary standpoint will not occupy much time or space in this study, that should not be construed to demonstrate a lack of interest in or attention to the literary aspect. The reality remains that the various schools of criticism have not devoted extensive attention to in this area of biblical criticism. There are exceptions that can be noted in the works on various wisdom books.[4]

Fourth, the question can and should be raised: can an in-depth study of wisdom literature be included in a biblical theological work such as this third volume of *From Creation to Consummation* purports to be? Some scholars have written studies of wisdom literature in a biblical theological context.[5] One's understanding of what a study of biblical theology should include has a definite bearing on this question. For example, if biblical theology is understood to basically address the subject of the history of the revelation of God, how is wisdom literature to be considered as divine revelation in view of its appearing to be the product of human observation and reflection?[6]

Fifth, another question that calls for an answer pertains to the use of New Testament revelation concerning wisdom in this study of Old Testament wisdom literature. An essay entitled "Christ, Our Wisdom" is subtitled "Israel's Wisdom and its Fulfillment in Christ."[7] To state our question differently: should one consider wisdom literature to be prophecies concerning Christ? Wisdom literature is distinct from prophetic literature, so how is the biblical presentation of Christ as the Wisdom of God (1 Cor. 1:18–31) to be understood in the context of the Old Testament?

Definition of Wisdom Literature

As one attempts to define wisdom as it is presented in biblical wisdom literature, one is cautioned to remember that a simple defining statement is not possible. One writer, after stating various ways the Bible refers to "Wisdom," wrote . . . "a precise definition of wisdom is well nigh impossible."[8] There have been recent efforts to come to a more definite understanding of wisdom.[9] It may occur to a reader to ask: is wisdom to be defined, or is wisdom literature to be defined? Both are, but one must realize that the concept of wisdom cannot be separated from wisdom literature since wisdom is the main subject and theme in wisdom literature. When the term *wisdom* is used as an adjective, various nuances are expressed, such as skillful, shrewd, cunning, prudent, and when used as a noun similar shades of meaning are expressed.

There are terms that are often closely associated with wisdom. One is discernment, derived from the verb *bîn,* to discern, perceive, and distinguish, to have insight. So also are the nouns *bînâh* and *tĕbûnâh,* which are correctly translated as understanding. Knowledge is also closely associated with wisdom. The Hebrew term *da'at* is translated, depending on contexts, as knowledge, perception, or understanding.

The term *hokmah* is a feminine noun. This may well have been the basic reason for speaking of "Lady Wisdom." In various contexts, wisdom is personified; she is born of God, she rejoices in the created world, and she is the source of life.

A consultation of what various scholars have written concerning the meaning of wisdom, and of wisdom literature provides a wide range of understanding of the term and literature and applications of them. Paul N. Tarazi, an Orthodox Church scholar expressed his view of wisdom as follows: "wisdom in literature expresses one collective voice indicating interest in the preservation of the flow of human life on earth. Wisdom is not religion nor linked to belief in a monotheistic god. Wisdom is a personal quality of understanding and a knowledge that endures that law will be put to its intended purpose.[10]

G. Von Rad summed up his understanding of wisdom as presented in wisdom literature as "experiential knowledge" that is very complex and vulnerable. Wisdom's invaluable service is that of enabling a person to function in what could be a totally strange world. Wisdom puts one in a position of understanding life in an ordered system.[11] Andre Caquot preferred to speak of wisdom as a human and divine capacity that enables one to cope in whatever circumstance, vocation, or profession one is involved.[12]

Ronald Murphy did not attempt to give a precise definition of wisdom and wisdom literature. He did, however, list characteristics from which a general conception of wisdom literature could be developed. He found no reference in it to salvation history, but much about creation theology. Furthermore, it reveals a search for order in creation and life that can be found by experience. It portrays life and its riches and honor and it is rooted in eternal life. It has limitations and many faces, various levels of authority, and some aesthetic qualities.[13] This widespread description of characteristics renders a precise definition all but impossible. Murphy, however, was not incorrect in describing the characteristics, but he gave reason for Dianne Bergent to write that a definition of wisdom as developed within ancient Israel is as diversified and elusive as the phenomenon itself. She wrote this in the earlier part of her career, but fifteen years later she noted that wisdom as recorded in the Old Testament could be defined as the meaning in life, a way of coping, a way to success, and the discovery of the order and uniformity of creation.[14]

The editors of a festschrift wrote that wisdom literature pays little attention to cult or covenant but witnesses to the religion of the Old Testament and its faith and to Israelite intellectual endeavors predicated on a belief in the orderly governance of the world by God. In a summary statement it is said the best definition is "wise conduct before God."[15]

An evangelical scholar in a book on wisdom literature stressed that wisdom books do not call for obedience and faith but for hard and humble thinking. They call for open eyes, use of conscience, and common sense to face the most disturbing questions in life. Wisdom literature is a distinctive voice that calls for the pilgrim (everyman?) to be related to the world at large as it is spread out on every side.[16]

In conclusion, it must be stated that it is difficult to formulate a consensus on what scholars say regarding the definition of wisdom as it is presented and applied in wisdom literature. Wisdom is a reality in life, but not many agree on how its essence and origin must be understood.[17] There seems to be more agreement about its applicability. The question to be asked now is: what methodological procedure should one follow to come to a fuller and richer understanding of wisdom as presented in wisdom literature? Should one consider adopting Von Rad's method, namely, selecting major aspects and themes for study and application?[18] This method may assist in avoiding some repetition that is possible if each wisdom book is studied individually. This latter method will be followed in this biblical theological study.

Once the various wisdom books have been studied, an effort will be made to present what should be considered to be the biblical definition and value of wisdom as presented in wisdom literature.

Sources of Wisdom Literature

It is not unusual to read books and essays written by critically oriented scholars that attribute the origins of wisdom literature to Near Eastern countries: that is, it has its roots in certain ancient Near Eastern forms, particularly Egyptian ones. One scholar wrote that a study of wisdom in the Old Testament resulted in "theories of common origins of traditions."[19]

It is commonly understood that wisdom is a native human attribute. Yet not all people demonstrate it in similar manners and ways. Since an evolutionary mindset is common among many scholars, the tendency is to seek the simpler forms and expressions of wisdom as the roots and earliest beginnings of sayings and writings. The questions raised are: who had experiences, insights, and reflections that could be characterized as evidences of wisdom being exercised? The Scriptures exhibit a higher and richer form of wisdom. From whence did these develop? A common answer is: from oral traditions, from early educational efforts in families and primitive schools.[20]

It would serve one well to consult some of the ancient texts that contain wisdom literature and that are referred to as sources for biblical wisdom literature. To do this at length in this study would detract from its basic intent of and motivation. Some references, however, to secondary sources should be made.

The editors of the *festschrift* in honor of J. A. Emerton[21] recognized him as a scholar who contributed to the study of wisdom literature. In this work the editors included three interesting chapters on Near Eastern wisdom texts. Editor Day wrote a brief survey of Egyptian so-called wisdom literature. He pointed out that

Egypt, feeling culturally superior, exerted wide influence beyond its borders. The Egyptian writers (sages) usually worked in schools attached to temples and they produced manuals for believers. These writings, calling on fathers to instruct and guide their sons, developed into proverbs and ethical observations. Themes included morality and justice; admonitions to respect motherhood and religion were also included. The masterpiece, according to Day, was the Wisdom of Amenemope because it included a treatise on moral responsibility. Day considers it to be similar to Proverbs 22:17–24:23. In general, an underlying theme was fate controlled by gods. After Amenemope, some more so-called wisdom literature was produced but this was of inferior quality. Day believes Egyptian wisdom was influenced by Aramaic, Iranian, Akkadian and Greek cultures.[22]

W. G. Lambert's essay entitled "Some New Babylonian Wisdom Literature" is also included in the Emerton festschrift.[23] Previously in 1966 Lambert produced a work entitled *Babylonian Wisdom Literature,*[24] which he described as a text edition "and touched only very lightly on the thought content and on comparison with other literature, such as the Hebrew texts."

Ancient Sumerian, Akkadian, and Babylonian texts[25] contain a wide assortment of proverbs, ethical sayings, moral thoughts and religious admonitions, all of which are summed up under the theme of wisdom. A few samples gathered from a cursory review follow.[26] The relationship between a "Man and his God" is to be maintained by a constant exaltation by man of his god whether this is done artlessly or in a lament. The gods will hear him, supply his needs, and heal him (ANES, 155). There is the admonition to avoid talebearers, do good and be kind every day, avoid prostitutes, be trusted with another's wealth, and have freewill offerings for your god (ANES, 159), and there is the advice to continue to praise the Lord of wisdom whose anger is irresistible but whose heart is merciful. Dreams can terrify one concerning his god; keep your voice low and hope that the god who abandoned you will give you help (ANES 160-64). One who will not work gains nothing; the strong man gains results from being hired, but a weak man gets a child's wage. Where is justice in the economic world? The evildoer will recompense with good, but keep your mouth shut. A large number of these ancient Oriental texts have been translated by G. W. Lamberts. His knowledge of the earlier as well as the later texts is quite impressive. His comments in his essay are worth noting.

The Babylonian idea of wisdom initially referred to skill in woodwork and metallurgy. Wisdom writings came to include piety, wholesome conduct in life and in the service of gods, and right living and reflections on it (30). The criminal bent of man was implanted by the gods at the time of creation and therefore doubt is cast on the gods as to their exercise of justice. The text entitled "Dialogue of Pessimism" is difficult to understand; the thrust, however, seems to be on the futility of all human endeavors. The activity of life seems not worth doing (36, 37). So, if the gods do not give satisfaction, they cannot expect worship (38). The Ugaritic and Syrian texts derived and created from the Babylonian texts express the futility of life; human achievement, once great, is later forgotten (40). Lambert referred to some parallels between Oriental wisdom texts and biblical texts, such as Ecclesiastes and some aspects of Job (33).

The question confronting a reader and scholar, who accepts the inspired, authoritative, infallible, and inspired inerrant Scriptures, is whether the views of many liberal and critical scholars should be accepted or not. These writers do not hesitate to draw parallels between the scattered Oriental wisdom sayings and those in the Scriptures. Some state outrightly that the Oriental documents were foundational for the biblical texts. In fact, it is outrightly stated that there was direct borrowing by the biblical authors.[27] Another scholar was careful not to stress the direct dependence. He referred to Israel's ceaseless search for knowledge, divine presence, meaning, and survival as part of a larger quest in the Ancient Near East.[28] Contemporary writers, as a rule, turn to Samuel Terrien who spent considerable time studying the relationship of Near Eastern wisdom and the scriptural material. He believed that the Ancient Near East contributed to biblical thought and literature.[29]

Some basic considerations must be kept in mind when one considers the relationship between Oriental wisdom and biblical wisdom.

First, all people of all races are image bearers of God. As such, they all possess basic aspects of that image. Wisdom is one aspect and therefore all people have the gift and virtue of wisdom. Not all exercise and demonstrate this virtue in specific similar ways, but that does not negate the reality of a degree of the presence of wisdom in each person.

Second, no person is able on his or her own initiative and effort to develop, practice, and demonstrate wisdom to its fullest possible degree. This is for two reasons. All people are finite; none have the full and perfect wisdom of God. And just as important is the reality that all people are sin infected. Sin, evil, and corruption have tragic influences in all people. Wisdom is therefore also deeply affected. No human being has and exercises wisdom perfectly. But all, regenerated or not, can exercise it to various degrees. This is because God by his common grace shown to all people enables them to do so.

Third, the people of the Near East, from Egypt to Greece and to the Mesopotamian valley, lived in a common world. In varying degrees, people influenced each other through their gifts, perceptions, and practices in all areas of life. Israel did not live in a hermetically sealed environment. Wisdom could and was developed and practiced in this interactive international setting.

Fourth, the Scriptures attest to the reality of the internationally known practice of wisdom. The book of Job gives evidence of this, as do Proverbs, Ecclesiastes, and some of the prophetic books.[30]

Fifth, the Scriptures make abundantly clear that Yahweh God is the source of all wisdom. Much human wisdom may be considered folly in the light of divine wisdom. Divine wisdom is the standard by which all human wisdom is to be measured and evaluated. And God gives and determines the measure of wisdom one receives and can practice. This should become evident as this study proceeds.

Sixth, a comparison of Oriental wisdom literature with biblical wisdom literature reveals that biblical wisdom literature far excels Oriental wisdom litterature. A few comments should be made in this regard. Oriental wisdom is crudely written. There are few thought sequences. It is atomistic. Theologically it is polytheistic; the gods are more like humans than of a divine character. Fate, not purposeful living, permeates Oriental wisdom literature.[31]

The question to be answered is: why the difference between Oriental wisdom literature and biblical wisdom literature? Did they not both come forth from the pens of human authors, all of whom were divine image bearers and who all lived in a Common Era and in a common Near East oriental setting? Do not some parts of biblical wisdom literature reveal a type and character of Oriental expressions of thought? Is it not true that it is not possible to discern a clear sequence of thought in some of biblical wisdom? In reply to this latter point, it can be confidently asserted that series of themes or approaches from different perspectives may give the impression of atomistic thinking. This factor will be more closely evaluated in the following chapters. It must be positively asserted that biblical wisdom literature is of a unique character.

The Revelatory Character of Biblical Wisdom Literature

All literature can be considered revelatory. It reveals the mind-set, character, methods, and purposes (in general) of the writers. Biblical wisdom literature however, has a unique character. It is divine revelation because it is divinely inspired. The Holy Spirit inspired the writers. This is the testimony of the entire Scripture concerning itself.

The legal, historical, and prophetic books have repeated assertions that Yahweh God spoke to men. He spoke to the inner man. As he did, the Holy Spirit was present, enabling men to understand in many situations and to write correctly what had been communicated.

A specific point must be made concerning how biblical wisdom's authors functioned differently from the authors of the other types of biblical literature. Poetical literature is basically response literature. True, a historical writer, as he records what took place, was responding to activities as perceived and understood under the Holy Spirit's influence. Authors of wisdom literature did not respond to direct communication or to specific events.[32] They reveal an awareness of truth; they reveal reflections, applications, values, and benefits of it. The Holy Spirit "carried" the authors as they responded to life's activities, whether these were events, speeches, or thoughts.[33] This reality of the Holy Spirit's presence and influence on the writers of biblical wisdom literature results in it being divine revelation given through human agents.[34]

In the succeeding study, further discussion of the Spirit's role in producing wisdom literature will be referred to. Suffice it to say at this point that it was the Holy

Spirit's presence and influence upon the authors of biblical wisdom literature that gave it the unique character of divine revelation.

Wisdom Literature and Theology

Does wisdom literature contain theology? Can a system of theological truths or doctrines be distilled from this genre of biblical literature? Even more pressing is the question, does Oriental Near Eastern wisdom literature have theological content? Since the truths in wisdom literature are said to be based on observation and experience that can be tested by honest and critical scrutiny, can it be said to even be religious, let alone theological?[35] These questions were raised concerning biblical wisdom. These can be raised more seriously concerning Near Eastern Oriental wisdom literature.

There are references to God, his attributes and actions, in biblical wisdom literature, but are these sufficient to provide a theology of wisdom? The reality is unmistakably clear that wisdom recognizes and proclaims God the Creator and governor of the cosmos. Clements made it clear that creation itself is the handiwork of wisdom.[36]

Creation reveals wisdom. Hence the conclusion is that wisdom literature is both revelatory and theological. How is this wisdom theology to be understood?

Joseph Blenkensopp has presented the position that wisdom (he employed the term *sapiential*) and law were two streams that flowed side by side throughout preexilic times; eventually, in the postexilic period they came together and found their outlet in rabbinic writings and early Christian theology.[37] Theological wisdom thus arose with the confluence of wisdom and law.[38] This view hardly answers the question concerning the relationship of wisdom literature and theology. The question remains, is there a real and obvious theological aspect or dimension in biblical wisdom literature?

Dianne Bergent has a specific answer to this question, which arises in the context of the development of feminism in contemporary society. Her study of wisdom literature, both biblical and apocryphical,[39] assured her that the cultural setting of this literature was patriarchal and therefore also hierarchical. Men were placed over women, free people over slaves, rich over poor, Hebrews over foreigners, and thus each person was appropriately relegated to a certain rung in the social ladder. Also determinative was a person's sexual status or prestige in a given society.[40] Bergent was correct when she pointed out that creation theology is dominant in wisdom literature. She stressed the integrity of creation. She went on to interpret and apply this motif as the basis of the sameness of all things. Integrity, she insisted, means that there are no ranks. There is no order of beings. Bergent critiques biblical wisdom revelation according to her contemporary conception of race, ethnic origin, class, and gender. Traditional exegesis is completely ignored.[41] A feminist creation theology, foreign to biblical revelation in all literary genres, is imposed on the biblical text. Bergent correctly understood that creation theology is germane to wisdom literature. Her interpretation and application of reformulated creation theology, however, are not based on the actual biblical wisdom texts.

The question remains. Does wisdom literature contain theology? Or is it basically anthropological and philosophically humanistically oriented? The intent of this book is specifically to make an extensive biblical theological study of this literature.

The Golden Cable in Biblical Wisdom Literature

The initial point to be emphasized is that biblical theological study presupposes the historical unfolding of divine revelation. Biblical wisdom literature is Spirit-inspired revelation. This literature is of a different genre than the legal, historical, and prophetic books. It, however, is to be considered equally divinely inspired, authoritative, infallible, and inerrant. It was written by Spirit-inspired human agents in the course of Israelite history. This means that all wisdom was not written simultaneously. Different authors wrote at different times. Solomon was a prodigious author, but he was not the only one. Also to be stated in unequivocal terms is that biblical wisdom literature was not developed in stages, in successive periods of time, that it grew, was defined, and refined within the Israelite culture as it was continually influenced by non-Israelite sources of nontheological material.[42] In the study of each wisdom book this question will be addressed.

This biblical theological study will determine if the Golden Cable unites wisdom literature within itself as in the other genres, the legal, historical, and prophetic. In the study of the three genres it was demonstrated that the threefold strands of the Golden Cable, the kingdom, the covenant, and the Mediator united them. The persistent question indeed is, are these three concepts present, and if they are, do they form a uniting cable within wisdom literature? Do they form and serve as an integral and integrating reality?[43]

Voices have been raised stressing that there is no *mitte*[44] in wisdom literature. R. E. Clement wrote "the place that should be assigned to the wisdom writings of the Old Testament in a world of Old Testament theology has not so far been accorded any widely held consensus."[45] Walther Eichrodt included a chapter entitled "Cosmic Powers of God" in which a subsection was entitled "Wisdom of God."[46] Scholars have not lined up to support Eichrodt's view. Rather, they noted that references to the concept of covenant are absent in earliest wisdom teaching.[47] Samuel Terrien, a renowned scholar in wisdom studies, wrote that attempts to center biblical theology in the idea of covenant ignored the diversity of its meaning in Israel.[48] Terrien, however, was interested in locating a theological unity of the Bible. It was not found in some form of biblical individualism. He stressed the importance of the individual in wisdom, but he located unity in the biblical theology of wisdom literature in the concept of "The Presence of God."[49]

A recent study by L. Perdue included a valiant attempt to set forth a theology of wisdom literature.[50] He considered it very difficult to locate it in the literature. He referred to a number of comprehensive articulations on prolegomena of wisdom literature that have not produced a *mitte* or a basis for the theology of wisdom. Also, the fragmentation of methods in Old Testament biblical theology studies have led to the view that there is no dominant paradigm.[51] He proposed to interpret wisdom literature through the paradigm of metaphor and imagination as he concentrates on the concepts of creation and providence that were at the center of sapiential sages' understanding. He proposed that four methodological considerations be examined in the study of the various wisdom books.[52]

As one reviews what various writers have written about the theology of wisdom and about a theological *mitte* or basis, one must conclude that if wisdom literature is indeed not inspired by the Spirit of God, but arose from humanistic efforts to reflect on the order of the world and life within it, then the following questions are indeed in order. Should wisdom be considered an integral aspect of the Old Testament? And, if so, is the search for a theological center even in order?[53]

Conclusion

I have spent considerable time reading books on wisdom literature. The material written in the preceding paragraphs should not give the impression that all issues have been referred to, much less solved. The above is meant to serve as an introduction to the studies of biblical wisdom literature with a biblical theological method.

A final comment in this introductory chapter is in order. A biblical theological study of wisdom literature is not to be considered a separate study from that of the legal, historical, and prophetical studies. The wisdom revealed in the wisdom books of the Old Testament is the wisdom that permeates the entire Old and New Testament revelation. The wisdom books concentrate on wisdom -both divine and human- and a study of these books should enlighten and increasingly enrich our understanding of the wisdom that permeates the entire Scriptures.[54]

ADDENDUM

How to Gain Wisdom:
How to put it altogether and doing so, to live and practice accordingly.

I. The first principle—re Scripture is the fear of God
  A. To know him personally
    through Scriptural revelation

through creational revelation which reveals wisdom of God
through reflection—meditation—prayer—fellowship
Meaning: factual knowledge
love God
live in and with God in Christ

B. To trust him
Fully assured re God
Fully committed to God
Fully surrendered
Spirit-filled and led

C. To obey him
To listen
To follow
To be assured his way is best way

D. To serve him
To recdognize God as sovereign Lord
To recognize will of God as highest good
To worship him
To work—slave—for him

II. The supporting principle is to have and exercise discernment

A. In regard to God's Word: refers to a constant effort for enterinag into it in its entirety, to evaluate, to relate, to see the parts and each part in relation to the whole.

B. In regard to life
To know life
to be open to a knowledge of all aspects of created reality
to be aware of complexity of life, seeing the unity as well as variety
to study—read, widely apprehend as much as one can
to observe how the Lord directs all aspects of creation.
Consider how a plant fuctions, an ant works and so on.
To understand, see into, see through, human nature
self first
humanity in general
calls for specific and wide knowledge (in addition to what said above) of psychology and sociology
To evaluate—weigh factors independently and collectively.
Determine relative as well as integral value of various facets.
Be sure you have a divinely given/sanctioned set of value standards

III. The co-ordinating principle is to practice, exercise, demonstrate wisdom

A. The necessity of "gifts" and "talents" to be recognized and the diversity in Distribution. But, all people, as a rule, have some—enough to be wise to a great extent.

B. The necessity of time for gathering facts, discerning, evaluating, relating. (Fools rush in.)
C. The necessity of appreciation for the good, the proper.
D. The necessity of a repulsion for the evil, the wasteful, the disastrous.
E. The necessity of being open to guidance, advice, admonition, encouragement, sharing.
F. The necessity of maintaining the proper reapport and balance between goals (whereto?) and means (how), between time (when) and the place (where) and above all between persons (who?) and things (what?).

Notes

1. The relationship between the legal, historical, and prophetic literature on the one hand with that of wisdom literature on the other has never been clearly understood and therefore not made definitely clear. This is the opinion of John L. Mackenzie who, in his essay "Reflections on Wisdom," *Journal of Biblical Literature* 86, no. 11 (1967): 1–9, opined that much of the biblical historical literature appeared for wisdom purposes, that is, to reflect on life and to give guidance to one wishing to understand life in its manifold manifestations.

2. Gerhard Von Rad wrote that the Joseph material, Gen. 37:1ff. should be considered wisdom material. See "Josephsgeschichte und Altere Chokma," *Gesammelte Studien zum Alten Testamentum* (Munich: Chr. Kaiser, 1958), 272–80. In his book *Wisdom in Israel* (Nashville: Abingdon, 5th printing, 1981), Von Rad refers to the Joseph narrative as didactic material; it is an historical saga in which dream interpretations and allegorical motifs dominate, 16, 44, 47. Few scholars agree with Von Rad that historical materials can be so altered that their genre is radically changed.

3. An incomplete bibliography presents a wide range of authors and approaches. Had John Mackenzie written "Reflections on Wisdom" in 1997 instead of in 1967 he may not have claimed that there was not much interest in wisdom literature on the part of scholars, nor even of many lay readers. J. A. Loader published an article entitled "Wisdom by (the) People for (the) People," *ZAW* 111, no. 2 (1999):211–33, in which he stated that a steady growth of interest in wisdom tradition began in the 1960s. He went on to write that since 1966 there has been a veritable flood of monographs, papers, and anthologies "on about every conceivable aspect of the sapiential tradition" 211. Works include Dianne Bergent, *Israel's Wisdom Literature: A Liberation-Critical Reading* (Minneapolis Fortress, 1997); *What Are They Saying about Wisdom Literature?* (New York: Paulist, 1984); Athalya Brenner and Carole Fontaine, eds, *Wisdom and Psalms: A feminist companion to the Bible,* 2nd series (Sheffield: Sheffield Academic, 1998); William P. Brown, *Character in Crisis: A Fresh Approach to the Wisdom Literature of the Old Testament* (Grand Rapids: Eerdmans, 1996); James L. Crenshaw, *Old Testament Wisdom: An Introduction* (Atlanta: John Knox Press, revised and enlarged, 1998); W. T. Davison, *The Wisdom Literature of the Old Testament* (London: Charles H. Kelly, 1984); Katharine J. Dell, "Wisdom Literature Makes a Comeback: Pursuing the Good Life." *BR* 13, no. 4 (August 1997), 26, 31, 46; John G. Gammie, ed., *Israelite Wisdom: Theological and Literary Essays in Honor of Samuel Terrien* (Missoula: Scholars Press for Union Theological Seminary, 1978); John Franklin Genung, *The Hebrew Literature of Wisdom* (Boston: Houghton Mifflin, 1906); Friedemann W.

Golka, "Wisdom by (the) People for (the) People: eine Antwort an J.A. Loader," *ZAW* 112, no. 1 (2000): 78–79; Robert Gordis, "The Social Background of Wisdom Literature," *HUCA* 18 (1944): 77–118; Michael D. Guinan, "Images of God in the Wisdom Literature," *The Bible Today* 38, no.4 (July 2000): 223–27; J. A. Loader, "Speakers Calling for Order," *Old Testament Essays* 10, no. 3 (1997): 424–38; D. B. Macdonald, *The Hebrew Philosophical Genius* (Princeton: Princeton University Press, 1936); Roland Edmund Murphy, "Form Criticism and Wisdom Literature" *CBQ* 31, no. 4 (October 1969) 475–83, *The Tree of Life: An Exploration of Biblical Wisdom Literature*, 2nd ed. (Grand Rapids: Eerdmans, 1996); Leo G. Perdue, *Wisdom & Creation: the Theology of Wisdom Literature* (Nashville: Abingdon, 1994); O.S. Rankin, *Israel's Wisdom Literature* (Edinburgh: T & T Clark, 1936); J. C. Rylaarsdam, *Revelation in Jewish Wisdom Literature* (Chicago: University of Chicago Press, 1946); Anthony J. Saldarini, "Human Wisdom is Divine " *Bible Review* 14 (April 1998): 18; Eben Scheffler, "Archaeology and Wisdom," *Old Testament Essays* 10, no. 3 (1997): 459–73; Richard L. Schultz, "Unity or Diversity in Wisdom Theology? A Canonical and Covenantal Perspective," *Tyndale Bulletin* 48 (November 1997): 271–306; Patrick William Skehan, *Studies in Israelite Poetry and Wisdom*, Catholic Biblical Quarterly Monograph series (1971); WillieVan Heerden, "A Bright Spark is Not Necessarily a Wise Person," *Old Testament Essays* 9, no. 3 (1996): 21–26; "Proverbial Wisdom, Metaphor and Inculturation," *Old Testament Essays* 10, no.3 (1997): 512–27; H. Viviers, *Roots of Wisdom: The Oldest Proverbs of Israel and Other Peoples* , (Nashville:Westminster/ John Knox, no date).

4. When individual wisdom books are discussed, references will be made to the literary critical efforts. Concerning Wisdom Literature, as a genre, Ronald E. Murphy, wrote an essay, "Form Criticism and Wisdom Literature," *Catholic Biblical Quarterly*, 31/4, 1967, 475–483. Murphy referred to a German effort to deal with the entire Masoretic text with a form critical procedure. The German effort was not easily or readily made available to an English audience. When German Form Criticism did become available, soon thereafter the suggestion was made to go beyond it to Rhetorical Criticism. But Rhetorical Criticism was not readily adopted. Succeeding Rhetorical Criticism scholars began to emphasize the Narrative Genre of the Biblical text. Wisdom Literature proves to be difficult and not helped by the Narrative approach.

5. Lindsay Wilson, "The Place of Wisdom in Old Testament Theology" *Reformed Theological Review,* 49/2 May–August, 1990, 60-69). Roland E. Murphy, "Wisdom Literature and Biblical Theology" *Biblical Theology Bulletin,* 24/1, (1994), 4–7. Walther Zimmerli, "The Place and Limit of Wisdom in the Framework of Old Testament Theology," *Studies in Ancient Israelite Wisdom,* ed. J. L. Crenshaw, (New York: Ktav Publishing, 1967). W. Eichrodt included a section entitled "The Wisdom of God" in his *Theology of the Old Testament*, trans. J.A. Baker, (Philadelphia: The Westminster Press, 1961). Vol. 11, 80–92. In the chapter entitled "The Cosmic Powers of God" Brevard S. Childs included a section entitled "The Wisdom Tradition," in *Biblical Theology of the Old and New Testaments*, (Minneapolis: Fortress Press, (1993), 187–95. It can be concluded that it is not a novice undertaking to produce a Biblical Theological book on Wisdom Literature.

6. Wisdom Literature as divine revelation will be discussed in a subsequent section of this chapter.

7. Graeme Goldworthy, *Present Truth*, 18–23.

8. Ibid., 20. Willie Van Heerden, living and working in the academic and social context of South Africa, wrote that he observed African wisdom was in a state of flux. He implies that biblically recorded wisdom developed likewise, hence to define wisdom as it developed

is well nigh impossible. He referred to the rigidification of wisdom traditions in a specific context. As the contexts developed, so did the wisdom tradition in that new context. Cf. his essay entitled "Proverbial Wisdom," 514–15. He also wrote the essay "A Bright Spark," in which he briefly developed his view that there is evidence in wisdom texts that the idea that wisdom means superior intelligence is not readily acceptable.

9. A review of the bibliography listed in note 3 will reveal an increase of studies in wisdom literature. See, e.g., Dell, "Wisdom Literature Comeback."

10. Paul Nodem Tarzi, *The Old Testament: An Introduction*, vol. 3: *Psalms and Wisdom,* (Crestwood: St. Vladimir's Seminary Press, 1996), 118–20.

11. *Wisdom in Israel*, 3.

12. Andre Coquot, "Israelite Perceptions of Wisdom and Strength in the Light of the Ras Shamra Texts," trans. K. Noweel, in *Israelite Wisdom: Theological and Literary Essays,* 22.

13. R. E. Murphy, *Wisdom Literature and the Psalms* (Nashville: Abingdon, 1983), 25–37.

14. Bergent, *What are They Saying*? Later, in 1997 she did try, in *Israel's Wisdom Literature*. In this more recent work she referred to John Gammia, Walther Brueggemann, W. L. Humphreys, and James Ward. She felt Von Rad's view could be summed up as "Empirical Knowledge of Order," Whybray's as "Intellectual Tradition," James Crenshaw's as "Quest for Self Understanding," S. Terrien's as "Effort to Establish Order," 3–15.

15. *Wisdom in Ancient Israel, Essays in Honor of Emerton*, ed. John Day, Robert P. Gordon, and H.G.M. Williamson (Cambridge: University Syndicate, 1990; ppb. ed., 1998), 1–2.

16. Derek Kidner, *The Wisdom of Proverbs, Job & Ecclesiastes* (Downers Grove: InterVarsity, 1985), 11, 12.

17. William Brown, *Character in Crisis*, when asking himself where the idea of "character" appears in the Scriptures, was surprised to find that wisdom books were the immediate home of character. He then proceeded to write his book attempting to demonstrate that character is the main issue as biblical wisdom confronts readers with ethics and ethos, VII, 1–21. It should be noted also that Brown finds that the narrative approach supports the theme of character as central in wisdom literature.

18. Cf. his method in *Wisdom in Israel.*

19. Bergent, *What Are They Saying?* 6, 7.

20. Murphy, *Wisdom Literature and Psalms,* 14–24. Eben Scheffler's thesis is that material concrete objects and matters of the mind are part and parcel of *one holistic reality,* (emphasis his). Hence, archaeology offers much insight, especially about the material concrete objects. Archaeology has much to contribute to the understanding of the origin and development of wisdom literature. "Archaeology," 459–61. Scheffler's efforts to provide evidence for his thesis are brief and not too convincing, but he does challenge scholars to consider the contributions of archaeology to a deeper and richer understanding of biblical wisdom literature, 461–70.

21. Cf. *Wisdom in Ancient Israel,* 17–29.

22. Sources Ray listed include, Miriam Lichtheim's *Ancient Egyptian Literature*, and R. O. Faulkner, E. Wents and W. K. Simpson, *The Literature of Ancient Egypt* and some sources written in European languages.

23. *Wisdom*, 36–42.

24. Published in Oxford, 1960.

25. Lambert, *Some New Babylonians,* 30.

26. Texts referred to are included in *Ancient Near Eastern Texts Relating to the Old Testament,* 3rd ed., ed. James Pritchard (Princeton: Princeton University Press, 1969), referred to henceforth as *ANET,* and in the Supplement, *The Ancient Near East,* ed. James Pritchard (Princeton: Princeton University Press, 1969), referred to henceforth as *ANES.*

27. Victor H. Matthews, *Old Testament Themes* (St. Louis: Chalice, 2000), 91.

28. Crenshaw, *Old Testament Wisdom, Introduction*, 205.

29. Cf. what James A. Sanders wrote: "The apparent tension between a history of religion method of the study of the Bible and an abiding quest for a valid biblical theology and a theological unity to the Bible is caught up in Terrien's appreciation of the contribution of international Ancient Near Eastern wisdom to biblical thought and literature." Cf. Gammie, editor of *Israelite Wisdom, 11.* Terrien's scholarship gives evidence of a basic critical approach to the Scriptures. He appreciated the biblical text, but considered it as basically only a human document in which man's seeking to know and live for God is recorded.

30. In the study of the various biblical wisdom books, evidences of acquaintance with Oriental wisdom will be considered.

31. These thoughts arose from my rather long and extensive readings of Oriental texts.

32. In our study of the books, it will be pointed out that at times historical references are included, e.g., Job 1, 2, 42.

33. J. Coert Rylaarsdam asked, "How did the men who produced this literature think that God and his ways became known to them"? He wrote that wisdom literature does not offer a single, static reply. *Revelation in Wisdom*, ix. Rylaarsdam severely complicates his quest for "revelation" in wisdom literature because he accepted the critical position concerning the human development of wisdom including apocryphal literature and biblical wisdom literature, which views it as the product of human effort. Rylaarsdam is correct to say that the wisdom concept was an instrument of revelation in relation to the Spirit (99). A very basic problem, however, is his concept of the development of wisdom from outside wisdom sources, its evolution in Israelite culture, and its eventual coalescing with the concept of spirit in Israelite religious tradition, which followed the coalescing of wisdom with word and law in Israelite cultural and religious tradition (99ff.)

34. O. S. Rankin in *Israel's Wisdom Literature* referred to biblical wisdom literature as documents of "Hebrew Humanism." Cf. heading of chaps. 1 and 52. He comments that "to refer to this literature as humanistic should not be considered a negation of the supernatural." He goes on to write, however, that a theology is founded in human thought (3). This human thought involved a growth of the "conception of Jahve as Creator" (35). D. Morgan, in *Wisdom in the Old Testament Traditions* (Atlanta: John Knox, 1981), also showed that biblical wisdom arose and developed through the ages as various writers contributed to the growth of wisdom. His chapter headings are evidence of his view that wisdom originated in popular contexts, and was boosted in an early monarchy setting in which all the prophets contributed to its development. In postexilic times, wisdom literature received its form as it is in the Scriptures. Morgan, very evidently, does not accept wisdom literature as divinely inspired revelation. An example of his views concerning prophetic influence is in his discussion of Amos's influence on the later wisdom tradition (66–72).

35. R. E. Clement raised these questions in the introduction to his book *Wisdom in Theology* (Grand Rapids: Eerdmans, 1992), 21.

36. Ibid., 177.

37. J. Blenkensopp, *Wisdom and Law in the Old Testament* (Oxford: Oxford University Press, 1983), 14.

38. Ibid., 130.

39. Bergent, *Israel's Wisdom.*

40. This summary of Bergent's views was written by Alice L. Laffey in the foreword (vii).

41. Cf. Bergent's chap. 1, "The Integrity of Creation," 1–12.

42. This view of wisdom growing, developing, and being refined is the basic view of critical writers, among whom are Rylaarsdam, Blenkensopp, Clement, Von Rad, and Terrien.

43. Lindsay Wilson reviewed various suggestions regarding the discussion of "wisdom" in some Old Testament theology books. His suggestion is, that in view of seeing the wisdom motif in various Old Testament books, whether it should be thought of as a strand of rope that unites the message of the Old Testament. See his "The Place of Wisdom in Old Testament Theology," *The Reformed Theological Review,"* May–Aug.,1990, 68.

44. *Mitte*—the term used to refer to a central uniting factor.

45. Clement, *Wisdom in Theology*, 13.

46. Cf. vol. II, 81–92, note 4.

47. Clement, *Wisdom in Theology*, 20. Richard L. Schutlz, however, wrote that Wisdom Theology presented a canonical and covenantal perspective. This issue concening the covenant serving as a part of the "*"mitte*" is discussed in chap. 36 in this volume.

48. Sanders, in *Israelite Wisdom*, 11.

49. Ibid., 8.

50. Leo G. Purdue, *Wisdom and Creation, the Theology of Wisdom Literature*, (Nashville: Abingdon Press, 1994).

51. Ibid, 19. See also his review of what G. Wright, G. Von Rad, and C. Westermann have proposed, 21–25.

52. With the presupposition that creation is at the center of wisdom theology, because creation integrates all other dimensions of God talk, Purdue examined four methodological considerations that he found necessary to articulate creation at the center of wisdom: (1) sapiential imagination, (2) rhetoric—how language was used, (3) description of the rhetoric of sapiential language, and (4) imagination and rhetoric in specific social locations.

53. Clement raised these questions in his essay titled "Wisdom and Old Testament" in *Wisdom in Ancient Israel*, 220–21. Clement conceded that in postexilic life, wisdom became an integral aspect of education in Israelite family life, in which virtue had a commanding role, 269–86.

54. Saldarni's brief but pointed essay states this truth succinctly. "Human Wisdom." See also Katherine Dell, "Wisdom . . .Comeback," who referred to the renewed interest in biblical wisdom literature in recent decades; the reason for it is the increasing awareness that the God of wisdom referred to is not necessarily in the foreground but is undeniably involved in human concerns at all levels, 30. This God is not the inaccessible Creator but is accessible through paths open to us, 31–32.

II

The Golden Cable in the Book of Job

34

The Character of the Book of Job

I. Introductory Comments

II. The Structure of the Book of Job

III. The Author

IV. The Message

34

The Character of the Book of Job

Introductory Comments

In this study of wisdom literature the book of Job calls for specific attention. There are a number of reasons for this. First of all, this study under the theme *From Creation to Consummation* is of a biblical theological nature. More specifically, in this type of study, the question that arises is: given the acceptance of the proposition that biblical theology's primary concern and task are to deal with the progress of divine revelation as it is given in word and deed (act), does the book of Job offer insights into this progress? The answer to this question will be uncovered as the study proceeds.

Second, there are numerous scholars who have set themselves the task of studying the book of Job or parts of it, to ascertain how to understand the work from a literary, historical, social, and religious/theological perspective.[1] To say that there is widespread agreement on the basic issues concerning these perspectives is an understatement. There is very little basic agreement. One should point out that historical and literary critical scholars are generally agreed that the Book of Job is one of many Wisdom Treatises that have come from the Levant, including Egypt.[2] In this study the author cannot concur with all these scholars. What then can be discerned from this study of Job concerning this issue? The answers will become evident as the study proceeds.

Third, the book of Job does not deal only with wisdom themes. There are theological, historical, and sociological issues included. What influence have these had on the wisdom themes that are the predominant aspects of the book? The question demands a clear, forthright answer.

Fourth, the book of Job has been given much attention by a wide variety of scholars because of its unique presentation of the subjects of suffering, God's justice, and human attempts to understand these. Furthermore, various subthemes have been discussed such as the hidden God, Job's patience (James 5:11) or impatience, whether the term *Satan* refers to a personal reality or a title, the book of Job as a link in God's unfolding revelation, the scriptural mind that permeates the book of Job, religion as disinterested or utilitarian, Job's radical challenges, and Job as not wisdom literature but utterly unique. The question before a student of the book of Job is: are these subthemes aspects of one or more of the strands of the Golden Cable, the kingdom, the covenant, and the Mediator? In this study it will be demonstrated that this is not only a possibility but also a reality.

The Structure of the Book of Job

The question concerning the structure of the book of Job is not easily answered. Involved in the concept of structure is the unity of the various parts. The matter concerning the classification of the book is also involved.[3] Is it basically a lament? Or is it basically a dialogue? Is it a disputation or a forensic process,[4] or are there other aspects of speech patterns integrally involved? Is the book of Job basically a drama? Westermann, employing a stringent form critical methodology, has helped readers to consider various possibilities regarding structure and classification. His position, however, regarding the author and origin of the book of Job is difficult to accept.[5] Carol Newsom, discussing the issues of structure and unity, found that the relationship between the prose and poetic sections poses the most intriguing questions about how the entire book is to be read.[6] She concluded, on the basis of what scholars have written since 1900, that one should consider the book of Job to have been structured in four stages with the final structure represented by a simple diagram.

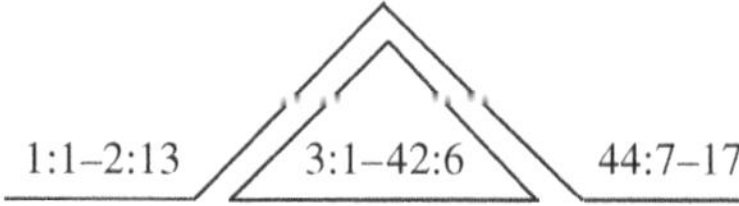

Newsom did not include the various parts that Westermann had in his diagram.[7]

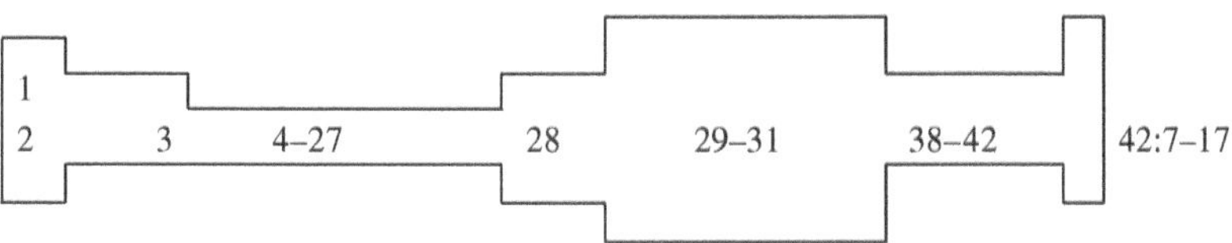

Critical scholars have indicated that if and when they employ critically determined methods for the study of the interpretation and comprehension of the message of the entire book, there is no consensus in their conclusions. The book of Job is a challenge for them but they are forced to deal with it, as it is included in Holy Scriptures.[8]

Conservative scholars have been either reluctant to accept the critical methodology and its consequences or ignore it entirely. W. H. Green accepted the book, as it is a reliable, well-written account of the historical person, Job. He considered the theme of the book to be "The Temptation of Job," which is recorded to have been experienced in three stages.[9]

Derek Thomas, in his commentary for the average reader, dealt with the book as an historical account. He did not discuss the structure or unity of the book of Job. He stressed that the historic person, Job, was the central figure in the biblical account of "the problem of suffering." Thomas implies that to dissect the book by means of various types of analysis detracts from or basically eliminates the God-given revelation concerning human suffering.[10]

Franz Delitzsch unhesitatingly accepted the position that the book of Job should be considered a "drama" that includes seven divisions, or eight if Elihu's speech is accepted as an integral part. That the prologue is in narrative form does not detract from the view that the book is a well-developed drama in which historic persons were involved and events are described.[11] The Dutch scholar, Kroeze, however, wrote that the structure of the Book of Job is not that of a drama with identified scenes. He apodictically stated that it contains or is comprised of events, speeches, and dialogue. These together form the structure of the book.[12]

There is also what could be termed mediating writers. Some of the critical views are accepted but a gallant effort is made to set forth the book of Job as an average ancient composition. It has a sandwich structure: prologue-prose, main body—poetry, epilogue-prose. This compilation is carefully constructed so that Job's lament and speeches are beautifully integrated by a composer.[13]

The Author

The book of Job does not give any indication whatsoever concerning the author. Job is the main character in the book. There is no evidence that he or the friends referred to in the book composed it. Neither is there any reference to time. Hence the book's place in wisdom literature, the origin and setting, according to Perdue, must be assessed by consulting ancient Israel and early Judaism.[14] Many scholars have done this. No consensus has been reached. If there is any agreement among critically inclined scholars it usually is that there were a number of composers with a final composer who gave the book of Job the form and content as it is in the Bible.[15] Those who consider the book to be a literary production by one composer consider him to be an uncommon genius.[16] One writer referred to the author as a highly educated person, a devout servant of Yahweh, indeed one of the great wise men of ancient Israel. He was skilled in proverbs and riddles. His knowledge of nature included animals and plants. He knew about gems, mining, and precious metals. He wrote of weather patterns and was knowledgeable about hunting and trapping. The foreign cultures of Egypt, Arabia, and countries near Palestine were not foreign to him.[17]

The question that must be asked is: was the author of the book of Job really one of Israel's wise men? That Ezekiel and James referred to Job as an historic person does not imply that either Job or the author was an Israelite. Evidence can be presented that both were Aramaens, living in ancient Syria. The many Aramaic words in the text are one evidence as is the geographical references to living near the great desert and to marauding bands.[18] The friends of Job were not of Israelite parentage.

The most plausible conclusion is that Job, the four visitors, and the author of the book were non-Israelites[19] but they all lived in areas not far from the borders of Canaan.

This conclusion raises another question: what was the time period of Job and the author? The answers are by no means unanimous. Dhorme has written, "What seems clear . . . is that the period the author had in mind was that of the patriarchs."[20] and Marvin Pope wrote that there is a characteristic literary excellence, particularly in the dialogue, which suggests the influence of a single personality.[21]

Summing up, the position taken in this study is as follows. Job and his four friends lived in the time of the patriarchs in areas bordering the land of Canaan. The author, a wise and accomplished writer, was an Aramean. He was the single author. His work became known in Israel. It was recognized to be of canonical stature and was incorporated into the Old Testament canon by Solomon, who was himself a Spirit-inspired author of Holy Scripture.[22]

The Message

Is there a message in the book of Job? One writer has written that it has been questioned whether the book has a determinate meaning at all, "suggesting that Job is nothing more than a self-deconstructing artifact."[23]

A reading of commentaries and studies of the book of Job can be a very exasperating experience although the reading of the book of Job itself may not necessarily be such. But the book can raise questions, particularly if it is considered a book that recounts ancient people's experiences, searchings, and discussion.

My reflections, after reading a wide variety of authors and carefully studying a number of these authors, are as follows:[24] (1) All agree that human suffering is a reality. Job suffered. What was missing in most writings was a clear reference to what characterized Job's suffering. Was it physical? Or psychological? Or social? Or spiritual? Or theological? Or a combination of two or more of these? One author was clear: the soul struggle of Job was spiritual[25] induced by physical pain. (2) The perseverance of the human spirit is lauded. But what was the basic factor in this perseverance? Was it the human spirit that had strength to endure? Very few authors referred to God's providential sustaining power. (3) The why of human suffering received very few helpful explanations. Why innocent people suffer was not clearly answered by most writers. (4) Only two or three referred to the covenantal relationship between God and humanity. Involved is the question "do the righteous suffer under the curse of the covenant?" No definitive answer was given in the many sources that were consulted.[26] (5) There was little reference to Satan as the arch enemy of God and his people. The relationship between the presence and action of Satan as a real living agent of evil and God and Job was not explained in a satisfactory manner by most authors. (6) There was very little, if any, thought given to the reality of the antithesis within the entire cosmic realm. (7) Only a few authors referred to or gave helpful insights into God's providence, his preservation of the saint (Job), and his justice in the exercise of his providence. (8) The relationship between Job's suffering and Christ's suffering, and between Christ's suffering and all human suffering, particularly of believers, was discussed by three authors. (9) What was missed, or touched on only very indirectly in most writers, was the sustaining power of faith in God.

It seems appropriate to give specific attention to four authors. W. H. Green's view concerning the theme of the book of Job is not the problem of suffering. It is rather the afflicting of the righteous. The adversary of God and his people has awesome power but it is conquerable even by a saint who is not aware of what is really happening. Hence the title of his book, *Conflict and Triumph*.[27]

Johanna Manley understood the church fathers, (Augustine, Ambrose, Basil, the three Gregories, John Chrysostom, and others) to write that Job dealt with man's spiritual combat and his integrity. The book deals with the fundamentals of man's relationship to God.[28]

Alex Luc wrote an essay entitled "Storm and the Message in Job." Luc's view is that the storm motif serves as a negative image of Job but gives positive portrayal of God's design. Storm, in respect to Job, related directly to his suffering. Job in his complaints implied that he was treated more oppressively than wicked men were. This thought magnified Job's inner turmoil, his inner storm. The storm with fearful and destructive power was the potent vehicle to describe Job's suffering and pain. Luc wrote "the storm stands for Job's unbearable pain."[29] In the storm, which God creates, his wisdom is expressed. God also uses the storm to address Job in a theophanic experience. In his conclusion Luc wrote, "Though sufferings often seem without purpose, unjust and destructive like storms, the reader is called to trust in God's control and design."[30]

D. Thomas also considered the pain and suffering of Job as a storm. When Satan afflicted Job in every aspect of his life, the storm came over Job and relentlessly buffeted him. While the storm lasted, friends intensified it. It ended when God spoke to Job and Job responded. But why did Job have the storm break over him? Thomas's answer is that the book of Job gives us insight into God's way of dealing with Satan, who accuses people of serving God for personal gain. In a real sense, then, according to Thomas, pain and suffering that people experience may not be the result of sin at all. Rather, as in the case of Job, pain and suffering are designed to demonstrate that these afflictions do not stop suffering people from having faith in and serving God.[31]

In conclusion to the section on the message of the Book of Job that human suffering is in reality a major theme— this suffering is not to be isolated from Satan's pernicious lies and efforts to discredit people of faith nor from God's justice and all his providence. The challenge before us now is to see these in the context of Yahweh God's kingdom, his covenant relationship with his people, and the role the Mediator has in revealing the sovereign will, purpose, and outcome of Yahweh God's dealing with Satan and with his faithful people in whatever experiences they may have.

Notes

1. A working bibliography should include the following titles. Undoubtedly some scholars would present a differing list.

Geoffrey J. Aimers, "The Rhetoric of Social Conscience in the Book of Job," *JSOT* 91 (December 2000): 99–107; Robert Althann, "Elihu's Contribution to the Book of Job," *Old Testament Essays* 12 no.1 (1999): 9–12; Francis I. Andersen, *Job: An Introduction and Commentary* (Downers Grove: InterVarsity, 1976); L. C. Bezuidenhout, "A Context to Frame the Book of Job" *Old Testament Essays,* 9 no.1 (1996): 9–19; John J. Bimson, "Who is 'This' in "Who is this . . . ? " (Job 38:2) a response to Karl G. Wilcox, *JSOT* 87 (March 2000): 125–128; William Bode, *The Book of Job* (Grand Rapids: Eerdmans, 1914); William P. Brown, "Introducing Job: A Journey of Transformation, *Interpretation* 53 no.3, (July 1999); 228–38; Lael O. Caesar, "Job: Another New Thesis" *VT* 49 no.4 (October 1999): 435–47; John Calvin, *Sermons From Job* (Grand Rapids: Baker, 1952); Joseph Caryl, *An Exposition of Job* (Evansville: Sovereign Grace, 1959); Cordon Christo, "The Battle Between God and Satan in the Book of Job," *JATS* 11 no.1–2, (Spring-Autumn 2000): 282–86; David J. A. Clines, *Job 1–20 Word Biblical Commentary* vol. 17, (Dallas: Word, 1989); James L. Crenshaw, *Old Testament Wisdom, An Introduction*, rev. ed. (Louisville: Westminster/ John Knox, 1998); Thomas F. Dailey, "The Wisdom of Irreverence: Job as an Icon for Postmodern Spirituality," *Interpretation* 53 no.3, (July 1999): 276–89; John Day, *Wisdom in Ancient Israel,* ed. John Day, Robert P. Gordon, and H. G. M. Williamson (Cambridge: University Press, 1995); F. Delitzsch, *The Book of Job,* 2 vols., trans. Francis Bolton

(Grand Rapids: Eerdmans, 1949); E. Dhorme, *A Commentary on the Book of Job,* trans. Harold Knight (Camden: Thomas Nelson, 1967); H. L. Ellison, *From Tragedy to Triumph* (London: Paternoster, 1958); Susan R. Garrett, "The Patience of Job and the Patience of Jesus," *Interpretation* 53 no.3, (July 1999): 254–64; Robert Gordis, *The Book of God and Man: A Study of Job* (Chicago: University of Chicago Press, 1978 [1965]); *The Book of Job: Commentary, New Translation and Special Studies* (New York: Jewish Theological Seminary, 1978); William Henry Green, *Conflict and Triumph* (Carlisle: Banner of Truth Trust, 1999 [1874]); Murray J. Haar, "Job After Auschwitz," *Interpretation* 53 no.3, (July 1999): 265–75; Norman C. Habel *The Book of Job* (Philadelphia: Westminster, 1985); John E. Hartley, *The Book of Job* (NICOT) (Grand Rapids: Eerdmans, 1988); "Job as Paradigm for the Eschaton" *JATS* 11 nos.1–2, (Spring-Autumn 2000): 148–62; J. H. Kroeze, *Het Boek Job* (Kampen: Kok, 1966); *Job* (Kampen: Kok, 1961); Andre LaCocque, "Job and Religion at its Best," *Biblical Interpretation* 4 no.2 (June 1996): 131–53; Tod Linafelt, "The Undecidability of *irb* in the Prologue to Job and Beyond," *Biblical Interpretation* 4 no.2, (June 1996): 154–72; Alex Luc, "Storm and the Message of Job," JSOT 87 (March 2000): 111–23; Johanna Manley, *Wisdom, Let Us Attend: Job the Fathers*, comp. and ed. Johanna Manley (Menlo Park: Monastery Books, 1997); J. C. Marnewick, and A. P. B. Breytenbach, "Die Boek Job Gelees Vanuit'n Ou-Testamentiese Verbondsperspektief," *Hervormde Teologiese Studies* 50 (November 1994): 923–35; Carol A. Newsom, "Job and His Friends: A Conflict of Moral Imaginations," *Interpretation* 53 no.3, (July 1999): 189–201; Michael D. Oblath, "Job's Advocate: A Tempting Suggestion," *Bulletin for Biblical Research,* 9 (1999): 189–201; Leo G. Perdue, *The Voice from the Whirlwind: Interpreting the Book of Job* (Nashville: Abingdon, 1992); *Wisdom and Creation: The Theology of Wisdom Literature* (Nashville: Abingdon, 1994); Tina Pippin, "Job 42:1–6, 10–17" *Interpretation* 53 no.3, (July 1999): 299–303; Marvin H. Pope, *Job* 3rd ed. (Garden City, N. Y.: Doubleday, 1974 [1993]); K. J. Popma, *A Battle for Righteousness: The Message of the Book of Job,* trans. Jack Van Meggelen (Belleville, Ont.: Essence, 1998); Henry Wheeler Robinson, *Suffering, Human and Divine* (New York: Macmillan, 1939); V. Sasson, "The Literary Theological Function of Job's Wife in the Book of Job as a Drama," *JSOT* (June 1999): 69–82; John H. Stek, "Job: An Introduction," *Calvin Theological Journal* 32 no.2 (November 1997): 443–58; *The New Interpreters Bible*, vol. 4, ed. Michael E. Lawrence (Nashville: Abingdon, 1996); David Thomas, *Book of Job* (rpt. Grand Rapids: Kregel, 1982); Derek Thomas, *The Storm Breaks: Job* (Darlington: Evangelical, 1995); William P. Thomason, *God on Trial: The Book of Job and Human Suffering* (Collegeville: Liturgical, 1997); Bruce Vawter, *Job and Jonah, Questioning the Hidden God* (New York: Paulist, 1983); Jaco Viljoen, " 'n PsigologieseVerstaan van die Boek Job: 'n beskouing van W. Brueggemann se bydrae tot 'n psigologiese verstaan van die boek Job, in die gesprek rondom psigologiese skrifverstaan," *Old Testament Essays* 11 no.1 (1998): 115–27; Gerhard Von Rad, *Wisdom in Israel,* 5th print. (Nashville: Abingdon, 1981); Larry J. Waters, "Reflections on Suffering from the Book of Job," *Bib. Sac.* 154 no.616 (October–December 1997): 436–51; Claus Westermann, *The Structure of the Book of Job,* trans. C. A. Muenchow (Philadelphia: Fortress, 1977); Roger Norman Whybray, *Job* (Sheffield: Sheffield Academic, 1981); Karl G. Wilcox, "'Who is This . . . ?': A reading of Job 38:2," *JSOT* 78 (June 1998): 85–95; Lindsay Wilson, "The Book of Job and the Fear of God," *Tyndale Bulletin* 46 (May 1995): 59–79 Walther Zimmerli, "The Place and Limit of Wisdom . . . of O.T. Theology" *SJTH* 17 (1964): 146–58; Bruce Zuckerman, *Job the Silent: A Study in Historical Counterpoint* (Oxford: Oxford University Press, 1991).

2. Critical scholars seek to find a common source for the book of Job in Egyptian, Hittite, or Akkadian literature. See, for example, Perdue, *Wisdom and Creation*, 125. Perdue wrote that he found Job to unite the various themes and motifs in Near Eastern wisdom literature, 126.

3. See Westermann, *The Structure*, who referred to scholars who question Job's classification as wisdom literature because it is so utterly unique.

4. Ibid, 3. Meredith G. Kline contends that the book of Job is to be considered a drama in which a legal conflict is depicted and developed. Cf. his chapter "Trial by Ordeal" in *Through Christ's Word,* a festschrift for Dr. Philip Edgecomb Hughes, ed. W. R. Godfrey and J. L. Boyd III (Phillipsburg: Presbyterian and Reformed, 1985), chap. 6, 81–93.

5. See 27–28.

6. Carol Newsom, *The Book of Job,* "Introduction" NIB, vol. 4, 319.

7. Westermann, *The Structure*, 6.

8. Two obvious examples of this lack of consensus are Norman Habels *The Book of Job,* who sees three movements, God afflicts Job, Job challenges God, God challenges Job, 27–33; and Bruce Zuckerman, a Jewish/Yiddish writer who employed a Yiddish story entitled "Bontsye Shvayg" as an analogy for his understanding of the book of Job which he considers a composition in counterpoint, *Job the Silent,* 4.

9. Green, *Conflict*, cf. outline, 1. In an appendix he gave his view of "The Place of the Book of Job in the Scheme of Holy Scripture," 157–72. He wrote that Job is an essential part of the Law in the Old Testament that portrayed the gospel of the New Testament.

10. Thomas, *The Storm*. Thomas referred to and accepted John Calvin's understanding of the book. For Calvin's understanding of the book of Job one can read the selected and translated *Sermons from Job*.

11. Delitzsch, *Book of Job*, 14–18.

12. Kroeze, *Boek Job*, 33.

13. See John Stek's essay "Job: An Introduction," as a prime example of this, esp. 447.

14. Perdue, *Wisdom and Creation*, 123.

15. Carol Newsom who wrote that different parts of the book were composed at different times for different audiences over a possible period of eight hundred years. "Introduction," 325. There is no specific or concrete evidence for such a position.

16. Green, *Conflict*, 3.

17. Hartley, *Job*, 15–17. Elmer Smick wrote that the place of origin, which includes Job's *Sitz im Leben,* was near centers of Aramaic influence. Just where, Smick did not indicate; he wrote that Uz was a wide region encompassing many tribes. See Smick's essay "Job," in *The Zondervan Pictorial Encyclopedia,* ed. Merrill Tenney (Grand Rapids: Zondervan, 1975), 602.

18. See Dhorme's discussion of this subject, *Commentary*.

19. Brown somewhat cryptically referred to Job as a *goy* from the indeterminable land of Uz. "Introducing Job."

20. Dhorme, *Commentary* (1965 ed.). Meredith G. Kline wrote that the events recorded belong to the patriarchal times. He disagrees with critical scholarship's view that has added perplexity to the problem by presenting dates from the time of Moses to the Maccabeans. See his essay in *The New International Dictionary of the Bible,* ed. J. D. Douglas, rev. ed. Merrill Tenney (Grand Rapids, Zondervan, 1987), 629–30.

21. Brown, *Job*, xxxvii.

22. I have taken this view in full awareness of what a neo-orthodox critically inclined Old Testament scholar wrote. He described the Mosaic age as the time of composition to be that of the far right and the Maccabean period that of the far left. Brevard S. Childs, *Introduction to the Old Testament as Scripture* (Philadelphia: Fortress, 1979), 526–33. Childs' mediating position and reasons for it are unacceptable to various critical scholars as well as to conservative students of Holy Scripture.

Another Old Testament theologian who had added to the confusion concerning the book of Job is Walter Brueggemann. In his *Theology of the Old Testament* (Minneapolis: Fortress, 1997) he wrote that the book of Job has important links with Jeremiah and the complaint Psalms, 386.

23. Brown, in "Introducing Job," quoted D.J.A. Clines, 9, but Brown himself wrote "the book of Job is a cauldron of contending theological positions," 229.

24. Consider the bibliography in note 1 and other sources quoted in previous notes. Should a reader desire to consult additional works on Job, he or she could review the lengthy notes in Alex Luc's essay, "Storm and the Message of Job," in *Journal for the Study of the Old Testament* 87 (2000): 111–23.

25. C. Van Gelderen, *Job's Soul Struggles,* trans. from Dutch (Kampen: Kok, 1935).

26. This issue will be discussed in chap. 36.

27. *Conflict,* viii.

28. Manley, *Let Us Attend*, VI, 653–80.

29. Luc, "Storm and Message," 111.

30. Ibid., 123.

31. Thomas, *The Storm*, see esp. the Introduction, 11–17.

35

The Kingdom in the Book of Job

I. Introductory Comments

II. God and Job

III. Kingdom and Creation

IV. The Kingdom Revealed

V. The Parasite Dominion

VI. Kingdom Victory

VII. Wisdom's Role in the Kingdom

35

The Kingdom in the Book of Job

Introductory Comments

The Idea of King in the Book of Job

The term *melek* appears eight times in the book of Job. It is translated as king(s). Job referred to kings and counselors of past times who had built palaces that were in his time in ruins (3:14). Earthly kings with their reign and domain did not continue. Kings had shackles put on them by conquering enemies. Kings were neither supremely invincible nor necessarily doomed to bondage (12:18). There was a higher royal power that determined the human king's destiny. Kings could be overwhelmed by circumstances even though they were prepared for battle (15:24). While a king was in power he could bring terror (18:14). Job referred to his pre-calamity and suffering days; he said he was then as a king in charge of troops who could comfort mourners (29:25). Elihu spoke of the Mighty One who can address kings and tell them they are worthless (34:18). God is this Mighty One according to Elihu. He evaluated and judged human kings and kept his eye on the righteous ones. He enthroned the kings, exalting them forever (36:7). The Lord, speaking to Job, referred to himself as unequaled by earthly kings. He looked on all who were haughty and proud and the king dealt with all those who were proud (41:34 [MT 36]). A quick review of these passages clearly indicates that the book of Job refers to proud human kings whose destiny was always under the control and purpose of the Mighty One, who was the King over all.

The passages referred to on the previous page give ample evidence that the author of Job was fully aware of the presence of royalty. Royalty was demonstrated by references to human kings, their character and reign. There is no reference to their domain but their relationship to their subjects is indicated in various ways. There is also reference to the throne, the seat of power. Men and God were ascribed royalty in various contexts.

The Idea of Kingdom in the Book of Job

The concept of kingdom, though not referred to by a term is certainly held forth in Job. The idea of kingdom includes four specific references: the king, the throne, the reign, and the domain. Hence to say the book of Job refers to and even speaks of kingdom is not placing an idea within the message of the book of Job.

It is to be admitted that the concept of kingdom is not clearly defined. It is referred to, but it is not explained. What concrete evidence is there in the book that could enable one to see and understand that God's kingdom is the all-inclusive concept? God is recognized as the Lord over all of creation. He is God. He is referred to by various divine names. *'ĕlôh*, the singular form occurs forty-two times, and the plural *'ĕlōhîm* appears eleven times. The brief form *'ēl* appears fifty-five times. *Shaddaî* in combination with *'ēl* appears thirty-one times. These names all express the thought of God as the greatest, the highest, the mightiest, the all-sufficient one. There should be no hesitation in accepting the truth that God, the God of Scripture, the Only Sovereign, Supreme, Almighty, all Authoritative Divine One was recognized, known, accepted, and honored as the Lord. He was the only King, whose throne, reign, and domain were known and recognized as the all-inclusive kingdom of God.

This kingdom concept, in its all-inclusiveness, is elaborated in at least five ways. These will now be discussed.

God and Job

God is King

God, the King, and Job, the kingdom man, interacted in the setting of the cosmic kingdom. God was the sovereign Lord and Job was an obedient kingdom servant. Job knew his royal Lord and he knew his kingdom status. He revealed this in the statements he made (1:21, 22). *'ārōm yāztî* "naked I came" . . . *wĕ 'ārōm 'āšûb* "naked I return." The term *'ārōm* is an adjective, derived from the verb *'ûr*, to be exposed, bare. As an adjective in this context it can be understood as bare but more specifically it refers to being without possessions of any kind. So Job spoke truthfully. As a newborn boy, he was not only bare, without covering of any kind, he had no earthly possessions. And if he were to die under his present affliction, he would be thus again.

Job, however, said more. Twice he referred to God by using the covenant name, Yahweh. It was his God who had *nātan* (given) and it was none other who had *lāqâh* (taken). It was his God who had dispossessed. Job did not hesitate to confess his faith in his Lord whom he recognized as the Ruler over all aspects of his life.

Commentators have discussed what Job meant when he used the phrase *'āšûb šāmmâh* (return there). He had come from his mother's *beten* (womb). Did he imply he would return to the womb? The answer is that he would depart thus to the womb of the earth, the grave.[1] Passages such as Psalm 139, Ecclesiastes 5:15, and 1 Timothy 6:7 are cited to support this view that Job referred to the grave. Appeal also has been made to God making man from the dust of the ground (Gen. 2:7). Job, with these words, acknowledged his creaturehood. He did not consider himself autonomous. As a man he was totally dependent on his Lord.

The question has been asked whether Job indicated that he was accepting common Oriental resignation. This resignation was evidence of pessimism that was expressed in Oriental wisdom.[2]

A consideration of the context in which Job's words are given presents a very different view of his emotional state as well as his religious convictions. Job expressed grief in the common Oriental way. As related in the Scriptures Job tore his clothes and shaved his head. This grief did not express pessimism or defeat nor did it demonstrate fatalism. With torn clothes and shaved head, Job fell to the ground in complete submission to his God. *yiśtāhû*[3] (prostrated in worship) Job, on the ground, worshiped his God. This was not an action of despair. Job knew and demonstrated that God was the source of all he had had and that his God could and did take away what had been given.

Glory to Yahweh God the King

A second point to consider is this: Job proclaimed, "May the name of Yahweh be blessed." In deed and word, Job demonstrated that God was worthy of praise. Job was not driven from God. Job "destroyed the suspicion of Satan."[4] Job truly honored and adored his God.

Commentators have correctly interpreted Job as ascribing glory to Yahweh God. They have referred to God's sovereignty. Habel wrote, "The sovereign activity of Yahweh's 'giving' (ntn) and 'taking' (lqh)" was proclaimed as a positive reality in the world.[5] A Dutch Old Testament theologian employed two terms, *vrijmacht* and *souverein* (literally translated "free power" and "sovereign").[6] Hartley wrote that Job both acknowledged God's lordship over all his possessions and sought consolation from the Almighty. He went on to write that thus Job acknowledged God's sovereignty over his entire life for both good and ill.[7] Job was resigned to God's will. The text stated twice, in all this Job did not sin (1:22; 2:10). Job's acknowledgment of God's sovereignty and power led to patience and perseverance. It motivated him to submission and gave him endurance.[8]

God's Cosmic Kingdom, the Setting for Job

The cosmic kingdom of God is the context in this initial revelation of God's dealing with Job. He blessed him with great wealth and a worshiping family. This cosmic kingdom included the world, all that was in it, and specifically, Job, his family, and his possessions. This kingdom over which God reigned sovereignly was the context *of all that is recorded* in the book of Job. To understand the entire book of Job, one must constantly keep in mind that all that is said and done is within the kingdom of God. God's dealing with Job should be an incentive for all people to submit to this sovereign Lord, irrespective of circumstances.

The Influence of Suffering on Relationship

The question to be considered is: did Job throughout the entire period of suffering continue to express faith in, devotion to, and full submission to his sovereign Lord? Habel, as noted before, wrote that Job denounced God's sovereign dealings with him as arbitrary, unjust, and cruel.[9] Is this truly the case?

It must be repeated. Job did not *nātan tiplâh* (give blame or fault) to God (1:22). He did not *hata* (sin) with his lips (or mouth). The emphasis is on what Job did *not* do. He did not blame God or accuse God of folly. He did not say a word against God. This should be noted particularly because his wife urged him to do so (2:9). The one person one would expect to stand by and support Job was his wife. But she did not. Job was alone, terribly alone, in his suffering.[10] This suffering did have a strong effect on Job, the kingdom servant. But did his relationship with his sovereign Lord break down?

To answer this question, a study must be made of what follows in chapters 3 to 42. The question arises concerning the approach one should take to the body of material that follows the prologue and precedes the epilogue. Should we accept Newson's approach and methodology? She proposed that the reader/student of Job should consider the Jobian material as presenting "A Conflict of Moral Imaginations." This conflict is developed by a series of narratives that Job's friends employed as a literary method of presenting their "imaginations." Job, however, employs a model of moral answerability. And at the end of the discourse God is presented as providing a different moral imagination that challenges both Job and the friends. What literary form God is said to employ is not developed.[11] A study of Newsom's essay reveals that the book of Job is considered the work of a poet. She developed that thesis in another context.[12] What could be considered a major problem in understanding Newsom's interpretation of the book of Job is her attempt to introduce Narrative criticism into a work that has a basic dialogic form in which theological and moral issues are discussed.

Critical efforts have not produced a unanimous approach to or interpretation of Job. While all agree that the prologue and epilogue have an historical episodal form, it is the body of the book of Job that has provided critical scholars with a plethora of divergent explanations and conclusions. While almost all critical scholars date the final composition of the entire book anywhere from the sixth to the second century B.C., few have given a precise historical context for the final composition. Some, as has Perdue, presented a finite historical setting. These appeared in three stages. The didactic prose arose in pre-exilic times to respond to the relationship between human suffering and behavior. The dialogues, dealing with laments and sapiential wisdom, were produced during the exile in response to Israel's suffering. Later some parts, the chapter on wisdom and Elihu's speeches, were added.[13] Perdue, evidently not wishing to accept the historicity of the Jobian material employed the concept of metaphor. He discussed metaphors for humanity, world-kingdom, for God, anthropology, reality, cosmology, slave, creation, and providence. He concluded that the metaphorical process, in which all participants were involved, resulted in transformation and re-stabilization. In the end the sovereignty of God over the world and forces of chaos was realized. Job cowered in submission to this sovereignty.[14] It seems very difficult when reading chapter 42 to see a cowering Job. Rather, Job is the restored cosmic kingdom man. This does not imply that Job was a strong confessing and worshiping man throughout his ordeal of suffering.

The Scriptures make clear that Job was an historical person. He was much more than a personality for a poet to visualize and present in varying situations and corresponding moods. Job was a real human being. He was a person, an image bearer of God. He was a kingdom man who faithfully worshiped and served his sovereign royal Lord. During his suffering, however, the relationship between Job, the royal servant, and God, the sovereign King, did not come to clear and positive expression on the part of Job.

The text states Job did not sin by charging God (1:22). After his wife advised him to curse God and die, Job rebuked her; he replied that good as well as trouble should be accepted from God. Then the comment follows: Job did not sin in what he said (2:10). Could it be implied that Job's words were correct but his heart was harboring complaints against God? That these came to strong expression after his friends had come and sat with him for seven days?

Job's soul struggles moved him to curse his day of birth, his every existence. He did not curse God (3:1). He did lose sight of his sovereign Lord although he referred to "God above" who seemed not to care about him (3:4). In reality Job said God was not with him. God was hidden,[15] out of reach and beyond reaching down to him. What in reality was hidden from Job was God's counsel and purpose. But, as Van Gelderen has helpfully written,[16] as Job interacted with his friends, he increasingly overcame the anguish of his suffering and increasingly realized he was in the reigning Lord's hands. He exclaimed that it was God who had devastated his entire household; God wore him out, bound him, and turned him over to evil men (16:1–14). Job, in sackcloth, knew his eyes were red from weeping and that his heart and prayers were pure. He nevertheless professed that he was assured that he would be vindicated. Job looked to his advocate and intercessor. He would be fully restored to fellowship with God, not in this life but when he departed from it (16:18–22).

Job's Assurance under God the King

Job reached the epitome of his assurance that his God had not forgotten or forsaken him. He, the kingdom man, knew his redeemer lived and that he would enter into the blessed presence of God (19:23–27). But Job did not have to wait until he died. After God, the creator, the providential ruler, of the cosmic King, addressed Job (38:1–41:34) Job confessed his unworthiness (40:4) and God's sovereignty. He said, "you can do all things, no plan of yours can be thwarted," and assured God he would listen (42:1–6). The cosmic Ruler then restored the wealth of the natural aspect of his cosmic kingdom to Job. His family and possessions were restored.

The concluding and summarizing statement that must be made is: the Ruler of the cosmic kingdom never left his throne, never turned away from his domain, and never withdrew his reign from over any person or aspect of his cosmic kingdom. Job was always in the King's hand.

Kingdom and Creation

Preliminary Issues

The question could arise: what is the relationship between kingdom and creation, particularly in the context of the book of Job? The discussion that follows should clarify this issue. But aside from what the text of Job reveals, it should be clear to all that God's cosmic kingdom came into existence when God created the heavens and the earth (Gen. 1:1). The two concepts are inextricably related. To speak of creation is to refer to God's cosmic kingdom.

Another question that arises is: when using the term *creation*, is the act of creating (the verb) stressed, or is the result of the act of creating (the noun) to be understood? Creation was an act of God. By this act of creating God brought forth the creation—the kingdom. It follows then, that when the term is used, both the verb (act) and the noun (object) are inseparably referred to. In the book of Job, as will be discovered, the result of the act, creation, the cosmic kingdom, is referred to in various ways, either to the whole, parts, or aspects of it.

A third question pertains to the theological emphasis of the book of Job. Involved in this issue is the conception of many biblical scholars that the Scriptures present a record of redemption. Conservative scholars prefer to refer to the redemptive message of the Scriptures that has come by way of divine revelation. Critical scholars prefer to speak of Israel's faith that had redemption as a central motif. Perdue addressed this issue. He pointed out that Gerhard Von Rad emphasized redemption as the first and basic concept of Scripture, including Wisdom Literature also.[17] Perdue went on to indicate that Claus Westermann gave a more constructive and significant place to creation in wisdom literature. Perdue, however, properly stressing the role of creation[18] erroneously accounts for this emphasis on creation because Israel inherited the idea of divine creation from "Ancient Near Eastern" sources, from which creation wisdom was gathered.[19]

The position taken in this biblical theological study is that the book of Job presents divinely inspired revelation in which the role of creation, both as act and noun, is emphasized. The reality is that creation is the setting of all that transpires as recorded in the book of Job. And since creation is the dominant motif, the cosmic kingdom is the setting in which the entire drama was acted out.

The Biblical Evidence

In the prologue (chaps. 1, 2), the terms *creation* and *kingdom* do not appear. The evidence, however, for the cosmic kingdom as context for all that transpires is irrefutable. Job's blessings (1:1–5) were in the natural (creation) realm. There are spiritual connotations, as will be discussed later. The creation/cosmic kingdom is the context. The interaction between God and Satan is in the cosmic kingdom setting. In the dialogue between Job and his three friends and in the speeches of Elihu, the references are numerous. Job spoke of kings, counselors, rulers and their fortunes (3:14, 15). He referred to caravans and merchants (6:19). The friends spoke of harvest, thorns, and wealth (5:5), of well watered plants in sunshine and shoots spreading in the garden over rocks and stones (8:16, 17). They spoke of wild donkeys' colts and of evil and deceit (11:11, 12). In the "Wisdom Chapter" the reference to a mine, to minerals and to the activities involved in acquiring them, provide further evidence of the natural/creation/cosmic setting of the book of Job.

The Kingdom Revealed

Was God the King a Just Ruler?

It is not only the references to aspects of the natural created world that indicate that the kingdom is a central and all-embracing concept. These aspects basically refer to the domain. What is to be stressed is that the reign of God, the King of the cosmic kingdom, is revealed. To state it plainly, the sovereign reigning Lord was in charge and in control. He was in control of Job's life and family before tragedies struck (1:1–5). And the Lord remained sovereignly in control when Satan challenged him.[20] God kept Job alive and able to dialogue with his visitors. God enabled Job to become more confident during the dialogues and enabled him to proclaim that he had an advocate and redeemer. Job was correct when he eloquently spoke of God's reign over all aspects of the cosmic kingdom. Consider what Job said after the three friends had had their say (26:1–31:4). God is in control of death (26:6) and over the skies, clouds, light and darkness, earthquakes, and storms (26:7–14). God allots the fate of the wicked (27:13–23). God is the Creator of all the riches in the cosmic kingdom and continues his reign over all these. He gives to mankind the insight and ability to discern and acquire these riches. Meanwhile God sees everything under the heavens and understands all forces and elements in the natural created world. This reign, control, and the directives of God are all carried out according to his wisdom (28:1–28).

The kingdom of God is revealed. The reign of God over his domain, the cosmic aspects of it, has been considered and acknowledged by Job and his friends. The text clearly indicates that God was present, in control, and his purposes were achieved.

Theodicy

Job, however, was not convinced that his God, the Creator and King, was just and righteous as he displayed his authority and his power. Job and his friends knew God was Almighty. The name *shaddaî* appears thirty-one times. It has been translated as Almighty in every case.[21] Job's friends believed God to be the almighty, just, and righteous one, who was punishing Job for misdeeds, sin, or evil he had committed. They had a logical theological view. A righteous and just God hates sin; he brings punishment upon sinners. Job was suffering; hence he was being punished for sin he refused to confess. The three friends considered God, the sovereign Ruler of his kingdom, to be consistently just. The problem was with Job, not with God.

Job, denying that he had sinned and thus brought judgment upon himself, conceded God was wise and mighty (12:13). But he could not understand why God in his wisdom performed deeds that were in reality unjust. Job referred to destruction, imprisonment of innocent people, and droughts. He spoke of poverty among faithful people and disruption in nations (12:14–25). Job referred to realities in life and questioned God's justice in his sovereign rule over the cosmic kingdom. He knew the wise and powerful God reigned. God's kingdom was manifest. But was this reign just and righteous when suffering and destruction were prevalent in all aspects of life?[22]

This problem of suffering under the reign of a wise, powerful, righteous, and just God has been referred to as theodicy. Tina Pippin has written that theodicy is one of the main questions in the book of Job.[23] No one should contradict that statement. What is necessary, however, is to keep in mind the *Sitz im Leben* in which Job suffered. Job was not aware of much that was involved. He knew that he was suffering. He was convinced he was not being punished as his friends insisted he was for evils committed. Job was not aware that the cosmic kingdom was under constant challenge by a parasite dominion.

The Parasite Dominion

Satan

When the term *parasite dominion* is used, reference is to both Satan and the sphere of his activity.

The text states that *wayyābô' gam haśśāṭān bĕtôkām* (and also the satan came in their midst) (2:6). God's angelic emissaries came together *lĕhithyaśśab* (to stand, to report) *'āl yĕhwâh* (before Yahweh). Satan was in that group. What the specific purpose for this gathering was is not stated. What is stated is that Yahweh God spoke to Satan, requesting him to report on his activities.

The term *haśśāṭān* has received much discussion. The prefix *ha* (the) has led some scholars to write that a "personal" being was not referred to but to a position or office.[24] The idea is that an angel is referred to who had been given the position of "adversary." Some of these critical scholars also hold that the idea of a personal adversary, Satan, was not known until after the exile. That idea is unacceptable, because the adversary of God and righteous humankind was present long before Job lived. He appeared as a serpent in paradise to Adam and Eve and tempted them.[25] Satan has been referred to as the prince of darkness, a spirit of malice, the enemy of goodness in men and women, having the subtlety of a fiend, with the power of an archangel by which he can exercise control over external aspects of nature.[26] Another scholar wrote that the mentality of Satan is a mystery whose depths can never be fathomed. He is a false accuser, a wanderer, a cynic, and a tormentor.[27]

The Parasite

Satan, as a fallen archangel, was banished from his position of administrator under God in the cosmic kingdom, but his power, ability, and authority were not taken away. Hence he was able to establish his dominion. But it was not a distinct kingdom that existed separately from God's cosmic kingdom. Satan was limited to function within this kingdom. Although his power and ability were great, they were always within God's cosmic kingdom and subject to God's sovereign rule and authority. The term *parasite* is therefore very fitting. A parasitic growth on a tree cannot function without the tree from which it derives a place and the necessities to grow and be an influence.[28] Satan's powerful influence is always under God's reign. God gave and gives Satan latitude to function. God did not give Satan complete freedom,[29] but gave him permission to act as the adversary. The text states that God said Satan incited him to ruin Job without any reason (2:3). Thus God was involved in Job's suffering, but he was in control. Satan could destroy Job's possessions, turn his wife against him, and cause him intense personal physical suffering, but Job, the afflicted, remained under God's reign and control. The parasitic dominion had tremendous influence on Job, but he remained a living member within the cosmic kingdom.

Conflict and Antithesis

Within the cosmic kingdom, ever since Lucifer, the archangel (who became Satan the adversary), was cast from his heavenly abode, there has been an ongoing conflict. God was fully aware of this at the time of Job. Hence he questioned Satan concerning his going about the cosmic kingdom. He had Satan report to him.

And in this context God inquired of Satan if he had observed the faithful, just, and righteous Job. Why did God ask Satan? One must be careful not to speculate. The text states that God spoke to Satan regarding Job as a blameless, upright man who feared God and shunned evil (1:8). Specifically God said to Satan *hăśamtâ libĕkâ* (*ha* represents an interrogative—have you set [*sîm,* to set or put] your heart on Job? (1:8). The usual translation is an interpretation, have you considered. Dhorme has been more specific; the phrase really means have you given attention to Job? The phrase also emphasizes that the heart, the very core of the personality, was involved.[30] To paraphrase then is to hear God saying to Satan, "Have you taken to heart that Job is a blameless and upright man ?" Satan's reply was definite. The conflict was joined. The antithesis established in paradise was real, dramatic, and forceful.[31] Satan opposed God with a vigorous accusation. Job was the man he was because God coddled him. Job responded as God wanted because he wished to be the rich and powerful hero in the land. Satan demonstrated that he was alert to the specific situation in which Job existed. Under God's providential reign Job had prospered. He had become rich; a man of influence and power in his social context. But Satan would not admit that Job's greatest virtues were his faith in God and his steadfast unswerving loyalty to God.

In this conflict between God and Satan, Job was given a central and pivotal role. He was a kingdom agent; he was a faithful servant of God. Satan used Job to attack God. He accused Job of being "bought" by God and sheltered by God. Job responded to these favors. Satan would not concede that faith in God was the all-sustaining and enduring reality in the relationship between God and Job. Satan could have known the true character of living faith. He chose to ignore it. He would rather accuse God of favoritism and using his sovereign power to keep Job as his "model."

Nefarious Realities

It must be emphasized that Satan is a reality. He is an angelic personal being. He has great administrative ability. He has unbelievable power and influence. He controls a vast army of loyal subjects in the angelic and human dimensions of the cosmic kingdom. Satan, however, always has been and is subject to God's sovereign will and reign. God always did have, and has, complete control. True, God did respond to Satan's challenge, which in effect was that man's faith in God was not durable and sustainable, that it was not genuine. Job suffered to demonstrate that Satan was radically wrong and that God knew in reality what faith was and what it could and would do.

The parasite dominion, controlled by the great adversary of God and believers, is a reality. It must be recognized. It must be opposed even when God gives Satan latitude to make vicious attacks on God's cosmic kingdom, upon which Satan is totally dependent himself. The parasite dominion will never be victorious in spite of many successes. Satan was very successful in causing Job to suffer. He was able to lead marauding bands, to cause natural calamities, and to cause personal physical suffering. But Satan could go only so far and do as much as God permitted him to do within the cosmic kingdom.[32]

Kingdom Victory

The victory of the cosmic kingdom was over the parasite dominion and its master Satan, the adversary of God and his kingdom. God proved victorious in his kingdom conflict with Satan. Questions, however, can and should be raised. Did Job fully share in this kingdom victory? And what was the role of the three friends and Elihu? Did God declare himself victorious over Satan? If not, how did God demonstrate this victory of the cosmic kingdom?

Job's Seeming Loss of Kingdom Victory

Job's Problem

Job did not speak of or consider himself a victorious kingdom agent once he was dispossessed of his wealth, his family, and his wife's confidence and support.[33] But he spoke as a victorious man when he rebuked his wife for not accepting God's ways with them (2:9, 10). When he was smitten physically, it is stated *bĕkōl zō't lo' hāṭā' ' iyyôb biśepāṭāyw* (in all this Job did not sin with his lips) (2:10). It is understood that Job did not speak a sinful word. But what developed in his heart could be understood as a deep depression. He spoke words that indicated that spiritually he was declining in strength, courage, and insight. For when his friends had sat with him silently for seven days, Job's words indicated he had descended to depths of hopelessness.

The text states his uncertainty. *pātaḥ. 'yôb 'et pîhû wayĕpallēl 'et yômô* (Job opened his mouth and cursed his day) (3:1). Two Hebrew words call for attention. The term translated curse is not the usual term for a strong absolute curse (*'ārar*). Rather, the term is *qālal,* which in its qal form should be translated "be slight." In other Semitic languages the term can mean "to despise." The term in the text is in the piel form. It signifies intensity: Job intensely despised his day. Translators have added "of his birth" because Job went on to refer to the day he was born (3:3). Job certainly did not speak as a victorious man, but as a smitten, defeated person. It can be correctly stated that he despised his life. All the blessings of the past were of no meaning or significance to him. He was bereft of all he had had; he suffered intense pain; he was completely humiliated as he sat on "the ash heap" before his friends. Job's faith had dropped to a very low level. In reality he spoke as a man without active faith.

Job's Assurance

As his friends began to address him an ascendancy became apparent. He climbed out of the pit of despair and began to speak confidently that he was not guilty of sins for which it was assumed he was being punished. Job was climbing upward. His faith in God was increasingly being asserted (4:1–19:20). Then, he ascended from expressing his faith to beholding God. He confessed his assurance in God's wisdom (chap. 28) and his own lack of full knowledge of God's ways (40:4, 5; 42:1–3).

Job proved to be a servant of God the cosmic King. His faith in God upheld him and he again, and more fully, reposed in the victory of faith. The victory of faith was in reality kingdom victory. God the King was honored; Job, the kingdom agent, experienced the victory of God's kingdom over all that the parasite dominion of Satan, the adversary, included.[34]

The sketch of Job's faith and kingdom victory should help clarify Job's faith and kingdom victory.

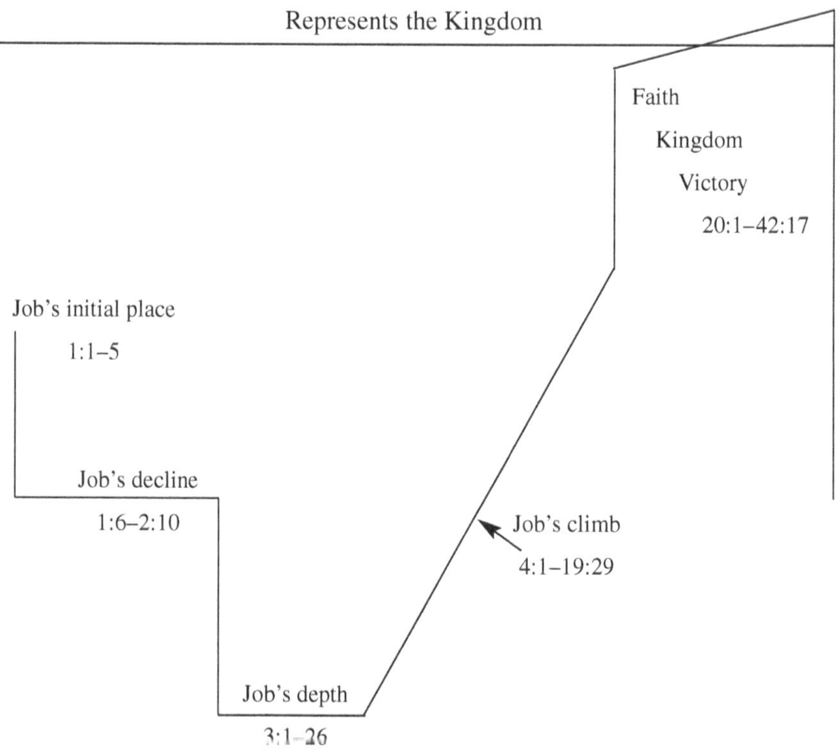

The struggle of faith—the victory of faith within the construct of daily life in the cosmic kingdom[35]

The Friends' Role in Job Regaining Kingdom Victory

The Friends' Intent

Job's three friends arrived some time after Job's sufferings began. They came from areas about three hundred miles apart. They had heard of Job's experiences and decided to go together. Their intent was *lânûd lô* (to sympathize with him) *wĕlĕnaḥâmô* (and to comfort him).[36] But did they become Job's enemies, as Clines wrote? It would seem more correct to say that they expressed their disagreement with Job as to the cause and purpose of his sufferings. The friends, believing in God sought to be spokesmen for him.[37] But the thoughts they expressed were not only inadequate, they were at times utterly wrong. Did this reality make the friends allies with Satan, and enemies of the recalcitrant and unteachable Job?[38] A brief survey of what each said and Job's response to each should provide an answer.

The Friends' Contribution

The three friends responded to Job's vehement outburst in which he had declared that he wished he had never been born even though he had had a good life.[39] After tragedy had struck he was confronted by the reality that the accepted orthodoxy of his day did not provide ease or rest (3:26). He was overcome by trouble that should not have come upon a faithful man. Job did not claim sinlessness that could bring chastisement. But he suffered as a chief of sinners and he knew he was not that. Why then did he experience "a hell on earth"? Job's vehemence conveyed that he had moved a great distance from God.[40] He did not deny God. He did not accuse God directly in a blasphemous manner. Basically he questioned God's justice. Why did God deal with him as he did? The friends had their stock answers. These answers in the end really helped Job back to peace with God in a unique manner. They increased his anguish.[41] Each speech by the friends was somewhat akin to someone turning the knife in Job's wounds.[42] Thus they drove him back into fellowship with God.

The Textual Evidence

Eliphaz demonstrated he was sensitive and wished to be helpful. But he spoke as a logical orthodox man. He asked "who being innocent has ever perished?" (4:7). One reaps as he has plowed. God knows what he is doing, he is righteous (4:8–21). Appeal to God, he can restore blessings to those whom he corrects. So do not despise the discipline of *Shaddaî* (Almighty God) (5:8–17). Job replied that his anguish was nigh immeasurable because *Shaddaî* had driven poisonous arrows into him (6:1–4). He longed for death and hoped he would not deny his God (6:8–13).[43] Job was deeply troubled that his "brothers" turned against him and were of no help to him (6:14–23).[44] Why, Job asked, do they not consider his integrity (6:24–30)? Job, having described his pain and anguish for months (7:1–6) called on his friends and God to ignore him for he would soon be gone (7:8–21).

Comments: (1) Job was fully aware that God was involved in his life, that God was the final arbiter in life and controller of it. (2) Job reflected his wide knowledge of cosmic kingdom life: a wild donkey and an ox are content when they have grass; food without salt is tasteless as is the white of an egg; strength and durability characterize bronze and stone; thawing ice swells streams; caravans in the desert disappear for lack of water; and men pay ransom to gain relief. (3) Job did not in any way confess to or admit being guilty of sin and evil as reasons for punishment.

Bildad was upset with Job's refusal to acknowledge sin in his life and his accusations against God (8:1–3). Job, if pure and upright, could expect God to restore him (8:4–7). Nature illustrates that one cannot tear oneself from God who does not reject innocent men. Comment: Bildad, revealing he is acquainted with nature, employs aspects of the natural in the cosmic kingdom to press upon Job his guilt and reason for suffering. Job responded, saying he knew God was righteous and no mortal could argue with the all-wise Lord of creation (9:1–4). He acknowledged God's sovereignty in his reign over all aspects of the cosmic kingdom (9:5–13). Job admitted that if he were entirely innocent he could not appeal to God's mercy. But he insists he is blameless of specific evil that could be the reason for his present pain and anguish. His friends have judged him definitely guilty (9:4–31). Job made a plea for an arbiter who could persuade God to take away his rod (9:32–35). Job continued speaking. In a real sense he addressed God. Though God seemed removed, yet Job considered him near and was searching for him. He boldly states that God knows he is not guilty of what the friends accuse him (10:1–7). Job spoke to God his Creator who gave him life (10:8–12), and Job knew God would be watching him wherever he went and whatever he did. And, in so doing, God increased anger against him (10:13–17). So, he asked God "Why was I born? Why, in the few days I have remaining will you, God, not give joy?" (10:18–22). Comments: (1) Job demonstrated that he knew God as the righteous, all-wise, sovereign Lord of the cosmic kingdom. (2) He knew he was entirely subject to God and his mercy. (3) God was his Creator and Lord of his entire life who knew all Job's activities. (4) Job requested God to give him a few days of joy and then take him out of life. (5) Bildad's sharp words against Job, while increasing his anguish, did draw him to consider more realistically that he was in God's hands.

Joseph Carlyle made an interesting observation when beginning his study of Zophar's reply to Job. "His name (Zophar) imparts a watchman, and his designation signifies pleasant."[45] In his reproof of Job and counsel for him, Zophar could hardly be considered pleasant. Directly or by implication he accused Job of being an idle, mocking talker (11:1–3). He lacked wisdom to comprehend God's mysteries (11:4–9). Job was guilty and witless (11:10–12). Zophar counseled Job to devote his heart to God, to remove evil from his dwelling, and then he would be able to lift his face without shame (11:13–15). Then trouble would be gone and he would again be secure and rest peacefully (11:16–19). Zophar's last words were an indictment of Job as a wicked man (11:20). Comments: (1) Zophar was an impatient man; he could not understand that Job could and would not confess his sin and evil, the basic causes of God's judgment on Job. (2) Zophar had God and Job boxed into a strict logical theological framework. Zophar, more than his two friends, expressed a certainty concerning God's justice; he punishes sin, deceit, wickedness, and evil; God forgives and restores the person who confesses that he is guilty of these. (3) Zophar also referred to realities in the cosmic kingdom life to make his point. God's mysteries are higher than the heavens and deeper than the grave, longer than the earth and wider than the seas (11:8–9) When speaking of the impossibility of a fool becoming wise, Zophar compared that to the impossibility of a wild donkey giving birth to a man (11:12).

The first round of the discussion was finished. Job had begun it by asking why he had been born, why he was devastated, and why God had dealt so severely with him. Job spoke as if God was far removed from him personally, but that from a distance God had brought disasters into his life. The friends responded "motivated by their view of divine justice"; tragedy, punishment come from God because of sin committed basically against God. Job in turn accused the friends of false accusations against him. He also, in various ways, accused God of punishing him for no specific evil in his life. Job called for an advocate; thus he expressed a glimmer of hope that he would be proven just before God. There was a small movement to the eventual victory Job was to experience. He, however, was far from savoring this when he initiated the second round of the dialogue on the ash heap. It began by Job's lengthy response to Zophar.[46]

Job responded by referring to the friends' lack of true and lasting wisdom and that he had knowledge of God that was not acknowledged by fellowmen (12:2). Job related evidence of his wide range of knowledge concerning things in the cosmic kingdom; these are all under God's control (12:3–12). God is truly wise[47] and powerful and demonstrates that as he reigns in the cosmic kingdom (12:13–13:2). So Job wanted to talk with God. In fact, Job wanted to have his day in court with God, in which the friends would be proven wrong, even deceitful (13:3–12). He commanded his friends to be silent, for he was certain that even if God slayed him, he still had hope in God (13:15). Job pled with God to remove his hand—Job considered God as the source of his trouble that frightened him. He asked God to indicate what wrongs, if any, he had committed (13:17–28). Again, Job expressed a wish to be removed to the grave. There he would be hidden from his troubles and appear to be gone for all time. A tree can be cut down and sprout; not so a person in the grave (14:1–12). Then surprisingly, Job expresses hope. "Hide me, 'til anger is past" and "I will wait for my renewal. Then I will be able to answer fully when my sin is covered" (14:13–22). Comments: (1) Job expressed an element of disdain for his friends; they were sure of themselves but lacking wisdom. He counseled them to be careful lest they come under God's judgment. (2) Job wanted a day in court with God so he could hear what sins, if any he had committed. (3) Job expressed a longing for eternal life. He would be assured of victory because in the final judgment he would be vindicated. (4) As the friends became more aggressive in their accusations, Job increasingly expressed assurance of God's vindicating him. He, more and more, began to sense victory.

As the dialogue progressed in the second cycle of speeches, insults were increasingly traded.[48] It is well to remember, however, what Dhorme has written: "Job and his friends are agreed as to the transcendence, the omnipotence, and the omniscience of God. They are divided in their opinions as to the application of his righteousness."[49]

Eliphaz accused Job of being full of wind that continued to be released. Eliphaz began an attempt to prove himself correct in his application of his theology. Sin brings punishment; Job, you are punished. Job, you have sinned. Repent. But you refuse to and act impudently, requesting a court with God (15:1–13). So doing, Job lacked dignity before God. Job was accused of a gross moral failure and he lacked wisdom (15:10–16). Eliphaz then proceeded, saying, "Listen to me . . ." He warned Job of the terrible fate of the wicked, and he described them (15:20–35), as if Job was guilty of at least some of these. Comments: (1) Eliphaz no longer tried to comfort Job; rather, he joined the other two friends in accusing Job. (2) Eliphaz increasingly sought to justify himself and prove his theology correct. (3) The description of the wicked and the sure judgment that would come was correctly stated. Thus there continued to be a vexing mixture of truth and incorrect theological expressions. (4) Job understood clearly that all three friends were serious, well-meaning men, but very wrong in their evaluation of him and his sufferings.

Job rebutted with an insult. You are miserable comforters. Your speeches contain nothing new and I could make even better ones than you. If I were to address you when in trouble I would encourage and comfort (16:1–5). Job called on God, who in anger assaulted him, his family, and his possessions (16:6–9). God gave occasion for fellowmen to scorn him when his Lord shattered and crushed him, humiliating him and causing him deep grief (16:10–16). Yet Job said that he had never done violence and had prayed pure prayers. He knew his advocate was his witness, his intercessor was with God (16:17–22). Job went on to express his hopeless situation on earth. God had forsaken him; fellowmen talked against him as he grieved. Job was certain that righteous men would prevail (17:1–9). But for him the grave, in which he would have darkness, corruption, and become dust, was his future (17:10–16). Comments: (1) Hartley has offered some incisive reflections. Job vented his agony and estrangement from God, who was the architect of his suffering. God had blinded his friends who became mockers, inflicters of suffering rather than sharers in his sorrows. But Job proved he had daring faith. He declared he had a witness in heaven who would verify his innocence and guarantee freedom from illness.[50] (2) Job was on an emotional roller coaster. His faith lifted him for a time above his immediate circumstances, but when he considered his present situation, he gave evidence of hopelessness and wanted to go to the grave. (3) The chasm between the friends and Job widened. They were convinced of his guilt; Job was equally convicted of his innocence. The friends were pushing him, or even motivating him to consider that there was victory for him in the all-embracing cosmic kingdom of God.

Bildad, having heard Job's many words had become impatient. He called for Job to stop making long speeches, to be sensible and join in a fruitful discussion. Bildad did not appreciate being considered as ignorant as cattle (18:1–4). Then he proceeded to relate what the calamities of the wicked were. He employed a long list of illustrations taken from the natural order of existence in the cosmic kingdom (18:5–20).[51] He concluded, having cleverly referred realistically to Job's recent experiences, saying that evil men do not know God (18:21). Bildad's words drew a passionate response from Job.

Job spoke *'ad 'ānâh* (until low long). Bildad had begun his first speech with these words also (8:2). He had begun his second speech with the identical words ('til how long). How long would Job give such speeches? Job asked the same exasperated question and added *tôgĕyûn* hiph impf of *yāgâh* (to cause grief and sorrow)[52] to *napši* (my soul or to my whole person). He added a stronger complaint; his friends *wetĕdakke 'ûnnanî* (piel impf. 2 masc.-pl. of *dācâ,* to crush). Job intimated that he had been completely shattered by his friends with their words (19:2). Job reproved them, saying if he had gone astray, that was his business. God had wronged him; the friends did not have to add to this wrong (19:4–6). Job then uttered a series of complaints. He had been wronged and received no justice. He had been blocked, shrouded in darkness, stripped of honor, uprooted like a tree. Enemies advanced against him, brothers were alienated, servants ignored him, his wife detested him (his breath), little boys ridiculed him, and he had been reduced to a living skeleton (19:7–20). He cried for pity from his friends and they did not join in God's pursuit of him (19:21, 22). His friends had driven him to the extremes of desperation. They had allied themselves with God. Then Job suddenly lifted himself from a desperate depth and rose to a lofty vision of his Redeemer and a sure future vision of God (19:23–27).[53] Job concluded his rebuttal to Bildad warning his friends that they should fear God's wrath—the sword—themselves (19:28–29). Comments: (1) Job expressed frustration, disappointment, and anger with his friends. They revealed no sympathy or compassion for Job even when Job reminded them of his losses, humiliation, grief, and suffering. (2) Job did, however, rise above his earthly situation. By faith he beheld his Redeemer. By faith he knew he would stand innocent before his God. From the lowest depths he had risen to a wonderful glorious height. He knew he was in the Redeemer's care and was innocent in God's sight. (3) Job expressed concern for the future of his friends; he could, for he had gotten a glimpse of God's righteousness and justice.

Zophar's response to Job was harsh. He objected to being rebuked by Job (20:1–3). Then he pronounced a series of calamities upon humankind that had come even in earliest times for pride expressed in mirth and abuse of the weak and poor fellowmen (20:4–22). Zophar assured Job that God vented his anger on such behavior for it was thus appointed by God himself (20:23–29). Comments: (1) Zophar by implication and direct references was accusing Job of social and cultural sin and evil. He gave clear evidence that he was well acquainted with everyday life in the cosmic kingdom. The rich and strong disappeared as dung, thus children must make amends and restitution. Evil men are poisonous as serpents. (2) Zophar continued to speak for God and doing so assured Job he was under God's wrath and judgment.

Job had his reply ready. Dhorme wrote that if Job had become impatient it was because he had to complain not of men but of God.[54] There was a strong contradiction in Job; he knew God would vindicate him, yet he also said that his affliction was from God. Job compared his lot with those who ignored or rejected God. The wicked had happiness, no misfortune, but prosperity, numerous offspring, and a "happy death." (21:1–15). These wicked people had no punishment. If a catastrophe struck them it was brief and isolated (21:16–34). Comments: (1) Job was deeply troubled. He knew his friends' contentions were absolutely incorrect. (2) Job reminded his friends that the openly wicked did not suffer. Hence their logic that sin, wickedness, and evil brought punishment was very incorrect. (3) Job was convinced that he, a righteous man, suffered at God's hand and the unrighteous were, as a whole, not punished before their death. (4) Hence, the views of the three men were nonsense and falsehood (21:34).

Eliphaz responded with his logic-driven view. God does not benefit or gain pleasure if a man is blameless; God does not punish men of piety (22:1–4). But Job was punished for great wickedness and endless sin (22:5). Eliphaz proceeded to describe Job's spiritual, social, and cultural sin (22:6–18).[55] The truly righteous see how such sinners are ruined and destroyed (22:19–20). Eliphas made an eloquent plea to Job: "submit to God, repent, accept God's word" (22:21–22). To do so would bring restoration; he would again be prosperous. His riches would be in God. Prayer and clean hands bring blessings (22:23–30). Comments: (1) Eliphaz expressed his impatience with Job because he thought Job considered himself useful to God but if that were so, Job would not suffer punishment. (2) Eliphas was convinced Job was a hidden yet blatant wicked man. (3) His words calling for submission, repentance, and prayer were expressions of deep concern. The problem was that Eliphas expressed these in a context of which he was totally unaware—namely, Job caught in the battle Satan waged against Job's God.

Job had a lengthy response to Eliphas. He repeated that he had a bitter complaint. God's heavy hand was upon him but he was not able to face God directly and could not state his case. If he could, he would be declared innocent (23:1–7). Job could not locate God, but God knew where he was. Job insisted he had followed God's footsteps (23:8–12). God carried out his decrees; no one could oppose him and that was why Job was terrified before God (23:13–17). Job asked a penetrating question. The Hebrew of 24:1 is difficult to translate.[56] The main thrust is that Job asked why God did not have a set time for judgment. Why cannot men, who know God, have knowledge of this? Job went on to describe unjust social conditions.[57] Evildoers reign; civil and criminal injustices abound (24:1–17) but the curse would come upon the wicked (24:18–23). Comments: (1) Job longed to know what was beyond human boundaries of knowledge, namely, God's timetable. He knew God as sovereign had his time. 2) There is less of a complaint against God for his suffering, but Job wanted to comprehend God's way of dealing with men in everyday life. (3) Job knew well what wicked people did and that God would deal with them—but when? And why did Job, as an innocent man, suffer the punishment of evildoers now? (4) Job insisted that his fellowmen could not prove him wrong. Their accusations of his wickedness were not proven. (5) Job reflected that he had confidence that he was not suffering as a result of evildoing. His vision of God was clouded, yes, but it was clear enough to express that his Lord was righteous and just in dealing with evildoers. But why was he, not an evildoer, punished as one?

Bildad made the last response to Job. He was brief, but sharp with his words.[58] God is sovereign, he is incomprehensible and righteous (25:1–3). No man can declare himself righteous and pure before a God who is beyond comprehension.[59] Compared to God man is a maggot, a worm (25:4–6). Comments: (1) Bildad, in a real sense, supported Job in his view of God's sovereignty and majesty. Even the sun and the moon cannot reflect God's full glory and splendor. (2) Compared to God, man represents corruption the *rimmâh* (a maggot) and a *tôlē'âh* (a worm). The one feeds on carrion (dead, spoiled flesh) and the other in the ground feeds on degenerating vegetation or food (e.g., on manna, Exod. 16:26). (3) Job, in Bildad's view, was corrupt; he had fed on greed and abetted corruption. (4) Bildad's words drove Job further from his friends and into a deeper realization of God's person and works.

Job benefited in a negative manner from his friends' speeches. Their common logical theological dictums, namely, sin brings judgment, Job, you are under judgment due to sin, pressed Job into closer fellowship with God. He, however, had not arrived at a full and complete relationship with God.

Job made a rather long reply to Bildad; his answer was also directed to the other two friends. He reflected anger and an element of scorn against them (26:2, 3). He had received no positive help from his friends. In fact, Job asked who it was that motivated Bildad to speak as he did (26:4). Commentators suggest Job scathingly implied Bildad didn't think for himself but was echoing Eliphaz.[60] Another wrote that Job was emphasizing that he had to deal with sinful and ignorant men.[61] Thomas wrote that Job implied that it was Satan.[62] Whether Job had it in mind that Satan was the direct influence is difficult to determine. That Satan was involved in the suffering of Job is known by what was written in the prologue (chaps. 1, 2). The three friends, who knew and honored God in various ways, could have been unknowingly influenced. Satan, after all, was doing his utmost to discredit Job. But, he ultimately did much to turn Job to God.

Job reflected his knowledge of God by referring to the "awesome mysteries" of God that are under God's sight and sovereign control. The entire cosmic order was established and ruled over by God. But Job added that God remained barely audible and hence incomprehensible (26:5–14). Job, in a wide-ranging address emphasized by oath his integrity (27:1–6) and warned his friends, who in reality were adversaries, that they faced the destiny of wicked men (27:7–23). But the man who feared God had wisdom and knew of God's sovereignty over the entire cosmos

(28:1–28).[63] Job continued to speak of his life as that of a covenant servant of God (chap. 29), of how he experienced aspects of the curse of the covenant (chap. 30), and of his innocence (chap. 31).

Elihu, the young angry man, was more in tune with Job than the three friends. He did not declare Job a sinless man but that there was sin hidden in him. God's intent with suffering was to draw out that hidden sin (chaps. 32–37). Elihu reflected that he was aware of God's righteous reign over his cosmic kingdom. In many ways Elihu revealed that he thought and spoke as a covenant man.[64]

Yahweh, the Kingdom Lord, Spoke

Job Rebuked (38:1–3)

Job did not reply to Elihu, neither did the three men. God spoke *min hasse'ārâh* (from the storm). It is to be understood that Yahweh (38:1) appeared theophonically in a "whirlwind" in response to Job's declaration that his covenant, sovereign, kingdom Lord would appear from the north in golden splendor and awesome majesty (37:22). And God spoke. He did not reply to Job's request for a day in court in which he would be exonerated (31:35). Yahweh did not answer Job's questions. He directed questions to Job instead which led Job to make two replies. What was the basic message in Yahweh God's questions?

The Lord rebuked Job for speaking as he had. God asked a rhetorical question: *mî zeh mahšîk 'ēṣâ* (who is this that causes counsel to become dark?) (38:2). Yahweh, in a real sense, accused Job of causing darkness. It could be said Job had blinded himself to Yahweh God's way of dealing with him. The Hebrew term 'esah has challenged commentators.[65]

One wrote: " *'ēṣâ*: counsel, design, plan, scheme, purpose, as applied to God's control of the world in the present context may quite appropriately be rendered providence."[66] Another wrote that "this counsel of God is the wisdom that permeates his creative acts and guides his governance of the universe."[67] This counsel of wisdom was caused to be darkened, obscured *bemillin* (by utterances) without knowledge. In other words, ideas that had been uttered on the ash heap were foolish; they were void of insight, discernment, and understanding.

Job Instructed

This speech of Yahweh was addressed to Job. It certainly did apply to the three friends and Elihu also. Newsom has written that Job's friends had spoken from a rich store of cultural resources.[68] Indeed, this speech indicated that they were aware of many aspects of life in the cosmic kingdom. But their knowledge of Yahweh God's wise counsel and governance in Job's situation was erroneous. Their words added to the obscurity of Yahweh God's providential governance of his cosmic kingdom. Hence Job and the four friends were strongly reminded that Yahweh God reigned supremely. Consider the questions that were put to Job. Where were you when I created the world (38:4–6)? Did you hear the song of the stars and the angels' shouts of joy (38:7)? Who controls the universe (38:8–11), gives orders to days and nights (38:12), and removes wickedness (38:13)? Yahweh God proceeded to ask questions concerning many aspects of the cosmic kingdom over which he reigned wisely and omnipotently, e.g., the rain, the snow, the frost, the stars and planets, the wild animals and ravens (38:14–41). God continued by questioning Job concerning life in the animal world. Who knows about goats and does birthing (39:1–4) and about the life of wild donkeys and oxen that are trained to work (39:5–12)? Who knows the way of the ostrich, who lays eggs in warm sand and mistreats its young (38:13–18)? Who made the horse, strong and excitable, serving well in battle (39:19–26) and gave the hawk its unique character and activities (38:26–30)?

Yahweh God's first address was concluded by an important question. In essence it was "Will you now submit?" (40:1, 2). Job had questioned the justice of God. He had protected his innocence and done so in a manner that had reflected on God as unjust. God questioned him therefore concerning his power, greatness, and wise providence demonstrated in his reign over many aspects of the cosmic kingdom. Had Job, in his suffering and turmoil, forgotten God's true character? *hărôb 'im šaddaî yissôr* (Will you take me to court? *rôb* derived from *rîb,* contend in court scene). "Will you accuse me Job?" is the question and added to it is the term derived from *yasar* (to make straight, correct). *'ĕlōâh* (God) referred to Job as one in court *môkujâh* (hiph. Ptc. of *yācâh,* who seeks a conviction or reproof). In a real sense, *'ĕlōâh, šaddaî,* Yahweh let Job know that he had taken the role of a prosecutor as well as judge. He had brought a charge against God's justice and pronounced him guilty. If Job was to truly experience kingdom victory, he had to realize how wrong he had been. To have and enjoy victory, Job had to repent! Job did not make a full confession.[69] He was moving toward repentance. He said, *hēn qallôt mâh' 'ăsîbekâ* (behold, or yes, I was too quick with what do I answer). Job confessed he had been too quick or thoughtless with his mouth.[70] He had no answer and added, "I put my hand on my mouth" (40:4, 5). He added that he would not say anything more.[71] Job admitted guilt but no sorrow. Commentators understand Job to mean that he was unworthy. Yahweh was not satisfied. Still present in the storm, he rebuked Job (40:6) *'eyêr nâ kĕgeber* (the verb is *'āyar* here in the imperative, meaning to gird oneself) Job had to prepare himself for Yahweh's attacks. "Do you attack my justice in order to justify yourself?" (40:7, 8). Yahweh, by referring to his power and deeds, humbled Job by asking him if he could be and act like God (40:9–14). Job, in questioning God's justice, had placed himself above God. To lead Job to full repentance and kingdom victory, he was questioned concerning the *bĕhēmôt.* Could Job make such an animal?[72] Job and the *bĕhēmôt* are creatures made by God. Man is wonderfully made; so are the very different type of creatures such as the *bĕhēmôt* and the *livĕyātān,* (41:1 [MT *40:25*]), usually referred to as a great sea monster.[73]

Job was instructed by Yahweh God that he (God) was just, and also powerful and awesome, as proven by the extraordinary creatures he had created. Job had to understand that Yahweh God was just, sovereign, powerful, and incomprehensible.

As such God always knew what he had done and was doing. And Job, "who are you to question and accuse me?" Job's answer explains that he understood what Yahweh God was communicating to him (42:1–6). He both heard and saw that he truly was the King of the cosmic kingdom.

Job's last words have to be carefully noted. *'al-kēn 'em'as* (therefore I despise [myself] 42:6). The translation, *despise*, according to Dhorme, should not be used.[74] In Job 7:5, 16, it was properly understood as melt away or sink down. Job said, "I mortify myself." Job was completely humiliated. Then he confessed, *wĕniḥamĕtî* (and I repent). His addition of the words in dust and ashes indicated that he truly was filled with remorse.[75] Job had come to complete and genuine repentance. He confessed he had sinned against Yahweh God. The point to be made is that the sin he confessed was not the cause of his suffering. He had not committed this sin before his suffering began. Nor had he when he was first struck (1:22, 2:10). His sin was committed by his disposition toward God and the words he had spoken once the three friends sat with him. His faith, though holding fast, had wavered. In the end, when he repented he achieved victory.

The Friends Addressed (42:7–9).

Yahweh God addressed Eliphaz. He said, "*hāvâh 'appî bĕhô*" (my anger burns against you). Five specific points should be noted. First, the three friends who knew and believed in God had erred in their expression of theological admonitions and accusations against Job. Their theology aroused Yahweh God's displeasure. Second, they had not been a source of comfort and strength to Job. They had assisted Job in directing his mind, heart, and hopes toward God but had done so in a negative and erroneous manner. They had, in a real sense, dishonored God. Third, intercessory prayer by Job was called for on behalf of the friends. Job had to pray for his accusers. This was acceptable to God. Fourth, the friends had to offer sacrifices for themselves to cover the sins they had committed. Fifth, the intercessory pray and sacrifices were efficient and effectual in restoring the friends. Thus they also were partakers in the victory of the kingdom.

Kingdom Victory Demonstrated

The restoration of Job's health and the attention his brothers, sisters, and acquaintances gave him demonstrated that Job was in reality recognized as a victor. He had been struck and he had endured. He had been exonerated. He was restored to his rightful place in society.

The covenant blessings Job received also demonstrated kingdom victory. Job did not earn or deserve these blessings. The context in which he had suffered is an important reality to remember. Satan, under the latitude God had given him, had taken away Job's blessings and that without cause. Yahweh God restored what had been wrongfully taken away. But not only was there restoration; there were added blessings given by a compassionate, forgiving, gracious, and sovereign Lord. Kingdom victory became Job's portion in a rich and full manner.

Wisdom's Role in the Kingdom

Understanding the Concept of Wisdom

In the preceding study an effort was made to define wisdom. A scholar was quoted who had written that wisdom reflects on life and gives guidance to one wishing to understand life in its manifold manifestations.[76] After much study of many sources, agreement was expressed with the author who had written that a single defining definition of wisdom was not possible. It was also noted that concepts closely associated with wisdom are discernment, understanding, knowledge, experiential knowledge, and perception. Since wisdom is such a rich and inclusive reality in life, no person is able to develop, practice, or demonstrate wisdom to the fullest extent. Wisdom calls for hard and humble thinking if there is to be an increase in understanding and demonstrating it.[77] In view of what is reviewed above, the pertinent questions now are: does the book of Job provide some clarity on the meaning of wisdom, and is there progress in divine revelation to be noted?

References to Wisdom

The term *wisdom* appears twenty-three times in the book of Job and the term *wise*, ten times. *Understanding* appears fifteen times; *knowledge*, nine times, and *discern/discernment*, two times.[78] There are thus approximately sixty references to wisdom and its corollaries in the book of Job.[79] There was a search for wisdom that would enable Job and his friends to assess Job's situation correctly.[80] The five men were not able to do this. That, however, does not negate the reality of wisdom as a unifying theme in the entire book of Job. That there is progress in the understanding of the concept is also evident.

A consideration of the speeches will reveal how the five men struggled to find, understand, and apply wisdom. Eliphaz, in his first reply to Job, implied that Job, in his outburst (3:1–26) indicated that he was lacking in wisdom. He had not gained insight into the spiritual values of life or the reasons for human mortality (4:21).[81] Eliphaz went on to say that crafty, wily, scheming people (like Job) may think they are wise but God sweeps them away. Job in reply asked if there was wickedness on his lips and if he could not discern (*yābîn*)[82] malice (6:30). Bildad, bothered by Job's refusal to acknowledge sin, told him to consult the former generations who could instruct with words *millibēm* (from their hearts). The heart is referred to because it is the heart that is the source of memory, attention, intelligence, and wisdom (8:10).[83] So for Eliphaz and Bildad, Job was lacking in wisdom and understanding. He could not discern his sin, that is, distinguish between good and evil.

Job responded that he knew God was *hākām lĕbâb* (wise in heart and mighty in strength) (9:4). God's wisdom and power go together as revealed in the work and wonders of the cosmic kingdom (9:5–13). Job went on to say that he could not understand, comprehend, or discern what God was doing with him in the context of the cosmic kingdom. Stated simply, Job knew he did not have the wisdom to deal with and learn the reason for his suffering.

Zophar responded to Job saying that though Job longed to have God reveal the true secrets of wisdom, it has two sides (11:1–6). One side reveals God's greatness, the other side, man's foolishness. Such a person, witless as a donkey, cannot be wise. Zophar informed Job that he considered Job to be stupid and foolish because he would not admit there was sin and evil in his life. Zophar was certain he had enough wisdom that enabled him to speak for God (11:7–12). Zophar was correct in the abstract when he said a heart devoted to God would have his shame removed and be at peace (11:13–20). He was incorrect and unwise when he applied his words to Job.

Job's response was sharp: will wisdom die with you (12:2)? He referred to himself as a ridiculed man (12:4, 5). But various aspects of the cosmic kingdom, animals and fish, are secure under God's reign and Zophar should learn from them (12:7–11). Furthermore, aged people and long life are blessed with *hākām* (wisdom) and *tĕbûnâh* (discernment/understanding) (12:12). God is the source of these as well as of *gĕbîrâh* (power) and *'ēṣâ* (counsel) 12:13). Job was convinced that if he could only get a court hearing with God, he would receive insight and answers. He longed for God's wisdom and counsel to be revealed. Wisdom, and its corollaries, were not present on the ash heap on which Job sat with his friends around him. The friends could show some wisdom if they became altogether silent (13:5). Job expressed a sense of security in the presence of God in either life or death (13:15–14:22).

Eliphaz replied that a wise man would not talk as Job did. He asked if only Job had access to God's counsel and therefore he alone had wisdom (15:2–9). Eliphaz went on to demonstrate that wicked men suffer—as Job did (15:10–35). Job responded with certainty. Though the friends, lacking in insight, discernment, counsel, wisdom, and knowledge, were miserable comforters (16:2–5), he had one who would intercede for him. He implied that the intercessor would exhibit true wisdom as a friend (16:6–22). Job challenged the three men to exhibit wisdom when he said he would not find a wise man among them (17:10).

As the three men became sharper in their words to Job, basically accusing him of unrepentant wrong, sin, and evil, Bildad ended his speech implying Job was an evil man who did not know God (18:1–21). Job responded asking how long men would torment him. He followed this up with a very unwise declaration: "God has wronged me" (19:6). He pleads for pity from his friends who pursue him as God did (19:21, 22). Then came the uttered wish, "Oh that my words were recorded engraved on a rock forever"(19:23, 24). When he declared that he knew his redeemer lived and he would stand before him eventually, Job suddenly revealed insight and faith. Zophar responded unwisely, describing the end of the wicked (20:1–29). He implied Job would die in his sin and misery. Job replied that he did not complain to men (21:4). But he did ask why the wicked prospered and he suffered (21:5–21). He accused his friends of trying to teach knowledge to God who omnisciently and powerfully judges and adjudicates his purposes. Job informed his friends that they unwisely, foolishly, tried to comfort him with falsehood (21:22–34).

Eliphaz replied that men like Job, who consider themselves wise, are of no benefit to God. In fact, Job is an unrepentant sinner; his wickedness is great (22:1–4). Job is told to submit to God and then he would be restored. He should receive instruction from God and he would be blessed. Eliphaz's view was that it would be wise of Job to repent and then he would be blessed again (22:21–30). In the discussion that followed Eliphaz's call to repentance, there is a struggle to achieve "wisdom" but it eludes the men on the ash heap because of their accusations and complaints. With exasperation Job began his final response. He, in effect, said that all that the men had said did not provide wisdom that they implied Job lacked (26:1–4). Job continued to acknowledge God's display of wisdom in creation and his rule over it (26:5–14). He continued stating his conviction that God denied him justice (27:1–6) as did his fellowmen who were wicked and did evil. They would receive their due just punishment (27:7–22). Justice can be observed in life. But can wisdom, the necessary virtue to discern, understand, and know God's mind and ways be found anywhere? Job soliloquized. He indicated that he had a wide profound knowledge of the natural aspects of the cosmic kingdom (28:1–22).[84] In the midst of these thoughts about creation's wonders, many of them found by means of mining (28:1–11) the question is pointedly rhetorical, "Where can wisdom be found?" (28:12). Not in mines or by mining precious minerals (although it requires wisdom to mine). Wisdom is not to be found in the marketplace where earth's costliest jewels can be acquired (28:13–17). Wisdom's price exceeds all (28:18, 19). So the question was repeated: where is wisdom to be found? It is to be found in a specific relationship with God who has revealed wisdom in his creating and providential reigning activities. *Yir'ēt 'adōnai* (the fear of sovereign [God]) is the relationship that identifies wisdom (28:28). This fear of God is positive and its necessary negative correlate is understanding that is demonstrated by shunning evil.

This passage, 28:27, 28, presents what is an absolute requirement for learning what the missing aspect in the dialogue on the ash heap is. Men searched and sparred with words, argued and made false accusations as they searched for the reason why Job suffered. Though, as reviewed above, they spoke of wisdom, it was not effectively present. There were slight hints regarding it, but it was not grasped. Job reached a sublime high point when he reflected on how the richest minerals on earth could be found and possessed, but that wisdom was not acquired in a similar manner.

In the progress of revelation, as recorded in the Old Testament, Job struggling for answers to his problems, was given insight to proclaim what was spoken also by others. The Psalmist (like David) referred to the fear of Yahweh as the *rē'šît* (beginning) of wisdom (Ps. 111:10). Solomon repeated this (Prov. 1:7). The term translated *beginning* is derived from the noun meaning head. At the head of, or in front of, or the source of wisdom is the fear of Yahweh. Wisdom has its origin in Yahweh God. Persons in relationship with Yahweh God have the means to achieve and demonstrate wisdom.

Four terms or concepts in this passage (28:27, 28) call for clearer comprehension. The term *fear* (Heb. *yârā'*) has three distinct references: to be afraid, to be or stand in awe of, and to honor and reverence. In the context being considered, the idea of being afraid is not apropos. The other two are. To stand in awe of Yahweh God calls for an acknowledgment of the sovereignty, majesty, splendor, and power of God. And to honor or reverence Yahweh God refers to the response one makes to Yahweh God. Thus to honor and reverence Yahweh God, one must stand in awe as one serves and worships him. These actions express a living reciprocal relationship in which God bestows blessings and virtues that open the way to receiving wisdom and understanding. Yahweh God bestows these undeserved gifts upon the serving, worshiping, reverencing, and honoring person. Stated simply, God gives his wisdom to such persons. A later classic example is Yahweh God giving Solomon wisdom (1 Kings 4:20–34).[85] But, in the Jobian context, such wisdom was not given; the fear of Yahweh God was missing. True, Job was afraid of God; he had said in effect that the rod of God was upon him and he was terrified (21:6–9), and his heart was faint because he was in terror before God because God had terrified him (23:15, 16). To be afraid and filled with terror does not serve to receive wisdom.

Of the various requirements to receive the gift of wisdom, along with fear of God properly understood (as discussed in the preceding paragraphs), is an open and humble heart that is submissive to God and the presence of the Holy Spirit.[86] These requirements are discussed more fully in following chapters.[87]

The term or concept of wisdom requires specific attention in this context.[88] Wisdom (*hokmâh*) is the noun derived from the verb *hakam* (to be wise). The adjective *wise* describes some integral aspects. To be wise is said to be skillful in technical and administrative affairs; to be shrewd and cunning in dealing with people, to be prudent in legal and ethical situations, and to be submissive to the Spirit in religious matters. The person who is wise as described above is said to have wisdom and demonstrates it.

There was no wisdom demonstrated on the ash heap; it must be stressed that wisdom and the exhibition of it were sought. But there was no Spirit-induced fear of God; the Spirit was ignored. Men sought wisdom as they were inclined to from their own context. They referred to God but were not submissive to him. They were not skillful and shrewd in interacting and dealing with each other.

A third term in this passage is *bînâh*. It is derived from the verb *bîn,* having the distinct meaning of to discern. When one discerns one considers all issues involved in a situation and seeks to understand and comprehend each issue as to their character, value, and contribution. To discern then is to separate the issues from each other; to put space between them so that each can be considered separately. In this way, truth, error, good, and evil can be considered and evaluated and the wise person who is skillful can be discerning and come to correct conclusions.

The fourth term is a phrase: *sûr mērâ'* (to turn aside from evil). To turn aside from evil is to reject or repudiate the wrong. This term carries various shades of meaning, for example that which is bad, wrong, displeasing, harmful, and unkind. It is the opposite of good, correct, right, pleasing, and helpful. A clear distinction had to be made. The discerning person, submissive in heart and mind to the Spirit of God, considering the various issues involved in a context of pain, misery, and grief would be able to observe the differences between the good and evil. That one would turn from the latter and take and hold up the good. So doing, one demonstrated discernment and exhibited wisdom.[89]

On the ash heap, where Job sat in abject sorrow and physical pain, he had not been in the frame of mind or propensity of heart to fully discern the right, the good from the wrong, or the evil. He was too deeply influenced by his tragic experiences. He, however, as a man of faith did know what he should do. He said it: he was at a high point in his spiritual attitude and relationship with God but he failed to fully apply what he said so eloquently and forcefully. His three fellowmen who accused him of sin and having a hardened, unrepentant heart were far greater offenders. They did not shun sin or evil because they were convinced, wrongly, they had discerned evil in Job's life.

Having attained a high point in his reflections, thinking, and speaking, Job again reverted to discoursing about his life before tragedy struck him. He had walked and served uprightly as a faithful covenant man in the context of the cosmic kingdom (29:1–31:34). He concluded with a cry for someone, God or any person, to listen to him as he defended himself (31:35–40).

Elihu Introduced

Elihu filled the void of silence. The four older men who had searched for discernment and wisdom had failed to properly discern Job's situation and to understand his complaints. They had given clear evidence they had no correct knowledge, for they lacked wisdom. So, Elihu the young man, angry because of the three men's false accusations against Job, declared that he had the Spirit to give him understanding and enable one to be wise (32:7, 8, 9, 13). He repeated that the Spirit of God was a powerful agent in his life (33:4). He rebuked Job for accusing God of finding fault with him (33:8–11). Elihu then orated on how God carries out his purposes and how God hears and answers prayer (33:12–30). Job had to listen to Elihu to learn wisdom (33:33). Elihu told the four men of learning, whom he referred to as wise, to test words and learn together for the good of all (34:1–4).

Elihu addressed Job specifically, saying Job had accused God unjustly. God does no wrong (34:1–10). God is just, repaying sinful men with what they deserve (34:11, 13). Elihu then became quite eloquent as he spoke of God's sovereign rule over life and death; he sees all men and is impartial in his judgment. He referred to Job as speaking without knowledge; rebellion added to his hidden sin (34:13–37). Elihu continued to extol God's virtues, his own insight, knowledge, and understanding, and to call Job to repentance (35:1–37:20). He concluded saying as one cannot look to the sun so one cannot see the Almighty God exalted in power, justice, and righteousness fully. But, this great God does not oppress men. Therefore God is worthy of reverence from the wise in heart (37:21–24)

Comment: Elihu revealed that he had insight into God's ways. He exhibited flashes of wisdom when he referred to God's rule over the cosmic kingdom. But

Elihu lacked wisdom to a great extent. He was not aware of the influence of the power and influence of Satan and his parasite dominion. Elihu, was not wise nor just in calling Job to repent of hidden sins that Elihu considered to be the cause of his affliction.

Yahweh's Theophanic Appearance

In a theophanic appearance (out of the storm, 38:1), Yahweh God spoke directly to Job but in the hearing of the four accusers who had not spoken correctly of Job (38:1–39:30). Job himself, however, had not spoken correctly or wisely either. He had darkened God's *'ēṣâ* (counsel, wisdom). He had not honored the King of the cosmic kingdom who revealed himself in many ways in his providential rule over all aspects of the created world. Yahweh God revealed his wisdom in the glories of the morning, in the springs of the sea , in the light and darkness that appear, in the rain that falls, in the stars and constellations that sparkle, in the lightning that flashes, in the mountain goats that reproduce, and in the stubborn wild ox, in the unusual ways of the ostrich, in the power of the horse, and in the soaring eagle. The open book of creational natural revelation had not been read correctly. Job and the four men had not observed God's sovereign and wonderfully wise control over the universe in which they lived. Their eyes had, as it were, blinders that hindered them; hence in their speeches they overshadowed and darkened their eyes, preventing them from seeing God's great deeds in everyday life in which divine wisdom was so brilliantly revealed and demonstrated.

Yahweh God then addressed Job asking him if he, in his contentions with his Lord would correct him? Would Job condemn God to justify himself and challenge Job to serve himself (40:1–14)? God then referred to the *Bĕhēmôt* and Leviathan that had been created by God and given its characteristics. The question basically was: do you challenge God, the creator, ruler, and provider of all aspects—even of great beasts, with injustice and lacking wisdom in his reign over the cosmic kingdom? Job's reply was that he knew of God's many virtues and he had not considered them correctly. Job repented. He confessed his lack of understanding. He confessed his lack of wisdom! Hartley has written that Job's concern for vindication was shifted to his need to prepare his heart for God. The integrity of Job's faith shone brightly.[90]

Notes

1. The bibliography of chap. 34 is intended to serve the following four chapters. See Dhorme's explanation. *Job*, 73. Also Kroeze, *Job*, 67.

2. Dhorme, *Job,* 73. Cf. Cline's *Job 1–20,* which suggested Job uttered a sentiment in tune with the generalization of pessimistic wisdom, 36. Pope, *Job,* wrote, "This utterance is a piece with other pessimistic observations on human fate," 16.

3. The verb is the hithpalel imperfect of *sāhâh,* to bow down (cf. *BDB*, 1005).

4. Delitzch, *Job*, vol. 1, 65.

5. Habel, *Job*. Habel went on to write, however, that Job later denounced God's sovereign deeds as arbitrary, unjust, and cruel. This comment should not be taken seriously, 93.

6. Kroeze, *Job*, 56.

7. Hartley, *Job*, 77, 78.

8. Thomas, *The Storm*, 45–48.

9 See note 5 above.

10. See Victor Sasson's article "Job's Wife." Sasson responded to an essay by D. Clines, who took an unconventional stance in discussing the role of Job's wife.

11. Newsom, "Job and His Friends," 239–53.

12. Cf. her Introduction, 321–22.

13. Perdue, *Wisdom and Creation*, 124–26.

14. Ibid., 136–42.

15. Bruce Vawter wrote concerning "The Hidden God." Job could not find him, much less reach him. Vawter considered Job's wife as a new invention to assume the role of tempter, doing Satan's work.

16. *Soul Struggle*, entire treatise, 75 pages.

17. Perdue, *Wisdom and Creation*, 23.

18. Perdue wrote that the view that redemptive history takes priority over creation cannot be defended by reference to the Hebrew Bible itself. Ibid. 34. He also wrote that images of creation abound in the Bible. Ibid., 133.

19. Ibid., 26.

20. See the next section on God and Satan's interactions.

21. The etymology of the term *shaddaî* is uncertain. The verb *shadad* means to deal violently with. In some cases it could be argued that Job, using that name, referred to the violence he incurred at God's hand. Another possibility is *shadâh*, but this is an unknown term. The name *shaddaî* in the biblical context should be understood to mean the all-sufficient, powerful One. The term *Almighty* can be understood to express this combination of terms.

22. Perdue understood Job to admit God was wise and mighty, but that Job denied God was just, *Wisdom and Creation,* 152. It is more correct to say Job questioned whether God was just rather than to say he denied it.

23. Pippin, "Job 42:1–6." Her statement is correct but her explanation, quoting an author, that Job in reality was a "scapegoat" calls for serious reconsideration, 300. E. W. Nicholson has defined theodicy as "a vindication of divine justice in allowing the existence of evil" and added that theodicy has limits in the book of Job. See his essay "The Limits of Theodicy as a Theme in the book of Job," in *Wisdom in Ancient Israel*, 70–82. It is true that the book of Job does not present the entire scope of God's justice in regard to human suffering.

24. Crenshaw, *Old Testament Wisdom*, 92.

25. See what I wrote about Satan, the origin of evil and the parasite dominion in my study of Genesis 1–3. *From Creation to Consummation*, vol. I, 98–104.

26. Green, *Conflict*, 22.

27. Thomas, *The Storm*, 27–31.

28. In natural life a parasite can destroy the very source it depends on.

29. The idea of permission basically includes the thought that the one who gives permission retains control.

30. Job 1:6.

31. See my various references to the antithesis in *From Creation to Consummation*. vol. I, 127–29, 450, where the absolute character of the antithesis is indicated.

32. It should be emphasized that because Satan was involved in Job's suffering, that it must not be concluded that all human suffering is satanically induced and controlled. The human condition in the cosmic kingdom is such that it readily is subject to pain, suffering, and loss.

33. Reference has been made to Job's initial experience in previous parts, e.g., chap. 2, and page 47 of this chapter.

34. Nicholson has written, "Job suffered unto a good end, he would prosper to an extent." "Limits of Theodicy," 70–82.

35. It should be repeated that I am indebted to the book written by C. Can Gelderen, *Job's Soul-struggles.*

36. Pope, *Job* (1965 ed.) quoted a Jewish tradition that the three friends entered together, seemingly each without knowledge of the others coming, 24. See also Clines, *Job 1–20,* on the coming and purpose of the three friends: they were wholly supportive in intention, 57.

37. Thomas wrote that they covenanted together to comfort Job. They believed in God. *Storm*, 60.

38. Cf. Clines, *Job*, 57.

39. Ellison, *From Tragedy*, opined that the friends may have been rising to leave after seven days of silent mourning when Job suddenly spoke. 30.

40. Ibid. 31.

41. Ibid. 32.

42. Thomas, *The Storm*, 75.

43. Habel stated that Job explained his personal hope. *Job*, 146.

44. Ibid. 148–50.

45. Carlyle, *Exposition*, 60.

46. Thomas, *The Storm* commences his study of Job by correctly observing that getting tired of his friends, Job really wanted to talk with them about his condition, 125.

47. See the next section on wisdom revealed.

48. Cf. Thomas, *Storm*, 131ff.

49. Dhorme, *Job,* LC.

50. Hartley, *Job*, 271–72.

51. Kroeze, *Job*, Bildad employed graphic language to describe his reaction to Job's speech, it was as a *stortvloed* (torrent) and an incomprehensible *woordenvloed* (flood of words), 206.

52. The NIV translation, torment, could be considered an overstatement.

53. This passage is studied in depth in chap. 37.

54. Dhorme, *Job*, LC.

55. Eliphaz basically accuses Job of covenant breaking. See chap. 36 for a full discussion.

56. Dhorme translated the first line: "Why have times been hidden from *Shaddaî*" *Job*, 353. Delitzsch, "Wherefore are not bounds reserved for the Almighty?" *Job*, vol. II, 15. Thomas interpreted the phrase as: Why does God not have a regular circuit for judging? *The Storm*, 189. Hartley: "Since times are not hidden from *Shaddaî*," *Job*, 343.

57. Cf. Hartley, *Job*, 342–43.

58. Some conservative scholars question whether this chapter is complete. Should the last part of the previous chapter be considered part of chapter 25? Also, in view of Bildad's two previous speeches he may have said more this time also. Cf, e.g., Kroeze, *Job*, 284.

59. Scholars inclined to resort to unnecessary textual criticism have transposed some verses, e.g., 26:5–9 to 25, thinking the description of the awesome mysteries of God should be added to Bildad's description of God. Dhorme, *Job*, 370; Habel, *Job*, 370. And, evidently insisting on symmetry, 27:13–23 is ascribed to Zophar as his last speech. Dhorme, *Job*, 386. Habel, *Job,* 383ff. The thoughts expressed in 27:13–23 are not inconsistent with Job's train of thought. Cf. Kroeze, *Job*, 289. Hartley ascribed these words to Bildad, suggesting that he drew heavily on Zophar's last speech, chapter 20, *Job*, 359.

60. Cf. Delitzsch, *Job* II, 50; Kroeze, *Job*, 286.

61. William Bode, *The Book of Job* (Grand Rapids: Eerdmans 1914), 198.

62. "The inference is clear: Bildad's contribution was inspired . . . by Satan."

63. This section, 26:4–31:40, is studied in more detail in chap. 36.

64. See fuller discussion of Elihu in chap. 36.

65. The verb root of *'ēśâh* is *yā'aś* which is usually taken to mean advice or counsel.

66. Pope, *Job*, 250.

67. Hartley, *Job*, 491.

68. Newsom, "Job—Friends," 239.

69. Thomas, *The Storm*, 297.

70. Kroeze, *Job*, 442.

71. Kroeze briefly discussed how textual critics have attempted to rewrite the text by reducing God's speech to one. Ibid. 442.

72. Commentators present different ideas concerning the *bĕhēmôt*. Habel saw the noun as an intensive plural meaning "The great Beast." It is purposefully described in ambiguous terms, thereby preventing any covert identification with known animals. *Job*, 564–65. Hartley, *Job*, 524–25, and Kroeze, (*Job*, 445–46), however, attempt to find the crocodile or the hippopatamus in the description.

73. Job had referred to Leviathan when he spoke of cursing his day of birth. Asaph used leviathan to refer to monstrous Egypt (Ps. 74:14). The Psalmist in 104:26 referred to leviathan as a sea or ocean creature; Isaiah did also (27:1).

74. Dhorme, *Job*, 646–47.

75. Kroeze, *Job*, 468. Habel wrote the meaning of the term *nḥm* is disputed but concludes that the term should be translated repent/relent *Job*, 376.

76. Chapter 34, note 1.

77. Chap. 34, 29–30.

78. Cf. the NIV.

79. At times when the word wisdom occurs in the NIV it may not be a translation of *hokmah*. An example is in 9:4. The Hebrew has *hakam*, an adjective, but the translation has *wisdom*.

80. Richard L. Schultz, "Unity and Diversity in Wisdom Theology," *Tyndale Bulletin*, 48 (1997): 271–306, esp. 285.

81. Hartley, *Job*, 115.

82. To discern is to be able to see and understand aspects of life as these are related and mutually influence each other. Discernment is a very necessary ability in gaining and demonstrating wisdom.

83. Dhorme, *Job*, 117.

84. Critical scholars have not considered chap. 28 to be an integral part of the discourse between Job and his fellowmen. A conservative writer, Hartley, wrote that chap. 28 does

not match well with any of the speakers. But it does serve as a bridge between the preceding dialogue and speeches that follow. *Job*, 373.

85. Solomon's wisdom is discussed in chap. 43.

86. Walther Eichrodt, in his *Theology of the Old Testament*, trans. J. A. Baker, 4th ed. (Philadelphia: Westminster, 1964) has written about the role of the Holy Spirit in applying wisdom and the law. Cf. 63 and other references in the index of subjects.

87. Cf. chaps. 46, 47.

88. Some comments on wisdom were made previously in chap. 33, 6–8, when wisdom literature was defined.

89. A practical application: I am a father of eight children—six are sons. They at times could get into a serious quarrel or fight. I felt I had to separate and adjudicate and do it with discernment and wisdom. To do that I had to determine *who* was the "main culprit," *who* was the innocent, *why* he was upset *when* he had become angry, *where* he was when he did so, and the *way* he felt was proper to settle the quarrel. With the five terms beginning with *w*, I usually was able to settle the dispute. Too often, when in haste I missed one of them (a *w* word) I finished up not solving the problem and feeling foolish.

90. Hartley, *Job*, 537.

36

The Covenant in the Book of Job

I. Introductory Comments

II. Understanding the Idea of the Covenant

III. Elements of Covenant

IV. Demonstration of Job's Covenantal Relationship

V. Covenantal Emphases in the Book of Job

VI. Conclusion

36

The Covenant in the Book of Job

Introductory Comments

Does the Book of Job Deal with the Covenant?

The question can legitimately be asked: is it correct to refer to the covenant in the book of Job? The phrase *bĕrît kārat* occurs once in the entire book (31:1), and there the meaning of the term *bĕrît* can be understood variously. Another question could be raised concerning the knowledge and use of the idea of a covenant in the times of Job. Was the knowledge of Yahweh God's covenant with Adam/Eve, Noah, and Abraham known in the land of Uz, Job's homeland?

Few Writers Refer to the Covenant

Very few commentators on Job refer to the concept or idea of covenant, except when a discussion of 31:1 includes a reference to it. Few biblical theology authors and students refer to the idea of covenant when writing on Job.[1] And if one is to develop the thesis that the book of Job includes covenant theology, the caution that Lindsay Wilson called for must be heeded. He urged that one dominant theme in the book of Job, namely, "the fear of God," should not be considered the inclusive theme that would serve as a basis and source for a covenant theology of the Old Testament. His basic point is that wisdom and covenant strands speak of the "Fear of the Lord." Job has it as an important theme. Since it does, covenant theology, dealing with "the fear of the Lord" should not be considered that the only and basic theme. Other covenantal themes are present.[2] In the study that follows, it will be demonstrated that there are a number of concepts and themes in the book of Job that are thoroughly covenantal.

Understanding the Idea of the Covenant[3]

At the heart of the covenant is the idea of a bond. This bond can be established in various social contexts, for example, in the legal, business, and social areas of life. Yahweh God's covenant with creation was established when he created the cosmic kingdom (the universe) and established himself as its King. Hence there is a royal bond between Yahweh God and the cosmic kingdom. Yahweh God established a special and specific bond (covenant) when he created male and female in his image. It was a bond of life and love, bonding himself to humanity. God gave them his mandates. Adam and Eve violated this creation bond (covenant of life and love), but Yahweh God immediately declared that his covenant (bond) with humanity would continue. He established the redemptive aspect of covenant, that is, through the seed of the woman (Gen. 3:14, 16) the bond of love and life would continue between Yahweh God and humanity.

Elements of Covenant

Survey of Basic Aspects

A short survey of what elements were involved in a covenant will assist in understanding that the book of Job is strongly covenantal.

A covenant always included two parties, the suzerain (lord, God) and the vassal (agent, man). A covenant included requirements, stipulations, and obligations on the part of each party. The lord was required to keep the stipulations and promises. The vassal was required to submit, obey, and carry out obligations involved in a covenant. Furthermore the assurance (promise) of blessing to be given by the Lord and curses to be executed were involved. Covenant keeping by the vassal, man, agent, would result in blessings—the continuity of life, love and friendship. Covenant breaking would have the consequence of Yahweh God expressing his wrath, that is, in executing the curse. A covenant was sealed by an oath and provisions were included for the continuity of a covenant.[4]

The Redemptive Aspect of the Creation Covenant

There is more to be said about inherent aspects of God's creation/redemptive covenant. These were integrally involved in the covenant with creation and sustained and upheld as integral aspects of the redemptive covenant. Reference is specifically to the three relationships and mandates. These relationships are the spiritual relationship between God and humanity; the social relationship between male and female, their offspring, and fellowmen; the cultural relationship between humanity and the natural/material dimensions of the cosmic kingdom. These three relationships must be seen as having a profound integral, mutually interdependent involvement with each other. That is to say, violating the cultural mandate has tragic effects on the other two relationships. Each has a direct bearing on and influences on the other two. Thus to violate one has the effect of violating, at least to a great extent, the others.

The Mandates

Each relationship has its unavoidable mandate. The spiritual calls for submission to, obedience to, and continual fellowship on the part of humanity with Yahweh God, the maker and sustainer of the covenant. The social calls for upholding the God-ordained demands for the male and female in marriage, procreation, and proper attitudes to and interaction with fellow men and women. The cultural relationship demands obedience to Yahweh God in cultivating and beautifying the natural aspects of creation.[5]

The brief delineation of the essence and aspects of the covenant as surveyed are found throughout Scripture. Again, the question can be raised: are these integral to biblical wisdom literature?[6] Are these integral to the book of Job? It is the intent of this chapter to demonstrate that the covenant is a definite factor in the book of Job, properly considered a wisdom book.

The Covenantal Lawsuit

The Biblical References

As we proceed to a detailed study of the covenantal theology in Job, still another important reality in the biblical revelation of the covenant must be clearly discerned. The covenant Yahweh God established is of such a nature that it often results in a type of lawsuit. The prophets have demonstrated this to be a reality. When the vassal, agent, participant violated his required role in the covenant Yahweh God "entered into a lawsuit" with the violators.[7]

The question again is: does Job exhibit a covenant lawsuit? That answer is that it does.[8]

The Scene of the Lawsuit Revealed in the Book of Job

The scene of the covenant lawsuit is not solely on earth or in heaven. It was initiated in heaven. The text does not indicate that someone received a vision. The reality is that God called the *bĕnê hā'ĕlōhîm* (sons of God) to come and stand before *Yĕhwâh*. Two comments must be made immediately. The phrase *wayĕhî hayyôm* indicates that a specific time (day) was set for the "sons of God" to *lĕhiṭyaśśēb* (stand before, report to Yahweh). The covenant name Yahweh indicates it is to be understood that this was a covenantal activity. Yahweh God, the covenant King, held court on a specific day on which those "who belonged to him"[9] were called to appear before him to report on their activities. The intent of calling the "sons" was not to have a court scene in which charges were to be made. Rather, the intent was that all those in service to Yahweh were to report what they had been involved in as they went about their covenantal duties. This scene presented the opportunity for a specific legal situation to unfold.

The Participants

Among those who belonged to God and who came to give an account of their activities was *haśśāṭān* (the satan), the adversary.[10] It is his presence that especially brings out the legal aspect, the covenant lawsuit dimension of the gathering of those "belonging to God." Yahweh God initiated the exchange of words. He inquired of Satan if he, in his going about the earth, as Satan said he had been doing, *hăśamĕtâ libbĕken 'al 'abdî 'iyyôb* (have you given your heart to my servant Job?) Yahweh God inquired of Satan if he had given attention to Job in the sense of setting desire on him. Yahweh God reminded Satan that Job was a faithful covenant man (1:8). The question and characterization of Job set the stage for Satan to make his twofold accusation—one against God, the other against Job. He accused God of supplying Job with an abundance of material possessions and thus putting a hedge,[12] a protecting barrier, around him. Satan accused God of buying Job's devotion. God had secured Job's allegiance with a generous bribe. The accusation against Job was that he really was not his own man. Material possessions made him a devotee to God. He served God as payment for his rich good life.

The contest has been set. Will Yahweh God put a countercharge against Satan? Is there to be an open legal discourse with an eventual winner—either God or Satan? The wisdom of God was vividly demonstrated. Let Job settle the dispute. He can do so by whatever means you devise. God said that he, the sovereign One, gave Satan the latitude to deal with Job, and with all that he had. God did not give Job freedom to do all he could. Satan did have the ability and power to bring devastation and suffering into Job's life. But he was restrained by God. Satan could not take Job's life. In a real sense, God set the stage for Satan to attack and devastate Job. To kill Job would not have settled the lawsuit. Job had to remain alive to demonstrate that he was not bought and influenced by material possessions, social and physical well-being. Job had to demonstrate that to be a covenant man was to be this whatever happened.

Job Revealed as a Covenant Man

Satan's Desire Regarding Job

It should be clearly understood that the legal contest was basically between God and Satan. Job's covenant relationship with Yahweh God was the central and crucial issue in this contest. Obviously Satan strongly desired to have Job in his service. Job could and would not be if his covenant relationship with Yahweh God held firmly.

The question to be answered is: how can the reader/student of the Scriptures be assured that Job was a covenant man? He is never referred to directly as such in the book of Job. There is no reference to God making a covenant with him as he did with Adam, Noah, Abraham, Jacob, and David. The evidence that Job was is spelled out. Covenant terms are employed to characterize Job.

Job's Covenantal Character

Four specific characteristics describe Job as a faithful covenant man. *tâm* is the first term that appears in the text (1:1). The adjectival form of this verb was used to describe Noah, who was said to be *tamin*. As a verb and adjective it refers to completeness, integrity, sound, blameless and innocent. These are terms that describe and qualify a faithful covenant man. Abram was called to be thus as Yahweh God confirmed his covenant with him (Gen. 12:1). Israel, the covenant people, when entering Canaan, a land filled with detestable practices and idols was called to be blameless (Deut. 18:9–13). David testified to his being blameless before God (2 Sam. 22:24, 25; cf. also Pss. 18:23, 25; 26:1, 11). Job was also described as a *yāšar* and the adjective refers to one being straight and right. In an ethical sense it refers to a person being straightforward and upright in attitudes, communications, and activities. Samuel, in his farewells, addressed to the covenant people, Israel, telling them he would pray for them and teach them the way that was good and *yāšar* (upright), that is, the covenant way of life (1 Sam. 12:22). Two other characteristics of the faithful covenant man were included *yârā' 'ĕlōhîm* (feared God)[13] and *sār mērā'* turned from evil). Job was consistently a covenant man. His covenantal relationship with Yahweh God was consistent with the spiritual mandate, as was his social relationship with his fellow human beings and his relationship with the entire cultural dimensions of life were complete, sound, and wholesome.

Demonstration of Job's Covenantal Relationship

Job, the Image Bearer

Job was a covenant man by virtue of his creation in God's image. He was described as a man who had and demonstrated covenant qualities and characteristics. Did Job in actual life's situations demonstrate this covenant relationship and character? There are evidences recorded in the biblical text that Job, in his daily life, was consistently a covenant keeping man.

In Regard to His Family

Yahweh God had blessed Job and his wife with offspring. His seven sons and three daughters were covenant seed. The sons, it is recorded, had feasts by turn in their homes and invited their sisters to join them in eating and drinking. There was obviously harmony in Job's family. As a covenant father, Job was concerned about this offspring's spiritual, social, and cultural attitudes and activities, particularly as these were expressed during the periods of feasting. Job did his parental duty.

In terms of Old Testament practices, Job sacrificed a burnt offering for them for the purpose of sanctifying them. The term *wayĕqaddĕšēm* (1:5) can be variously translated. The verbal root, *qādaš*, has the basic meaning of to set apart or to consecrate. In its piel form in the text the specific thought is that Job, by sacrificing on their behalf, meant to purify them and thus consecrate them to their covenant Lord. Thus Job performed a priestly function. As a father he knew he had a covenant duty on behalf of his sons and daughters.

The text holds before readers and students an intriguing question. Job did not say that he expected his children to openly sin against the Lord. He said that possibly they did so *belebabam* (in their hearts). That Job so thought indicated that he was concerned for the entire person; he realized that as there were sins committed in words and deeds, so also in the inner person—by thoughts, inclinations, and desires. Job realized that in the inner person it was possible that they had sinned *wŭbērăkû* (and blessed?) God. The term *bārak*, which appears in a piel stem (1:5, 10, 11; 2:5, 9; 31:20; 40:12), in the pual (1:21), and once as a noun (29:13), has the primary accepted meaning of to "bless" when used with God as object. When so used it usually has the intent to express praise or worship. The question therefore is, why is it translated as curse in some instances, as in 1:5, 11, but bless in 1:10? Dhorme has called attention to some textual variants where the term *qillĕlû* appears. This term is best translated as curse, but the sense of curse is not as absolutistic as *'ārâr* is. *qālal* expresses a mitigated sense of curse. The reality to be faced, nevertheless, is why the Masoretic text employs the term *bārak* if the context quite readily calls for the term *qālal* in one stem or another.[14] One common explanation is the standard euphemism theory. This theory is based on the idea that the author or a later editor did not wish to give even the impression or a hint of a curse directed to God.[15]

It would seem preferable to consider the use of the term *bārak* in a euphemistic way. The context strongly suggests that Job, knowing the sinful propensities of the human heart, believed it possible that one or more of his children sinned against God. As a priestly, covenant father, he did his parental duty. He sacrificed on their behalf, believing that thus he would bring sanctity and blessing into his family—should it be necessary. Job thus demonstrated by his sacrificing activity that he was a faithful covenant father.

In Regard to His Possessions

Job is described as a wealthy man. His possessions, in terms of patriarchal times, were numerous. He had cattle, sheep, donkeys, land, and houses (his children lived in these). He was recognized as a wise, wealthy, and influential man in his community. He had a prominent role in his community. He testified in his last speech that he had led a useful life in his community. God was his intimate friend and drenched his pathway with cream (29:6). He sat as a leader and judge in the gate of the city. He served in the public square (29:7). He was honored and praised. He used his wealth to "rescue the poor" and "help the fatherless." He brought joy to widows and helped the blind. He was a father to the needy and befriended strangers. He opposed the wicked and rescued their victims (29:8–17). Job, the wealthy and honored man, had demonstrated how a blessed man could and did serve his covenant Lord in the social and cultural dimensions of covenant life.

In Regard to God

Job maintained his covenantal, spiritual relationship with God.[16] The loss of his children and material possessions did not influence this relationship in a negative manner. Rather, learning of his losses he honored his covenant Lord.[17] His testimony gave a strong expression of Job's awareness that all he had and was, was a gift from God. He said "*yĕhwâh nātan, wahwâh lāqaḥ*" (Yahweh gave, Yahweh took away). He recognized the sovereignty of his Lord. He added that in his losses *yĕhî sēm yĕhwâh mĕbōrak* (let the name of Yahweh be praised, worshiped). The pual stem of *bārak* expressed a strong, fervent desire to praise and worship Yahweh God his covenant Lord who had dealt with him by giving and taking possessions.

When Job became afflicted and suffered terrible pain he was in agony. His relationship with God became cloudy and tenuous. Yet, throughout the entire period of suffering, Job did not disown his covenant Lord. He did not understand why he, as a faithful covenant man, had to endure agonizing pain, physically, socially, and psychologically. And when his friends accused him of sins, whether done secretly, inadvertently, or unconsciously, Job sank into deep despair. But slowly he rose and recovered his awareness of being in a living relationship with his covenant Lord.[18]

In Regard to His Wife

Job's wife is referred to twice in the book of Job. She told Job to curse God and die (2:9, 10). And Job referred to how, in his sickness and pain, his breath had become "offensive" to his wife and he had become loathsome to his own brothers (19:17). The term translated offensive is *zārâh*. The verbal root is debated.[19] The phrase "his own brothers" is the translation of *libĕnê bitênî*.[20] The main point is that Job, a covenant man, brother, and husband, had become offensive and repulsive to his immediate family. He was a covenant outcast.

His wife, the closest and most intimate covenant person in his life, spoke in an unexpected manner. Scholars are not agreed on how to interpret her role.[21] It would seem proper to speak of her positively to begin with. As Sasson has written, Job loved his wife and remained faithful to her (31:9, 10). He was not enticed by young virgins (31:1). Job's wife had given birth to ten children before Job's trial and ten afterward. This mother must have been an attractive lady; she gave birth to six beautiful daughters.[22] The text does not give many particulars about her; tradition recorded that her name was Dinah. Some writers try to explain her words as evidence of sympathy. It was very difficult for the wife to observe the person closest and dearest to her wracked with pain, suffering, and humiliated. She may have known what the Scriptures (Lev. 24:17) prescribed: death for the one who blasphemed God. Commentators are not agreed on how to relate "curse" and "die" in the wife's comments. Could it be she meant "curse and be put to death" or "curse and your death will come soon"? It would seem proper to consider her to think, "you are suffering, for whatever reason, the curse of the covenant. Accept that reality. So respond with cursing and die. There is no hope for you."

Commentators have asked: why Job's wife was not taken from Job when he lost all his possessions and his children. Satan did not take her away. It is doubtful that Satan considered that a covenant marriage should not be dissolved by a tragic death. Rather Satan was fully aware of the covenant relationships between God and man, between husband and wife and their children, and the male and female relationship to the cultural dimensions of the cosmic kingdom. Involved in these relationships are the divinely posited mandates. Man/woman, in the image of God, were called to maintain their covenantal relationship with Yahweh God. They likewise were called to submit to, obey, and carry out the mandates regarding the covenantal social and cultural relationships. The point to be stressed now is that these three relationships and the mandates involved in each are closely, firmly, and mutually integrated. That is to say, to disobey and violate the cultural relationship and mandate places a strain on the other two. Thus, if the intent is to break the spiritual relationship and its requirements, a real effort to do so can be made by attacking and seeking to thwart one or both of the others.

Satan had not been able to break or destroy the covenantal relationship between Job and God by dealing with Job's cultural relationship. Satan was given the latitude to totally dispossess Job. Likewise, Satan attacked Job's spiritual relationship with God by taking away his social heritage—his covenant seed. Job's comment, "The Lord has given and the Lord has taken," testifies to Job's full awareness of the Lord's involvement in the social and cultural areas of covenantal life.

What was the last and hopefully most effective way of breaking Job's covenantal spiritual relationship with Yahweh God? Satan knew how he had broken and devastated Adam's spiritual relationship with God. He used the covenantal relationship between husband and wife. He had used Eve to cause Adam to fall. Satan had used this tactic to cause covenantal trouble for Abraham. Sarah gave Hagar as wife to Abraham (Gen. 16); Zipporah attacked Moses (Exod. 4:24, 25; Delilah was a source of tragedy for Samson (Judges 14, 15); Jezebel was an evil in king Ahab's life (1 Kings 21); Bathsheba caused untold trouble in David's life (2 Samuel 11); Solomon's wives became a snare for him and through this social relationship's influence Solomon's heart was turned away from Yahweh, the God of Israel (1 Kings 11:1).[23]

The early church fathers did not hesitate to refer to Job's wife in very unflattering terms. Pope referred to Augustine's phrase to describe her as the *diaboli adjutrix* (devil's adjunct) and to Calvin's phrase *organum Satannae* (organ of Satan). Chrysostom opined Satan had not taken her so he could use her as a scourge by which to plague Job more acutely than by any other means.[24] The question has been implicitly referred to: was Job's wife aware of her role as a covenant-breaking wife of a suffering covenant-keeping husband? There are those who would refer to her as a victim of patriarchal dominance and to her forced submission to a wealthy and powerful man, her husband.[25] Others, as mentioned, considered her a "tool of

Satan," and she readily submitted to his influence and became guilty of treachery against her husband.

The basic point of this section, however, is Job's demonstration of his covenantal relationship to his wife. How, in the tragic situation that developed, did he deal with her? Job did not curse God or her. He did not disown her. He did tell her that she did not speak as a faithful, wise covenant partner. He told her she spoke like "one foolish woman."[26] What she said was senseless. She, in effect, had renounced God's ways for Job and all he had. A covenant woman/wife did not make sense at all when she spoke of cursing God and dying. Rather, a couple united in the marriage covenant should know that in life not only good could be experienced at the hand of God but also *hārâ'*. The lexicon has a rather long list of explanations for this term. As an adjective *bad* and *evil* are given; as a noun it can refer to evil, distress, misery, calamity, injury, wrong, or adversity.[27] The definitions that would indicate bad, evil, or wrong should not be considered acceptable in this context. Job spoke of God giving good; he referred to the covenant blessings he and his family had received. The deprivation, pain, and agony he also considered as coming from God. He did not refer to himself as being under the curse of the covenant. He refused his wife's counsel; it was a false way of escape from his suffering. He expressed unwavering trust in God. Job demonstrated his total submission to God in this time of ill and calamity. Hartley wrote correctly that Job accepted an active and positive submission to God "for good or ill." His was not a mere passive reception but a positive participation in what God decreed.[28] This is clearly implied in the comment that Job did not sin.

In conclusion it must be stated in most positive terms: Job demonstrated his covenant relationship with God. Loss of possessions and children did not deter him from expressing his submission to his covenant Lord's ways with him. His wife's foolish comments did not influence his spiritual relationship with Yahweh God. In reality, she gave him occasion to express his submission to and confidence in the blessed covenantal relationship he knew existed between him and Yahweh God. This submission and confidence was severely tested when the three friends sat with him.

In Regard to the Three Friends

The role of the three friends in Job's experiences as a cosmic kingdom man was discussed in the previous chapter. The question to be answered now is: did the three friends come as fellow covenant servants? How did they influence Job's covenant relationship with God? with society? and with the cultural dimensions of life?

The biblical text refers to the three men as *re'e* (a term that depending on the context can be understood to refer to a friend, a companion, or a fellow). Since they lived some distance from Job and conversed together about going to Job, the idea of friend is dominant. The concept of friend has various connotations in the Scriptures but for Job a friend was a close, intimate person on whom he could rely. A strong bond between men (and women) could exist. It may not have been thought of as a covenant bond in all circumstances as it was between David and Jonathan (1 Sam. 20:42). Job, however, considered that a close intimate bond existed between him and his friends. The friends also did. They considered that as close friends they should prove they were by visiting Job. Their intent as friends was *lanûd lô ûlĕnaḥamô* (to condole or show sympathy, from the verb *nud,* which has a distinct reference to "showing grief and to comfort, piel ptc. of stem of *nāḥam*). The friends desired to help Job to be strong as they sympathized with him. But when they actually saw Job they expressed their grief in an Oriental manner—they wept, tore their clothes, and sprinkled dust on their heads and sat speechless with him for seven days and nights (2:11–13). They were overwhelmed at the sight of Job. They were unable to express their shock, they were unable to sympathize with him. They were unable to demonstrate compassion—that is, they were unable to really suffer with him. If there was a friendship covenant, the friends did not know how to express it.

In the dialogue that ensued after Job's outburst of agony and despair (3:1–26), the friends made it very obvious that they considered Job to be under the curse of the covenant. Job was unrighteous (4:7). Job, in various ways, hidden though these were, was a covenant breaker. He had transgressed in deed, words and thoughts.[29] This absence of true sympathy and comfort added to Job's trouble, pain, and grief. Job pled for his friends' devotion (6:14, *NIV*).[30] He specifically called for *hesed.* This word can also be translated mercy or faithful kindness. It is one of Scripture's main terms to express Yahweh God's loving compassion and kindness to his suffering covenant people. Job pled with his covenant friends to reveal they were spokesmen and agents of Yahweh God's covenant love and mercy.

Consider Job's longing for understanding and love from his three friends. He expressed his loneliness and expectation of compassion when he said *ti'ăbônî* piel of *tā'ab (*regard as an abomination) (19:19) *kōl mĕtê sôdî* (all my confidants). The *NIV* translates the phrase as intimate friends. Job went on to groan in words *wĕzeh 'āhabtî* (and those I love) *nehpĕkû bî* (niph. Impf. of *hāpâh*, to turn). In the niphal the emphasis is on turning oneself away from another. His covenant fellows, his confidants, his intimate friends, as they sat with him on the ash heap, had turned away from him, abhorring him as an abomination who had become thus under Yahweh God's covenant curse on covenant breakers.

Consider also Job's deep pathos when he appealed to his "former confidants." *Ḥānnunî ḥānumî 'attem rē'ê* . Job uttered a piercing cry pleading for *ḥānan.*[31] The term has the basic idea of favor or graciousness. Corollaries listed are long for, merciful, and compassionate. Job expressed his deepest agony, saying God's hand had struck him. His covenant Lord had placed a terrifying curse upon him. Why, Job pleads, do his former confidants do so also? In Job's mind Yahweh God was joined by his friends. There was no intimate covenant friendship bond anymore.

Satan had not only turned Job's wife against him. Satan, diabolically using the three friends to rely on a faulty theological premise, had also turned them away from Job. It is in this context that Job appealed for a friend that would not turn against him—his Redeemer—and Job could do so rightfully. There was one, a friend who stuck closer than a brother (Prov.18:24). That friend is none other than the Lord Jesus, the covenant Mediator and Redeemer (John 15:15).

The conclusion to this section is clear. The three friends, used by Satan, led Job to refer to his one and only abiding covenant relationship—with his Redeemer. Human covenant relationship motivated the three friends to visit Job. They were not true to that relationship but, in spite of what they intended and said, they influenced Job to seek, find, and depend on his abiding covenant relationship/bond with his Lord.

In Regard to Elihu

Elihu's role in the life and struggles of Job and of his speech in the book of Job has given reason for various opinions.[32]

The basic questions that are raised are in regard to the continuity of the Jobian experience. Do Elihu's four speeches contribute to the debate of the three men with Job? How do Elihu's thoughts tie in with what God says to Job after Job's audacious avowal of his innocence? Had Job not challenged God in his final words? Why is Elihu interjected between Job and God?

A consideration of the context is important. Job had eloquently spoken about wisdom and discernment. He pronounced with conviction that the fear of *Adonai* (sovereign master) and the shunning of evil were the sources of these (28:28). He followed this up with a statement on the blessedness of man's covenant life, how he had been honored for his faithfulness to it (29:1–25). He then proceeded to refer to the mockery he received from unworthy sources (30:1–15). He went on to describe how his life was ebbing away and that God was choking and rejecting him (30:16–19). He vehemently stated that he had cried out "to you God" but received no answer; instead God turned ruthlessly against him in his brokenness, pain, agony, and despair (30:20–31).

Job then presented a challenge. Or, as has been written, "he swears an oath of innocence" (31:1–40).[33] Job stated he was a faithful covenant man in regard to his sexual relationship and his attitudes to women were blameless (31:1–6). He went on to express his conviction that he had not sinned with regard to seventeen additional possible vices (31:7–39), and if he had, let "curses" befall him.[34] But he had absolute confidence that he was not a covenant breaker in relation to the spiritual, social, and cultural mandates.

In a real sense, there were two responses to Job's last words. The three men were silent. There is a debate concerning why they were. Was it because they finally concluded that Job would not listen to them? Did they come to a conclusion that man who was righteous in his own eyes would never confess his sins they had accused him of committing? Should they continue to dialogue with a man who insisted he was right with God? A man who insisted he was justified in God's sight even though God punished him as a sinner who, upon confession, would be justified?

There is another view concerning the silence of the three men. Dhorme, for example, referred to what he said in the "original text" *bĕ 'ênêhem* (in their eyes).[35] The three friends came to realize that Job was right with God after all. Hence their silence. This view has not been widely accepted. It is difficult to harmonize this view with what God said to them after he had addressed Job. Yahweh addressed

Eliphaz and rebuked him and his two friends. He said he was angry with them for not speaking correctly of him. They had scorned the covenant Lord. Sacrifices and intercessory prayer on their behalf was required (42:7–9).

The silence of the three men gave a fourth friend the opportunity to speak in response to Job's final words. He was the young Elihu.[36] It can be assumed that he had been present and heard the three men tell Job that he had sinned. He had displayed proper decorum; he had not interrupted the older men. Once he began to speak, he was vociferous,demonstrating that he was an impatient man with a tempestuous character (32:19, 20).[37] He was angry with the three men because they had accused Job and had given no acceptable reason for their accusations. Hence he stated boldly that he would not repeat their useless arguments (32:14). Job had responded to them. He had proved the three men to be ineffective because they were incorrect. Elihu spoke. He said he had the breath of God, the Spirit, that gave him understanding (32:8). And he was full of words that the inspiring Spirit compelled him to speak (32:18).[38] The older men had not revealed wisdom nor had they understood what was right (32:9). Thus he in effect informed the three men that they had nothing more to say. It was his duty to instruct Job and vindicate God.

Elihu addressed Job (33:1). He felt he should serve as a moderator.[39] He repeated that he, a man with an upright heart and with sincere words from his mouth, was influenced by the Spirit of God (33:1–7). It is clear that Elihu was certain he had a specific message for Job. He was angry with Job because Job justified himself rather than God (32:2). If this is the correct interpretation, then it follows that Elihu's speeches, as a whole, were not included in the book of Job as a later addition. But the question remains. Do Elihu's speeches serve an integral purpose in the book of Job? The answer is yes! The three friends/men had failed in their accusations against Job. Elihu had heard these fallacious accusations. Claiming inspiration by the Spirit, Elihu "functions as God's forerunner both by his position between Job's avowal of innocence and Yahweh's answer and by the content of his speeches."[40] So what did Elihu say as the moderator and forerunner of Yahweh God who addressed Job after Elihu was finished? Elihu filled the role of a covenant mediator—at least to an extent. It bears repeating, Job may not consciously have regarded Elihu as such. Whether Job did or did not, does not alter the reality that Elihu served as such to the advantage and benefit of Job. But, it must be stated clearly, Elihu also considered Job guilty of sin, but spoke of this differently than the three men had. And Elihu spoke concerning Yahweh God correctly, as will be discussed in what follows.

After the introduction in which Elihu was referred to as angry at Job and the three men, he had acknowledged his youth, claimed the Spirit's inspiration, and assured all before him that he was important (32:20). He addressed Job. In the initial address to Job Elihu rebukes Job for saying he was pure and sinless but God had punished him (35:5–13). He then proceeded to speak "wise words" (33:33) concerning God revealing himself in various ways and does so mysteriously with the intent to preserve humble men (33:14–22). And God specifically reveals himself in various ways to those who confess their sins (33:23–28). Thus God saves one from the pit and shines the light of life on that one (33:29–33).

In the second speech, Elihu addressed those in his presence. He repeats most of what he had said to Job. Job had insisted he was innocent and right but God was unjust to him (34:1–6). Job is not innocent, consider his sins (34:29). Elihu proceeded to defend God's goodness and justice (34:10–12). God reigns sovereignly, he upholds life in the world (34:13–15). In his righteousness and justice God governs without partiality. He knows the inner thoughts and covert evil deeds (34:16–30). Elihu then calls for a confession and repentance by Job who spoke without knowledge and thus added rebellion. Job should be tested more than he was (34:31–37). Thus Elihu served as a covenant counselor to Job. This was to assist Job the covenant man.

Elihu addressed Job again asking him if it was to God's advantage when men sinned. Of course not, it only affects the sinner. Pleas to men instead of to God are to no avail (35:1–9). God deals wisely and does not listen to Job who speaks empty words (35:10–16). Elihu then continued with a long discourse (36:1—37:24). First, he exalted God who is mighty and justly gives rights to the afflicted. The righteous are exalted, but the suffering ones experiencing prison and affliction receive these for purposes of correction, repentance, and service. God was blessing Job and had justice and judgment come upon him because of discreet sinful deeds (36:22–26). He sovereignly rules his creation (36:27—37:13). Elihu concluded by asking Job to consider God's wonders—the clouds, lightning, winds, and rain (37:14–18). And should a man like Job correct God who comes in awesome majesty, power, justice, and righteousness? Job should revere God for he does have regard for the wise in heart (37:19–24).

What now did Elihu, as a moderator and covenant mediator, do for Job? The text, as indicated previously, does not include Job's response. Elihu, in spite of his verbosity, self-esteem, and confidence, had some wise words but not all he said was evidence of wisdom. He was wise to extol and exalt God, assuring his hearers that this sovereign, powerful and omniscient God was righteous and just in all his deeds. As a faithful covenant man, he extolled and exalted his covenant Lord. This was to Job's benefit.

It was also to Job's benefit that he was reminded that all men are sinners. Job was not the pure one he said he was. Elihu, not aware of the antithetical situation between Yahweh God and Satan, was true to the general covenantal principle: sin brings punishment. He did not do Job justice when, he was, as his friends were, controlled by that principle. He considered Job to have sinned—furtively. God was humbling Job by afflicting him and calling him to consider these sins, and repent of them as he confessed them.

It bears repeating. Job may not have fully realized that as a covenant man, he was being benefited, to an extent, by a covenant spokesman. So, whether Job realized what Elihu said was for his benefit, or not, did not alter the reality that Job was.

Covenantal Emphases in the Book of Job

Progression in the Revelation of the Covenant

A basic presupposition in the study of the revelation of the theology of the Scriptures is that there is a progression in divine revelation. Basic concepts revealed in the earlier stages of revelation are not only repeated but expanded and applied as life progressed. One of the outstanding concepts revealed in Genesis 3, regarding the Redeemer and his activity, are expanded, more fully explained, and presented in more definite historical sequences. The same is true concerning the concept of seed—seed of the woman, Abraham, and David. The question before us pertains to the covenant. It was revealed to Adam and Eve, to Noah, and to Abraham, Isaac, and Jacob. Is this revelation of the covenant included in the book of Job? In the preceding, in section IV, the covenantal relationship's Job had in various contexts were studied. These, his relationship's with God, his family, wife, and friends, do not clearly reveal that there was a distinct progression in the revelation of the covenant and covenantal life A consideration of five specific themes is in order.

As we consider the five concepts it must be kept in mind that Job is considered to have lived during the patriarchal period. He was indeed a patriarch, but he was not one in the seed-line of the woman that eventually brought forth the Messiah. Job is recorded to be a resident "in the land of Uz" (1:1). Cartographers attempting to locate places on maps of ancient places often omit indicating where the land of Uz was precisely located. Biblical scholars have considered Uz to refer to a wide geographical area east and south of the Jordan. Countries in the north (e.g., Syria) and in the south (e.g., Edom) were considered to be included in the area of Uz. One factor is clear: Job, living in the land of Uz, was not living in the area of Abraham, Isaac, and Jacob, west of the Jordan.

Job is also considered to be a descendant of Shem. He lived in the area that is recorded to be that of either the son of Aram (Gen. 10–23) or of Uz who was the eldest son of Nahor (Gen. 22:21–23), the brother of Abraham.[41] The point to be observed is that Job lived in the area where the covenant could have been widely known and its implications for life in service to Yahweh were evident. The conclusion must be stated positively. The knowledge of Yahweh God, the covenant Maker and Lord, was widely known beyond the immediate *Sitz im Leben* of the patriarchs. The question can be answered with assurance: did Job know about Yahweh God's covenant established at the time of creation, given elaboration in the garden, and confirmed to Noah (Gen. 6:18; 9:9–11), and to the patriarch?[42] Job lived in covenant with Yahweh God and when smitten as he was, he expressed uncertainties regarding Yahweh God honoring his covenant to which he was submissive and had been obedient.[43] Evidence of this submission and obedience that also indicate a progression in the revelation and comprehension of the covenant are discussed in succeeding paragraphs.

Worship

Job worshiped God as a covenant man. There is evidence that he did this in ways not recorded concerning his predecessors and contemporaries. Job was a covenant *family* man (1:4–6). His sons and daughters shared in his wealth. Job realized they could be guilty of some unsanctified behavior. So, he offered regularly sacrifices on their behalf. And when offering sacrifices he undoubtedly interceded for them in prayer. Job worshiped his covenant Lord as a covenant father of his covenant offspring. Consider also what the text states. When he learned of his losses (1:13–19) Job got up, tore his robe, shaved his head, and fell to the ground and worshiped (1:20). The verb *yišetāḥû* receives translation as prostrated or kneeled. Translators consider the term to mean obeisance before God, that is, worship.

In the course of the dialogue Job uttered sporadic statements that could be considered acts of worship. He said he had called upon God (12:4b). He confessed that he knew that to God belonged power, strength, and victory (12:13, 16). Other statements of worship can be gleaned from Job's words such as "I have treasured the words of his mouth more than my daily bread" (23:12).

Faith

The question concerning the authenticity of faith in the book of Job has been debated. A scholar unhesitatingly wrote that the book of Job deals with authentic faith.[44] He is correct as will be briefly discussed in the following.

An integral aspect of a covenant man's life and general relationship in life is faith. Faith is more than belief, although it is an important element of faith. Faith includes knowledge, acceptance, assurance, and expression of it in words and deeds. Job had faith. It may have wavered at certain points in his experiences on the ash heap. But as a covenant man he never denied his knowledge of God. Nor did he radically refuse to accept what God did. He had no problem with faith in God when he lost his possessions, family, and the loyalty of his wife. When prolonged affliction overcame him, he questioned and begged God to explain to him why he had to suffer as he did. Through all his suffering, aggravated by the accusations of his "friends," he knew, accepted, and was assured that his covenant Lord knew the what and why of his suffering and was assured that only God could relieve him and restore him. Consider some of his words: " The Lord has given, he has taken, the name of the Lord be praised"(1:21). To his wife he said that they should receive good from God and also trouble (2:10). Job had faith he would be exonerated by the Redeemer he knew lived (19:25).

The question is: did Job demonstrate progression in understanding God's covenant ways with his people? Or does the text give evidence of progression in the revelation of God to his people? The answer is affirmative.[45] Noah and Abraham had experiences in which faith was tested. Noah spent years building an ark and waiting for the Lord to carry out his plan to bring on the flood while fellowmen mocked him. Abraham had to endure tension in Egypt regarding his wife and later had to wait for a male heir. Job, however, had a far greater and intense experience, losing his possessions and then his health through which he suffered excruciating pain and mental anguish brought on by friends who insisted they spoke on behalf of God. Noah and Abraham maintained their faith (Heb. 11:7–12). Job certainly was a hero of faith also—in a real sense more so. As Yahweh God's revelation progressed, Job demonstrated how faith, the gift of his covenant Lord, was proven to be a greater anchor than had been demonstrated before his time.

Submission

Submission in everyday life's circumstances was expected, in a covenant context, whether in a social or legal context; the vassal would submit to the sovereign lord. In Yahweh God's covenant he is the sovereign Lord. He determined the historical situation, the prerequisites for promises made by oath, to be fulfilled. He had determined the continuity and heirs of Job. Job, the covenant man, when confronted by mysteriously executed losses and nigh inhuman psychological and physical suffering, initially expressed total submission. He did not sin when informed he had lost all his possessions and family. He spontaneously submitted to his Lord, saying that the Lord had given and taken. He praised God (1:21, 22). When his wife called on him to curse God, his reply expressed total submission (2:9, 10). But, when enduring pain and suffering overcame him, he raised his voice in questioning why he had to suffer as he did. Job reflected the tension that a thinking man can have endeavoring to understand the mysterious ways of Yahweh God's dealing with his covenant servant/vassal.

Job revealed his true covenant character and relationship to his Lord when he had been rebuked by his Lord's question to him. Yahweh asked Job if he, who had a problem with God would try to correct him (40:2).[46] Most translators think of Job contending, arguing with God, who is referred to as Yahweh (his covenant name), *Shaddaî* (expressing his sovereign lordship), and *ĕlōâh* (a form of *ĕlōhîm*). Confronted by his sovereign, almighty, powerful, authoritative covenant Lord, Job submitted immediately. He admitted his unworthiness and confessed he had no more to say. In this submission to his Lord, Job confessed he had not been as submissive as he should have been. He expressed complete submission. Job repeated his complete submission (42:2–5) and openly confessed his unworthiness when he said he despised himself.[47] And he repented of his past attitudes, uncertainties that had led him to question God's dealings with him.

Job clearly expressed genuine remorse as was not recorded before him. Indeed, there was progress in the revelation of genuine remorse, repentance, and submission in a living covenantal context. A true covenant servant expresses genuine worship (worthiness of his Lord), faith, and complete submission.

The Fear of the Lord

The theme "the fear of the Lord" requires careful attention. It is the central concept in the book of Job. It is also prominent in other wisdom texts and is an aspect in the covenant strand. The book of Deuteronomy refers to it repeatedly, calling Israel to this covenantal requirement. The concept is also common in historical and prophetic books.[48] Was the fear of God known before or at the time of Job? It certainly was. Fear is a term that can refer to various human experiences.

The idea of fear referring to being afraid is included in the account of Noah (Gen. 9:2). When Abraham interacted with Abimelich, living in the Negev, we read that because he sensed there was no fear of God in that place, he lied concerning his wife. Abimelech took her into his harem but when he learned Sarai was Abraham's wife, through the word of the Lord, he and his officials were "sore afraid" (Gen. 20:8). In this context the difference between being afraid of God (Abimelech) and not fearing the Lord becomes clear. Abraham realized there was no acknowledgment of reverence for, submission to, nor a true worship of the Lord. Abraham did not exhibit God-honoring fear in the Abimelech interaction but demonstrated it by obeying Yahweh, when commanded to sacrifice Isaac. He truly feared the Lord. Hence, in the patriarchal times, God-honoring fear of the Lord was present, known, and exercised. This fear of the Lord was a constituent aspect of faithful covenant life.

Job knew what it was to fear the Lord. There is no evidence he was called to it as Abraham had been, who had been commanded by Yahweh to be blameless when the covenant was confirmed with him (Gen. 17:1). Job was described as blameless and upright—he was this because he feared God and shunned evil (Job 1:1). There can be no doubt, after considering what was discussed in the preceding, that the fear of the Lord was an integral constituent aspect of Yahweh God's covenant with his people and their response to it. Covenant people feared Yahweh God. It was their very nature to do so.

Scholarship dealing with the book of Job has tended to omit a study of the concept of fear of God. The reason for this is thought to be the critics' preference to deal with the book of Job as a literary phenomenon.[49] A consideration of some passages that refer to the fear of God in the book of Job will support the proposition that it is in reality a central concept in it.

Satan acknowledged that Job feared God. He implied that Job did so because Yahweh God had been most gracious to him, providing him with wealth and protection (1:9). Satan was correct when he spoke of Job fearing God but very incorrect when he gave his insulting and wicked reason for it.

Job feared God (1:1). Job, as a covenant man knew that being bonded with God was a blessed covenant reality. Fearing God, he honored God as his covenant Lord and benefactor. Job obeyed his Lord, not because he was afraid of God but because he believed in God, appreciated his lordship, and respected him as his covenantal Master. God's covenant love is not referred to directly.[50] There is evidence of this love. Consider the blessings Job received before and after his affliction and Yahweh God silently and mysteriously upholding Job during his varied painful ordeals.

Job's fear of God was genuine; Job demonstrated it in life and words. God acknowledged it; God said it was a basic and true reality in the mind, heart, and life of Job. Yahweh openly and directly told Satan of Job's fear of God (2:3). Satan took this aspect of God's description as the key to the relationship between God and Job. Satan did not refer to God's description of Job as blameless, upright, and fearing evil. Satan knew that if he could disqualify Job's fear of God, the other virtues mentioned would no longer be true and applicable. It must be concluded, then, that fearing God meant to know, honor, obey and serve God and do so in a blameless, upright manner in which no evil had even a lurking part.

It is of interest to note that Eliphaz knew that Job feared God (4:6).[51] He asked Job if his fear of God should not give him confidence in God. Eliphaz was correct to ask that question. True, fear of God inspires confidence and hope. Job had expressed a deep uncertainty and lack of trust when he broke his silence and expressed his anguish and despair (3:1–26). He had said he had no peace, quietness, or rest, the very experiences that true fear should inspire. As indicated before, Job had sunk into a deep spiritual abyss. He did not deny his faith in God. He was understood, and correctly, to question whether he demonstrated his fear of God to be his basic virtue and if faith in God was truly his anchor.

When Job replied to Eliphaz he referred to the fear of *Shaddaî,* the Almighty Sovereign Lord (6:14).[52] The thrust of this passage is that Job has a twofold accusation against Eliphaz (and friends?). He replied that Eliphas forsook or refused to be loyally kind to his friend, Job. Doing this Job contended that Eliphaz forsook the fear of *Shaddaî.*[53] There should be no doubt that in Job's reply we hear of his further pain because his friends accuse him of no longer fearing God. Job's reply is interpreted in two contradictory ways. One is that a stricken man such as he is should have "the devotion of his friends" (6:14, *NIV*), even if they think he no longer fears *Shaddaî.* The preferred interpretation is that friends who do not demonstrate support and comfort to a stricken man have forsaken the fear of *Shaddaî.* Job, so understood, accuses Eliphaz of not speaking as one who had the fear of *Shaddaî.*" He spoke from his own mind, not from the mind of God. Job understood that the fear of God/Yahweh/*Shaddaî* included and was the source of compassion for a stricken man. The friends, not knowing what the prologue revealed, wrongly accused Job of forsaking his all-inclusive relationship (fear) of God. This passage further elucidates what is to be understood by one's fear of God. It also gives added support to the thesis that a central theme in the book of Job is the covenant man's attitude to and relationship with his covenant Lord.

Job did not refer to the fear of God in his direct reply to Eliphaz. But Eliphaz continued his accusation against Job. He accused Job of unwise and valueless words because he broke away from the fear of God (15:4). And because he had done this, Eliphas further accused Job of sinning with his mouth, condemning himself, and thus testifying against himself (15:5, 6). Eliphas correctly understood that that man who truly feared Yahweh/God/*Shaddaî* would keep his mouth clean. It would guard against and keep one from speaking untruth, especially concerning God. Eliphas, however, as stated before, did not know what the prologue revealed.

As he spoke objective truth, in his ignorance he falsely accused Job of lacking the fear of God and sinning grievously with the words he had uttered.

Eliphaz spoke again about the fear of God. He answered Job when he called on the three men, after they had continued to accuse Job of sins. Job had said: listen carefully to my words. He ended with a rebuke, "how can you console me with nonsense and falsehood?" (21:4–34). Eliphaz asked if a man, for example, Job, could be of benefit to God. Of course not was the implication, especially not Job. God was rebuking Job not for his fear of God but for charging God was indifferent to him. Eliphaz, still totally unaware of what the prologue recorded, did not realize that Job was suffering precisely because he did fear God. God himself had assured Satan that Job was genuine in his fear of God (his piety).[54] And God knew that God-fearing Job was righteous.[55] In a real sense, it was Eliphaz who blasphemed. One must conclude that the reality is that God knew Job feared him and did so as a righteous man. Fearing God and living a righteous and just life were completely and mutually compatible. Indeed, the man who fears God has righteousness reckoned to him. Eliphaz was wrong, confused, and unfair to Job. He did not realize that the piety/fear of God Job had, was the very reason for his suffering.

Elihu concluded his long contribution to the dialogue on the ash heap (37:24). Commentators are not agreed on the thrust of Elihu's final words.[56] One commentator pointed out that, like other verses which conclude speeches, they have "a succinct bicolon with a tight parallelism." The *lā* should not be read as *lô* "not," but as an assertive "surely." Then the two terms "*yr'h* is a repetitive parallel of *yr'whw.*"[57] The correct translation thus is "Therefore men fear him, surely all the wise of heart fear him." This translation coincides with what Job had asserted. The fear of God and wisdom are totally compatible and are mutually interrelated and integrated.[58]

One must conclude then, to study 28:28 properly, the two concepts fear of God and wisdom should not be discussed separately. But to discuss these two concepts, the preceding discussion should be considered to determine if a strong desire to have and demonstrate wisdom was present in each participant in the dialogue on the ash heap.

Wisdom

Wisdom and its closely related concepts, understanding and discernment appear frequently in the book of Job. In some instances the term may not appear in the Hebrew text but a phrase appears, such as *wĕmillĕbam yâẓ'û millîm* (and from the heart go words). Translators and commentators understand the phrase to refer to understanding arising from the heart and mind (9:10). In most instances the terms *hōkmâh* (wisdom) *hăkamîm* (wise ones), *yabîn* (discern), and *tĕbûnâh* (understanding, discernment) appear.

To follow the dialogue and to try to discern what each speaker meant to convey should give an indication of how men, created in the image of God and indicating in various ways that they knew of and believed God, struggled to convey what it was to possess, illustrate, and exhibit what wisdom was, how it was to be understood and applied in the covenant man's life.

Eliphaz, in his first response to Job's outburst (3:1–26), referred to Job's assistance to others (4:3, 4) but tells Job he does not do for himself what he has done for others. He intimates that Job is really without a sense of what God is doing. Eliphaz referred to a dream he had in which he saw men who considered themselves to be pure before God or more pure than God who lost all they had and died without wisdom. Eliphaz's point was that those who despise God's ways do not have the necessary insight into the spiritual values of life or into reasons for human mortality (4:21).[59] Eliphaz went on to say that God blesses the humble but thwarts the plans of crafty and scheming men (5:11–13). Eliphaz revealed that he understood the wise person to be humble who admits the wrong in his life for which punishment is given. In Eliphaz's words, there is the thought that the man who truly fears God has access to and practices wisdom. Bildad added his word of admonishment to Job. He should consider what the fathers had learned and taught in former generations. They had learned from God's ways that he upholds the pure and upright (8:6) and does not reject the blameless. These fathers had true understanding in their hearts and minds (8:10). These covenant fathers had been and still were models and teachers of true piety and wisdom.

In the response of Job to Bildad, Zophar's response to Job, and Job's to his, the terms *wise*, *discernment*, *understanding,* and *wisdom* were spoken eleven times. Job spoke of God's profound wisdom revealed in his providential rule over and care of the created natural world (9:1–13). He employed a unique phrase *hokam lebab* (wisdom of the heart). The wisdom God revealed in creation was seated in and expressed from the very heart of God. Job knew that the created world was a revelation of the "inner person" of God's wisdom and thus revealed the inner and all-pervasive nature of God. And this wisdom is inseparable from God's righteousness and *kōah* (power). Job gave expression to what later biblical personages expressed about Yahweh God's revelation of himself and his wisdom (Pss. 19; 104:24; Rom. 11:33). Job reflected that he had indeed been obedient to the covenantal cultural mandate and had learned he could not resist God (9:4).

Zophar was upset by Job's confession of God's righteousness, wisdom, and power that was followed by an insistence he was innocent of sin and evil committed against God. Zophar wished that God would speak, informing Job of divine secrets of wisdom that could include God forgetting some of Job's sins (11:6). Zophar went on to accuse Job of being an *'îš nābûl* (a senseless or foolish man) (11:12), who cannot become wise just as a donkey cannot give birth to a human being. Zophar continued to plead with Job to devote himself fully to God and turn from all evil. God demanded that and if Job obeyed, he would no longer be ashamed, would no longer have trouble, and would be secure (11:13–20). Zophar revealed a basic sentiment: repentance, devotion, wisdom were requisites to covenantal blessings. To this Job replied that his companions on the ash heap had a conception of wisdom that was unique to them. When they died wisdom would disappear from the earth (12:2). To be noted here is that Zophar correctly understood that a person's submission to God was requisite to wisdom. Job understood Zophar's point. But Job was convinced that Zophar was not correct or justified to accuse Job of having broken his relationship with God. For Zophar, Job was no longer fearing God and revealing true piety; hence, as a man without wisdom, he was suffering.

Job continued to lament his losses but was assured that aged persons had acquired wisdom and understanding of God's dealing with his creation (12:7–12). This wisdom that the aged had known was from the sovereign Lord. Job attributes four virtues or attributes to his covenant Lord (12:12, 13). These four are mutually interdependent. To God belong wisdom, power, counsel, and understanding. God reveals these attributes in his reign over and control of his entire creation. The point is: God understands and guides as he with sovereign power and authority rules over, directs, and providentially dispenses blessings for the good of his entire creation. God covenantally administers the totality of his creation in full accordance with his promises and determined purposes. But, Job insisted, God dispossessed and removed kings, priests, advisers, nobles, and also removed discernment from elders (12:17–25). This loss of discernment was demonstrated by a lack of ability to honor Yahweh God in all his work and to recognize that trouble, disappointments, and losses are also aspects of Yahweh God's purposes and activities. Since the three disputants were very incorrect in their accusations against Job and were speaking wickedly and deceitfully on God's behalf their silence would demonstrate wisdom (13:5–7).[60] Eliphaz answered Job with more harsh criticism. He appealed to the former fathers who had taught that wicked men suffer (15:17–20) and for Job to deny that his suffering was not due to his sins against God was to taper[61] the "fear of God" and to restrain or diminish devotion[62] before the face of God. Eliphaz outrightly accused Job of causing piety/fear of God and devotion/meditation before God to be pulled down, broken, and destroyed (15:4).

It is important for the purpose of this study to emphasize what Eliphaz said. A wise man would not employ useless words by which he violated piety, fear of God, devotion to, and meditation before God. A wise man would not do such a thing (15:2). Eliphaz was correct to stress that the fear of God and wisdom are integrated and correlated. The wise man fears God. The man who fears God demonstrates wisdom. In his response to Job, Eliphaz, while he spoke correctly of the integral relationship between "the fear of God" and wisdom, foolishly denied that Job had either one (15:8). Here was a situation in which a man exhibiting ignorance and folly did speak the truth. He did so objectively, revealing that he had prior knowledge of God and man's covenant relationship with Yahweh God.

Job replied to Eliphaz but doing so he appealed to God to reveal himself to the three men of whom God had closed *libbām* (their hearts, minds) and *śekel* (understanding) (17:4). Job was correct to refer to the heart of a man being the seat of understanding and wisdom. Since their minds were closed, not one of them was a wise person (17:10). Zophar in turn replied that, hearing a rebuke, the spirit (*rûaḥ*) inspired him to give a discerning reply. Zophar insisted he had discernment and would give a wise reply (20:3). He told Job that the joy and mirth of wicked people was brief, their dreams fly away and the sweet words of their mouths would turn sour in their stomachs (20:1–29). After Job had asked for careful attention to his words (21:2, 3), Eliphaz sarcastically asked if a wise man, as Job claimed to be, was of any benefit to and give pleasure to *Shaddaî* (22: 2, 3). Job's response was from a deep-seated heart's desire: "where can I find God, and as an upright man present my case before him and be declared innocent?" (23:3–12). Bildad had a brief answer. God is pure; man who is a maggot and worm is not (25:1–6).

Job gave a lengthy reply. He referred to wisdom seven times (26:3, 12; 28:12, 18, 20, 27, 28) and understanding four times (26:14; 28:12, 20, 23). He asked the three men if they had helped him a powerless and feeble man whom they considered to be without wisdom (26:3). What help had they given him to understand "the power of God's thunder"? Job had described the revelation of God's power in creation in beautiful terms and phrases.[63] Job demonstrated that he knew, discerned, and understood his sovereign Lord's power and was filled with awe and wonder. But, what was the answer to his grief, pain, and losses? He had heard aspects of the answer when wisdom, discernment, understanding, and knowledge of God, his reign over his created world had been mentioned. He himself had uttered some very relevant and important truths. But his riddle, his puzzle, his problem continued to baffle him. His companions on the ash heap had falsely accused him and had exhibited that though they knew God and believed in him, they revealed a fatal error. Their theological logic kept them from grasping Yahweh God's wise ways of dealing with a righteous man who was in the depths of suffering and anguish. Much less had they discerned and understood why Job, as accusations against him were upheld with vigor, slowly rose from the spiritual and psychological depression he experienced and exhibited. During the lengthy dialogue, Job had come to understand more clearly that his covenant Lord had not forsaken him even though he did not heed Job's pleas and calls for explanatory answers. When the men did not know what more to say to Job, whom they considered to be self-righteous, they kept their silence. But, Job had his final climatic speech.

Job spoke of God's omniscience and omnipotence that were clearly revealed in his sovereign reign over the cosmic kingdom (26:5–14). He then made a clear and powerful statement. He said that God had denied him justice and caused him bitter pain. He had not sinned. He maintained he was righteous in regard to the accusations made against him. He had a clear conscience (27:1–5). Those who were really wicked would in time experience punishment in varied ways and be helpless under it (27:6–23). But what about wisdom that had been repeatedly referred to as the men sought to come to grips with the issues before them on the ash heap? Where could it be found? Yahweh God, their covenant Lord, revealed himself in varied ways. Through all of creation through mines, fields, forests, oceans, marketplaces, foreign fields, and countries, Yahweh God had revealed his glory, divinity, and power (28:1–22; Ps.19:1; Rom. 1:19, 20). How could a man gain wisdom? It had been hinted before (15:4). Job, undoubtedly inspired by the Spirit of God, proclaimed the way to achieve wisdom! It was in an abiding covenantal relationship with *Adonai* (the covenant master/lord) (28:28).[64]

Solomon later taught that the fear of the Lord was the beginning of knowledge (Prov. 1:7). This knowledge is an essential, foundational aspect of wisdom. The Psalmist also repeated what Job had expressed (Ps. 111:10) and included a reference to the keeping of all covenantal precepts as a way to achieving wisdom. But Job, living in patriarchal times, gave positive expression to the key to achieving, and exhibiting wisdom. To fear God was and is to continually live in a close relationship with the covenant Master, to know, love, honor, obey him and to be totally submissive to him. It is to have security, peace, and joy. Living with and serving God thus reveals to the searching heart and mind of man the heart and mind of the all-knowing, loving, caring heart of God. This covenantal relationship is the door and path to being a person of knowledge, understanding, discernment, and wisdom.

After Job had reached lofty spiritual heights as expressed by his words concerning the fear of God, wisdom, and understanding, he recalled the security and joy when he lived in an abiding covenantal relationship with God. He spoke of his intimate friendship with God. This joyous experience was no longer his. He made a strong apologetic defense of himself and again expressed a strong desire to have someone hear him explain his situation (29:2–31:40).

Elihu made his contribution to the dialogue. He referred to wise (three times), understanding (five times), discernment (one time), and wisdom (two times). He gave no basic additional insights concerning these terms. In a real sense he summed up and applied what had been said before he spoke (32:7, 8, 9, 13; 33:33; 34:2, 4, 10, 13, 16, 24; 36:26, 29; 37: 5, 24). In these references a basic agreement with what Job had said can be seen.

When Yahweh God addressed Job (38:1) he spoke to him . He asked if he understood Yahweh God's creating power and work (38:2). Job was asked if he really understood that God endowed the heart with wisdom and understanding to the mind (38:36). Did Job really understand that it was God who kept wisdom from the ostrich (39:13–18) but gave it to the hawk so it could find its way south and to the eagle who builds its nest in heights (39:26–30)? These statements by God should be taken to assure Job that Yahweh God is the dispenser of wisdom to all aspects of creation as he administers it according to his covenant plan and purpose.

Conclusion

Recall that the first statement in this chapter asked the question: is the covenant referred to in the book of Job? The study, endeavoring to determine the correct reply, revealed that although the term *bĕrît* is present only once, the covenantal concept, relationship, virtue, and inclusive relevance to all of life in the cosmic kingdom constitute a very important and central reality in the life of Job and hence in the book of Job.

Satan knew of its presence in Job's life. Yahweh God knew it was an abiding reality. Nothing that Satan could do would break and destroy the love/life bond that held Job securely in the fellowship of Yahweh God. Erstwhile friends did not fully comprehend its reality and influence in Job's life. Job did not always have a full grasp of it. But his losses and sufferings and accusations of would-be friends increasingly had the result of Job residing confidently in the reality that he was indeed in covenant with Yahweh God.

Notes

1. Commentators such as Hartley, *Job,* Habel, *Job,* and Kroeze, *Job*, refer to the covenant a few times but do so without a full or clear explanation. An exception is Meredith G. Kline; his covenantal view will be referred to in the development of this chapter. See the developed bibliography in chap. 34 to which repeated references will be made. Note should be taken of what may appear as repetition or duplication. References and some comments with some detail were made in reference to Job, Job and God, and to one in the previous chapter. What was written there was considered germane to the study of Job and kingdom. These are also thus to the theme of Job and the covenant.

2. Wilson, "Fear of God," 78.

3. In previous studies, the idea of covenant has been repeatedly referred to and discussed. Cf. the indices of *Messianic Revelation in the Old Testament* (Grand Rapids: Baker, 1990) and *From Creation to Consummation,* vol. 1 (Sioux Center: Dordt, 1996).

4. It is quite unanimously agreed by biblical scholars, students, and readers of the Scriptures that these elements were present and functioned, be it in various ways, in the biblically revealed covenant Yahweh God made and upheld with his cosmic kingdom, particularly with humanity (male and female) as the basic agents of the creation/redemptive covenant.

5. I again refer the reader to the material I have written and published in the books referred to in note 3 above.

6. Cf. Richard L. Schultz's essay "Unity of Diversity in Wisdom Literature," *Tyndale Bulletin* 48 (1997): 271–306. Schultz stressed that there is a unity of wisdom theology from a cononical and covenantal perspective. An important conclusion to his presentation is that wisdom theology does not reflect a distinct and separate tradition from the canonical/covenantal "traditions" embodied within the totality of the Scriptures, 306.

7. Cf. Isa. 1:2–31, esp. vv. 18–20; Amos 3:1–4; Mic. 1:1, 2.

8. Meredith G. Kline, in a unique manner has given ample proof that the book of Job's covenantal character is exhibited in "a legal drama." See his "Trial by Ordeal," chap. 6 in *Through Christ's Word. A Festschrift for Dr. Philip Edgecomb Hughes*, ed. W. R. Godfrey and Jesse L. Boyd (Philipsburg: Presbyterian and Reformed, 1985), 81–91.

9. Kroeze emphasized that the phrase should be interpreted not as *bĕnê* (sons) but as those belonging to Yahweh. They were covenant agents called to report to their covenant Lord. *Job*, 50, 51.

10. See my discussion of Satan in *From Creation to Consummation*, vol. 1, 99–116. Kroeze reminded his readers that the term itself means "*voet dwars zetten*" (set foot cross way), accuse, resist. Ibid. 51.

11. See Dhorme, *Job*, for a brief discussion of this phrase, 6.

12. Satan employed the term *śakēta*—derived from *sûk*, to place a protection *ba 'ădâ* (around him).

13. The phrase "fear of God" will be discussed in a subsequent context.

14. Tod Linafelt has presented a study entitled "The Undecidability of ברק in the Prologue to Job and Beyond," in *Biblical Interpretation*, 4 no.2, (1996): 155–71. He pointed out that one translation used blaspheme.

15. Ibid., 157. Linafelt has concluded that as Plato in his dialogue Phaedrus used a term that could either mean cure or poison, 155, so the author of Job has turned the term " *barak:* on "its strange and invisible pivot, 171. Kroeze attempted to explain the use of the term *bless* when a curse or ill will was intended in the context of the parting of two people at odds with each other. The term *bless* could be used to convey, "I hope you are not." *Job*, 50.

16. See also the discussion of Job's relationship to God, 38–42.

17. Geoffrey J. Aimers raised the issue of Job being in covenant with the God of wisdom on the basis of his honor as a man of wealth and nobility. But Job could not understand why God did not honor this covenant and why God did not indicate he owed Job redress. See his essay "The Rhetoric of a Social Conscience in the Book of Job," *Journal for the Study of the Old Testament*, 91, (2000): 99, 100. Aimers stated at the outset of his writing that he extrapolated to make his points. It would seem that Aimers did less of that than he thinks. Had he placed Job in the wider context of the Old Testament revelation of the covenant he would have found himself on a firm biblical basis.

Thomas, *Storm*, writing of God's friendship quoted Ps. 25:14, which speaks of God's covenant being made known to those who confide in him, 225. Though shaken, Job, the covenant man, remained confident in God.

A writer who did place Job in a wider context of the Old Testament is Robert Gordis. What is definitely unacceptable in Gordis's interpretation of Job is that he did not ascribe spiritual growth and relationship with Yahweh God exhibited in the book of Job to Job, but to an imagined author who lived in the 6th or 7th century B.C. This author, according to Gordis, reflected ideas of the Prophets and Torah and these helped mold the spirituality. Gordis obviously will not accept that Job had a deep covenant relationship with Yahweh God. See his book *The Book of God and Man, A Study of Job* (Chicago: University of Chicago Press, 1965).

18. Cf. the discussion of Job's spiritual experiences in chap. 35, esp. sections II and V and in section IV of this chap.

19. *BDB* lists *zur* as the root (279, 6) but Dhorme wrote that *zur* means to turn aside, be a stranger to but *zur* is the root, meaning to feel repugnance or repulsive toward. *Job*, 277.

20. The phrase literally means sons of my belly. Was Job referring to his own children—they had been killed (1:19). Was he referring to his brothers who came from the same womb he had come from? Or did he use the phrase as a reference to his fellow human beings? The context gives some support for the "brothers." Reference is to the covenantal relationships: wife and brothers.

21. In the following paragraphs references will be made to the following, Dhorme, *Job* 19, 20; Hartley, *Job*, 83–84; Delitzsch, *Job*, vol. 1, 70, 73; Kroeze, *Job*, 60, 61; Pope, *Job*, 22, 23; Sasson, *Job's Wife*" 86–90; Habel, *Job*, 427–32. Habel intimates that Job was aware

of the curse of the covenant. Thomas wrote commenting on Job's covenant with his eyes, 31:1–4, that Job, a covenant man, knew about the power of temptation. *The Storm*, 237.

22. Sasson wrote that Job's wife married a man much older than herself since she had ten children after the loss of the first ten, 89.

23. What was written in preceding paragraphs is not acceptable to feminists who stress the dominance of the patriarchalism.

24. Pope, *Job.* 22. Cf. also comments by Dhorme, *Job*, 19.

25. Cf. Sasson "Job's Wife," 90.

26. Dhorme wrote that *năbālôt* were foolish women who had neither brains nor moral principles, *Job,* 20.

27. The NIV translates the term as *trouble*. The term *misfortune* appears in various comments on this passage.

28. Hartley, *Job,* 84.

29. Cf. chap. 35, page 49.

30. This text, 6:14, is considered to present textual problems; cf. Dhorme, *Job*, 84, 85; and Hartley, *Job*, 13:1–8.

31. Dhorme wrote, "what could be vehement, more piercing than the twofold cry." *Job*, 280.

32. Dhorme has presented a review of what various critical scholars have proposed concerning the authors/editors of the book of Job and how various distinct parts, like Elihu's speech were included. Ibid.. The omission of a reply to Elihu has led some scholars to suggest that Elihu's speech is a later insertion into the text.

33. Cf. Hartley, *Job*, 426,

34. Note that Job used the term *'im* (if) seventeen times and followed these with a readiness, if guilty, to be cursed.

35. *Biblia Hebraica*, edited by K. Kittel, reads *''saddîq bĕ 'ênōyû* (righteous in his eyes).

36. Elihu is identified more specifically than the other three men. The name means "My God is He." He was a son of a Buzite, the family of Ram whom scholars have not been able to identify with any specificity. Barakel and Elihu were Aramaeans. Cf. Delitzsch, *Job*, vol. II, 206, 207. A specific implication of Elihu's heritage is that Yahweh and faith in and service for him, were prevalent beyond Abraham's family and descendants. Cf. also Kroeze. Elihu was not an Arab but an Aramaean, *Job*, 360.

37. Cf. what Hartley wrote: "the youthful bombastic man was verbose and overly apologetic," *Job*, 427. Kroeze referred to Elihu's anger, calling attention to the unique phrase *wayyihhar 'aph 'ĕlîhû* (Elihu's nose became hot) and the three more references to his anger (32:2).

38. Cf. what Hartley wrote about the Spirit and Elihu. Ibid., 434.

39. Carlyle, *Job*, referred to Elihu as moderator telling the three men they were foolish for condemning Job and that Job had been presumptuous and demonstrated ignorance, 249.

40. Hartley, *Job*, 427.

41. It cannot be established with certainty that the Uz referred to, as descendant of Shem and son of Nahor, is the same person.

42. Cf. my book *From Creation to Consummation*, the first seven chapters.

43. Cf. comment by G. Aimers, in his essay "The Rhetoric" "Job had a grievance with God—he thinks God owes him redress for not honoring the covenant," 100.

44. Wilson, "Book of Job and Fear," 60.

45. Cf. Bruggemann, *Theology*, who refers to Job as the counterpoint to Abraham. Job gave a fuller expression to being blameless, 489–91.

46. Hartley correctly commented that the verb, prefixed by *hā* (interrogative) *rôb* has various interpretations. Cf. his note 1, 514.

47. Dhorme read *'amĕ'am* as *'amĕ'as* (I sink down) *Job*, 646, 647. He interpreted the term to mean "I mortify myself."

48. See Wilson, "Fear of God," 65.

49. Ibid., Wilson believes that the concept "fear of God" when properly studied offers a key to one's understanding of the shape of the book of Job, 86.

50. Elihu referred to Yahweh God's love for his created world by referring to the rain that God gave to water the earth (37:12). Job, as a man, living on and from the land, having pastures for his livestock benefited from Yahweh God's love for his created world.

51. Some biblical translators translated the Hebrew term *yir 'ālĕka*, literally "your fear." Others interpreted it as piety, reverence, religion. Again, these differing translations indicate the rich and extensive meaning of the term.

52. Dhorme has referred to 6:14 as *crux interpretation.* A review of what he surveyed gives one an overview of how this passage has been interpreted. Dhorme concluded the passage should be interpreted as "His friend has scorned compassion and forsaken the fear of *Shaddaî*," *Job*, 85. Kroeze has also discussed various interpretations and entitled t 6:14–20 as the *"ontrouw"* (*unfaithfulness or disloyalty*) of the friends. *Job*, 103.

53. Hartley, *Job*, 136–38.

54. Note that piety (NIV) is the translation used rather than a literal translation.

55. Cf. Francis Andersen, *Job* (Downer's Grove: InterVarsity, 1976), 202–3.

56. Cf. Dhorme, *Job*, 573. God does not even look on all the wise in heart because he is surrounded by a very formidable glory, 573. Hartley wrote that Elihu meant to say that the wise in heart fear God and do not dispute with him, *Job*, 484.

57. Andersen, *Job*, 268.

58. Ibid., "We have come full circle to Job 28:28," 268. Hartley also wrote Elihu's conclusion parallels Job 28:28. It is difficult to understand how Hartley reached that conclusion when one considers his comments on 37:24. *Job*, 484.

59. Hartley, *Job*, 115.

60. Commentators draw attention to Prov. 17:28 where Job's words are explicitly stated "Even a fool who keeps silent is considered wise." Cf. e.g., Dhorme, *Job*, 183.

61. The verb *parar* appears only in the hiphil and is variously translated as break, destroy, undermine, violate.

62. The term *sihah* means complaint but in various contexts it refers to meditation or devotion before God (cf. Ps. 19:97, 99).

63. Andersen has described Job's words as recorded in 26:5–14 as one of the grandest recitations in the whole book. It is a magnificent description of God's power in creation. *Job*, 216.

64. Note that Andersen correctly wrote that many commentators do not like this verse because it is a platitude expressing banal moralism. *Job*, 229. Gordis, having posited that Job was written in the era of the 6th to 4th centuries B.C., wrote that Job 28 was written by the author of Job and reflected the spirituality of the Torah and the Prophets, 30. Wilson wrote that "the statement of 28:28 is clearly the peak of the fear of God idea in the whole book." *Job*, 69.

37

The Mediator in the Book of Job

I. Introductory Comments

II. Job: A Type of Jesus Christ

III. Studies of Relevant Passages

IV. Conclusion to Study of the Book of Job

37

The Mediator in the Book of Job

Introductory Comments

Is the Mediatorial Strand in the Golden Cable in the Book of Job?

In my biblical theological studies of the Old Testament,[1] the Golden Cable was seen and set forth to be the unifying reality of Old Testament revelation.

The kingdom and the covenant were seen as two strands of the cable. These two are present in the book of Job. The question to be addressed in this chapter is: is the mediatorial strand present, thus indicating that the book of Job is and contributes to an integral part of the Golden Cable? Objectively observed, one should conclude that it is present because the Mediator is the Lord in the kingdom and the Administrator of the Covenant. From the biblical theological perspective, then, it should be understood that this strand is an integral unifying reality also. The questions to be answered are: does the text of Job include it? And is the book of Job, usually referred to as a wisdom book, an integral and contributing reality in the progressive revelation of the Mediator as recorded in the Scriptures? In this chapter it will be demonstrated that the mediatorial strand is indeed present and contributes to the unity of divine revelation as recorded in the Scriptures.

Is the Messianic Mediator Himself Revealed?

Accepting the reality of the presence of the Golden Cable's messianic/mediatorial strand in the book of Job, the pertinent question confronts the reader/student: is the personal Messiah presented or referred to in the book of Job?

The terms *māšaḥ* (anoint) and *māšîaḥ* (Messiah) do not appear in the book. Other terms, found in the Old Testament, do appear and refer to the messianic Mediator. In this chapter terms such as *listener*, *advocate*, and *redeemer* will be discussed.

Another important factor must be kept in mind. Old Testament scholars have pointed out that there are two conceptions of the *māšîaḥ* (Messiah). The narrower refers to the person, the king, and the bliss he offers. The wider concept includes promises, work, and results—that is, all that is included in the entire reality of salvation and redemption.[2] In the study that follows it will become evident that the wider conception appears in various contexts. The narrower concept is not absent either.

In the study of the book of Job it becomes evident that Job knew and believed in a person who was divine and available to persons as a friend, helper, and deliverer.

Is Redemption from Sin Stressed in the Book of Job?

One would look in vain for statements such as "Job, are you saved?" or "Have you accepted the Lord as your personal savior?" What are referred to repeatedly are the ideas of sin, evil, judgment, and punishment. The need for repentance and confession of sin is repeatedly stated. Deliverance from earthly troubles and woes is repeated as a blessed reality. Faith in God as the one who can remove pain and grief and bring healing and joy is presented as an absolute requisite. Many of the basic ingredients of a personal faith in the Triune God can be detected in the book of Job. The blessedness of having this faith is not omitted. So, the question "does the book of Job present the covenant Lord as Savior, Redeemer, and Lord? should not be answered in the negative. The blessings of having and living out a personal relationship between the covenant Lord and his covenant people are taught in the book of Job. This is done in the Old Testament historical context. Fuller revelation concerning redemption is given as the Triune God makes himself and his works progressively known.

What Has Scholarship Done?

There are a variety of approaches to the study of the book of Job. Most of these would be classified with one of the two main approaches—the critical and the conservative.

The Critical Approach

Michael O. Oblath can be considered a recent representative of the critical school, both from a critical literary and critical historical approach to the Scriptures.[3] He gave evidence that he is acquainted with a series of critical biblical scholars who have done extensive work on the book of Job.[4] In his introductory note he listed key words: *advocate*, *witness*, *protector*, *messenger*, *haśśāṭān* (the satan), *oath*, *formula*, *indirect question*, *divine retribution*, *literary construct*.[5] He presented a specific study of advocate, witness, protector (he chose this term instead of Redeemer), messenger/angel.

Oblath addressed what he considered to be the initial and central issue: the search for the identity of Job's advocate. He accepted the literary critical view concerning the writing, editing, and final production of the book of Job in postexilic times. Hence he saw the need to peel away "the centuries of biblical interpretation that cover and influence most analyses." Having done this to his satisfaction, he concluded that he was faced with two broad categories: "either the character in question is God, or is *not* God"[6] Oblath stated his view clearly: he accepted the proposal that one can speculate on Satan's possible identification as the advocate.[7] In his conclusion Oblath wrote that Satan was Job's advocate and he worked with God "to create the entire Joban scenario." He also wrote that Satan was not proved wrong because he helped demonstrate that the world does "not operate in a context of a retributive system."[8]

Comment: it is striking how critical scholarship attempts, and can, alter the basic message of the Scriptures. By adopting the view that the book of Job was written, edited, and re-edited repeatedly, and that the final production came in post-exilic times, the appeal can be made to the view that *Satan* was introduced to biblical writers in the Persian period. Satan, considered to be the adversary in Jesus' time, was now construed as God's helper among the heavenly hosts.

The Conservative Approach

The commentators and essayists that have written concerning the Mediator in the book of Job are not consistent in their acceptance of the Hebrew text as it is available. Some give evidence of uncertainties. An example of this is a New Testament scholar who wrote concerning "The Patience of Job and the Patience of Jesus."[9] Garrett does not give an indication that she accepted the revisionist view of the book of Job. But when she discussed the reference to the patience of Job (James 5:11), she relied quite heavily on intertestamentary/apocalyptic sources. These she indicated provided the setting and sources for James to quote Job and write of "patient endurance and steadfastness."[10]

In this study concerning the Mediator in the book of Job, the conservative approach to the text and to the subject is taken. This approach leads one to conclude that Job refers to a divine person. He made no specific distinction between the Father and Son but did indicate certainty regarding one who is God.[11]

Job: A Type of Jesus Christ

The Issue of Typology

The question basically is what, if any, relationship did Job have to the promised seed of the woman (Gen. 3:14, 15) and to Noah's son Shem who was particularly and specifically blessed (Gen. 9:26)? Is there any special relationship between Job and Abraham? The seed, Shem, and Abraham have been correctly understood to have had a specific future relevance in regard to the promised Messiah. Does Job have a role also in Old Testament pointing to, foreshadowing of, and prophesying concerning the promised Mediator, Messiah, Servant? These questions arose anew when the essay "The Patience of Job and the Patience of Jesus"[12] came to my attention. Is Job in some way a type of Jesus Christ?

An Old Testament type was a truly historical thing, event, or person. These could serve as symbols at the time of their presence but they had a definite prospective aspect regarding what would become real or applicable in the future.[13] Furthermore, a type could function in three specific ways. First, a person who was a type was to be and became an ancestor of Jesus Christ. Abraham, Joseph, and David are outstanding ancestral types. Second, a person was a type of Christ, not by ancestry but by positions held, for example, priests, prophets, kings, and by deeds performed. Prophecies often highlighted and clarified the typological significance of a given person, object, or event. Third, a person or experience of a person could have typological significance by analogy. A specific relationship of some kind was present at an earlier point in history with what became present at a later stage in history. It must be repeated, both the earlier and later had to be historical realities.

Job should be considered a type of Jesus Christ. Both were persons who existed in history. Both suffered extreme pain and anguish. Satan had a role, be it very different, in each situation in the suffering and anguish. Job suffered near indescribable physical, psychological, and spiritual uncertainties, troubles, and anguish. Satan had a definite role in this when he challenged Yahweh God concerning Job's faith and covenantal integrity. Satan had a definite role in the suffering of Jesus Christ in various ways. He, by tempting Adam and Eve, opened the way to Christ's suffering. Satan, throughout history and especially when Christ was on earth, added immeasurable depth to Christ's suffering. We can properly conclude that Job was a type of Christ by analogy when the Satanically induced increasing depths of suffering are considered and compared.

Job can be considered a type of Christ by analogy also in regard to his endurance under suffering. Job, even when he cursed his day and uttered bitter complaints, never cursed God or denied his faith in and reliance on his covenant Lord. Likewise Jesus Christ, though never complaining or struggling in doubts as Job did, did have his Gethesamane experience. He prayed God to have his suffering pass from him (Mark 4:35, 36). He prayed that God the Father's will be done. Job did not come fully to that point of submission but he did remain steadfast in his faith.[14]

The Role of the Three Friends[15]

The point to be considered in this context of Job as a type of Jesus Christ is how the three men, dialoguing with Job, influenced him.

The initial question to be considered is: were the men representing, be it unwittingly, Satan? They accused Job of sin and evil. They accused him of unfaithfulness. They implied that his previous wellbeing and security was in reality undeserved. They implied, as Satan had said outrightly, that God had blessed Job but had done so with partiality. The three men accused Job of a reliance upon God that was not correct or justified.

The three men on the ash heap with Job increased Job's anguish and suffering. Their false accusations, however, strengthened Job in his steadfastness, endurance, and patience.[16] Job was sorely tried as he maintained his integrity. Job's suffering increased by his friends was minor compared to what Christ suffered when Judas betrayed him, Peter denied him, Jewish leaders falsely accused and condemned him, and the Romans tortured and crucified him.

Job's Experiences

In the preceding discussions references were made to Satan's role and the friends' role in Job's experiences of losses, pain, anguish, and spiritual turmoil. He had given explicit verbal expressions concerning these. Before we proceed to a study of individual passages that refer in one way or another to the Mediator, it is helpful to keep the following in mind.

First, when Job heard of and experienced the losses of his possessions and his family, he knew and said that he knew that what he experienced was at God's hand. He confessed that Yahweh, his covenant Lord, had given what he had had *wahwâh lāqāḥ* (and had taken) (1:21). Job experienced loss at Yahweh God's hand and according to his purposes. Job had confidence in Yahweh God's deed when he experienced losses and also in his physical well-being. He rebuked his wife because she did not acknowledge God as the cause of his trouble (2:10). Job expressed his faith and confidence in his sovereign heavenly father and covenant Lord.

Second, throughout the entire period of his trouble, pain, suffering, and anguish, Job knew that what he was experiencing was included in his sovereign Lord's will and purposes. Whereas Christ knew why he suffered, Job did not. This lack of knowing why did not indicate that he ever denied that it was his covenant Lord who was involved in bringing on his awful experiences. The reality is, as has been discussed before, his suffering, the accusations directed against him, influenced him to become more steadfast in his awareness that he was in his Lord's hands and that he suffered according to his purposes. Job experienced crises in his faith and confidence in Yahweh's dealing with him but he continued steadfast, patient, enduring deepest trouble and turmoil, in the assurance that Yahweh God knew what was happening and that only Yahweh God could deliver him.

Third, Job, amid his suffering and being ignorant of why he suffered, expressed hope and confidence in his Lord. He continued to appeal to him. He knew that the resolution to his tragic experience was with his Lord. In spite of an expression of uncertainty and calls for explanation, his hope in his heavenly Father, at times dimmed, but never extinguished.

The conclusion that one must accept is that Job was a type of Jesus Christ. Their suffering in the final analysis was incomparable. But Job's sufferings, in various ways, were harbingers and foreshadows of the experiences that the Mediator would experience. Both knew they were in the Father's hand and were secure in his sovereign power and righteousness.

Indeed Job's suffering must be considered typical of that of Jesus Christ in an analogous manner.

Studies of Relevant Passages

Job 3:1–26

Two comments should be made in a study of passages in which there may be a reference to or implication concerning the messianic Mediator. First, it should be kept in mind that all but one such reference and/or implication came from the mouth of Job. Elihu also made a reference to a Mediator (33:23–33). Second, Job's extreme suffering, unbearable for human beings to endure, motivated Job to refer to someone who would speak to him and explain to him why he was suffering. Job himself felt helpless and hopeless. He needed someone. And he knew that that someone was to stand between himself and God. Human helpers, fellowmen, even friends were not able to represent God to him. He knew he needed more than human insight, discernment, knowledge, and wisdom. He knew he needed divine power and authority to come to his relief from severe problems and troubles. He knew it was not only human powers and capabilities that had not brought disaster, loss, pain, and grief to him.

Job's first utterances speak clearly and effectively concerning his awful plight. He revealed how he had sunk to a deep level of spiritual desperation.[17] His questions, why was I born? Why was I not still-born? Why was I given milk of life? express this depth of hopelessness. Why do others experience peace and prosperity while I am given to sighs and groanings? Why can I not have peace, quiet, and rest?

Job, the covenant man, who had known the blessings of living in a covenantal relationship with his sovereign Lord, was in dire need of a covenant Mediator between himself and God.

Job 9:29–35

In his reply to Bildad's first speech, Job agreed that he knew he, on his own, could not stand before God. He posed the question *mah zizdaq 'ĕnôš 'im 'ēl* (how can a human being/man be righteous with/before God?) No one can dispute with God, whose wisdom is profound and who has vast power (9:2–4). Yes, who can stand before the Creator of the cosmic kingdom (9:5–13)? Job knew he could not win in a court case even though he knew he was innocent of the charges his friends brought against him (9:14–28).

After Job had begun his answer to Bildad as referred to above, Job brought in his desire for a Mediator again. He referred to how his friends considered him guilty. He was accused of sin and evil (9:29). Job insisted that his hands were clean, as if washed with soap and soda, but he nevertheless was cast *băššahat* (into a filth)[18] by God. If he would remove himself from this and redress himself, even his clothes would detest him. Dhorme has referred to a commentator who interpreted that friends would detest him. Another commentator wrote that clothes were endowed with "feelings of horror and aversion from such a sullied body."[19] Job was deeply troubled. Not only did his friends accuse him. God also did. He believed he was suffering under God's hands in which was the rod that afflicted him. He himself could not remove it. But how could it be removed? Or even, how could he come to understand why he was under it and be relieved?

Verse 33 has been considered an important statement. There may be some difference in detail, but there is agreement that Job looks beyond himself or his friends. Does Job say he needs someone or that there is no one? Does Job call for someone who will enable him to attain a right relationship with God who "makes existence in suffering holy and acceptable?"[20] The term *môhîah* must be properly understood. It does not refer to a judge who would stand above God and Job. That was not in Job's mind. The term must be understood to refer to an umpire[21] or to an arbiter between God and Job. This latter term is preferable. Arbitration takes place in a legal context. An arbiter knows both sides of the problem. Job believed an arbiter would understand him and also God. The arbiter, speaking anthropologically, would lay his hand on both God and him and in that way the rod of affliction would be removed from him. Once that was gone, the terror that frightened Job would be removed. Then he would be free to speak without fear. But, as Job continued his speech (10:1–20), he did not indicate that an arbiter was active between himself and God.

What conclusion should be drawn from Job's reference to his need for an arbiter? First, Job knew he needed more than a human person who could or would serve as an effective arbiter. He knew he needed a heavenly umpire to effect a reconciliation. Job's genuine yearning for divine help "shines through this line."[22] Second, Job gave undoubted expression to his knowledge that his sovereign Lord was involved in his suffering. Only a divine one could and would remove God's rod upon him, remove his terror, and restore his relationship with God. It should be noted, however, that from God's perspective, his relationship with Job was not broken or dissolved. Job knew nothing of the cosmic battle between Satan and God in which he was the chief and central issue. Third, Job spoke prophetically[23] concerning the great and absolute need every sinner had. This need was to have an arbiter, in fact, a mediator between the sovereign covenant Lord and mankind, the covenant servant, who in sin and its results requires a divine mediator and deliverer. Fourth, Job did not refer directly or implicitly to the arbiter or mediator who would take the punishment for sin upon himself. Job did think the mediator would remove the rod, remove terror, and restore a righteous relationship between the Lord and his suffering agents. Job did not refer to a substitutionary mediator.

Job 13:13–19

Job made a rather long response to Zophar, who had spoken harshly to him as if he were as dumb as a donkey's colt (11:12). He began by addressing the three men with him (12:1–13:19). Then he addressed God (13:20–14:22). In the last part of his words to the men Job again referred to his innocence and expressed assurance that he would be vindicated. The phrase in the Hebrew text *yâda 'tî kî 'ănî 'ezdaq* (I know that I am righteous) calls for special attention. First, note that Job has stated with confidence that he has prepared his case (13:18a). He is ready to go to court. He is confident that he is fully aware of his situation. Second, in the legal context he made a strong statement referring to himself. The Hebrew use of *'ănî* indicates Job placed strong emphasis upon himself, *I*. This emphatic personal pronoun is followed by the first-person prefix to the two verbs that he used. Job was prepared. Third, the verb *to know* is used. Job was certain concerning the aspects of his case. He had listened to his companions. He had reflected on his past. He knew, without doubt, what the truth was concerning himself. Fourth, Job said *'eẓdaq*. The form of this denominative verb is first-person qal perfect. Literally translated it means "I am righteous."[24] But, Hartley translated "I will be acquitted."[25] He considered the court setting and as often is done, when the term *righteous* is employed, it refers to being declared righteous. Delitzsch also kept the court scene in mind when he translated "I shall maintain the right."[26] Ellison wrote "I know I shall be justified."[27] This was clear evidence of Job's strong faith that he stood before God as an innocent man. Fifth, in this passage Job refers to his own status before God. He does not indicate what God does other than at most imply that God knows he is innocent and considers Job righteous. Sixth, there is no direct reference to a vindicator who serves as a mediator. The stage has been set for Job to be more explicit in his reply to Eliphaz.

Job 16:18–21

After Job had addressed his friends and directed his thoughts to God (12:1—14:25), Eliphaz accused Job of empty words and having a belly full of wind. He also accused Job of lack of wisdom and thwarting piety or devotion to God (15:1–6). Job's response was in a real sense a cry for pity when he moaned that he was dressed in sackcloth and had dust on his head. His eyes with deep rings around them were red from weeping. But the cry was followed by strong assertions. His hands were free from violence and his prayer was pure (16:15–17). This was followed by a call to the earth not to cover his blood, that is, he did not want to die (16:18). Why not? He was assured that there was one in heaven who would vindicate him. Before he was assured of this vindication, acknowledgment of his righteous status before God was needed. Now he identifies that one who stands before God on his behalf. He has three names for him.

The first name or description is *'ēdî* (my witness). A witness is one who appears in a court setting and repeats what the accused one has said. The witness declares that what was said in defense is true.[28] Job was convinced that in heaven there was one who had seen what really had taken place. That one, a heavenly, divine being, stood before God also and spoke the truth

The second name Job employed is *śāhădî*. This is an Aramaic term. Dhorme used a phrase to interpret it, "he who testifies on my behalf."[29] Job had no one on earth who would testify on his behalf or to defend him. Job is convinced that a divine one is his steadfast supporter. Hence the *NIV* is correct to translate "my Advocate" (16:19). On earth a defense lawyer is an advocate; in heaven there is an advocate for the innocent; he testifies on behalf of the innocent and thus defends him.

The third name Job mentioned is *mělîẓâi.* This term is another difficult challenge. Some translate it as scorner[30] but Hartley rejected that translation and wrote that other passages in Scripture translate the term as interpreter or intecessor.[31] Meanwhile Dhorme has reminded students that various early translators wrote "brothers and friends" and then went on to demonstrate his readiness to employ radical textual criticism by rewriting the Hebrew words and translating 16:20 as "my claim and word has reached even *Eloah.*"[32] Job, however, must be understood to refer to his witness and advocate as his intercessor or mediator. This heavenly one is also his *rē'êy,* his friend.

Job, it must be concluded, came to a more clear comprehension of what great benefits he had as his thoughts turned heavenward. God was sovereign in his dealing with him. He did not understand why God dealt with him as he supposed he did. Job, however, was convinced he had a friend in heaven. This friend would testify on his behalf, defend him as advocates do, and intercede for him. Job has no personal name for this friend. He is convinced concerning the help he has in heaven.

A final comment. Jesus Christ is spoken of in the New Testament as the One who at the Father's right hand intercedes for his people (Rom. 8:34). The writer to the Hebrews reminded his readers that Christ always lives to intercede for his suffering people (Heb. 7:25). Job does not identify his witness, advocate/defender, intercessor, and friend as the New Testament writers later did. But Job declared with assurance and conviction that he, a faithful covenant man, had a faithful, fully dependable covenant Mediator.

Job 19:21–29

As one follows Job's increasing insistence on his innocence and as he spoke more forcefully of one in heaven who represented him as witness, defender, and intercessor, one comes to realize that Job was becoming psychologically and spiritually stronger. He would still have weak moments and would express uncertainties. But in this passage, Job reached the heights of his assurance and faith. He knew he had a covenant mediator who was his Redeemer.[33]

Chapter 19 records Job's reply to Bildad, who concluded his second speech by intimating that Job was an evil man who didn't know God (18:21). Job's reply reflected his pain, "How long will you torment me crushing me with words?" (19:2). As Job considered his fellowmen he told them that if he had indeed sinned that was between him and God who he was assured had *'iwwětānî.* This verb *'ût* in the piel is as a rule translated made crooked, to falsify, to subvert justice or to deprive one of it.[34] Job had sunk to a very low state of mind and heart. He was assured that God was involved in his stricken condition (19:3–6). Not only did God deny him justice, he moved fellowmen to do so also (19:7–20). Job cried out to his accusers to pity him because the hand of God *nāgě'âh (ñagâ)* struck him. Job did not curse God. He did unjustly accuse God when he said God's hand had smitten him. Job was completely unaware of Satan's role in challenging God. Thus, in a real sense, Job was not entirely incorrect for God had given Satan the latitude and freedom to smite Job. The point to be stressed, however, is that Job had sunk to deepest despair as he considered what God had done. Job called out twice *ḥonnûnî* (imp. of *ḥānan,* to be gracious). Some translators wrote "have mercy on me."[35] Job called for grace. He was accused of being guilty. If indeed he was guilty in his fellowmen's eyes and mind, they should show a concern for him. Could they not deal with him in love? Should they not show that there was forgiveness in their hearts, a readiness not to accuse him when they were not sure of what evil he had committed?

Job felt forsaken. He suffered physical pain and psychological anguish. His spiritual suffering was more profound and devastating than any other suffering, great as these were. Considered from any and all perspectives, Job had fallen to the deepest depths of pessimism. He had called for a witness, an advocate, a defender. They had not appeared. His friends proved to be his accusers, as if speaking for God.[36]

Then came light! Job rose swiftly to heights of assurance. His words, carefully considered, are an inspired response even to his own despairing words. Job spoke truth, theological affirmation with definite eschatological emphases.[37] Job's contribution was indeed a positive reality in the progress of divine revelation. As one considers these truths that Job spoke, it must be remembered that there is little unanimity in the interpretation of Job's words, even among conservative scholars.[38]

The Written Defense, 19:23, 24

Job expressed his deep heart's desire: *mî yetēn 'ēpô* (who will give then). This optative form of *nātan* (give, do) preceded by *mî* (who) and followed by *'ēpô* (then) expressed Job's realization that no one in his immediate company, or even God, would carry out his deepest desire. Job wanted someone who would act on his behalf, declaring his innocence. Since he had expressed the possibility that he might die before he would be exonerated, he made clear what should be done. He employed the niphal form of *kātab (yikkatebûn)* (be written) *millây* (my words). He deeply desired a written account of all he had said, defending himself against the accusations the three men had repeatedly expressed. Job was convinced he was innocent. His suffering was not due to specific sins. This conviction led him to add thoughts that expressed durability far beyond his lifetime.

mî yetēn that they (my words) *bassĕpher* (in the book) and *wĕyuḥāqû* (hophal form of *ḥāqaq,* to inscribe or engrave). Job wanted a record that would be more durable than if written in a scroll, tablet, or book. These might not be as permanently durable as inscriptions on monuments or rocks. Job called for the most reliable means to keep his record of innocence for posterity. This posterity should be considered, not only for personal descendants but for all time and for all people. Note that Job used the term *lā 'ad* (the *la* indicating the direction, *'ad* indicating perpetuity). Job certainly expressed his desire that his lament, his declaration of innocence, his affirmation of trust in God, and his appeal for vindication[39] be available to all who came after him. The translation that renders Job's statement that an iron be used to inscribe his words on rock so that they would endure forever is certainly correct (NIV, 19:24).

Job, living as he did in partriarchal times, was quite evidently not aware of Yahweh God's intention to have an inspired written record of his experiences. Job called for an inscription on rock, the most durable material he knew. He was totally unaware that in due process of time, written records would be written with the Holy Spirit's inspiration, thus producing a lasting and durable record—yes, on paper. It is amazing to reflect on what was said on the ash heap. Job, without his personal awareness, made prophetic[40] statements that would certainly be fulfilled. Today, the permanent record of Job's life, words, and experiences as a covenant servant of Yahweh God has been kept and it has and will endure.

Job's Faith (19:23–27)

Job gave eloquent expression to his faith. He spoke personally; that is, with conviction, he declared what he was assured of was truth and he himself would see his faith come to actual reality in the future. He employed three words, *wā 'ŭnê yāda 'tî* (and I know) (19:25). Job used the emphatic term for *I* that was followed by usual personal reference affixed to the verb. Thus the correct translation should read "and *I* know." The verb *yādâ'* can convey various nuances. It can refer to having actual knowledge; it can refer to a person having a very intimate relationship with another. It can also refer to what a person has experienced. And it can refer to a conviction that has arisen in a person's mind and heart through what was heard or portrayed or given by the Holy Spirit. Any one of these nuances are relevant in this context.

Knowledge is an integral aspect of faith. Thus when Job said "I know," he essentially said "I believe." This belief or faith, however, was more than "head knowledge." Job was convinced and absolutely assured of the truth of what he knew. He was prepared to surrender himself completely to what he was assured was true knowledge. This knowledge had relevance for his entire being, even in his present circumstance. Suffering, anguish, false accusations, a sense of aloneness and even forsakenness did not detract from the core and essence of his knowledge and faith concerning his God.

Job's knowledge and faith were the basis for what he went on to say. *wĕ'ahăron 'al 'āpār yāpûm* (and afterward upon dust he shall stand). The term *yāqûm* is the qal imperfect third person of *qûm,* to arise or to stand.[41] Job was convinced, with his knowledge as a firm basis, that his vindicating Redeemer would arise and stand upon the earth. Job said this because he was assured that he would be totally exonerated of all the accusations brought against him. He was convinced that he could be in the presence of the Arisen One, and be declared righteous.[42]

Job said more. Twice he used the verb *'ehĕyeh* (qal. Impf. first person of *hāyâh,* to see) (19:26, 2S7). Job's faith led him to say with conviction that he would see God. The Scriptures record that Abraham, Moses, and Isaiah saw God. Job was convinced that he would share in that experience. He fully expected, that as a person, with skin, eyes, and flesh, he would see God. He emphatically referred to himself as one who would have the blessed experience of being in the presence of the arisen Lord.

In conclusion to this brief discussion on Job's faith it must be emphasized that real and genuine as Job's faith was, it should not be thought that Job retained the lofty stance he exhibited. He never lost his faith. He maintained it and it fortified and guided him in his further experiences on the ash heap. It must also be stressed that through Job's knowledge and faith he gave the revelation of the Mediator a very applicable quality to the human experience.

The Gō'ēl *Lives*

Job spoke with conviction and assurance when he said, "*gō'ĕtî hay*" (my *gō'ēl* lives). Before a study is made of the term and its relevance, it should be clearly apprehended that Job made a personal claim. He referred to himself three times in a brief phrase. Consider the emphatic pronoun, *'ani*, I, with *ti* as suffix to the verb *know*, and the suffix *I* added to the noun *gō'ēl*. Job thus gave an eloquently positive statement not only of his sure knowledge but also of his close, intimate relationship with the *gō'ēl*. He was confident that he had not been completely deserted. His friends were against him, his wife had spoken against him, God was not answering but continued the "punishment" of Job. Job was alone on the ash heap; he complained about it bitterly. Yet he knew there was one who was there for him, a Living One—the *gō'ēl*" translated by many as redeemer, kinsman-redeemer,[44] but also as vindicator by some.[45]

The verb *gā'al* and its derived terms have the root meaning of redeem, that is, to buy back, to pay the price, whatever it may be, to regain possession, to gain freedom and/or to restore a prior relationship that has been broken. The term as verb, participle, or noun occurs often in the Pentateuch, the Psalms, and among the prophets, especially Isaiah. It appears in the New Testament approximately eighteen times. Dhorme pointed out that early church fathers and early translations saw an eschatological aspect in the term, mostly because of what they understood the context to say concerning the resurrection.[46]

A well-known reference to the *gō'ēl* is found in the book of Ruth. The inheritance (property) that had once belonged to Naomi's family had been taken by another person, not a kinsman, when Naomi's family had gone away to Moab. When Naomi and her daughter-in-law Ruth returned to Bethlehem, they could not retake the family's property since the men of the family had died, and the two women did not have the means to buy back, or redeem, their property. It was, however, the duty of a kinsman, the nearest relative, to pay the price of the property and thus restore it to its original and rightful owners. The account informs readers that such a relative/kinsman was present and able to purchase the property and restore it to Naomi and Ruth. It was Boaz who served as a faithful kinsman and carried out what had been prescribed in Leviticus 25:25–49.

There are, however, other contexts in which the term *gō'ēl* as a verb or noun appears. In Exodus the Lord promised Moses that he would bring Israel out of

Egypt and free them from slavery; with acts of judgment upon Egypt he promised that *gō'altî* (I will redeem) you (Exod. 6:6). Here the idea of redeem refers to doing great deeds on behalf of the covenant people to free them from slavery. The concept of kinsman is not clearly present, but the emphasis is on what the covenant Lord would do on behalf of his covenant people. In this context then one could consider Yahweh God serving as the kinsman benefactor on behalf of his people, to whom he was bound with covenant life and love.

In another context Yahweh God commanded Israel, his covenant people, to pay shekels (money) in order to retain the firstborn of nonconsecrated animals. The common translation for this verb, *pādâh* is to pay, to redeem. In this context the idea of redeem referred to the giving of money in order to give what the Lord claimed as his. Thus, redeem here referred to rendering possession by making payment. In a real sense, a substitution was called for: substitution of money for an animal (Num. 15:15–17).

In the translated version of the Psalm, the English term *redeem* appears repeatedly. It is often the translation of the verb *pādâh* (to buy, to pay the price, to do on another's behalf). Isaiah also used the term *padah* to refer to what Yahweh God had done or would do to deliver his people. It should be noted, however, that the term *pādâh*, in various forms often appears in the same context as *gā'al*. Hence the two terms should be considered synonymous in various contexts.[47] It should also be kept in mind that *pādâh* emphasizes purchase, paying a price on behalf of someone or something. *Gā'al* has that connotation in various contexts, but the idea of a kinsman purchasing, repossessing, and substituting expresses the heart of the term *gā'al*.

The problem to be solved is: how did Job use the term *gā'al?* A survey of the book of Job reveals that he used it two ways. When he first spoke, he referred to darkness and deep shadows as *yīgĕ'āluhû,* the day of his birth (3:5). *BDB* has "claim as kinsman," that is, let darkness and shadow claim the day of my birth as kinsman. This interpretation suggests a possessive relationship. It could suggest that Job's birth day belonged to darkness, so let darkness claim it.[48]

A review of commentaries confirms what one commentator wrote, "The choice is a matter for continued debate."[49] A basic difference is due to the two specific and divergent meanings of the root *gā'al*. A second meaning is to defile or pollute. Job is understood, then, as he "curses" the day he was born, to say it was a defiled day.[50] There are differences in the understanding of how *gā'al* is to be interpreted among those who do not accept the second meaning, to defile. One wrote that Job called for darkness to purchase back that day.[51] This hardly makes sense; how could darkness carry out the act of purchasing? Another wrote that Job called for darkness to take control of his birthday.[52] It is obvious that there is no clear understanding of what Job meant when he used the term *gā'al*. It can be said with much assurance that he did not wish darkness and shadow to "redeem" the day. Rather, Job seems to have said that darkness was a characteristic of that day. If so, then the idea of claiming it could be understood to have relevance.

It can be stated with assurance that Job had quite a different connotation in his mind when he stated with conviction *gō'alî hây* (my . . . is living). A careful study of what Job said and the context in which he said it does not tend one to interpret Job to place emphasis on the idea of him having a kinsman. In no other context did Job give expression to that thought. Rather, he expressed conviction that, although friends, wife, and seemingly, God convicted him as a guilty person, there was one who would totally exonerate him. He would be declared innocent. Job gave expression to his certainty that he was and would be involved in a court situation. There was One who would defend him. More, there was One who would completely vindicate him. Job did not include the thought that a price was to be paid for him.[53] Rather, this was to be done by the issuing of an innocent verdict.[54] Job was very ready for judgment day. Job had an eschatological vision that gave him assurance and comfort.

This eschatological certainty is embedded in the term *hây*, an adjective derived from *hāyâh*, to live. Job exclaimed that his *gō'ēl* was alive. He is a living one. Job was assured that though he had said he was ready to die, there was One who would not. His Vindicator was alive. He knew what the true situation was with him. He knew Job was innocent and would so declare him. He would surely do so in the future. Job did not directly imply that this would happen after his death. The latter part of the book informs us that Job, though never declared innocent, nevertheless was restored in his present lifetime. What Job went on to say, however, does give a definite futuristic thrust. Job spoke eschatologically.

Before we proceed to further discussion of eschatological references, the question to be answered is: who is the *gō'ēl*? Who is Job's defender, vindicator, redeemer? Commentators are generally agreed that the Living One Job refers to is God. But a question arises. If God is the One who brought on Job's losses and suffering, is this same God also his vindicator and deliverer? There can be little doubt that Job spoke of God in two ways.[55] He was convinced that his God would vindicate, deliver, and restore him. Why can it be posited with certainty that Job referred to God as the Living One? Job knew his God as alive; though he would die, his God would not!

The Gō'ēl *Stands*

The Hebrew text reads *wĕ'ahărôn 'al 'apār yāqûm* (in the future/end, he will arise/stand) (19:25b). The verb *yāqûm* is the third person imperfect of *qûm*. The text reads he will arise/stand. To arise is to stand. One should not consider the verb to refer directly to Christ's future resurrection. Job is convinced that his divine defender, vindicator, deliverer will stand! He, the Living One, will stand upon the earth. He will be present in the court of judgment. He will act on behalf of Job.

Job was convinced that the Living God would be present in the future. Job might die, in fact, he knew he would, but in the eschaton there was a sure future for him in the presence of the Living One. Indeed, Job was convinced of his future life.

Job's Future[56]

Job spoke of his eventual death (19:26). But that reality did not dim his assurance. In the grave he would lose his skin; he would return to dust. His Living defender/vindicator/deliverer/redeemer would not. He would be present on earth where he, not a stranger,[57] would see him with his own eyes. These words of Job have been interpreted in two ways. First Job having suffered terribly, all but become "skinless," would be restored. He, in his present life, would stand before and see God.[58] The other preferred interpretation is that Job, with assured faith in the Living God, would see God after he had died. He spoke with assurance that after he had been in the grave, he would be in the presence of God himself. He would actually see him! This undoubtedly must be understood to mean that Job, a covenant man of faith, spoke prophetically. Job would be resurrected; it is not explicitly stated that he would be, but the thrust of the passage leads one to believe he did.[59] The Mediator would stand upon the earth. Job too would be there. He would stand as a resurrected man and that in the presence of his divine, living, redeemer. His redeemer would vindicate him completely, deliver him and restore him fully.

Job, while on the ash heap, stated what his inner reactions were. The phrase *kālû kilĕyôtây bĕḥāqî* has given interpreters a vexing problem. One translated "my reins grow faint within me."[60] Hartley understood the phrase to reflect how weak Job had become. He wrote the correct translation should read "my kidneys fail (or are consumed) in my bosom."[61] It is a strange expression for readers who do not think of kidneys as seats of emotion, much less that kidneys are in the bosom. The thrust of the passage seems quite obvious: Job was in deep emotional stress. It radiated throughout his whole being. His breath, his quickened heart beat, his innards were in turmoil. He, reflecting on and speaking of a redeemed life as a risen man, expressed a deep longing to be in the presence of his covenant deliverer who was his covenant Lord.

In conclusion to this study on Job's statement that he knew his redeemer was the Living One, one should realize that a person in deep distress when overcome by trials in whatever circumstances these may be, he or she is not alone. On the ash heap Job came to the realization that his redeemer was with him and through him he would receive full redemption. This might not come in the present life, but it was a surety for the future. Various central biblical teachings were alluded to, such as the work of the covenant mediator as the defender and deliverer of his people, the return of the Lord, the resurrection of believers and the final judgment. These, recorded in incipient terms in the *Sitz im Leben* of patriarchal Job, were progressively unfolded as divine revelation continued throughout the subsequent historical events. In the study of the Psalms that follows this study of the book of Job, the progression will be noted. The Old Testament covenant people, exercising their faith, received blessed assurance that their covenant Mediator was with them, upheld, guided, protected, and supplied them with their basic needs in all aspects of their lives.

Job 23: 1–17

As Job concluded his prophetic speech he had challenged his fellowmen to consider their sins and the judgment on these (19:28, 29). Zophar did not appreciate the rebuke (20:1–20). Job then replied, saying, mock on; I know how wicked people live. You do not console me with your nonsense (21:1–34). Eliphaz responded asking how Job was of benefit to God. He again accused Job of transgressing the covenant social mandate (22:1–30). To this charge Job made reply. He did not maintain the high level of faith he had expressed before. He was confident he would be exonerated, but why did he have to wait? Why could he not go to court and present his case before his God? He did not directly refer to the *gō'ēl*, but keeping in mind what he had confessed previously, it can be concluded that Job had both God and his *gō'ēl* in mind. He referred to the Almighty who terrified him, who knew the way of life he took but nevertheless carried out his decree against him (23:14, 15). Job went on to ask why God did not set a day for judgment (24:1). Considering what Job had spoken before, one must conclude that Job again asked why his *gō'ēl* would remain silent so long. Job believed that in Yahweh God's court, his defender and vindicator would bring him deliverance. Bildad had a last word. In effect he told Job, a worm, a maggot, should not challenge God who sovereignly ruled. Job should be in awe of him (25:1–6). To this brief speech, Job gave a lengthy reply (26:1–31:40).

Job 28:27, 28[62]

In a previous chapter this passage was studied in conjunction with the concept of the fear of the Lord. A brief consideration of the concept of wisdom under the general theme of the Mediator follows.

We have considered various passages in which reference to wisdom was included. There have been no direct indications that wisdom was in one way or another related to the Mediator of the covenant. The question, however, should be raised in view of the role of wisdom in poetic literature: did Job introduce a connection between wisdom and the mediator?

The question "Where can wisdom be found?" was raised (28:12, 20). Wisdom was not found to be a product of nature. It did not have a material essence. It was to be found with God. God understood where its source was. He knew its role in the cosmos (28:23–26). God is said to have considered and appraised it. He also *hĕkînâh wĕgam hăqārâh* (hiph. pf. of *kûn*, be firm). In the hiphil the verb should be rendered "he established it" and the verb *hāqar* has the sense of search through, to explore. The idea of testing can be included). The thought expressed implicitly is that on consideration God determined that wisdom should have a role in creating and ruling the cosmic kingdom. One must be careful not to have Job convey what was revealed more explicitly later. Wisdom was given a personality (Prov. 8:12–31). Wisdom had a role in the work of creation (Ps. 104:24; Prov. 3:19; 9:1; Jer. 10:12). John, the apostle, wrote that the Logos, the Word, brought forth the cosmos. (John 1:3). The Logos of John is the same as the Logos/Wisdom of

Proverbs 8. One can rightly conclude that Job was used of God, prophetically, to set the scene for further revelation concerning the Mediator of the covenant who is the Word by which all creation, the cosmic kingdom, came into existence , was organized and ordered by Wisdom, who is the Firstborn over all creation (Col. 1:15–17).

A final comment. Job added that the fear of the Lord is wisdom. By a true fear of the Lord, a person comes into a direct and lasting relationship with wisdom/the Word/the Mediator of creation and of the covenant.

Job 31:35

Job concluded his lengthy oration in which he rose to heights of spiritual discernment and expression on a lower note. He was still on the ash heap. His suffering continued. He received no consolation from his fellowmen. God was quiet. His defender, vindicator, deliverer had not spoken. Job made a passionate statement. It was a cry from his heart. "Oh, that I had someone to hear me" (31:35a). Job, in a real sense, challenged God. He called on *Shaddaî*, the All-Sufficient sovereign God, to answer him. Job called for a written statement from *his* accuser (31:35a). He was confused. Who would stand up to accuse him and who would defend him? He did not repeat what he had boldly confessed before. He did not call on the *gō'ēl*, but on *Shaddaî*, but calling on *Shaddaî*, he also, in reality called on his *gō'ēl*, the Living One.

Job 33:23–33

The immediate question to be asked is: did Elihu speak concerning the messianic mediator? (33:23). He referred to a *mal'āk* (angel) and *mēlîẓ* (hiph. ptc. of *lîẓ*). The verb *lîẓ* is said to mean scorn, but in various contexts it is used to express turn aside, speak indirectly; in the hiphil it also means to interpret ([Gen. 42:23; Isa. 43:27] and thus to be an intermediary between God and man). The term *kōpar* comes from *kāpar*, which in the piel means to cover over, make propitiation, provide ransom (33:24). This combination of terms in the pericope under consideration has produced a wide variety of suggested interpretations. The basic issue is to identify the *angel.* Hartley has written as follows: "There have been numerous suggestions (1) another human being, e.g., a covenant friend, a prophet, or a teacher; (2) the sufferer's own conscience; (3) one of the angelic hosts; (4) the heavenly witness mentioned in 16:19; (5) the special angel or messenger of Yahweh (*māl'ak yhwh*, e.g., Gen. 21:17; 22:11, 15; Judg. 6:11–22; 13:2–23; (6) the concealed Christ."[63]

The broader context sheds light on the problem confronting the reader/student. Job had spoken of a vindicator, a deliverer, redeemer. This One would stand and defend Job (19:21–27). Eliphaz had responded saying in effect that there was no such a One who would deliver Job. Job had but to accept the instruction of the Torah and *tāšûb 'al sāddaî* (return to the sovereign Lord) (22:21–23); then there would be gold and silver for him and Job would find delight in his sovereign Lord

(22:25, 26). Job insisted he had not disobeyed Yahweh God's instructions yet he was punished as if he had.

Elihu had sat throughout the dialogue on the ash heap. He had heard what the three men and Job had said. He was assured it was his duty to reply to them. In answer to Eliphaz's position that repentance and confession by Job would be the way to restoration, Elihu asserted that a mediator was required.. There was such a One. The angel is an intercessor. He commands the "death angel" to release Job. A ransom has been found, though not necessarily money. Whatever it was would compensate for Job's failures and meet the demands of divine justice.[64] Elihu also posited the need for Job to pray to God and thus be restored. He had to confess he had sinned, gotten more than he deserved, but had been spared going to the pit (hell?) (33:25–36).

In summary of what Elihu said, the following should be noted. Job had been correct to call for a defender, vindicator, or redeemer. There was such provided by Yahweh God, the sovereign Lord. A messenger, an angel, the Angel of Yahweh, coming from God provided the ransom, whatever that might be, to satisfy God's justice and to provide for Job's restored righteousness. But, to have the gracious benefits Yahweh God provided, Job had to pray, and confess his sins (hidden as they might be), and then he could rejoice in his deliverance. What Elihu said can be considered a progress in revelation and a partial clarification concerning the messianic Mediator. He, however, not being aware of what the prologue recorded, was incorrect concerning the cause of Job's suffering. A final note: Elihu reflected a theological awareness that was definitely germane to patriarchal life and thought, particularly in regard to the Angel (of Yahweh) and the need for divine deliverance and redemption.

Job 42:1–9

This passage introduced Job's last words as he responded to Yahweh God's address to him. Job was reminded that his covenant Lord was sovereign in his providential rule over the cosmic kingdom. The Lord did not explain to Job the reason he had suffered at the instigation of Satan who had received latitude to afflict Job. The self-revelation of Yahweh God led Job to confess that he had obscured divine counsel without knowledge and that he had spoken about that which was beyond his comprehension. He repented, having gained a vision of his sovereign Lord (42:1–6).

Eliphaz was addressed by the Lord. He was admonished for speaking about God in relation to Job in an incorrect and sinful manner. Eliphaz and the other two needed sacrifices to cover their sins and also were in need of intercessary prayer. Job was to offer that prayer so that the three men would be cleared of their sin and guilt.

Job prayed for them. Yahweh God accepted Job's prayer. Job prayed effectually.

The basic point to be stressed is as follows. In a previous section the question was raised, should Job be considered a type of Jesus Christ who is a sure and reliable intercessor for redeemed people (Heb. 7:25)? Job was not a type of Christ as an ancestor or as an appointed priest. But he was commanded by God to intercede for his friends who had wrongly accused him and spoken incorrectly about him and God. This prayer was heard and effectual. Thus, in a real sense Job can be considered to be a suffering and interceding foreshadowing of Jesus Christ, the Mediator of the covenant.

Conclusion to the Study of the Book of Job

Job lived in patriarchal times. He was a covenant man, husband, and father. He was a man of faith and he lived an upright life. He was a kingdom man; he obeyed and served his sovereign Lord. When God gave Satan latitude to afflict Job, he proved to be an adversary of God and his people in a most disastrous manner. Job was totally unaware that Yahweh God was demonstrating to Satan that a covenant man, such as Job was, would not falter, curse God, and turn away from him. Satan led Job's wife and friends to be allies with him. Though Job sank to deep levels of despair and agony, he never cursed God or broke covenant with God. His suffering increased when his wife and friends spoke to him. But in that context of suffering, Job's faith and hope in his sovereign Lord was restored and increased.[65] Job became an agent of revelation concerning Yahweh God's cosmic kingdom, the covenant, and the Mediator. He particularly emphasized the role the promised Mediator has in vindicating his people who are attacked by Satan and falsely accused by fellow people.

What does the book of Job offer the contemporary reader, student, scholar? The answers to this query are not unanimous. One writer, having studied various commentaries, ancient-medieval, particularly Calvin's sermons of Job, has summed up what these commentaries on Job offers: layers and depths of suffering , the inexplicity of evil, the incompleteness of human existence, and the noetic nightmare of history. Meanwhile Job exemplifies vindication, endurance, and survival, as well as transcendence, insight, and wisdom.[66]

The attached sketch demonstrates Job's spiritual itinerary.

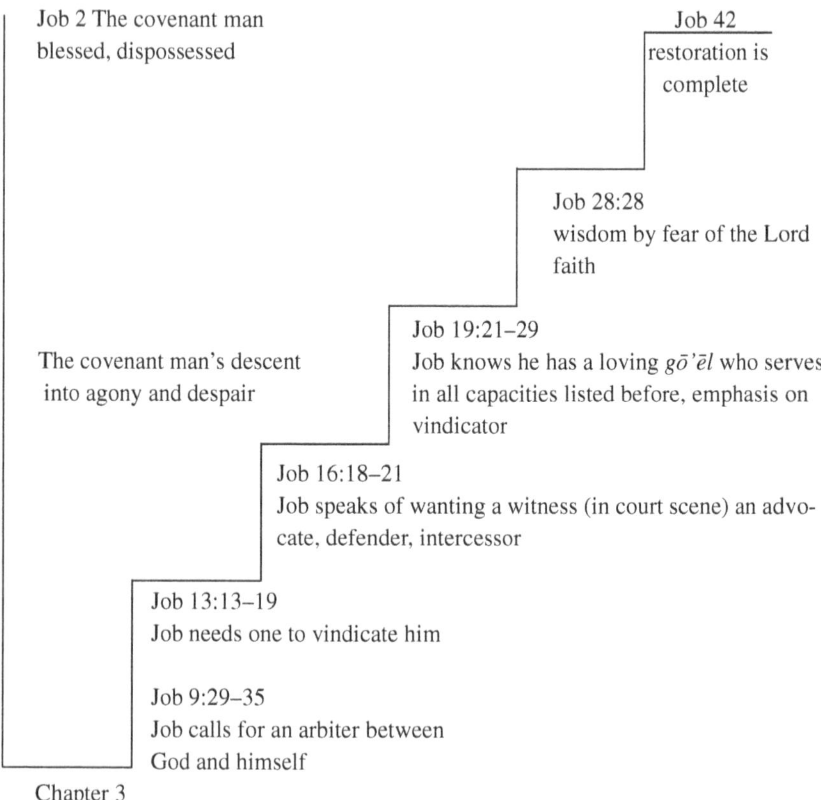

Notes

1. Cf. the author's works entitled *From Creation to Consummation*, vol. II, and *Messianic Revelation in the Old Testament.*

2. Cf. my discussion of these two concepts in *Messianic Revelation*, 19–23.

3. Michael O. Oblath, "Job's Advocate: A Tempting Suggestion," *Bulletin for Biblical Research* 9 (1999): 189–201.

4. Ibid., Cf. his note 4, 190, in which he lists scholars who wrote commentaries and essays. He referred to these as sources that "offer clear presentations and references for background material surrounding" the discussion concerning Job's Advocate, 790. It is of interest to note that he does not include a single reference to a conservative scholar. Oblath made particular reference to W. A. Irwin, "Job's Redeemer," *JBL* 87 (1962) as a source for his thinking.

5. Ibid., 189.

6. Ibid., 190.

7. Peggy L. Day, *An Adversary in Heaven: Satan in the Hebrew Bible* (Atlanta: Scholar's, 1988).

8. "Job's Advocate," 200.

9. Susan R. Garrett, "The Patience of Job and the Patience of Jesus" *Interpretation*, 53 (1997): 254–64.

10. Ibid., 255–57. One must not conclude that an appeal to nonbiblical historical and literary sources in the interpretation of a New Testament quotation from Job necessarily implies that the text of Job is considered to have been taken as the result of critical textual editions and revisions. It should be added, however, that there is clearer and positive evidence that the original Jobian text was accepted.

11. Two comments should be made: first, commentators such as F. Andersen, *Job*; Delitzsch, *Job*, vol. 1; Ellison, *Tragedy-Triumph*; Hartley, *Job*, Kroeze, *Job K.V.* 755; and Youngblood and Smick (note in NIV Study Bible), consider passages to refer to the divine person. Second, these, and other authors, will be referred to in the study that follows.

12. Garrett, "Patience."

13. See my study of typology in *MROT*, 153–67.

14. Garrett wrote that patient endurance should be considered, rather than just patience alone. *Patience*, 255.

15. The role of the three friends was discussed in a preceding context. Cf. chap. 35, 49–56.

16. Cf. chap. 35, 51–52.

17. Reference has been made to this in a previous chapter. Cf. chap. 35, page 47.

18. The verb *šāhat* in the niphal means be spoiled or corrupted. The noun derived from it correctly can be interpreted as ruin, or filth or slime pit (NIV).

19. Dhorme, *Job*, 143.

20. Andersen, *Job*, 151.

21. Ibid.

22. Hartley, *Job*, 151. Ellison has written: "Here is a broken man who has lost all, yet he refuses to listen to either his fellow townsfolk or to his friends. He knows he is a sinner, yet he cannot believe that God has cast him off." *Tragedy-Triumph*, 47.

23. Cf. Kroeze, *Job, K.V.*, 92.

24. Cf. translation of Dhorme, *Job*. 188: "It is I who am right." Kroeze, "*dat ik rechvaardig ben*—that I righteous am," *Job K.V.*, 109.

25. *Job*, 224, 5.

26. *Job*, vol. 1.

27. *Tragedy–Triumph*, 53.

28. The term *'ed* could be a derivative from the verb *'ûd,* which expresses a number of nuances of the thought to repeat, return, do again.

29. Dhorme, *Job,* 239. *BDB* lists *šāhâdû* as testimony. Hence one who gives testimony is a witness. See also Hartley, *Job* note 3, 267.

30. Cf. Kroeze, *Job, K.V.*, 127.

31. Hartley, *Job*, note 6, 263.

32. Dhorme, *Job,* 240.

33. Recall what Van Gelderen wrote in his book title succinctly translated *Job's Soul's Struggles*, See chap. 35, 6, B.

34. Hartley wrote that the term refers to an unjust prejudicial decision that denies a defendant his rightful due. *Job*, 284.

35. Here is a case in which a strict difference between grace (favor to guilty) and mercy (pity on a stricken person) is not observed.

36. Cf. Andersen's summation: "Job's dignity and composure are lost." He is broken under God's blows and the words of men. His appeals to the human and divine sources of help are ignored, *Job*, 192.

37. It is of much interest that Walter Brueggemann revealed an anticonservative line in his study of the theology of the Old Testament. In his index of scriptural references there is no reference to any of the passages that refer to the messianic/mediator explicitly or implicitly. Nor does he seem to consider that Job may have spoken prophetically. Cf. *Theology . . . Old Testament*, 758. He did refer to chap. 13, the first part, in which he saw a concern to speak of God correctly, 136, but made no reference to the second part of that chapter.

38. Cf. Andersen: "This passage (19:23–27) is notoriously difficult." The central problem is how to interpret "My Redeemer Lives." *Job*, 193. Andersen provided an excellent summation of what the passage clearly conveys and what difficulties must be considered as not open to definite solutions.

39. Cf. Hartley, *Job*, 291. Note that Job spoke of his words being written in a book. One commentator wrote that for Job the word *book* did not "necessarily imply extensive content" but the point Job made was durability, hence he spoke of lead, a tablet, and an iron stylus on a rock. See S. R. Driver and G. B. Gray. *The Book of Job A Critical and Exegetical Commentary,* vol. 1 (New York: Scribner & Sons, 1921), 170–71

40. See, e.g., Kroeze, who in his unusually lengthy exposition of Job's testimony, wrote that Job presented a prophetic consideration when he had not yet come to a clear understanding (*Job K.V.*, 148). Kroeze went on to write that the struggling Job began to see more clearly the prophetic character of his words—words that would come to fuller clarity (Dan. 12:2). Kroeze emphasized that the book of Job was written before the book of Daniel, 149.

41. The verb *qûm* carries the concept of firmness, of an abiding quality, and this can translate to establish and/or to confirm which in certain contexts is the preferred rendition.

42. Further reference to this "arising " will be made in subsequent sections.

43. See Andersen on Job's saying he would see God. *Job*, 1934. David Wolfers, *Deep Things Out of Darkness* (Grand Rapids: Eerdmans, 1995), wrote that Job expressed a craving for immortality, 404, 488, 89.

44. Hartley, *Job*, 292. Cf. Hartley's rather extensive bibliography on the term *gō'ēl.* Notes 8, 9, 292.

45. Dhorme, *Job*, 282.

46. Ibid., 283.

47. Compare uses of each verb in Leviticus, Deuteronomy, and Psalms.

48. Cf. Kroeze, *Job*, 45; Hartley, *Job*, 90, note 5.

49. Cf. Andersen, *Job*, 103. Cf. what Habel wrote, *Job*, 305–7. He opted for a celestial witness, a sympathetic member of the heavenly court who would serve as arbiter and vindicator, 306. Cf. also what Cline wrote, *Job* 1–2, 459.

50. Cf. Dhorme, *Job*, 26.

51. Delitszch, *Job I,* 77, 78.

52. Kroeze, *Job*, 45.

53. In the progress of theological revelation, it was revealed that a price—of blood/death—would be paid to remove sin.

54. Cf. Zechariah 3; the Angel of the Lord, the messianic Mediator, as judge, declared the priest innocent because his filthy garments were removed.

55. Cf. Hartley, *Job*, 295.

56. Some phrases in 19:26, 27 are difficult to translate and interpret. Yet, interpreters are quite confident that Job includes a reference in a very vague and general way to a future resurrection.

57. Cf. Andersen on the phrase "not another." *Job*, 194.

58. Cf. e.g., Hartley, *Job*, 295.

59. Ibid., 297.

60. Dhorme, *Job*, 285.

61. Hartley, *Job*, 297.

62. Chap. 36, 92–93.

63. *Job*, 447. Dhorme accepted the translation "interpreter" who as a prophet stood between God and man. *Job*, 501. Andersen opts for mediator, an agent of revelation, but he did not provide a specific identification of this angel who could be one of many thousand. *Job*, 250. Walther Eichrodt *Theology of the Old Testament,* held the view that this mediating angel "may be identified with the angel of Yahweh," vol. II, 23–29.

64. Hartley, *Job*, 446.

65. David L. McKenna, in *Job, The Communicator's Commentary* (Waco: Word, 1986), correctly referred to the book of Job as "a journey in faith" and exhibited that faith is not static, 20, 21.

66. Susan E. Schreiner, *Where Shall Wisdom Be Found?* (Chicago: University of Chicago Press, 1994), 1, 2.

III

The Golden Cable in the Psalms

38

Introductory Comments on the Psalms

I. Are the Psalms Wisdom Literature?

II. Challenges

III. The Role of the Psalms in the Revelatory Process

38

Introductory Comments on the Psalms

Are the Psalms Wisdom Literature?

An initial affirmation must be made. The book of psalms was Israel's songbook. The Hebrew title for the book is *Tĕhillîm,* the plural of the noun *tĕhillâh*, a nomative derivitive from the verb *hālal*. This verb in the qal is translated as boast, but in the piel, it is translated praise. In a real sense, then, to praise God is to intensely boast of Yahweh God, the Sovereign Lord of Israel. Korah, the director of music, brought boasting and praising together in a parallel expression. He led Israel to sing "In God *hillălēnû* (we make our boast) all day long and we will praise (sing of) your name forever" (44:8 [MT 44:9]). Since there are various warnings against boasting in the Old Testament (Pss. 12:3; 52:1; 75:4; 94:4; Prov. 20:14; 25:14; 27:1), should Israel's boasting in their God be considered wisdom? This question is impertinent. Israel was called to glorify their covenant Lord, to proclaim his wonderful deeds graciously and mercifully performed on Israel's behalf. To intensely boast, that is to sing praises to Yahweh God was obedient worship. It was wise of Israel to heed Yahweh God's call to praise him, to sing of his character, to rejoice musically in his goodness, and to give heartfelt thanks to him.

Indeed, it was wise to obey Yahweh God using the Psalms in various ways, for worship, meditation, and instruction. These were acts of wisdom, but that did not mean that all the content of these Psalms are to be considered as explicit wisdom literature.

There are two more considerations to mention under the heading "Are the Psalms Wisdom Literature?" Many of the Psalms have specific wisdom motifs and some have explicit wisdom content.[1] Consider Psalms 19, 36, 37, 49, 51, 78, 90, 107, 111, 119, 121, 127, 128. These Psalms, or parts of them, could also be included in categories such as history, law, confession, and admonition as well as praise and prophecy, but wisdom is integrated in these. Another consideration is that the Psalms can hardly be included in the other major divisions of the Old Testament-Law (Mosaic), historical, or prophetic.[2] The Psalms share literary styles with other wisdom books although some of the literary aspects of the Psalms are unique to them.

Challenges

Literature

The literature on the Psalms is extensive. No effort will be made in this biblical theological study to consult even a greater part of it. In a previous work, an introduction to the Psalms was included.[3] Some of the more recent publications will be consulted in the course of this study on the Psalms.[4]

Literary Aspects

The Psalms will be considered from a biblical theological perspective. This is not to be construed as simply or basically considering the Book of Psalms as a source book for theology. While the Psalms present a full array of theological themes, they do not do so in a systematic manner. Nor is there a specific methodology revealed. Rather, the Psalms are largely prayers, songs, and meditative reflections on a wide range of personal experiences, historical events, divine interventions, and promises.[5] While they are such, they served to express praise and adoration to God, to confess sins, to revel in the wonders of cosmic kingdom, to exhibit a recognition of the many promises Yahweh God had given, and to include strong statements of expectations that the sovereign covenant Lord would achieve his purposes for his people.

The Psalms, as mentioned, can be considered songs, prayers, and personal reflections, to be used in public and private worship and as instructional material. It is universally accepted that the Psalms exhibit a wide and varied array of Hebrew poetical features.[6]

More relevant than specific literary aspects for this biblical theological study are consideration of other features of the Psalms. A Scandinavian scholar wrote an essay subtitled "Hermeneutical Remarks on the Language of the Psalter." His title revealed his main thesis "The Mythic Dimension." That writer, studying various Psalms, concluded that the language of the Psalms was different from ordinary daily language. When Psalmists attempted to express reality they employed images and figures from a "makebelieve world." In his conclusion he wrote that mythology had been discarded; it had been exchanged "for a world of freedom." But the language of the Psalms is "intimately involved in the world-view of myth and mythology." Thus the language is a curious admixture of poetry, drama and myth.[7] Another scholar has appealed to Ugaritic poetry for comparison, illustration, and explanation.[8] Still another scholar, writing before Dahood, Hirsch, and Mowinckel had considered Egyptian sources referring to their use of parallelism, women singers before the countenance of gods, and other such aspects of Egyptian worship, contends that content determined the literary expressions of the Psalms.[9]

The question before a student of the Psalms, particularly seeking to determine the biblical theological role of the Psalms is: to what extent is a knowledge of Israel's contemporaries' methods of worship, use of songs, and their content and features a requirement for the understanding of the literary aspects of the Hebrew Psalms? There should be no doubt that Israel lived, worked, and worshiped in a *Sitz im Leben* that was an integral aspect of the world in which they lived. But did this reality determine their way of expressing themselves and their understanding of their covenant Lord, their Redeemer, their providential sovereign Triune God? Some aspects of cultural life, poetical features, and settings for worship were undoubtedly adopted. The position taken in this study, however, is that these external aspects did not influence the internal—that is, the content and message. In this respect, the Psalms are a unique literary phenomenon.

When considering the literary aspects of the Psalms from a biblical theological perspective, should attention be given to what scholars have referred to as the individual praises, struggles, and laments in distinction from communal or national? Whereas each Psalm had an individual author (except eleven Psalms attributed to the sons of Korah), these authors had their own spiritual, social, personal, and cultural experiences and reflections. But that did not limit them; that did not mean they did not see, participate, and reflect on what the community and nation experienced. While the authors, as individuals, wrote they did so as persons of their times and they were individually inspired by the Spirit of God to record what they saw, experienced, understood, and believed. Thus the Psalms of the Old Testament have a unique literary character. They are inspired, trustworthy, infallible, authoritative literary productions. They reveal truth.

In this context in which the inspiration of the Psalms is referred to, one should remember that although the Psalms arose from the hearts and minds of various authors, their writings were not just personal products. As they wrote they were led by the Spirit and this gave the Psalms their authority. One conservative author felt led to accept the view that Psalms have authority and received it when they were included in the canon.[10] It should be emphasized that the Psalms that were included in the canon were accepted because their inherent authority was recognized.

Another literary aspect to consider is as follows. Do these individual and communal reflections and expressions of praises and laments exhibit and reveal a theological core? Stated differently in this context, if there is a theological core, did it influence or even determine the types and character of literature that the Psalms exhibit? Or, stated more concretely, does theology per se have its own unique literary genre that employs specific literary features? In reply to these questions, the correct response is, or should be, that God revealed himself through Spirit-inspired writers who, being people of a given cultural mileau, employed literary features and characteristics that were apropos to the individual authors' experiences, insights, and abilities.

In conclusion to this brief discussion it should be stated emphatically that the Psalms are steeped in theology.[11] And it is expressed in literary forms, some of which are quite unique to theology but also in more common social and cultural literary expressions. There are unique theological terms; it is hardly correct to say that theological expression comes only in specific theological literary forms.[12]

Authors of the Psalms

Another challenge a student of the Psalms faces is in regard to how authorship is determined. Some Psalms refer to the name of the authors. Seventy-two refer to David, twelve to Asaph, eleven to sons of Korah, two to Solomon and one to Moses. Forty-nine do not include a reference to an author. Scholars have not come up with a unified position concerning this phenomenon. Nor is there agreement concerning what has been referred to as the *lamedh acctoris.* Does the *lamedh* preceding a name mean written by or written for, or in honor of ? It seems proper to accept "written by." Consider Psalm 18, *lĕdawid* (by David). The setting of this Psalm is recorded in 2 Samuel twenty-two. The heading relates that David sang this song when Yahweh delivered him from the hand of all his enemies and from the hand of Saul (v. 1). Another very specific reference to David, as author, is found in 2 Samuel twenty-three. David referred to himself as a man exalted by the Most High, a man anointed by God. He was Israel's singer of songs. The words he sang (produced) were given him by the Spirit of Yahweh. He stated that the God of Israel spoke when he sang concerning what the Rock of Israel was and did for him (vv. 1–3). This passage not only reveals that David himself was the author, but he was a divinely inspired author.[13]

In regard to the other authors, some information concerning them is recorded. Asaph was of the priestly line of Kohath; he served at the right hand of Heman the chief musician in the temple (1 Chron. 6:33, 39). In David and Solomon's time he led the service of music. Some writers interpret 1 Chronicles 25:1, 5, 6 to say that Asaph participated in the work of a seer and was involved in the ministry of prophesying.[14] Asaph is recorded as the author of Psalm 50 (calling the covenant people to worship) and Psalms 73–83. Asaph exhibited a comprehensive knowledge of Yahweh God's revelation in the Law and through historical events. And his style revealed he was forceful and spiritual.[15] He did not refer to himself as inspired but his ministry and Psalms clearly reflect that he was Spirit-led.

Psalms 42–49, 84, 85, 87, 88 have a superscription indicating these belong to the sons of Korah. Little is known of them other than they participated in the worship of the temple (2 Chron. 20:19). The message of these Psalms reflect a deep spiritual, heartfelt tone (cf., e.g., 42: 1, 2; 84:1, 2; 87:2). Solomon, the inspired writer of Proverbs, Ecclesiastes, and Song of Songs wrote Psalms 90 and 127. Ethan is referred to as the author of Psalm 89 and Moses of Psalm 90. These authors also, reflect a deep spiritual tone and a desire to be faithful to the covenant Lord of Israel.

The Psalms are indeed an integral part of the inspired, infallible, and inerrant revelation of Yahweh God as recorded in the entire Scriptures.

Historical Settings

Many of the Psalms, especially the forty-nine that have no superscription, have no direct reference to the historical situation when they were written. Some do, however.[16] Moses reflected Israel's journey through the desert from Egypt to the promised land (Ps. 90). Thirteen Psalms are directly related to David's personal life. Most of these reflect dire circumstances;—when he fled from Saul, 57; when Nathan informed him of Yahweh's reaction to him causing Bathsheba's husband to die in battle and he tried to cover up his adultery, 51, Psalm 137 was written at the time of the exile. The Psalmist wrote and sang this plaintive Psalm when he had not yet returned from exile.[17] Bitter memories were clearly disturbing the poet. He undoubtedly recalled the Psalm (30) David had written for use when eventually the temple was to be dedicated.

The Psalms can be said to cover the entire life of the covenant people as a theocratic nation. They refer to times from before their entry into the promised land (1360 B.C.) to the time when Jerusalem no longer served as the center for worship and government. During the entire span of approximately one thousand years, Israel had been under Yahweh God's keeping. They sang concerning this. When they were troubled they sang; when they sinned, they confessed and sang; when they thought of how their covenant Lord loved them and that they loved him, they sang. These songs of Israel were reflective of personal and communal life. Undoubtedly they were written, collected, and used basically for worship.[18] As they were developed and used, they reflected Israel's response to Yahweh God's revelation to them.

The Role of the Psalms in the Revelatory Process

A Summary Statement

It should be obvious to all readers and students of the Psalms that the poets who composed them did not consciously attempt to set out their literary production as representing stages in the progress of Yahweh God's revelation to his people. Nor did the poets attempt to present a definite system of truths or religious confessions.[19] Rather, the poets reflected an awareness of their contemporary situations. They expressed knowledge of what Yahweh God had said and done in times past.

They portrayed a real need to be aware of what Yahweh God would have them be and do as his covenant people. The Psalms thus reveal how the covenant people lived, worshiped, and served Yahweh God in their daily lives.[20] And, as they wrote, their constant source of truth and guidance was Yahweh God's past revelation in words and deeds. The Psalmists knew the Torah. They were well acquainted with what Yahweh God had done in the past. They knew that the Torah and Israel's early history contained Yahweh God's revelation to his people throughout the ages.

Summing up, the role of the Psalms in the progress of Yahweh God's revelation was to make known Yahweh God's past revelation, what it meant and required for daily life, and the consequences of acceptance and obedience as well as of rejection and disobedience. In this context, revealed truths were repeated, explained, developed, and applied.[21]

The Golden Cable in the Psalms

While one cannot state that the Psalms exhibit a systematic theology, one who is acquainted with the Psalms is well aware that theology permeates them. Scholars of varying perspectives and insights include either a rubric entitled a theology or sections with theological themes as headings.[22]

The main question for this biblical theological study is: do the Psalms exhibit a role in the presentation and development of the Golden Cable? Recall that the three continuing and integrating theological strands in the Mosaic, historical and prophetic literature, have been demonstrated to be the Kingdom, the Covenant, and the Mediator. Stated simply and pointedly, do these three "theological strands" reveal how they were integral to the revelatory responses to God's historical revelation?

A word of caution: no attempt will be made to place a theological grid upon the Psalms. Rather, a careful consideration will be made of the Psalms to discover and highlight what their central and uniting realities are. Since the three mentioned above were dominant, central, integrative themes in the Mosaic, historical, prophetic, and Jobian literature, the method to be followed will be to discern what role these themes/strands have in the Psalms as a whole. And to be determined, also, is whether all that is revealed in the Psalms can be seen as integral aspects of one or more of the three strands.

Notes

1. Cf. the discussion of wisdom and wisdom literature in chaps. 32, 33. Repetition of that material in this context should be unnecessary. A recent effort however, has been made to consider wisdom as a feminist concept.

Cf. Athalya Brenner and Carol Fontaine, eds., *Wisdom and the Psalms: A Feminist Companion to the Bible,* 2nd series (Sheffield: Sheffield Academic, 1995). I have decided that this essay makes no real contribution to the biblical concept of wisdom.

2. In my earlier years, when a pastor and in the initial years of my teaching career, I thought of the Psalms as included in the "Writings of the Old Testament." The Psalms were

also considered poetic literature, unlike any other book of the Bible although some books were recognized to have some poetic features. In the 6th and 7th decades of the 20th century a few essays came to my attention that called for a consideration of wisdom in the Psalms. Robert Bennett wrote "Wisdom Motif in Psalms 14 –53—*nabal* and *'esah." American School of Oriental Research*" 220, (Dec. 1975): 215–221. Sigmund Mowinkel's essay "Psalms and Wisdom," *Vetus Testamentum,* Suppl. III, 1955.205–24, also came to my attention. While not finding some emphases in these essays acceptable, I did come to realize that I could freely include the Psalms in the category of Wisdom Literature. One argument I found persuasive was that Psalms were also employed for teaching purposes.

3. Cf. *Messianic Revelation in the Old Testament* (Baker, Grand Rapids: 1990, reprint, Eugene: Wiph and Stok, 1997).

4. Joseph Addison Alexander, *The Psalms Translated and Explained* (Grand Rapids: Baker, 1975 [1873]); Arnold Albert Anderson, *Psalms 1–72* (Grand Rapids: Eerdmans, 1983 [1972]) (New Century Bible); and *Psalms 73–150* (Grand Rapids: Eerdmans, 1983 [1972]) (New Century Bible); G. W. Anderson, *The Psalms* (London: Thomas Nelson, 1962); W. E. Barnes *The Psalms,* (London: Methuen, 1931); Christopher F. Barth, trans. R. A. Wilson, *Introduction to the Psalms* (Oxford: Blackwell, 1966); Herbert W. Bateman, "Psalm 110:1" *Bib Sac* 149 (October-December 1992): 438–53; Roger T. Beckwith, "The Early History of the Psalter," *Tyndale Bulletin* 46 (1995): 1–27. Robert A. Bennett, "Wisdom Motifs in Psalm 14 *nabal* and *'esah ." BASOR* 220 (December; 1975): 215–22; James Montgomery Boice, *Psalms*, 3 vols. (Grand Rapids: Baker), n.d.); Theodore Booij, "Psalm CX: Rule in the Midst of your Foes!", *Vetus Testamentum* 41 (1991): 396–407; and "Psalm LXXXIV: A Prayer of the Anointed." *Vetus Testamentum* 44 (1994): 433–41; and "Royal Words in Psalm XXXIV 11." *Vetus Testamentum* 36 (January 1986): 117–21; P. J. Botha, "The Enlightenment Psalms: A Claim to the World-wide Honor of Yahweh." *Old Testament Essays* 11 no.1, (1988): 24–39; Marc Brettler, "Images of YHWH the Warrior in Psalms," *Semeia* 61 (1993): 135–65; Walter Brueggemann, *Abiding Astonishment: Psalms, Modernity, and the Making of History,* (Louisville: Westminster/John Knox, 1991), and *The Message of the Psalms: A Theological Commentary* (Minneapolis: Augsburg, 1984); C. Hassell Bullock, *Encountering the Book of Psalms* (Grand Rapids: Baker, 2001), and *An Introduction to the Old Testament Poetic Books: The Wisdom and Songs of Israel* (Chicago: Moody, 1979), and *An Introduction to the Old Testament Poetic Books: The Wisdom and Songs of Israel*, rev. ed. (Chicago: Moody, 1988); John Calvin, *Commentary on the Book of Psalms* (Grand Rapids: Eerdmans, 1949); F.M.A. Cassiodorus, *Explanation of the Psalms* (New York: Paulist, 1990–1991); Walter Chantry, *Praises for the King of Kings* (Carlisle, Pa: Banner of Truth Trust, 1991); Peter C. Craigie, *Psalms 1–50* (Waco, Tex.: Word, 1983); James L. Crenshaw, *The Psalms, An Introduction* (Grand Rapids: Eerdmans, 2002); Keith R. Crim, *Royal Psalms* (Richmond, Va: John Knox, 1962); Mitchell Dahood, *Psalms I: 1–50* (Garden City, N.Y.: Doubleday, 1965, 1966) (Anchor 16), and *Psalms II: 51–100* (Garden City, N.Y.: Doubleday, 1968) (Anchor, 17); and Psalms III: 101–150 (Garden City, N.Y.: Doubleday, 1970) (Anchor, 17A); Franz Julius Delitzsch, *Commentary on the Psalms* (London: Hodder and Stoughton, 1888); Basil De Pinto, "The Torah and the Psalms" *JBL* 86 no.2 (June 1967):154–74; Pieter De Villiers, "The Psalms and Spirituality," *Old Testament Essays* 12 no.3 (1999): 416–439; David Dickson, *The Psalms*, (London: Banner of Truth Trust, 1959); J. Du Preez, "Uitsig op Sending in 'n Israelitiese 'oeslied' : Psalm 67," *In die Skriflig* 32 no.3 (September 1998) 259–76; John H. Eaton, *Kingship and the Psalms,* 2nd ed. (Sheffield: JSOT, 1986); and *Psalms: Introduction and Commentary*

(London: SCM, 1967); Helen Efthimiadis, "Is There a Place for Women in the Theology of the Psalms? Part I: An Investigation into the Female Imagery of the Ancient Hebrew Psalter," *Old Testament Essays* 12 no. 1 (1990): 33–56; Peter W. Flint, "The Book of Psalms in the Light of the Dead Sea Scrolls," *Vetus Testamentum* 48 no.4, (October 1998); 453–72; David Neal Freedman, *Pottery, Poetry and Prophecy* (Winona Lake: Eisenbrauns, 1950); Sue Gillingham, "Messianic Prophecy and the Psalms," *Theology* 99 (1996); 114–24; J. Gray, "The Kingship of God in the Prophets and Psalms," *Vetus Testamentum* 11 (1961); 1–29; F. W. Grosheide, *De Psalmen* (Kampen: Kok, 1952); H. H. Guthrie, Jr., *Israel's Sacred Song* (New York: Seabury, 1966); Allan M. Harmon, "The Continuity of the Covenant Curses in the Imprecations of the Psalter," *Reformed Theological Review* 54 (1995) 65–72; S. R. Hirsch, *The Psalms* (New York: Philipp Feldheim, 1960); David M. Howard Jr., "Psalm 94 among the Kingship-of-Yhwh Psalm," *CBQ* 61 no. 4 (October 1999): 667–85; A. R. Johnson, *Sacral Kingship in Ancient Israel* (Cardiff: University of Wales Press, 1955); Walter C. Kaiser, *The Journey Isn't Over: The Pilgrim Psalms for Life's Challenges and Joys* (Grand Rapids: Baker, 1993); Derek Kidner, *Psalms 1–72: An Introduction and Commentary on Books I and II of the Psalms* (Downers Grove: Inter-Varsity, 1973), (Tyndale OT, 14a); and *Psalms 73–150: An Introduction and Commentary on Books III-V of the Psalms* (Downers Grove: Inter-Varsity, 1975) (Tyndale OT, 14b); Elmer A. Leslie, *The Psalms: Translated and Interpreted in the Light of Hebrew Life and Worship* (New York: Abingdon-Cokesbury, 1949); Clive Staples Lewis, *Reflections on the Psalms* (London: Wyman & Sons, Ltd., 1958); Alex Luc, "Interpreting the Curses in the Psalms" *JETS* 42 no.3, (September 1999): 395–410; James Luther Mays, "The Language of the Reign of God," *Interpretation* 47 (April 1993): 117–126; and *The Lord Reigns: A Theological Handbook to the Psalms* (Nashville: Westminster/John Knox n.d.); Patrick D. Miller, Jr., *Interpreting the Psalms* (Philadelphia: Fortress, 1986); and *They Cried to the Lord: The Form and Theology of Biblical Prayer* (Minneapolis: Fortress, 1994); Signumd Olaf Plytt Mowinckel, *The Psalms in Israel's Worship*, 2 vols. trans. D. R. Thomas (Nashville: Abingdon, 1962); Philip J. Nel, "The Theology of the Royal Psalms," *Old Testament Essays* 11 no.1, (1998): 71–92; A. Noordtzij, *Het Boek der Psalmen* (Kampen: Kok, 1925) (Korte Verklaring der Heilige Schrift, vol. 2); Greg W. Parsons, "Guidelines for Understanding and Proclaiming the Psalms" *Bib Sac* 147 (1990): 169–187; William Swan Plumer, *Psalms: A Critical Commentary* (Carlisle, Pa.: Banner of Truth Trust, 1978); Matthew Ploome, *A Commentary on the Holy Bible*, vol. 2 (Edinburgh: Banner of Truth, n.d.); Patrick Henry Reardon, *Christ in the Psalms* (Ben Lomond, Calif.: Conciliar, 2000); Jan Ridderbos, *De Psalmen*, vol. 1, (Kampen: Kok, 1955–58) (Commentaar op het Oude Testament); and *De Psalmen,* vol. 2 (Kampen: Kok, 1955–58) (Commentaar op het Oude Testament); Helmer Ringgren, *The Faith of the Psalmist* (London: Fortress, 1963); Theodore H. Robinson, *The Poetry of the Old Testament* (London: Duckworth, 1947); Leopold S. J. Sabourin, *The Psalms* (New York: Alba House, 1974); Calvin Seerveld, "Reading and Hearing the Psalms: The Gut of the Bible" *Pro Rege* 27 no.4, (1999): 20–32; P.J.N. Smal, *Die Universalisme in Die Psalmen* (Kampen: Kok, n.d.); David Starling, "The Messianic Hope in the Psalms," *Reformed Theological Review* 58 no.3, (1999): 121–134; Marvin E. Tate, *Psalms 51–100* (Dallas: Word, 1990); T. K. Thordarsan, "The Mythic Dimension," *Vetus Testamentum,* 24, (1974): 212–220; Gregory Vall, "Praying in the Messianic Spirit," *The Bible Today* 38 no.3, (May-June 2000): 156–161; Carlos G. Vallas, *Psalms for Contemplation* (Chicago: Loyla University Press, 1990); B. Vanderwaal, *Job—Song of Solomon*, trans. Theodore Plantinga (St. Catharines, Ont.: Paideia, 1978) (Search the Scriptures, vol. 4); Willem A. Van

Gemeren, *Psalms* (Grand Rapids: Zondervan, 1991) (The Expositor's Bible Commentary, 5); John D.W. Watts, "Yahweh Malak Psalms," *Theologische Zeitschrift* 21 (1965): 341–48; Artur Weiser, *The Psalms*, trans. Herbert Hartwell (Philadelphia: Westminster, 1962) (OTL); Claus Westermann, *The Praise of God in the Psalms*, 2nd ed., trans. Keith R. Crim (Richmond: John Knox, 1965); and *The Psalms: Structure, Content and Message*, trans. Ralph D. Gehrke (Minneapolis: Augsburg, 1980); Donald M. Williams, *Psalms 1–72* (Waco: Word, 1986) (The Communicator's Commentary, 13) and *Psalms 73–150* (Dallas: Word, 1989) (The Communicator's Commentary, 14); W. Norris S. Wilson "Happily Dashing Babylon's Infants Against the Rocks: The Use of Imprecation in the Psalms," *Reformed Theological Journal*, 15 (November 1999): 57–65; Erich Zenger, *A God of Vengeance? Understanding the Psalms of Divine Wrath* (Nashville: Westminster/John Knox, 1996).

5. Scholarly work on the Psalms reveals a wide difference on how to categorize and evaluate the Psalms. T. Robinson, in *Poetry*, discussed H. Gunkel's twelve categories of Psalms, 125. Ringgren, *Faith of Psalmist*, followed Gunkel in 1963, as did J. L. Crenshaw, *Psalms-Introduction,* 80–95. S. Mowinckel presented a far wider range of types of Psalms, *Psalms . . . Worship*, cf. his 15 (unnumbered) pages of content. A noted Old Testament scholar, writing in the 6th decade of the 20th century, Weiser, *Psalms*, considered the Psalms to have a cultic foundation, especially in the presupposed covenant festival. He listed five types, hymns, laments, thanksgiving, blessing, and curse, and wisdom and Psalms, 23–36, 52–90. H. Guthrie categorized the Psalms according to dominant themes; he decided there were 8 categories, *Sacred Songs*, 10–13. M. Dahood, *Psalms*, wrote that he would not join in the categorizing efforts but concentrate on translation and philology and doing so utilizing the linguistic information offered by Ras Shamra tablets XVIII.

Some recent students/writers on the Psalms have reduced the basic number of categories to 4 (plus collection). Cf. e.g., Van Gemeren "Psalms," to praise, lament, enthronement, wisdom, and miscellaneous forms such as Zion songs, creation, praise, penitential, and hallel, 28–33.

6. These accepted poetical features can be found in commentaries on the Psalms and in introductory studies to the Old Testament. Not all commentaries present a list of these features; e.g., Mitchell Dahood rather than presenting specific poetic features, discussed comparative psalmnody, authorship, theological character, Hebrew grammar, and lexicography. Sigmund Mowinckel produced an extensive presentation of poetic and other features of the Psalms in his *Psalm's Worship,* cf. table on contents, 15 unnumbered pages in vol. 1. The various authors of the Foreword in Samuel Raphael Hirsch's *The Psalms*, wrote general comments but did not include specific poetical features. A recent commentator who did consider the inclusion of literary features of the Psalms is Van Gemeren, "Psalms." Cf. his Introduction, which includes an extensive bibliography, 5–47.

The students of the Psalms are also faced with differing approaches to the interpretation of the Psalms. Bruggemann wrote "The Psalms are a strange literature to study." *Psalms . . . Theological*, 9. He went on to write that there are two traditions, the devotional tradition of piety; it is pre-critical, and there is the scholarly tradition that is often arid because of excessive attention to formal questions, 15. The devotional is represented by writers such as Vallas, *Psalms for Contemplation*, (he does accept critical views); Lewis, *Reflections*; Chantry, *Praises*, and Parsons, *Guidelines . . . Understanding*. Parsons, representing the critical authors such as Miller, *Interpreting . . . Psalms;* Barth, *Introduction Psalms* and Johnson, *Sacral Kingship.*

7. Thordarson, The Mythic," 212–20.

8. Dahood, *Psalms XVII.*

9. Leslie, *The Psalms*, 24–26.

10. Williams, *Psalms 1–72*, 20.

11. The issue raised in this discussion was brought to mind rather forcefully when a few years ago I read an essay by Calvin Seerveld entitled "Reading Psalms: The Gut . . ." 20–32. The terminology and literary features of this essay exhibited the character of the author as well as his adopted cultural context. Consider also that Brueggemann, in his *Theology*, has more than twice as many textual references to the Psalms as to any other Old Testament book, 758–62.

12. Consider what Dahood has written concerning the Psalmists' use of commonly known "mythical terminology" in the Psalms. The use of these did not reflect acceptance of what nonbiblical writers portrayed, but these terms were employed in a context to give expression to Yahweh's abilities and character. *Psalms I*, xxv–vii.

13. Grosheide has written that this Psalm was written at the end of his life. That he referred to great deeds in his life was not unusual in the broader context of his times. The difference, however, between his contemporaries was that they boasted of what they had done; David knew that Yahweh had rescued and kept him, thus the Psalm ends praising Yahweh, who lives and is David's Rock, his Savior, who is to be exalted. *Psalmen*, vol. 1, 52.

14. Cf. article by C. L. Feinberg in *The Zondervan Pictorial Encyclopedia of the Bible*, 5 vols., general ed. M. C. Tenney (Grand Rapids: Zondervan, 1975), vol. 1, 345.

15. Ibid.

16. G. Parsons, "Guidelines . . . Understanding" advised that three steps be taken to determine the historical setting of a Psalm: (1) utilize superscription; (2) examine internal evidence for clues; (3) explore the general historical and cultural background, 172. Parsons explained further that the expositor of an unnamed Psalm or one that has some reference to a person or time must distill the teaching of each stanza into a single sentence. Comment: is this distilling really necessary?

17. Some commentators have suggested that this Psalm was composed after the exiles returned to Jerusalem and were faced with the ruins of Zion and the temple.

18. Various studies on the origin, compilation and uses of the Psalms can be read in introductory studies to the Old Testament. R. K. Harrison has presented a commendable study in his *Introduction to the Old Testament* (Grand Rapids: Eerdmans, 1969, reprint, 1979), 976–1003. For a critical view of the origin and compilation of the Psalms, cf. C. F. Barth's *Introduction to the Psalms*, esp. 2–4.

Recent scholarship has continued to study the historical context in which the Psalms were sung. R. Beckwith, "Early History," pointed out that the postexilic books, Chronicles, Ezra, and Nehemiah, testify that the Psalms of David were sung in the 2nd temple, 5. The collection had been in three books but were later divided into five when postexilic Psalms were added, 24, 25. P. Flint, "Psalms and Dead Sea Scrolls," reported that 126 Psalms are represented in the scrolls, 454, 471. Flint pointed out that the Psalms predated the period of the scrolls. He, following J. Flanders, opined that the Psalms were collected in four books, 458ff. P. de Pinto already in "Torah . . . Psalms," wrote that the Psalms gave evidence of the presence of the Torah (Law and Israel's history). These Psalms were sung to maintain covenant union with God. Thus Israel, as a nation, sang in loving response to and in thankfulness to God.

19. Cf. Harrison, ibid., 1000, and Barth, ibid., 55.

20. The Psalms have been referred to as windows into Israel's faith. Van Gemeren, "Psalms," 5. For many Psalms it would be more correct to say they were doors that opened to Israel's covenantal life and worship.

21. See my introductory comments to the study on the messianic revelation in the Psalms. *MROT*, 327–33. A brief reference is included concerning how form critical scholars have attempted to place the songs, sayings, and so on, as the initial writings, before the historical, prophetic, and legal parts of the Old Testament.

22. Delitzsch has written a lengthy paragraph under the title of "Theological Preliminary Considerations," in which he reminded expositors of the Psalms to place oneself on the poet's standpoint or of the O.T. church's standpoint, or of the church in the present era. As they do, regardless of which standpoint is taken, the development of revelation must be acknowledged. Why? ". . . because redemption itself has a progressive history." *Psalms*, vol. 1, 64, 65. Cf. also writers such as Dahood, *Psalms*, vol. 1, xxxv–xxxvii; Van Gemeren, "Psalms," Section 3, 14–18, included in their introductory comments.

39

The Kingdom in the Psalms

I. Introduction

II. Kingdom—Kingship Terminology in the Psalms

III. The Kingdom Psalms

IV. Study of the Four Aspects

V. The Duration of the Kingdom

39

The Kingdom in the Psalms

Introduction

Literature

Research in various older commentaries revealed that the idea of the kingdom in the Psalms was not considered a dominant theme. One commentator referred to it in the context of his discussion of the messianic references and eschatological implications.[1] These and twentieth- century writers included extensive discussions of the enthronement of the Lord and of a newly anointed king. A reigning monarch was recognized as lauded by songs and prayers.[2] Recent studies reflect a deeper and more consistent awareness of kings and of Yahweh as King than of kingdom.[3]

Necessary Distinctions

The authors of the Psalms did not make careful distinctions between various terms that can be understood to refer to the entire, that is, to the broad and inclusive ideas of kingdom, kingship, and kings. Scholars of all schools of interpretation have recognized that this concept is present in the Psalms. That critical scholars resorted to the theme of enthronement is but one evidence of their uncertainty regarding the biblical intent and meaning of kingdom.

Traditional scholarship representing conservative approaches to and understanding of the Psalms has not presented a consistent understanding of the kingdom concept either. There has been a rather homogeneous understanding of a promised royal Messiah. His relationship to kingship has not been clearly explicated, nor has his role within the context of kingdom.[4]

Reasons for not readily making distinctions can be mentioned. The Psalms were written in many instances within the crucible of, or after, impressive and challenging experiences in daily life. They became the songs to be used in personal and communal worship. They became the sources for reflection, meditation, and general instruction. They became sources for encouragement and assurance in personal and communal life's experiences.[5]

The basic intent of this chapter is to discern what the Psalms reveal concerning Yahweh God's kingdom, that is, concerning Yahweh as King, his throne, his domain, and his sovereign rule (reign).

Kingdom—Kingship Terminology in the Psalms

The Psalms in the Hebrew Bible include the following royal terms: *mālkût* (kingdom), appears five times. In each instance, 45:6 (MT 7); 103:19; 145:11, 12, 13, the term *kingdom* refers to Yahweh God's kingdom. The noun *melek* (king) in singular or plural form appears seventy times. Judging from a cursory review, the term *king* refers to Yahweh God twenty times. The verb *mālek* (reign) appears six times; in each instance the subject of the verb is God (47:8 [MT 9]; 93:1; 96:10; 97:1; 99:1; 146:10). The term *kissē'* (throne) appears seventeen times; eight of these are references to God's throne (Pss. 9:4, [MT 5], 7 [MT 8]; 11:4; 45:6 [MT 7] 47:8 [MT 9]; 93:2; 97:2; 103:19).

The Kingdom Psalms

There are six Psalms that have been widely recognized to give "full throated praise" of Yahweh's kingship. They are 93 and 95–99.[6]

Psalm 93:1, 2

Psalm 93:1, 2 summarizes the constituent aspects of the kingdom of Yahweh God. It should be stated immediately that human kingdom and kingship are derived from and exemplify the over-all, inclusive kingdom of Yahweh God revealed in Psalm 93:1, 2. The four aspects will be briefly outlined and then a detailed study of the other Psalms that support and expand these four aspects, will follow. The term *malkut* (kingdom) does not appear in these two verses but the four aspects identify and describe the reality of the kingdom.

The Four Constituent Aspects of Kingdom

The King

Yahweh is the King. He is Yahweh *bammĕrôm* (the one on high), the great King, the great Lord (95:3). He is the Creator (96:5), and he is the judge (96:13). He is the Savior (98:3) and the holy one who is worthy of worship (99:5).

The Throne

The throne is the seat of the king. It has been established from eternity (93:2). This throne is wholly compatible with the great King. Judgment and grace issue forth from this seat of authority and power (94:2; 97:8; 98:9). The throne is between the cherubim (99:1) who are Yahweh's faithful, invincible representatives and agents.

The Reign

Yahweh God reigns in majesty (93:1). This actual exercise of his power, authority, and ability extends over all the world (96:10). His reign is absolute and because it is, he can and does judge and carry out his judgments with justice and equity (99:4).

The Domain

The term *tēbēl* appears in 93:1. The root of this noun is *yābel,* used only in the hiphil expressing the sense of conducting or bearing along. *Tēbēl*, the noun, is understood to refer to the world, that is, all that it bears or carries along. In some contexts (e.g., Job 37:18; Prov. 8:31) *'erez* (the earth) can be judged to be its synonym. In the context of the kingdom Psalms, the term *tēbēl* obviously refers to the entire cosmic kingdom. As the study of the domain proceeds, it will become evident that nations, Israel, the natural world, the heavens with stars, galaxies and the environment of the divine King's throne are all included in the cosmic kingdom.

Study of the Four Aspects

Yahweh the King

His Name

Yahweh, the covenant name of him who is King, appears five times in Psalm 93. The emphasis is on Yahweh the covenant Lord; he is the reigning King. Psalms 94–99 also refer to Yahweh as King twenty-eight times. While the name Yahweh appears repeatedly, it must be noted that Yahweh is referred to as *'ĕlōhîm* (God) nine times. He is acknowledged as my God (94:22) and as our God (94:23; 95:7; 98:3; 99:5, 8, 9). Yahweh is God.

The Psalmists, as they wrote and sang about Yahweh God, their king, referred to him as the Scriptures recorded him to be. Yahweh God's attributes as described by Moses in the Pentateuch and as he was known and referred to in the history of the kingdom of Judah and Israel appear repeatedly in the Psalms. The covenant people were taught and led to sing of, meditate on, and educate concerning Yahweh God as he had revealed himself in times past and in their own times.

His Attributes

Consider the attributes the Psalmist ascribed to Yahweh God in Psalm 93.

Majesty. He is robed in majesty (93:1). The Hebrew term is *gē'ût* (also *ge'ûn*). His entire appearance is majestic because he is fully robed with it. Majesty raises the conception of royalty, stateliness, excellence, dignity, and grandeur. The term has been translated as pride or arrogance (Ps. 17:10) when used to describe wicked men who present themselves as lords over God's people (Ps. 10:2). This false demonstration of would-be majesty arises from calloused, hardened, and haughty hearts. There is another context in which the term appears: that of the sea with its waves rising high. The raging or surging sea (Ps. 89:9 [MT 10]) presents a scene and sound of majesty. Try as one will, to think of and describe Yahweh God as a majestic God is impossible in human terms. His majesty is far greater than human terms can convey.

Strength. Yahweh God is described as deity with strength (93:1; 96:7). The Hebrew term is *'oz*.[7] A close synonym is the adjective *'addir*. It is translated as mighty (NIV), excellent (Ps. 8: 1[MT 2], 9 [MT 10]; 16:3; 76:4 [MT 5]; and as famous (Ps. 136:18). The Psalmists, however, indicated that they preferred to use the term *'oz* when they thought, spoke, and sang of Yahweh God's strength, might, power, and ability. Moses had sung of Yahweh God's strength (Exod. 15:2, 13). Deborah had called on herself to be with strength (Judg. 5:21). Hannah had sung of Yahweh giving strength to the promised king (1 Sam. 2:10). David sang of Yahweh as a source of strength for the covenant people (1 Chron. 16:11). Job had spoken of his God's strength (Job 12:16). This strength gave Yahweh God victory. The Psalmists joined their predecessors more than forty times in singing of Yahweh God's strength, might, ability, and invincibility. In theological terminology, God is spoken of as omnipotent; God is all powerful and powerful overall.[8]

Eternal. Yahweh God is referred to as eternal; it is in the parallel phrase in which his throne is said to have been established long ago. The phrase *mē 'ôlām 'āttâh* is specific. Yahweh God is addressed as "you are from eternity." The term *'ôlām* is translated variously as long duration, antiquity, futurity, indefinite time, unending future, or everlasting. In the context of Psalm 93:2 the term emphasizes that Yahweh God is without beginning or end. He will endure throughout all time and beyond. The Psalmists gave expression to Yahweh God's eternal being and presence more than 125 times. Not only is Yahweh God himself praised as eternal, so are his virtues, promises, and covenant.

The Psalmists, as they recalled the past, reflected on God's past deeds and ever-present virtues[9] and were assured of the continual existence and presence of their Lord, Yahweh God. He would never cease to exist. He had been, was, and would always be present with all his virtues, executing his promises and carrying out his purposes according to his never changing will.[10] References to Yahweh God's eternal existence as well as of his attributes, word, and deeds are in passages such as Psalms 9:7 [MT 8], 10:16; 29:10; 33:11; 41:13 [MT 14]; 66:7; 100:5; 103:17; 118:1; 145:13.

Holy. Holy is a prevalent term in the Old Testament. As a denominative verb, *qādaš* refers to being set apart, to consecrate. As a noun *qōdeš* usually refers to apartness or sacredness and as an adjective *qadoš* reference is to sacred and holy. These three terms appear in quite a number of psalms.

To be emphasized is that the source of and reason for holiness is that Yahweh God is holy (Pss. 22:3; 71:22; 78:41; 89:18; 99:3, 5, 9; 105:3; 145:21). Yahweh God's name is holy. His name identifies him. Because he is holy as the divine one, his name is holy (30:4; 33:21; 97:12; 103:1). His majesty is holy (110:3). The second person of the Trinity is holy (16:10) and the Spirit is holy (51:11). To be holy is to be totally and distinctly separate. It is to be pure, to be without defilement and sin, evil, and iniquity. To be holy as Yahweh God is holy is to be transcendent, above all else and incomparable. That Yahweh God, the Father, Son, and Spirit, is holy as described above, however, does not mean he was unapproachable and beyond reach for his people. The Psalmists knew they could fellowship with him, pray to him, praise and thank him. They could and should worship him as the holy one. To do this, however, demanded the worshipers and all things involved in this worship and service to be holy. The Psalmists exhibited a good awareness of what Moses had prescribed "as the Lord your God is holy, you be holy" (Lev. 19:7).

Holy worshipers were to acknowledge the holiness ascribed to Yahweh God's house (93:5). Not only was the house such, but the place and the hill were holy. Beyond a doubt, the Mosaic prescriptions for the tabernacle (temple), its furnishings, and the officials performing their duties in it were well known (cf. the book of Leviticus) and were a source of joy, thanksgiving and praise (cf. Pss. 2:6; 3:4; 5:7; 11:4; 15:1; 20:6; 24:3; 28:2; 43:3; 46:4; 65:4; 68:5; 77:13; 78:41; 96:9; 98:1; 99:9; 105:42; 138:2).

Omniscient. Yahweh God, the King, is omniscient; he knows all people, their lives, their circumstances and their experiences. The Psalmist reflected on the reality that God knows the thoughts and futile character of man (94:11). David knew that the Lord searched him and knew him; knew his thoughts, yes, all his ways (139:1–4, 23). He had also found comfort knowing that Yahweh God knew the anguish of his soul (31:7) and that the Lord knew that he proclaimed divine righteousness and salvation (40:9, 10). But David also confessed that Yahweh God knew *lĕ'iwwalĕtî* (my folly), *wĕ'asĕmôtî* (the root is *'āšam,* to offend, be guilty) and guilt was not hidden from his Lord (69:5 [MT 6].

God's omniscience had been revealed and recognized in the life of Abraham (Gen. 20:6; 22:12). Joshua had assured the tribes of Reuben and Gad, and half tribe of Manasseh that God knew they had proper motives for returning to their inheritance given them on the east side of Jordan (Josh. 22:22). The Psalmists knew their Lord; he had revealed himself as all-knowing. Yahweh God's omniscience had proven to be a source of confidence and assurance. Nothing had been, was, or could be kept secret from Yahweh God. The divine King knew his people, their lives, their hopes and intentions.

Additional Attributes. The Psalms, referred to in this study as the kingdom series, include a number of divine attributes not yet studied. These, such as Yahweh God's greatness (95:3, 9), faithfulness (97:1–4; 98:3), love (98:3), righteousness and justice (96:13; 97:2; 98:2; 99:4), anger (95:10, 11), and his glory (96:8) can be discussed profitably under one or more of the other three aspects of kingdom.

Yahweh's Throne

Psalmists' Assurance

There are three references to Yahweh God's throne in the kingdom Psalm series. The throne referred to as your throne (93:2) gives assurance that Yahweh God has a throne. And the Psalmist sang with confidence that God was on the throne (99:1) and that it was founded on righteousness and justice (97:2).

Moses had demonstrated confidence that God was on his throne when the Amalekites attacked the Israelites at Rephidim in the desert. He had gone to the top of the hill from which he could observe the battle. When he lifted up his hands to God on his throne, Israel was winning the battle. After the battle was won, Moses built an altar to Yahweh God on his throne (Exod. 17:15, 16).

David sang of Yahweh God sitting on his throne (9:4, 7). So did the sons of Korah (45:6; 47:8). Ethan, the Ezrahite, led Israel to sing of the durability of David's throne (89:4, 29, 36), because it was established by Yahweh God who was upon his eternal throne (89:14).

Metaphorically

Why is it significant that Yahweh God has a throne and that he is seated on it? It must be immediately stressed that when we speak of Yahweh God's throne we do so metaphorically. Yahweh God does not have a literal throne made of silver and gold. He never had, and never will have, a material throne such as David and Solomon and their successors had. To speak of God's throne is to say with conviction that there is a royal center in the cosmic kingdom. This center is not on the planet earth, or on any other planet or on the stars. It exists because God does. In a sense, the throne is also ubiquitous as Yahweh God because the Lord is always on his throne. He always has his royal seat; he has it everywhere because he is everywhere!

It should not confuse anyone to think of or speak of Yahweh God's throne in his kingdom. One must realize that an inherent and integral aspect of a kingdom is its throne. And for one to actually be king, he must have a throne. So what does a throne basically signify? A throne represents royalty. To occupy a throne is to be royal. It means the one on the throne is recognized as king (or queen). The throne represents authority, power, sovereignty. It exhibits majesty and grandeur and generates awe, respect, and submission.

Enthronement Psalms?

Commentators on the Psalms refer to these Psalms that refer to Yahweh God's throne as enthronement Psalms. Not all of these scholars agree on what is meant by enthronement or even if it is correct to refer to them by that descriptive title. Some writers refer to Mowinckel's study produced in 1921. He is said to have originated the theme of "Yahweh has become king."[12] Mowinckel, in a subsequent study, informed readers that he employed the form critical method in his study of the Psalms.[13] He concentrated on the festivals he discerned as the historical setting for the production of these "enthronement Psalms."[14] As one considers various writers on the Psalms it certainly is not clear whether Yahweh God is perceived as coming onto his throne, being on his throne, and/or acting like a king.[15]

Conservative scholars indicate that they all are not prepared to refrain from using the ascription "enthronement" for some Psalms. Did Israel also thus annually re-enact Yahweh's enthronement? A scholar wrote that Yahweh becoming King was not entirely in conflict with the Old Testament thought world. Referring to Hengstenberg and Delitzsch, he agreed with them that a newer and richer development of Yahweh's kingship was indicated in an eschatological understanding of the enthronement of Yahweh in Old Testament times.[16]

A careful consideration of issues surrounding the entitling of any Psalm as enthronement brings a series of problems to the fore. The very term *enthronement* indicates that a king becomes king and ascends to his throne. He becomes a reigning king when he seats himself on his throne. This clearly implies that when applied to Yahweh God, that he was not always a reigning king. The Scriptures make clear that from the very moment of creation, Yahweh God was on his throne. The throne is as eternal as Yahweh God himself (Ps. 93:2). As Yahweh God's attributes are eternal so are they as foundations of God's throne (97:2).

A second consideration is grammatical. The kingship texts emphasize that God *is* King. He has his throne. He is not presented as becoming king, or that he began to reign. The Hebrew text clearly states: Yahweh God is King and his throne therefore always existed. [17]

A third consideration is that the Psalms clearly indicate that God the Creator was King from the very beginning of creation. Hence his throne was clearly established before and during the time of God's creation activity.

A fourth consideration is that those who set forth an enthronement activity for and by Yahweh appeal to extra biblical sources. These pagan enthronement acts often included divine suffering and death. Israel's divine kings could not and did not re-enact divine suffering. The biblical text never records nor implies this.[18]

The conclusion must be stated clearly. The concept of enthronement applied to Yahweh God is definitely not biblical. Hence, the term should not appear, in commentaries and theological studies. If it is included, it should, as in this study, be properly interpreted and negated as a helpful ascription of Yahweh God as King.

Attributes of Throne and God

It was stated in the preceding paragraphs that the throne of Yahweh God represented royalty, authority, power, and sovereignty and that it exhibited Yahweh God's majesty and grandeur. The biblical text gives more information concerning the throne of Yahweh God. What is said of the throne are in reality attributes and virtues of Yahweh God himself.

The Psalmist revealed that God and his throne are eternal—never-ending (93:2). The throne is from eternity through all eternity. The sons of Korah sang concerning this eternal character *kiś'ăkâ ĕlōhîm 'ôlām wā'ed* (your throne, God, forever and perpetual) (Ps. 45:6 [MT 7]). To stress this reality, two terms are employed. The emphasis of the first adjective stresses duration, from beginning to end. The second stresses a close synonymous concept, perpetuity. The first term stresses the time aspect, the second stresses the durability character.[19] This throne has this perpetual and ever enduring character because the Psalmist was as convinced as Moses was that God himself was a rock (Deut. 32:4, 13, 15, 18, 31, 37). David sang of God as his rock (Pss.18:2, 31, 46; 19:14; 28:1; 61:2; 62:2). The sons of Korah also sang of God as a rock (42:9).[20]

The idea of God and his throne being a rock led the Psalmists to sing that as a *rock*, God was a refuge (18:2), a fortress (31:3), and a savior and redeemer (18:2). The rock concept stressing refuge spoke of security and protection. As a fortress it spoke of sure defense and well-being. As a savior and redeemer the basic thought was that God, on his throne, was a wholly, totally, and absolute certain and dependable source of salvation from evil and redemption from sin and guilt. As a rock, Yahweh, on his throne, is ever faithful, he will not reject his people (93:2). The salvation for his people is as assured as this throne is stable as a rock (95:1, 98:3).

The Psalmists express assurance that Yahweh's throne will never be moved. It will always serve its purposes because this throne is founded or based upon the justice and righteousness of Yahweh God (89:14; 97:2). Yahweh God is righteous; he maintains his will and his purposes according to his own character. As a holy God he never forgets nor thwarts his character as he has revealed himself, particularly in the promulgation of his Law.[21] Yahweh God remains true to himself in character and deeds. Hence his throne is secure, based on righteousness and justice (99:4; 45:6, 7).

Yahweh's Reign

Textual References

The Hebrew text reads *yĕhwâh mālak* (Pss. 93:1; 96:10; 97:1; 99:1). Yahweh reigns (reigned). The imperfect *yimlōk* (shall reign) (146:10) does not imply he is not reigning but shall begin at some time, rather the entire phrase stresses the future. He will continue to reign forever as he is now reigning.[22] Another verb *yāšab* is employed to indicate Yahweh God reigns. The usual translation of this Hebrew verb is to sit, remain or dwell. In certain contexts it refers to Yahweh God reigning as he sits on his throne (2:4; 9:8; 55:19; 102:12).[23] In these passages an emphasis is on Yahweh God's constant reign. He sits, dwells eternally on his throne.

A study of the terms referring to Yahweh God's reign reveals how inseparably connected the concept of throne and reign are when referring to Yahweh God as the King. As the throne is eternal, so also is Yahweh God's reign. Scholars who have sought to posit the view that the royal Psalms were composed to meet the requirement of a court festival prefer to consider that these psalms refer to a human king.[24] It is true that human kings began their reign by ascending and sitting on a throne.

There were celebrations when David and Solomon began their reigns but there is no historical record of an annual festival of human kings' repeated enthronements. Furthermore, it must be stressed that human kingships arose under Yahweh God's abiding and sovereign reign. These human kings in Israel/Judah were representatives and agents of their eternal divine reigning covenant Yahweh God.

Aspects of Reign

The Psalms include various aspects and characteristics of Yahweh God's reign. In the preceding, the eternal, abiding, ever-present reign of God was referred to when considering Yahweh God's throne. The terms employed in the Psalms describe this eternal reign. These should be briefly considered because it is necessary to grasp the full and rich meaning that the Psalms reveal. A scholar has written that he considers that the "reign of God" is the central concept, the *mitte,* of the Psalms.[25] It certainly is true that the Psalmists related much of life to Yahweh's eternal reign.

Authority and Power. The biblical concept of reign is the exercise of authority and power by the eternal King who is on his ever-abiding throne. In the exercise of the reign, immeasurable ability is demonstrated. And this reign always demonstrates Yahweh God's omniscience and wisdom, righteousness and justice. Yahweh God's reign exhibits how faithful God is to himself and all his virtues and characteristics. He is absolutely sovereign over everything. This will be more fully developed under the fourth aspect—the domain.

To say Yahweh God reigns is to say he controls and directs all aspects of his cosmic kingdom. He provides and withholds according to his perfect will and plan. Nothing escapes his care and concern. His reign always demonstrates his love for truth, righteousness, justice, and all aspects of his cosmic kingdom. His people particularly enjoy being under Yahweh God's reign of love (Pss. 31:7, 8; 40:11; 98:3). As he reigns Yahweh God is exalted (47:9; 92:8; 97:9), and his people call for this continual exaltation (18:46; 21:13; 40:16; 57:5; 70:4; 92:8; 108:5), for they know that they are finite and dependent on an abiding, faithful, loving, reigning God. They know they are secure under this authoritative and powerful reign of love.

Helper. There are additional aspects of Yahweh God's reign that have to be considered.[26] The Hebrew term *'azer* in various verbal forms and its derived noun *'ēzer* appears more than fifty times in the Psalms. The meaning of both the verb and noun is help. *BDB* also gives the Hebrew term the meaning of succor, which as a verb means to run up to, to aid, to help, or relieve when in difficulty, want, or distress; and to assist and deliver from suffering. As a noun it is understood to mean aid, help, assistance, relief and deliverance from difficulty, want, or distress.

The Psalmists repeatedly called on their reigning Lord to hear their cries for help and to come to them in their various needs. Consider such calls as "Listen to my cry for help, my God and King" (5:2; 12:1; 18:6; 22:19; 28:2; 30:2, 10; 38:22; 39:12; 40:13; 44:26). The remaining one hundred psalms repeat the call, the cry, the plea for help. The testimony of the crying and pleading Psalmists was that they know Yahweh God could help them. Yahweh God has the strength to help (22:19) and to be a shield and deliverer (40:17). Yahweh had said "I am an ever present help in trouble" (46:1). The Psalmist responded, "Surely God is my help who sustains me" (54:4). Since the help of man was worthless (60:11; 107:12; 108:12), the Psalmist repeated his confession, "You are my help and deliverer" (70:5), "come quickly O my God, to help me" (71:12), and added "My help comes from Yahweh" (121:2). The psalmists acknowledged that with Yahweh God's presence and help, they are protected, for he is their shield (31:20; 115:9, 10, 11). Thus they can advance against a troop (enemies) and scale a wall (18:29). Under the reign of Yahweh God they can and will have help, deliverance, and victory.

Judge. Yahweh, the reigning and helping God, was also acknowledged as judge. The Psalmist called on Yahweh as the *šōpēt* (judge) of the earth and to deal with the proud as they deserved (94:2). And Yahweh God's people sang before him because he will *yōdîn* (qal impf. of *dîn,* to judge) (96:10) the peoples *bĕmêšarîm* (in uprightness).[27] The root term *yāšar* expresses the sense of straight and right (98:9). Both verbs must be understood as expressing action according to the Law Yahweh God has revealed and upholds. All of Yahweh God's judging activities are in a real sense revelation of his Law. It is the standard by which all people and their life's activities are to be evaluated. Hence, in some instances the judge can be understood as the giver as well as the one who upholds and applies the Law. The term *mispāt*, judgment, refers to what the judge decides, executes, and administers according to the demands of the law. The Psalmist sang of judgment based on righteousness (94:15).

As Yahweh God is known and honored as the eternal, omniscient, authoritative, and loving reigning One, the Psalmists do not express fear, in a sense of being afraid, or of terror, but fear in the sense of awe, submission, and full dependence. The Psalmist sang that Yahweh God had upheld his right and cause as he sat on his throne judging righteously. Note how the concept of God the King, reigning on his throne, is confessed as judging a man according to the righteous character of the law (9:4).

And there was no doubt that it is God himself who is the judge (58:11; 75:7). The Psalmists knew that from prior revelation. Abraham, pleading for Sodom and Gomorrah, had based his plea on God the omniscient judge (Gen. 18:25). And Moses had faithfully recorded that blessed truth also (Deut. 32:36).

As saints in earlier times had called upon Yahweh God to be judge, between people, (Gen. 31:53; 1 Sam. 24:12, 15) so also the Psalmists called upon God to judge them personally (7:8). The psalmist called on God to *šāpĕtēnî* (judge me)[28] and to plead his cause against ungodly nations and to rescue him (43:1). But more often the psalmists, in the songs and prayers, called on Yahweh God to judge his people (50:4; 72:2) and especially the nations and the world (7:8; 9:8; 58:1; 82:8; 110:6). This desire for Yahweh God to judge cannot be separated from a God-fearing and God-honoring person and his deep longing that the Law be known and executed. He wants justice and righteousness to triumph in all aspects of life.[29]

Avenger. In close correlation with the inclusive aspects of judging-vindicating is the idea of avenge. The Hebrew term *nāqam* is translated avenge or take vengeance and *nĕqāmâh* is the derived noun *vengeance.* These terms appear in the Psalms. The verb appears quite often in the Pentateuch (Gen. 4:15, 24; Exod. 21:20, 21; Lev. 19:18; 20:25; Num. 31:2; Deut. 32:35, 41, 43, 45). Samson is recorded to have prayed to Yahweh to give him strength to revenge the Philistines for his two eyes (Judg. 16:28). The translation of the Hebrew term can vary—to punish, or to pay back. In the kingdom Psalms the idea of avenge appears three times. Yahweh God was called upon as the One who avenges (two times). As judge he was called to rise up, shine, and pay (back), avenge the proud and wicked who are arrogant and boasting evildoers. These people crush the covenant people; they slay widows and murder the fatherless (94:1–6). The Psalmist did not ask if he himself should do it, but appealed to his covenant Lord to do so. The term, in participial form *nōgēm* (the avenging one), appears in 99:8. This psalm refers to Yahweh God's reign; it adds that he was great, exalted, and holy. A mighty God, he loved justice. He had communicated with Moses, Aaron, and Samuel and had spoken to the covenant people from the cloud (99:1–7). He had forgiven his people (99:8b) but he was *nōgēm* (an avenging God.[30] The text, taken seriously, states that Yahweh God, an avenging Lord, executed vengeance upon his people. Translators prefer to translate the term punish. The question was raised by commentators: is it compatible to laud and praise Yahweh's goodness and mercy exhibited in forgiveness and then to add he is an avenging God?[31]

In three psalms written by David he referred to enemies, the foe, who he referred to as *mitĕnaqqem* (hith. Ptc. of *nāqam*, avenging ones). David rejoiced that Yahweh God, the glorious One, silenced the ones who sought to execute vengeance on his people (8:1, 2 [MT 2, 3]). David also knew Yahweh God was the *hannôtēn nĕqamot* (one who gave vengeance) to him (David). The parallel lines read, who subdues nations under me and saves me from my enemies (18:4, 47, 48a [MT 48, 49a]). Not only would David praise God for "being avenged" by him, he praised Yahweh God for giving joy to the righteous person, *kî hâyâh nāqām* (when he sees the vengeance). This vengeance will overcome the wicked through Yahweh God's "judicial interposition."[32]

Asaph, a Levitical musician, wrote Psalms. In one of them he called for God "our Savior" (79:9) who for the glory of his name would have his people see *niqĕmat dam 'ăbōdîkū haššapûk* (the avenging of the outpoured blood of thy servants) (79:10). The sons of Korah gave reason for such a call. They called on God, their King, who had decreed victory for Jacob (44:4[MT 5]). He had given his people over to taunting enemies *metĭnaqqem* (hith. Ptc. of *nāqam*, avenge who are bent on revenge NIV 44:16 [MT 17]). According to Deuteronomy 32:35 the Lord said, "It is mine to avenge, I will repay." Anderson, commenting on 44:16, wrote that "while vengeance and recompense belong to God," the sons of Korah wrote, in their song, that Yahweh God had given them into the hands of those who would execute vengeance upon them.[33]

In conclusion to this study on Yahweh God's reign including judging and executing vengeance on his peoples and their enemies, it must be stated emphatically that Yahweh God, the avenging judge of all people, gave latitude to Israel's enemies to execute vengeance on the covenant breakers. In the final analysis Bible readers must accept that an integral aspect of the covenant curse was the carrying out of vengeance on Israel by their enemies. Yahweh God employed vengeful enemies to punish covenant breakers.

Warrior. A consideration of Yahweh God's reign should include his involvement in *milḥāmāh* (war, battle). Moses had sung of Yahweh God as *'îš milḥāmāh* (man of war, warrior) when he witnessed the destruction of Pharaoh's army that was pursuing Israel (Exod. 15:3). Hannah, when she had given her promised child, Samuel, to the Lord, sang of her God shattering those who oppose him (1 Sam. 2:10). David continued the train of thought when he sang that Yahweh, his God, trained his hands for war (Ps.18:34 [MT 35[) and Yahweh, his God, armed him with strength for battle. But he added that his God made the adversaries bow at his feet (19:39 [MT 40]; 144:1). He also sang of the King of glory who was strong and mighty in *milḥāmāh* (battle, war) (24:8), and called on worshipers to seek his face (24:6). The sons of Korah led Israel to sing of God as their refuge, strength, and ever-present help in trouble. This God, reigning over all of creation and kingdoms, brought desolation on earth and made wars to cease (46:9 [MT 10]).

The Psalmists do not outrightly refer to or speak of Yahweh God as a warrior. They, however, do set forth that he, as the reigning, helping, judging, avenging God, is very much involved in war.[34] He was with his people in war and gave them victories (2 Sam. 5:19; 8:6; 2 Chron. 13:15, 16). These were for the purpose of demonstrating his righteousness, justice, and faithfulness to his covenant promises that he would keep and bless his covenant people and uphold their cause. But, the Psalmists fully realized that victories were given to obedient and faithful covenant people. They were also for Yahweh God's honor and glory.

Yahweh's Domain

Created by Yahweh God

The psalmists who composed the kingdom Psalms (93–99, 45) did not use the verb *bārâ* (create) in any of its possible forms. But in other psalms the verb does appear. Ethan sang that the heavens are yours (Yahweh's), and also the earth; Yahweh *yĕsadtam* (established, founded them). In the parallel line that follows, the verb *bĕrâlām* (created them) is used, (Ps. 89:11[MT 12], 12[MT 13]). He also referred to Yahweh *bārâ'tā* (he created) all men (47 [MT 48]). The psalmist, composing Psalm 148, called on beings (angels) in the heavens and in the heights, and on the sun, moon, stars and waters above the skies, to praise Yahweh because *hū' suurwâh wĕnibĕrā'û* (he commanded and they were created) (148:5). Note that the Psalmist unhesitatingly referred to "fiat creation," creation by command. Nothing in all of creation came by chance. The author of Psalm 104 stated another insightful and important truth. He referred to Yahweh's many works that *bĕhākĕmâh 'asîta* (in wisdom had made them) (104:24).[35] Then he added *tĕšallâh ruhākā yibbār'ûn* (he sent his Spirit and they were created) (104:30), and a despondent poet wrote that *'am nibrâ'* (people to be created would prove him) (102:18 [MT

19]). In another instance in which the verb *bārâ'* occurs is in David's prayer for forgiveness. He pled that Yahweh *lēb tāhôr bārā-tî* (a heart clean create me, i.e., in me—51:10).

A review of the appearances and uses of the verb *bārâ'* in various Psalms reveals that the verbs *founded, established,* and *made* are synonomous in specific contexts. Furthermore, this creating work was done in wisdom and through the Spirit whom the Father had sent forth. No one should doubt that what is written in Genesis 1:2, "The Spirit hovered over the waters," was truly a reality. He was active in the creating activity. It is also correct to say that the concept of wisdom in which creation came into existence refers to the Word, the Son. The Psalmist thus spoke of the creating activity of the Triune God. This was repeated in Psalm 33:6, "By the word of the Lord were the heavens made and their starry host by the breath of his mouth."

The Cosmic Kingdom

The term *cosmic kingdom* refers to the kingdom Yahweh God created and over which he reigns. He created this kingdom. It is all-inclusive. All that exists in the heavens, on and in the earth, and in the waters are integral parts of this kingdom that Yahweh God has brought forth by command according to his will, purpose, and plan.

The term *cosmic* is derived from the term *cosmos*. It in turn is derived from the Greek word *kosmos* that is defined as order and harmony. "Cosmos refers to the universe as an embodiment of order and harmony; the system of order and harmony combined in the universe."[36] The Psalms refer to many aspects of the cosmic kingdom. These many parts all have their role and contribute to the order and harmony that is very obviously displayed.

Yahweh God reigns over this cosmic kingdom (Ps. 103:19). He maintains it as a universe. It is one entity and has its numerous integral aspects. Yahweh God, with sovereign power, guides and directs every one of the diverse elements that comprise the universe. They exhibit Yahweh God's glory. They do this because the stars, moon, flocks, herds, beasts, fields, birds, fish , and people are all the work of Yahweh God's fingers (Ps. 8). One of the grandest expressions of the relation of Yahweh God with, and involvement in, the cosmic kingdom, the universe, is Psalm 104. It repeats how great he is; a God of splendor, majesty, and light. Clouds, wind, fire, and water serve him as he controls them (3:10). The beasts of the field are supplied, as are the birds of the air. The grass in the fields respond to him. He provides fruit from trees, wine from vineyards, and oil from orchards. These also provide a place for birds' nests, a place in high mountains for goats, and refuge for the coneys[37] in the rocks (11–18). The moon and sun obey Yahweh God as they control light, warmth, and darkness (19–23). To reflect on all the creatures Yahweh God made and to think of the sea with its abundant life and the ships that sail on it, fill one with wonder at all of Yahweh God's works (24–32). The Psalmists, living in a small country, with a sea to its west, deserts to its south and east, and mountains to the north were able to gain an insight into what Yahweh God had made and ruled: the all-embracing cosmic kingdom.

The World

In the Psalms we have referred to specifically as the kingdom Psalms, the Hebrew term *tēbēl* appears six times. It also appears in nine other Psalms. The verbal root is *yābal,* which appears in the hiphil and denotes the idea of conduct or bear along. The derived noun *tēbēl* is variously translated as world or earth. In Job 37:12 an unique phrase is employed *'al pĕnê tēbēl 'ārīzâh* (upon face of world the earth). The sense here is that the earth, that is, the land, is the face of the world. Face suggests the outward cover of the world that gives it a specific appearance and identity. The basic concept is *tēbēl* (world), with the earth as a basic and constituent part.

According to the kingdom Psalms the *tēbēl* (world) is said to be firmly established (93:1; 96:10). Earth is used as a synonym of world (97:4; 98:9; cf. also 19:4 [MT 5]; 24:1; 33:8). The seas, oceans, that is, bodies of water, are included when world/earth is the subject (93:1, 3, 4; 97:7–10). Other Psalms also include the sea and rivers with the earth/world (18:15, [MT 16, 17]; 89:8–11[MT 10–12]; 90:2). The Psalmists were also clear that they understood the earth/world to include all that was created in it and continued to exist (96:1, 9; 97:1; 98:3).

Note should be taken of some aspects of the world/earth/waters that are inherent aspects of Yahweh God's domain. The mountains, valleys, and fertile fields (97:5; 98:4), trees and produce (65:9–13 [MT 10–14]; 72:16; 96:12) are integral parts of Yahweh God's created world/earth. The Psalmists ascribed greatness, splendor, and majesty to Yahweh God the Creator who providentially reigns over his creation that includes clouds, wind, fire, thunder, springs, ravines, beasts, wild donkeys, goats, singing birds, grass, cattle, wine, and bread. These are all the works of God (104:6–26), made in wisdom and continuing to depend on their Maker. To read the Psalms that extol Yahweh God's creation and all that is included, moves one to realize that every aspect has its place and role. The *tēbēl* (world/earth) is a grand and glorious display of order, integration, harmony, and beauty.

A special aspect of the *tēbēl* are the people whom Yahweh God has created, placed on earth, and over whom he reigns and for whom he provides their needs. Limiting the passages to be considered to references in the kingdom Psalms, one soon realizes that Yahweh's domain includes various designations of people. The first reference is to all people among whom the senseless and the foolish live (94:8). All people are to hear of Yahweh God's glory and marvelous deeds (96:3, 7; 97:6), and know they will be judged by him (96:10, 32; 98:9). Second, included among all peoples are the nations that are in Yahweh God's domain (96:7; 99:1, 2). A third category of people that are included are the covenant people. Those are referred to as your people (94:5, 14; 95:7, 10). All peoples, of whatever designation, are included in the *tēbēl* (earth/world). Yahweh God know these and rules over them. They are an integral part of the created domain and are called to live orderly and in harmony within the whole *tēbēl*. And each person, people, nation, including Yahweh God's "own covenant" people will be judged in righteousness and with justice (9:4; 98:9).

The Rich Testimony Concerning It

In the preceding three sections references were made to and quotations taken from Psalms 8, 19, 24, 33, 45, 47, 72, 89, 90, 93–99, 102, 103, 104, 148. It bears repeating. Integral and essential truths regarding Yahweh God's created cosmic kingdom and particularly the world or earth, the dwelling place of people, were repeated in songs of praise and worship. The kingdom Psalms also included references to ears and eyes (94:9), to false gods and images people made and worshiped (95:3; 96:4, 5; 97:7, 9); to Yahweh's wicked foes (97:3, 10), to Zion, Yahweh's city (97:8), and to the towns and villages in the countryside (97:8). Psalmists sang of leaves and chaff (Ps. 1), of chains, iron sceptors, and pottery (Ps. 2). References were made to shields, teeth, and sleep (Ps. 3); to sacrifices, wine, the heart, and the face (Ps. 4). The Holy Temple was reverently acknowledged, as was the open grave (Ps. 5). Poets reflected on bones and the soul, on one's bed and tears (Ps. 6); on lions, dust, hearts, minds, sword and bows, to holes and pits (Ps. 7). Children and infants were ordained to praise God (Ps. 8). David reflected on the endless ruin overtaking enemies and the perishing of their memories because Yahweh avenges blood as he in justice returns the wicked to the grave (Ps. 9). The proud and haughty wicked paid to be prosperous for a time, but their mouths are full of curses. Those who crush their victims are under the Lord, who is King forever and ever (Ps. 10).

As one studies the Psalms and reflects and meditates on their rich message concerning Yahweh God's domain he or she should be led to realize that all of life, every aspect of it, belongs to God. He rules, guides, and preserves. Humans, however, have the glorious privilege to be beneficiaries of Yahweh God's manifold works. But more also, people are called to be caretakers of the environment and to do their part to assist in the exhibition of the integrality, order, and harmony of Yahweh God's cosmic kingdom.

The Duration of the Kingdom

The question to be answered concerns the Psalmists' understanding concerning the beginning of Yahweh God's kingdom, its duration, and its end. In a preceding section[38] the reality and character of Yahweh God's reign was studied which included the examination of Yahweh God's domain. Reference was made to the cosmic kingdom and the world as integral parts of the domain.[39] In this section the question of the duration of the kingdom is more specifically addressed. To answer this pointedly, it is necessary to distinguish between the psalmists' references to varying conceptions of the kingdom.[40]

Kingdom References

Cosmic

The Psalmists speak and sing of the cosmic kingdom. Reference is to the entire created world with all of its diversities, the stars, sun, plants, people (cf. 24:7, 8, 9, 10; 47:2[3], 6 [MT 7], 7 [MT 8]; 99:4).

Nations

Nations and kingdoms are repeatedly referred to. The kings, the people, their relationship to Yahweh God and to the covenant people as a nation (10:15; 33:16; 46:6 [MT 7], 10 [MT 11], 47:1[2], 8 [MT 9]; 89:18 [MT 19]; 136:19, 20).

Israel/Judah

The Psalmists indicated a deep interest in and concern for their covenant people's political presence. They spoke and sang of the kingdom of the people but also as Yahweh's special kingdom (2:6; 18:50 [MT 51]; 20:9 [MT 10]; 48:2 [MT 3]; 61:6 [MT 7]; 63:11[MT 12]; 98:6; 149:2).

Eternal Kingdom

The psalmist, in their songs, referred to the eternal reign of Yahweh God over all that he had brought forth *ex nihilo*. The emphasis in this category is to more than the cosmic (natural) kingdom or all human kingdoms. Included in this conception of kingdom is the spiritual role of Yahweh God, particularly over his image bearers, his servants, and his worshipers (2:6 [MT 7]; 24:9, 10; 45:1[MT 2] , 5 [MT 6],11[MT 12], 14 [MT 15], 15[MT 16]; 47:2 [MT 3]; 72:1; 145:11–13; 146:10).[41]

Personal

The Psalmists include a definite personal dimension. They do not consider themselves to be an individual kingdom but members of Yahweh God's kingdom. Whether they refer to the eternal, or cosmic, or national, they know themselves to be under the reign of Yahweh God. They know they are part of his royal dominion. They sing of *my* or *our* king (21:1[MT 2]; 44:4 [MT 5]; 47:7 [MT 8]; 68:24 [MT 25]; 72:1; 74:12; 84:12 [MT 13]; 145:1)

This consideration of the various references to kingdom, kingdoms, personal involvement, leads one to understand and appreciate the wide and inclusive extent of Yahweh God's royal domain. An added factor must be clarified.

Time Reference

All the Psalmists were assured of Yahweh God's reign. But they made a distinction regarding the time aspect.

Temporal

Human kingdoms that were reflections, exhibitions, demonstrations of Yahweh God's eternal reign and kingdom were not established to last forever. It cannot even be said that the Davidic or messianic kingdoms were conceived of as existing before, or after time. These were all limited in time. The cosmic kingdom began when Yahweh God created. It will no longer be a separate kingdom in the eschaton. The messianic kingdom on earth was initiated when David was anointed. Its earthly existence was for a time. But it blended with the eternal kingdom (2:6; 45:1–15; 72:1).

Eternal

The Psalmists do not envisage that the Davidic/messianic kingdom will continue or return for a period of time.[42] They do express a confidence that the Lord, the messianic King, will reign forever. His name will endure forever. This ever enduring kingdom will include all nations (45:6 [MT 7]; 12:17 [MT 18]; 99:2; 103:19; 145:13; 146:10).[43]

An attempt to sketch what was written above could produce the following:

Cosmic Kingdom
Originated at Time of Creation

National Kingdoms
(came & disappeared;
continues to arrive and disappear)

Messianic Kingdom
(initiated with David's reign)

Eternal Kingdom

All-Inclusive

Fully realized when

Christ sat at Father's Right hand

FOREVER

Notes

1. Delitzsch, *Psalms,* vol. 1, 70, 71.

2. Cf. Leslie, *Psalms*, 63–107; cf. also Barth in *Introduction . . . Psalms*, under the heading of "Royal Psalms," who wrote that Israel did not possess royal Psalms until the time of their kings; Barth limits kingship to humans primarily, 23–26. A. Johnson, *Sacral Kingship*, the title suggests, had a very limited view of kingship, much less of kingdom.

3. Brueggemann's *Theology . . . Old Testament* refers to Yahweh's governance and his sovereignty but the term *kingdom* is scarce, if present at all. Cf. his discussion of nations under governance of God, 492–97.

4. A good example of this is Chantry, *Praises for King*.

5. Cf. Goldingay, *Songs . . . Strange Land*, 68–70.

6. Howard, "Psalm 94" included Psalm 94 in the kingship group because he perceived that the perspective in 94 was similar to that of 93, 95–99, 483.

7. The term *'oz* is a noun, its corresponding adjective is *'az* (strong). The Psalmists are recorded as using this noun only two (2) times (Pss. 18:17 [MT 18]; 59:3 [MT 4]).

8. Vallas, in his book *Psalms for Contemplation,* contemplates Yahweh God's omnipotence as he watched in awe the eternal mighty waves as they rumbled and crashed upon unyielding rock, 177.

9. Moses, writing his five books had repeatedly referred to Yahweh God's ever abiding presence and promises. The historical writers had repeatedly referred to and were assured of Yahweh God's eternal character, of his everlasting presence, promises and care. Cf. e.g., Josh. 14:10; Judg. 2:1; 1 Sam. 3:15; 2 Sam. 7:13–20; 1 Kings 10:9; 2 Kings. 5:7.

10. Note that the Psalmist sang of Yahweh's statutes standing firm and that his holiness adorns for endless days, 93:5.

11. The word translated folly has an Arabic root *'wel,* to grow thick and thus become foolish, despising wisdom and discipline, to be quarrelsome and licentious. The wise wrote that folly bound up in the mind could be removed only by the rod of discipline (Prov. 22:15).

12. Cf. Tate, *Psalms 51–100*, 472. Tate referred to Mowinckel's *Psalmenstudien*, II, 6–8, who initiated the enthronement motif. Tate went on to review problems scholars have raised in regard to the enthronement concept.

13. *Psalms . . . Worship*, 23–28; Anderson implied that Mowinckel's approach and method was acceptable by suggesting that the Feast of Tabernacles was the life setting of royal Psalms. *Psalms 73–150*, 665.

14. Cf. Watts "Yahweh Malak," 341, who in 1965 pointed out that there was a fundamental difference in how Yahweh's rule is concerned, 344.

15. Cf. Mays "Language . . . Reign" who wrote that the Yahweh Malak Psalms are to be associated with a basic scenario or narrative plot that explicates Yahweh becoming, being, or acting as king, 118. Uncertainty is not dispelled by a consideration of other writings. Brueggeman, *Theology—Old Testament* wrote that Mowinckel's view that "Yahweh has just become king in a moment of liturgical enactment," is a possible view, 239, note 23.

Crim, *Royal Psalms*, reviewed various views propounded by writers and concluded that the idea of kingship may have come in with an initial knowledge of the Hittite covenants, the suzerain, that the Sinaitic covenant reflected it. During the initial settlement of Israel in Canaan some efforts were made to establish a kingship, but it was in David's time that the concept of kingship became established. Human kingship was emphasized. Israelite/Judahite kingship came under stress when the concept of Messiah came to the fore. This Messiah concept was seen then as having the covenant as its context. Crim followed H. J. Kraus in his acceptance and development of this theme.

Cf. also Gray, "Kingship of God"; Howard, "Ps. 94 Among . . . Kingship"; Johnson, "Sacral Kingship; Nels, "Theology . . . Royal Psalms." Brueggemann, in his *Message—Psalms,* does not present a clear distinct view concerning "enthronement," as for example, "The new king—god" is not simply there but comes in triumphant procession, 148.

16. Ridderbos, *Psalmen*, 42–106, 419.

17. Consider Dahood's reference to this truth—although he does equivocate somewhat. His reference to Kitchen, who has written a defense of Yahweh Malak, should be understood to imply he agrees with Kitchen, *Psalms 51–100*, 340.

18. Cf. Van Gemeren, "Psalms," 31, 32, esp. considerations 3, 4.

19. Williams' commentary on this Psalm asked "Whose throne, a king's? the Messiah's?" He concluded it was God's but the context includes reference to the king and to the Messiah, *Psalms 1–72*, 329.

20. Cf. also Pss. 62:6, 7; 71:3; 78:35; 89:26; 92:15; 94:22; 95:1; 144:1.

21. Cf. what I wrote discussing God's righteousness and justice. God is righteous, he ever upholds and applies his Law and he is just, revealing his justice in the carrying out of the stipulations and requirements of the Law. *FCTC*, vol. 1, 122.

22. The NIV correctly translates "The Lord reigns forever" and the parallel phrase indicates continuity for all generations.

23. Commentators such as Ridderbos prefer to employ terms such as *zetelen* (reside), *Psalmen,* I, 76, but others, e.g., Delitzsch prefer to use the term *enthrone*, *Psalms*, I, 158, and list *abide* as a synonym.

24. Cf. Crim's study of Psalms 2, 18, 20, 21, 45, 72, 81, 101, 110, 144 in which he basically limits royal ideology to human kingship. *The Royal Psalms*. In the foreword to this work, J. M. Myers posits the view that the annual Feast of Tabernacles was the setting, 48. A. R. Johnson in *Sacral Kingship*, 20, agreed. Mowinckel, Gunkel, Kraus were basic sources for Myers and Crim. J. Gray stated that Yahweh emerges as king, "Kingship . . . Psalms" and liturgies were prepared appropriate to the epiphany of Yahweh as king at the New Year festival, 3. Cf. what was written in the preceding section concerning the concept of enthronement.

25. Cf. J. L. Mays, "The Lord Reigns." He accepted the critical position concerning a complex history of the composition of the Psalms. But he asked if there was some one central, organizing characterization of God out of which much unfolds and to which all the variety in the Psalms can be related. He specifically asked: do the Psalm texts themselves provide such a center? Do they provide clues to the fabric of relations that connect and arrange the rest around this center? 12. His answer: Yahweh Malak, 13. He quoted Mettinger, who posited the idea that Yahweh as king is a root metaphor, a generic code for a broad complex of ideas. Brueggemann has a problem with the concept of *mitte*. To hold to a *mitte* as Eichrodt did, calls for an intellectual, cognitive, and conceptual approach that does not allow as fully as necessary for the emotional, aesthetic, rhetorical, and cultural realities that do not easily accommodate the cognitive. *Theology,* 28.

26. Under the section title of Yahweh's domain additional aspects of Yahweh God's reign will be considered.

27. The two verbs *šāpat* and *dîn* can be considered synonymous in various instances. There does seem to be a distinction in *šāpat,* which expresses the idea of to judge and to govern while *dîn* is employed to emphasize the ministering of judgment and vindicating.

28. The NIV, RSV, NASB, translate the term as vindicate, KG has judge. The term *vindicate* places emphasis on being proven correct, righteous.

29. In addition to the twelve psalms referred to above, various commentators refer to fifteen more psalms that imply that Yahweh is active as judge: 1; 10; 11; 14; 32; 34; 36; 37; 53; 73; 91; 112; 119; 146; 147.

30. The NIV weakend the idea—translating "punished."

31. Ridderbos, *Psalmen II,* wrote that God's gracious forgiveness was not "in strijd" (in battle) or was contradicted by his punishing wrath. The history of Israel as recorded revealed

Yahweh God's anger and vengeance and also his mercy and grace. These are interwoven, 459.

Anderson, *Psalms 73–150* commented that Yahweh God was an avenger of Israel's wrongdoing, their breaking and neglecting the terms of the covenant was punished—because the covenant was not a one-sided affair. It brought blessing on obedience, curse (vengeance) on the disobedient, 697.

32. Delitzsch, *Psalms II,* 184.

33. *Psalms (1–72),* 342.

34. Brettler, in his essay "Images—Warrior," wrote that early studies had not assisted in trying to understand what Yahweh as warrior really meant in Israel, 135. Brettler considered Psalms such as 3 to portray God as a warrior because he demonstrated power to deliver people and nations, and 83 called for a deliverer for Israel, the covenant partner of Yahweh, 144.

35. It is correct to say that the concept of wisdom in which creation came into existence, refers to the Word, the Son.

36. Cf. *Webster's Collegiate Dictionary.*

37. The coney is thought to be either a shrewmouse or rockrabbit or some small animal distinct from these but nevertheless closely related.

38. See 150–54.

39. See 155–57.

40. Some Psalmists refer to more than one aspect of Yahweh God's kingdom.

41. Goldingay, commenting on Psalms 45 and 47, wrote that the Old Testament does not present two kingdoms, that is, of church and state. There is only one kingdom, its throne is occupied by David' s son. Goldingay added a confusing statement about that throne of Yahweh's kingdom over Israel. *Songs from a Strange Land, Psalms 42–51*, (Downers Grove: InterVarsity, 1978), 88.

42. Chantry wrote, "Jehovah spoke from his throne of universal and absolute dominion." He said to his Son, upon return from his earthly mission to sit at his right hand and was thus given a position of supreme dignity and dominion, *Praises . . . King*, 52.

43. It is most difficult to know and understand what Brueggemann's view of the Psalmists' presentations concerning the *Kingdom of Yahweh.* E.g., his discussion of the kingdom Psalms, 93, 97, 98 is introduced by indicating these are enthronment psalms. *Message Psalms*, 148–48. The same should be said of Eaton, *Kingship—Psalms.* In his introduction he expressed some disagreement with Gunkel and some with Mowinkel but he nevertheless accepted their basic premise concerning the royal psalms as enthronement Psalms, 1–26.

40

The Covenant in the Psalms

I. Introductory Comments

II. The Psalmists' Acknowledgment of the Spiritual Mandate

40

The Covenant in the Psalms

Introductory Comments

The idea and reality of the covenant Yahweh God established with creation and his people is a major theme in the Old Testament and New Testament. That the Old Testament has been referred to as the Old Covenant and the New Testament as the New Covenant[1] surely testifies to the supreme and central significance of the covenant in Yahweh God's revelation, the Scriptures.[2] It should therefore surprise no reader or student of the Psalms to be confronted by the covenant and its various aspects.

The Term **bĕrît** *in the Psalms*

The term *bĕrît* appears twenty-one times in the Psalms. As this study proceeds it should become quite evident that although the term itself does not appear that often, aspects of the covenant and involvement with it permeates the Psalms. Where the term does appear one finds reference to God making it (89:3 [MT 4]) and maintaining it (25:14; 89:28 [MT 29]); 105: 8, 10; 106:45; 111:5). There is the call to Yahweh God's people to keep his covenant (25:10; 103:18; 111:9; 132:12). There are references to and warning against breaking the covenant (44:17 [MT 18]); 55:20 [MT 21]); 78:10, 37).

Understanding the Covenant

The Old Testament conception of the covenant is that it is a bond (cf. Ezek. 20:37) of life and love that Yahweh God established between himself and his image bearers.[3]

But Yahweh God also established a covenant, a bond of goodness and love, with the entire creation.[4] In the context of and working from within this bond, Yahweh God functions in relation to his covenantal partners—mankind and creation.

The scope of the covenant[5] involves several dimensions. Yahweh God, the bond between himself and his cosmos, he rules, guides, provides, and cares for his creation. Thus God covenantally administers the work of his hands.

Yahweh God also redeemed and restored his fallen creation after Adam and Eve sinned; they brought ruin and death; there was brokenness, pain, and grief. There were tragic consequences for the love/life bond. But Yahweh God brought in the redemptive dimension of his covenant relation with mankind and the cosmos.

There is a third dimension that the Scriptures refer to. It speaks of the bond that people, within the context of the administrative (creation) bond and the redemptive bond, make between themselves. It has been referred to as a bond of friendship or a legal treaty.[6] These were also considered to be binding and of great advantage and good for the parties involved.

Yahweh God, when establishing his life/love bond to make the bond a living and productive reality, included three mandates for covenant people to know and obey. The first is the spiritual that deals with the specific I-you relationship between Yahweh God and covenant people. The second is the social that is directed to give motivation to the development of God-honoring and people-edifying relationships. The third gives direction concerning the relationship of covenant people with the natural and cultural aspects of the cosmic kingdom. These mandates are recognized and responded to in many Psalms as will be demonstrated in the ensuing study.

As is widely acknowledged, the covenant as it functions and holds mandates before people also has a series of important elements. First of all one must realize that the covenant maker and Lord must be recognized, known, and honored. People with whom the covenant is established and is to function are to be identified.

Promises, privileges, responsibilities are included as is the Lord's oath and the giving assurances of blessing or curse. The continuity of the covenant is also an important feature.

In conclusion it should be emphasized that Yahweh God, the covenant maker and keeper, is central and pivotal in the Psalmists' minds and hearts. So also are their responsibilities to know, obey, and live within the divinely ordained covenant relationship. In the study that follows, the three covenantal mandates will serve as the context in which the Psalmists' responses to Yahweh God's covenantal revelation were recorded. In these contexts, the other features, the scope, and elements will be indicated as having important parts, influences, and results.[7]

The Psalmists' Acknowledgment of the Spiritual Mandate

Yahweh God's Self-Revelation in Regard to the Spiritual Mandate

The Psalmists exhibited a wide and good knowledge of what Yahweh God had spoken and done in times past. The Psalmists were historically oriented as they thought, meditated, and reflected on what Yahweh God as King and covenant Lord had revealed.

The Revelation of His Virtues

It must be repeated again and again. The Psalms are verbal responses in songs, prayers, meditations, reflections, and expressions to Yahweh God's self-revelation.

Royal Virtues

The Psalmists responded to Yahweh God's specific royal virtues: his sovereignty, authority, strength, majesty, everlastingness, holiness, omniscience, righteousness, and justice.[8] These virtues were also revealed in various ways in the spiritual covenantal relationship between Yahweh God and his covenant people.

Faithfulness

The noun *'ĕmûn* (faith) does not appear in the Psalms. The verb *'aman* appears in various forms. As a qal participal, it is translated the faithful one, the one who exercises faith (12:1[MT 2]; 31:23 [MT 24]) and it also appears as a niphal participal (19:7 [MT 8]; 111:7). In the hiphil in the past tense, it is translated believe (27:13; 78:22, 32; 116:10; 119:66). In these instances the reference is to mankind's exercise of or lack of faith.[9] That Yahweh God is said to be faithful, that is, exercising it, is expressed in various contexts (18:25; 33:4; 145:13; 146:6).

Yahweh God's faithfulness to his covenant is extolled in Psalm 89. The Psalmist, Ethan, led worshipers of Yahweh God to express their assurance that he was absolutely reliable in keeping his covenant with David and his house. Yahweh would not fail or break, ignore or forget what he had said and done covenanting with David. Yahweh's *'ĕmûńâh* (faithfulness) was established in the heavens (vv. 2 [MT 3]); it is praised there (vv. :5 [MT 6]). Faithfulness surrounds mighty Yahweh and goes before him (vv. 14 [MT 15]). Yahweh's covenant faithfulness will never fail (vv. :28 [MT 29]) for Yahweh would never betray it (vv. 33 [MT 34]). As the moon is always in its place, never failing to be present, so is Yahweh God's absolute faithfulness. Yahweh God is absolutely reliable (vv. 37 [MT 38]). Ethan composed Psalm 89 after a tragedy, due to the people's unfaithfulness, had overcome Judah. He then inquired concerning Yahweh's faithfulness to David (vv. 49 [MT 50]). He understood it did not fail, but it was no longer evident to a disobedient people. But Yahweh God was faithful when he had to execute the curse of the covenant.[10]

The faithfulness of Yahweh God was acknowledged and commemorated for various reasons and in differing circumstances. David sang of Yahweh God's faithfulness, shown to those faithful to him, when his covenant Lord delivered him from Saul (18:25; 57:3 [MT 4]). When David celebrated the covenant blessings he had received, he sang of Yahweh's faithfulness (25:10). When he composed a song for the dedication of the temple, he questioned that if he would be destroyed would he then proclaim Yahweh's faithfulness (30:9 [MT 10], cf. also 88:11[MT 12])? But when he sang from his heart, David rejoiced that Yahweh's faithfulness reached to the skies –it was limitless! (36:5; 57:10[MT 11]). So David unhesitatingly spoke of his Lord's faithfulness in the great assembly of Yahweh's people (40:10 [MT 11]; 71:22) and prayed that Yahweh's faithfulness would always protect him (61:7 [MT 8]). A consideration of three more Psalms could be considered a summation of Yahweh God's faithfulness. David prayed Yahweh to hear his cry for mercy. He added, in your faithfulness come to my relief (143:1). David was assured that Yahweh was a hearer of prayer and answered that prayer so that David, the covenant man, would not have to fear his pursuers. Yahweh, the covenant Lord, exercised and demonstrated that he could be depended on fully. David added a specific assurance. Yahweh God, the King of his everlasting kingdom, was faithful to all his promises (25:13). David referred to all the covenant promises Yahweh had given: about his ever-continuing throne and reign, about Yahweh's love and protection for him, about the goodnesses/blessings he would receive as Yahweh's royal agent. Indeed, this ever-continuing faithfulness was as certain as the truth that Yahweh God had created heaven and earth and all that was in them (146:6).[11]

Yahweh's Love

The Psalmists acknowledged and praised God for his love demonstrated in various ways. Yahweh loves justice because he is righteous (11:7). The Psalmist extols Yahweh God's righteous character; he is absolutely true to himself and his will. Because of this love, Yahweh God loves the righteous deeds of his covenant people.[12]

Yahweh God's love (*'āhab*) was extolled in other Psalms also. The Psalmist called for righteous and upright people to sing joyfully, play skillfully on the harp and lyre, and thus praise Yahweh, who *'ōhēb* (loves, act. Qal. ptc.); that is, he is always loving righteousness and justice (33:5). David corroborates that by singing that Yahweh *'ōhēb* (loves, act.ptc.) the *mišpāt* (the just), that is, just people, who are Yahweh's faithful people (37:28). The Psalmist calls for praise for Yahweh the King's greatness, awesomeness, holiness, and might; more, *'āhāb* (he loves) *mišpāt (justice)*, proven by Yahweh's establishment of *meśārim* (uprightness or equity) (99:4).[13] Psalm 146 also calls for praise to be given to the Maker of heaven and earth who ever remains faithful in his care for the hungry, blind, prisoner, alien, widow, fatherless, and those bowed down with burdens. Yahweh is to be praised, sang the Psalmist, because *'ōhēb saddîqîm* (he is loving the righteous ones). In a real sense, Yahweh God is praised for ruling in love[14] over those in great need. These are called the righteous ones, not because of their needs and problems, but because they look to and depend on Yahweh God.

Yahweh was also praised for loving the pride or excellency of Jacob (47:4 [MT 5]). The setting of Psalm 47 is an acknowledgment of Yahweh God subduing nations, whom he calls to clap their hands and to acknowledge that Yahweh had given special attention to his covenant people. He had chosen them as his special people, that was their privilege and excellency. He had also chosen their inheritance. Thus the love of Yahweh God was demonstrated.[15]

Yahweh God was praised also because of his love for Zion.[16] It should be immediately noted that in Psalms 78:68; 87:2, Zion is identified with Judah and is distinguished from Jacob, the nation of Israel. Zion represented Yahweh God's dwelling among his people. There his glory appeared. There he met with his covenant people. To say Yahweh loved Zion was to sing he loved his people, he loved to be present in their midst. Zion also represented Yahweh God's choice of David and his descendants and the promise of the eternal king who would reign eternally in the heavenly Zion. Thus, to love Zion was to exhibit his love for David and the coming of the promised Messiah.

As one reflects and meditates on what the Psalmist wrote and sang about Yahweh God's love, one comes to realize that the concept of love was not defined. It was spoken of particularly in regard to its character and function. Yahweh God's love is expansive and inclusive. He loves his creation and his covenant people. He loves the promises given to them as also the inheritance he gave them. He loves his righteousness, justice, and equity that are revealed in his will, his Law, and his governance of the entire creation. He loves the righteous and just deeds his people perform. This expansive and inclusive love unites, integrates, and harmonizes all realities mentioned above. It particularly unites Yahweh's heart with his people who are responsive to his love and live faithfully as his obedient covenant people. To describe it in its relationship and deeds leads to an increasing wonder of and adoration for Yahweh's love. To know this love as to its essence is nigh incomprehensible. To say, however, that the essence of love is a bond that unites Yahweh's heart to the hearts and lives of his covenant people, gives us a clue. Indeed, love is a bond that attracts, holds, perseveres, and serves as the channel through which all of Yahweh God's gifts flow into the hearts and lives of his people. This bond is, in a real sense, with the entire cosmic kingdom. He created it; he remains bound to it. He serves it, providing for it. And at the very heart of all this are Yahweh God's imagebearers –male and female.

Grace

The term *ḥēn* does not appear often in the Psalms. The sons of Korah, singing concerning the king, extolled Yahweh God's blessing on him. Evidence for this was that his lips were anointed by grace (45:2 [MT 3]). They also referred to Yahweh God as a sun and shield who bestows grace and honor on those whose walk is blameless (84:11[MT 12]. *Ḥēn* is translated as favor in various Old Testament contexts.[17] The basic thought expressed by the term is the bestowing of love upon those who are not deserving of it. Sinners received grace; Yahweh God's love is not meritorious.

The adjective derived from the noun *ḥēn* is *ḥannân* (gracious). David and other Psalmists were fully aware of Yahweh God revealing his gracious attitude toward undeserving sinners. They repeated what Yahweh God had said to Moses when the Lord renewed and confirmed his covenant with Israel at Mt. Sinai. Israel had sinned worshiping the golden calf. Yahweh the covenant Lord had proclaimed that he was gracious, compassionate, slow to anger, and abounding in mercy (*hesed*) and faithfulness, maintaining his mercy and forgiving wickedness, rebellion and sin (Exod. 34:6, 7). The Chronicler (2 Chron. 30:9), Neh. (9:17) and the prophets Joel (2:13) and Jonah (4:2) reminded their contemporaries that Yahweh God, their covenant Lord, never ceased to be gracious. Undoubtedly the Psalmists had done their part in keeping this virtue (attribute) before the covenant people. David sang of it (51:1, 103:8; 145:8) as did the composers of Psalms 111:4 and 116:5. The historical context of each specific reference varied slightly. The basic thought, however, was the same: God's unmerited love was shown and given to undeserving sinners.

Grace was demonstrated by Yahweh God being compassionate (*rahûm*). The verb *rāham* in the piel stem is translated as mercy or pity in various contexts. Compassion, however, expresses the basic thought of this term. The term *rehem* (womb) is derived from the verb *rāham*; this supports the preference for compassion, which means suffer with. Think of a mother whose child is in pain or deep trouble; her womb aches for what was formed in it. A mother suffers with her child. The covenant Lord, in his love for his child/son/daughter, suffers when he or she suffers. When Israel danced before and around the golden calf, Yahweh God suffered pain and grief,[18] knowing how his covenant people deserved chastisement, pain, and suffering.

The phrase *'erek 'appîm* (long breath or nose) indicates that Yahweh God's anger does not flare up. He keeps control of himself. He takes long, deep breaths before he reacts and responds to sin, rebellion, and wickedness. And David rejoiced that this anger of Yahweh lasted but a short time but his grace endures for a long time (30:6 [MT 7]).

Mercy

Moses had heard Yahweh, when he confirmed the covenant with Israel after their disobedience, that Yahweh God was abundant in *hesed* (mercy) to thousands (Exod. 34:6) The term *ḥesed* appears over 120 times in the Psalms. It is translated mercy/mercies, lovingkindness, and goodness. The basic thought of the term is that Yahweh God reveals and demonstrates his love to those who are needy, hurting, and suffering. It is important to note that mercy is a distinct concept.[19] It differs from grace, which refers to Yahweh God's love revealed to the guilty one. Mercy is that same love bestowed on those who are afflicted and suffering due to sin and wickedness.

Note should be taken of the adjective *rab* which describes Yahweh's mercy. It is great. Yahweh's mercy is abounding, absolutely abundant for the covenant person whatever his or her circumstances and needs may be. And note that the term *'emet* (faithful) was also described as *rab* when Yahweh spoke to Moses. The Psalmists do not repeat the adjectives in the context of *ḥesed.* They realize that Yahweh's covenant mercies are indeed very great and faithfully bestowed.

David realized that Yahweh God, the covenant Lord of his people, was a forgiving God. He remembered that Moses had heard that Yahweh God forgave wickedness, rebellion, and sin (Exod. 34:7). When, he, the king, was guilty of deceit, murder, and adultery, he pled with his covenant Lord that according to his unfailing mercy and great compassion Yahweh blot out transgression, wash away iniquity, and cleanse from sin (51:1, 2 [MT 3, 4]). David, acknowledging Yahweh God's virtues, also praised his covenant Lord for not always accusing, harboring anger forever, or repaying according to sin (103:8–10). Yahweh God was good to his covenant people (145:8, 9). Other Psalmists recorded that Yahweh God, according to his virtues, caused his wonders to be remembered and, according to his covenant, provided food for those worshiping him (111:4, 5). And Psalm 116:5–8 records that the gracious, righteous, and compassionate covenant Lord protects and delivers the simple hearted, saves them, restores them, and gives them rest.

Goodness

The Hebrew word *tôb* appears as a verb (to be pleasing, good), as a noun (a good thing, benefit; welfare), and as an adjective (good, pleasant, agreeable). The feminine form *tôbiâh* has similar references (good, good things, welfare, benefits).

Yahweh God, the covenant Lord, is described as good, the source of good, and the rewarder of the good that is performed or demonstrated (25:7, 8; 34:8 [MT 9]; 51:18 [MT 19]; 73:1; 100:5; 106:1; 107:1; 118:1, 29; 125:4; 135:3; 136:1; 145:7).

It is important to remember that Yahweh God's goodness must be kept distinct from his love, grace, and mercy. Goodness is a correlate to love. Grace and mercy are revelations or exhibitions of God's goodness.[20] To say God is good is to say God is true to himself and to his will and his promises. God is good as he proves himself and makes himself and all his virtues available to his imagebearers and especially to those who love, obey, and serve him and seek his fellowship.

The Psalmist knew he could not expect "the good" or "goodness" referred to as peace, light, joy from evil sources of whatever kind they might be (4:6; 14:1, 3; 53:1 [MT 2], 3 [MT 4]). They knew that good/goodness was the very opposite of evil that could be expressed or exhibited in various ways (34:12–14 [MT 13–15); 36:3 [MT 4]; 37:27; 38:20; 53:1[MT 2], 3 [MT 4]; 109:5).

The Psalmists expressed repeatedly that they were recipients of Yahweh God's goodness. When they asked for Yahweh's goodness, saying, "do good to your servant" they added that by teaching good *tā'am* (judgment)[21] and knowledge (119:65, 66), they were blessed. Yahweh also was praised for affliction, for through it his precepts, decrees, and commands were proven to be good. They gave knowledge, guidance, assurance, and hope that were needed in the midst of life (119:57–71). So the Psalmist summed up by saying Yahweh's *mišpāteká* (judgments, laws, precepts) (119:30) are good and are more precious to the Psalmist than silver or gold (119:72).

The Psalmist's also realized that seeking good as revealed by Yahweh God and doing it was required (34:12, 14). And they did so knowing that goodness would come to them only from God (16:2; 84:4; 103:5; 104:28). They praised God for that goodness (13:6 [MT 7]; 54:6 [MT 7]) as they sought to be near him (73:28) and have rest (116:7).

As love is a virtue that is very difficult to define, so also is goodness. The Psalmists used metaphors to give meaningful expression to these virtues. Consider the following.

David sang of Yahweh God, his covenant Lord as *rô'î* (my shepherd) who cared for him and provided his needs (Ps. 23). He prayed that Yahweh be the shepherd of his people and that he *naśśĕ'îm* (piel, impf. of *nāśa,* to carry) carefully carry them. The scene of the lost sheep hurt and crippled being picked up by its shepherd, when he found it and carried it to safety, comes to mind. The good shepherd does this; he provides the good that is needed for restoration (28:9).

Asaph, poet and director, had Israel sing, "Hear us, O Shepherd of Israel." The Shepherd enthroned was called upon to come, save, restore, and make his face shine upon his people (80:1–3 [MT 2–4]). Asaph described David as a human shepherd who, with integrity and skillful hands, led the covenant people (78:72). The New Testament took up this metaphor and revealed that Jesus was the fulfillment of the Old Testament presentation. He was indeed the good Shepherd (John 10:2–16; cf. also Heb. 13:20; 1 Peter 2:25; 5:4).

David also sang of his covenant Lord as *'ôrî* (my light) (27:1). The term *'or* serves both as a verb (to be or become light) and as a noun (light). The idea of God being a light or providing light was well known for those who knew and remembered how Yahweh God had been and provided light for Israel as they marched from Egypt and through the desert (Exod. 13:21). God had banished darkness with his light. So the Israelites sang asking God to let the light of his face shine upon them (Ps. 4:6; cf. also Num. 6:24–26) because God turns darkness into light (Ps. 18:28 [MT 29]) and by his light the sinner can see light (36:9[MT 10]). The word is the lamp by which light is given (119:105, 130). This light that only Yahweh God is and can reveal and give, is an absolute necessity for salvation, truth (43:3), and life (56:13 [MT 14]). Yahweh God in his goodness reveals and gives light.

The Psalmists also gave expression to Yahweh God's goodness by the use of terms such as shade, shelter, and cloud. Yahweh God watched over his people; he had been a shade (121:5) so that the sun would not harm his people by day. He provided a cloud (105:39; 78:14) to protect them. He was shelter for, and provided one, for his people (91:9). David sang of God's wings as his shelter (61:4[MT 5]) and also of God's presence as his shelter (31:20 [MT21]). He also considered the tabernacle, the dwelling place of Yahweh God, to be his shelter (27:5) It is interesting to note that the Psalmist spoke of Yahweh God as the One who protected them. He was identified with the very means he employed (metaphorically) to demonstrate that he personally and reliably was a shelter, a hiding place, a refuge for his people. So, whatever the threatening circumstances in life might be, Yahweh God in his goodness proved he was a covenant Lord, protecting and keeping his people safe,

Another metaphor that appears often is the rock. In a real sense, the metaphors referred to in the preceding paragraphs express what the rock is and does. But the idea of rock contributes the concepts of stability, durability, and complete reliability. The Psalmists knew from the covenant people's history and from their own experiences that their covenantal Lord was absolutely faithful to his promises and was totally dependable in all circumstances of life, whatever these were. For David, when he was delivered from Saul and other enemies he sang *sēlĕ'î.* This term is usually understood to refer to a crag or cliff. David sang literally, Yahweh (is) my crag or cliff (18:2 [MT 3]; 31:3 [MT 4]; 42:9[MT 10]; 71:3). The idea of *miśûdâtî* (fortress) appears as a synonym. The context suggested by rock/fortress is that of battle or wars in which safety and security was experienced. Yahweh God personally was that as he provided it (31:3 [MT 4]; 71:3).

The term *śûr* (rock) appears more frequently when Yahweh God was considered to be the needed support and defense of his people (18:31 [MT 32], 46 [47]; 28:1; 62:2 [MT 3]; 73:26; 92:15 [MT 16]; 144:1). Translators have translated *śûr* as strength in various contexts (19:14[MT 15]; 62:7 [MT 8]; 73:26, 144:1). As a correlate to the idea of rock, the term *savio*r (95:1) and *redeeme*r (19:14 [MT 15]) appear. The rock was also used to refer to Yahweh God as a source of life when reference was made to the rock that was smitten to provide water (78:15, 20, 33; 105:41; 114:8).

It was pointed out in the preceding that Yahweh God's goodness is to be clearly understood to be distinct from mercy and grace. That, however, does not negate what the Psalmists sang when they combined goodness and mercy (23:6) and that Yahweh God revealed his goodness when he was merciful (118:29).

A final thought: when Yahweh God created the cosmos his activities and the result of them were good (Gen. 1). That same goodness was revealed after mankind sinned. Yahweh God did not change. He continued to be good as the covenant Lord of his covenant people by being a shepherd, a light, a shade, a shelter, a cloud, and a rock for and to them. The Psalmists knew that their covenant Lord had so revealed himself. They acknowledged this revelation and with joy and praises they responded in songs, prayers, meditations, and admonitions.

The Holy Spirit's Role

The Term

The term *rûaḥ* (spirit) appears approximately forty times in the book of the Psalms. The first thought that comes to mind when translating it is that of spirit. The contexts in which the term appears calls for one of the acceptable four translations. It is translated as wind, the chaff before the wind (35:5), or he causes the wind to blow (147:18). It is translated as breath (104:29). When you take it away they die and return to the dust. Closely related in thought is the spirit of a person. Spirit in this context refers to the nature of man, who consists of body (the outer man) and spirit (the inner man). The Psalmists referred to this makeup of mankind by referring to "into thy hand I commit my spirit" (31:5 [MT] or "such as he of a contrite spirit." (34:18 [MT 19]).[22] It should be understood that in the Hebrew understanding of a person, to lose one's breath was to die as also when the spirit of a person departed, he or she died. Breath and the human spirit were considered very close correlates.

The fourth reference of *rûaḥ* is Spirit, the Holy Spirit, the third person of the Trinity. In some instances the phrase "breath of his [God's] mouth" is used to refer to the Holy Spirit (33:6).[23] That the Psalmists knew of and referred to the presence and influence of the Holy Spirit should not be doubted.

The Holy Spirit's Activities

The Sinners' Need

The covenant Lord, Yahweh God, had included the spiritual mandate in his covenanting activities. His imagebearers had been given the privilege to serve as his agents within the totality of creation. They had been instructed and led into spiritual fellowship with their Maker before their fall (Gen. 1, 2). Their fall did not take away the spiritual mandate or any other covenantal responsibilities. The fallen ones were totally and absolutely unable to fully know, much less obey, the spiritual mandate. The covenantal Lord did not forsake them. As the Holy Spirit had been the life giving agent in creation (Gen. 1:1, 2) so he was also the life restorer.

In Revelation

The Psalmists indicate in various ways that they were aware of the Holy Spirit's presence and work and their complete dependence on him. David gave clear expression to the role of the Holy Spirit in revealing to and through him the revelation of Yahweh God in the Psalms (2 Sam. 23:1–9). This passage referred to as a *nĕ'um* (oracle),[24] has a poetic structure, but it has not been included in the book of the Psalms. Nor is there a direct reference to the Spirit's presence and activity by the Psalmists regarding his involvement in revelation to and by them. There should be no doubt, however, that the Holy Spirit enabled the Psalmists to recall, repeat, and make numerous references to previous revelations of word and deeds. What Peter wrote centuries after the Psalms were composed applied to prophets and prophetic Psalmists (2 Peter 1:19–21). It must be stated positively: the Holy Spirit made known to the Psalmists that Yahweh God, their covenant Lord, maintained the spiritual mandate that they had to know, understand, and obey.

In Creation

The Psalmists did not restrict themselves to special or word revelation. They were very much aware of the natural world about them.[25] And they were aware of and referred to the Holy Spirit's role in creation (33:6) and in the cycles of life in nature. The Psalmist reflected his appreciation of what Moses had written concerning the Triune God's cooperative action in the act of creating the cosmos. God the Father spoke, the spoken Word brought creation into existence, and the breath—the Spirit—gave life and enriched it (Gen. 1:1, 2). The Psalmist repeated the Triune God's creating activities. He referred to the heavens and the stars as brought forth by the Triune God. He took one part to represent the whole. Note should be taken, however, of the following context in which the sea (33:7) and the earth (33:8) are referred to as is the commanding and creating Word (33:8). Thus by the Father's Word, and breath (Spirit), is activity, the setting for the revelation of and obedience to the spiritual mandate came into existence.

The Psalmists were also aware of and gave praise for the Spirit's continued involvement in the created cosmos, thus sustaining the environment for the spiritual mandate to be known and obeyed. In a specifically praise Psalm (104), the Spirit, sent by the Father, renews the face of the earth (v. 30). The song writer understood the full import of (vv. 27–35)

Thy creatures all look to Thee for their food;
Thy hand opens wide, they gather the good;
Thy face Thou concealest, in anguish they yearn;
Their breath Thou withholdest, to dust they return.
Thy Spirit, O Lord, makes life to abound,
The earth is renewed, and fruitful the ground;
To God ascribe glory and wisdom and might
Let God in His creatures forever delight.

My soul, bless Jehovah, His name be adored,
Come praise Him, ye people, and worship the Lord.[26]

In Human Lives

The Psalmists, aware of the role of the Holy Spirit in revelation, creation, and providence for their knowledge of and fulfillment of the covenantal, spiritual mandate, were conscious of their need for the Holy Spirit in their own lives. They expressed their innate knowledge of their inability to meet the demands of the spiritual mandate: to know, love, obey, and serve their covenant Lord. The Psalmists were not as explicit about this as the New Testament writers and some Old Testament prophets.[27]

David, realizing he composed Psalms under the Holy Spirit's inspiration, also referred to his need of the Spirit in his sinful life. He pled with Yahweh God not to withdraw the Spirit from him when he confessed his sin of adultery and murder (51:10–13 [MT 11–14]). He realized he depended on the Holy Spirit to renew his heart and spirit and to give him joy in his life. David indicated his need of the Holy Spirit also when he spoke of his need of redemption (31:5 [MT 6]; 34:18 [MT 19]. Asaph implied the same need of the Holy Spirit to renew and refresh his personal spirit (77:3 [MT 4], 6 [MT 7]). David also expressed his personal total dependence on the Holy Spirit to be known by Yahweh God and to know himself (139:7).[28] He also prayed that Yahweh God's good Spirit, in a real sense, God himself would refresh him (143:4, 7) and lead him (143:10).

The conclusion concerning the Psalmists' awareness and reliance on the Holy Spirit must be stated positively. As the Holy Spirit was known to be active in revelation and creation, so was he in the personal lives of redeemed sinners. They were conscious of the Holy Spirit's work of convicting them of sin, of being the agent of their redemption, restoration, and guidance in daily life. As the Holy Spirit had revealed the Spiritual mandate, so he also led the redeemed in knowing and obeying it. The Holy Spirit was active in the upholding the covenant and leading a life according to it.

Universalism/Missions in the Psalms

Two initial questions are: do the Psalmists give evidence of the Holy Spirit's role in "missions"? and was the spiritual mandate postulated only for Israel or for all peoples, nations, and races? A positive answer must be given to the second question[29] when one remembers that the spiritual mandate was an integral aspect of the covenant of creation. All people are in and under this covenant. Hence it was and is obligatory for all to know, understand, and obey this covenantal mandate. When Adam and Eve sinned the covenant was not abrogated by Yahweh God although it was broken. Immediate divine revelation and action kept the covenant as a definite reality for all people. The history of the human race is replete with the ignorance concerning the rejection of, and the disobedience of the spiritual mandate. Yahweh God, continuing to uphold it, revealed it in Noah's time, and made the patriarchs hearers and bearers of the divine demand to know, obey, and live out the spiritual mandate. It was specifically revealed to Israel and in its national theocratic situation this mandate had to be lived and demonstrated. It is interesting to note that Israel, as a theocracy, was never commanded to communicate the spiritual mandate verbally.[30] Theocratic Israel had to demonstrate its adherence and obedience to it in their daily lives. They were called to live it and thus lead nations to observe and to follow it also. Hence, it is correct to speak of universalism in the Old Testament and particularly in the Psalms.

A South African scholar has produced a specific and detailed study on universalism in the Psalms.[31] After a consideration of more than fifty Psalms, he stated three conclusions. (1) Most obvious is the particularism in the Psalms. Theocratic Israel particularly was called to know and obey the spiritual mandate. (2) There is a general universalism in the Psalms. (3) There is a universalism in the pregnant sense. By this latter conclusion he referred to those Psalms that do not outrightly call for it or refer to it, but it is embedded or implied in them. In this category are such Psalms as 47:1 [MT 2] "clap your hands, all you nations"; 66:1, 4, 8, all the earth is called to sing Yahweh God's praises; 68:32 [MT 33] "sing to God, O kingdoms of the earth."[32]

The general universalism came to expression in a wide variety of Psalms.[33] A brief consideration of a few of these is in order. The poet who composed Psalm 2 acknowledged the rebellion of nations (vv. 1–3) and the sovereign lordship of Yahweh's Anointed One (vv. 4–9). The kings and rulers are warned and urged to serve Yahweh with fear and joy. They are commanded to kiss the Son and find blessedness in his refuge (vv. 10–12). The threat of judgment is clear and definite. The call to redemption and blessed life is an Old Testament gospel message.

The Psalmist who composed Psalm 67 did not specifically address all nations, he did express a strong desire, a fervent longing, that as Yahweh God was gracious to his covenant people and had his face shine on them, so also the nations might know Yahweh's salvation. Then all peoples would praise Yahweh and be glad and sing for joy. This is followed by an implicit call to all peoples and nations to submit to the rule of Yahweh.

Commentator Grosheide wrote that the *Evangelie* (gospel) is sung in Psalm 87: "Not without reason do we write gospel."[34] In this Psalm it is stated that the peoples of nations shall have a part in the salvation "granted to Israel first." Israel was called upon to let this salvation be known but the nations have to grasp it.[35] Hirsch, a Jewish commentator, gave a very different interpretation. Yahweh is the Lord of Zion, for Israel only. Other nations were mentioned because they could refer to one worthy member but Israel sang that everyone worthy of mention, that is, "the great spirits" in Israel were born in Zion. For Hirsch, there is no gospel for other nations.[36]

Other Psalms, in various ways, include this blessed truth: the spiritual mandate must be made known to all peoples, nations, tongues, and races. At the heart of the spiritual mandate is the gospel, and at the heart of the gospel is the Messiah.[37] And Scripture progressively elucidates that the Holy Spirit is the motivating and directing and enabling people to realize the universal intent of the spiritual mandate.

The Torah Extolled in the Psalms

Its Inclusive Reference

The Hebrew term *Torah* appears ten times in various Psalms but twenty-five times in Psalm 119. The term is derived from the verb *yārāh* (to throw or shoot), but the derived noun refers, depending on its context quite often to direction, instruction, or law. When David praised Yahweh God for his Torah that was *tămīniâh* (perfect), he used synonyms—*'ēdût* (statutes), *păqqûdê* (precepts), and *mišewat* commandments)—to express how inclusive Yahweh God's covenant laws were. Whereas the very heart of the Torah was Yahweh God's Ten Commandments, these were expanded, elucidated, and made relevant in all aspects of life for the covenant man and woman. It was stressed in a former work that Yahweh God's covenant law applied directly to the three mandates; commandments 1 to 4 to the spiritual, 5 to 7 to the social, and 8 to 10 to the cultural mandates.[38]

Its Implied Knowledge

The Psalmists do not repeat the Ten Commandments verbatim. Nor is there a direct reference to the covenant mandates. The Psalmists, however, give much evidence that they were very aware of what Yahweh God had revealed in his Law, testimonies, statutes, precepts, and commandments. It is by being attentive to their responses to this previous specific revelation that the reader can readily discern that the Psalmists knew the requirements of the spiritual mandate and what was involved in knowing and obeying it.

The Promised Blessing

The author of Psalm 1 stated emphatically that knowing, obeying, and delighting in Yahweh's Torah (his instruction and direction) was the divinely determined way to a blessed life. The Hebrew term *'āšer,* derived from the verb *'āšar* (to go straight), is found only in the plural construct form (*'āšrey*) and has a double meaning, happiness and blessedness. Hence various translations have either one or the other. The basic thrust of the term is that of a life in fellowship with Yahweh God, the source of all that is good, is pleasing, enriching, and fulfilling.

The term *bārak* appears often in the Psalms.[39] It means to bless and in its various forms it refers to God as the source and object and likewise to the Psalmists as the ones who bless or are the ones who are blessed.[40] The feminine noun *bĕrākâh* refers to what was expressed, given, or received.

The spiritual mandate required that Yahweh's people know, serve, and worship their covenant Lord. The Torah was given to instruct them in who their Lord was, and what he had done for his creation, particularly his people. The Torah explicitly revealed what Yahweh God demanded of his people. In all of life and especially in their worship they were to know and serve the One True God, Yahweh their covenant Lord. The manner of worship was clearly stated. There were to be no idols or any kind of material forms of the infinite Lord. They were to honor him, especially by using his name properly and they were to set apart one day out of seven for worship of him.

Blessings were sure to follow the faithful covenant people (25:10). The character of the Torah was an assurance for this. Consider what was revealed concerning it. It gives water and power to productive lives (1:3; 23:2). It gives light (119:105), peace (4:8; 23:4), and hope (119:43, 49, 81). It revives the person (19:7 [MT 8]; 23:3), gives comfort (119:52), and gives wisdom (19:7 [MT 8]; 119:98). It gives joy (19:8 [MT 9]; 119:15, 16, 24, 35, 47, 77, 174). It guides into and teaches truth (25:5, 9; 27:11; 32:8; 73:24; 78:1–6; 86:11; 119:30) and reveals Yahweh God's faithfulness (33:4; 111:7; 118, 119:93). Yahweh's Torah warns against sin and evil and the sad results of violating his law (89:30–32 [MT 31–33]).

The Psalmist wrote a very assuring reality. Yahweh's Word and his righteous laws are *lĕ'ôlām* (eternal) (119:89, 160). The Torah is an abiding, trustworthy revelation for all times and for all situations. The divine demands that are revealed are steadfast, unchangeable, even as are its virtues and promises. It follows then that careful attention be given to the call for obedience. The Psalmists were aware of what actually was required.

The Required and Confessed Human Response[41]

Worship

The Psalmists realized that throughout history Yahweh God called for and had provisions made for his people's worship of their covenant Lord. Hence there is the call by the Psalmists to the choir in the Temple:[42] *hābû* (qal imper. masc. Pl. of *yāhab*, to give) praise to Yahweh God. To give praise meant to acknowledge and ascribe Yahweh's glory and strength. Ascribing glory to Yahweh, the singers also acknowledged Yahweh's holiness and strength (29:1, 2; 96:6, 7). The Chronicler, who repeated the call in these Psalms, added that this call was to all families of the nations. In addition to ascribing glory and strength they were to bring offerings to Yahweh. This singing and bringing was summed up in *hištahāwû* (to worship) Yahweh in splendor and holiness (1 Chron. 16:27–29).

The verb *kābēd*, from which the noun *kābôd* (glory) is derived carries various nuances. It can mean to honor (15:4). The word as a verb, however, is mostly translated glorify—the worshipful act of recognizing Yahweh's glory and proclaiming it. This is very specifically an act of worship. It was considered a command to do so (50:15, 23; 86:9). The Psalmist vowed to glorify Yahweh, praising him with all his heart, and to do so *lĕ'ôlām* (for all time) (86:12). Another form of the verb *kābēd* is the niphal participle, plural, *nikĕbādôt* (glorious things) are said of Yahweh's city in which the people of various nations are citizens (87:3). The gathering and presence of peoples from various nations was a God-glorifying reality and Yahweh's people praised their Lord for this reality in their worship.

By far the most dominant aspect of worship was to bless[43] Yahweh God. The Psalmist used three correlative terms that demonstrated the close interaction between acts of worship. Three main verbs are concerned with getting low before God (95:6); come, lie prostrate (*mištaḥaweh*), and kneel. Thus the worthship of God is demonstrated.[44] They express "the proper attitude of adoration."[45] The term *bārak* (kneel) appears often in various verbal forms in the Psalms. As a qal passive participle *bārûk* is used repeatedly to express adoration to Yahweh God because he is my rock (18:46 [MT 47], and strength (144:1). He hears prayers (28:6; 31:21 [MT 22]), and does not reject them (66:20). He alone does wondrous deeds (72:18).[46] Collectively Yahweh's people sang that they blessed God zealously and fervently from the house of Yahweh (118:26)[47] Mutual calls to bless the Lord intensively in worship appear repeatedly to the people (66:8; 134:1), of the congregation (68:26[MT 27]), of the house of Israel (135:19), of the house of the priest Aaron (135:19), and of the house of Levi (135:20). A strong call comes to all servants that fear Yahweh (134:1). Thus the people were led to sing, "Bless Yahweh, O my soul" (103:1, 2, 23; 104:1, 35), and the angels and all the works of Yahweh were called to join in this song blessing Yahweh (103:20, 22). The Psalmists vow saying "I will bless Yahweh." This personal act of worship is expressly stated (16:7; 26:12; 34:1[MT 2]; 63:4 [MT 5]; 145:1, 2). Yahweh God, receiving the blessed acts of worship, will in reply bless his worshipers (5:12 [MT 13]; 29:11; 67:6 [MT 7]; 115:12, 13). A final call to worship Yahweh is fervently expressed: "let all flesh bless his holy name" (145:21).

Love

The people of Yahweh God, who honor him by worshiping him as required by the covenantal spiritual mandate, must realize that love for their Lord is an absolute requirement.[48] Yahweh's covenantal love is the basis, source, and motivation for his covenant people's love for him.[49] Hence we read that the Psalmists verbally expressed their love *'āhablî . . . yĕhwâh* (I love Yahweh). The Psalmists sang and led worshipers in singing Psalm116. This expression of love came from the heart of those who were assured Yahweh heard their prayers. They called for deliverance from trouble and sorrow. They called for salvation when they faced death. They were assured that their prayers were heard and *answered!* He revealed that by demonstrating grace, righteousness, and protection (116:2–9). To exhibit love for Yahweh the singers sang about walking before Yahweh, believing him, and fulfilling their vows in the house of Yahweh (116:9–19).

David repeatedly sang of his love for Yahweh. When delivered from his enemies, especially Saul, David sang, using an unusual word, *'arĕhemēkâ.* The root term *rāḥam* can indicate affectionate. The derived noun, *reḥem,* means womb and is "associated with a mother's care for her children."[50] Commentators have not been united in explaining why David used this unusual term. Was it because David had experienced care and protection, as a mother gives her child, which responded with this expression? "It was so good to have Yahweh as my rock, strength, and deliverer." It expressed a special relation with the Lord.[51] David also sang of that relation with Yahweh when he gave joyful expression of his love for Yahweh's house (26:8), Yahweh's salvation (70:4), and Yahweh's Torah, his Law (119:97, 163), his commandments (119:47, 48, 127), and his precepts (119:159). For David, love for Yahweh God included and involved love for Yahweh's Torah, his Law (119:97, 163) his commandments (119:47, 48, 127), and his precepts (119:159). For David, love for Yahweh God included and involved love for Yahweh's name and his revealed Word. All saints were called to share in this love that was all consuming, involving Yahweh and all that pertained to him (31:23).

Faithfulness

As with Yahweh God's love, demanding a response of love, so Yahweh God's faithfulness[52] required a response of faithfulness by covenant people. There are some instances in which the Psalmists' awareness of this requirement was included in the Psalms they sang. Asaph led Israel to sing of their lack of faithfulness (78:8). This had been demonstrated after Yahweh God had redeemed them from slavery and provided for them in the desert (78:9–20). They had put God to the test and rebelled against him (78:56).

In a kingdom Psalm, however, there is an acknowledgment of faithful ones. They are the ones who, loving God, hate evil. These faithful ones are guarded. If caught by evil hands they are delivered; light and joy are shed upon their upright hearts (97:10–12). The reward of faithfulness is great and wonderful. The Psalmist spoke of Yahweh's hating faithless men who have perverse hearts. But Yahweh's eyes will be on the faithful. They are those who do not slander neighbors and do not have proud and haughty hearts. They walk blamelessly. They are assured they dwell with their covenant Lord (101:3a–6).[53] They were assured that Yahweh preserves *' emûnîm* (the faithful ones) who love him (31:23 [MT 24]).

The Psalmists gave expression to their faithfulness in various other ways. The poet who wrote Psalm 119 confirmed *derek 'ēmûnâh bāhāetî* (the way of faithfulness[54] I have chosen). This faithfulness was exhibited by setting his heart that had been set free on Yahweh's laws, statutes and commands (119:30–32).

Obedience

A major and grievous complaint or accusation against the covenant people was their disobedience. Asaph spoke for Yahweh: "If you would but listen to me" (81:8[MT 9]). He went on to say that "my people would not listen (*śāma'*) to me and *lo'âbâh lî* (not submit to me) (81:11[MT 12]; 106:25). Obedience to Yahweh God's covenantal spiritual mandate demanded that Israel hear the demands of the Torah, submit, obey, and do them. Israel, as a nation, would not obey. They were punished by exile (2 Kings. 17). Judah, likewise was exiled (2 Kings. 25). The Psalmists reflect various aspects of this disobedience that led to the exile (Ps. 137). But there was the remnant that clung to Yahweh and his city. Psalmists also reflected on the punishment received for disobedience.[55] David gave a classic example of this saying Yahweh's hand was heavy on him; he wasted away and groaned (32:3, 4).

Yahweh God's covenant people had had specific instruction regarding obedience. Moses had repeatedly called for obedience (Deut. 4:30; 6:3, 24, 25; 11:13, 27, 32; 12:28; 13:4, 18; 15:5; 27:10; 28:1, 2; 30:2, 10, 14). The Psalmists repeated Moses' call and admonition to obey. To be faithful to the covenant, one was to obey Yahweh's precepts (103:18) as the angels obey his word (103:20). Psalm 119 repeatedly refers to *śāmar* (keep, obey) the decrees, word, Law, commands, statues, and precepts. Indeed, the Psalmist vowed to hear, keep, the Law of Yahweh *bekāl lēb* (with all [my] heart) (119:34).

Confession

The Psalmists gave much evidence, as studied in the preceding paragraphs, of Yahweh as their covenant Lord and King and of his self-revelation. They knew what was required of them in their relationship with their Lord.

Of Sin. The Psalmists were very much aware of their need to confess that all was not right with themselves, their relationship with Yahweh God, and in regard to what was required of them in obeying the spiritual mandate. A series of terms are employed to give expression to this sad reality. These are as follows.

The term *'āwen* (iniquity)[56] appears often to describe those who perform evil deeds. The phrase "workers of iniquity" appears repeatedly. David pled *timšekēnî* (do not draw, or drag)[57] me with the wicked (28:3). He did not wish to be seen or characterized as a man of iniquity. A Psalmist (66:18) wrote that if he had cherished *'āwen* in his heart, Yahweh would not have answered him. He, however, is assured that Yahweh had listened to him. Conclusion: he was not a man of iniquity.

When David had been confronted by the prophet Nathan concerning his deeds of murder, adultery, and cover up (2 Sam. 12:12) and confessed that he had done as accused, he used various terms to refer his situation before God. He confessed he did not cover up his iniquity; he had acknowledged the wrongness of what he had done. He referred to his crimes as *pěsâ'* transgression (32:1). He had stepped over and gone beyond the boundaries of Yahweh's Law. He acknowledged he had broken the Law of God and had offended his Lord in doing so. David also, in a synonymous manner, spoke of *hātâ'âh* (sin) (32:5). He confessed he had missed the mark, and had not met the full requirement of the Law. In reality, it referred to an opposition to Yahweh's Law. David had known the Law; he ignored it, more, he opposed and violated it. Thus he confessed the guilt of his sin. Guilt is the translation of *'âwon*, which is also the root of the term translated iniquity. Guilt, however, stresses the status of the person who is considered iniquitous. Guilt places one before the Law that requires punishment (cf. also how the term is used in 7:3; 38:4). David used the term *'ašam* (derived from the verb *'ăšhōm)* that expresses the sense of offense and fault rendering a person guilty (69:5 [MT 6]).

A term that occurs often throughout the Old Testament is *râ'* (evil).[58] To do evil is referred to by *rāsā'*. David taught what is included in the idea of evil by the descriptive synonyms he used: wicked, arrogant, doing wrong, telling lies, being blood thirsty and deceitful (5:4–6 [MT 5–7]). David confessed he had not done evil when pursued by enemies (18:21 [MT 22]). He wanted nothing to do with evil. He insisted he abhorred the assembly of evildoers and would not sit with the wicked (26:5). Evildoers he knew never learn (53:4 [MT 5]). So he prayed, deliver me from evildoers and save me from blood-thirsty men (59:2 [MT 3]). He called on God to hide him from the conspiracy of the wicked and from the noisy crowd of evildoers (64:2 [MT 3]). Other Psalmists joined David. The poet who composed the song for the Sabbath Day rejoiced that God's enemies would perish and all evildoers would be scattered (92:9 [MT 10]). The author of Psalm 119 commanded evildoers to be away from him so that he might keep the commands of his God (v. 115). Another one called on those who love Yahweh to hate evil (97:10). David joined him urging those who love life to keep their tongue from evil, to speak or do no evil but to do good and seek peace (34:13, 14 [MT 14, 15]).[59]

David's confession of sin was referred to in the preceding section when terms he employed were considered (32:1–5). After a review of David's confession and his acknowledgment of the prevalence of sin in life and his strong desire to avoid all aspects of breaking the Law of Yahweh God, a brief study of Psalm 51[60] should be considered. This Psalm has received very much attention from a wide variety of scholars and it has been characterized as a penetential Psalm.[61]

The structure of the Psalm reveals David's complete awareness of what he had done, what he needed, what God demanded, and what a forgiven sinner should and could do.

A review of this sketch leads to the conclusion that Psalm 51 does not lend itself to a neat outline.[62] There are three statements of confession of sin (3–5). There are three statements that acknowledge Yahweh's demands (vv. 6, 8b, 16 [MT 17]). The greater portion of the Psalm could be considered a plea for mercy applied. These

Psalm 51

Sinner's Plea
Sinner's Confession
God's demand
Saint's Response
For mercy,
Compassion
cleansing 1, 2
Transgression
Sin anti God
Sinful from birth 3, 5
Truth,
Wisdom 6
Cleanse with
hyssop, wash me,
make white,
give joy 7, 8a
Crushed bones, 8b
Hide not face from sin
Blot out iniquity
Create pure heart
Do not cast away
Do not take Holy Spirit
Restore joy of salvation
Give willing spirit 9–12
Teach sinners, 13
Save me, 14a
Tongue sing, 14b
Open lips, 15a
Mouth declare,15b
No delight in
sacrifice
broken heart
Good pleasure
Build Zion
Sacrifices brought

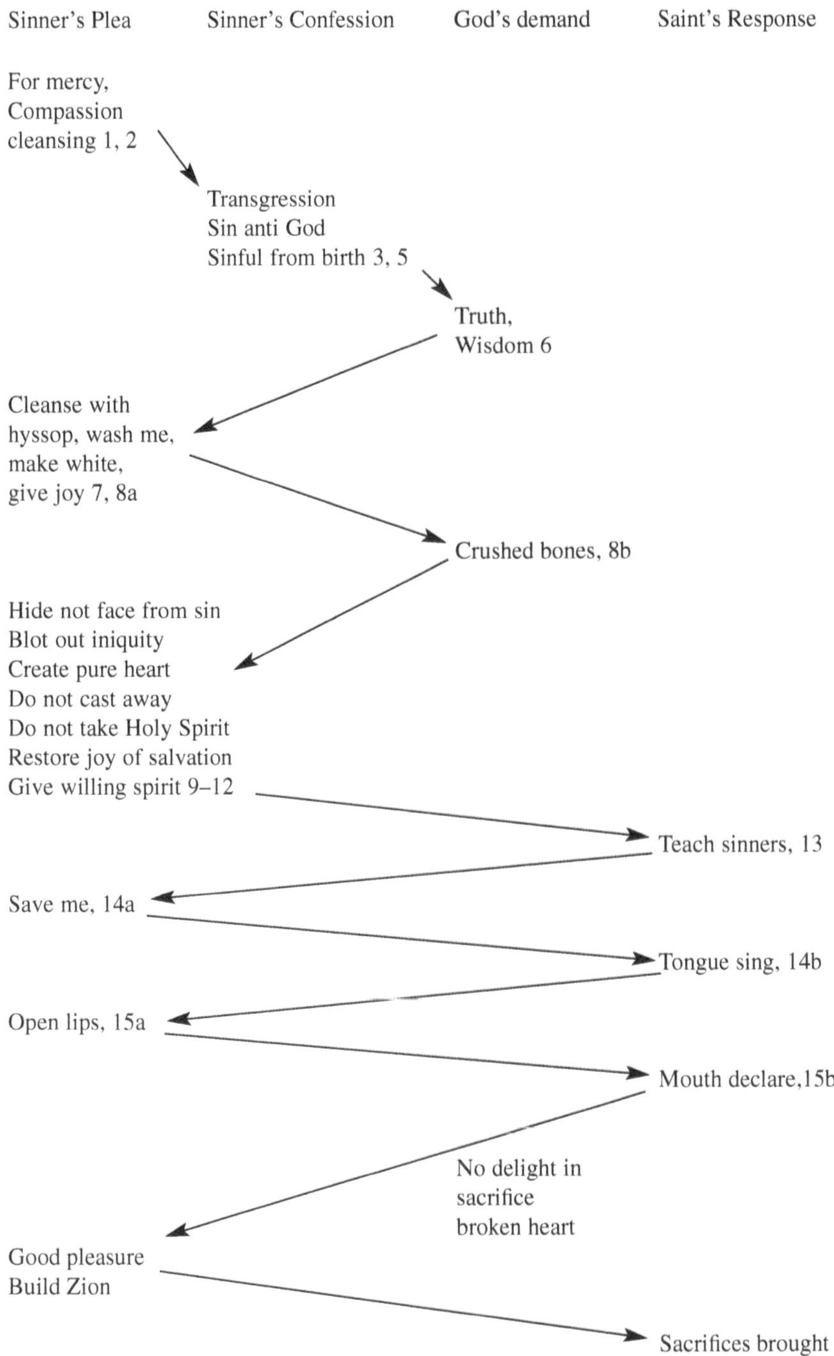

pleas, however, are saturated by evidences of repentance, sorrow for sins committed, and Yahweh's remedies. Consider what David said, "Have mercy and compassion, demonstrate this by cleansing me" (vv.1, 2, 7, 8a). "I have forfeited your blessed presence and the joy it gives, but do not hide your face, cleanse and renew my heart so it may be fit for the Holy Spirit's presence. Renew my spirit and joy; enable me to open my lips so that I can continue to prove you and teach sinners your demands and have them return to you."

Psalm 51 must be considered pentential. Repentance is not referred to, but the Psalms breathe sorrow for sin committed against Yahweh God. Repentance motivated confession. Psalm 38 records David's confession of iniquity and sin (v. 18). He expresses pain and affliction caused by these (vv. 2, 6, 8, 17), as well as estrangement from friends, companions, and neighbors. In Psalm 143, also considered penetential, David confessed he was not righteous (v. 2); thus he knew he did not merit Yahweh God's attention. But he needed it, enemies pursued him (vv. 3, 9). Yahweh was his only hiding place. David also referred to enemies as an indirect source of his need for mercy. He implied, however, that he had brought on Yahweh's rebuke, anger, and discipline (6:10 [MT 11]). An unknown poet, joining the throngs that went up to Yahweh's house to worship, led his companions to confess that because of sin they could not stand before Yahweh God. They, however, acknowledged that sin brought them into the depths of despair. They knew, however, that Yahweh would hear, forgive, and, in his unfailing love, redeem his people (Ps. 130).

Of Need. In the preceding discussion of the Psalmists' confession of sin, one could not avoid the repeated reference to the needs sinners have. If the covenantal spiritual mandate was heeded and obeyed, there would be far fewer references to needs. But, living in a sinful world, in which evil environments were almost unavoidable, the obedient covenant person had specific needs.

The need for mercy was repeatedly noted in the context of repentance and confession of sin, evil, iniquity, and transgression. We have studied the Psalmists' sure knowledge of Yahweh God's *ḥesed* (mercy).[63] The Psalmists knew they did not deserve or merit Yahweh's mercy because they by sin had offended their Lord. They had become unworthy of Yahweh God's covenantal lovingkindness.[64] But the poets sang "let your mercies come to me" (119:41). They knew it was available: the earth O Yahweh, is full of your mercies (119:64) and these would endure forever (118:4, 29). Yahweh's mercy was a real need for sinners as they realized what their situations were. Their own sin caused misery and guilt (32:3–4; 78:40–42, 56–64). Their fellowmen made life difficult for them. Natural phenomena could afflict them, famine (33:19; 37:19; 105:16), floods[65] (69:2, 15 [MT 3, 16] ; 124:4); and storms and tempests (55:8; 83:15; 107:25). The covenant people knew and confessed their need for mercy and freely called upon their sovereign merciful covenant Lord.

The Psalmists confessed their need for help for they realized their sinfulness, weakness, and inability to deal with the problems and vicissitudes in life. They admitted their weaknesses before wicked men (10:1–11), and pled with Yahweh their king (vv. 16–18) to rise up and not forget the helpless (vv. 12–15). David had cried out *hosi 'ah* (hiph. imp. of *yasa,* to deliver). Translators correctly wrote "Help!" (12:1[MT 2]).[66] When Yahweh heard his cry, the Psalmists exclaimed, "Praise be to Yahweh . . . for I am helped (28:7; 86:17).

Of Faith. In a preceding section the faithfulness of God was studied.[67] Yahweh God is faithful. He faithfully upholds his covenant promises. He is utterly reliable and dependable. He does not change (110:4). The Psalmists knew and believed that. It was an abiding assurance and comfort for them. And they knew that Yahweh's covenantal spiritual mandate required that they, in response to their faithful covenant Lord, were to be faithful. They were to be men of faith and demonstrate it in all aspects of their lives.

It is interesting to note that the term *faith* does not appear in the Psalms in the English Bible because it does not appear in the Hebrew version of the Psalms. The concept of faithful, an adjective, appears (18:25 [MT 26]; 33:4; 78:37; 89:19).

The noun *faithfulness* occurs repeatedly. But phrases such as "my faith" or "I have faith" or "I believe" do not occur in the Psalms. They do occur in the New Testament. Is one now to assume that the Psalmists did not exercise faith? Was it an unknown spiritual concept and requirement for them? The answer: the Psalmists confessed and declared their faith in Yahweh God in a variety of ways.

Consider how often the Psalmists spoke of their God. You God are my shield (3:3 [MT 4]); deliver me O my God (3:7 [MT 8]); listen . . . my king and my God (5:2 [MT 3]); O Lord my God, I take refuge in you (7:1 [MT 2]); O Yahweh our Lord (8:1 [MT 2]). The personal expressions of the Psalmists claiming the covenant Lord as their God, Savior, rock, refuge, are too numerous to list. The point is, however, these expressions of my Lord, my God, are clear and positive confessions of faith in Yahweh God. The Psalmists knew their covenant Lord. They were assured of their fellowship with him. They submitted to him and fully trusted him.

Trust is an essential element of faith. Consider how the Psalmists expressed their submission to God, their fully trusting him. The verb *bāṭâḥ* meaning trust occurs in various verbal forms. It does not occur as a noun. Consider the various personal testimonies. David sang, "I trust in your *ḥesed* [mercy] and my heart rejoices in your salvation" (13:5 [MT 6]). David had true faith. He knew he was a saved man. He lifted his soul to Yahweh, an act of worship, and trusted in him when enemies sought to triumph over him. David went on to say that trusting in Yahweh he had hope and would not be put to shame. He went on to sing that he trusted in Yahweh without wavering. He called on Yahweh to test his trust that was upheld by Yahweh's ever-present love for him (26:1–3).[68] David knew his heart, and boldly said he would trust Yahweh God in the future (55:23 [MT 24]) and this trust would keep him from being afraid (56:3 [MT 4]). Other Psalmists joined David in confessing their trust (faith in Yahweh 91:2). These Psalmists also sang that trust brought blessedness into their hearts (84:12 [MT 13]). Hence, it was in their hearts to call upon the covenant people to trust in Yahweh (e.g., 4:5 [MT 6]; 11:9, 10, 11; 37:3; 62:8.

Another expression of faith must be considered. The Psalmists unashamedly and boldly expressed their love for Yahweh God. To love their covenant Lord was the highest, fullest, and most comprehensive way to express their adhering to and obeying the covenantal spiritual mandate. The spiritual mandate called for a deep and abiding relationship between Yahweh God and his covenant people. Since the term *love* expresses a heartfelt continuing bond the Psalmists readily gave expression to their being bound to God with ties of love. Two Hebrew terms are used to express love: *'ahab* refers to the bond that unites and holds hearts and lives together; *rāḥām* refers to a compassionate relationship and is correctly translated as love. David was passionately in love with Yahweh when he was delivered from the hand of his father-in-law, Saul (18:1[MT 2]). But when the Psalmist reflected on Yahweh God hearing his prayer and revealing his grace and compassion to him, he realized how he was bound to Yahweh, for his Lord held him securely (116:1–8). This love for Yahweh motivated the covenant people to express love for his habitation (26:8). The people loved to be in Yahweh's immediate presence. Love for Yahweh's revelation was repeated by the Psalmist who sang about his love for Yahweh's Law (119:97, 113), commandments (vv. 47, 48, 127), testimonies (v.119), and precepts (v. 159). He expressed love for Yahweh because the covenant people were secure within the will of their Lord.

Notes

1. The prophet Jeremiah made the distinction between the Old and New Covenants (34:13–18).

2. Walther Eichrodt wrote that the covenant was retained (sic) as the central concept by which to illuminate the structural unity and unchanging tendency of the Old Testament message. *The Theology of the Old Testament*, vol. 1, 6th ed., trans. J. A. Baer (Philadelphia: Westminster, 1961), 13.

3. See my *From Creation to Consummation*, vol. 1, 67.

4. Ibid., 24, 25.

5. Consult the diagram of "The Covenant in Scriptures," ibid., 148.

6. E.g., reference is to the bond between Jonathan (1 Sam. 20:42) and Solomon and Hiram (1 Kings 5:1–12).

7. The elements or essential aspects of covenant are widely recognized and studied in most Old Testament biblical theological studies. Some introductions to the Old Testament also include these and/or give a broader discussion of the covenant. Cf. R. K. Harrison, *Introduction to the Old Testament* (Grand Rapids: Eerdmans, 1969) 476–79.

A careful survey of Brevard Childs' *Introduction to the Old Testament as Scripture* (Philadelphia: Fortress, 1979) will not enable one to discover a discussion of one of the central themes, or strands, of the Old Testament, much less of the Psalms. Childs does have a short segment on promises, but he does not place it in the context of the covenant, of which it is a central motif, 130.

8. See especially chap. 39, 146–48.

9. See discussion of faithful in the following section, 195–96, as applied to people.

10. See chap. 42, 219–21 on the administration of the curse of the covenant.

11. Cf. other Davidic Psalms in which Yahweh God's faithfulness was acknowledged and praised (33:4; 115:1; 117:2; 138:2; 143:1). Other Psalm composers also referred to it (85:11; 91:4; 92:2; 100:5; 111:7, 8; 119:75, 90).

12. Cf. comments of Ridderbos, *Psalmen*, 97,101–2. A reading of the Hebrew text clarifies. The term *śaddîq* describes Yahweh God; the feminine plural form *śidaqôt* refers to righteous deeds a covenant man performs; these deeds Yahweh loves.

13. This term is derived from the term *yāšar* which denotes either smoothness or straightness and uprightness. As a noun *mêšār* is often translated equity (NIV).

14. Cf. Delitzch, *Psalm III*, 396.

15. Grosheide, *Psalmen*, commented that some commentators found it strange that nations cast down were at the same time called to covenantal life and worship, 133.

16. For a full yet succinct discussion of Zion, see A. A. MacKae's article in *The Zondervan Pictorial Encyclopedia of the Bible*, ed. M. C. Tenney (Grand Rapids: Zondervan, 1975), 1063–67.

17. See *FCTC*, 124 for a succinct discussion of the term *hen* .

18. It is important to remember the descriptions of Yahweh God's emotions are basically anthropological.

19. Andersen, in his essay, has written that Yahweh's *ḥesed* is the central and pivotal virtue. "Yahweh, the Kind and Sensitive God," in *God Who is Rich in Mercy,* ed. Peter T. O'Brien and David. G. Preston (Homebach West: Lanner, 1986), 41–86.

20. See my discussion of God revealing his goodness when he created. *FCTC*, 19, 20.

21. The noun *tā'am* is derived from the verb *tā'am* (to taste, perceive); as a noun it is understood to refer to judgment, that is, by tasting one examines and comes to a conclusion-judgment. Allen translated the word as discernment, *Psalms 101–150*, 129.

22. Cf. also 32:2; 51:10 [MT 12], 17 [MT 19]; 77:3 [MT 4]; 78:6; 143:4, 7.

23. It is difficult to know precisely what David referred to with (the breath of your nostrils). The context suggests David was rescued when Yahweh, his strength, intervened and delivered him (18:15[MT16]). Yahweh is said, allegorically, to have employed various means. Did David refer to a tempest, a fierce wind storm, or to the Holy Spirit who brought judgment upon his enemies?

24. *BDB* has "utterance" as the basic meaning, but also adds as proper translations, declaration, revelation. As a verb *nā'am* is translated "to utter a prophecy."

25. Cf. discussion of the cultural mandate in chap. 42.

26. Composed by Charles H. Gabriel, 1856–1932, in the *Psalter Hymnal* (Grand Rapids: Publication Committee of the Christian Reformed Church, 1959) #209, 246–47.

27. Cf., e.g., Ezek. 37:1–14; Zech. 4:6.

28. David clearly understood that the Holy Spirit and the Father was one God; in his parallel comments he referred to the Holy Spirit and Yahweh God's presence as the same God.

29. The first question is answered on 176–77.

30. Cf. Gerhardus Vos, *Biblical Theology* (Grand Rapids: Eerdmans, 1948, 11th ed. 1980), 79, 105,106.

31. P.J.N. Smal, *Die Universalisme in Die Psalmen* (Kampen: Kok, no date [latest source quoted publisher in 1951]).

32. Other Psalms understood to reveal a "pregnant universalism are 33, 49, 67, 96, 97, 98, 100, 110, 117, 145.

33. Smal referred to Psalms that lauded Yahweh God as Creator, Owner, Keeper of all things created; Yahweh as monotheistic, transcendent, king and world Judge.

34. *Psalmen II*, 45, 46.

35. Grosheide used the term *aangegrijpt*, translated in common language "grasp it."

36. Hirsch, *The Psalms,* vol. II, 113, 114.

37. This is a basic point underlying my work *MROT* and will be briefly discussed in chapter 43.

38. Cf. *FCTC*, vol. 1, 338.

39. The verb *bārak* appears in the qal, especially in the participial form, in the niphal, in the piel, and pual stems.

40. It is interesting to note that the consonants *b r k*, when pointed with seghols, becomes a segholate referring to knees. The question can be asked: does the covenant person, when on his knees, bless his Lord and/or receive the blessing from the Lord?

41. In the study of the human response, one should keep in mind that the response is to the revelation Yahweh God has given concerning himself and the covenant mandates. One should take issue with Brueggemann's position that Psalms are basically a "saving recital of Israel's Creed." *Message—Theological*, 140–43. Weiser wrote that the Psalms were a reflection of Israel's history and its cultus. *The Psalms*, 24.

42. Ridderbos understood that this call to the singers in the temple to praise Yahweh was directed above all to the heavenly choir. *Psalmen* I, 215.

43. The verb *barak* was introduced and briefly discussed in an earlier section.

44. Kidner, *Psalms 73–150*, 345.

45. Delitzsch, *Psalms,* vol. III, 86.

46. Cf. also Pss. 41:13 [MT 14]; 68:19 [MT 20], 35 [MT36]; 89:52 [MT 53]; 106:48; 119:12; 124:6; 135:21.

47. The verb *bārak* appears here in piel, ptc. Form; cf. also 129:8.

48. In the piel imperative.

49. Consider what was studied concerning Yahweh God's love in the preceding section.

50. Van Gemeren, "Psalms," 168.

51. N. A. Van Uchelen translated "hartelijk lief" that is, love that is heartfelt, cordial, *Psalmen I* (Nijkerk: Callenbach, 1971), 113, 148. Ridderbos explained that David gave expression to "a feeling of inner thankfulness," *Psalmen I,* 149; Anderson did not explain the term; rather he referred to it as gloss because 2 Sam. 22:2 did not include the phrase "I love you" *Psalms (1– 72),* 154.

52. Cf. discussion of Yahweh God's faithfulness on 180–81.

53. When I was a child, a verse the class had to learn went as follows: On the good and faithful, God has set his love. The author was Spencer Lake, cf. *Psalter Hymnal*, No. 7. Spencer interpreted the Hebrew term *ḥesed* (godly, saint) as "good and faithful."

54. The NIV translated *'ĕmūnâh* as truth, possibly because the Law, Statutes, and commands are truth. Allen, however, translated it as "way of faithfulness" *Psalms 101–150*, 301. Delitzsch, *Psalms,* vol. III, has helpfully pointed out that the context presents the way of faithfulness or perseverance standing in opposition to the way of lies or of treachery, 248.

55. Psalm 44:9–18 [MT 10–19] records that Yahweh's people complained that he had rejected them. They had been given over to their enemies. There is, however, the insistence that the covenant was not forgotten. The Psalm concludes with a call for help and redemption. Delitzsch concluded that God's people suffered defeat and shame for their infidelity, *Psalms II,* 71. Van Gemeren wrote that the people suffered vicariously like "sheep to be slaughtered" because of their infidelity, *"Psalms,"* 341.

56. The word *'āwen* is translated iniquity in the KJV. Other versions have sin, evil, mischief. The term has also been suggested to mean trouble, sorrow, idolatry, emptiness, unjust, imbalanced.

57. Commentators have interpreted this Hebrew word as rank—i.e., do not rank me with the wicked, Dahood, *Psalms 1—50*, 172, and do not carry me away with the workers of iniquity, Delitzsch, *Psalms 1*, 361, 62.

58. The term, in its various forms, occurs more than 575 times.

59. Asaph led Israel to sing that Yahweh God accused the wicked of using their mouths for evil purposes when they quoted the Law of the covenant but refused instruction, cast Yahweh's word aside, joined thieves, and adulterers, and slandered their brother (50:16–21; cf. also 10:7). The references to evildoers—men of evil words and deeds occur repeatedly in the Psalms (22:16 [MT 17]; 27:2; 34:16 [MT 17]; 35:11; 36:4; 37:9; 38:20; 52:3[4], 54.5 [MT 6]; 55:15 [MT 16]; 64:5 [MT 6]; 71:4; 73:7; 109:5, 6, 20; 125:3; 139:20; 146:1, 2MT [2, 3]).

N. H. Ridderbos wrote his thesis on "De Werkers der Ongerechtigheid in de Individuale Psalmen" (The Workers of Unrighteousness in the Individual Psalms) (Kok: Kampen, 1939), in which he evaluated Mowinkel's position that most Psalmists referred to foreigners when they referred to "workers of unrighteousness" and not to the Psalmists' fellow Israelites, 2, 3. Ridderbos considered that references were to Israelite evildoers, in life, worship, and special situations.

60. It is disappointing that critical scholarship would consider that David is not the author, but that it be considered, in part or the whole, as a postexilic Psalm. Tate, *Psalms 51–100*.

61. Psalms 6, 32, 38, 102, 130 and 143 have been referred to as penetential Psalms. Anderson, *Psalms 1–72*, 389.

62. Kidner presented a breakdown, History Appeal 1, 2; Confession, 3–5; Restoration, 6–9; Inward Renewal, 10–13; Humble Worship, 14–17; People's Prayer, 18, 19.

63. Cf. the study of mercy as a virtue of Yahweh God above, 170–71.

64. *Ḥesed* is often translated as lovingkindness—mercy is love revealed with kindness, tenderness, to the afflicted ones.

65. Floods are employed metaphorically but the Psalmists undoubtedly knew what damage floods of water could and did do.

66. David wrote that he called to his king and his God to listen when he called for help. The Hebrew text records the piel inf. construct form *sawe 'i* of the verb *sawa'* used only in the piel, to cry out for help (28:2, 3; 31:22 [MT 23]).

67. Cf. 167–68.

68. David's confession of absolute trust (faith) in Yahweh his covenant Lord appears repeatedly. Cf. 28:7; 31:6 [MT 7], 14 [MT 15]; 52:8 [MT 10]; 56:4 [MT 5], 11 [MT12]; 143:8.

41

The Covenant in the Psalms

The Social Mandate

I. Introductory Comments

II. The Psalmists' Societal Context

III. Marriage and Family

IV. Classes of People in the Covenant Community

V. Social Justice

41

The Covenant in the Psalms

The Social Mandate

Introductory Comments

The Inter-relationship of the Three Mandates

In this study of the Psalms the inter-relationship of the three mandates, the spiritual, the social, and the cultural, has become very evident. The Psalmists gave positive expression to the reality of the unity of life for the covenant person living within the cosmic kingdom. Under each mandate, in every aspect of life, the sovereign Lord of the kingdom and covenant was acknowledged. This unity of kingdom life and covenant service was not divided and compartmentalized. Under each mandate the other relationship could not be ignored nor denied. Since Yahweh God was Creator and ruler over the entire cosmos, the covenant person had, by divine design, a personal spiritual relationship with the King! This relationship came to expression also in the covenant person's interaction with people and society as a whole.[1] Likewise the spiritual relationship with Yahweh God was integrally involved with the covenant person's life and interaction within the creational, natural, cultural dimension of cosmic kingdom life. And as the spiritual was integral to and impacted on the other two mandates, they had their influence on the spiritual. It must be emphasized that the cosmic kingdom was an integrated unity. This unity, however, does not give reason to ignore or deny the reality, presence, and influence of the three specific covenantal relationships.

Understanding the Torah

To understand the social mandate, it is imperative that Yahweh God's revelation in the Torah be known and understood.[2] Major points that must be seen reflected in the Psalms is that Yahweh God created both man and woman in his image. They were created sinless, in fellowship with their covenantal kingdom Lord. They were created to be a pair uniting in flesh to reproduce and bring forth a family. The family is a divine creation. Sin brought radical divisive influences between man and woman, and between siblings. Yahweh God, brought immediate possible restoration, but sin and evil continued to have drastic effects. Punishment for sin was also immediately promulgated.[3] Yahweh God also provided guidance for social living when the commandments were spoken; and when commandments 5 (family), 6 (preservation of life), and 7 (preservation of marriage and family) were written.

The Psalmists' Reference to Evil

The Psalmists referred to sin, wickedness, evil, and iniquity often. The sad results of these in their personal lives were revealed and lamented repeatedly. The calamities resulting from sin and rebellion in all of life were described. These, however, were always followed by expressions of confidence in Yahweh's mercy and forgiveness. These in turn led to thanksgiving and praise.

Awareness of the Antithesis

The Psalmists were deeply aware of the antithesis in life. They knew Yahweh God posited it.[4] The core of the antithesis was between the seed of the woman and Satan and his followers. There is no direct mention of Satan or the devil in the Psalms and only a few references to the seed of Abraham (47:9; 105:6), who are also included in the general seed of the woman in distinction from the seed of Satan (Gen. 3:15). The Psalmists' words reveal clearly that they were aware of the ongoing antithesis between God's people and the evildoing followers of Satan. Consider what the Psalmist wrote. Those persons, who are distinguished by not walking according to the advice or influence of the wicked and are not taking their stand with sinners and are refusing to fellowship (sit) with mockers, are blessed persons (1:1). They delight in Yahweh's Torah, are refreshed by living water, and are watched over by Yahweh (vv. 1, 2, 3, 6a). In distinction from these righteous kept ones, are the wicked, driven away like chaff and perishing in their ways (vv. 4, 5, 6b). In a real sense, Psalm 1 introduces the life and conduct of believing covenant followers. And the rebellious covenant breakers are likewise introduced. The two absolutely distinct ways of life, are set before worshiping Israel as they sang and lived according to Yahweh's revealed will for and governance of the world. Two distinct and absolutely separate pathways of life and the end of both are infallibly recorded. Believing Israel of all times and ages sing of it and do so rejoicing they are walking on the pathway of life that is forevermore.

In what follows, various Psalms will be studied or referred to as three themes in the Psalms are considered: (1) the Psalmists' social context; (2) marriage and family; and (3) classes of people.

The Psalmists' Societal Context

Royal Mankind's Place and Role

David wrote and sang for believers in all times and places. He was Yahweh God's covenantal agent in the midst of social life. Throughout his entire life he had many experiences—in Jesse's family, in Saul's family, in his own family, and in the family of Israel over which he was king.

David knew that Yahweh God was his sovereign Lord. He knew that his Lord had placed him where he was and had given him what he had. He sang, *yĕhwâ mĕnât hālĕqî wĕkôsî* (Yahweh portion of my portion[5] and my cup) (16:5). There is no agreement on whether Yahweh did the dividing of portions or if the Psalmist considers Yahweh himself to be his portion-heritage.[6] The text says that David praised his covenant Lord because he had received a delightful inheritance (16:6). He felt secure within what he referred to as boundary lines within pleasant places. The entire social context, in which he lived, served, and reigned was a gift from his covenant Lord.

In Psalm 8 David glorified his Lord because of the exalted place and role Yahweh God had given him in the cosmos, and especially among his fellowmen. He asked, "what is man that you are mindful of him and care for him?" (8:4 [MT 6]. In the midst of life, man and woman are image bearers of God himself. Human beings are remembered (*tizkĕrennûi*, qal impf of *zākar*) as (*tĕhassĕrehû mĕ'at me'ĕlōhîm,* to be lacking little of God) (v. 5 [MT 6]). The verb *haser* is a stative verb that expresses condition or status of a person. It means to be lacking. People were made to be lacking divinity, they are a little less than God.[7] They are not gods; they are not divine. As created human beings they are of the highest order of living beings and as such they have been *tamešilôhû* (hiph impf of *masal*, rule) caused or made to rule over everything Yahweh God has made (v. 6 [MT 7]). Yahweh God alone is majestic. Can a human being share that majesty with him? They can acknowledge it and adore their sovereign covenant Lord as they consider his majesty. They can exclaim, how majestic is your name, your glory is above the heavens (v. 1 [MT 2]). Note how majesty and glory are correlates. David recognized Yahweh's majesty in his powerful voice that swept over and echoed across all creation (29:4; 104:1, 2). He insisted that Yahweh's majestic power be proclaimed (68:34 [MT 35]). The poets who composed the kingdom Psalms adored Yahweh's robe of majesty (93:1) that was beheld in his sanctuary (96:6). Yahweh's majesty, along with his glory and righteousness, were revealed in his deeds (111:3; 145:5). The question is repeated, can human beings partake or share that majesty? The Psalmists answer "yes."

Consider what is recorded in various Psalms. David sang concerning himself as king under Yahweh. He acknowledged that the victories Yahweh gave him bestowed splendor and majesty upon him. This was accompanied with blessings and joy. The king, in fellowship with his Lord, trusted in Yahweh and through divine love he was kept secure (21:5–7).[8] David also referred to holy majesty adorning Yahweh's faithful willing servants (troops). One must conclude that at most, Yahweh's servants could, to quite a measure, reflect Yahweh's majesty, splendor, glory, and righteousness (110:3).

Yahweh's covenant people could approach and behold the majesty of their Lord. They were called to come before their Creator, who was God the Lord. They were urged to enter his gates/courts/dwelling with thanksgiving and praise. If they did they could behold his majesty (96:6; 100:2–4). David professed that he did and had seen Yahweh's power and glory there (63:3 [MT 4]). Asaph does not stress that when he was in the sanctuary he saw the divine majesty, power, splendor, and glory. Rather, he expressed his awareness of the tremendous gulf that existed between those who went to the sanctuary where Yahweh God revealed himself and those whom he described as arrogant, prosperous, and wicked (73:18–28).

In summary to this section on royal mankind's place and role, it must be emphasized that the Psalmists, knowing they were sinners and had to have cleansing, acknowledged they were royal imagebearers of Yahweh God. They knew that their love for and faithfulness to their covenant Lord was the way for them to receive the inestimable privilege of knowing, seeing, experiencing his majesty, glory, and splendor. And more, they knew these divine virtues influenced them and were strong forces in developing their character. They knew they were a different people distinguished from many people in their social environment.

The Wicked Ones

The Psalmists' repeated references to the wicked, arrogant, foes, and fools surely indicate that they were very much aware of the antithesis in all areas of social life. They knew they had to struggle with their own sin, evil, iniquity, and guilt. They, however, pled for forgiveness and cleansing (sanctification) and were assured they received these. Their struggles, however, were repeatedly intensified because of what fellowmen within Israel/Judah were and did. David gave eloquent expression to his struggles (6:6–10 [MT 7–11). His foes were the cause of being worn out, groaning, and weeping during the night. He knew that the future of his foes would be shame and disgrace. But in the course of daily life, especially before he became king, he had to face the fierce opposition of pursuing foes who intended suffering and death for him.

There are so many references to the wicked and evildoers in the Psalms that it would be needless repetition to list them all. A consideration of a few Psalms should suffice.

This sketch demonstrates how David kept before him the need to be continually aware of his involvement in life in which he was in constant interaction with wickedness and evil. He knew the wicked plotted, drew swords, and laid in wait

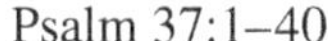

Psalm 37:1–40

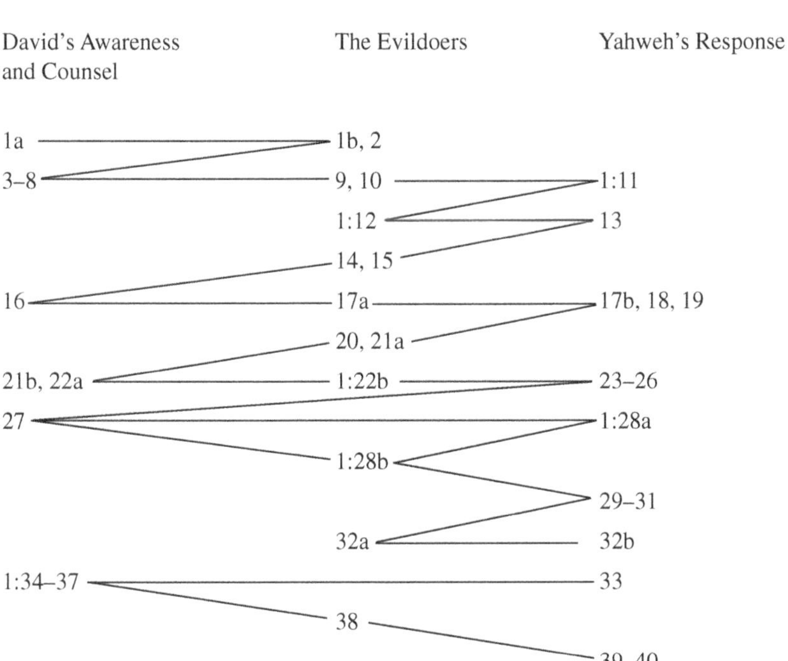

for the righteous to destroy them. He knew they borrowed and did not repay. He knew how he had to be constantly aware that he not *titĕḥar* (hith. Impf. of *ḥārâh*, to burn with anger) (37:1, 8). David knew he was tempted to hurt himself in vexation[9] because of the wickedness of fellow Israelites. He also knew that he had to resist *tĕqânnâ'* (piel of *qânâ'*) being intensely jealous or envious. His comfort and assurance was that Yahweh his covenant Lord would sustain, protect, and uphold him. But he had his responsibilities; he had to commit himself to Yahweh; he had to trust him. He had to be still and quietly wait for the Lord as he turned from evil and did the good and right. So, although, as the sketch illustrates, the wicked and evildoers seemed always to be between the righteous ones and the Lord, they could not draw the seeking and praying ones from the presence of Yahweh God.

Asaph, Israel's song leader, knew what experiences the covenant children of Yahweh faced and experienced in their social situation. Neither Asaph nor David asked to be separated from the wicked and evildoers. They did not ask God to lead them into the life of a hermit or into monastic living.[10] Consider how Asaph constructed his Psalm that exhibited how he went from darkness to light (73:1–28). This Psalm is didactic;[11] it demonstrates how in the daily activities of life, the prosperity of the wicked and the pressure under which the pious live are to be understood and resolved.

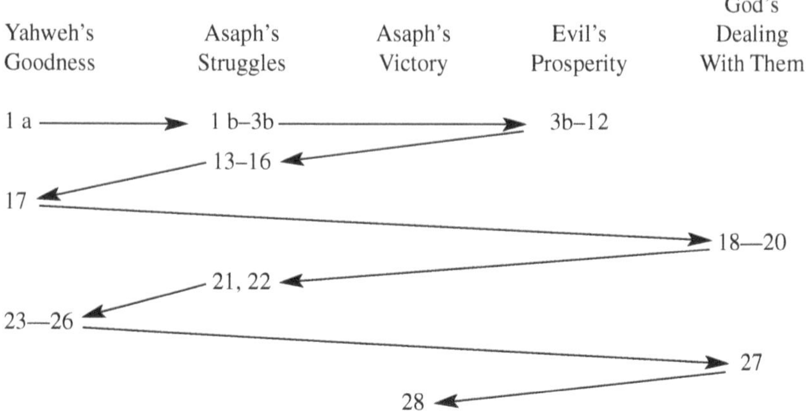

As Asaph struggled, almost slipping and falling, the wicked prospered. They had no struggles; they exhibited pride. There was no limit to their scoffing and threats. It was as if God was absent and silent. Asaph confessed he was senseless and ignorant when he thought of his God not paying attention or caring. The wicked had their good life. They seemed not to have illnesses, their calloused hearts led them to violence and to say God the Most High did not concern himself with them. Asaph, however, knew where to get the proper solution to his seeming dilemma. His good Lord, Yahweh God, did not forget the pure in heart. Nor did he ignore the evil ones. Asaph, in Yahweh's house, submitting to his Lord's word and teaching, was reminded that evil would be punished. The wicked had no enduring future. But he did; his sovereign covenant Lord was his refuge. He, Asaph, realized that Yahweh God revealed his goodness to those who in his presence worshiped him in his house.

The Psalmists knew there was an unbridgeable chasm between those who sought and served Yahweh God and those who in many ways exhibited a disdain of the righteous and who rejected the God of Israel who had created them and given them the good things in life. The antithesis was so absolutely clear. It was impossible for those who feared Yahweh God not to see it. They were convinced their good, their peace, their comfort, their strength was theirs only when they were in his presence and they took their refuge in him, their covenant Lord.

The Psalmists had a variety of terms they employed to describe or characterize the sinful, the evildoers, and the wicked. The NIV has the word *arrogant* twelve times. It is the translation of *hôlĕlîm* (qal. act. Ptc. of *hālâh*) that refers to people who are boastful or braggerts.[12] Asaph referred to those who troubled him as *hôlĕlîm* (arrogant) (73:3, 8). He called upon these arrogant not to boast with outstretched necks or to lift up their horns against heaven (75:5, 6 [MT 6, 7]).

Arrogance is also the translation of the Hebrew term *gā'ăwâh* (10:2).[13] It is also translated as pride. Pride is a characteristic of an arrogant person. They speak proudly (31:18 [MT 19];17:10), and pride encompasses the arrogant (73:6). A synonym *ge'he* (proud) also refers to the wicked who are jubilant in their way of life (94:2, 4). These proud and arrogant people ridicule the worshipers as they go up to meet with their Lord on his holy hill (123:4). These proud men also lay hidden snares, nets, and traps along the paths of Yahweh God's servants (140:5 [MT 6]). The Psalmist who loved Yahweh God and his Word was deeply troubled by the *zēdîm* (proud). He knew Yahweh God rebuked them (119:21). They have smeared the Psalmist with lies (119:69) and have dug pitfalls for him contrary to Yahweh's laws (119:86). These proud ones (also referred to arrogant ones, NIV 119:51) mock without restraint as the Psalmist hopes in Yahweh and remembers his word. He prayed that Yahweh would ensure the well-being of his servant by preventing the *zēdîm* (proud, arrogant) from oppressing him (119:122). The Psalmist prayed, "I know your laws are righteous . . . and they are my delight" (119:75, 77). Having thus confessed, he prayed that the proud/arrogant be put to shame. He did not pray that he himself do that but that Yahweh would. He trusted that he would uphold his word and sustain him and that he would *yāšûirû* (put to shame) the *zēdîm* who wrong the Psalmist (and all his people) without cause. David had prayed thus also.[14] He invoked Yahweh's covenant virtues, compassion, grace, love, faithfulness, and slowness to anger when he appealed to his covenant Lord when the *zēdîm* (a band of ruthless men) were attacking him, seeking to end his life (86:14, 15).

In various contexts, the Psalmists refer to the boastful and the arrogant as fools or foolish. It is the *nābāl* (fool) who says there is no God. The fool is described as corrupt, vile and one that can do no good (14:1; 53:1[MT 2]). They are evildoers who frustrate the plans of the poor who have Yahweh as their refuge (14:6). The fool stands ready to scorn the person whose transgressions are known, though they have been confessed and forgiven (38:18). These biblical references reveal how a *nābāl* can be known in the course of social life. In reality the fool has no common sense; he is senseless. He has no insight into ethical and religious concepts or principles. He is the opposite of the man who is wise and understands the basic realities of life.

A study of the Psalmists, inspired writers and poets that they were, reveals how they understood and unhesitatingly expressed what the person who rejected Yahweh God and his Word revealed themselves to be. They were arrogant, proud, and foolish. They *ni'ăsû* (spurn and condemn) spurned and reviled Yahweh's name. These foolish revilers were *'ôyêb* (enemies) (74:10) of Yahweh, and spiritual enemies of Yahweh's faithful serving covenant people.[15]

There certainly was and is an unbridgeable gulf, a chasm in the social aspect of the cosmos. The antithesis stands out clearly, boldly, and unmistakably.

The Nations

The Psalmists referred to *gōîm* (nations) many times. What role did these nations have in the life of the Psalmists and in the life of the covenant people? Did they have an adverse influence on Israel's social life? Were they considered to be the evildoers/enemies? In an effort to determine the correct responses to these questions, it is important to remember that the Psalms were composed at different times and in varying circumstances.

Various Psalms do refer to or reflect adverse influences by neighboring nations. These nations created very difficult social situations for the covenant people. It is not readily apparent from a consideration of some Psalms if reference was only to foreign nations. That these were referred to in some instances is apparent.[16]

A summary review of Psalms that include references to *gōîm* (nations) follows.

Psalm 2. The nations (heathen) rage, conspire, plot; kings and rulers together take their stand against Yahweh's anointed—the king of Israel, the type of Jesus Christ. These nations will be ruled and dashed as they become the inheritance of the covenant Lord.

Psalm 9:5–20 [MT 6–21]. David, serving as spokesman for Yahweh, spoke of his enemies who were wicked nations (heathen): Yahweh rebuked and blotted out their names so that the memory of them has perished.

Psalm 10. Yahweh, who is King forever, causes nations (heathen) who afflict the covenant people to perish from the land.

Psalm 18. David, when delivered from the hands of Saul who was his enemy, sang prophetically that he would be the head of nations (heathen) (43 [MT 44]. He referred to these as his foes (vs. 17 [MT 18]) as crooked (vs. 26 [MT 27]) as adversaries (vs. 39 [MT 40]), and violent men (vs. 48 [MT 49]). But he knew that with Yahweh as his rock, fortress, and deliverer, he would be delivered from both evildoers among his own people and from foreigners.

Psalm 22. David felt forsaken by God, for fellow Israelites, evil men, and nations surrounded him like bulls, roaring lions, dogs, and wild oxen. These motivated him to call upon Yahweh and to proclaim his name to his brothers.

Psalm 33. The Psalmist rejoices that Yahweh foils the plan and thwarts the purposes of nations. A sharp distinction is drawn between these and the nation Yahweh blesses and has chosen as his inheritance.

Psalm 43. The Psalmist calls on Yahweh to vindicate him against a nation of deceitful and wicked men who oppress him.

Psalm 44. The sons of Korah reflected on how God had driven out nations (heathen), crushed them, and made the fathers flourish. They had had victory over them.[17] Israel had become a reproach, a scorn, a derision. They had been scattered among the nations (heathen). But the Psalmist insisted that he and the people had not forgotten God or been false to his covenant (v. 17). Brought down by enemies, they in their misery and oppression had called fervently on Yahweh (v. 26).

Psalm 46. The sons of Korah also sang of Yahweh God as their refuge and strength while nations (heathen) raged. But Yahweh would be exalted among nations (heathen), yes, in all the earth (v. 10 [MT 11).

Psalm 59. David, being watched by Saul's men, called on Yahweh to rouse and punish nations (heathen) who were traitors. But David clearly referred to his personal enemies as included in nations (heathen).

Psalm 66. The director of music led worshipers to sing the glory of Yahweh's name. He rules forever by his power and his eye is on all nations to see if rebellion might rise up against him. The Psalmist prayed that Yahweh God, shining his face upon his people, would have his way and salvation be known among all nations (67:2) and that they would be glad and sing under Yahweh's just rule and guidance (67:4). Solomon, in his Psalm, sang of all nations bowing down and serving Yahweh and being blessed by his Royal Servant, would bless Yahweh (72:11, 17).

Psalms 78, 79. Asaph referred to the Caananites as nations (heathen) whom Yahweh dispossessed in order to keep his promise to the sons of Abraham that they would possess the land (78:55). Asaph referred to a reversal, the nations (heathen) having invaded the land defied the temple (79:1). He called on Yahweh to pour out his wrath on these nations (heathen) (79:6) so that they would not mock God (v. 10). Asaph referred to the casting out of nations (heathen) again (86:8 [MT 9]). Yet Asaph knew that all nations (heathen) whom he mentioned (83:5–8 [MT 6–9]) sought to destroy Israel as a nation (83:3 [MT 4]).

Psalm 86. Verse 9 expressed an eschatological hope that all nations would come, worship, and bring glory to Yahweh's name.

Psalm 94:10. The Psalmist acknowledges that Yahweh, chastening nations (heathen), punishes them. Yet Yahweh's glory is to be declared among nations (heathen) (96:3) because Yahweh God reigns over them (96:10) and his salvation and righteousness has been made known to the nations (heathen) (98:2).

Psalm 102:15 [MT 16]). An afflicted man, crying for help, knows Yahweh God will come to his aid. The nations observing this will fear Yahweh.

Psalm 105. The Psalmist recounted the history of how God's people went from nation to nation in their wanderings (v. 13) but eventually received the land promised to Abraham (v. 44).

Psalm 106. The Psalmist called for the people to share in the joy that they inherited in their land as a nation (v. 5). But the covenant people came to despise their inheritance; Yahweh caused their seed to fall among nations; they mingled with the nations (heathen) (v. 25) and were ruled by them (v. 41). The Psalmist concluded by calling on Yahweh to save and gather them (v. 47).

Psalm 110. David recounted how Yahweh, through his appointed Ruler, would judge the nations (heathen) and bring about their destruction.

Psalm 111. The Psalmist sang about Yahweh God who, remembering his covenant, gave his people the land (heritage) of the nations (heathen). Yahweh did this as the exalted One above all nations (113:4).

Psalm 115. The Psalmist rejoices that all glory be given, not to people, but to Yahweh God. He calls on his fellow covenant people to do so in order that the nations (heathen) not ask "where is their God?" (vv. 1, 2).

Psalm 117. The Psalmist called for all nations to praise Yahweh.

Psalm 118. The Psalmist thanked Yahweh for enduring love (v. 1) and in the name of his loving Lord he would be able "to cut" off all nations who surrounded him (v. 10).

Psalm 128:2. Worshiping pilgrims as they ascended to worship rejoiced that it was said among the nations (heathen) that Yahweh had one great things for his people.

Psalm 135. In this Psalm the history of Yahweh's people is reviewed. There is reference to Yahweh striking great nations and their kings and smiting their idols (vv. 10, 15).

Psalm 147. The Psalmist praises Yahweh for dealing with his people as he has not done with any other nation (v. 20).

Psalm 149. The Psalmist called for praises to be sung unto Yahweh and as they did, to acknowledge that Yahweh God alone executes vengeance on nations (heathen).

This review of those Psalms that include reference to nations (heathen) certainly make clear that the covenant people were aware of the reality that they were not the only nation in the cosmos. They were repeatedly made aware, and repeatedly sang of Yahweh God's call for the nations to know and serve him. The covenant people were not called to carry out missionary work. Rather, by their life and witness in the social environment the nations were to learn from them and come to know, serve, and worship Yahweh. The Psalms do not in any way or at any time refer to people of other nations, who did serve and worship Yahweh with them, as strangers to Yahweh God and that they should be excluded from the worship activities of Yahweh God.

There is, however, repeated warning against having "heathen" practices and influences upon Yahweh's people. The idols of nations were to be banished from all aspects of covenant living. It was in the social dimensions of life that "heathen" practices and influences had their initial infiltrations. For these reasons, Israel had to learn and be reminded by the singing of their Psalms, that idolatrous and Yahweh rejecting people were under the curse of the covenant.

David gave repeated expression to wicked men and evildoers. These sought to destroy him. Underlying these efforts by enemies was the Satanic effort to dethrone David and to prevent him from serving as the messianic type and forerunner of the promised Messiah.

The considerations of the references to nations (heathens) in the Psalms give clear evidence of the integrality of life. The social aspects of life impinged on the spiritual and cultural dimensions and these in turn on the social.

Neighbors and Companions

Neighbors, companions, and friends are living realities in social life. The Psalmists revealed how real these were and their roles in life.

The Psalmist referred to himself as a friend. He had considered his ways and walked according to Yahweh's statutes. So doing, he was a friend to all who feared Yahweh and followed in his footsteps. The bond of friendship arose and was upheld by a mutual love for and obedience to Yahweh (119:59–63). David also indicated how painful it was to learn that a friend, in whom he had trusted, betrayed him (41:9; 55:13 [MT 14], 14 [MT 15]).[18] He referred to Ahithophel, who had been a companion and a close friend. To have companions, that is, loved ones, taken away, the Psalmist says, is to make darkness his only friend (88:18 [MT 19]). When David experienced Yahweh God's wrath he was wounded and afflicted. He complained that his friends, companions, and neighbors remained far away from him. This added to his pain and darkness (38:1). His heart was "fever-racked."[19] He suffered in body and soul.[20] Commentators do not try to refer to an historic situation in which David experienced his loss and pain. They do discuss the relationship of sin and affliction and pain.[21]

In addition to friends and companions, the Psalmists refer to neighbors. They are important in the daily common experiences of social living. When the Psalmists referred at times to nations as neighbors they lamented that Yahweh had sold his people, having rejected them and scattered them, thus giving cause for reproach and disgrace by these people living near them (44:13[14]). These neighbors, who had invaded Yahweh's people, reproached Yahweh. The Psalmist prayed that Yahweh "pay back seven times" these neighbors. Then his people, the sheep of his pasture, would praise him forever (79:12, 13). David, however, was also aware that among the godly pious people could vanish: proof? They lie to their neighbors, with boastful tongues and flattering lips (12:1–4 [MT 2–5]). But he knew that those who live on Yahweh's holy hill, walk blamelessly, speak the truth, do not slander, and do his neighbor no wrong (15:1–5). Thus, the antithesis could come to a positive demonstration in the social environment in which Yahweh's faithful people lived.

Maintaining Confidence and Obedience

We have seen that Yahweh God in creating man and woman made them royal. in the midst of a fallen humanity. The wicked evildoers outnumber Yahweh's saints. They harass, reproach, attack, persecute, and take many of Yahweh's people captive. In the midst of such turmoil, uncertainty, and devastation, can a covenant person maintain confidence in and obedience to Yahweh God? Cries of despair and pleas for deliverance were repeatedly uttered. Had desperation overcome Yahweh's people in these social circumstances? The Psalmists gave clear and positive responses. They maintained their confidence in and obedience to Yahweh God. This testimony is recorded in various Psalms.[22]

David had confidence in Yahweh his covenant Lord. He realized his enemies had set a trap for him but he knew his Lord was the rock of his refuge and his fortress. He committed his spirit into his hands (31:1–5 [MT 2–6]). When fleeing from Absalom, David referred to his many foes who had risen up against him but he confidently prayed (in song) that Yahweh was his shield and bestowed glory upon him and lifted his head (3:1–3 [MT 2–4]). In a climactic manner, David, when false witnesses rose up against him, said *hĕ'āmantî* (I am confident) that I will see the goodness of Yahweh in the land of the living (27:12, 13).[23] And consider how David praises Yahweh his Savior when he was delivered from attacks of the people (18:43[MT 44], 46[MT 47]). He repeated saying, "In God, whose word I praise . . . In God I trust, I will not be afraid," when he was in the hands of the Philistines who lived in Gath (1 Sam. 21:10–15; Ps. 56:10, 11 [MT 11,12]).

Other Psalmists joined David in expressing confidence and obedience when in the midst of social adversities. The sons of Korah, experiencing a seeming rejection by their Lord because of adversities brought on by enemies, called on Yahweh with confidence "Rise up, and help us; redeem us because of your unfailing love" (44:26 [MT 27]). Asaph taught the covenant people to sing when they felt rejected under Yahweh's anger, "you, O God my king . . . bring salvation upon the earth" (74:12).

Obedience was a specific covenantal requirement. Yahweh demanded that the three mandates, spiritual, social, and cultural, be obeyed. The Psalmist who composed Psalm 119 acknowledged that he had gone astray and was afflicted. He realized he should have obeyed Yahweh's word. He pledged to do so (v. 67). He admitted it was good for him to have been afflicted because it led him to learn Yahweh's decrees (v. 71). Yes, it was Yahweh's faithfulness that motivated his affliction (v. 75). The wonderful effect this had was that Yahweh's love for him was his comfort and his continual hope in Yahweh's Word (vv. 75, 76). Knowledge of Yahweh's love and mercy, and of his law, commandments, statutes, and decrees motivated the Psalmist to obedience whatever his circumstances in life might be.[24] Indeed, the arrogant would mock without restraint (v. 51). They would dig pitfalls for him contrary to Yahweh's law (v. 85). But in spite of them Yahweh's Word and his Law was his delight (v. 92). He sang from the heart, "O how love I your Torah!" (the entire revealed Word) (v. 97; cf. also vv. 47, 48, 113, 119, 127, 159, 163, 167).

The many references by Psalmists to their struggles and pains in the social aspects of their lives did not drive them away from Yahweh and his Word. If it did, it was only for a time. Yahweh, knowing their social environment, restrained them, revealed his love and comfort to them. And they responded obediently and with confidence that they loved Yahweh. Difficulties in life increased their love, their confidence, and their obedience.

Marriage and Family

Marriage and family are at the very heart and core of the social mandate. When Yahweh created the male he said that it was not good for man to be alone (Gen. 2:18). Yahweh God ordained that the male and female become one flesh. He mandated that the male was to leave father and mother and become one flesh with the female (Gen. 1:27; 2:24), and nothing was to separate the male and the female once they had united as one flesh. Thus God ordained marriage and family and the basis of the social mandate was established. When Satan sought to bring disharmony and division between the male and female, Yahweh God made immediate provision for the continued unity of the man and woman and sanctioned their reproduction. They were to produce seed. Thus marriage, family, their continuity, and redemption was provided for humanity.

The Psalmists reflected their awareness of this entire revelatory message recorded in Genesis 1–3. Some Psalms will be considered.

Psalm 45. The sons of Korah intended this Psalm to be used in a liturgical setting.[25] Problems continue to be raised and various answers are presented.[26] Does this Psalm present a wedding song (song of love, KJV, NIV?) for a wedding context? Or is war the context (vv. 3–5 [MT 4–6]). Indeed, the military language supports that. But, though the predominant emphasis is on the military involvement of the king (Messiah), the scene presented in this Psalm is that of the king on his wedding day. Hence the military and marriage are combined.

The king, nobly and splendidly dressed, was prepared for marriage. Daughters of kings were present. They brought gifts. The princess (the royal bride) was gloriously dressed in her gown that was embroidered with gold. Virgin companions followed the bride. Sons to be born would take the place of fathers.

We must conclude that marriage was extolled. It was a central factor in royal life as Yahweh, Creator God, intended it to be. The king and his royal bride not only set an example for the people of the kingdom but also emphasized marriage's fundamental role in society. David and Solomon's taking multiple brides and concubines proved to be a blemish on their lives and had tragic consequences in their lives and that of their families.

Psalm 128. This Psalm was sung as pilgrims walked to Zion to worship Yahweh. The men who feared Yahweh, walking in his way, would be blessed. A specific blessing was emphasized. The wife of that God-fearing man would be like a fruitful vine. She would be a mother of sons, who metaphorically referred to as olive shoots, would be sources of blessings. Olive trees produced fruit and oil; olive wood was excellent for building and cabinetry products. The wife was thus portrayed as a very rich and absolutely necessary partner in life. Her unique role as wife and mother was of inestimable value. Her sons were to be considered as a heritage from Yahweh. They would enrich her life as mother in the family but also provide security for her and for future offspring (Ps. 127).

Psalms 127 and 128 certainly do hold in high honor the wife and the mother and their role as such in ancient society. The men, the partriarchs, had their specific roles. But these could and would never be filled if the wives and mothers did not carry out their duties in the roles Yahweh God assigned them.[27] The Psalmist praised Yahweh the Lord exalted over nations who stoops down to look on the heavens and the earth. He sees the barren woman in her home and *mĕwôsbîbî* (hiph. ptc. of *yāsab*—to remain, dwell causes her to be settled) (NIV) or content to dwell in her home[28] as a happy mother of children (113:6, 9). The Psalmists, in the course of composing their songs, reflected the importance of children being prepared for a fruitful life in society. Parents were to teach and train them so they could declare Yahweh's wonderful deeds (71:17). Fathers were to teach their children in the ways of Yahweh in such a way that generations to come would benefit from the great-great-grandfathers' instruction (78:1–8). Faithful covenant members of Israel were expected to train their young males to be like well-nurtured plants. Their daughters were to be prepared to serve as pillars in society.[29] Thus the role of the female was set out as a basic and fundamental influential role in society (144:12). Yahweh thus laid out the way for the land to be blessed (144:15). He would still the hunger of his cherished people; their children would have plenty and wealth could be stored up for their offspring (17:14).

The Psalmist acknowledged that families experienced difficulties. David confessed that as a youth he committed sins and had been guilty of rebellious ways (25:7). David also referred to dissension in his family. He endured scorn and was a stranger to his brothers because of his zeal for Yahweh God and his house (69:8 [MT 9]).

A review of Psalmic passages certainly does inform one that marriage and family had very important influential roles in the covenant community. Yahweh did not open the door to the wishes, desires, or preferences of individual groups of people regarding marriage and family. Yahweh God kept reminding his worshiping people of what was involved in knowing and obeying the covenantal social mandate.

Classes of People in the Covenant Community

Various categories or classifications of certain people were considered. The fool or foolish ones and the arrogant were seen to be a blemish among Yahweh's covenant people.

These were but a comparative few among the many wicked people, often referred to as evildoers and workers of iniquity, of whom the Psalmists wrote and often complained. Some who opposed covenant believers were neighbors, to whom the Psalmists knew they had to show compassion and give aid. In addition to the foolish, the evildoers, the arrogant, and the neighbors, the Psalmists refer to two other classes or categories of people who lived among Yahweh's covenant people.

The Rich

Asaph addressed the sick and poor, the low and high, calling all of them to listen to words of wisdom so that they might get understanding (49:2 [MT 3]). He went on to counsel the rich people's fellowmen not to be overawed by the riches of a man and the splendor of his house. These assets were temporal. He can take none of his treasures with him to the grave (49:16, 17 [MT 17, 18]). And, should a person be rich and have no *yābîn* (understanding or discernment) he is compared to *běhêmmôt* (large beasts) that perish (49:20 [MT 21]). They have no eternal future of blessedness (49:20 [MT 21]). It will be consumed like a moth in a flame (39:11[MT 12]). The wealth that they heaped up has no purpose (39:11[12]), although they say it is for children (17:14)

Riches can be a blessing. Yahweh God enables a king who rejoices in the strength of Yahweh to live royally for many days. He will be victorious on the battlefields. Riches will not prevent him from trusting in Yahweh who, in unfailing love, will keep the king steadfast (Ps. 21).[30] Thus he will be qualified to serve and represent his people in a God-honoring manner. And the rich people under the reign of the king will be able to feast and worship. Their offering, posterity, the future generations will learn about Yahweh and serve him (22:29–31 [MT 30–32]). But this wealth and riches can be a strong temptation to trust in them more than in Yahweh. David knew that well enough. He sang, "Better the little the righteous have than the wealth of the wicked" (37:16). And when he thought of Doeg, going to Saul to betray him (David) to gain favor with the king, David reflected on the strong man who did not make God his stronghold but trusted in his wealth that gave him power to destroy others (52:7 [MT 8]). Asaph also reflected on wicked men with wealth who asked if God knew and had knowledge of them—as if God didn't, so they could live carefree irresponsible lives (73:3–12).

In conclusion to this summary of what the Psalmists wrote concerning riches and wealth, one must realize that wealth and riches as such were not condemned. They were gifts from Yahweh who in love supplied his people with the abundant means so that the rich people could and would be a blessing in the kingdom. That these gifts could and were misused for self-glory and advantage was condemned. The rich people were in a position to be generous to the poor among the covenant people.

The Poor

The Psalmists knew that there were the *ānî* (translated variously as poor, humble, meek) and the *'ebyôn* (translated as in want, needy, poor). The term '*ānî* is derived from the verb '*ānâh* (to be afflicted). It appears thirty times and is translated to be humble and poor. There always were those among the covenant people who had to be recognized as requiring help.

Psalmists referred to themselves at times (88:7 [MT 8];[31] 116:10; 119:67, 71, 75, 107)[32] as being afflicted and suffering. Sometimes they indicated that God brought this on them (88:7 [MT 8]; 90:15; 102:23 [MT 24]), and at other times they brought it on themselves (35:13; 132:1). They also refer to enemies and evildoers who cause affliction and suffering (89:22 [MT 23], 94:5; 107:17). These passages referred to the activity of affliction and suffering as caused by self, others, or God.

There are references to the people that were afflicated. They were the '*ānî* (poor, humble, afflicted, and needy). As one reads the Psalms, one can ask: why were they? What caused these people to be afflicted and in various conditions of poverty and distress? Arrogant and wicked men caused schemes so that they could satisfy the cravings of their hearts for prosperity and happiness (10:2–6). In their strength they rob the poor (35:10). They are fools who say in their hearts that there is no God. They seek to prove to themselves that they, the proud, the self-sufficient, and the corrupt, can frustrate the plans of the poor (14:1–6).

Another question can be asked: what specifically do the *'ānî* consider to be the precise nature of their condition? Is it spiritual? social? cultural? or some other condition? When the cries for help, relief, and deliverance were uttered the nature of affliction, need, and/or poverty could be a combination of all three. Asaph referred to the social rights of the destitute and fatherless that were violated. He called for their vindication and their justice (82:3).[33] The afflicted man who composed Psalm 102 referred to his spiritual and physical distress[34] because *'ôyĕbî* (my enemies) taunted him, railed against him, and used his name as a curse (102:1 [MT 2], 8 [MT 9]). This social stress was exacerbated by his awareness that he had brought Yahweh *zā' ām* and *qesef* indignation and wrath) upon himself (102:10 [MT 11]).[35] There is no reference to or indication of what had aroused Yahweh's displeasure. The Psalmist was spiritually distressed because he had offended Yahweh. He was socially mocked and taunted when his enemies undoubtedly perceived his affliction.

The Psalmist did not lie down and give up. He called upon Yahweh God his Lord, who could relieve and deliver him from his spiritual and social distress. David had pled with Yahweh to turn to him and be gracious for he was lonely, afflicted and in anguish (25:16). So also the unknown Psalmist (102) called on Yahweh to hear his prayer (his lament). He knew Yahweh sat enthroned. He would arise and have compassion on Zion.[36] This assurance that Yahweh saves his people when afflicted was expressed by others also (18:15 [MT 16], 27 [MT 28]; 22:24 [MT 25]; 140:12 [MT 13]).

The Psalmists, referring to themselves and others as afflicted, also referred to themselves and others among Yahweh's people as the *ebyôn* (poor). The question again is: were they poor spiritually, socially, or culturally? In modern parlance the poor, as a rule, refer to those who have little in the way of money and possessions (i.e., culturally). A brief consideration of a number of references by the Psalmists to the poor follows.

David, when he reflected on his experience in the Philistine town and acted insane before Abimelech (Achish) (1 Sam. 21:10–15), wrote *zeh 'ānî* = this? (NIV poor [man] (Ps. 34:6).[37] Commentators prefer to translate *'ānî* as poor because of David's circumstances. He had no possessions; he sought refuge after "horrid experiences and adversities." He needed protection and deliverance in the social circumstances in which he lived.[38] In other circumstances David, calling on Yahweh, wrote he was poor and needy (70:5 [MT 6]; 86:1–7; 109:16, 22, 31) and in great need of deliverance. He was also concerned about his fellowmen whom he knew were oppressed, weak, and groaning in their need to be protected from lying and flattering neighbors (12:5 [MT 6]), and from robbers and other strong foes (35:10). Similar concerns were expressed (37:14); Asaph pled with Yahweh to rescue the weak and needy (poor, 82:4). An unknown Psalmist praises Yahweh God enthroned on high, for he stoops down to look on the heavens and earth and raises the poor from dust and the needy from the ash heap.

Included among the afflicted, poor and needy, were the widows and the fatherless (94:6). David asked that those who hated and attacked him be punished by having his wife become a widow and his children fatherless. David asked for the death of his enemy and that his family be cast into poverty and insecurity (109:9–12). This prayer was in keeping with the statement in the decalogue "unto the third and fourth generation" (Exod. 20:5). The references to the widows and fatherless are in the context of having compassion on them and asking for help for them (82:3). Yahweh was called upon to be the helper of them (10:14, 18; 68:5; 146:7).

Social Justice

For Israelites

The term social justice does not appear in the Psalms. The term *mispat* appears over twenty times. It is translated as just, when referring to the person who is just (37:28); the man whose tongue speaks what is just (37:30). Just is understood to refer to doing what Yahweh wills. The term *mišpāt* is often translated judgment, that is, a decision that accords with Yahweh's will and Law. The preferred translation, however, of *mispat* is justice. Its basic meaning is that what is done and said by a person who is right (righteous) with Yahweh God and performs according to his Law. Hence, it is written that Yahweh God loves justice (11:7; 33:5) and he secures justice for the poor (140:12). Yahweh's agent on earth, the king, has a scepter of justice (45:6). The scepter refers to a king's rod or staff that represents royal authority.

Psalm 72 has a royal context. Scholars have discussed how to classify this Psalm. Is it a prayer or is it a prophetic song concerning the messianic king?[39] The reigning king, as a type and forerunner of the messianic king, is to execute justice over his kingdom and its inhabitants. Houston has presented a schematic structure of this royal prophetic prophecy and prayer.

Just Rule 72:1–4
Long Rule 72:5
Fertility of the Land 72:6, 7
Universal Rule 72:8–11
Just Rulc 72:12–14
Universal Rule (Prayer for the king) 72:15
Fertility of the Land 72:16
Longevity (prayer) 72:1[40]
Call to Praise Yahweh 72:18, 19

The title of his essay Preferential Option for the Poor," emphasizes what he has shown to be the climactic statement, indicating specifically what characterizes the just reign of the typical messianic king. He has a preference for the afflicted, the needy, and the poor (*'ānî,* the *'ebyôn),* 72:12. The king will be well supplied to bestow care upon them because his fields are fertile (vv. 6, 7, 16), and distant kings bring tribute to him (vv. 10, 15). Thus qualified he will show pity (v. 13), save the poor and needy (vv. 12, 13), and rescue them from oppression, violence, and death (vv. 12–14).

The afflicted, the humble, the meek, and the poor are considered to be the special recipients of Yahweh God's covenantal love. This love is to be exercised by providing protection and the basic necessities for a God-honoring life within the kingdom. The king is to be the sovereign King's representative and agent. The people are to support the king in his ministry to the poor. Thus social justice will become and actually be a blessed reality.

For Foreigners

Social justice was a major benefit for the poor, humble, meek, afflicted, oppressed, the widow, and fatherless. This was Yahweh's demand. He commanded the king, the leaders, and the people of the Israelite/Judahite kingdoms to exercise and apply justice among the covenant people. They also were always to be alert to those who were aliens, foreigners, strangers, and sojourners. Moses had commanded that the *gēr* (alien) who wished to be with the Israelites and wished to celebrate the Passover (Num. 9:14), or present an offering or sacrifice (Num. 15:14) could do so. They would have to follow the rules and meet the requirements the Israelites did. The Psalmist led the covenant community to sing "*yĕhwâh sōmer 'et gōrîm*" (Yahweh keeps watch over the aliens) as he sustains the fatherless and widow (146:9). When Israel "were few" in Canaan, and had wandered from place to place, Yahweh God had not allowed anyone to oppress them. They were protected *gōrîm* (sojourners, 105:12). But the covenant people were led to pray for deliverance from the hands of their *nākĕû* (foreigners, aliens) whose mouths were full of lies and hands were full of deceit (144:11). The Psalmists indicated that Yahweh's covenant people had to be alert to foreign gods (44:20; 81:8, 9 [MT 9, 10]). Social justice, however, was for all people. It especially had to be carried out by the covenant people to their fellowmen and women and to those from outside who, as aliens and strangers, desired to join the covenant community in worship to Yahweh God.

Notes

1. See de Villiers who emphasized in his essay "Spirituality-Psalms" that spirituality comes to expression in all aspects of life. The complete bibliographical information of the abbreviated references in this chapter is listed in chap. 38, note 4.

2. A study of Basil De Pinto's article "Torah-Psalms" is recommended.

3. Gen. 1:1–9:29 records divine revelation that cannot be ignored in the study of the social mandate that the Psalms refer to so repeatedly.

4. See my discussion of the antithesis, its establishment, its extent, its nature, *FCTC*, 127–29; 450.

5. Commentators have struggled to translate this phrase. The Lexicon *BDB* translated both *mĕnât* and *hōleq* as portion. As commentators tried to interpret this phrase in the Hebrew text, some quoted others without presenting a clear interpretation. Cf. Van Gemeren, " Psalms" quoting P. Craigie, *Psalms 1–50*, 157, n. 5. Most commentators refer to passages that record either the dividing of land to tribes and to daily supplies for priests. B. Gemser, *De Psalmen*, 127, wrote that what God gives is expressed in a double metaphor referring to a host who according to Near Eastern custom selects the best and divides this among his guests. Dahood translated "you have portioned out . . . my cup of smooth wine and my cup." Dahood appealed to Ras Shamra sources, *Psalms I*, 89.

6. Cf. Alexander, *Psalms*, 67: "Jehovah (is) my allotted portion and my cup." Hirsch translated "The Lord is the portion of my inheritance," *Psalms 1*, 106.

7. Most translations and commentators translate *'ĕlōhîm* incorrectly. There is no contextual basis for the translation "heavenly beings or angels." Mankind was created in the image of God. Angels and seraphim were not. A human being is the highest of all beings. They are more like God himself than any other being in heaven or on earth.

8. It should be acknowledged that this Psalm reveals messianic motifs. Cf. *MROT*, 349–53.

9. Kidner, *Psalms I*, calls attention to Prov. 24:19, where the same admonition is recorded, 148, 49.

10. Monasteries became hiding places. Centuries later monks and nuns sought to separate themselves from social contacts in everyday environments. David did express a wish to fly away and be at rest in the desert (55:6–8 [MT 7–9]) but concluded that a call on God enthroned in heaven would sustain him as he cast all his cares upon his Lord (55:19 [MT 20], 22 [MT 23]).

11. Ridderbos, *Psalmen II* , wrote that Psalm 73 carries a lyrical and didactic character, 288, 289.

12. *Hālâh*, when in the piel stem is translated praise. Yahweh God is repeatedly praised. But one who praises himself or herself is boastful or arrogant.

13. A closely related term *gâ'wôn*, is translated excelling as well as pride.

14. David prayed the same prayer when Doeg, the Edomite, joined Saul in his pursuit of David (52:1–4).

15. There are more passages that could be considered that reveal how those who oppose Yahweh God and his people are considered. They have a flattering life and boastful tongues by which they seek to triumph (12:2, 3 [MT 3, 4]; 31:18[MT 19]). David knew that Yahweh provided for him even in the presence of his foes (23:5) and those that gloated over the saints' distress and exalted themselves would be put to shame (35:26).

16. The NIV according to *The* NIV *Complete Concordance*, ed. E.W. Goodrick and J. R. Kohlenberger III (Grand Rapids: Zondervan, 1981) does not have the word *heathen* as translation for *goim*. *The Englishmans Hebrew and Chaldee Concordance of the Old Testament*, 5th ed., translated *gōîm* as heathen 35 plus times and as nation(s) 20 times. In Pss. 9 and 106 nation and heathen appear as synonyms. In the study that follows, nation will be the main translation and where others have heathen it will be placed in parentheses.

17. Mowinkel made some references to the evil influences of foreign nations. *Psalms—Worship*, vol. 1, 201.

18. David referred to Ahithophel, a trusted friend and counselor who deserted and betrayed him (2 Sam. 16:15–17:14).

19. See Dahood, *Psalms I*, 236.

20. David Dickson reflected on how the Lord can be pleased to make "children sensible of their sins and of his terrible justice." *A Commentary on The Psalms* (London: Banner of Truth Trust, 1959), 210. Alexander wrote that suffering and distress was aggravated by the neglect of friends and the spite of wicked enemies, *Psalms*, 167.

21. See, e.g., Ridderbos, *Psalmen I*, 330–31.

22. In previous discussions, e.g., under the heading of the "Wicked Ones," (196–99) references were made to the responses of covenant people who had experience with them.

23. Mowinkel, who considered Ps. 27 to be a song of lamentation, stated that worshipers who sang this Psalm had the assurance of being heard, *Psalms-Worship I*, 234.

24. The Psalmist vowed to obey Yahweh and his Word repeatedly (119:8, 17, 34, 44, 56, 57, 60, 67, 88, 100, 101, 129, 134, 145, 158, 167, 168).

25. See my interpretation of Psalm 45 in *MROT,* 362–70.

26. Cassiodorus, *Explanation . . . Psalms,* understood this Psalm to speak of the spiritual marriage of Christ who was the anointed king and priest and his incarnation was proclaimed (438–52). Christoff Schroeder considered Psalm 45 to be a Love Song and interpreted it in the light of Near Eastern Marriage Texts. *Catholic Biblical Quarterly* 58 no.3 (July 1996): 412–32.

27. Helen Efthimiadis asked in her essay "Is There a Place for Women in the Theology of the Psalm?" Part I, *Old Testament Essays* 12 no.1 (1999): 33–66. She seems not to be content with passages such as Pss. 45, 127, 128.

28. It is difficult to accept what the editors of the *BDB* offered as the reading of Ps. 113:9. They wrote, "giving a dwelling to her that is barren of house" (445).

29. The metaphor employed for daughters were the specially prepared pillars that adorned the palace.

30. The king referred to in Psalm 21 is David and is seen as a type and forerunner of the royal Messiah. Cf. *MROT,* 349–53.

31. The Psalmist wrote *'innîtâ* (piel pf. of *'ānâh,* afflicted me intensely); NIV translator wrote overwhelmed me.

32. NIV translated the niphal form as suffered very much.

33. Commentators intimate that in the courts the offended poor, weak, needy, be vindicated and have justice administered. Dahood, *Psalms 51–100*, 268, 269; Delitzsch, *Psalms*, vol. 11, 402–3.

34. Kidner wrote that the Psalmist referred to fever, frailty, wasting, pain, sleeplessness, melancholy, rejection, and despair. *Psalms 73–150*, 360.

35. Anderson commented that the singer of this Psalm is fully aware that his misfortune is the result of a just divine punishment. *Psalms 75–150,* 707.

36. The Psalmist was assured that he would have the blessing of compassion as a member of Zion.

37. Dahood, *Psalms 1–50*, 204, translated poor. In Ps. 86:1 *'ebyon* is translated poor.

38. Van Gemeren, *Psalms*, 283.

39. Houston, "King's . . . Option," considered which was correct and after weighing the evidence concluded this Psalm needs to be understood both as a prayer for the reigning king and as a prophecy of a future king, 345.

40. Ibid.

42

The Covenant in the Psalms

The Cultural Mandate

I. Introductory Comments

II. The Psalmists Understanding of Creation

III. The Covenant Stipulations

IV. Knowledge Involved in the Cultural Mandate

42

The Covenant in the Psalms

The Cultural Mandate

Introductory Comments

The Cultural Context of the Other Two Mandates

Reference was made to the close correlation between the covenant mandates in a preceding chapter.[1] This factor comes to specific and clear expression and in an illustrative manner when the aspects of the cultural mandate in the Psalms are studied. It is vitally important that the reality of the cultural mandate, expressed in many ways, be considered. There are especially two reasons for this.

The Cultural Mandate Provides the Historical Perspective.

This reality must be emphasized. The Psalmists lived and wrote within the course of Israel's history. They were not isolated from their past. They gave concrete expressions to their heritage. They had roots. They had had personal experiences in times past. These had made a definite impression on them. They knew that they were not autonomous personalities. They had a covenant Lord who had revealed himself to their ancestors. Their God was leading and guiding them as he had their forebears.

The Cultural Mandate Provided the Daily Setting

This factor has become increasingly relevant to this author as he studied the Psalms. When the hymns and choruses that are so prevalent in contemporary worship are evaluated, it becomes obvious that many of these are lifted out of the course of human history and daily experiences.[2] Many sermons by evangelical ministers also reflect an attention to the spiritual needs; some focus on the social dimensions but very little on the cultural settings and influences. The cultural aspects and elements are regarded as secular in distinction from the spiritual desires, needs, and experiences.

The Psalmists, especially David, presented a wide variety of personal daily experiences. Their songs arose from a crucible of life's challenges, concerns, distresses, and pain. They also arose from a redeemed heart and an assured mind that their covenant Lord was personally present with them. And this assurance was fortified by their steadfast knowledge that their Lord was the sovereign Master over their lives and over all the aspects of their environment, whatever these may have been.

The Psalmists' Understanding of Creation

The cultural dimension with its many aspects did not arise spontaneously. The created cosmos had a sovereign Lord reigning over it after he had brought it into existence.

The Creator

Moses had recorded that Yahweh God, by fiat (command), had brought the entire cosmos into existence (Gen. 1:1). The Psalmist acknowledged this historic and cosmic truth when he called for all aspects of creation to praise Yahweh God, "for he commanded and they were created" (148:5). When Ethan sang that he would praise Yahweh for his *ḥesed* (great love, NIV) forever (89:1 [MT 2]) because he had *takun* (established) his faithfulness (98:2 [MT 3]) when he *yĕsidtem* (*yāsad,* founded) the *tēbēl* (the world) and all that is in them (89:11[MT 12]). Ethan continued his praise of Yahweh referring to the reality that *bĕrā' tem* (created) the boundaries (north and south) of the cosmos (89:12 [MT 13]). He also referred to Yahweh God having "created all men" (89:47 [MT 48]). David knew Yahweh God had created him (139:13). And the Psalmist reflected his knowledge of the Spirit's role in the creating activity (Gen. 1:2) when he sang "when you send your Spirit they (all aspects of the cosmic kingdom) were created" (104:30). The second person of the Trinity, (the Son, who is the Word, John 1:1), was also praised as an agent in the creating activity (33:6).

The truth has to be acknowledged, confessed, and proclaimed. When Israel sang the Psalms and when contemporary worshipers sing, they obediently worship the Creator who is the Triune God, Father, Son, and Spirit.[3]

The Cosmic Kingdom

The Psalmists sang of Yahweh God's *tēbēl* (world). He had created it, the world, with its totality of aspects (18:15 [MT 16], 89:11[MT 12]—note the phrase "the fullness thereof," 50:12). This *tēbēl* (world) is Yahweh God's kingdom. David sang of this cosmic kingdom of Yahweh. He was not merely referring to the kingdoms of Israel and Judah. David referred to all people Yahweh had made, calling them to tell the glory of his kingdom, the splendor of his kingdom which is an everlasting kingdom and endures through all generations (145:10–13).

Yahweh God reigns and will reign over all aspects of his kingdom (103:19). And this reign over the entire cosmos is a rule that is described as under Yahweh's (and the Messiah's) sceptre of justice (45:6).

Yahweh God's Providential Reign over All Creation

Justice has, is, and always will be a dominant factor characterizing Yahweh's reign over the cosmic kingdom and all that it includes. This just reign has been, is, and always will be providential. The sovereign King will uphold and cherish every aspect of his kingdom. Indeed, all the Psalmic references that will be reviewed are under his care and control.[4] A few examples should suffice in this context. Yahweh God makes grass grow for cattle and plants for man to cultivate so that food is available to them (104:14). Lions also seek for and receive food from God (104:21). The blessed truth is that sovereign reigning Yahweh God is good to all and has compassion on *all he has made*. God, being compassionate, certainly means that all he has made, not just people, are dear to his entire being. He loves and cares for everything. When troubles and difficulties arise, his tender concern and care is extended, to animals and plants as well as to people.

The Covenantal Stipulations

All the commandments have relevance to the cultural mandate. Because Yahweh God is Lord and keeper of all things he must be honored and praised. He must be recognized as the only God of creation; no part of his creation is to take his place or role. His name is to be the name above all and only his name is to be exalted (148:13) and worshiped. The commandments that specifically address social aspects of life, parentage, family, and protectors of human life have relevance also in obeying the cultural mandate. Commandments 8, 9, and 10 specifically speak to possessions, to speaking the truth at all times, especially in courts, and the attitude of the heart to material things, that is, all that is in the cosmic kingdom.

Commandment 8

The eighth commandment reads *lô' tignōb* (do not steal). The verb does not occur in the Psalms but the noun *gannab* (thief) is derived from it (50:18). The verb *gōyal* (to take away violently) occurs in 69:4 [MT 5]. In the broader scriptural context this term is translated rob, tear away, seize, and plunder. Objects referred to as taken away violently are flocks, women, children, wells of water, and houses. David, when calling out to Yahweh God to save him, cried out that he was worn out seeking help. He needed assistance; enemies, hating him, were seeking to destroy him. They were forcing him to restore what he had not stolen or taken violently from others (69:4 [MT 5]). David did not specify what he was accused of robbing violently from others.

Asaph gave some insight when he reminded the congregation that as they sang of Yahweh, *'el* (the Mighty One [NIV], *'ĕlōhîm* (the sovereign God), they should remember and worship him as such. Their God needed no sacrifices because bulls in stalls, goats in pens, cattle on hills, and animals in forests were his. If the covenant people brought the prescribed sacrifices and fulfilled their vows Yahweh, the all sufficient One, assured them that he would deliver them. Thus the worshipers *tĕkābbĕdēnî* (will glorify me). To the evildoers who refuse his instructions, violate the covenant, join the thieves and adulterers, Yahweh said he would rebuke them and accuse them openly (50:16–18, 21). He will tear them to pieces (50:22). The thief would go down with those guilty of other deeds of evil.

At the root of stealing, thievery is *qānâ'*. This verb appears only in the piel, hence it basically refers to an intense jealousy or envy. Asaph spoke for those who knew God was good but found themselves slipping and losing foothold. He knew that was his situation because he envied the prosperity of the arrogant wicked ones (73:3). These people were carefree as they increased their wealth (73:12). David knew that he should not fret or be envious of such people for they would pass away as grass and green plants (37:1, 2).

The eighth commandment draws attention to the cultural materials and aspects in the created world. But one can be guilty of violating this commandment by resenting the excellence and superiority of another. Saul was guilty of this because he recognized these virtues in David. He begrudged the basic advantages David had. Saul was envious.

David knew that Saul would take extreme measures, even kill, so that even by violent means he would possess the advantages, powers, and abilities David had been given by God. Saul would kill to take and have what God had given to David. Hence David prayed for deliverance and protection from a would be violent thief (cf. e.g., Psalms 56, 57).

Commandment 9

The ninth commandment is acknowledged by the Psalmist as speaking to personal relationships (e.g., with neighbors) and to judicial aspects in the public areas of life.

A personal note: when I was a ten-year-old child we were required, as part of our Bible class assignment, to memorize Silas J. Vail's rendition of Psalm 15. Words that now seventy years later still resound in my mind and heart are as follows:

Who, O Lord, with thee abiding,
In thy house shall be thy guest?

He that ever walks uprightly,
Does the right without a fear.

He that slanders not his brother
Does no evil to a friend,
To reproaches of another
He refuses to attend . . .

David, the author of Psalm 15, was a covenant man. He knew that if he was to be in a healthy and vibrant relationship with his Lord and his brothers and fellowmen, it was incumbent upon him to obey the ninth commandment.

Various Hebrew words have been translated as slander. To understand these terms certainly helps one to realize various aspects of slander. David vowed he would not have *rogal*[5] on his tongue. A commentator wrote that this verb "seems strictly to denote the act of busy, or officious tale bearing." Moses had written that the Israelites were not to go about spreading *rākîl* (slander) about someone among your people (Lev. 19:16). Another Hebrew term translated slander is *dabbat,* derived from the verb *dābab* (to move gently or to glide). The noun is understood to mean defamation or an evil report. David wrote that he heard the *dabbat* (slander) from many enemies and neighbors, causing terror. The slander spoken led to conspiracy against him and a plotting to take his life (Ps. 31:13 [MT 14]). David also used the denominative verb *yiśtĕnûnî* (to satanize me). The verb is derived from the noun *sātān* (adversary, esp. Satan). His enemies, who hated him when they knew and saw his good, sought to repay him with evil. David had confessed his iniquity and sin (38:18 [MT 19]), but his enemies continued to gloat over him. He did not in turn seek to slander them or hurl imprecations at them. He spoke to Yahweh, imploring his Lord not to forsake him but to make haste to help him (38:22, 23 [MT 23, 24]).[6]

David, however, did not hesitate to pray to Yahweh his Lord to destroy those who *lĕšorĕraî* (slander me, 54: 5 [MT 7]). The term *sorer* can be understood to mean slanderer, defamer, foe, enemy, and adversary (5:9 [MT 10], 27:11, 56:3, 59:11).[7] As a covenant man he had experienced pain and grief because of the violation of the ninth commandment in various ways.

It was not only David who sought to be obedient to the ninth commandment. Asaph referred to those who slandered their brothers, their mothers' sons (50:20). The composer of Psalm119 knew that the arrogant rulers and kings, when they sat together, *nidbārû* against him. The verb is the niphal of *dābar* (to speak). When it appears with *b* it is understood that men together spoke against one. The Psalmist wrote that though a group of royal and authoritative personnel talked[8] about and against him, he would continue to keep Yahweh's statutes, delight in them, and meditate on his decrees (119:21–24). Kidner wrote that Yahweh's testimonies (his counselors) gave the Psalmist stability when men plotted against him.

The Pslamists revealed that they were very aware of how the ninth commandment was ignored and disobeyed in the society in which they lived, worked, and worshiped. The arrogant despisers of Yahweh's will regarding how each person was to honor and uphold the good name of fellowmen was flagrantly violated. Since the despisers could not deny God's will, they attacked and sought to humiliate those who strove to be faithful to Yahweh's will. In spite of what the Psalmists experienced, the slander, reproach, ridicule, and opposition, they sought, with the help of Yahweh and his Word, to obey the command to speak and uphold the honor of their fellowmen.

The Psalmists were also aware of what Yahweh God's ninth commandment required in the legal or jurisprudential aspect of everyday life and affairs. They knew that they had to be fully aware of being judged. Their thoughts, words, and deeds were and would be weighed and evaluated in Yahweh God's tribunal (7:1–11). Yahweh would judge in righteousness and with justice (9:8; 50:6; 51:4; 75:2; 96:10, 13; 98:9, 110:6)

The tragic situation in the judicial arena was that rulers did not judge uprightly. They devised injustice in their hearts and carried out violence (58:1, 2 [MT 2, 3]) and David experienced that among his fellowmen there were also false accusations. When he tried to befriend troublemakers, he was accused without cause. They repaid him evil for good (109:3–5).

Commandment 10

The tenth commandment repeats *lô' taḥmōd* three times (Exod. 20:17). It is the qal imperfect of *ḥāmad* (to desire or take pleasure in). Whereas there can be a healthy desire, this commandment forbids an inordinate, ungoverned, or selfish desire.[10] The term *covet* expresses this type of desire. When Moses repeated the Ten Commandments before Israel crossed the Jordan river, he employed the verb *ḥāmad* when he referred to the neighbor's wife and when he concluded by saying "anything of your neighbors." But in regard to the neighbor's house, servants, or animals, he said *titĕ'awweh* (hith.of *'āwâh*, to desire), commentators have written that whereas the verb can mean to incline to, in the hithpael it refers to a longing for or a lusting after what is forbidden.

The verb *'āwâh* appears in the piel in Psalm 132:13, 14. Yahweh expressed a strong desire to have his chosen Zion as his house and the place for his throne. Likewise the king greatly desired the beauty of his bride (45:11 [MT 12]). But, the Psalmist also used the verb, in the hithpael, to describe Israel's craving for water and food when Yahweh God tested them in the desert (106:14). These Psalmic references demonstrate that it depends on what was strongly desired if this verb referred to sinful coveting. Things, situations, and hearts' longings determined if a strong desire was sinful or to be praised.

The verb *ḥāmad* does not appear often in the Psalms. It is used of God desiring (choosing, NIV) Mt. Zion rather than the majestic mountains of Bashan for his dwelling place (68:16 [MT 17]). It is used also (in the niphal) when the Psalmist expressed his keen delight in Yahweh's commandments, more so for them than for desired (precious, NIV) gold (19:10 [MT 11]). It is interesting to note that the verb *ḥāmad* (to covet) does not appear in the Psalms referring to men and women. The Psalmist did admit to being envious of those who had prosperity, that is, much wealth (73:3). There is no doubt that envy should be considered as a root of or motivation for evil desires/coveting.

David had wise counsel for those who did not possess material advantages and wealth. He sang "Better than the little the righteous have than the wealth of many wicked" (37:16). Wealth was not unknown among Yahweh God's covenant people. In fact, a Psalmist sang *hôn wāōšer* (wealth and riches) are in his house. This was sung of the faithful covenant man who found great delight in Yahweh's commandments and whose children were mighty, upright, and blessed (112:2, 3). And having this prosperity, the covenant man's righteousness endures forever (112:3). Abraham, Job, Solomon, and David had not coveted wealth. They received and had it because Yahweh God had bestowed it upon them. As rich and wealthy men they had been enabled to serve Yahweh God and his kingdom with efficiency and fruitful work. Wealth and riches were and can be wonderful assets for one in the kingdom of Yahweh God, ones fellowmen, and the cause of the kingdom. To be rich and wealthy was not a sin and to have become so was not necessarily because of greed, coveteousness, or violence.

The Psalmists reflected on various pitfalls as well as the blessings of prosperity. David referred to the callous, hard-hearted men who pursued him but who stored up wealth for their children. David also referred to men, who, in reality were mere phantoms who vainly heaped up wealth; they cannot retain their wealth because Yahweh consumed it like a moth in a flame (39:5, 11). The sons of Korah also expressed the vanity and foolishness men who boast of their great riches but leave their wealth to others. These rich boasters do not endure for like beasts they perish (49:6–12).

David gave wise counsel. It was better to be like a green olive tree flourishing in the house of God, trusting in Yahweh's unfailing love, than to be like those who did not make Yahweh God their stronghold. Those who instead trusted in their wealth, having gained it by destroying others, will be uprooted from the land (52:7, 8 [MT 9, 10]). Asaph agreed: to envy the rich, to covet their wealth gave no assurance for a happy life and future. He found the answers to life and its blessings in the house of Yahweh God (73:3–12; 17:23–28).

In summary, it must be stated clearly. Yahweh God blessed his people as a whole with many cultural advantages and blessings. In the midst of this blessed covenant life, sin could have and did have devastating effects. Sinners sought advantages by stealing, speaking untruths, and coveting for themselves what Yahweh God had bestowed on others. In this *Sitz im Leben* the Psalmists knew that the covenant people trusted in their Lord, received gifts graciously given, and praised Yahweh God for all the evidence of his goodness to them. Indeed, the Psalmists knew very well that they were not to seek after wealth and fame but live obediently according to the revealed will of their covenant Lord.

Knowledge Involved in the Cultural Mandate

The Psalmists revealed a very broad and comprehensive range of knowledge that was involved and integral in the cultural mandate. As discussed in the preceding they knew the mandate itself, creation, and the covenant stipulations that pertained specifically to the cultural mandate. In this section specific aspects of the cosmic kingdom will be studied.

Israel's Inheritance

The Hebrew term *nahălâh* translated as possession, property, or inheritance appears often in the Pentateuch, particularly in Numbers, Deuteronomy, and Joshua. likewise. In Jeremiah and Ezekiel, prophets during the exile, the term appears also. This noun and its derived verb, *nāḥal,* appear frequently also in the psalms. It has been pointed out that *nahălâh* has four distinct references: (1) the inheritance God gives the godly, (2) the social and legal regulations governing the land, (3) Yahweh's possession, that is, the earth, its inhabitants and especially Israel, and (4) God as the heritage of the godly.[11]

Israel as Yaweh's Inheritance

David eloquently expressed the reality of the covenant people being Yahweh's inheritance. He called on Yahweh God to save and to bless his people, his inheritance. He called on Yahweh to be their shepherd and to carry them forever. David's intimate knowledge of shepherding flocks that were the possession of his family enabled him to metaphorically sing of Yahweh caring for his own possession (28:9). The Psalmist knew that Israel was Yahweh's inheritance because he had chosen the nation, Israel (33:12; 106:5). And they had the assurance, that even when the arrogant and envious wicked ones sought to crush and oppress the covenant people, Yahweh would not forsake his inheritance (94:5, 14). Israel, as a covenant people, was blessed in a very specific way. They were chosen, graciously and effectually, to be Yahweh God's possession. It was not that Yahweh God had this possession handed down to him. He did not receive it as a right by means of primogeniture. Israel is to be construed as Yahweh's inheritance because this reality could not be undone. Normally an inheritance once possessed could and would not be taken away unless some condition to retain it was not met. Yahweh was and is faithful. By grace he elected Israel as an inheritance to be that forever (94:14). Israel had to fulfill the requirements of the covenant. They failed to do so.[12] As a nation with its own legal and social system it was disinherited. But, Israel as an ethnic entity continued to exist so that the promises made to Abraham and David could and would be fulfilled. Their seed, the messianic king, came to the world through them.[13]

The Land as Israel's Inheritance

The Psalmists reminded worshiping Israel that Yahweh God had promised Abraham and his seed that they, as obedient covenant people, would inherit the land of Canaan. Included in this inheritance were Yahweh's judgments (that were in all the earth), and his word that he had commanded for a thousand generations (105:6–11). To be emphasized (because many devotees of the modern Israeli state ignore the reality) is that the land, as inheritance, was given with its attendant legal, social, and spiritual requirements.[14]

It cannot, however, be ignored that Yahweh promised the "land of Canaan" as an inheritance to Abraham, Isaac, and their descendants (25:13; 69:36 [MT 37]);105:6, 9, 42. "The land" that was Israel's inheritance (47:4; 68:9, 10 [MT 10, 11]); 78:55, included Zion and the Temple (79:1). David knew what was required to inherit the land. Those who had their hope in Yahweh (37:4) and were meek (37:8) and righteous (37:29), would participate in the promised inheritance.

The Psalmists readily revealed that they were not only aware that "the land" was Yahweh's inheritance for them, they reveled in the blessings they received as inheritors. They demonstrated that particularly by their knowledge of inherent aspects of the land.

Of Nature

Yahweh God, the Creator of the cosmic kingdom, included various aspects that enriched the land. The covenant people lived in houses but they were surrounded by the living and natural world. And the Psalmists readily made references to this.

Plant Life

The Psalmists sang of trees, planted by stream of water, yielding fruit and having ever green leaves (1:3; 104:16). David compared himself to an olive tree flourishing in the house of God (52:8 [MT 10]). The composer of Psalm 92 was assured that the righteous would grow like a cedar tree and flourish like a palm tree. Those planted in the house of Yahweh would bear fruit in old age and stay fresh and green (v. 12–14 [MT 13–15]). The trees also praise Yahweh God (96:12; 148:9). Trees were seen as symbols of faithful, righteous, and prosperous people who worshiped and served Yahweh God as they were called to do. Trees were also referred to as metaphors of the wicked that could cause damage and pain (120:4).

Grass was also employed to refer to various aspects of life. Yahweh made grass to grow on hills (147:8) and for cattle to feed on (147:9). Man was likened to grass that grows (72:16; 90:5) but whose days are like grass that withers (102:4, 11 [MT 5, 12]).

Animal and Bird Life

Lions were heard to roar as they sought for their food from God (22:13 [MT 14]). But lions were considered dangerous and were to be feared. Wicked men who pursued fellowmen were often referred as lions (22:21 [MT 22]; 35:17; 57:4 [MT 5]). David pled with his Lord that he would tear out the fangs of the lions (his pursuers). He also called for these lions to melt away as slugs do under a hot sun (58:6, 8 [MT 7, 9]).

The deer, that Moses had ruled were clean and therefore could be eaten (Deut. 12:15, 22; 14:5), were not referred to as such in the Psalms. Rather deer were seen as having abilities that compared beautifully with what God's enabled people do—to be strong, stand in commanding position to observe (18:33 [MT 34]). The deer panting for water reminded the Psalmist of how he at strenuous times had deep strong longing to be in fellowship with his Lord (42:1 [MT 2]).

Sheep were well known animals in Israel. They added to the wealth of their owners (144:13). The habits of sheep were not unlike a wandering personal soul (119:176). Sheep, however, were considered to represent people, even of the covenant community. They needed guidance in the desert as sheep would (78:52). Covenant people needed knowledgeable, dependable, and caring leaders as sheep needed shepherds (78:70, 71; 79:13; 100:3). Yahweh's people were often in danger, as sheep would be because of wild animals (44:11, 22 [MT 12, 23]; 49:14 [MT 15]). Hence the Psalmist sang of Yahweh as his shepherd (23:1) and called on him, their shepherd, to hear them (80:1 [MT 2]). Yahweh demonstrated his loving care for his people, the sheep of his pasture, by giving them David as their king (78:9, 71).

Bulls and goats were prime animals for sacrifice according to Mosaic legislation. The Psalmists referred to bulls and goats as Yahweh God's possessions; yet they were prescribed as fit for sacrifice to Yahweh God. But Israel had to remember that Yahweh God did not prescribe them because he needed them. Yahweh said bulls in stalls, goats in pens,[15] and cattle on a thousand hills and every creature of the forest were his (50:8–11). Note that Asaph, the song writer and musician in the temple, was well aware of animal life. Animals were owned by God but placed under man's control for purposes of personal wealth and sacrificing. Note that oxen were well known to the Psalmists. Sirion, another name for Mt. Hermon, was seen as skipping like a wild ox or a calf freed from its stall.[16] Animals considered domesticated in contemporary life were not always so considered by the Psalmists. Wild donkeys were grouped with beasts of the field who drank from streams (104:11). Dogs were considered as lowly and bad creatures. David compared a ruthless evil band of men to snarling dogs (22:16, 20 [MT 17, 21]; 59:6, 14 [MT 7, 15]). Dogs sought their share of blood when Yahweh destroyed his enemies (68:23 [MT 24]). Jackals who had their haunts (44:19 [MT 20]) were like dogs that sought the carcasses of enemies for food (63:10 [MT 11]).

Horses were known for strength. Yahweh, the Psalmist sang, delights more in those that put their hope in his unfailing love than in strong horses (147:10, 11). Horses were often considered in a military context (76:6 [MT 7]). But Israel was reminded that they should place their trust in the name of Yahweh God and not in horses and chariots (20:7 [MT 8]). Horses, like mules, needed bridles to guide them since they lacked understanding (32:9) and were therefore a vain hope for deliverance (33:17).

The Psalmists also demonstrated a knowledge of birds. David objected to fleeing like a bird to the mountains for refuge. Yahweh God was his refuge (11:1). Asaph rejoiced to know that Yahweh God knew every bird (50:11). But that reality did not motivate David to take the wings of a dove and fly away; he knew Yahweh was his refuge (55:6 [MT 7]) and that therefore he could escape as a bird did from captivity by a fowler (124:7). Yes, Yahweh beautified the wings of the dove

(68:13 [MT 14]) and the dove therefore may have been used as a term of endearment for Israel (74:19). But the bird, sitting alone on a roof, also reminded an afflicted man how lonely he could be and was (102:7 [MT 8]).

Natural Phenomena

The Psalmists reveal an intimate knowledge of nature. They reflect Yahweh God's cultural mandate to subdue and rule over the earth. To do this effectively and efficiently they had to know about birds, fish, and living creatures.[17] As seen in the preceding study, they were well aware of various types of life and their general characteristics. These types of life lived in and off their environmental surroundings. And the Psalmists give ample proof that they understood the natural environment and aspects involved in it.

There are references to mountains and hills. Mt. Zion is particularly referred to, if only because of its spiritual and social relevance (48:2, 11 [MT 3, 12]). It was considered the place where Yahweh had dwelt (74:2) because he loved it (78:68 [MT 69]).[18]

The references to mountains in general are found in various Psalms. Yahweh God made them (30:7 65:6 [MT 7]). He can make them smoke (83:14 [MT 15]; 97:5; 104:32; 144:5). They provide habitat for birds (50:11). Mountains were seen as majestic (68:15 [MT 16]; 76:4 [MT 5]) but were symbolically heard to sing (46:3 [MT 4]; 98:8, 9; 114:4). The mountains brought prosperity (72:3) and water fell upon them and flowed to refresh the earth (104:13).

Hills were also spoken of at times as a synonym of Mt. Zion (2:6: 3:4; 15:1; 24:3). Hills were said to be clothed with gladness (65:12). Cattle grazed on them (50:10) because grass was made to grow on them (147:8). They were seen as a symbolic source of security (121:1) and of righteousness (72:3).

The Psalmist called great sea creatures and all ocean depths, lightning, hail, snow, clouds, winds, wild animals, cattle, small creatures, and flying birds to join the kings, princes, rulers, young people, and older ones to praise the name of Yahweh. His name is exalted and his splendor is above the earth and heavens (148:7–13). It was indeed a universal call; all of creation, animals, natural phenomena, and people everywhere were called to praise Yahweh God. He was their Creator and Sustainer who ruled and provided for all according to his will and wise counsel.

Attenton should be given to one more phenomenon that is referred to more than any other. The Psalmists, especially David, spoke of the *sûr* (the term appears in the Psalms twenty-six times). The synonym used nine times is *sela'*. Both mean rock, cliff, or cave. Yahweh is claimed to be a *sela'* (18:2 [MT 3]; 31:3 [MT 4]; 71:3; 92:15). He is referred to as a *sûr* more frequently (18:2 [MT 3], 31 [MT 32], 46 [MT 47]; 19:14 [MT 15]; 28:1; 31:2 [MT 3]; 62:2 [MT3], 7 [MT 8]; 73:26; 78:35; 89:26 [MT 27]; 92:15 [MT 16]; 94:22; 144:1).

Rocks and cliffs were well known in Canaan. Mountains and hills covered a large part of the country. Rocks were in the desert wilderness. Yahweh was said to split the rock in the wilderness (78:15, 20) so that water came out of it (106:41). Honey was found in the rock, a safe place for a beehive (81:16 [MT 17]). Conies had their homes in rocks (104:18) and rocky places and cliffs could become scenes of judgment and death (137:6; 141:6).

David, however, referred to the rock and cliff as a symbol of what Yahweh God was for him.[20] During his flights from Saul and during military campaigns, as well as being a shepherd, he had become very well acquainted with cliffs, caves, and rocks. He found shelter and security in them; they became a refuge for him. A rock, or cliff, became a place of strength and advantage. He expanded on how Yahweh was as a rock (19:1–3 [MT 2–4]). He referred to Yahweh God as *sel'i* (my rock, cliff) and *suri* (my rock, cliff). His use of both terms for rock may have a specific purpose. Dahood made a distinction. He translated *sel'î* as rock and *sûr* as mountain. The first reference was to fortress and the second to mountain.[21] It is true that David could have thought of Yahweh God as a rock. The stability and strength of a huge rock gave him security as a fortress did in a battle context. The rock/fortress was a place of deliverance from pursuit and capture. But David also thought of overhanging cliffs or caves in which he found refuge. The basic point is that rock, cliff, or cave were actual means of escape and security in David's life when threatened by Saul. But he made it very clear that his protective natural phenomena were means by which Yahweh God protected, delivered, and kept him safe. Thus David thought of actual rock, cliff, and cave as not only a means Yahweh God provided; they were symbols of Yahweh God's strength, stability, care, and protection.

Metaphors and Symbols[22]

The Psalmists certainly demonstrated their intimate knowledge of nature's plants, animals, and inanimate aspects. Even Asaph, the temple musician, revealed a wide-ranging awareness of and a good insight into the natural aspects of Yahweh God's cosmic kingdom. The Psalmists employed their poetic and musical talents, in obedience to the cultural mandate, to demonstrate their awareness of the close relationship that exists between the Creator and the creation. They knew that that what had been created did not become divine. The Psalmists were no animists. They did, however, see that the created plants, animals, and natural phenomena possess unique qualities that reflected the virtues and abilities of the Creator. They demonstrated this close relationship between the Creator and aspects of his creation. The Psalmists revealed an uncanny awareness of how to express this with metaphors, symbols, and analogies.[23]

Consider how Asaph employed the vine as a metaphor for Israel. The vine was brought out of Egypt, planted in cleared ground, and filled the land (80:8, 9 [MT 9, 10]).

The heavens declare the glory of God and thus reveal the majesty of God. The sun and other heavenly bodies were not considered divine, as, for example, Egyptian religionists did. Rather, they were created and placed to reveal some of Yahweh's glory and majesty. God, who is light, made the sun give light. The sun thus is a metaphor of God who gives light. The mighty waves and breakers that pound the shores of seas and oceans reveal the power of Yahweh God who is armed with incomparable might (93:1–4).

The thrones of human kings (122:5) were symbols of Yahweh God's eternal throne (45:6 [MT 7]). The sons of Korah echoed a meaningful analogy when they sang of their souls panting for the Lord as deer pant for streams of water (42:1 [MT 2]).

The chief author of the Belgic Confession, Guido de Bres, understood the relationship between the Creator and the universe. He wrote that the universe before our eyes is like a beautiful book in which all creatures, that are as letters, make us ponder the invisible things of his eternal power and divinity. God has given all creatures their being, form, and appearance and various functions for serving their Creator.[24] And, serving as they do, they demonstrate their inherent qualities that reflect divine qualities, characteristics, and virtues. The Psalmists demonstrated that the better they knew and understood all aspects of the created universe, the better they perceived Yahweh God's revelation of himself.

Environmental Care

The terms *environment/environmental* are often heard, or referred to, in contemporary society. They do not occur in the Psalms or in any other part of Scripture. The absence of these terms, however, should not lead to the conclusion that the Scriptures are silent on people's attitude toward and care for the natural aspects of the cosmic kingdom. They give various leads and indications of how all natural environmental aspects of the cosmic kingdom should be considered.

It should be noted that the Psalmists thought of Yahweh God's created world wholistically. When referring to God's created works and care for them, they may refer to them with general inclusive terms and at other times single out one or more aspects.

First to be noted is that the Psalmists proclaimed that every animal of the forest, the cattle on a thousand hills, every bird in the mountains, and all creatures of the field are claimed by Yahweh God as mine (50:11). To be clearly understood is that the environments referred to, namely, forests, hills, mountains, and fields, belong to Yahweh God also. So does the sea with ships and teeming creatures in it. These are all works of Yahweh God's hand. In wisdom he made them all. And he provides food and meets all needs with good things (104:24–28; 147:9).

Second, the Psalmists extolled Yahweh God for his works (deeds) in the cosmic kingdom. Asaph wrote he would meditate on them (77:12 [MT 13]) because they were performed on behalf of the covenant people. Another Psalmist wrote he would sing for joy at the works of God's hands (92:4). David called for praises to God for all his works everywhere in his kingdom (103:22). And another Psalmist called for angels, sun, moon, stars, sea creatures, mountains, trees, hail, and snow to praise Yahweh God.

Third, a review of how the Psalmists revealed that they understood that all aspects of the cosmic kingdom, the animate and inanimate ones, were created by

God, provided for by God, and being what they were, to praise God. Although the Psalmists do not refer directly to the command of God to humankind, to cultivate the cosmos, this blessed truth is the basis for what the Psalmists composed and sang. The culturally mandated image bearers of God were to be agents for and co-workers with Yahweh God, the covenant Lord. They were to join in its care and protection. They were to work with Yahweh God so that all plans, purposes, and possibilities would be actualized and carried out. Indeed it meant people had to care for, protect, and work for the development in Yahweh's created environment.

Fourth, there is a reference to the desolations Yahweh God has brought on the earth (46:8). He did these among hostile nations. This desolation was wrought for the well-being of Yahweh's covenant people. It should be noted, however, the people were not encouraged to join in causing desolations. In reality, the call is for wars to cease and battle equipment to be broken.

Of Domestic Aspects of Life

In the preceding chapter the social mandate was studied. In this section various aspects of domestic life that are quite closely related to social issues will be reviewed. Two domestic realities referred to in the Psalms were the daily needs and possessions.

Daily Needs

Three factors were referred to as inherent needs in daily life; home, food, and clothing.

Various terms were used to refer to the place where people lived. The Psalmists referred metaphorically to the sparrow's nest *(bayît)* (84:3 [MT 4]) and the stork's (*beytah*) as home (104:17). The barren woman becomes a fruitful mother and Yahweh settles her in her home. There she has security and peace. Asaph referred to nations destroying the covenant people's homes and lands, implying that homes were ruined and made uninhabitable (79:7). So, for the faithful and fruitful family, a home was their assurance of peace, security, and well-being.

The term *house*, the usual translation of *bēt*, appears when a man's family and progeny are the subject (45:10 [MT 11]). It also appears very often as a reference to the building prepared for Yahweh. David spoke of *bētî* (my house) when he stressed that in his house of habitation, in which his family would live, there would not be a place where deceit was practiced (101:7). He sought to walk in his house with a blameless heart (101:2). The term *bayet*, as it appears in Psalm 127:1 and Psalm 120:3 has, in a real sense, a double reference referring to the building (house) and to the family. Yahweh is said to be the sure and capable builder of the family that dwells in the house in which a fruitful wife lives.

The term *miškān* (dwelling) appears as a reference to Yahweh God's tabernacle and temple. *Hêkāl* is the preferred term to refer to Yahweh's house.[25] *Miškān* refers a few times to people's dwellings (49:11 [MT 12]; 78:28). The term *'ohel* is usually translated tabernacle when the reference is to Yahweh's dwelling. It is translated as tent when referring to human habitations (52:5 [MT 6]; 69:25 [MT 26]; 78:55; 84:10 [MT 11]; 91:10; 106:25).

This brief survey of the terms the Psalmists used indicates that they were well aware of the different types of habitations extant in their past and present. Yahweh God had dwelt in a tabernacle and then in a temple. People dwelt in tents (in the past) and were considered to be living in houses, also referred to as homes. These were cultural assets in which social and spiritual realities could be and were realized.

The Psalmists also included references to their cuisine. Yahweh brings in showers and supplies the earth with *māṭār* (water); thus vegetation grows (147:8). Yahweh thus supplied the food for people to eat in their land as he had supplied food in the wilderness, the bread from heaven (78:25 [MT 26]; 105:40). They knew about honey; it came from the comb (19:10 [MT 11]) and Yahweh could supply it from a rock (81:16 [MT 17]). They reveled in its sweetness (19:10 [MT 11]; 119:103). They referred to *se'er* (meat, flesh) that had rained upon them in the wilderness (78:20, 27) but make no reference to meat as part of their daily cuisine in Canaan. They knew of fish but did not refer to them as food. The Psalmists do refer to grain as abundant (4:7 [MT 8]; 65:13 [MT 14]; 78:24) and to bread as a necessary staple for children (37:25; 105:40). The three specific blessings that Yahweh God is praised for providing are bread that sustains the heart, wine that gladdens it, and oil that makes the face shine (104:15). Oil is not referred to as a food; it is for anointing (23:3; 133:2). Wine was known but was not referred to as food but as a providentially supplied drink.

Food was referred to metaphorically. Tears and ashes were food for the persecuted and mourners (42:4 [MT 4]; 102:9).

Various terms were used to refer to clothing. The term *beged* occurs in various Old Testament Scriptures and is translated as garment, covering, wrapping, clothing, raiment, and robe. *Beged* refers to garments or clothes that are taken from a victim and divided among persecutors (22:18 [MT 19]). These garments can become old (102:26 [MT 27]) but the king's garments smell of myrrh, aloes, and casia (45:8 [MT 9]).

A synonym of *beged* is *lĕbâš*. Ity also has been translated as vesture (22:18 [MT 19]; 102:26 [MT 27), and garment, made of sackcloth (69:11 [MT 12]; 35:13). It was also used to refer to the bride's clothes of wrought gold (45:13 [MT 14]). This term also appears as a metaphor; the Psalmist sang that at the time of the flood, then waters were as *lĕbôs* (a garment) around the earth (104:6).

Possessions

Wealth. It may seem inappropriate to include possessions under the heading of daily needs. Reference in this section specifically will be to wealth. The Psalmists were well aware as they considered the cultural mandate and aspects involved in it that in addition to land, houses, food, and clothing, people required means with which they could buy, sell, and bartar, in contemporary language, "do business." Wealth, in whatever amount, was therefore referred to as an integral aspect of covenant living.

The Psalmist sang that *hôn* and *'ošer* are in the house of the righteous; the children of the house are mighty, upright, and blessed (112:2, 3). The term *hon* is translated as wealthy or sufficiency;[26] *hôn* appears only two other times. The Psalmist who complained bitterly because of the woes that had befallen Israel said that Yahweh God had sold his people "for a pittance" (NIV 44:12 [MT 13]) or without getting money.[27] Yahweh God did not profit from the sale of his people into the hands of enemies. The author of Psalm 119:14 used the term *hôn* to refer to great riches. He wrote that he rejoiced in following Yahweh's statutes as one rejoiced in great riches. The passage certainly suggests that wealth or riches could be a source of well-being and joy.

The term *'ōšer*, derived from the verb *'āšor* (to be rich), appears only three times. Riches were considered to be a blessing for the righteous family (112:3). The Psalmist also considered riches to be a snare; to boast of them brought no peace to the wicked (49:6 [MT 7]). To exchange Yahweh for riches brought disaster upon the boaster of evil (52:1 [MT 3] who had become rich by destroying others (52:7 [MT 9]).

The term *ḥayil*, derived from *hûl* (to be firm and strong), also carries the idea of wealth as well as strength and army. It appears as a synonym of *'ōšer* (49:6 [MT 7]). Covenant people were urged not to put their hearts on riches even if they increased (62:10 [MT 11]). Increasing wealth can be a snare for the covenant man when he sees how carefree the wicked are as they increase in *ḥayil*.

Two terms that refer to wealth are *keseph* (silver) and *zēhāb* (gold). That these precious metals were available is demonstrated by the references to idols made of silver and gold (115:4; 135:15). The believing covenant person knew the value of gold, not necessarily because he had it but because he had Yahweh's word and commandments which he treasured more than gold (19:10 [MT 11]; 119:72, 127). God was, as a rule, associated with royalty (45:13 [MT 14]); but the Psalmist sang of all Israelites being given gold and silver by the Egyptians when the exodus took place.

As gold was known and not necessarily possessed by most covenant people, so was silver. It is often referred to in the same context that gold was. But non-royalty could possess *keseph* (also translated money) for they are warned not to speculate with it (15:5). It is quite obvious that the average covenant person knew how *keseph* (silver) was processed and purified by fire (12:6 [MT 7]; 66:10).

Land and Livestock. The Psalmists did not make references to individual ownership of pieces of land or farms. Land had been apportioned to families and that gave ownership of land to people (Josh. 13:8–21:43). The Psalmists readily sang of our land that will yield its harvest (85:12) or the land will yield its harvest (67:6). This land was happily referred to as an inheritance from Yahweh God (25:13; 37:11; 136:21).

Abraham and Job had been blessed with livestock (Gen. 13:2; Job 1:3). The Psalmists knew of livestock (78:48). Cattle were referred to (50:10; 104:14; 147:9). Cows and bulls were not referred to as individually owned although the Pentateuch referred to individuals owning them and offering them as sacrifices. The Psalmists referred to prescribed sacrifices but did not elaborate (66:15). Sheep were individually owned but these were referred to more as metaphors or symbols of people (44:11 [MT 12], 22 [MT 23], 49:14 [MT 15]; 74:1; 79:13).

One can summarize as follows: the Psalmists recognized that the culturally covenant people had been richly blessed. They inherited the promised land and families enjoyed the products of the land. They were able to bring the prescribed sacrifices. All their daily needs were supplied and they had the wherewithal to lend to and help the poor as they were commanded to do (68:5 [MT 6]; 82:2, 3; 107:41; 112:9: 113:7).

Idols. Possessions often gain and claim more attention and devotion than Yahweh God. Possessions thus become idols. The Psalmists had some poignant phrases to describe what translators referred to as idols or false god. The phrase in 31:6 [MT 7], "I hate those who cling to worthless idols," is an adversative parallel to "I trust in the Lord" (NIV). Yahweh was referred to as the complete opposite of *habele sawe'* (empty vapor or worthless breath). The phrase is translated "worthless idols"[28] in various commentaries. The main point to be observed is that for David idols were ephemeral and worthless. In another Psalm he wrote *wĕśāṭêy kazat* (those falling away to falsehood), i.e., to false gods (40:4 [MT 5]). Asaph supported the concept of how wealth or riches were ephemeral for the man who trusted in them (49:12). Wealth may be in terms of silver and gold and when these become the center of a person's longing and devotion, they become idols. Silver and gold can be formed into an image (78:58; 115:4 135:15) but they need not become idols. Whatever the case, worshipers are warned not to set their hearts on them. Riches, silver and gold, are not referred to as evil, nor is having them sinful (62:10 [MT 11]). The wicked can have wealth, riches, silver, and gold but these will not give them eternal life (37:16, 17; 73:3–12, 17). The righteous person's trust is in Yahweh God. To have wealth, silver, gold, or other riches can be a blessing enabling Yahweh's worshipers to serve in beneficent ways in the social and cultural spheres of daily life.

Broader Aspects

Government. Government is an aspect of Yahweh's reign over his entire cosmic kingdom.[29] In this section, the question to be answered is: did the Psalmists reflect their understanding of government in everyday life as they sought to give expression to kings' and rulers' responses to the cultural mandate particularly?[30]

To be emphasized is that the Psalmists extolled the reality of Yahweh God's kingship over everything. Human kings and rulers were all subject to him whether they knew and honored him or not (2:10, 11; 47:9 [MT 10]; 68:14 [MT 15]; 79:6; 102:22 [MT 23]; 105:14; 11 0:5; 135:11). The Psalmists knew that human kings and rulers were not autonomous. There were kings who sought to be totally independent, but the worshiping people of God were reminded that whatever they experienced at the hands of human kings, they had to find comfort and peace in the knowledge that they and all kings were under the sovereign reign of their covenant Lord.

The Psalmists led Yahweh's worshipers to pray, in song, for a long life for their king (David and successors). They were to call on Yahweh to appoint love and faithfulness for their human king's protection (61:7 [MT 8]). And the composers also drew attention to the human king's duty to honor Yahweh God, to bring gifts and render homage to him (68:29 [MT 30]; 72:8–11, 15).

In summary, it is correct to say that the Psalmists were very much aware of the lordship of their covenant God over all aspects of their lives. Human kings and national government were to represent the sovereign rule of Yahweh God. If they did not, ruin and disgrace would befall them (46:6). Blessings in everyday life and in specific situations would become reality for those who honored, obeyed, and prayed for their rulers/kings.

Warfare. The Psalmists knew that covenant people lived in a hostile world. The antithesis between Yahweh and Satan, between Yahweh's people and Satan's followers, was absolute.[31] Yahweh's cosmic kingdom is universal and is the context of all that transpires in time. Satan, the powerful antagonist of Yahweh, has sought to maintain his parasite kingdom. No peace ever was or will be established or come to any form of expression between Yahweh's kingdom and Satan's parasite efforts. The Psalmists expressed their awareness of this tragic reality. Satan had his agents and forces demonstrate their abilities and strategies and too often the covenant people were tragically affected by these. The Psalmists, however, led the worshipers of Yahweh in their awareness of the hostility and what their expected role was. While the warfare was at root and essentially a spiritual warfare, it was often executed in the social and cultural realms of covenant life. The reality is that this pervasive warfare was expressed in social terms and more often in cultural terms.

Social warfare was initiated by evil men. They opposed the covenant people. They sought to take advantage of, subdue, and overpower them. This sad reality will not be discussed under a separate heading but in the study that follows the spiritual and social aspects of the covenant people's struggles and wars will be unavoidably included.

First of all, the Psalmists' awareness of weapons and places of warfare should be noted. The weapons were considered deadly when Yahweh entered the fight (7:13). These weapons—sword, bow, and arrows—were used metaphorically to give a sense of reality to Yahweh's battle. In this context Yahweh provides a shield for his people when the wicked and evil men draw their swords (37:14). David prayed that Yahweh would rescue him by his divine sword (17:13). The term *sword* was used to refer to either victory (44:3) or defeat (63:10 [MT 11]; 78:62). Such was the case also when other weapons of war were referred to.

Terms that reflected places in the contexts of war were citadels, used metaphorically of the temple (48:3 [MT 4], 13 [MT 14]; 122:7). A synonym of citadel is fortress, which was often used to speak of the safety and security Yahweh provided for his covenant people (46:7 [MT 8], 11 [MT 12]; 48:3 [MT 4]). The Psalmists also sang of Yahweh God being their personal fortress and it is used as a synonym for rock (18:2; 31:2 [MT 3], 3 [MT 4]; 71:3).

If one is aware of what David experienced when Saul and his henchmen pursued and sought to kill him (1 Sam. 16:1—30: 31), one can understand why David as a Psalmist, used culturally oriented terms of warfare to express his spiritual, social, and especially cultural circumstances.

Notes

1. See chap. 40.

2. There are exceptions indeed. A classic example is the hymn "How Great Thou Art."

3. Cf. *FCTC,* chap. 12–14, in which the plurality of the Persons involved in creation is discussed.

4. In a following section, many of these aspects will be reviewed and some briefly considered.

5. The consonants *r g l* when pointed with *segoletes* refers to foot. The denominative verb, derived from this noun is translated "foot it" or "go about." Alexander, *Psalms*, 64.

6. See comments by Sabourin, *Psalms,* 238.

7. Dahood, *Psalms* 11, 25.

8. Commentators are not consistent in their translation of *nibār*. Van Gemeren follows the NIV translators, with "slander," *Psalms*, 741, Dahood wrote "gossip" *Psalms 101–150*, 176. Hirsch, wrote "talked against me," *Psalms 11*, 335. Allen wrote "plotted in session against me," *Psalms 101–150*, 127.

9. Kidner, *Psalms 73–150*, 422.

10. *BDB*, 326, col. 1.

11. See *Nahala* in *Theological Wordbook of the Old Testament*, ed. R. Laird Harris (Chicago: Moody Press, 1980), vol. 11, 569.

12. Israel, as a national entity, was disinherited. The Psalmist wrote that Yahweh was angry with his people; he abhorred his inheritance (106:40).

13. In addition to giving Christ, the promised messianic king through Israel as a people, the Scriptures and the church also came through them to the world. Hence the promises to the forefathers were fulfilled and the purposes Yahweh God had were met. Furthermore, people of Israeli descent today can continue to consider themselves as the Israel of God by being incorporated into the church (Gal. 6:16).

14. A contemporary example is a son of a wealthy man losing his inheritance because of failing to meet his ancestors', or even father's, condition/demands.

15. Note how the Psalmists were aware of how bulls and goats were kept—in stalls and pens. They knew the aspects of husbandry.

16. I, the author, grew up on a dairy farm. We all enjoyed watching calves leaping and running when they were released from their closely confined pen and led into open pasture.

17. Birds are, as a rule, not classified as animals. They are included here for convenience.

18. Cf. also 43:3; 68:16; 87:1 [MT 2]; 99:2, 9.

19. Overhanging cliffs in mountains often covered entrances to deep cavities in mountainsides.

20. Andersen, *Psalms 1–72*, denies David wrote this Psalm, 18, so the use of these terms, says Andersen, was not due to David's experiences. But Ridderbos reminds his readers that Psalm 18 is also recorded in 2 Samuel 22. David composed it in the latter days of his life. The terms he employed reveal what Yahweh God had meant to him and did for him, *Psalmen*, I, 144.

21. Dahood, *Psalms 1–50*, 101, 105. He commented that *sûrî* answered to Ugar, *gr,* (to the Ugaritic), mountain, one of Baal's appellatives. Here is an instance in which Dahood's knowledge of various Semitic languages leads him to posit a very dubious comment—not that he refers to mountain but to a Baal context.

22. A metaphor is the transferring to one word the sense of another or it can be considered a figure of speech in which one thing is likened to another. A symbol is understood to be a token, pledge, or sign by which one infers a thing; a symbol is something that stands for and represents another thing.

23. Cf. the study of these in chap. 39, 154–57, esp. 155–56.

24. The Belgic Confession, art. 2, 12. *Psalter Hymnal* (Grand Rapids: CRC Publications, 1987), 818, 827.

25. The Hebrew term *hăcāl*, appears thirteen times in the Psalms and is, as a rule, translated temple ten times and palace three times.

26. The noun *hun* is derived from the verb.

27. Ridderbos translated "you sold your people for no money," *Psalmen II*, 20.

28. Thus the NIV tranlsation, Delitzsch, *Psalms I*, translated vain idols, 380. Ridderbos translated *afgoden* (false god or idol). He, following an MT alternate, posited Yahweh as hating false gods. *Psalmen I*, 264.

29. See chap. 39.

30. Persons involved in government also had responsibilities in regard to the spiritual and social mandates.

31. See this author's study of the antithesis in *FCTC*, vol. 1, 127–31.

43

The Covenant in the Psalms

Additional Integral Covenantal Realities

I. Understanding the Broader Scope of the Covenant

II. Integral Covenantal Aspects

43

The Covenant in the Psalms

Additional Integral Covenantal Realities

Understanding the Broad Scope of the Covenant

The Psalmists' Indications

The covenant has been defined and discussed in previous chapters. The Psalmists gave much evidence that they knew Yahweh God, the Lord of the covenant. They revealed that they were aware of the various dominant aspects of the covenant as a bond of love and life between their covenant Lord (suzerain) and themselves as bonded people (vassals). As developed in preceding chapters they were fully aware of the covenantal mandates and the spheres of life they addressed.[1]

The Psalmists also revealed that they, under the Holy Spirit's guidance, understood and gave expression to various broader issues involved in the covenant. They knew the Lord, their role, the mandates, the privileges and requirements that were integral to covenant life and service. They also revealed that these realities involved more than formal aspects. They realized that the scope of covenant life was as broad and inclusive as kingdom life itself.

In this chapter a number of aspects of the broader scope of the covenant will be studied.

The Vital Necessity

Of primary importance was to know, love, and serve Yahweh God, their covenant Lord. To know the formal aspects was undeniably crucial. To live, however, in full awareness of the relevance and influential roles these formal integral realities had, was absolutely important and fundamental. To be covenantally alive demanded faith. Faith included knowledge, agreement, consent, and submission while seeking to be fully involved in the wider, fuller dimensions of the covenant. To be a faithful and alert covenantal person involved living and serving fully and wholeheartedly in the cosmic kingdom of the Lord.

Since many aspects of covenantal life that are revealed or reflected in what the Psalmists composed, only some important ones are selected for specific attention.[2]

Integral Covenantal Aspects

Relating to the Three Mandates

These integral aspects that are selected for study have deep and broad ramifications for covenantal life. They relate equally to the three mandates. That this is so indicates the close relationship that exists and functions between the mandates. To disobey, ignore, or abuse a facet in the area of one mandate has a negative impact on the others.

Promised Blessings

Yahweh God's blessing and promises of continual blessing are recorded throughout the Old Testament Scriptures. When Adam and Eve were created they were blessed (Gen. 1:28).[3] They received a benediction that expressed Yahweh God's good pleasure and his assurance that they were enabled to be what God intended them to be and to do Yahweh's will. The form of verb *wayĕbārek* (qal impf.) stresses continuity[4] not only for Adam and Eve but also for their offspring. This covenantal promise was not always realized because of the fall into sin. But as Yahweh upheld his creation covenant and established the redemptive restorative covenant, as an integral element of the creation covenant, his blessing continued for faithful obedient covenant servants. Yahweh blessed Noah and his sons (Gen. 9:1) and had blessed Abraham in every way (Gen. 24:1). Yahweh God remained faithful to his covenant; he continued to bless his people. The Psalmists knew this and they called for and claimed Yahweh God's blessing on themselves and Israel.

The verb *bārak* (bless) occurs twenty-five times in the Psalms. It is interesting to note that the subject of the verb is either Yahweh, or the Psalmists, or the saints. This surely indicates that there is more than one specific meaning of the term. Psalms that exhibit these differences will be considered. The noun *berakah* (blessing) derived from the verb appears nine times. The Hebrew term *'ašerê,* which appears over twenty-five times, is derived from the verb *'āšār* (to go on, go straight, advance); it appears in the plural construct form and is defined as blessedness or happiness. Translators have used both "bless" and "happy" as the translations of this Hebrew term.

The first word in the entire collection of the Psalms is *'ašerê*. One commentator preferred the translation "happy" or "the happiness of "because the separate term *bārak* exists for the translated term *blessed*.[5] Scholars agree that the term *'ašerê* should be considered as distinct from *bārak*. The former indicates that man has to do something, usually positive,[6] but also some negatives.

Consider Psalm 1. The covenant man faces two ways of life. One way leads to life, the other to death. The way of life is characterized by *not* walking in the ways of the wicked, nor standing with sinners, nor sitting with mockers. The wicked are like chaff that blows away. They, in life, are distinct from the righteous over whom Yahweh watches. The wicked perish. The righteous man has delight in the Torah of Yahweh and meditates on it. Thus he is like a tree planted by streams of water; he is fruitful and prospers. The man who walks in the way of the covenant advances; he goes forward. His life is enriched with divine protection. He is truly *'ašerê*—a happy man who has an ongoing life with Yahweh his Lord. Happy in this context is to be understood as more than a passing emotion. The biblically described happy man experiences delight, security, and well-being because he is in constant fellowship with his covenant Lord. He advances in the covenantally prescribed covenantal way of life.

What Psalm 1 reveals as the "happy" way of life is repeated, emphasized, and developed further in other Psalms. The happy man trusts, resting securely in Yahweh (34:8 [MT 9]; 40:4 [MT 5]; 84:12 [MT 13]). He knows he is a forgiven man; his sin does not separate him from his Lord (22:1 [MT 2]). This happy man finds his strength in Yahweh with whom he dwells (84:4, 5 [MT 5, 6]). He received discipline as he received instruction from the Torah (94:12; 119:2). He fears (reverences and worships) Yahweh (128:1, 2). What an individual person can experience, the covenant community as a whole, can also (89:15 [MT 16]).

The brief consideration of various Psalms' use of *'asere* supports what a scholar wrote.[7] To be a happy man calls for a positive way of life that is in accord with Yahweh's revealed covenant prescribed way of life. This man/community truly experiences happiness having Yahweh as his/their God (144:15) and whose help is in Yahweh, the God of Jacob (146:5).

The verb *bārak* (bless) occurs over fifty times in the Psalms in various verbal forms, qal participle, niphal past, piel infinitive and imperative, future, pual future. Yahweh God, the covenant Lord, is the subject in almost all of these instances. Repeatedly the covenant persons are the objects/recipients of Yahweh God's favor. He fulfills his promises to bless his people and their seed. But there are instances when the Psalmists wrote that they would bless the Lord.[8]

The author of Psalm 115 emphasized that Yahweh God is the source of blessings on the house of Israel, Aaron, and those, great and small, who fear him because he *zĕkārānû* (remembers us). This assurance was expressed in the context of nations asking where Israel's God was. Their gods of silver and gold, made by man's hands, were seen but were helpless. Yahweh God, however, was to be trusted because as a help and shield for his people he would bless them. In this context *bless* certainly refers to Yahweh God being present always, upholding his people, fulfilling their needs and demonstrating his grace and mercy to his covenant people.

The covenant people, as they marched to the house of Yahweh, sang of Yahweh's sure faithfulness to his people. They sang quoting their royal King that he would bless[9] them abundantly and this abundant blessing included bread for the poor, clothing for he priests, and songs of joy for the saints, (132:13–18). The author of this Psalm of ascent gave striking evidence that when Yahweh God blessed, he not only remembered every class of people but also the individuals in their specific roles (cf. also 72:17). Yahweh God's blessing to his people included his being a shield and strength for his people, a fortress of salvation, and being an ever caring shepherd (28:8, 9).

The noun *bĕrākâh*, derived from the verb *bārak,* appears a number of times. The source of blessing is none other than Yahweh God. The phrase *birĕkôt tôb* (blessings of good) has been translated as *rich* blessings (NIV 21:3 [MT 4]). These blessings of good for the king include victories, a crown of pure gold, and life everlasting. This passage, considered an implicit messianic Psalm, exhibits how all-inclusive Yahweh God's blessings are; they are for all his people (3:8 [MT 9]; 133:3). These blessings are not intended for or given to those who hate Zion and oppress Yahweh's worshipers (129:1–8).

It has been correctly stated that the Psalmists considered Yahweh God to be the source and dispenser of blessings. There are, however, various passages that almost seem to indicate that people are also dispensers of blessings. Consider such passages that have *bārak* in Hebrew but translate it as praise in the NIV (16: 7; 26:12; 64:4 [MT 5]; 66:8; 68:26 [MT 27]; 96:2; 100:4; 103:1, 2, 20–22; 104:1, 35; 145:1, 2, 10, 21). The subject in these instances is either *I*, my soul, the saints, or all flesh. The verb is often in the imperative. It is considered a duty to "bless" Yahweh God. How is the term *bārak* to be understood in these passages in which the call is to "bless" Yahweh God? The NIV translators, in almost all contexts have translated *'ăbārăkâh* as I will extol (34:1 [MT 2]) and as praise (66:8; 68:26; 96:2; 100:4; 103:1, 2, 22; 104:1, 35; 145:1).[10] In Psalm 145:1 *'ăbārăkâh* is a synonym of *'ărômimkā* (I will exalt). This parallelism provides an indication of what the Psalmists meant when they sang that they would bless Yahweh.

Commentators, however, are not all agreed that the translation "bless" should be replaced by "praise." One wrote "since God is the source of all that is good . . . "man can add nothing to the power and majesty of God. Yet man can bless God in the sense of acknowledging his blessings."[11]

One can conclude that when the Psalmists sang that they would bless Yahweh God and called on worshipers to bless, that they, as many indicated, acknowledged Yahweh God as the source and giver of a wide inclusive range of good. Yahweh God, their covenant Lord, provided them with the necessities for life and very much more. Their lives were enriched; they had assurance and joy acknowledging that their Lord upheld and carried out his promises to bless his people. And as they acknowledged Yahweh God as the source of promised blessings they praised, extolled, and exalted him.

Finally, note should be taken of the Psalmists' use of the qal possessive participial form of *bārak* (*bārâk*)[12] (18:46 [MT 47]; 28:6; 31:21 [MT 22]; 41:13 [MT 14]; 66:20; 68:19 [MT 20], 35 [MT 36]; 72:18, 19; 106:48 [MT 49]; 118; 26; 119:12; 124:6; 135:21; 144:1). In all but one instance (115:15), Yahweh God is the object. He is acknowledged as a rock and strength for his people; he hears their cries; he showed wonderful love to his besieged people; and he is the source of truth that is revealed in his Word. This passive form of the verb emphasizes that Yahweh's people acknowledge who Yahweh God is; he is the great beneficent One. He does as he does because of who he has revealed himself to be. This Yahweh God's covenant people joyfully acknowledge him with thanksgiving and praise.

In conclusion to this study of "bless," "blessings," one must marvel at the revelation of Yahweh God's faithfulness and grace. His sovereignty as the Lord of his covenant is demonstrated in every instance and the covenant people, the recipients of all of Yahweh God's beneficent gifts and deeds, respond in song, prayers, and worship to their blessed and blessing covenant keeping suzerein, their covenant Lord.

Acknowledgment of the Divine Curse

In a preceding chapter it was pointed out that the Psalmists should not be considered as the original revelatory agents for their covenant Lord. They were largely respondents to what Yahweh God had revealed in word and deed to preceding generations. As they responded they repeated, explained, developed, and applied revealed truth. And, in various ways they added to this revealed truth as inspired writers. As they reflected on their own situations and the relevance of Yahweh's past and present revelation, they exhibited that divine revelation was progressive.[13] The Psalmists' knowledge of and explication of covenantal promised blessings to their forebears was studied in the preceding subsection. These inspired writers acknowledged how Yahweh God's promised blessings continued to be revealed, unfolded, and applied to their specific life situations. The question should now be asked: did the Psalmists also refer to the covenant curses and their relevance for their people and their fellowmen? This will be researched in this subsection and the prayers and calls for the application of the curse will be considered in the following subsection.

The Anger and Wrath of God Recognized

Whoever decides to study the imprecatory prayers of the Psalmists cannot avoid the subject of Yahweh God's anger or wrath[14] against sin and his judgment on it. Many Old Testament passages can be cited that specifically record that Yahweh God's anger burned. It did against a remonstrating Moses (Exod. 4:14). A person seeking to invoke a promised blessing when he continued in sin would come under the burning anger of Yahweh God. Thus the curse that Yahweh God had warned about would be carried out (Deut. 29:20–28 [MT 19–27]). One cannot ignore that the Scriptures recorded thatYahweh God's anger and fierce wrath burned against those who were guilty of sin and evil.

Historical Evidences

The Psalmists did not hesitate to speak or even sing of the *'aph* of Yahweh God. Various passages refer to how Yahweh God was seen in expressing his anger. Moses had proclaimed that Yahweh God is a consuming fire (Deut. 4:24). David, when hunted and pursued by Saul, perceived that his Lord, by consuming fire could and did bring deliverance (18:8 [MT 9], 15 [MT16]). Asaph asked, when crying out to God for help, if Yahweh had forgotten his promised love and mercy and had withheld, or shut up, these because of his *aph* (anger) (7:7–9 [MT 8–10]). But the Psalmists also knew that in the past Yahweh God demonstrated his grace to his sinful people (Exod. 34:6) and was slow to anger (Ps. 103:8).

Yahweh God had also demonstrated his anger against those who refused to serve him and who opposed him and his people. David was assured Yahweh God would rise up in his *'aph* (anger) and swallow up, and with his fire consume the enemies of the king (21:9 [MT 10]). Asaph, when referring to God's anger and fire against Israel in the wilderness (78:21) for gluttonous behavior, recalled how Yahweh God had also wreaked his anger, wrath, indignation, and hostility against Egypt before Israel was let go (78:49).

As the Psalmists referred to the *'aph* Yahweh God had shown and visited upon people and the world so also they referred to his *ḥāron* (the burning anger or wrath).[15] Yahweh God, in wrath, could and did quench the wrath of enemies that was kindled against his people (124:3, 8). But his wrath was also against Israel when they defiled themselves and prostituted themselves to idols. Then they were cast off and exiled (106:40). The Psalmist also acknowledged that in the past Yahweh God forgave the iniquity of his people, and called on God to "set aside all your wrath and to turn from your fierce anger" (NIV 85:3 [MT 4]).

A stark reality that the Psalms present cannot be ignored. The Psalmists knew and did not hesitate to recognize that the world of their forefathers and their world was filled with enmity and violence.[16] In addition to the six Psalms that are categorized as imprecatory Psalms,[17] other Psalms have been listed as having an element of imprecatory expressions or they may be listed as "laments."[18] Any careful reader or student of the Psalms cannot avoid entering into the Psalmists' world of anger, enmity, violence, grief, pain, and cries for help and understanding.

Consider some of these.[19] David composed Psalm 5. He wrote that God did not take pleasure in evil, nor would he dwell with the wicked. God hates those who do wrong and abhors bloodthirsty and deceitful men. He will not have arrogant men stand in his presence; God destroys those who lie (5:4–6). David called all doers of evil to be away from him; he knew they would be ashamed, dismayed, and disgraced (6:8–10). His trust was in his righteous Judge who expressed his wrath every day, he is a shield to the upright in heart (7:10, 11). David also gloried in the reality that Yahweh God reigned and as a righteous Judge rebuked nations, destroyed the wicked, uprooted their cities, and brought endless ruin upon the wicked (9:5, 6, 17, 20). The Psalmist sang that Yahweh who is King for ever and ever (10:16) sees grief and trouble caused by arrogant wicked men who reviled Yahweh (10:2–13). The prayer arises "break the arm of the wicked and evil man" (10:15). These prayers or calls for Yahweh God to deal with the enemies of believers did not arise from angry, vengeful hearts; rather they lifted their souls to Yahweh and trusted in him (25:1–3).[20]

Basic Theological Considerations

The imprecatory Psalms were composed with an acknowledgment of Yahweh God's anger and wrath against sin, evil, wickedness, and those who were guilty and unrepentant of these. The Psalmists also gave ample evidence, as seen in the preceding, that they were fully aware of the historical contexts in which Yahweh God revealed his anger and wrath. Before a study is made of the imprecatory Psalms, two considerations should be discussed: first, the widely differing interpretations of these Psalms and second, the basic biblical presuppositions that control the proper understanding and interpretation of these.

Review of Interpretation

Reference has been made in the preceding to Erich Zenger's attempt to understand "the Psalms of Divine Wrath."[21] He commenced his study of imprecatory Psalms by stating that they presented a complex problem because they are unpleasant and repulsive and they speak of the "Constant Presence of Enemies."

Alex Luc has written his *Interpretation of the Curses in the Psalms.* He understands the imprecations (curses)[22] as the Psalmists' call or wish for divine punishments on the enemies. He reviewed three interpretations. First, the imprecations are only the Psalmists' own sentiments before God. Harsh statements were made that cannot be purified. These Psalms merely report that there were expressions of vindictiveness and hatred.[23] Luc realized that this view cannot be defended in view of the New Testament's reference to these as "God's Word."

The second interpretation Luc found unsatisfactory is that the covenant is the basis for Psalmic curses.[24] He readily agreed that there were some points to be made in favor of this approach but he considered the covenant concept to present only a general framework. Therefore, it does not provide a specific and particular explanation. The preferred interpretation according to Luc is to approach these imprecatory Psalms as prophetic predictions. They are, he states, divine pronouncements. He appealed to some references to these Psalms as prefiguring the life of Christ. He also considered the Psalmic imprecations as "Parallels to Prophetic Speeches."[25]

A consideration of what a sampling of commentators have written about the imprecatory Psalms does not provide much clarity as to how precisely to consider these. A. A. Anderson includes Psalms 35, 69, and 109 as laments by individuals and 83 and 137 as national.[26] J. Ridderbos considered these Psalms as more than laments. Commenting on Psalm 35, he wrote that the Psalmist with *felle* (grim or fierce) words expressed the wish that his enemies would be punished by a complete *Ondergang* (going down, i.e., perish).[27] Thus what the Psalmist uttered meant more than a lament or complaint. "They were cries for vengeance," so different from the humble devotion that characterizes many Psalms.[28] No, wrote another commentator, the Psalmists cried for help with "war words."[29]

We refer to one more commentator who, it would seem, wishes to be considered more evangelical than liberal in his approach to the imprecatory Psalms. In his classification he wrote that the "lament psalms" include the imprecatory prayer. He added that the expressions of hatred and "the desire for vindication" are not limited to the Psalms and went on to refer to prayers by Jeremiah and Nehemiah. He quoted W. Brueggemann, C. S. Lewis, and his bibliography includes quite a few critical authors. The conclusion to the appendix contains an exhortation to Christians to uproot selfish passions, judgmentalism, and personal vindictiveness. Unfortunately these imprecatory Psalms are not considered in the context of the theology of the Old Testament.[30]

An Old Testament scholar revealed a good understanding of the place and role of the "Imprecations of the Psalter." A subtitle is "The Covenant Context of the Imprecatory Psalms."[31] This reference introduces the consideration of the biblical theological realities that serve as a basis for understanding the place and role of the imprecatory Psalms in the Scriptures.

Basic Biblical Theological Realities

An introductory comment is in order. When one reads and studies the Psalms, he or she has the inspired, revealed Word of God. This revealed Word records, in various ways, the responses to this Word of God. We are not justified considering the entire Scriptures to be human testimony. And to consider the Psalms to be expressions of faith only is incorrect.[32]

The Antitheses. When Adam and Eve fell into sin, Yahweh God cursed Satan and declared that there would be enmity within humanity. The seed of the woman would experience extreme hostility from the seed (followers) of Satan (Gen. 3:15, 16). We have noted in the preceding that Zenger was correct to describe the world of the Psalmists as full of enmity and violence.[33] Yahweh God's covenant people were constantly reminded of this tragic reality. This was briefly referred to in a preceding paragraph.[34] It must be acknowledged that the antithesis came to glaring expression between Israel as Yahweh's covenant people and neighboring nations. Indeed, the scope of the antithesis was international. The Pentateuch recorded how Egypt demonstrated its antithetical attitude to the seed of Abraham. The Amalekites did so as Israel passed through the Sinai desert. The antithesis was clarified when Israel was exhorted to remove the Canaanite nations from the promised land. And they were strictly forbidden to intermingle with any remnants of these nations that remained in the land. These people, and the relative nations of Israel (Edom, Moab, and Ammon) expressed and demonstrated enmity against Israel and when possible committed violent acts against them.

The greater tragedy was the antithesis that came to expression within the community, the nation, the seed of Abraham. Consider the tragedy of Korah, Dathan, and Abiram in Moses' time (Num. 16:1–15). The antithesis became sharply defined between king Saul and anointed David. Consider also how it was expressed between father David and son Absalom (2 Sam. 15). The antithesis became a stark reality within the covenant nation when Jereboam rebelled and led nine tribes to form a separate nation (1 Kgs. 11:26–40).

The inspired revelation of Yahweh God recorded in the Scriptures presents a clear and definite historical context of Yahweh God's placing the antithesis within humanity and maintaining it throughout the history of the covenant people. The Psalmists demonstrated that they were very much aware of this reality and the influences of this theological reality. If one is to gain a truly biblical perspective and interpretation of, and application of the imprecatory calls, prayers, and psalms, the divinely implanted antithesis must be considered a basic and determinative theological presupposition.

The Covenant Curse

The second theological affirmation the inspired revelation, the Scriptures, records is that Yahweh God pronounced the covenant curse on all covenant breakers and opponents of Yahweh God's covenant people. A view of various commentators and theologians reveals that either they completely ignored or minimized the role of the covenant curse in the Psalmists' imprecatory prayers and/or calls. One must ask: is there really "continuity of the covenant curses in the Imprecations of the Psalter?"[35] To answer this question a brief summary of what preceded the Psalmists is necessary.

Yahweh God pronounced a curse on Satan in the garden of Eden and immediately followed that pronouncement with stating that enmity would be placed between the followers of Satan and the offspring of the woman. Hence, followers of Satan were under cursed leadership. The first murderer, Cain, was cursed (Gen. 4:11). Abraham was assured that whoever cursed him would be cursed by his covenant Lord (Gen. 12:3). This assurance was repeated to Jacob (Gen. 27:29). The episodes concerning Barak's intention to have Israel cursed make very clear that the covenant people who were delivered from Egypt were not cursed or to be cursed (Num. 22:6–24). In the interchange between Balak and Balaam, Balaam quoted Yahweh: "May those who curse you be cursed" (22:9). Moses made it clear to the Israelites that Yahweh God's curse would come upon those in the covenant community who violated the law of God (Deut. 27:15–29:19). Moses repeated this (Deut. 29:27). Joshua told the Gibeonites they were under a curse for their deception (Josh. 9:23). The Psalmist who composed Psalm 119 wrote, "Open my eyes that I may see wonderful things in your law. I am a stranger on earth; do not hide your commands from me. My soul is consumed with longing for your law at all times. You rebuke the arrogant who are *'ărûrîm* (cursed) and who stray from your commands" (119:18–21). The Psalmist knew the Torah. It called the covenant curse to be on the arrogant and straying ones.

This brief survey confirms what Harmon wrote. He pointed out that the concept of cursing was inherent in the Abrahamic covenant.[36] This covenantal cursing came to fuller expression in "the dual sanctions included in the covenant at Sinai." He also stressed that the concept of covenant cursing is embedded in the Decalogue and is clarified in the conclusion of the book of the covenant (Exod. 23:20–33). He correctly referred to the fullest expression of these when the covenant was renewed (Deut. 27–30). A convincing statement regarding the covenant as a basis and context for the imprecations is "The Psalter forms the songbook of a people bound in covenant to their God. " This relationship lies behind much of the language of the Psalms. The Psalmist, when he spoke the curses against his and God's enemies, was echoing "agreed conditions from the covenant term."[37] It would appear that those biblical students who do not refer to the covenant, or say that the covenant is not the basis of the covenant curses, or say that the covenant merely serves as a general framework for them, have not grasped the entire and inescapable role of the covenant in all of life within the cosmic kingdom.[38]

The Imprecatory Psalms

Various Psalms

It was pointed out in the preceding that the Psalmists were very aware of the enmity, hostility, and violence present in their contemporary situations. It should be stressed even more that the Psalmists were aware of and assured by the truth that their covenant Lord was King over the entire cosmic kingdom and that he also was the Judge of all men.

A brief consideration of various Psalms not included in the usual list of "imprecatory Psalms" but which include what can be considered an imprecatory prayer, follows.

David referred to the many foes that surrounded him. He called on Yahweh, his covenant Lord, to arise and deliver him (3:7 [MT 8]). He was assured that Yahweh was his shield and would bestow glory on him and lift his head (3:3 [MT 4]). So doing Yahweh was requested to strike the enemies and break their teeth (3:7 [MT 8]). David realized and believed that if Yahweh God, his King, was to deliver him, his enemies would have to be dealt with severely. David also called on his covenant Lord, addressing him as *malkî* (my King) *wê'lōhî* (and my God). He was assured that the wicked could not dwell with him because his God hated all who do wrong (5:2, 4, 5,[MT 3, 5, 6]). David therefore called on God as judge to declare his enemies guilty and to banish them (5:10 [MT 11]).[39] Take note also of how David called on his shield and righteous judge when he prayed that Yahweh would rise in anger against the rage of his enemies (7:6, 10, 11 [MT 7, 11, 12]).[40]

Asaph called on his covenant Lord by addressing him as *'ĕlôhîm* (79:1) and as Yahweh (79:5). In these Psalms, with imprecatory calls, the Psalmists do not request of Yahweh God, their covenant Lord, to be their agent in carrying out judgment and punishment upon enemies. They knew it was not their prerogative to punish and destroy their personal enemies. If, for example, David executed punishment as king for hating evil and attacking enemies, he did so as a covenant agent of his sovereign Lord and King.

Psalm 35

David is the author of this Psalm. He called on Yahweh his covenant Lord, the King, and addressed him as "warrior."[41] This was undoubtedly based on the first word of the Psalm, *rîbâh* (qal imp. of *rîb,* to strive, contend). Dahood was dramatic in his translation: "attack . . . who attack me."[42] Commentators are agreed that the term should not be taken literally.[43] David called on Yahweh God to defend him from enemies who attacked him. He had more than a law court in mind. He used battlefield terms such as *shield, spear,* and *javelin.* The historical context in which this Psalm was composed is believed to be during the time that Saul was pursuing him. Various commentators suggest that this Psalm should be understood in conjunction with the preceding Psalm, because of verbal affinities. It also reflects an anxious waiting for darkness to be dispelled.[44] If it is to be understood that Psalm 34 speaks of darkness being dispelled, then it ideally should be placed after Psalm 35.[45]

The structure of Psalm 35 should be carefully noted. Most commentators consider this Psalm to have three distinct parts. The following sketch may challenge that view.

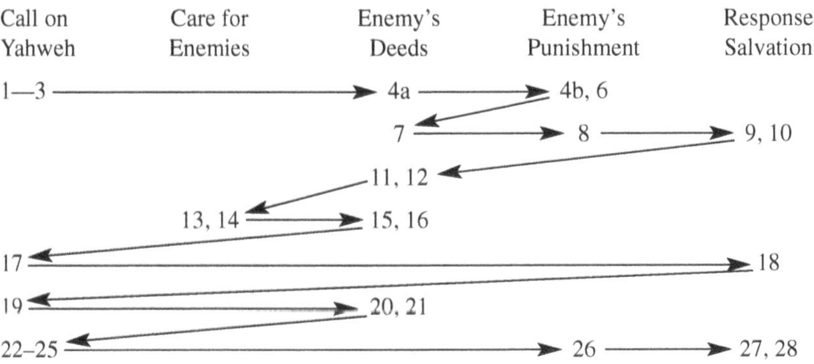

A close consideration of this sketch indicates that there are five emphases or parts in this Psalm. David called on Yahweh God, his covenant King and defender, four times. Between these calls he stressed that he was kind to his enemies. Five times he referred to what his enemies did to him. Three times he spoke of the punishment the enemies deserved and three times he expressed confidence in his God. He gave thanks, praised Yahweh, and called on his listeners and fellow singers to praise Yahweh all day for his righteousness.

There is evidence in this Psalm that David asked to have his enemies punished. He, however, never expressed the thought that he be permitted to wreak vengeance upon and perform violent acts against his enemies. Rather, he tried to care for them and show his concern for them. In his entire behavior, when he was pursued and persecuted, he trusted Yahweh God to demonstrate his righteous character and to execute just judgment upon those who in reality defied Yahweh God when they sought to destroy him.

This Psalm speaks clearly and strongly concerning the antithesis in life. The unbridgeable chasm between Satan and the Triune God is not mentioned per se. It is however, definitely present in the Psalmist's mind when he posits what enemies do and what Yahweh God is and can do. And because the Psalmist has a full awareness of Yahweh God's past revelations of himself as *King* and as a *covenant Lord,* he readily prays and calls on his Lord to keep his promised covenant love and security. He also prays that the covenant be revealed in the execution of the curse on willful disobedient covenant breakers.

Finally, the expressions of joy (vv. 9, 27a), adoration (v. 10), exaltation (v. 27b), and praise give this Psalm a tone of faith, trust, submission, and jubilation. In view of this inherent tone, this Psalm should not just be considered an imprecatory prayer and lament.

Psalm 58

David is recorded as the author of this Psalm. There is no reference in it to an historical context. Some commentators have suggested that this Psalm was written much later than in David's time. A main question concerning the judges who are referred to as corrupt is: were there such in David's time? Undoubtedly there were. Absalom certainly was an example of these.[46]

Psalm 58 is recognized as an expression of passion for justice.[47] It has also been characterized as a type of prophetic Psalm. The early church applied it to Jesus' trial before the Sanhedrin..

Commentators have not been in agreement in analyzing the structure of this psalm.[48]

A sketch of this Psalm can be helpful:

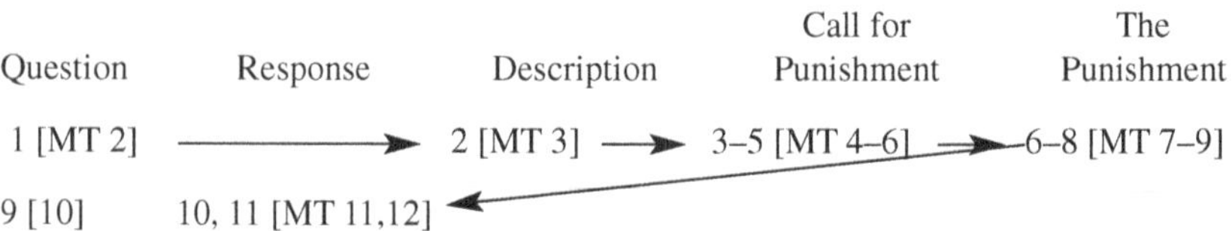

The conclusion of the Psalm extols righteousness. Righteous people are avenged and rewarded. God, the Judge of the earth, judges righteously. The antithesis between Yahweh God's royal righteousness and justice, and the unjust decisions by earthly judges[49] who from birth stray, is a stark reality. Wicked human judges devise injustice in their hearts and bring violence in the earth. They are covenant breakers. They condemn the righteous but a greater condemnation awaits them. The curse of the covenant will be executed fully upon them. They will receive in greater measure than they have given.

The righteous, the obedient and serving covenant people, are given reason to be glad and to be assured that they have victory. They will experience their triumphs when feet are bathed in the blood of the wicked. Readers and students have considered this phrase ghoulish and offensive. The phrase, however, is said to reflect the imagery of the literary conventions of the Ancient Near East.[50] Kidner's explanation may be helpful. "Not corrupt followers but victorious warriors on the battlefield walk in the blood of fallen enemies."[51] David was in reality a man of his times who knew the Scriptures and his sovereign covenant Lord. He was not ghoulish; he was rather a rejoicing servant who had to struggle against evil and violence. And his victory was real because his righteous covenant Lord carried out the curse of the covenant upon those who defied him. Years later Isaiah prophesied concerning this righteous Lord who would trample nations and with his own arm work salvation. To illustrate, Isaiah referred to a well-known activity by wine makers; when they trampled grapes their garments became stained. This portrayed Yahweh trampling victoriously over nations as their blood spattered his garments (Isa. 63:1–6). Commentators have reminded readers that the apostle John, the disciple of love, described heaven's victory over sinful earth by referring to the enemies of Yahweh God in the winepress of God's wrath from which much blood flowed (Rev. 14:17–20).

One misses the central thrust of the Psalm if one concentrates on how the results of righteous Yahweh's victory over defying violent enemies are described. The thrust of this Psalm is twofold: Yahweh God is victorious and his righteous people are glad and spontaneously say that there is a righteous God who judges the earth (58:10, 11, [MT 11, 12]).

Psalm 69

According to the heading, this Psalm was written by David. Liberally inclined commentators are hesitant to accept this. One wrote that this Psalm, a national lament, was composed in the exile.[52] Another wrote that the zeal for the house of God (v. 9 [10])[53] indicated that David, during a time of great trouble, is the author. Kidner's title for this Psalm is "Persecution." He noted that the Psalmist, king David, was in a "sea of trouble" and suffered the "sting of insult" and expressed "a zeal for justice."[54] Mowinkel commented that David was persecuted for his piety in the context of the struggle between two parties—the righteous and evildoers. He referred to the debate between those who consider the Psalm as personal or as national. That is, are the parties who are struggling the righteous persons and the evildoers? Or is the reference to the "Jewish community" and the Gentile nations?[55] The biblical evidence for the personal setting and reference is strong. The Psalmist confessed his folly; he knew his God knew it. He acknowledged Yahweh God to be the Lord of the universe, Lord of the covenant, and the divine warrior. To be considered also are the New Testament references to this Psalm.[56] These present a definite messianic interpretation of this Psalm; David was considered by inspired writers to be a type, a forerunner, of Jesus Christ in his suffering.

The structure of Psalm 69 has been considered from different perspectives. Is it unified or does it reflect two or more authors? Should parts of this Psalm be ascribed to Hezekiah or to a musician who prepared (edited) the Psalm for worship? Is the Psalm to be divided into lament and praise? Can a pattern be gathered from a sequence of headings?[57]

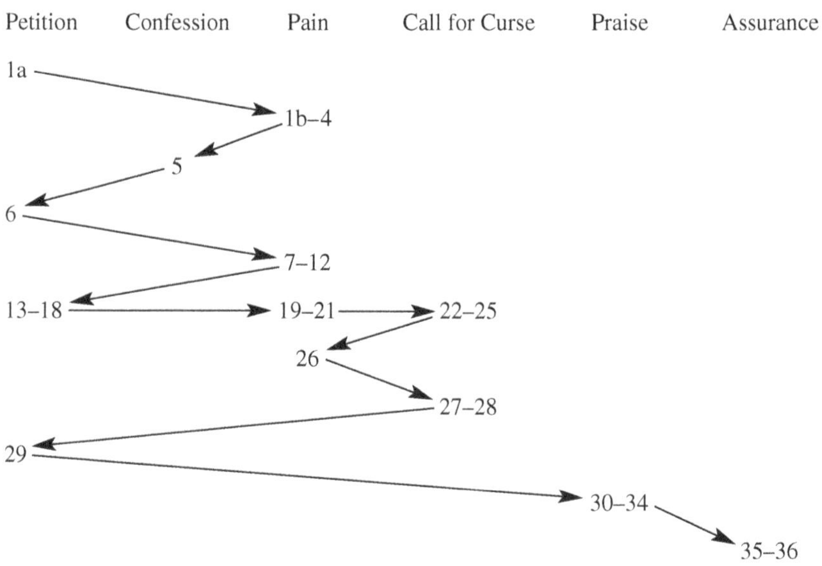

A survey of the sketch reveals how the Psalmist did not express a logical progression. He began with a petition to God, then reflected on his near hopeless situation because of severe circumstances that his enemies caused without reason. He confessed his folly and guilt. He referred to his pain in service to Yahweh God and among his brothers. He pled that Yahweh in his covenant favor, love, goodness, and mercy would rescue and redeem him from what enemies did to persecute and torture him. He then called on his Lord to execute the covenant curse on those who were so antithetical to him and his God. The curse applied on foes would bring salvation and protection for him. As a redeemed and protected person he, as a covenant man, would praise his Lord and all restored people would join him.

Theological affirmations recorded in this Psalm include the following.

Yahweh God, sovereign King and Lord, is indeed a divine warrior. He alone can and does bring redemption and salvation.

Yahweh God's covenant people are caught in the antithetical situation that exists. The foes of the earthly king are in absolute opposition to the Psalmist and his divine sovereign covenant Lord. The antithesis between the followers of Satan and the covenant seed is unbridgeable.

The sovereign ruler of the universe and keeper of his faithful servant will uphold his promises. He will execute his curse upon those who disobey and reject him. The Psalmist is assured he may call on his faithful covenant Lord to redeem and protect him by bringing the curse in many ways on his and his people's enemies.

Not to be overlooked is the reality that a petitioning and dependent servant of Yahweh praises, and calls all servants of Yahweh to join him in thanksgiving and praise.

This Psalm has been and is characterized as an "imprecatory Psalm." In reality, the emphasis is on the great redemption Yahweh God accomplishes for his people. This redemption will be fully revealed and given through him who was typified by David, namely, the Messiah, the Christ, the royal Son of God.

Psalm 83

Asaph, a worship leader in the temple, is the author of this Psalm. It has been suggested it was used in a service of intercession.[58] Those commentators who suggest a postexilic context for this Psalm,[59] ignore the superscription as well as historical factors such as the reference to the nations that surround Israel and the role of Assyria. Conservative scholars consider that the Chronicler presented a very likely setting, that of Jehoshaphat when he was confronted by some neighboring nations (2 Chron. 20). Kidner's comment calls for consideration. He wrote that this Psalm is concerned with more than a single threat or a "particular alliance," rather it deals with the perennial aggression of the world against God and his people.[60]

Commentators are quite agreed that Asaph had no doubt that Israel's enemies were Yahweh's enemies.[61] Thus Asaph did not pray just for the removal of his nation's enemies. He was concerned about the honor of his covenant Lord, Yahweh God who, as Lord of all nations, was hated by the whole world of humanity.[62]

A sketch can highlight Asaph's emphases. There is progression of thought and a final prayer.

Call on Yahweh	The enemies	Their destruction	Their salvation
v. 1	vv. 2–8	vv. 9—17	v. 18

Asaph clearly indicated to whom he should go when he considered the covenant people's plight. He called on *'ĕlōhîm* (God) (v. 1 [MT 2]), whose name is Yahweh (v.18a [MT 19]). He is the covenant Lord who also is *'elyôn* (Most High), the Lord over all the earth. Asaph knew his covenant Lord to be King over all nations, yes, over the whole cosmos.

Asaph knew that the antithesis between Yahweh God's people and the enemy nations was as a chasm, deep and wide, that was unbridgeable for humans. In their own strength they could not cross it. He knew that the covenant people in the world were not of the world and cohorts with Yahweh God's enemies.

Asaph knew how God's enemies, the nemesis of God's people, demonstrated their anger and violence. They formed alliances and cunningly conspired and plotted to destroy Israel as a nation.[63] The nations that historically and presently opposed the covenant people were listed. Some of them were relatives via Lot.

The means that were referred to, to destroy the enemies, were elements of nature. The wind that blew chaff and tumbleweeds away, fire that burned forests and mountain sides, and storms that terrified people were means literally and figuratively at Yahweh God's disposal to execute the curse of the covenant upon them. But Asaph did not pray for total destruction. In shame they could perish but there was always the possibility that as Yahweh dealt with the enemies, they would acknowledge Yahweh God as their exalted ruler.

Finally, commentators have observed that Asaph did not include an admission of guilt. He did not consider himself as speaking contrary to Yahweh's grace and mercy. He appealed to Yahweh God's power as well as to his saving grace that was available to all people in the world.

Psalm 109

This Psalm expresses a malediction, a curse, more strongly[64] than others heretofore considered. The language is fiery and ferocious. David, the author, expressed a sense of outrage that is measured by the deeds performed by the opponent.[65] While some commentators have suggested a postexilic date, Dahood was correct to posit an early preexilic date.[66] Delitzsch considered David to be the author but is uncertain about the specific historical date or situation. He asked, was David outraged because of Doeg or Cush?[67] These are possible, but not all of David's experiences are recorded. Hence, it is unlikely to refer to a precise person and his cohorts. Whatever the situation was, it must be emphasized that while David was fierce in expressing anger against whoever it was that persecuted him, he remained faithful to his covenant Lord whom he praised (vv. 1, 30, 31).

The thoughts or themes in this Psalm do not progress in a logical order. Commentators have attempted to exhibit an order by producing an expository structure in an acrostic formation.[68]

A sketch that highlights five elements and the order in which they were referred to, exhibits the various emotional issues that poured from his troubled heart and mind.

Comments

The Psalmist, David, knew, believed in, and trusted his covenant Lord. He expressed his assurance that Yahweh God heard his prayer. He knew Yahweh God was his defender (v. 31a) and Savior (v. 32b). He was assured that his sovereign Lord would know him as a man of prayer (v. 4b), would bless him (v. 28b), and his opponent(s) would be disgraced and put to shame.

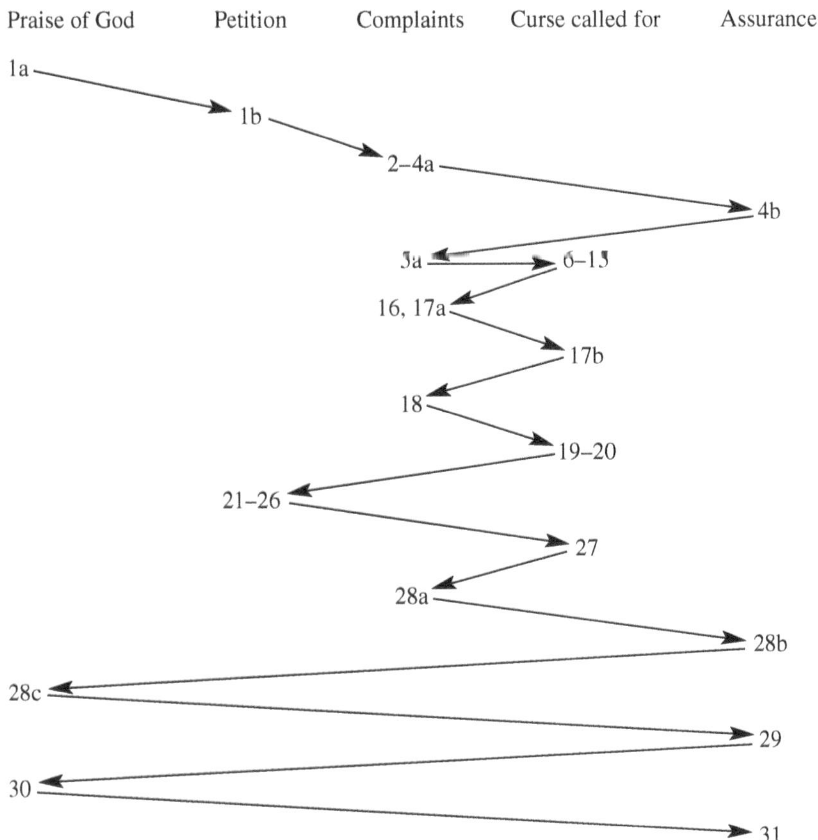

Commentators have correctly referred to what could be considered a problem. Was David referring to a corrupt judge[69] or to slanderers and various false accusers? The Psalm seems to intimate a court setting (vv. 6, 2, 29) but some other public setting is a possibility. A theological factor is definitely at the heart of the issue—the antithesis between truth and falsehood, between the righteous one (David) and his false accusers. At a deeper and more basic level, there is the antithesis between Satan, represented by false accusers of David, and David who was a representative, type, and forerunner of the Messiah.[70]

David's language has been considered sharp and harsh. Out of context, he has been considered brutish and mean-spirited when he called for the curse of the covenant to be carried out on the false accusers, and that (wives) become widows and his (their) children become orphans, beggars, and homeless. He went further, calling for the curse on parent(s) resulting in the demise of his/their offspring, (v. 13). They must not be shown kindness or pity (v. 12). Thus the iniquity of the father(s) and sins of the mother(s) should never be blotted out or forgotten. It should not be overlooked that, when considering what David prayed, Yahweh God had declared that punishment would be visited to the third and fourth generation of those who hate him (Exod. 20:5). David, thus, as a covenantal agent prayed and petitioned, and called for a curse in a definite covenantal context.

David demonstrated that he was aware of the full scope of the covenant. He prayed that spiritually his accuser(s) have their prayers condemned (v. 7); that socially their families, wives, and children share in the curse, and that culturally they be robbed, plundered, and shunned (vv. 9–12). This curse should come because his opponent(s) and accuser(s) loved to pronounce a curse on others; in reality cursing was ever present as were the garments and belts that were worn (vv. 17–19). This cursing life included rejecting kindness but hounding the poor, needy, and brokenhearted (v. 16). David thus called for the covenant curse to be brought upon those who sought to bring curses on others. Again, it should be strongly emphasized that David, a royal person, who had been anointed king, did not consider himself as the one to execute the curse. He called on Yahweh God, *covenant Lord* and *sovereign Ruler* over all, to keep his covenant. The promised blessings were expected and called for; the curse that Yahweh God had said would be executed on covenant breakers and rejected was likewise called for.

Finally, it must be emphasized that David himself was not a cursing man. And although he did not outrightly confess his sins, he confessed that he needed the love of Yahweh God to deliver him, a poor, needy, and wounded man (vv. 21, 26). Praying David, trusting in his sovereign covenant Lord, prepared to publicly praise and extol the righteous advocate who stands at the right hand of needy ones who are in dire need of salvation (vv. 30, 31).

Psalm 137

The author of Psalm 137 is unknown. He was undoubtedly aware of what was in the hearts and minds of the people with whom he lived.[71] There is uncertainty among scholars concerning the specific time and where the author lived when he composed this Psalm. Kidner commented that this Psalm does not need a title to announce the historical setting. It was the Babylonian exile. Most commentators, however, place the composer as a member of the small community that had returned but had not yet seen the city of Jerusalem and temple restored.[72]

Grosheide asked: why, once freedom had come for the exiles, did they sing this song? Did they want more than freedom? Could they not leave vengeance in the hands of their Lord? Grosheide wrote that these questions place one above what God would have readers and singers acknowledge. The question to be asked is: what is God saying to us? To ask this, one submits to the authority of God's word. And as one does that, he recalls what God had revealed before. Various prophets had spoken of the anger of Yahweh that was to be demonstrated to those who did evil to his people. The main point is: God maintained his covenant with his people and the composer asked for the fulfillment of all the covenant promises. Indeed,

God had begun to fulfill his promise but all his promised deeds had not yet been carried out.[73]

This Psalm has three distinct parts. And there is a very obvious progression in the emotional response to the events that the exilic community had experienced.

A consideration of what had been prophesied and what happened when the Babylonians captured Jerusalem is necessary. The historical context of what the Psalmist referred to helps us to understand this Psalm.

When Israel, under Moses, was being prepared to invade the promised land, the people were reminded that Yahweh God would destroy those who hated him. Yes, he would repay them (Deut. 7:10). Yahweh, through Moses, had assured Israel that it was God's prerogative to avenge and to repay those who sought to bring doom upon the covenant people (Deut. 32:35). Isaiah had also written that Yahweh God repaid sin, of covenant people as well as of all idolaters (Isa. 65:6). Jeremiah had been specific. He prophesied that Yahweh God would destroy defiant and rebellious Babylon (Jer. 51:56).

A quick review of what is recorded concerning Babylon's actions when it captured Jerusalem and destroyed the temple assists us in understanding what the Psalmist wrote. A lengthy siege of Jerusalem led to starvation of the inhabitants of Jerusalem (2 Kings. 25:3). The Chronicler wrote that the king of Babylon killed young men and spared neither young women nor old, aged men (2 Chron. 36:17). Jeremiah described what the people of Jerusalem experienced under the Babylonians: starvation, revelry of women, torture of princes, and slave labor exacted even of boys (Lam. 5:10–14). Isaiah prophesied that the men of Babylon would loot the homes of the people of Jerusalem; they would ravish the women and dash infants to pieces before the parents' eyes (Isa. 13:16). Hosea had prophesied that the children of Israel living in Samaria would have their children dashed to the ground by conquering armies (Hosea 10:14).[74]

A brief consideration of what the covenant people's prophets proclaimed and the historical events they experienced leads one to reflect on the following.

The punishment that was executed on the covenant people was under the hand of Yahweh God who in wrath brought enemies against his covenant-breaking people. Yahweh God had aroused enemies to attack Jerusalem and capture its inhabitants. The covenant people certainly were not innocent. The composer of Psalm 137 did not refer to evil his forebears had committed, much less confess their sin and admit their guilt. Isaiah had prophesied, however, that Yahweh God would have compassion on his people after they had suffered and would resettle them in their land (Isa. 14:1).[75]

The composer of Psalm 137 expressed a deep pathos as he reflected on what his people had experienced. He was aroused to pity, sympathy, compassion, and sorrow. He expressed this in a poignant manner while sitting on the banks of the rivers (streams, canals) lined with poplar trees; they wept. Their captors tormented them. They were asked by them to sing of Zion, their beloved city that had been destroyed (vv. 1–3). It was impossible to sing as they suffered deep humiliation and grief in the foreign country in which they existed. How could they sing when the city of their highest joy was in ruins? How could they sing when the city that represented Yahweh's reign over his people had been destroyed? They had seen the ruins. All the glorious representations of God's promises of grace, love, prosperity, and a definite future were gone.

The Psalmist, however, did lead the worshipers who sang this Psalm to remember what Yahweh God had given his people. They had a glorious heritage. Jerusalem was an earthly symbol of this. It represented the sure future Yahweh God had prepared for his people: an eternal inheritance in which the Lord himself was present. To sing of Jerusalem when in ruins was to sing of Yahweh God's unfaithfulness to his people and in regard to the glorious future he promised them.

If the grieving, humiliated covenant people were indeed to again have peace, prosperity, and an assured future from Yahweh God, the destroyers and annihilators would have to be removed. They would have to be punished as the covenant-breaking people had been. The Edomites, whose anger would never be abated, much less disappear, would have its heritage burned and consumed (Amos 1:11, 12; Obad. 7–10). Babylon would have its power broken and its city, the country and its people annihilated.

Thus, correctly understood, in the context of Old Testament revelation, the Psalmist did pray for restoration of covenant promises, life, and blessings. This restoration, however, called for Yahweh God's anger to be turned from his inheritance, the people and all they had received, and to be inflicted on the enemy of Yahweh and his people. This punishment could and should be as severe and awful as what the nations had brought on Israel.

The Psalmist's words, on their own, out of context, can be interpreted as hateful, vengeful, and unmerciful. In the biblical context, however, this Psalm calls for Yahweh God's righteousness and justice to be demonstrated. Thus Yahweh God's mercy and grace to his people could and would be revealed and be realized.

In conclusion to the discussion of the six psalms it is important to remember what a biblical scholar wrote. Imprecatory Psalms do not concentrate on imprecatory statements. This is not a chief element in them. Usually, a couple of verses in a Psalm are imprecatory. And these Psalms, often causing perplexity, are inspired by the Holy Spirit. God-fearing and truth-loving composers did not merely express personal vindictive attitudes and wishes. They impressed the heart of the covenant community who, faced with hatred and violence, looked to their covenant Lord for relief and deliverance. And not to be forgotten is the truth that behind the composers was One whom the New Testament informs us is the Christ.[76]

Notes

1. Cf. chap. 30, 384–86.

2. Cf. the outline on which blessings, curses, imprecatory prayer, education, worship, and duration are listed.

3. See discussion of this verb in *FCTC*, 57, 58

4. The consonants *b r k* with various consonants also appear as the name of a place in 2 Chron. 20:26, and as a name for various persons in Jer. 32:12 and Neh. 3:20; 11:5.

5. Kidner, *Psalms 1–72* , 47.

6. Hamilton, *Theological Wordbook of the Old Testament*, ed. R. Laird Harris (Chicago: Moody, 1980), 91.

7. Ibid.

8. These instances will be studied after passages that refer to Yahweh as the subject have been considered.

9. The form of the verb is piel infinitive.

10. As do Ridderbos, *Psalmen I*, 123, and Van Uchelen, *Psalmen II,* 99, who in their language wrote *prijzen* (praise).

11. Anderson, *Psalms 1–72*, 144, and Delitzsch, *Psalms,* I, 216, 227.

12. NIV translators were consistent; they translated *bārak* as the passive participle "praise be to," Dahood translated "praised be," *Psalms 1–50*, 171.

13. Cf. chap. 38, esp., 131–34.

14. The Hebrew term *aph* is translated anger, as a rule, but in various contexts it is translated wrath. Commentators have also translated it as ire, cf. Dahood, *Psalms 1–50*, 7; Anderson, *Psalms 1–72* acknowledges Dahood's translation but he prefers wrath, 67. The Hebrew term *ḥāron* derived from the verb *ḥārâh* to burn, to be kindled, is translated as wrath, or fierce wrath, or fierce anger, sore displeasure or wrathful anger.

15. To study the biblical concept of God's wrath is not a pleasing or welcome activity. This is especially true when Yahweh God's wrath is not considered in the context of covenant breaking. A case in point is Erich Zenger who entitled his book *A God of Vengeance?* and included the subtitle "Understanding the Psalms of Divine Wrath." The first part of his book covers the protests and rejections to these Psalms (1–23). The second part is devoted to "A Look at the Psalms Themselves." He set himself the task of seeking to derive "a series of observations regarding the profile, intention, and function of the violence-laden image of God that shapes these Psalms," 25. In the third part Zenger attempted to develop a hermeneutic of the Psalms of enmity and vengeance, 63–86. One hermeneutical problem he discussed is to consider the semantics of these Psalms. Semantics does not solve the problem of the "Unpleasant and Repulsive Psalms" but can liberate readers from some misunderstanding, 69.

16. Zenger's introductory comment is correct. The biblical Psalms confront us with a world full of enmity and violence. Ibid.

17. These are Psalms 35, 58, 69, 83, 109, 137 and will be discussed in a following section.

18. Cf. Van Gemeren who wrote that lament psalms (he listed 17) include *imprecatory* prayer. "Psalms," 830, 831.

19. In my reading of the Psalms in a devotional approach, over 60 Psalms, not including the "imprecatory Psalms," were noted to refer to the painful experiences of the Psalmists in their world.

20. Cf. also similar references and prayers in Psalms 11:8; 12:3 [MT 4]; 17:9–14; 21:8–12 [MT 9–13]; 26:4, 5; 28:35; 31:17 [MT 18]; 32:10; 36;1 [MT 2]; 37:1, 10, 13, 28, 38. Many more Psalms include references and prayers such as these.

21. Zenger, *Vengeance*, 1–13.

22. "Interpreting Curses," 395.

23. Luc quotes Craigie, 397.

24. Ibid., 399.

25. Ibid., 398.

26. *Psalms* (1–72), 38, 39. Anderson preferred to quote Mowinkel and Gunkel as reliable sources.

27. *De Psalmen*, 298. Grosheide, *De Psalmen,* referred to the imprecatory Psalms as *vloekpsalmen* (curse Psalms), 100.

28. Kidner, *Psalms 1–72,* 25.

29. N. A. Van Uchelen, *Psalmen I* (Nykerk: Callenbach, 1991), 233, 234.

30. Van Gemeren, "Psalms," 830–32.

31. Harmon, "Continuity of the Covenant Curses." Harmon has also indicated his interest in the Psalms and their role in the Scriptures in an essay "Aspects of Paul's Use of the Psalms," *Westminster Journal*, 32, Nov. 1969; 1–22.

32. As set forth by Ringgren's book, *The Faith.* His references to the Psalms characterized as imprecatory will be noted in the following.

33. Cf. note 16.

34. Cf. 242–43.

35. Cf. note 31.

36. Harmon "Continuity . . ." 68.

37. Ibid. 69, 70.

38. Cf. Luc's discussion concerning his problem with the covenant as a basis for the curse. He does agree that the covenant idea provides an important biblical basis. "Interpreting . . . ." 399. Luc's preference is to consider the imprecatory Psalms as prophetic statements. This reveals a lack of a full comprehension of the difference between direct prophecies and analogies.

39. Cf. Harmon, "Continuity . . . Covenant," 66, who emphasized that David used God's covenant name as done in all "imprecatory Psalms."

40. Cf. also other Davidic Psalms (28, 31, 37, 40, 54, 57, 63, 139), that record that he called on God not on Yahweh.

41. The phrase "divine warrior" appears in Stek's note on Psalm 35, NIV *Study Bible.*

42. Dahood, *Psalms 1–50*, 210.

43. Dahood wrote "the martial language is purely figurative." Ibid. Delitzsch wrote that "the psalmist begins in a martial and anthropomorphical style," *Psalms I,* 412. Kidner stressed that the use of the verb *rîb* should be understood in a legal sense as if the scene is in a low court, *Psalms 1–72*, 142.

44. Kidner, *Psalms 1–72,* 142. Delitzsch, *Psalms I*, 416.

45. Psalms are not always placed in an historical order. E.g., what is recorded in Ps. 51 preceded Ps. 32, but Ps. 32 is logically followed by Ps. 33.

46. See comments on context by Ridderbos, *Psalmen II*, 125.

47. Kidner, *Psalms 1–72,* 207.

48. Kidner, ibid. saw 4 parts; the challenge, vv. 1, 2 [MT 2, 3]; the charge, vv. 3–5 [MT 4–6]; the curse, vv. 6–9 [MT 7–10]; the purge, vv. 10, 11[11, 12]). Van Gemeren, "Psalms," produced an acrostic.

A. Concern for Justice (1, 2, [MT 2, 3])

B. The Lies of the Wicked (3–5, [MT 4–6]).

C. Prayer for Justice (6–8, [MT 7–9]).

C. Expectation of Justice (9, [MT 10]).

B. The Joy of the Righteous 10, [MT 11]).

A. Affirmation of Justice 11, [MT 12]).

49. The Hebrew term *'ēlem*, v. 1 [MT 2]), is translated god. The verb is plural, hence the translation "gods." Judges were given authority to speak God's will as revealed in the Law. They were placed to represent God the righteous and just Judge of the earth and all people. Delitzsch suggests that "gods" as such be understood to refer to men who are superhumanly proud and assumptive in their bearing. *Psalms II*, 130.

50. Psalm 68:23 [MT 24], has a similar statement. God will crush the heads of his enemies.

51. Kidner, *Psalms 1–72,* 210.

52. Dahood, *Psalms 51–100*, 156. He also wrote concerning the northwest Semitic influence he saw in the Psalm. Reference to captive people and the rebuilding of cities of Judah (vv. 33 [MT 34], 35, [MT 36]) have been considered evidences of an exilic setting.

53. Ridderbos, *De Psalmen II*, admitted that there is some evidence for an exilic setting, but concluded that he accepted the title, ascribing the Psalm to David the king, 205–6. Delitzsch did not hesitate to ascribe the Psalm to David, written when persecuted by Saul, *Psalms II*, 275.

54. Kidner, *Psalms 1–72*, 245–46.

55. Mowinkel, *Psalms,* I, 207.

56. Van Gemeren, "Psalms," 456.

57. Kidner, *Psalms 1–72,* 245–49, suggested a sequence of headings: Seed of Trouble, vv. 1–5; Sting of Insult, vv. 6–12; The Cry, vv. 13–18; The Cup, vv. 19, 20; The Curse, vv. 22–28; Praise from the Heart, vv. 29–33; and Praise from the Host, vv. 34–36. These headings indicate a progression that the Psalmist revealed from petition to pain, to prayer, to praise.

58. Anderson, *Psalms 73–150*, 595.

59. Cf., e.g., Leslie, *The Psalms*, 227.

60. Kidner, *Psalms 73–150*, 300. See also Grosheide, *De Psalmen II*, 30.

61. Anderson, *Psalms 73 –150*, 596.

62. Grosheide, *De Psalmen II*, 30.

63. Psalm 2 emphasized this antithesis also.

64. Delitzsch, *Psalms III,* 176, justified the extreme language.

65. Kidner, *Psalms 73–150*, 27.

66. Dahood, *Psalms 101– 150*, 99. Why Dahood considers the opponent to the Psalmist to be a venal judge is not clear.

67. Delitzsch, *Psalms III*, 176.

68. Van Gemeren, "Psalms," 689.

69. Dahood, *Psalms 101–150*, 93, referred to a venal judge who would not hear the complaints of the aggrieved but threw him out and listened to the perjurers.

70. Some writers have considered David, who was attacked, accused, and cursed, to be prophetic of his descendant, the Messiah. Luc "Interpreting Curses," 398, 400ff. Cf. Delitzsch also, *Psalms III*, 177.

71. Kidner, *Psalms 73–150*, 459.

72. Cf. Van Gemeren "Psalms," 826. He suggested this Psalm was composed during the time after the first group returned and before the rebuilding of the temple. He quoted A. A. Anderson, who classified this as a "Communal Lament" by the returned exiles, *Psalms 73–150*, 897. Mowinckel referred to Psalm 137 as a congregational song in which singers identified with a "former time of enslavement," *Psalms II*, 130. Delitzsch, referring to the past tense of the verbs, wrote that the Psalm was not composed during the time of the exile

but later in memory of the exile, *Psalms III*, 332. It is interesting to note that neither Leslie, *The Psalms*, nor Ringgren *Faith . . . Psalmists,* discuss or even refer to Psalm 137.

73. Grosheide, *Psalmen II*, 164, 165.

74. Kidner referred to a series of historical and prophetic passages. *Psalms 73–150*, 140.

75. Other prophets had prophesied likewise, e.g., Jer. 32, 33.

76. Wilson, *Happily Dashing*, 57–59.

44

The Covenant in the Psalms

Covenantal Education

I. Pentateuch Prescriptions Regarding Covenantal Education

II. The Psalmists' Desires

III. Content and Means

IV. Wisdom

44

The Covenant in the Psalms

Covenantal Education

The Old Testament is a covenantal book. The covenant Yahweh God established with Noah, Abraham, and Israel as a nation whom Moses served as the primary agent is a major integrating theme. This covenant between Yahweh God and the people had ramifications for personal, familial, and national life. Individuals were inextricably involved; families were at the heart of it and the entire nation of Israel was included.[1] Education, that is, teaching, training, and discipline—were and are major elements for an understanding of the covenant and its continuity from generation to generation.[2]

Pentateuchal Prescriptions Regarding Covenantal Education[3]

Genesis 18:16–18

The context of this passage included the account of Yahweh God confirming his covenant with Abraham and his seed (Gen. 17:1–27). This account was followed by referring to three visitors, one who was the preincarnate Lord, who came to Abraham to inform him his son Isaac was to be born within a year (18:10). The visitors also informed Abraham that Sodom and Gomorrah, the dwelling place of nephew Lot, was to be destroyed. The preincarnate Lord, however, assured Abraham that he (and his seed) would become a great and powerful nation. All nations would be blessed through him. He was elected to serve in that role. Added to this statement was a directive, which if carried out, would surely result in the continuity of the covenant and the blessedness derived through it for his seed and all nations.

This directive included two specific and meaningful terms, *yĕda'tîw* (I have known him). In translations of this verb, the term *chosen* is preferred. But the term *yādâ* (to know) refers to a close, intimate, personal relationship. Abraham was Yahweh God's intimate companion and agent. Abraham was chosen for that relationship. The Lord proceeded to instruct Abraham concerning his prerogative and responsibility as the Lord's covenant agent (*yĕṣawweh* [piel. Impf. of *ṣāwâh*, to lay a charge upon or give a charge], often translated "command") Abraham's covenantal duty pertained to *banayw* (his children), *w'et bêt* (and his household), extended family, all his children, and those over whom he had authoirty, and their descendants.

The charge included very important aspects. The descendants were to keep the way of the Lord. they were to know about the covenant, its involvements and demands. They had to be informed by word, deed, and example regarding the right and just relationship and duties they as succeeding covenant people had received and were to uphold. And if they followed this, Yahweh God would carry out his promises into the future for generations to come. Thus, for the continuity of Yahweh God's gracious covenant with Abraham and his progeny, education that included the imparting of knowledge, training, and discipline was imperative. Education is a covenantal privilege and duty.

Deuteronomy 6:1–12

The historical context that this passage reveals must be clearly understood. The covenant people had marched to and captured the territory east of the river Jordan (Deut. 1:1–4:10). Before proceeding to the west side of the Jordan, Moses *be'er* (3rd person sing. Piel., to make plain) the *hâttôrâh*. The term *Torah* can refer to a large accumulation of truths that include historical accounts along with legal materials. In this context, when the succeeding materials are considered, it becomes clear that the Torah included accounts of what Yahweh God had done for and revealed to Israel at Mount Sinai and during the forty years that Israel had spent in the desert.

Once the review of the past was completed, Moses proceeded to repeat the stipulations, decrees, and laws he had given before. The Ten Commandments were repeated in which he included a reference to their redemption from Egypt (5:15). He then stressed the heart of the entire Torah: love Yahweh your God "with all your heart, with all your soul, and with all your strength" (6:5). This love had to be in the hearts of the people. That this love would be possible and real was stressed by the words Moses spoke: "These commandments . . . are to be upon your hearts." The people, the older ones, parents had to know Yahweh God's truth and with their will and with their minds have them condition and control their hearts and influence all their efforts and activities. The parents had to know Yahweh God personally; they had to know his revealed truth and will. They had to learn all that Yahweh God made known to them. This parental knowledge was an absolute requirement for what parents were instructed to do.

Šinnanĕtem lĕbāneká. This phrase has been translated as "impress them on your children' (6:7). The verb *šānan*, (to whet, sharpen) here in the piel form stresses that the teaching of the Torah has to be done carefully and incisively. In order to so instruct or educate, parents, elders, and teachers must make it an effort in every aspect of life. They are to talk, that is, teach, at home and on the road. This is to be done before retiring for the night and after one rises. The truths to be taught and demonstrated should adorn the lives of parents, counselors, and teachers. Even homes should reflect that the Torah is the light and the guide. After giving this instruction to the parents and leaders Moses went on to add that as the Israelites occupied houses and took over wells, vineyards, and groves and became prosperous and ate well, they were to be careful to not forget their Lord who had redeemed them (6:10–12).

Summing up, it must be stressed that knowing Yahweh God and obeying his prescribed covenantal instructions for the continuation of faithful covenant living by all succeeding generations was and is an absolute requirement. Covenant education was the sure way and method for the continuation of a loving, serving, and worshiping people throughout all generations.

The Psalmists' Desires

Verbal References

The Psalmists used various terms that reveal their desires, intents, and requisites in regard to covenantal education. Some of these terms are *hôdî'enî* (hiph. impf. of *ŷādâ'*) "cause me to know," often translated as show (25:4), "make me to know" 39:4 [MT 5], "teach" (90:12), and the hiphil form past tense has been translated declared (77:14, 98:2). Two other verbs used as parallel in Psalm 25 to "show" are *lāmad* (to learn), in the piel intensive form translated teach (25:4, 9; 34:11; 51:13; 94:10, and repeatedly in Psalm 199) and *hadĕrîkēnî* (hiph. impf. of *dārak*, to tread or march), translated guide or lead me (25:5; 27:11; 119:35). Other translated terms are instruct, counsel (32:8), hear (95:7) and listen (81:12). The use of these terms by the Psalmists certainly indicate that they desired to be obedient to Yahweh God's covenantal demands to know him and his will and way for their lives and to have succeeding generations come to have that same knowledge.

Heartfelt Expressions

The Psalmists repeatedly and sincerely expressed their desire for the need of knowledge concerning Yahweh God's revealed word and will for their and progenies' lives. They declared a heartfelt motivation to be taught, to know, to teach, and to be guided.

Love for Yahweh God

In preceding discussions reference was made to the love of Yahweh God for his covenant and people.[4] The Psalmists repeatedly spoke in response to this love of their love for Yahweh God. Yahweh was addressed *'erăhāmĕkā* (1st sing. qal impf. of *rāham*, to love). I love you. This love for Yahweh was repeated in various ways. David said he did not conceal the love of Yahweh among his fellow worshipers (40:10 [MT 11]). He confessed his trust in Yahweh God's unfailing love (52:8 [MT 9]). He referred to his singing in the morning of Yahweh's unfailing love 59:16 [MT 17]; 92:2 [MT 3]; 101:1). The clear and bold statement *'āhabtî* (I love) is made by a Psalmist who is assured that Yahweh God hears and answers his prayers (116:1, 2).[5] These statements of love for Yahweh God came from the heart. This love for Yahweh, the covenant Lord, is a great and powerful motivation to speak and teach; to counsel and guide others. Indeed, covenantal education is firmly rooted in and is motivated by a heart that loves Yahweh God.

Love for Yahweh's Word

To love Yahweh included a love for his Torah, the Word. It was the Psalmists' conviction that this Word was rich and influential in life. Psalm 19, written by David, describes the Word he loves.[6] The word is *tĕmîmâh* (perfect). It is without blemish, it is blameless and upright. It provides renewed life because it reveres the *nepheš* (the inner man) (v. 7 [MT 8]). The statues included in the Torah are *ne'ĕmānâh* (niph. pf. of *'āman*). This term can be understood to stress sureness, firmness, trustworthiness (v. 7 [MT 8]). The simple, heeding, and following the Torah, become wise. The Torah's precepts are *yĕšārîm* (adj. of *yāšar*, to be straight). There is nothing crooked in these biblical precepts. As they give instruction, they impart gladness, enabling one to enjoy the fullness of life.[7] And the Torah's commandments are *bārâh* (pure). They are as bright as the sun. The enlighten and give understanding to the one who learns, considers, and applies them.

The author of Psalm 119 expressed his love for the Torah in a positive manner. He wrote that he delighted in Yahweh's commands because he loved them (vv. 47, 48). He exclaimed *māh 'ahabĕtî tôrāhtekā* (how I love your torah) (v. 97). This love is repeated in verses 113, 119, 127, 159, and 163. Yahweh's commands are greatly loved and are obeyed (v. 167); they are a source of hope (v. 74). Worshipers on their way to Zion also sang of the hope received through the Word as they waited on Yahweh God (130:5).

Love for Yahweh's People

The love for Yahweh and his Word would not be complete and well rounded if that love did not extend to Yahweh's people. It is crucial for our understanding of education in the Psalms to realize that as Yahweh loved his people, so his servants, the leaders and Psalmists, were to reflect him as his agents and spokesmen in expressing love for the people of God. The question is, however, did the Psalmists outrightly say, sing, or even refer directly to Yahweh's love for his people and more important, to their love for Yahweh's people? The answer is that there are no direct statements that express the love for Yahweh's people but the thought is nevertheless present.

The Psalmist sang of Yahweh God loving the righteous (146:8). These righteous form the assembly of Yahweh's people (1:5). Hence the Psalmists sang of love for Yahweh's house. There his glory dwelt (26:8) but there also the Psalmist's proclaim Yahweh's righteousness to the entire assembly (40:9). This righteous assembly is assured of Yahweh's love for them and their children (103:17). Thus to think of or to refer to Yahweh's assembly or house, that he loves, is to think of and refer to the people, the obedient and righteous people who enter and are in Yahweh's house and who form the assembly. And it is in this house, among the assembled people, that Yahweh's love, will, and righteousness are proclaimed. As one reflects on this reality it comes to mind that Moses instructed the redeemed assembly (from Egypt) at Sinai (Exod. 20), on the east side of the Jordan (Deut. 1:5).

The Psalmists reveal that they were fully aware of Yahweh's love for parents and their children. His dealings with Abraham included covenantal love and concern for children, that is, for families. This love and concern was also in the hearts and minds of the Psalmists as they sang of Yahweh building the *bayît*. This term is repeatedly used to refer to "family."[8] The context of Psalm 127 that records Yahweh building the family refers to children as a heritage and reward (v. 3). Yahweh's blessings rest upon the family that he builds. And how does Yahweh build families? Parents are his agents and his appointed builders.

The Content and Means of Covenantal Education

Introductory Comments

By reading, re-reading, reflecting on, and studying the Psalms it becomes very apparent that to separate the content of education and the means of education is not feasible. The Psalmists realized that what was to be the content of education could not be separated from the educators. These were the Lord himself, leaders in the community and in the assembly, and parents in the family.

The Psalmists, when referring to the recipients of instruction, guidance, and counseling, repeatedly focused on their own needs. Thus, as they asked for instruction they also indicated that the people, the assembly in the house of Yahweh, and the families in their homes needed education in the Word and works of Yahweh God, the cosmic King.

Three Psalms are selected for specific attention in the following paragraphs. Other Psalms could be included but references to some of these have been included[9] in the preceding discussions.

Three Psalms

Psalm 8

Psalm 8 has been and can indeed be considered a creation Psalm.[10] This Psalm not only extols creation but also the Creator and Yahweh God's covenant kingdom agents. An analytical sketch sets out the main aspects of this Psalm.

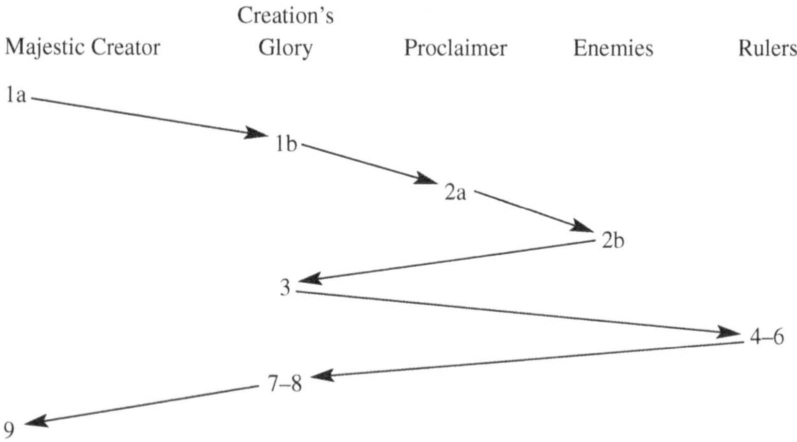

This Psalm extols the *'addîr* (majesty) of Yahweh *'ădōnênû* (v. 1 [MT 2]). Yahweh is proclaimed as man's sovereign covenant keeper who has revealed himself as the majestic King over all creation. This creation reflects, more, reveals Yahweh's majesty because it radiates the glory of the Creator. Creation includes the heavens, moon, stars, flocks, herds, beasts, birds, air, fields, fish, and the sea. These all came from the glorious, majestic Creator's hand.

David knew that not all people recognized and honored Yahweh. Mankind was created *tĕhassĕrēhû mĕ 'at me'ĕlōhîm* (piel impf. of *hāsar*: thou didst make him lack little of God).[11] The Divine One created mankind but they were not made divine. Men and women, created in God's image, lack God's divinity. They were, however, endowed with God-like qualities and abilities. To exhibit and manifest these, Yahweh God placed them, crowned with glory, to be rulers (the term *tămēšilēhû*, hiph. pf. of *māšah*, to rule, or have dominion or reign). In reality Yahweh God, the sovereign Creator and King, made men and women to be royal servants of Yahweh; they were made and placed to be viceregents, ruling over all of creation.

The Psalmist expressed a keen insight into the tragic division within mankind. Enemies, foes, and avengers made him realize that the antithesis was real. There were those who opposed Yahweh God the Creator and supreme Ruler. And they also opposed those who knew, honored, and served the Creator.

Within this antithetical situation, mankind had its responsibilities. They were to acknowledge Yahweh God's majesty. They were to know themselves as rulers who were divinely created but were not divine. They were to consider all that Yahweh God had placed under them. They were to silence the enemies, foes, and avengers. And they were to serve as Yahweh's agents in another very important role, which if carried out would *hašŭbît* (hiph. pf. of *sûb*, to cause to sit down) cause to be silent. The amazing reality that is set forth is that little and older children would do this. They would speak with their lips. They would declare the truth, the works, and the praises of their Creator Lord. Yahweh God "has placed the mouths of children . . . as a strong defensive controversive power.[12]

The question to be considered is: how was it possible for young children, to speak, to declare, to convey the truths, the will, the works of their majestic God? And specifically, how could they do this effectively in the world of enemies who demonstrated vengeance? The answer is given in other Psalms. Parents and spiritual leaders were to instruct them. They were to guide and counsel them. They were to lead the young into an appreciation of who their God was and what he had made and done. The young, according to this Psalm, were to praise their majestic God. They were to consider, with their parents, Yahweh God's natural revelation, that is, his revelation in nature. They were to be instructed concerning the fields and seas; concerning animals, birds, and sea creatures. And children, at a very young and tender age, were to learn to appreciate their environment, to know about it and to praise their majestic God who, having created it, made them his stewards over his handiwork.

Psalm 78

Psalm 78 has been referred to as a *leerdicht* (teaching poem).[13] It is interesting to note that this Psalm complements Psalm 77 in a unique manner. Asaph, the composer of both Psalms, expressed a degree of dismay and distress. The call came from a grieving heart, "will Yahweh reject us forever?" (77:7 [MT 8]). Had God forgotten his covenant promises of unfailing love, of his mercy and compassion? Asaph answered his own questions. Upon reflection on the past, he gladly recorded, "I will remember the deeds of Yahweh and the miracles he performed." He vowed to meditate on all Yahweh's mighty deeds (77:11, 12 [MT 12, 13]). Yahweh God had revealed himself as holy when performing miraculous deeds by which redemption had come. Asaph had but to think of the great exodus event of the past, of what Yahweh God had done through his covenant servants Moses and Aaron. And the question undoubtedly arose in his heart and mind. How can Yahweh God's redemptive deeds performed in the past be recalled, remembered, and inspire future generations? He answered his deep concern with his call *he'ăzînâ* (denominative hiph., give ear), listen to my torch (instruction, 78:1). He will proclaim things of the past that had been heard and told them by their fathers. The twofold emphatic intent was: (1) to have the future be assured by knowing the past;

and (2) to have the fathers through coming generations repeat the past to their progeny so that their covenantal future with Yahweh God would be assured.

Asaph, a spiritual leader in the Old Testament community, placed the responsibility for the future upon the parents of each generation. Consider how he developed this.

1st generation: fathers had told (v. 3b)
2nd generation: we have heard, known, and will not hide from them (v. 3a)
3rd generation: the praiseworthy deeds, his power, wonders, statutes proclaimed and commandments to be taught to the fourth generation (vv. 4, 5)
4th generation: tell the children yet to be born (v. 6b)
5th generation: they tell to the not yet born, who would trust God, remember his deeds, keep his commandments and not be like their stubborn and rebellious ancestors whose hearts were not loyal nor faithful to their covenant Lord (vv. 6c–8)

Asaph set forth a true, tried, and tested pedagogical method. Parents were to learn and know whom their covenantal Lord was and what he had promised, done, and commanded. They were to impress these upon their children (Deut. 6:7) so that the fifth generation after them would be taught, learn, know, obey and serve Yahweh God their covenant Lord.[14]

A number of specific emphases should be noted.

First, note the call to the covenant people who are addressed as *'ammi* (my people). Yahweh God claims the people addressed by Asaph as his own possession. Covenant people are not an autonomous unclaimed people. They are Yahweh God's redeemed people who are under Yahweh God's reign.

The appointed instructors are the *'ăbâtêmû* (our fathers). The fathers are commanded to speak and teach as Yahweh God's agents. It is their responsibility that the Torah be taught.

The children, in each succeeding generation, are to be taught so that their children will be taught. If the fathers are faithfully obedient as Yahweh God set forth, their grandchildren and great-grandchildren will be taught.

Second, note the verbs that are used to indicate the complete range of methods of instruction. Fathers are to open their mouths so that truths will be spoken. Fathers are to utter and not hide what they had heard, known, and been told. They are to tell and teach. They can use parables and stories.

Third, note the emphasis on what is to be known, taught, and heard: the things of old, that is, the history of Yahweh God's dealing with his covenant people. Yahweh God had performed praiseworthy deeds; he had performed wonders and miracles on their behalf. He had given them statutes and commands to guide their corporate and personal lives.

Fourth, the teaching of the past had a specific purpose for the present and the future. The positive effect would be to put their trust in God, remember his deeds, and obey his commands. The negative effect would be that they would learn not to be like their stubborn, rebellious, disloyal, and unfaithful forefathers.

Asaph presented an historical review to illustrate the importance of listening, learning, and obeying. A brief survey reveals the people's folly and sin, the results of these, and Yahweh's response to them. He began by referring to the northern tribes who did not keep God's covenant. They forgot what Yahweh God had done for them in Egypt, their deliverance and their experiences in the desert. Yahweh God had provided for them (vv. 9 16). But the people rebelled and complained (vv. 17–20). Yahweh God in wrath brought fire among them but the people did not believe or trust (vv. 21, 22). God nevertheless was gracious and merciful by supplying food and meat (vv. 23–29). God punished their gluttony but the people continued to sin (vv. 30, 31). Only punishment turned the people to God but as they did they flattered him with their mouths and continued to be unfaithful to Yahweh's covenant with them (vv. 32–37). Yahweh, however, was merciful and forgave them (vv. 38, 39). Asaph reflected on how often the covenant people rebelled against their covenant Lord; thy grieved him and put him to the test (vv. 40, 41). They did not remember his redeeming power and displayed in Egypt when he redeemed them from slavery(vv. 42–52). They did not remember their safe passage through the sea and the desert, or how they were given land (vv. 53–55). Once in the land God tested them and they proved to be disloyal, faithless, and unreliable (vv. 56–57). Yahweh God, in anger and with jealousy, rejected his people and gave them into the hands of their enemies (vv. 58–64). This rejection was for a time. He delivered his people; he chose Judah and Zion and gave them David, who proved to be a shepherd of integrity and skill (vv. 65–72).

Fifth, the teaching of the history of Yahweh God's people had and has a definite purpose. It teaches that Yahweh God is merciful, gracious, and compassionate. It teaches the folly of sin, rebellion, and deceit demonstrated when people ignore, disobey, and reject Yahweh God's covenant stipulations and promises. It teaches that Yahweh God in wrath will punish covenant breakers but that he is above all a forgiving Lord who in his boundless love provides for his people and keeps his covenant promises. He gave an undeserving people a king who was a forerunner and type of the promised covenant Mediator, Redeemer and King.

Psalm 119

Psalm 119 set before parents and teachers Yahweh God's revelation in the created world. Natural revelation must be taught. The authors of Psalms 33, 104, and 105 augment and amplify what is revealed concerning the Creator and the created world. Psalm 78 emphasizes the importance of teaching the history of Yahweh God's deeds on behalf of his people. The sad consequences of ignoring or rejecting Yahweh God as covenant Lord must be recalled as warnings. His mercy, grace, and forgiveness must be taught to encourage and strengthen covenant people to live in fellowship with their Lord. Psalm 119 emphasizes the vital importance of learning and knowing Yahweh God's word revelation.

Commentators have a wide range of ideas concerning Psalm 119. One considers the author as a young man.[15] The historical setting is uncertain. No commentator mentions a name. Did the composer live in the postexilic era?[16] Was he a persecuted man suffering scorn and contempt? Did enemies surround him?[17] As a teacher was he oppressed because he maintained his fidelity to Yahweh God in an alien world?[18]

The Psalm has been called superficial because there is no confession of sin and there is not the slightest reference to Christ's redemptive work. The covenant name of God, Yahweh, does not appear often. But the Torah, the Law of Yahweh, is set forth as wonderful and glorious.[19] Van Gemeren, in his introductory comments, wrote: "This is a Psalm not only of law but of love, not only of statute, but of spiritual strength; not only of devotion to precept, but of loyalty to the way of the Lord."[20]

Psalm 119 is concerned with the Law of God. Eight words are used to refer to it. The chief term is Torah. Kidner correctly wrote that its parent term means to teach or direct. The term therefore can mean either law or revelation.[21] Kidner added other terms that spoke of God's self-revelation, that is, "thy ways," "thy name," "thy faithfulness."

The question has been asked if the Psalmist was worshiping the Word. A careful look at what the Psalmist wrote gives assurance that the composer was worshiping the Lord, reflecting a true piety, a love of God that is refreshed, informed, and nourished by the Torah.[22]

The content of Psalm 119 has been briefly reviewed above. The question this study is particularly seeking to answer is: does the author indicate an awareness of or even the necessity of teaching the Torah? And if so, who is to be taught and by whom?

Implied in what has been written above, the composer considers Yahweh God, his covenant Lord, to be the author of the Torah. He is first of all called upon to instruct, teach, and guide. And who is to receive instruction?

A consideration of terms referring to "instruction" as a verb would be helpful. These terms are as follows.

The term *lāmad* in the qal stem means to exercise in or to learn. In the piel it is translated to teach while in the Paul it is translated as trained or taught. In Psalm 119 the verb appears in the qal infinitive translated as I learn (v. 7) and as a qal imperfect twice, translated as might learn (v. 71) and to learn (v. 73). It appears ten times in the piel stem, eight times in the imperative translated as teach (vv. 12, 26, 64, 66, 68, 108, 124, 135). The usual subjects the Psalmist asked to be taught were Yahweh God's decrees and once "thy laws." As a piel participle it is translated teacher and as a piel future it is translated "for you teach me." This future teaching will lead to lips overflowing with praise (v. 171). But what really does the Psalmist want to be taught so that his lips overflow with praise? The text repeatedly records that the Psalmist wants Yahweh God to teach the decrees he has had Moses and other biblical writers record. The Hebrew term *huqqim* (decrees or statutes), appearing twenty-one times, is derived from the verb *haqaq* (to inscribe).

When writers inscribed they cut into solid permanent materials such as rocks, monuments, walls, or slates. These inscriptions or engravements gave permanence to what was intended to be communicated. Thus, whether *huqqim* is translated as statutes or decrees, in Scripture and referring to Scripture itself, the sense of permanence and of abiding authority is communicated.

Yahweh God is the author of these *huqqîm* and in promulgating them he revealed his royal sovereignty in nature and in the covenant community.[23] The Psalmist, repeatedly asking to be taught Yahweh God's decrees, is in reality requesting to learn and live according to Yahweh's will for all areas and aspects of covenant life and service.

The Psalmist employed a variety of synonyms that reveal his earnest desire to be taught by Yahweh God by means of his written revelation. He prayed *gal'ēnay* (open my eyes) (v. 18). He readily confessed that by himself, with his own efforts, he could not turn his eyes from worthless things. In this context he pleads that his heart be turned to Yahweh's statutes and then his eyes could and would be opened (vv. 36, 37). By nature his eyes would fail to look for covenant promises (v. 82) and for salvation according to Yahweh's righteous promise (v. 123).[24]

The Psalmist prayed *hādĕrikênî* (hiph. imp. of *dārak*, to tread or march). He prayed that he be caused to march on the path that Yahweh God had commanded (v. 35). This pathway was the way of truth. Yahweh's word was a lamp and a light for those walking in Yahweh God's ordained way of life (v. 105). He acknowledged that without the understanding of Yahweh's *piqqādîm* (precepts), he would not hate every wrong path (v. 104). He longed to walk the covenant way of life.

The Psalmist prayed for understanding. In the context of asking for instruction to follow Yahweh God's decrees and resolving to obey the Torah with all his heart, he pled *hăbînēnî* (hiph. of *bîn*, to discern), cause me to understand or give me understanding, give me discernment (vv. 34, 73, 125, 130, 144, 169). To understand, or to discern, is more than mere knowledge. To discern is to see and identify the various aspects of what is taught. Discernment includes making distinctions and realizing the relationships between these. To understand is to comprehend the purport or meaning of what is being conveyed. The Psalmist desires to gain full, rich insight and comprehension of Yahweh God's revelation. He wrote that to receive understanding and discernment is to commit himself to keeping and obeying he Torah with all his heart. He will find delight in walking the way laid out before him (vv. 33–35). Others will rejoice with him also (v. 74).

The Psalmist made it clear and definite. He was in real need of instruction, teaching guidance, discernment, and understanding of the covenant life he was called upon to live and follow. He did not have innate truth. It had to be given him by Yahweh God through his revelation to him. He knew he was by nature sinful and that sin would rule over him (133). He, by nature walking in darkness, needed light as David had confessed also (18:28). And in a world in which sin, evil, and grief surrounded him, he needed comfort (to be with strength) (vv. 50, 52, 76, 82). He knew that Yahweh's decrees and statutes were a source of joy (v. 111).

The Psalmist expressed various responses to the Torah that taught, guided, comforted, an filled him with joy. He exclaimed, addressing Yahweh God, that he greatly loved his Torah.[25] This love motivated him to *'sîaḥ* (a denominative verb that is translated, depending on the context, to complain, muse, or meditate). Repeatedly he said he would or did meditate (vv. 15, 23). He thoughtfully reflected and mused on aspects of the Torah. He referred to Yahweh's wonders (v. 27), precepts (v. 78), statutes (v. 99), and promises (v. 148) as subjects or sources for his study and growth in comprehending and obeying Yahweh's instructions for the covenant way of life. And he added *dābaqtî* (qal pf. of *dābaq*, to cling). Translators have used the phrase hold fast, that is, to the decree or statues. This holding fast is an insurance against shame. As a covenant man he is convinced he should exhibit determination and strength in his obedience to Yahweh God's prescriptions for a God-honoring covenant life.

Questions are in order after a study of education according to Psalm 119. Who is the educator? The Psalmists repeatedly indicated that the word, the revelation of Yahweh God's will, was the instructing means. Yahweh God himself supplied this. Thus, the sovereign covenant Lord, Yahweh God, is the educator. Submission to him and to his revealed will is the fundamental requisite to be educated.[26] In a real sense, the motivation for and involvement in being educated with and in Yahweh God's Torah is the covenant person's responsibility. He or she has a basic role in being taught and guided by Yahweh God by means of his divine revelation.

This responsibility lies upon the *na'ar* (the young person) also.[27] Young people must keep their way pure. They have the duty to live sanctified lives. The word, the revelation of Yahweh's revealed will, must be the standard by which to be guided and judged. There is no direct reference to the role of parents or spiritual leaders and educators in Psalm 119. This absence by no means gives adults a reason not to be involved in the teaching, guiding, and applying of the teachings in the Torah to the younger generation. The role of parents is clearly set forth in the Old Testament,[28] as well as New Testament revelation.[29]

Three final comments in summary are: first, Yahweh God's revealed word, the Torah, is an absolute requirement for the God-honoring, sanctified life; second, there must be a motivation, kindled by love for Yahweh and his revelation, to be educated by the word; third, personal responsibility on the part of the educands, be they young or old, to submit to the instruction of Yahweh God's revealed will and way for covenant life is an absolute necessity if one is to have peace, joy, comfort, assurance, and untold blessings.

Theological Doctrines

Various doctrinal references have been made in the preceding study. As one reads and studies the Psalms it becomes apparent that the Psalmists did not intend to spell out doctrinal issues or to present an outline of biblical theology. In their prayers and praises, however, they certainly did exhibit a theological awareness of what had been recorded before their time and what they discerned and learned in their covenantal relationship with Yahweh God.[30]

Concerning God

Yahweh God is a personal Father to the king installed in Zion. The king is called a son to whom God is Father (2:3). He is father to those who may have been forsaken by earthly parents (27:10, 68:5). David, referring to Yahweh God as his Rock and Savior, called out to him "my father" (89:26). In this context the Father is claimed as a faithful covenant Lord whose love will never fail.

Yahweh God is sovereign. He rules by his power and watches over nations (66:7). Nations submit to him, for the kingdoms of the earth belong to him (68:31, 32 [MT 32, 33]). His son, the king, will rule from sea to sea (72:8). All the earth bows down to him (66:4 [MT 5]). As sovereign Lord his providence extends widely. His care for creation is evident (65:9–13 [MT 10–14]). He is omnipresent (139:7); he assures his servants he is always with them (73:23). He is eternal, enduring as the sun and moon (72:5) Yahweh's love is from everlasting to everlasting to those who fear him (103:12). His Spirit is present for people (57:11 [MT 12]) and he is active in creation (104:30).

Yahweh God is the saving God. He forgives sin (32:5; 103:3). He ransoms his struggling servant (55:18, 19 [MT 19, 20]). He revives those who call on him and restores them (80:18, 19 [MT 19, 20]). He is addressed as Savior who performs deeds of righteousness and is thus the hope of all the ends of the earth and the farthest sea (65:5 [MT 6]). The people of the covenant addressed Yahweh as Savior; he bore their burdens and brought escape from death (68:19, 20 [MT 20, 21]).

Yahweh God's unfailing love is known and extolled by David when Doeg the Edomite betrayed him (52:18 [MT 19]) and when Saul pursued him into a cave (57:3 [MT 4]). And David rejoiced because with steadfast heart he sang of Yahweh God's love and faithfulness (108:3 [MT 4]).

Other Doctrines

The wrath of God was known when he rose up to save the afflicted, who then praised him (76:7–10 [MT 8–11]). Individuals knew how heavy God's wrath could be (88:7 [MT 8]) but also knew that confession was the way to relief (32:15; 40:12; 106:6). Rebellion by the covenant people resulted in the wrath of Yahweh God (78:9–22). They knew that as a covenant people they were subjected to bitter labor when they rebelled against the word of God and despised the counsel of the Most High (107:11–17). They referred to judgment. They confessed that the wicked would not stand in the judgment and that the way of the wicked would perish (2:5, 6). They knew God was a righteous judge (7:11) and would judge the world in righteousness (9:8 [MT 9]). They confirmed that God, who himself was judge, would judge his people (50:4, 6). David confessed that Yahweh God was justified when he judged (51:4 [MT 5[). They unhesitatingly quoted their Lord who said that it was he who judged uprightly (75:2 [MT 3]) and the covenant man responded singing, "rise up, man of God, judge of the earth" (94:2) and judge the earth (96:10) in righteousness (98:9). David, prophesying concerning the Lord at the Father's right hand, said he would judge the nations and crush kings in the day of wrath (110:5, 6).[31]

The Psalmists were not pessimists. They taught there was a future beyond the grave. There would be a resurrection of the dead. Jubilantly the Psalmists taught the people to sing "I will not die." It is not the dead who, going down in silence, praise Yahweh but we (your covenant people) who extol him forever and ever (115:17, 18). So the anticipating believer sang, "open the gates that he righteous may enter" (118:17–21).[32] People going up to Jerusalem sang this psalm and it has been interpreted as a hope for the resurrection.

David sang with assurance that Yahweh would not abandon him to the grave and he would be filled with joy in Yahweh's presence (16:11). So also the sons of Korah sang that God would redeem me from the grave and take me to himself (49:15 [MT 16]).

To teach and sing of the resurrection from the dead was accompanied with eschatological assurance. It was noted in a preceding paragraph that he living ones would extol Yahweh God both now and forever more (115:18). When one considers that the term *ôlām* occurs 136 times in the Psalms it becomes impossible to deny that the Psalmists were eschatologically minded, oriented, hopeful and assured of a non-ending future. Consider a few references. Yahweh shall endure forever (9:7 [MT 8]; 48:14 [MT 15]); he is King forever (10:16; 29:10); his throne is forever (45:6 [MT 7]). His name endures forever (72:17, 19). The Psalmists also referred to covenant seed as enduring forever (89:36 [MT 37]; 116:5–9). Yahweh remembers the covenant made with his people forever (105:9, 14). His covenant mercy endures forever (136:1–26; 138:8). And because Yahweh God's kingdom is forever (145:13) his people can and will praise him forever (145:1, 2). Indeed, Yahweh God who keeps truth forever shall reign forever (146:6, 10).

Wisdom

Are Wisdom Psalms Included in the Psalter?

The question to be considered initially is: do the Psalmists include the concept of wisdom in their Psalms? If so, are they then to be considered as "teaching Psalms"? In other words, did the Psalmists seek to educate the people who sang the songs they composed in which the concept of wisdom occurs? The debate among commentators does not present a unified approach or a general agreement on whether Psalms (at least some) should be considered wisdom Psalms or not. Some do not consider "wisdom" as a type of Psalm. Anderson, under the heading of "Minor Types," includes eight Psalms in this category. He wrote that these could be characterized as reflective "poems." He listed Psalms 1, 37, 49, 73, 112, 127, 128, and 133 as such.[33] Van Gemeren, referring to L. G. Perdue,[34] lists twenty-five Psalms as wisdom Psalms.[35] If one is inclined to consider a number of Psalms as specifically "teaching life" poems, one could agree that many Psalms are wisdom Psalms. A consideration of when the concept of wisdom is referred to and in what context may be helpful to draw some conclusions.

Folly

The Psalmist referred to people who did not have or exhibit wisdom. David confessed that he was a guilty man; he had festering and loathsome wounds because of his sinful *'iwwaltî* (folly), (Ps. 38:5 [MT 6]). It is not clear if David referred to some disease due to lust or excess.[36] In another context David, surrounded by enemies, confessed that Yahweh God knew his folly and that it had brought guilt upon him (69:5 [MT 6]). The sons of Korah sang of Yahweh God's favor, restored fortunes, and Yahweh's forgiveness of the iniquity of his people. This expression of thanks and praise is followed by the prayer that Yahweh God's covenant people not be permitted to return to *kisĕlâh* (stupidity, foolishness), (85:9 [MT 10]). These references to folly and stupidity were acknowledged to have been present among Yahweh God's people. Sin and guilt were root causes the Psalmists confessed. And they knew that they needed forgiveness, healing, and restraining influence exerted by their Lord.

The Psalmists also referred to the *nābāl* (fool). A fool was one who said there is no God (14:1; 53:1 [MT 2]). They are corrupt and lack understanding. The fool scorns people, David wrote, when they seek to live the sanctified life, who say "I will watch my ways and keep my tongue from sin" (39:1 [MT 2], 8 [MT 9]). It is not only God-fearing men who are mocked and reviled by fools or foolish people. Yahweh God is even more so (74:18, 22). Asaph called on God to rise up and defend his cause and have regard for his covenant (74:20).

Wisdom Antithetical to Folly

In the context of men's folly, foolishness, and stupidity, the antithesis comes powerfully to expression. Wisdom is antithetical to folly. To be wise is antithetical to being a fool who has no perception of ethical and spiritual realities. The terms *hokmah*, *hokmot*, and *hokam* refer to wisdom and to the man who demonstrates it. To have the gift of wisdom, or to be wise, one had to fear Yahweh God (111:10). This meant one had to know God, to reverence and worship him. The wise person considers Yahweh's great love (107:43) and turns to him in the midst of turmoil and strife (107:28). David said he keeps Yahweh God's Torah in his heart and he is then enabled to utter wisdom (37:30, 31). Yet, he, in the midst of life's problems needs Yahweh God to teach him wisdom in his inner being. Thus he will have truth in his heart (51:6 [MT 7]).

Teaching Wisdom

Do the Psalmists indicate that the teaching of wisdom is necessary? The sons of Korah called "all you peoples" to heed words of wisdom spoken to them and to receive understanding from Yahweh God's revelation (49:4 [MT 5]). This revelation of wisdom is embedded in creation; all men can learn from it (104:24). But the act of teaching is referred to, be it briefly. Pharaoh commissioned Joseph to teach Egypt's princes and leaders wisdom (105:22).[37] Moses, reflecting on the brevity of life, prayed that Yahweh would teach his people while they lived[38] so that a heart of wisdom would be gained (90:12).

The conclusion of the matter of teaching wisdom can be stated briefly. Mankind, fallen in sin, often surrounded by folly, living in a world in which there are many foolish people, needs to be taught the wisdom that comes from Yahweh. It is revealed in creation; it is taught in his word. Those who have received the gift of wisdom through these sources indicate that they have received it and teach it. Yes, the Psalms include "education in wisdom. They introduce it. The author of Proverbs expands on it.

Notes

1. In various preceding chapters the core elements and ramifications of the covenant have been studied. Cf. e.g., chap. 40, 165–66.

2. An indication of the important role of education in biblical life has been demonstrated. See the extensive article "Education in Biblical Times" by A. W. Morton in *The Zondervan Pictorial Encyclopedia of the Bible*, vol. II, ed. M. C. Tenney (Grand Rapids: Zondervan, 1975), 206–223. This essay, however, is not too helpful for a study of "Education in the Psalms." There are only fourteen scattered references to the Psalms in this extensive essay.

3. There are some direct references to it and many indirect or implied references. See Morton's essay.

4. Cf. chap. 40, Yahweh's love.

5. Commentators have referred to the similarity between the words of this Psalm and David's, thus saying David may be the author of this Psalm.

6. Anderson wrote that four different aspects of the Law and the influence they exert were set forth primarily following a literary device. *Psalms 1–72*, 170–71.

7. Ibid. 171.

8. Cf. what David said when he referred to Yahweh's covenantal promises concerning his children. David said *bētî*, my family (2 Sam. 7:18).

9. References to Psalms that have been made in the preceding are: 1, 19, 25, 29, 32, 34, 39, 40, 41, 47, 51, 52, 59, 60, 77, 81, 90, 92, 94, 95, 98, 101, 103, 116, 127, 130, 146. References could also have been made to 17, 18, 20, 24, 25, 27, 48, 50, 71, 115, 132, 143.

10. Brueggemann refers to Pss. 8, 33, 104, 105 as hymns of creation praise, but Van Gemeren prefers to refer to Ps. 8 as a hymn of praise. "Psalms," 109.

11. Cf. this translation in *BDB*, 341.

12. Delitzsch, *Psalms I*, 152. Delitzsch went on to quote Paul's comment to the Corinthians (1 Cor. 1:27), that God has chosen that which is foolish and weak in the eyes of the world to put to shame the wise and strong.

13. Grosheide, *Psalmen II*, 22.

14. The pedagogical method Asaph spelled out is applicable in modern times. Examples of this can be given. In the author's own experience, (1) grandfather Cornelius was a faithful trusting, God-fearing man. He instructed his son Hendrik (2), who, in turn, instructed his son Gerard (3), who in turn instructed his six sons and two daughters (4), who are instructing their children.

15. Delitzsch, *Psalms III*, but Anderson, *Psalms 73–150* considers it impossible to judge his age, 807.

16. Van Gemeren, "Psalms," 736.
17. Anderson, *Psalms 73–150*, 807.
18. Kidner, *Psalms 73–150*, 425.
19. Grosheide, *Psalmen II*, 124.
20. Van Gemeren, "Psalms", 736, 737.
21. Kidner, *Psalms 73–150*, 417, 18. He lists the seven other terms that are used to refer to the Torah; testimonies, precepts, statutes, commandments, ordinances, word, and promise, 417–19. Cf. also Van Gemeren, "Psalms" 737, 738.
22. Ibid.
23. Van Gemeren, "Psalms," 738.
24. David had prayed thus also, requesting Yahweh God to show the way and to guide in truth (25:5).
25. Cf. reference to his love in the preceding paragraph.
26. There is no reference in Ps. 119 to the Holy Spirit's role in the learning, understanding, and applying of Yahweh God's verbal revelation.
27. This reference to the young man should not be taken as the composer's reference to himself.
28. Cf. e.g., Ps. 78.
29. Cf. e.g., Paul's admonition in Eph. 6:1–4.
30. This presentation of doctrinal issues is not the fruit of a specific study of this theme, but of a reading and reflection of the Psalmists' thoughts. John H. Stek was correct when, in the Introduction to the Psalms he wrote that the Psalter is not a catechism of doctrine. Its theology, however, is confessional and doxological. *The NIV Study Bible*, 784.
31. The Psalmists referred to the Messiah in various ways. This messianic element has been studied in length and detail in the author's work entitled *Messianic Revelation in the Old Testament*, 327–414. A subsequent study is made in chap. 45.
32. Psalm 118 has been discussed by scholars giving rise to various interpretations. Kidner wrote that the historical context was the Passover feast, *Psalms 73–150*, 412. Anderson opted for the feast of tabernacles, *Psalms 73–150 II*, 787; Van Gemeren referred to various possibilities, e.g., sung when a Davidic king led pilgrims in a thanksgiving service. Or, it may have a post-exilic context, "Psalms," 729, 730.
33. *Psalms 1–72*, 40.
34. Perdue, *Wisdom & Cult*; cf. Van Gemeren, "Psalms," 32, 33.
35. Van Gemeren, "Psalms," 32, 33.
36. Kidner, *Psalms 1–72*, 154. Delitzsch referred to the wrath of God (38:3) and opined that David suffered mental and physical illness after his adulterous affair with Bathsheba, *Psalms II*, 26.
37. Scholars who have praised Egyptian wisdom are not quick to refer to this order given to Joseph. Many consider the Egyptians to have had their own wisdom. As God's imagebearers they could have some innate knowledge of wisdom but not divinely revealed wisdom.
38. Cf. also Ps. 49:10 [MT 11].

45

The Mediator and Eschatology in the Psalms

I. Introductory Comments

II. The Mediator in the Psalms

III. Eschatology in the Psalms

IV. Conclusion to the Study of Psalms

45

The Mediator and Eschatology in the Psalms

Introductory Comments

Various Presentations of the Two Themes

The two themes discussed in this chapter are included in the Psalms in various ways and in differing contexts. They are integral aspects of the revelation Yahweh God gave previous to the Psalmists' writings and also in the Psalms. As the Psalmists gave expression to revelation they also revealed their own faith in what Yahweh God made known.

The Inseparable Relationship

The two themes, the Mediator and eschatology, are inseparably related in the Old Testament Scriptures. The first refers to a person, the second to time and/or eternity. The person exists and is a central reality in the Scriptures. He is an eschatological person; he has no beginning and has no end. He is present throughout all ages. He shares the attributes of eternity with the Father, the first person of the Trinity.[1]

Prophetic Themes

Both the Mediator and eschatology are basically prophetic themes. Both were referred to in Old Testament times, but references to them in the Scriptures are such that they are revealed as already present but not fully revealed. This revelation of both is progressive, ever more fully expressed but never fully and finally. To comprehend the scope and depth of the ever-increasing revelation of the Mediator and eternity (eschatology) is a tremendous challenge. It requires careful reading, reflection, thought, and expression. Because of this unique character of "prophetic revelation," scholars have attempted to explain prophetic realities in various ways. The concept of "myth" has been introduced[2] or reference has been made to the Scripture's use of mythological language.[3]

The integral relationship between the concepts of Mediator and eschatology is expressed in various Psalms in which the Mediator is particularly presented.[4] A representative Psalm is Psalm118. An analysis of this Psalm can be presented by a sketch (see page 285).[5]

Consideration of Major Subthemes

The following major points in Psalm 118 as analyzed are as follows.

1. Yahweh God's goodness and love are extolled as forever. The Psalm begins and ends with these attributes and their eschatological character.
2. There is much interaction between the Lord and the Psalmist(s).[6] They have Yahweh as their helper against enemies.
3. Salvation is the blessing received.
4. The Mediator is the central reality within the eschatological context. The Messiah, Christ, is prophesied.[7]

In answer to the question whether the Mediator and eschatology are major themes in Psalm 118, the answer is *yes* in regard to both. Yahweh God's eternal goodness and love revealed by the Mediator, the salvation granted by the helper are constant. They are always present and available; they will never fail.

The Mediator in the Psalms

The Third Cable

The integrating and uniting reality of Old Testament revelation is the Golden Cable. This cable, as explained in many previous contexts, consists of three strands, the kingdom, the covenant, and the mediator.[8] It has been repeatedly demonstrated that the kingdom is the setting and context in which the covenant is present and functions. The covenant was established by Yahweh God within his cosmic kingdom and sets out the relationship between Yahweh God and his created cosmic kingdom with all of its inherent aspects. The covenant is administered by Yahweh God, particularly by the Messiah, the Mediator of the covenant. The Psalmists demonstrated a definite awareness of the promised Messiah and referred to him in various ways and contexts.

The Previous Study

In the study published in 1990[9] an attempt was made to consider the historical context and author of each Psalm that was in whole or part considered messianic.

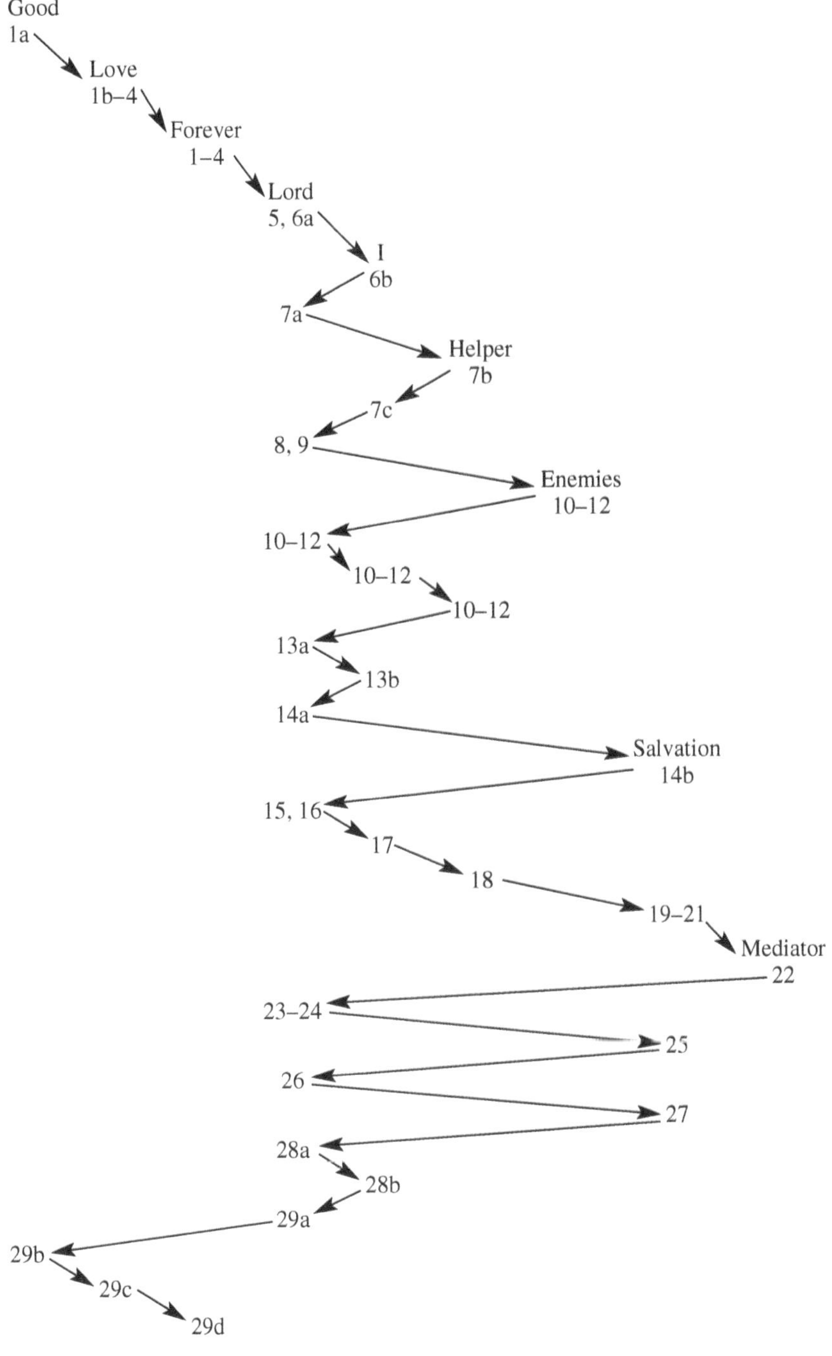
Good
1a
Love
1b–4
Forever
1–4
Lord
5, 6a
I
6b
7a
Helper
7b
7c
8, 9
Enemies
10–12
10–12
10–12
10–12
13a
13b
14a
Salvation
14b
15, 16
17
18
19–21
Mediator
22
23–24
25
26
27
28a
28b
29a
29b
29c
29d

A careful exegetical study of each messianic passage brought insights after which various conclusions were formulated. Plus a study also confirmed the proposition that, as in much of the Old Testament, so in the Psalms there are narrower and wider conceptions of the promised Messiah.[10] The narrower presents the person(s) and the wider concept includes promises of salvation to be fulfilled by a coming messianic person. A review of this previous study led to the conclusion that these messianic passages in the Psalms refer to or present the Messiah by using four categories of reference.

Four Categories of References

Direct Prophetic References

The author of Psalm 2 is not recorded in the superscription, but Peter and John related that David, inspired by the Holy Spirit, wrote this Psalm (Acts 4:25). The Psalmist proclaims that conspiring nations vainly plot against Yahweh's anointed One (v. 2). This Messiah was referred to as the King whom Yahweh installed and identified as my (Yahweh's) Son. Earthly kings are urged to kiss the Son—that is, to submit to him who is truly the King.[11]

The term *anointed one* does not appear in Psalm 110. The terms Yahweh and *'adoni* (my Lord, or Master) appear as referring to two divine persons. Yahweh spoke to David's Lord (the Messiah), referring to him as a royal One who is also eternal priest. This Psalm is directly prophetic; it speaks of Yahweh's King-Priest. The wider view of the messianic concept is obviously present also because qualifications and activities of the King-Priest are included.[12]

Indirect References

There are at least five 5 Psalms that include indirect references to the Messiah-Mediator. These all are included under the rubric of wider messianic conceptions.

Psalm 8 records David's praise of Yahweh's majesty and glory in the cosmos, that is, the earth and heavens. There are differing views concerning the interpretation of the phrase *ben 'ădām* (son of man). The context can be understood to refer to man as the imagebearer of God. Man has been made *mĕ'at* (little lower) *me'elōhîm* (than God) (v. 5 [MT 6]),[13] and the New Testament reference (Heb. 2:6–8) need not be considered contradictory. Jesus Christ is fully human yet as the incarnate Son of God fulfills the Messiah's task in the redemption of mankind.

Some commentators consider Psalm 12 to be prophetically messianic. David, the author, expressed a desire that wicked enemies be cut off and destroyed and that thus the afflicted and the poor receive salvation according to Yahweh's promises. The conclusion following a study of this Psalm is that there is a messianic element but it is very general.[14]

Psalm 45 has received close attention; one could say it has been given very close scrutiny. It has been entitled a wedding song (NIV, title) and according to the KJV it is a song dedicated to the king (v. 1 [MT 2]).[15] The "sons of Korah, listed as the authors, have combined a number of themes that do not seem too congruous. The king, most excellent, with lips anointed by grace, is called upon to have his sword on his side and to have his sharp arrows (5 [6]) pierce the hearts of enemies. God's everlasting throne and scepter of righteousness will last forever, as will his throne from which his love for righteousness and hate for wickedness flow. He and his bride are adorned and nations will praise the king forever. The psalm has been characterized messianic in a "prophetically allegorical sense" and as "typically messianic." A study of the psalm, however, does not give one certainty that the coming of the Messiah/Mediator is predicted. He may be assumed as present, ruling, and occupying the throne of Yahweh.[16]

David composed Psalm 101 and the conclusion stated after a discussion of the Psalm is that it can be regarded "messianic in only a very general sense."[17] Many commentators term this as a "royal Psalm" because it refers to David's reign. David gave expression to what he knew Yahweh God expected of him as the ruling royal anointed one. Thus there is no direct reference to the mediatorial predicted or expected role but the Psalm does include a general reference to the character of the reign of David, the king who was a type of the Messiah.

The messianic significance of Psalm 129 is very difficult to determine. Some have interpreted verses 3 and 4 to refer to Christ's suffering.[18] The terminology gave some interpreters an insight into how Christ was made to suffer. They resorted to allegory or analogy to arrive at their view.

Symbol or Metaphor

The Old Testament reveals that in Old Testament times various objects, persons, activities, or entities were, in a real sense, used to portray prophetically the Mediator in his messianic position and role. These symbols or metaphors were sacrifices, the temple, Isaac on the altar, the priestly robe, stone, and shepherd. The Psalmists also employed these. There is, however, not much evidence that the Psalmists, to refer to or to represent the Messiah/Mediator, employed these symbols or metaphors.

The concept "shepherd" should be considered. Jesus, the Messiah, is referred to as the shepherd of his people in the New Testament (John 10:11, 14; 1 Peter 5:4). In the Old Testament, as in various Near East contexts, kings were referred to as shepherds (cf., e.g., 2 Sam.5:2; Ps.78:71, 72; Jer. 3:15). David referred to Yahweh God as his Shepherd (Ps. 23:1). The messianic Mediator is not referred to prophetically as a shepherd in the Old Testament. Yahweh God is however (Pss. 80:1; 95:7; Isa. 40:22; Ezek. 34:11). Since the New Testament writers did refer to Jesus the Mediator as the "Shepherd" one can conclude that at least by analogy, the Old Testament concept of shepherd was a metaphor for him.

In Psalm 118 the use of the term *stone* is considered as a prophetic symbol of the Messiah. The stone, also referred to as the capstone (NIV) or "chief cornerstone" (NASB) or head stone (KJV), served a very important role in the construction of buildings. They were used to bind together rows of stones. Kidner wrote that "the New Testament leaves no doubt that this stone foreshadowed Christ (Matt.

12:42; Rom. 9:32ff; Eph. 2:20)."[19] As the "cornerstone" bound other stones together, so Jesus Christ, the Mediator, is the binding force of the church, his redeemed people.[20]

In the phrases "open . . . the gates . . . , this is the gate of Yahweh " (vv.19, 20), gates is considered a metaphor that points to or foreshadows the resurrection of Jesus Christ and of his believing followers.[21] David gave expression to a strong assurance that his body would rest secure because he would not be abandoned to the grave. He went on to say prophetically that, as he, the king, would not remain in the grave, so the Holy One would not see corruption.[22] He continued to speak of his assurance concerning the path of life on which he would have joy and eternal pleasure being in the Lord's presence—yes, being at the right hand of his Lord.

In Psalm16:9–11, the resurrection of the Messiah is prophesied but also of himself, David the king. David thus referred to himself as a type of Christ, foreshadowing his assured future as a resurrected servant of Jesus Christ.

Types

In the two preceding paragraphs reference was made to David as a foreshadowing, forerunner, or type of Christ. There are at least ten other Psalms that portray the king of Israel as a type of Christ.[23]

Psalm 20 is widely regarded as a royal Psalm. A commentator was explicit: this Psalm speaks directly concerning the king in the midst of his people. He is a type and shadow of the King.[24] The emphasis in this Psalm is on the seed-line that would extend from David on Israel's throne to David's Son who is to be enthroned eternally. Yahweh's people are led to pray for victory for Israel's king and ultimately for the eternally enthroned King.

David also composed Psalm 21. It is said to be a followup to Psalm 20 because thanksgiving is sung for the victory achieved by David under Yahweh's guidance. Yahweh enriches the life of the human king of Israel by gifts that are partially received by him but will be completely fulfilled by the eternal King. The eight gifts recorded are deliverance; enthronement; eternal life; attributes of glory; splendor, and beauty; joy; trust and faith; victory; and a worshiping heart and life. This Psalm is not prophetically predictive but the messianic concept is filled out more than before in both the narrower and wider views.[25]

A number of Psalms refer to the suffering endured by messianic types that foreshadow and point to the suffering the messianic Mediator will experience when he, as antitype, appears in flesh. These and other psalms express victory, well-being, and even joy.

Psalm 22 is widely recognized as a predictive experience of David that his Lord will experience to a deeper and greater extent when on the cross. The New Testament Gospel writers quoted this Psalm when they wrote about Christ's crucifixion and events surrounding it. The Psalm, however, while it refers to desertion, humiliation, despair, and death, also expresses praise to Yahweh God and acknowledgment of his universal reign.[26]

David, in Psalm 41, expressed his disappointment, sorrow, and pain when he learned that a trusted friend had betrayed him. Jesus quoted this Psalm when he, at the last passover meal, told his disciples that he was going to be betrayed (Matt. 26:21). These words of Jesus indicate without a doubt that David's experience was typical, a clear foreshadowing of the Mediator's suffering and pain.[27] The unknown composer of Psalm 102 gave expression to suffering and pain by an individual who experienced the tragedies accompanying the exile. This Psalm is considered messianic because it is quoted in Hebrews 1:10–12 as referring to the Son of God who experienced bitter anguish because God's absence was thought to be real.[28] It should be noted that Yahweh God is addressed; it is he that is eternally enthroned.[29] Botha is definitely correct when he wrote that it has become clear that the enthronement Psalms are not about the enthronement of Yahweh but about Yahweh's kingship, power, and worldwide honor.[30]

The Psalms that express victory and joy may have references to suffering and pain, but the emphasis is on the glorious aftermath of suffering and pain. Psalm 68 expresses the joy that Israel experienced when the king, powerful and victorious, returned from battle with gifts and captives. David returned to his throne because Yahweh God was securely and eternally enthroned. David's triumphant return was one of a series of successive stages in the Messiah's eventual coming, work, and ascension to heaven.[31] Psalm 72, considered to be an outstanding messianic psalm, holds up the theocratic reign over Israel as a model for the eternal kingdom of Yahweh. The messianic reign of the universal kingdom is proclaimed. The royal person is vividly portrayed as both human and royal. Verses 18 and 19 are a doxology of praise to Yahweh God, the God of Israel.[32]

Three Psalms, considered messianic, can be referred to as priestly. The emphasis in these Psalms is on what priests were and did as foreshadowing and typifying Christ. In some Psalms the royal and priestly aspects are included as in Psalm 110.[33] The reference to the priestly aspect is clear. Yahweh is prophesied as saying to David's Lord, the messianic Mediator, that he is a priest forever after the order of Melchizadek. And he is to be so forever. Priestly character and functions are not mentioned, as are the royal ones. Those mentioned refer to the scepter by which he will rule in the midst of enemies and do so with majesty. The Messiah is a royal priest.

Other psalms that have a priestly reference are 40, 69, and 109. Psalm 40:6–10 [MT 7–11], is quoted in Hebrews 10:5–7 in reference to Christ's priestly work. Yahweh did not call for blood sacrifices but for obedience throughout one's whole life. Christ was obedient as prescribed.[34] The New Testament writers quoted Psalm 69 more than any other, except Psalm 22, when writing of Christ's sufferings. David experienced this suffering spiritually, mentally, physically, and socially when persecuted by Doeg. These experiences of David, the ancestor and type of Christ, were experienced with greater pain and anguish by Jesus the Messiah. Psalm 109 reveals what David suffered due to Doeg's actions. These Davidic experiences were a foreshadowing of the Messiah's suffering under the cruel treatment of his enemies.

Concluding Comments

Scholars have written much about the Mediator, who is the Messiah, as he is portrayed and described in the Psalms. After a study of all the Psalms that include references to the Messiah[35] and the preceding review of messianic references, the following conclusions should be considered.

The covenant Yahweh God made with Abraham and David and their seed is considered fundamental for what the Psalmists composed concerning the messianic Mediator (Ps. 89:3; 132:11, 12). Abraham and David had been assured that one from their seedline would serve as the covenant Mediator. Redemption was to come through these seedlines. The Psalmists believed this and wrote concerning this for the benefit of all people, present and future.[36]

Yahweh God's faithfulness in regard to his promises was repeated. The Psalmists were assured that an eternal dynasty was promised. It had been established. Yahweh God would not fail to have the descendants of Abraham and David serve as central and fundamental agents in that dynasty. Their offspring would be an eternal king. Yahweh God's promises concerning them would not fail. This was the basis of the hope that the Psalmists repeatedly expressed.[37]

The Psalmists exhibit a wide variety of expressions concerning the hope they had concerning the promised covenantal messianic Mediator who would reign eternally. In the midst of persecution, pain, and sorrow, they expressed an assurance that Yahweh God reigned and that this reign was firmly established and would continue. The messianic Mediator was King and would be forever. Hence there are, amid various circumstances, thanksgiving, joy, and praise.

The Psalmists, as inspired writers, responding to past promises concerning the messianic Mediator and reflecting on past revelations concerning him, were led to keep the promises made by Yahweh before the covenant people. And what was the best way to do that? They composed songs and Psalms that the people could learn and sing. In worship, both private and public, they reassured themselves of what the future held in store for them.

Eschatology in the Psalms

The Scope of Eschatology in the Psalms

Creation

The Scriptures testify to the reality that time began when God created the cosmos. Moses stated, "In the beginning" God created (Gen. 1:1). The Psalmist refers to this in poetic terms (104:1–6). David sang of Yahweh God's fingers crafting the moon and stars and placing them in the heavens (8:3 [MT 4]) and making man ruler over all the works of his (God's) hands. All animals, birds, and fish, made by God, are under mankind's feet (8:6–8 [MT 7–9]). Yahweh God, the ever reigning Lord, firmly established the cosmos (93:1, 2).

Providence and History in Time

The Psalmists reveal an intimate knowledge of people and events since creation was completed. There are intimations concerning the flood (29:10; 124:4). The patriarchs and the role in their covenant life and that of their progeny are known to the psalmists (47: 9 [MT 10]; 105:6, 9, 42). Jacob is referred to thirty-four times and his descendants are also mentioned (22:23 [MT 24]; 77:15 [MT 16]). Yahweh God's provision of a homeland was recorded (105:11). Reference to priests, prophets, and kings were included (74:9; 99:6; 105:15; 132:9). A review of what the Psalmists recorded can assure one that they knew their history, their ancestors, and how Yahweh God their Lord called and led them to carry out his purposes and plans. Yahweh God's providential rule and care upheld and directed his people so that they could and would be his agents throughout all time.

Beyond Time

The Psalmists exhibited a lively awareness that there was a future for them, their progeny, and Yahweh God's program. As was discussed in the preceding section, they were assured that the Mediator of the covenant would appear in due time and that his presence and work would continue beyond time. Indeed, there was "eschatology" in the hearts and minds of the psalmists.[38] Accompanying this intimation of an ever-continuing future were expressions of faith, hope, and expectation.

The basic point that is to be understood when considering the scope of eschatology in the Psalms is to realize that "eschatological time" began when Yahweh God created the cosmos and that all future events in time had a definite eschatological movement. There was to be an ever progressive outworking of Yahweh God's ultimate goal—a restored, perfect, fully consummated kingdom to the glory of God.

Terminology in the Psalms

The verb *'āḥar* is defined "to remain behind, to tarry or delay." Nouns, adjectives, and adverbs derived from this verb are often employed to express the thought of what follows. *Behind*, *after*, *afterward*, and *end* are terms that express nuances of what the verb intends to communicate. For example, children come from, or are after, their parents. Posterity follows previous generations.

The Psalmists, David and Asaph, expressed an eschatological thought when they wrote that the end of man is peace (37:36, 37; 73:17). Asaph also expressed an eschatological certainty when he wrote that Yahweh God guided him with counsel in life and afterward "you will take me to glory" (73:24) and he would be with Yahweh, his portion, forever (v. 26).

The verb *bô'* (to come) appears in various Psalms to express a future coming or entering. David led Israel to sing about the King of glory coming into the present fellowship of his people and abiding with them continually (24:7–9). The Psalmist sang about Yahweh's coming to judge the earth (96:13; 98:9). Asaph also referred to God's[39] coming with a devouring fire before him, summoning the heavens and earth which he, the judge, would bring into judgment (50:3–6).[40] This Psalm, with its theophanic opening, has a prophetic character; it points to a future time and beyond.[41] The composer of Psalm 118 also introduced a future perspective using the phrase "I will enter" (v.19) and "he who comes" (v. 26).

The term *'ôlām* according to a concordance appears more than 140 times. It is used in the Psalms to refer to the far past, ancient (24:9) times. The perspective of the Psalmists, however, using the term is predominantly future, that is, indefinite future or continuous existence. Translations of *'ôlām* vary, according to contexts and translator's choice; forever, forever and ever, everlasting, never ending, enduring, eternal. The phrase *bĕ'ad* and a term derived from *nāzaḥ* are also translated eternal.

The conclusion to this review of eschatological terms and phrases is that the Psalmists were conscious of past, present, and future time and beyond time. They were assured of their future whether in time or beyond time—in eternity.

Subjects of Eschatology

Eschatological terms used by the Psalmists were applied to two distinct personages, Yahweh God and people.

Yahweh God

Personally. There are not many passages in the entire Scriptures that apply eschatological terms directly to Yahweh God. He is described as eternal or everlasting in various ways.[42] Moses had included the ascription of "everlasting to everlasting" when he acknowledged God (90:2). Asaph led worshipers to sing that God is our God forever and ever and will be our guide even to the end (48:14). The Psalmists readily proclaimed that Yahweh God's word was eternal (119:89) and that his laws are also (119:44, 160). Yahweh God's name is forever and ever (145:2, 21).

Yahweh God's Attributes. The verb *'āhab* and noun *ăhābâh* do not appear often in the Psalms. Yahweh is said to love his people but no eschatological terms are used to qualify this love. The noun *ḥesed* is translated love, lovingkindness, mercy, and goodness. This attribute of Yahweh God is particularly described in eschatological terms. *Ḥesed* will endure forever (51:1 [MT 2]; 106:1; 107:1; 118:1, 2, 3, 4, 29; 138:8).[43] *Ḥesed* will always follow the believer (23:6). It shall be built up forever (89:2 [MT 3]) and is everlasting (100:5). *Mišpāt* and *zēdēq* (justice and righteousness) are the foundation (89:14 [MT 15] of his throne that will last forever (45:6; 89:29; 132:12).

Yahweh God's Covenant. The Psalmists gloried in the reality of being members of Yahweh God's covenant that is remembered forever (105:9; 111:5). This covenant will never fail, it will stand fast (89:28 [MT 29]) and will not be broken (89:34 [MT 35]).

Messiah. Yahweh God's Messiah, the Mediator, was not promised for a time or specific period. To David, the type of the Mediator, it was said that Yahweh God gave him life, length of days forever and ever (21:4 [MT 5]). David's descendant will sit at Yahweh's right hand until all opposition is crushed and his "priestly" office will be forever (110:1, 4). David's own descendant is the covenant Mediator, the Messiah, who would come in time and then return to the Father's right hand (118:19–24; Matt. 26:64; Mark 12:36; 14:62; 16:19; Luke 22:69; Acts 2:34).

Reign. The reign of Yahweh God before the Mediator's sitting at the Father's hand and his reign through the Son/Mediator is an everlasting reign. The Psalmists rejoiced and sang that Yahweh God reigns forever (9:7; 146:10). This eternal, everlasting, never ending reign is over the earth (97:1), among the nations (96:10), and over the nations (47:8).

Conclusion: Yahweh was the one and only God the Psalmists knew and believed in. He was their eternal God of whom they wrote and sang. His name, attributes, and reign were, are, and will be as everlasting as Yahweh God is himself. He, the ever-enduring One, is, was, and will be sovereign Lord in time and will bring all aspects of the cosmic kingdom to its final state of perfection. The Psalmists, directly and indirectly, sang of this covenant God as the eschatological sovereign Lord.

People

All people, male and female, created in the image of God have an eschatological existence. This means that once persons are conceived and born their existence will never end. All people are created for eternity. The writer of Ecclesiastes wrote *hā 'ôlām nātan bĕlibbām* (eternity he set in their hearts) (3:11), and went on to write *hōlēk hā 'ādām 'el bêt 'ôlāmô* (the man goes to home eternal) (12:5). Solomon is understood to have written the book of Ecclesiastes.[44]

Solomon is also the author of Psalm 72. He clearly exhibited an acceptance and understanding of "eschatology." Referring to the messianic King, he used similies comparing the King's endurance with the sun and moon (v. 5), that is, may he live for all time. And he added his name endures *lĕ 'ôlām* (forever) (v. 17). The point to be noted here is that as a Psalmist, Solomon spoke of life—a human life, enduring temporally and eternally.[45]

The Psalmists were fully aware that the antithesis was unavoidably present within all of humanity. There was and is a great divide. On one side are the wicked who are condemned forever and on the other side are those blessed forever. Indeed, there is an eschatological divide within humanity.

The Condemned. The wicked are referred to more than one hundred times in the Psalms.[46] The wicked are referred to as arrogant and proud who revile God (10:2,4, 13). They strut about freely (12:8 [MT 9]); they devise wicked schemes (21:11 [MT 12]; 37:7; 119:118) and plot against the righteous (37:12) and draw their sword against them (37:14). These characteristics, attitudes, and deeds of the wicked are repeated throughout the Psalms. And the composers know that Yahweh

God knows about them and will deal with them in time and for eternity. The Psalmists led Yahweh God's people to pray for and sing about their destruction in time and beyond time. They knew the wicked would perish (37:20) and that in the future of the wicked would be cut off (37:38). They would be rebuked and accused by Yahweh God (50:21), they would be brought down (55:23 [MT 24]) and swept away (58:9 [MT 10]). So the Psalmist prayed "may the wicked perish before God" (68:2 [MT 3]) but he also spoke with assurance that Yahweh God would destroy the wicked (145:20).

Most of the Psalmic references to the "end" of the wicked could be understood to refer to their life on earth. But there are statements and intimations that this end "destruction" is beyond time. Consider these statements. Salvation is far from the wicked (119:155) and there is no mercy for them (59:5 [MT 6]). Their way will perish (1:6). The arrogant wicked are cursed (119:21). There is no statement by the Psalmists as one is made by Paul, "eternally condemned" (Gal. 1:8, 9). But the Psalmists did indicate that they knew there was no future life with God beyond time, that is, in eternity for the wicked. What the wicked will not have or experience is clearly perceived when one considers what the believer (the righteous), will receive and experience.

The Blessed. The Psalmists were assured that for them and believers there were blessings for them in their lives in time and beyond time. Indeed, they expressed a strong eschatological hope. David wrote of the blessings through life that Yahweh his Shepherd gave him. Goodness and steadfast love would be his all the days of his life. And he would dwell in Yahweh's house *lĕ'orek yāmîm* (for length of days) (Psalm 23). This phrase is "in itself not an expression for eternity."[47] The Christian understanding of this phrase is that nothing will separate us "neither in death nor life" from the love of God in Christ Jesus our Lord.

David reflected on all time when he addressed Yahweh his Lord (31:1 [MT 2]). He wrote "let me never (*lĕ'ôlām*: forever) be put to shame." Surrounded by enemies, he praised Yahweh, saying *bĕyādkâ 'ittōtî* (in your hands [are] my times) (31:15 [MT 16]). David was assured his covenant Lord was in control of his life at all times because of Yahweh's ever-present love (*hešedīkâ*) for him. He went on to glory in the blessed reality that he was *yazzîbēnî* (hiph. pf. of *yāzab*) set or stationed before the face of Yahweh *lĕ 'ôlām* (forever) (41:12 [MT 13]). In this passage, David presented an eschatological perspective that stretched from the very day he was surrounded by enemies and onward through all of life and into and through all eternity.

Asaph wrote as David did. He too had been surrounded by the wicked that prospered and were proud and violent (73:2–9). He was despondent, thinking his efforts to be innocent and pure were not recognized by his Lord. When he entered into the sanctuary of God, where he was in the presence of Yahweh (73:17a), who was his refuge (73:28), he realized he had been senseless and ignorant. This blessedness gave strength to his heart, in present time. But he included that what he had in time was also *lĕ 'ôlām* forever. It was to be ceaseless through time and eternity. It should be emphasized: Asaph was aware of his security and peace, in both time and eternity, when he sought and was in the presence of God, his Lord.

The unknown author of Psalm 135 also gave expression to eschatological assurances. In time he knew and experienced that Yahweh is good and greater than all gods (v. 5). He had done great things in the past, in Egypt, in Transjordan, and for his people (vv. 8–12). The covenant Lord of his people is renowned *lĕdōr wĕdôr* (for generations and generations (v.13b). The Lord's fame was and would endure through all generations, that is, for all time. The Psalmist was definitely eschatologically sensitive for he praised *semĕkâ* (your name) that endures both in time and eternity (*lĕ 'ôlām*).

Conclusion to the Study of the Book of the Psalms

The Book of Psalms is truly the Old Testament Book of Praise, Prayer, and Petition. The three themes (Golden Cable), unite to present a rich and integrated message. It reveals the great love, compassion, and providential care of Yahweh God. It reveals his righteousness and justice. It also reveals how those who know, trust, and obey him rejoice in having Yahweh God as their personal sovereign ruler, redeemer, and provider.

The book of Psalms teaches Yahweh's covenant people to express their need of him, their security in him, and an assured eternal future with him.

More than any other biblical book, it leads the trusting and honoring believer to sing: To God be the Glory, now and forever.

Notes

1. Cf. chap. 39, 145–48.

2. Various scholars have spoken of "myth" when referring to biblical or religious persons or phenomena. They do so when a story of unknown authorship seems to reflect some historical basis and is used to explain some phenomena of nature, the origin of man, or religious rites or customs and the continuing and future aspects of these.

3. Thorir Kr Thordarson attempted to present a degree of understanding of what the psalmists meant when using certain terms that are somewhat elusive but suggest a deeper meaning. He did not accept that "mythology" is included in the Psalms. He did, however, conclude that "the language of the Psalter is . . . intimately involved in the world-view of myth and mythology" because the psalmists are concerned with "the depth aspect of the human psyche. . ." Cf. "The Mythic Dimensions," *Vetus Testamentum,* 24, 1974, 212–220.

4. Cf. Van Groningen's detailed studies of all the Messianic Psalms. *MROT,* 333–414.

5. Cf. *MROT*, 397–407. This Psalm can be analyzed in various ways. Compare sketch on p. 399 with a second one here.

6. Kidner referred to "the many voices that are heard in this Psalm." *Psalms 73–150*, 412–16.

7. Note what Kidner wrote, ibid. 415. "The New Testament leaves no doubt that this stone foreshadowed Christ." Ps. 118:21–23; Matt. 21:42; Rom. 9:32; Eph. 2:20; 1 Peter 2:6–8. Grosheide, *De Psalmen*, wrote "De steen bij uitnemendheid is de Christus (the stone by excellency is the Christ)," II, 123.

8. The preceding chapters of our study of the Golden Cable in the Psalms discuss the kingdom and the covenant.

9. In 1990 my book *Messianic Revelation in the Old Testament* was published after more than 20 years of study of the many references to the Messiah in the Old Testament Scriptures. In the past 12 years, some other authors have discussed aspects of the Old Testament references to the Messiah. Some of these were included in the bibliography included in the notes of chap. 38.

10. Ibid., 19–22.

11. Ibid., 333–339.

12. Ibid., 390–397.

13. Ibid., 339–342. See also article by W. O. Walker Jr., "The Origins of the Son of Man Concept as Applied to Jesus," *Journal of Biblical Literature* 91 (1972): 482–90. Walker wrote that scholars agree that the phrase "Son of Man" is "kind of messianic." He suggested that the concept was derived from Jewish apocalypticism, particularly as it arose in Hellenistic circles in Jerusalem in distinction from Hebrew people who held to "Son of David Christology."

14. *MROT*, 342–43.

15. C. Schoeder has written an analysis of Ps. 45, and entitled his essay "A Love Song: Ps. 45." *Catholic Biblical Quarterly* 58 no. 3, (1996): 417–22. His appeal to Akkadian and Sumerian marriages led him to write that the words of Ps. 45 were not addressed to Yahweh but to a human king with Godlike features. This marriage reflected in Ps. 45 revealed that war and love were twin pillars of the God-like king's marriages. The studious efforts of critical scholars to find extra biblical sources for specific biblical concepts exhibit a lack of confidence in the unique character of biblical revelation. It is not to be denied, however, that biblical authors reflected aspects of their culture. These cultural aspects did not dominate the content and meaning of the cultural terms that were used.

16. Carefully review what is presented in *MROT*, 367–68 and take note of sources cited in the notes.

17. Ibid., 385, 86.

18. Ibid., 403.

19. Kidner, *Psalms 73–150*, 415. Cf. also Anderson, *Psalms 73–150*, 803.

20. Grosheide, *De Psalmen*, II, wrote that the stone was Jesus Christ on whom the entire building, the church, rests, 123.

21. Delitzsch intimates that there is some indication in vv. 19, 20 to the resurrection. *Psalms*, III, 230. He also intimates that Ps. 81 likewise has an indirect reference to it; note his title "Easter Festival Salutation and Discourse" to his comments on Ps. 81. *Psalms*, II, 390.

22. In *MROT* reference is included to Peter, who preaching on Pentecost, referred to Ps. 16:10 as a prediction of the resurrection, 393.

23. Cf. discussion on "Messianic Typology" Ibid., 153–67.

24. Ibid., 348–49.

25. Ibid., 349–53. Note should be taken when considering a Psalm such as 21 that there is thanksgiving and joy expressed; hence W. Chantry in his *Praises for the King of Kings* gave proper recognition of the praises Israel rendered to their human and divine kings.

26. *MROT*, 353–58.

27. Ibid., 361–62.

28. Ibid., 386–87.

29. Ps. 102, as do other Psalms, gives tribute to the worldwide honor due Yahweh for he is the eternally enthroned one.

30. Botha, "Enthronement Psalms," *Old Testament Essays*, 11 no.1, (1998): 24–39.

31. *MROT*, 371–73.

32. Ibid., 379–85.

33. Ps. 110 was briefly discussed in the preceding under the heading "Direct Prophecy."

34. *MROT*, 358–61.

35. *MROT*, cf. 333–414. One should take notice of the extensive bibliography included in this study.

36. R. M. Shipp, in his essay, "The Chronicler's Use of the Psalms," *Restoration Quarterly* 35, no. 2 (1993): 29–39, referred to the Chronicler's references to the Psalmists' assurance that David was assured an eternal dynasty. Indeed, in the postexilic times, the expectation for a covenant messianic Mediator was present. Cf. also Sue Gillingham, "Messianic Prophecy in the Psalms," esp. the first part in which she reviewed how this prophecy was believed and preached in the former two centuries, 1800–2000. *Theology* 99 (1996): 114–24.

37. See the article "The Messianic Hope in the Psalms" by David Starling, *Reformed Theological Review* 58, no.3 (1999). Starling refuted writers such as S. Mowinckel and others who were under "the influence of the anti-supernaturalism of the Enlightement" and under form critical methods espoused by H. Gunkel, 122–34.

38. T. K. Thordarson wrote concerning an element of eschatology in Ps. 84:2–8. There is the expectation of natural phenomena, e.g., rain, to come. But, he wrote that there is a mythic way of looking and considering this expectation—it is the spirit of expectancy and waiting on the Lord, expecting God's power and glory to be manifested "as a wonder-working agent in and through the events of nature and history." *Mythic Dimension*, 215. Thordarson was correct to see an eschatological perspective, but he errs when he limits it to nature and history.

39. Asaph, the author of this Psalm (and eleven others), when referring to God, uses only the name *'ĕlohîm*.

40. Commentators differ on a precise explanation of this Psalm. Delitzsch considered verses 1–3 to be a theophany. Israel is called before the divine tribunal. *Psalms II*, 126, 27. Kidner would have readers reflect on Israel before Mount Sinai. *Psalms I*, 186. He did not present the occasion. Alexander, likewise, refrains from indicating any occasion. *The Psalms*, 294. Van Gemeren also refers to a theophany, a Sinaitic type of setting, in which the covenant people are called into judgment. "Psalms," 373, 374.

41. Cf. Anderson's comment. He wrote that this is reminiscent of the oracles of classical prophets and therefore this Psalm has been described as a prophetic liturgy. *Psalms 1–72*, 381.

42. Cf. chap. 39, 146.

43. Each of the 26 verses of 126 has the term *la 'ôlām* and is translated endure in the NIV, KJV, and RSV, but everlasting in NASB and BV.

44. See D. Kidner, "Introduction to Ecclesiastes," NIV *Study Bible* (Grand Rapids: Zondervan, 1985), 991. Cf. also chap. 47 in this volume.

45. This Psalm is a typical messianic prophecy in which realistic concepts are employed to refer to eschatological realities.

46. This is in the NIV.

47. Kidner, *Psalms,* 1–72, 112, 113.

46

The Golden Cable in Proverbs

I. Introductory Comments to Part IV

II. The Book of Proverbs

46

The Golden Cable in Proverbs

Introductory Comments to Part IV

The Unique Character of Each of the Four Books: Proverbs, Ecclesiastes, Song of Solomon, and Lamentations[1]

This study on the four books is part of a biblical theological study. The Pentetеuch, the Former Prophets, the Prophets, and postexilic writings all were theologically oriented writings in which major theological subjects appeared. These were often woven into and integrated with historical events. Those could be, and were traced, as the progress of Yahweh God's revelation was discerned and discussed.

In the preceding chapters, it was without much difficulty that the historical contexts of the book of Job and of many Psalms could be discovered and included in the biblical theological discussion. The situation with Proverbs, Ecclesiastes, Song of Solomon, and Lamentations is uniquely different in that historical contextual references are lacking. And more challenging is the effort to discern if these books can correctly be classified as wisdom books.

Can These Books be Considered Theological?

The challenge before a student of these books is to discern and spell out the theological content of each. There is no direct reference to Yahweh God revealing himself, his purposes and relationship with persons or events. So can it be presupposed that there is the biblical theological content seen in the study of thirty-five other Old Testament books? One commentator wrote that one can think of Proverbs in two ways in terms of theology. It can be said to be untheological because it does not speak directly about theological issues. It can be considered very theological because it teaches about the very foundation of wisdom, " The Fear of the Lord."[2]

The Search for an Integrated Theological Message

The basic question, since these four books reveal "practical issues for life," is: would one be guilty of imposing a theological framework or "system" if one proceeds to study these books as the other Old Testament books were interpreted and presented? It is the firm belief of the present writer that to proceed with a biblical theological study of these four books should be in accordance or agreement with previous studies.

The issue or problem can be stated simply and clearly. Are the three strands of the Golden Cable—the kingdom, the covenant, and the mediator—the coalescing themes of the revelation Yahweh God has given in these four books? Are these three themes the central cords that unite, integrate, and more fully expose the divine revelation Yahweh God has for mankind living in various ages, times, and places?[3]

Is the Gospel Presented in These Four Books?

The gospel of redemption from sin is an integral part of Yahweh God's inerrant and infallible revelation as recorded in the Scriptures. Can it be truthfully and sincerely stated that this gospel is an integrally embedded and influential aspect in the very heart of these four books?[4] It will be shown in the studies that follow that one can be assured that it is.

Is There to be a Consistent Presentation of Wisdom?

The four books considered in Part IV are included in the category of wisdom literature. One must not conclude from this that these four books share wisdom characteristics to any great extent. Authorship differs, as does literary style. Life's issues are discussed in various ways. Amid these differences there nevertheless is a common dominant interest in life as it is experienced by the human race and particularly by those who are included in the chosen people of Yahweh God.

The Book of Proverbs

Literary Aspects

Authors

Most of the commentators and theological writers on Proverbs who have included an introduction found it necessary to include the structure of the book under the heading of "The Authors of Proverbs." The reason for this is obvious. The book itself indicates that there were various authors and that the writings of these were not presented in any specific order.

The problem of discerning authors is not difficult. But, when a survey is made of the different parts, one is faced with unexpected complexities. The author of the prologue (1:1–7); cf. 1:8–9:18) and of the epilogue (31:10–31) is not included. Nor are the names of the two groups of wise men (22:17–24:34). Solomon is referred to as the author of 10:1–22:16, and Hezekiah is listed as collecting more of Solomon's proverbs (25:1–29:27).[5] Two men are mentioned as authors, Agur (Prov.30:1) and Lemuel (31:1–9). Agur was not an Israelite; he is thought to have been an Ishmaelite. Lemuel, sometimes identified with Solomon, is an unknown writer. His words have been seen as an introduction to 31:10–31, that presents the "ideal woman" because he discussed sex and wine as well as good government.

So what is one to conclude concerning the structure? A consultation of studies reveals different divisions. Kidner in the "NIV Introduction" listed nine divisions but in his introduction to his commentary he listed eight.[6] There is no agreement on how to divide the material of Proverbs.[7] Again, the question arises, is there a unified, integrated message in the book of Proverbs? Did these different authors agree and were the various parts joined because of this agreement?

Sources

The question to be answered is: did the writers of Proverbs use and depend on various sources that came from neighboring countries? We should consider the two-fold biblical wisdom first. Solomon is considered the author of most of the Proverbs because superscriptions record that he is the author. The first verse states that the Proverbs are "of Solomon son of David, king of Israel." Proverbs 10:1 repeats this "The Proverbs of Solomon," 25:1 records "these are more proverbs of Solomon." There is no textual evidence that would indicate that these superscriptions can be considered incorrect. It is true that, according to the text, not all of Solomon's proverbs were collected at the same time. There is good reason to accept that view. Solomon did not speak all his wise sayings in one "presentation." The writer of 1 Kings gives us helpful information.

A consideration of 1 Kings 4:29–34 brings the following realities before the reader. First, it is stated plainly that God gave Solomon wisdom, great insight, and a breadth of understanding. Second, he was wiser than the men of Egypt and the men of the east. He was wiser than recognized wise men (v. 31). Third, in his many wise sayings and songs he spoke concerning aspects of nature. The natural realm of the cosmic kingdom was well known to him. Fourth, men of all nations came to listen to Solomon (v. 34). There is no biblical reference to Solomon learning from his fellowmen; rather, the text states that other wise men learned from him.

The question that is asked, basically because of chronological realities is: did Solomon, writing the Proverbs, make use of foreign sources? Did he make use of Egyptian wise men's sayings, that is, of Amenemope who lived at least a century before Solomon's time? It is not uncommon to read that evidence has been "greatly strengthened if not clinched, by chronological factors that Solomon did make use of Egyptian sayings."[8]

It is well known that Solomon was a man of many interests and international contacts and relationships. Being wise, he readily recognized "truth" that was known and spoken in non-Israelite contexts. All people of all nations have God-given talents. In and before Solomon's time, wisdom was a known virtue. Expressions of wisdom in foreign contexts need not be considered contrary to revealed truth. The point to be stressed is that Solomon, with his God-given talents and abilities, recognized truth in various areas of life. He evidently did not hesitate to take sayings of others as sources for his own. And as he adopted and adapted, he was led by the inspiring activity of his Lord.[9]

Characteristics

Many Forms. Delitzsch has referred to the "manifold forms of the Proverbs." One factor, however, must be kept in mind: the sayings in Proverbs are not to be compared with many popular "one-line" sayings in Arabic literature.[10] These various biblical forms indicate a specific element of originality. Topics and themes found in other cultural wisdom writings can be found in the Bible, but the manner of expression and various forms do indicate a biblical originality. Commentators have pointed out that the "original literary vehicle" is the "unit-proverb" that often comes in parallel form, but not to be overlooked are the many longer and involved forms that are developed in the Bible.[11]

These "manifold forms" do not detract from the overall message and submessages. The diversity of forms spells out the richness of the message. These enable the reader and student to discern and appreciate the wide ranging presentation of the theological content embedded in the Proverbs. Yahweh God's revelation did not come only in historical, legal, and prophetic forms of revelation, as was pointed out in the study on the Psalms. Psalms can best be considered to be response literature that inspired poets composed. Proverbs can also be included in the category of response revelation, but it differs from the Psalmic response in that the Proverbs reveal an inspired reflective activity on the part of the writers. These men combined a vision of the fullness of human life and knowledge of the richness of Yahweh's revealed will for this life. And they demonstrated their ability, as they were led and carried by the Holy Spirit, to express themselves in remarkably diverse ways as they wrote their contributions to the book of Proverbs.

It should be repeated, the manifold forms of the Proverbs do not detract from the theological message, but enhance the fullness and richness of the divinely inspired revelation Yahweh gave to his people, the theocratic kingdom, the church, and the world.

Poetic. It is necessary to bring to the attention of readers and students that Proverbs can be included in the "poetic genre." Robert Alden has written that the text of Proverbs is basically poetic rather than prose. He considers poetry to use a larger vocabulary; it "scrambles the word order for subtle effects and meanings are implied rather than stated directly."[12] Kidner revealed good insight when he wrote, "Modern hands itch to smooth irregularities, often overlooking the fact that an asymmetrical proverb can be richer than a symmetrical, by containing both an implied antithesis and a stated one." He referred to Proverbs 15:2 as a good example.[13] Scott referred to some poetry and some proverbs in the book of Proverbs.[14] Toy first presented a discussion of characteristics of poetry, and then he offered an example of the lines in Proverbs that are arranged almost without exception in couplet (distichal) and triplet form.[15]

One can readily be confirmed in accepting the conclusion that rather than hinder the effort to discern and understand the theology, and for this work, the Golden Cable (kingdom, covenant, Mediator) of the book of Proverbs, this effort is abetted and enriched.

Didactic. Most commentators, in one way or another, emphasize that the book of Proverbs is didactic. It teaches. A father teaches his son concerning vital aspects of life. The wise men teach whoever will listen. Often the call to listen and learn is issued. Longman wrote that Proverbs bombards the reader with pithy advice about a host of subjects.[16] Another student and writer on Proverbs made a list of the subjects the book refers to in various ways and at differing lengths.[17] These all are presented in a didactic manner.

The teaching concerning these many themes may not be readily absorbed. One reason for this may be that, as a commentator wrote, "proverbial" sayings are like pearls without a string.[18] An effort to categorize these sayings, proverbs, and themes has not been very successful.[19] Added to the difficulty of grasping the message, or messages, are the highly symbolic presentations. Many of these have deeper meanings than is initially apparent.[20]

The conclusion to this brief reference to the didactic character of Proverbs should be readily apparent. The book of Proverbs is very rich in content that is expressed often in poetic manner and in many forms. Thus, a reader and student cannot only learn the content but also the literary richness of Yahweh God's revelation given through inspired wise men. It takes time and it requires patience and perseverance to read, study, and grip the richness of the Book of Proverbs, as it does all wisdom literature.[21]

Content: Three Main Themes

Three subthemes should be considered. It hardly seems necessary to repeat that Proverbs refers to many aspects of cosmic life and existence. This rich collection of *mislêy*[22] are not exclusively religious. Its teachings apply to human problems in general and not to major theological themes such as election and redemption.[23] The "proverbs," however, do reflect a number of foundational themes.[24]

The Relationship of Man with God

Proverbs does not use the term *God* often.[25] That, however, cannot be construed to mean that the writers of Proverbs did not have their God in mind or that there was no basic concern about God as they wrote. That Proverbs is said to be not exclusively religious does not mean God was considered to have a minor role. Rather, what is pervasive throughout the book of Proverbs are God's Law and God's wisdom. And these are developed so that man can know and live with God in his daily life.

The book of Proverbs is not a book of laws. The relationship of the Law to wisdom sayings has been discussed from various perspectives. It must be stressed, however, that one must not separate Law and wisdom. Wisdom is not merely the "fine tuning" of the Law. It has been correctly stated that the "principles of the Mosaic law" apply to new and changing circumstances.[26] For example, David and Solomon lived and reigned in a period long after Moses lived and after the theocratic kingdom had been established. The New Testament religious, social, and legal *Sitz im-Leben* had changed considerably from David's time. But the principles and intent of the Law did not basically change.

The people living in contemporary society must realize that the principles of the Mosaic Law abide and are directly applicable to daily life. Wisdom literature provides a rich resource for knowing how to understand and apply the basic principles and directives of the Mosaic Law to the ever-changing aspects of modern spiritual, social, and cultural life considered in its widest ramifications.

One purpose then of Proverbs is to illustrate and demonstrate how the basic principles of the Mosaic Law are divine revelation for ever progressing and enriching modern life. And it must be emphatically stated: as cosmic life progressively changes, the principles of the Mosaic Law do not! And, it must also be emphatically stated that the development of the principles of the Law, as revealed in Proverbs, is to be considered divine instructive revelation for all ages and circumstances. Indeed, the writers of Proverbs had a deep and abiding concern about man's relationship with God. God's Law and wisdom were and are key components in man's relationship with God.

The Relationship of Man with Fellowman

The writers of Proverbs were men embedded in societal life. Their purpose, in co-ordination with their stressing the relationship with God, was to call attention to Yahweh God's revealed will concerning how his imagebearers relate with and influence their fellowmen. The relationship of husband and wife and the relationship of parents with children are particularly and emphatically set out. The social relationship the Proverbs teach is also very dependent on the living and functioning relationship between God and mankind. To honor God, husbands are to be faithful to their wives and they are to refuse to pay attention to harlots/prostitutes. Children, young as well as older, are to honor parents.

The authors of Proverbs also emphasized the tragic reality of much human wickedness.[27] This wickedness was not abstract. It was the character of those who were evil, defying God, and seeking to divert men's attention and devotion away from God. The tragic effects and results of wickedness are demonstrated in words[28] as are the passages on love.[29]

The Relationship of Man with the Cosmic Kingdom

The authors of Proverbs were men who gave much evidence that they were inhabitants of God's created world. The earth particularly with its natural elements and assets were widely known. Hence, as the authors sought to teach the importance of the relationship of people with God and fellowmen, they stressed the importance of all aspects of the created world. These were God-given gifts for the enrichment of human lives. The misuse or neglect of these were referred to as contrary to God's will and purposes for human life as well as his own honor.

In conclusion to this brief discourse on the purpose of Proverbs, one should realize that the three basic covenantal mandates and relationships are the very warp and woof of life in the cosmos.[30] In a succeeding section of this study, the covenant in Proverbs will be studied in more detail.

The Kingdom

Are There Direct References?

Kingdom is the initial strand that is observed in the Golden Cable that unites the biblical message. In preceding studies the concepts of kingdom and king were quite dominant. The kingdom provided the context, the setting for the other two strands, the covenant and the Mediator. In the book of Proverbs, the term *malkuth* (kingdom) does not appear once nor do the terms *mālkâh* (queen) or *melek* (reign). The term *king* appears more than thirty times in various contexts. Thus, the idea of kingdom as a domain, whether considered geographically or spiritually, is not a central issue. The poerson, however, who has royal status, position, power, or influence as he lives among and reigns over people is considered a major factor in life as portrayed by the authors of Proverbs. And, the reference to the presence of the king and his character and his influence certainly indicates that the authors were very aware of the concept of kingdom. A king without a kingdom was not considered. So, in this study the kingdom is considered the context in which life is lived and the character of the kingdom is described and understood to be demonstrated by the king under God who rules over all aspects of the kingdom.

Aspects of the Kingdom

The King

God. Yahweh God is referred to by his two names, God and Yahweh.[31] The name *'ĕlōhîm* (God) appears five times, 2:5, 17; 3:4; 25:2; 30:9. These references indicate that God is recognized as sovereign. Reference is to his knowledge (2:5), his covenant (2:17), his presence (3:4), his glory (25:2), and his name (30:9). The references to his covenant name, Yahweh or Lord, are more numerous.[32]

Passages that refer to God (*'ĕlōhîm*) indicate that God is mysterious; it is the glory of God to conceal a matter (25:2), but kings who reign by God's wisdom (8:15), are to search out these mysteries. The majority of the *'ĕlōhîm* passages speak to what God will do and does to the king who fears him (24:21).

Human. The practical aspect of Proverbs is demonstrated by the repeated emphases on what God the King does for his vicegerents, the human kings reigning under him. This king's throne is established through righteousness, that is, under God and in accordance with God's Law; he thus detests wrongdoing (16:12;

20:26). He speaks truth (oracle) and maintains justice (16:10). Love and faithfulness keep the king and his throne secure (20:28). He will be stately as he leads and stands before his army (30:31). A study of Proverbs assures one that as all servants of Yahweh God are called to fear God and attain wisdom, it is the king who is called to demonstrate this in every aspect of his personal life, his relationship with kingdom people and the world.

The Cosmic Kingdom

Neither *cosmic kingdom* nor *natural world* is found in the book of Proverbs. Nor do the Hebrew terms that refer to creator, creation, or creatures appear in Proverbs. The term *'ām* that refers to people is translated creature (NIV, 30:25, 26). Yet commentators and biblical theologians do not hesitate when discussing Proverbs to develop themes such as creation theology. Perdue referred to it as a central concept.[33] He wrote the Creator (God) shapes, directs, and sustains cosmic, social, and individual life.[34] Bostrom likewise referred to "Creation Theology."[35] He maintained that creation theology underlies wisdom, especially wisdom literature.[36] He went on to write that the concept of God in creation is dominant. He is the sole and sovereign Creator and Ruler of the universe. He is a God of order, a supreme, sovereign, transcendent, and personal God.[37]

Another student of Proverbs wrote that empirical knowledge of animals is revealed in the book of Proverbs.[38] Fauna, also the flora, come in for close analysis.[39] He considers that for the writers of Proverbs animal images operate as figurative elements.[40] Forti continued to develop his thesis by a study of what the "Sages" wrote about the ant (6:6–8); the bear (17:12), the lion (22:13); the dog (26:11, 17), and birds (26:2; 27:8).[41]

The writers of Proverbs reflected that they lived in a creational setting in which animals, domestic and wild, had their habitat and role. The cosmic kingdom created and ruled by God also included grain (11:26; 27:22) and grass (19:12; 27:25). Trees were referred to as symbols of life (3:18; 11:30; 27:18). Vineyards were regarded as evidence of initiative (31:16) or the lack of it (24:30) on the part of men and women.[42] And as the authors wrote referring to animals and plants in the cosmic kingdom, they considered all these to be God-given and controlled by God the Creator and Sustainer. Those who would separate the book of Proverbs into two parts, one that is theological "having the names of God or religious language" and the other that presents secular aspects, do violence to the integrated messages of Proverbs. The theological and religious is integrated with all aspects of the cosmic kingdom.[43]

The Theocratic Kingdom

The authors of Proverbs wrote for men and women of all times and places. But the evidence is clear that the reign of the theocratic King of Israel is the immediate and direct context in which the book of Proverbs was written and assembled.

Solomon, the king, son of King David, is a main author. He wrote for the people of the kingdom over which he ruled. He specifically addressed all the people whom he knew were members of the theocratic kingdom that had been established with David as the ruling king before him.

It is important to remember that the theocratic kingdom of Israel was an inherent part of the cosmic kingdom. And its place and role in that all-inclusive and embracing kingdom was to serve as a living and influential "model" or "example" of how the cosmic kingdom and all other kingdoms within it should consider themselves as under Yahweh God's sovereign rule.[44] The principles of the revealed Law explicated, demonstrated, and applied for theocratic kingdom living were and are intended as Yahweh God's instruction for all people. The theocratic kingdom members had the duty to demonstrate in all of life's situations how all aspects of life were to be influenced and governed by Yahweh God's detailed explanations for living a rich and blessed life.

The Covenant

Are There Direct References?

The term *bĕrît* occurs once in the Hebrew text (2:17). It is translated covenant in the various English texts. The use of the term is in the context of the warning against the wayward wife, who having left her husband became an adulteress, using seductive words to draw men into an adulteress relationship.[45] To be noted is that the text speaks of the wife *śākĕhâh* (*śākâh*, to forget or ignore) the *bĕrît* of her God. The implication is that marriage is a covenant ordained by God (Gen. 2:20–24).

This passage introduces the biblical student to the divinely ordained human marriage covenant that in turn introduces the divinely ordained bond between Yahweh God and specifically his elect people. Indeed, the marriage covenant is a symbol of and represents the intimate relationship Yahweh God established and upholds with his covenant people. This covenant includes the various aspects.[46] In what follows in this study are six selected covenantal issues directly referred to or implied.[47]

Select Covenantal Issues in Proverbs

Yahweh God and Human Relationship. The covenantal relationship of Yahweh God is stressed in various ways. Some of these, as for example, the Law and fear of Yahweh God, will be in sections following. In this section the specific emphasis is on the covenantal relationship between Yahweh God and his people.

To be noted immediately is that the names *'ĕlōâh* (3:7); *'ĕlōhîm* (30:5), and *'ĕl* (2:5, 17; 3:4; 25:2; 30:9) refer to the only true deity who is almighty, strong, powerful, and sovereign. The writers refer to their God by these names: omniscience, omnipresence, glory, and name. It is clear that the writers felt secure in life because they knew and honored their God who protected them, kept them, guided them, and controlled all of life.

The covenant name, Yahweh, appears more than seventy times in the book of Proverbs. The idea of Yahweh God's relationship to the covenant is not stated. It is clearly understood. Yahweh God has bonded himself to his people. Thus people are to respond, or are called to, or are expected to acknowledge this bonded covenant relationship that Yahweh God established and maintains. In the five following sections specific themes that express this relationship will be discussed.

The authors of Proverbs wrote concerning the Maker.[48] Yahweh God was referred to as the One who established or laid the foundation of the earth and put the heavens in place (3:19). Yahweh, Maker of heaven and earth, is also the Maker of the poor people (14:31; 17:5)[49] and of people's ears and eyes (20:12). Indeed, all people, both rich and poor, have this in common, namely, *'ōśêh kullām yĕhwâh* (maker of all of them [is] Yahweh). God has created (made) all people and he bonded all people together as one humanity.[50] Not all human beings will recognize this bond between Yahweh God and themselves nor the bond between all people. But there is a universal call to all people. They must trust Yahweh God, regardless of status, position, and possessions.

All people are commanded *bătaḥ* (qal. imper. of *bātāḥ*, to trust). Yahweh with all their hearts. The verb *trust*, in Hebrew, emphasizes the act of full commitment, surrender, and reliance. Yahweh calls for the covenant bond he established to be recognized and honored. This is done by trusting. Thus the human and divine relationship becomes a true reality in the lives of covenant people.

Consider what more the writers urged their readers to do. People are to receive teachings today (each day) so that they may trust in the Yahweh (22:19). Instruction by word and example is necessary because sinners by nature do not trust Yahweh. A person is not to trust in himself. If he does he is a fool. Likewise greed brings dissension but prosperity will be the lot of him or her who trusts in Yahweh (8:18). And safety is given to those who truly trust in Yahweh (29:25). The trusting person is blessed (16:3).

At the very core of the covenant bond that Yahweh God established between himself and his people is love. The Penteteuch teaches it, the Psalmists reflected on the love of Yahweh and love for him. The authors of Proverbs indicated that they too are aware of the role of love in their relationship with Yahweh God. They referred to many men who claim to be unfailing, but the question is raised: "who can find faithful men?" (20:6). People, however, are urged to bind love and faithfulness around their neck and have them written on their hearts (3:3). This advice is evidence that the authors of Proverbs were aware of the Penteteuchal teaching concerning "love and faithfulness" (Deut. 6:5; 7:9, 10, 13; 10:12; 11:1, 13, 22; 13:3; 30:16). So they counseled their readers to pursue righteousness and love and thereby find the covenantal blessings of life, prosperity, and honor (14:22b; 19:22; 21:21) and Solomon added that by love and faithfulness sin is atoned for.

The relationship between Yahweh God and his people is enriched by the *torah* (law) and the *yir'ât Yĕhwâh* (fear of Yahweh).

The Law *(Torah)*. The term *Torah* occurs eleven times in the book of Proverbs. At times it is translated as teachings or instruction (1:8; 3:1; 4:2; 6:20; 7:2; 13:14). The term *miswâh* (command) is also used as a synonym of torah teaching (3:1; 6:20, 23; 7:1, 2; 13:13). When considering these terms one is led to reflect on what

Moses taught Israel when the covenant was renewed on the plains of Moab.[51] The authors of Proverbs indicated an intimate knowledge of covenantal prescriptions intended to enable people to enjoy a living relationship with their covenant Lord, Yahweh God.

When considering how the authors encouraged the covenant people to respond to the Torah, the covenantal instruction used various terms. A seeming preferred term is *keep*, but other terms—obey and *listen*—appear also. The covenant person thus is addressed and called to respond positively to the Torah, understood mainly as instruction in the word and way that Yahweh required his people to live.

What, according to the authors of Proverbs was the purpose or goal that Yahweh the covenant Lord had for his people to achieve? It was not merely the acts of obedience, keeping, or listening that Yahweh God had in mind. These were human means to gain and receive what Yahweh intended for his people. Life, true covenantal life, an active living fellowship with Yahweh God was one of Yahweh God's desires and will (2:19; 13:14).[52]

The life that Yahweh God intends for his covenant people is a wise life, a life of wisdom (1:2; 2:6; 3:13; 4:5, 7, 11; 9:10; 13:10, 14; 16:16; 19:8). A life of wisdom brings joy (29:3). The life of wisdom has assurance for safety (28:26), and the living wise person has the qualification to recognize and deal with folly and wickedness (2:12; 9:12; 17:24; 23:4).

The preceding discussion, under the subject of the Torah (law), opens one's mind to discern the integration of the Law, wisdom, and the life of the listening, discerning, keeping, and obeying covenant person. Indeed, the covenantal prescription summed up in the Ten Commandments is the divinely ordained guide and motivation for the joyous and secure life of Yahweh's covenant people.

The Fear of Yahweh God. The *yir'ât yĕhwâh* (the fear of Yahweh) is a covenant theme in the book of Proverbs.[53] This phrase serves as a key to understanding the entire book. This reality must be understood clearly. The opening verses of the book state that for attaining wisdom and discipline, a prudent life, knowledge and discretion for the young, and the understanding of proverbs, parables, and riddles of the wise the *yir'ât yĕhwâh* (fear of Yahweh) is the beginning.[54] It should be understood that the phrase refers to more than a principle.[55] This term has strong formal, legal, intellectual, and order intimations. The phrase is a thoroughly covenantal phrase. It refers first of all to a relationship[56] between Yahweh and his people. It is a relationship that is intimate and inclusive. The phrase evokes a sense of humility, awe, respect, admiration, piety, and reverence. The term *yīrâh* often refers to afraid or terror but in this passage (1:7) it does not.

This phrase holds before the reader that the covenant life is impossible if this "fear of Yahweh" is not present and functions as it is intended to. The Hebrew term *rê'šît*, a noun having *rō'š* (head) as its root, is translated ordinarily as beginning or chief. In the present context it stresses negatively that without the "fear of Yahweh" there is no possibility of acquiring that what it involves. It stresses positively that all that the phrase "fear of Yahweh" connotes is not only possible but that these aspects are incipiently present. The full, rich, divinely intended covenant relationship between Yahweh and his people is no longer hoped for. It is a present reality with all its ramifications and involvement. It is for the covenant person to understand, grasp, appropriate, and exercise these. The authors of Proverbs make it clear that there are those who do not choose or intend to be recipients of his blessed covenantal reality (1:29). It is to their loss.

Various consequences or blessings are enumerated when the "fear of Yahweh" is present and influential. As referred to before it leads to knowledge of Yahweh and a prudent life (1:1–6) that is not afraid of sudden disaster (3:25). It motivates to hating evil (8:13). It leads to a long life (10:27; 19:23). It is the fountain of life (14:27).

The Family. The book of Proverbs is a family book.[57] It refers to parents and children and their relationships and interactions. The family is addressed either through the mouth of the father, through wisdom personified, or through other spokesmen for the Lord.

The Hebrew term *'āb* (father) appears twenty-five times. The term *'ēm* (mother) occurs fifteen times and *'îššah* is translated either as woman, or wife, fifteen times. Children are referred to as *ben* fifty-five times. The term often includes daughters but is usually translated son. The term *na'ar* (child, lad, or youth) appears seven times. The many references to these family members present the reader and student with a number of theological and social issues. The social issues will be studied in the following section.

The theological issues are basically covenantal in character. First of all, it should be noted that Yahweh God's work in instituting the family as a covenantal entity underlies all that is presented. Consider the following.

The father is given a definite headship role. He is the dominant leader and spokesman for Yahweh God. He repeatedly, as he counsels and instructs his offspring, expresses his authoritative role saying "*my* son(s) (4:1; 5:7; 7:24; 8:32). The father also indicates his headship role when he refers to the dangers and temptations his offspring will face and which they must not surrender to at any time. The father gives positive guidance on social and cultural issues.[58]

The mother is set forth as a very positive partner in the covenant family. Twice the "sons" are urged not to forsake their mother's teaching. This counsel certainly stresses the teaching role of the mother in the family. It is interesting to note that the *mûsâr 'ābîkâ* (command of father) and the *tôrat 'immeka* (teaching, instructions, rules) of the mother are both stated in a synonomous parallel verse (1:8). Mother's role in the growth of the knowledge of God and his word and will is not secondary to what the father sets forth for his offspring. The roles of the father and mother, the husband and wife, are definitely complementary; the wife and mother does not have a subordinate or secondary role. But there is also reference to the unhappy and quarrelsome wife and mother. Divorce is not referred to. The advice is to share the same rooms in a home but suggests that a husband is better off if he lives in a corner of the flat roof of his house (21:9). There is one passage specifically that speaks concerning the important role the wife and mother in the covenantal family has. In the epilogue to the entire book of Proverbs, the character, role, and influence of the wife, mother, and helpmate, is brilliantly described. She is noble, trustworthy, wise, diligent, compassionate, charming, discreet, and blessed by her children and praised by her husband (31:10–31). But there will be those who curse their fathers and refuse to bless their mothers because they are haughty and filthy (30:11–14). They are also foolish sons and a grief to their mother (10:1). They go on to despise their mother (15:20). A son may drive her out and bring shame and disgrace upon himself (19:26). The counsel given is clear: listen to your father who gave you life and do not despise your mother when she is old (23:22). These instructions by the authors of Proverbs reveal that they took the fifth commandment to honor father and mother (Exod. 20:10) seriously as a divine injunction.

The son, child, children, can be correctly stated to be main characters in the book of Proverbs. It should be noted that after the prologue (1:1–7) that states that the attaining of wisdom, discipline, understanding, and prudence are absolute virtues for the covenant people, the son is addressed (1:8). This address is in complete agreement with revelation given prior to the time of Solomon and his fellow authors.

Yahweh God had spoken with assurance to Abraham (Gen. 18:18, 19). He had chosen him to direct his children and household in the way of Yahweh, their covenant Lord. The goal was to carry out what Abraham had been promised. To be clearly understood is that Yahweh God laid out his intentions and the method for realizing these promises. They would only be realized through his offspring. Hence, Abraham was commanded to prepare his offspring for the realization of the promise that all nations would be blessed through him (12:1–3).

Moses, when he renewed the covenant with Israel after they had been redeemed from Egypt and had been led out of the wilderness, instructed the people to impress upon their children that they love Yahweh, receive his instructions, and obey his commandments. So doing, the coming generation would inherit the land and prosper in it (Deut. 6:4–9).

Asaph, a leader in the house of Yahweh composed Psalm 78. He had parents resolve not to hide but tell to their children what Yahweh God had revealed in word and deed (vv.1–8). This instruction was to be so given that the fifth generation following them would hear Yahweh God's covenantal promises and obey the prescriptions included in that ever abiding covenant.

Solomon, who undoubtedly was the original and main author of the message given in the book of Proverbs, was entirely consistent with all previous revelation concerning Yahweh's intentions, deeds, and demands that the generations following should receive and obey. Solomon lived and reigned during the most golden era of Israel's history. In that period of opulence and national liberty, the instruction of the coming generation was of paramount importance. A golden future awaited the covenant people for generations to come. They had but to hear, learn, and obey the entire historical and theological message repeated in the writings already available in Solomon's time.[59]

The authors of Proverbs are direct in their address to their offspring and followers. They spoke with the imperative voice of the fathers or wise counselors to those they were addressing. But a parental bond is repeatedly revealed indicating that a covenantal duty was exercised. The "son"[60] was warned against the enticements of the wicked (1:10, 15; 5:20) and is urged to listen to his parents (2:1; 3:1; 4:10; 5:1; 6:3, 20; 7:1; 13:1; 23:15, 19). A "son" who listens brings joy to his parents (3:13: 10:1) but one who does not is a fool who brings grief (17:25) and ruin (19:13) to his father. Along with instruction a "son" may need discipline (19:18; 29:17) that can include the rod (13:24). Among various warnings given and the expression of joy and comfort that the wise "son" can give comes the challenge to not despise the Lord's discipline or rebuke (3:11; 24:21). The parents or counselors reveal clearly that they consider themselves as spokesmen for Yahweh God, the covenant Lord.

The authors of the book of Proverbs, as indicated in the preceding, directed attention to fathers and mothers teaching and counseling their offspring. They also wrote concerning what the *mûšâr*[61] *a bēn, na'ar* requires. The root of the term *mûšâr* is *yāsor,* translated as discipline, chasten, or admonish. The noun *mûšâr* emphasizes that its basic reference is to morality and godly living. The term *disciple* is derived from *discipline.* A disciple is one who has been taught and obeys what is taught and required of him. The offspring, to be a truly faithful covenant person, requires discipline in the sense of correction because folly is bound up in the heart of a *na'ar* (child or youth) (22:15). A child is not without sin; he or she is born in sin. Thus instruction and correction is required. It is not without purpose that the context includes the injunction *hānok* (qal imper. of *ḥānak,* to train up or dedicate) *lanna'ar 'al-pî darkô* (the child according to its way) (22:6). This passage has often been translated as "in the way he should go." Commentators have written that the correct translation is that a child should be trained according to his or her individuality and vocation.[62] The implication is that a child should be psychologically understood to determine his or her inherent potentialities and inclinations. But not to be forgotten is the theological factor, namely, that a child is affected by original sin, the root of folly in its heart. This folly must be removed and parents and counselors are instructed to use the *šebet mûsâr*. The term *šebet* is translated as rod, staff, club, or scepter. The unanimous interpretation of the term *šebet* is rod. Corporal punishment was universal in antiquity.[63] The rod of discipline is necessary to remove foolishness, not childishness.[64]

In the context of the entire book of Proverbs, the idea of training up a child is developed from various perspectives. A summary is in order. First, children are by nature not able to develop into covenantally alert kingdom members without instruction, training, and guidance. Sin and folly that are inherited by nature must be addressed, exposed, and, by God's Spirit, graciously challenged. Second, the instructed and trained child is to develop wisdom. It is the wise son or daughter that honors and obeys Yahweh God. Their covenantal relationship with their Lord is thus developed, strengthened, and matured. Third, the parents will be honored and blessed as a result of their offspring's receiving and living according to the wise instruction and counsel they were given. If sons and daughters did not receive instruction and were left to themselves they would be a disgrace to their mothers (10:1; 29:15) and bring grief and ruin to their fathers (17:25; 19:13). Fourth, in submitting to instruction, training, and discipline the "son" brings joy to his father (10:1) and becomes or is wise heeding his father and brings delights to him (23:24). Fifth, Yahweh God calls for the heart of the son (23:26). The heart is known to be the center and mainspring of life. If the heart is committed and dedicated to Yahweh God, the entire person in all the various dimensions of life is also.[65] Sixth, this instruction and training that must be given to each generation must not be limited to the personal covenantal relationship between a son and Yahweh God. Every aspect of the son's life is involved.[66] The social and cultural dimensions of life must be recognized as spheres of the kingdom. Covenant people are mandated to address these dimensions.[67]

Social Relationships. The primary social relationship presented in the book of Proverbs is the *family*, man/father, woman/wife/mother, and offspring. The authors of Proverbs indicated that they were fully aware that the covenant family was not an isolated island in the entire ocean of life. There were many other people with whom covenant people could (or should not) have a close relationship. A number of these will be highlighted.

The youth are counseled not to have the *wicked* as friends or companions. Do not enter the path of the wicked (4:14). They do evil, for their souls desire evil (21:10) and with perversity in their heart they continually devise evil (6:18; 26:25). They drink the wine of violence (4:7) and have a false mouth (6:12). They love and spread strife (17:19). It is to be remembered that the Lord has made the wicked for the day of evil (16:4) but the years of the wicked will be shortened (10:27). The curse of the Lord is on the house of the wicked (3:33). In contrast, seek the righteous and upright because the Lord blesses their dwellings. They, the upright will live in the land (2:21).

Among the wicked there are the fools; they are foolish and folly controls their hearts. The Hebrew term *'ĕwîlîm* (fools), a noun or adjective, appears eighteen times in Proverbs and the noun *'iwwel* (foolish) appears twenty-four times. These terms have been interpreted to refer to a thick-brained or stupid person who exhibits moral perversion and/or insolence. A fool is a grief to his father and bitterness to her who bore him. Neither have joy because of him (17:21). The fool is spoken of at length in 26:1–10. As a whip is for the horse and a bridle for the donkey, so a rod is fitting for the fools back (26:3). There is no future for the fool, because with his babbling he will be thrown down (10:10).

There are many references to and descriptions of the fool or the foolish person.[68] He is to be shunned and avoided. Social relationships with such persons can and most likely have an unwanted and possibly a deleterious influence on the righteous person. The antithesis is clear and sharp. Wickedness and folly are diametrically opposed to wisdom and righteousness. In the social arena of life these are to be increasingly gained and developed.

The wicked person whom the young men are to avoid is the adulterous woman especially. She may be a stranger (2:16) or one who has left her husband (2:17a). She is a covenant breaker whose house and life lead to death (2:17b–19). The adulteress's lips drip with honey and her speech is smoother than oil, but in reality her end is bitter as worm wood. She is sharp as a two-edged sword; she leads one on the way to death (5:3–5). Sons are therefore urged to listen to wise counsel (5:7). Keep away from the adulteress's door, don't give your vigor to a foreigner or let her be a cause of your groaning when your flesh and body are consumed (5:8–11). The wise man (young or older) should drink from his own cistern and spring; he must consider his own fountain blessed (5:16–18). He is urged to be faithful to his wife, be exhilarated with love, and let her satisfy him (5:18b–19).[69]

The authors of the book of Proverbs often referred to love and its opposite hatred. Love is not defined nor is hatred, jealousy, or anger. These social emotions are described and their consequences are made quite clear.

In previous studies it was pointed out that love is basically a covenantal bond between persons with various ramifications. In the preceding paragraph reference was made to married love and the violation of it with adultery. Love, however, is referred to as a bond in other relationships.

The Lord's love is set forth as a powerful inducement or motivation for his covenantal people to emulate. The father loves his son in whom he delights; this love is a God-given bond between parent and offspring (3:12). Parents' love is demonstrated in the disciplining of their children (13:24). This disciplining by parents of offspring exhibits love for knowledge (12:1). Thus both parent and son are enriched by this exercise of love.

Love, be it at a different level, is a powerful reality in various aspects of social life. In adversity suffered by one, a friend's love is healing (12:18) and such a bond between two persons results in a closer bond between friends than between brothers (18:24).[70]

Love between friends and neighbors is referred to in various ways. It assures honesty and mutual confidence (3:27–29; 6:1–3; 12:26). A person's love for understanding can be of benefit to a neighbor (11:12; 12:26). And love for purity of heart and gracious speech flowing from it is known by a king to heal and strengthen friendship (22:11).

To read the Proverbs and to take specific notice of how the covenant is exhibited as a bonding force is to be reminded that Moses taught the people to love Yahweh God (Deut. 6:4) and one's neighbor (Lev. 19:18b). Jesus repeated this law to love the neighbor (Matt. 19:19) as did Paul (Rom. 13:9). And one need not go further than the book of Proverbs to learn and be admonished to love fellow people in many situations and circumstances in life.

Cultural Dimensions. The God-directed integration of all aspects of daily life is strongly exhibited in the book of Proverbs. This reality cannot be dismissed lightly.

One may wish to neatly categorize the various elements in or facets of life. The truth is that although there are the three covenantal mandates, these can be distinguished but the relationship between them cannot be avoided. All of life is spiritually oriented, guided, and often driven. The social dimensions of life are influenced by the spiritual and vice versa. And equally important to recognize is the interaction between the cultural and social dimensions of life. Life is an integrated whole; thus reality does not negate the need to emphasize the cultural dimensions.

The authors of Proverbs reveal that they are fully aware that the social world is influenced in various ways by the cultural. Ancient as well as contemporary society was and is divided by "classes" of people. One cannot avoid the reality of social stratas. The rich, the wealthy are clearly recognized as distinct from the poor. In the eyes of Yahweh God, however, there is no basic distinction between the rich and the poor. He is "the Maker" of them all. They have a common bond (22:2). In society, however, wealth is a cultural reality. It is a blessing of Yahweh God (10:22). God-given riches, however, do not profit anyone as does righteousness in the day of death (11:9). In life wealth gives security (10:15) and Yahweh God can be honored through it (3:9, 10). In contrast, the person who trusts in wealth will fall (11:28a). Hence the prayer of Agur includes a wise petition, "Give me neither poverty nor riches." If I receive too much "I may disown you" Lord; if I become poor "I may steal and disown you" (30:8, 9. Greed, bribery, and deceit are often fostered by wealth (11:26; 17:23: 30:8a).

Work is a cultural phenomenon. It is incompatible with laziness. The sluggard is known for laziness (6:10) and he is as a hedge of thorns (15:19a). He does not plow his field when he should (20:4) and his untended vineyard becomes overgrown with thistles (24:30, 31). He refers to lions as an excuse for his laziness (22:13; 26:13). He is counseled, however, to go and consider the ant who prepares food in summer and gathers provision in the harvest (6:6–9). They (the ants) have no negligent hand (10:4) nor are they slack in their work (18:9). It is not stated outrightly in Proverbs, but within the entire context of Scripture, obedience to the cultural mandate is the divinely ordained means to relieve hunger (12:11) and feed the poor (25:21).

The authors of Proverbs are very much aware that there is a blessing Yahweh provides that can be tragically misused. It can become a serious detriment to all facts of life. It is alcohol. It is not referred to in the book of Proverbs by that term. The reference, however, to it is by wine that is spoken of twelve times.[71] A father counsels his son not to be with heavy drinkers lest he come to poverty (23:20, 21). Wine leads to mockery (20:1) and causes eyes to see strange things and the mind to express perversity (23:33).

Justice is an inherent and integral reality in the legal world. It has strong ramifications for the social sphere of life as it also has for the spiritual. It is in the legal dimension of life, however, that it is expressed. Kings decree justice (8:15) and partiality in judgment is not good (18:5; 24:23; 28:21). Yahweh God desires the execution of justice more than the bringing of sacrifices (21:3). Evil men do not understand justice, as do those who seek Yahweh God (28:5). They know that justice for man comes from Yahweh God (29:26).

"Flora and fauna of all natural phenomena are two dimensions which come in for close analysis in wisdom circles."[72] The authors of Proverbs do not refer to trees. They do refer to fields that God produced when he created the world (8:26). Fields can be the possession of the fatherless (23:10) and husbandmen are counseled to finish outdoor work and get their fields ready before they build their houses (24:27). The produce of the fields was more necessary for life than a house. Priorities in the cultural aspect of life were an important consideration. Grass[73] was considered a blessing for thus hay could be provided for lambs that provided material for clothes and for goats that provided milk for the family and servant girls (27:25–27). Rivers were not mentioned but the sea is (8:29) as are the oceans (8:24).

Animals were highly esteemed because of their enigmatic sense of direction and the way they move gracefully in space, be it on earth, in the sky, or in the sea.[74] The proverbial writers found analogies between facets of the social order of people and the manners and habits of animals. A fool in his folly is to be avoided more than a she-bear robbed of her cubs (17:12) The bear has more reason to do what she does than a fool who lacks common sense. A sluggard, not wanting to work, pulls a lion out of his stock of excuses. He thus evokes incredibility (22:13).[75] A fool who repeats his folly is analagous to a dog that returns to its vomit (26:11).

Birds were known to be faithful to their nest, and young (27:8). Men's useless and groundless curses were said to be like a bird that does not alight (26:2). Locusts having no king are known "to march in perfect formation"[76] (30:27) demonstrating wisdom and order.

There was and is much to learn of Yahweh God's wisdom by observing the animal world. Animals, whether large or small, coy or fierce, all instinctively reflect their character and individual propensities. They reveal the manifold wisdom of Yahweh God. They are present in the cultural/natural world in their own rights. And they are there for man and woman to know so that their own life can be enriched as they live and serve their Creator, Redeemer, and Lord.

The Mediator

Are There Direct References?

The Hebrew term *māšîah,* messiah, does not appear in the book of Proverbs. Nor does reference to the Messiah as Mediator appear.[77] This absence of specific terms that translate as mediator should not be understood to mean that the concept of one standing between or on behalf of is absent.

Mediatorial Agents

The reader/student of the book of Proverbs cannot avoid the reality of voices speaking on behalf of Yahweh God, the covenant Lord, to both covenant keepers and covenant breakers. Whose voices are these? An obvious answer is "the authors" are inspired spokesmen. They serve as mediators. They stand between God and the people to present Yahweh's word and counsel, and to explain and apply them. As the Old Testament prophets were mediatorial agents who represented Yahweh God and in various ways typified the Christ, the second person of the Trinity, the Word that became flesh, so also the wisdom writers served as agents, spokesmen, and types of the "promised Mediator." The authors, however, indicate that they are aware of other voices that represent Yahweh God.

Solomon was one of these authors. He is known to have been and serves as a type of Christ. He did so as ruler of the covenant people. His reign extended over much of the Mideast area (1 Kings 4:24, 25). His wisdom exceeded that of all wise men (1 Kings 4:29–34). "The whole world sought audience with Solomon to hear the wisdom God had put in his heart" (1 Kings 10:24) and part of this God-implanted wisdom is recorded in the book of Proverbs. Thus to read Proverbs is to read what Yahweh God revealed through his anointed agent. He ruled and taught as Yahweh God's Old Testament mediator.

Solomon addressed his wise instruction to "my son" in his opening address (1:8–19). He is understood to refer to himself as the son's father. The mother, however, is immediately referred to as teacher (1:8). She and the father are equally responsible to teach, train, and guide the youth. Both parents therefore should be considered mediators between Yahweh God and their children. Parental responsibilities as Yahweh's spokespersons include strong warning. Avoid the mockers (1:22; 30:17). Wine is a mocker (20:1) and whoever loves wine will never become rich (21:17). They will experience woe (23:29, 36). Parents warn against adulteresses (2:16; 5:3, 20; 6:26; 22:14). Work is encouraged (12:14; 14:23; 18:9; 21:25) but warnings against laziness are repeated (10:4; 12:24; 19:15). Laziness is a vice of the sluggard (26:15, 16).

Wisdom

The greatest challenge the reader, the student, or interpreter of the book of Proverbs faces is to understand what the authors intended to convey with the term *ḥokmâh* (wisdom) (1:2, 7). In the opening verses of the book, it is presented as an independent reality. It also is set forth as a synonym for correlating of discipline, understanding, prudence, knowledge, and discretion.[78] In Proverbs, wisdom can be understood in three ways.

An Attribute. Wisdom is a virtue, attribute, or characteristic. The term *ḥākam* (wise) serves as a verb and as an adjective. The son is counseled to be wise and will be when he hears instruction (8:33; 10:8; 19:20; 23:19). The simple person can become wise (21:11)[79] as he walks with wise men (13:20). The heart, the core and fountain of life, is to be wise (23:15). The wise heart of a son brings joy to the father (10:1) and enables the son to answer anyone who treats him with contempt (27:11). Being wise one will be rewarded (9:12); he will inherit glory (3:35).

The question that is pertinent in the context of this discussion of the Mediator is: is the wise person fulfilling a mediatorial role or serving as a mediatorial agent? What specifically indicates mediatorial activities on the part of a wise person?

The first passage to consider in response to the question raised above is 11:30. The NIV has translated *lâqâḥ. niphšôt ḥācām* as "he who wins souls is wise." This phrase has been interpreted to say that a wise person wins souls for the tree of life or the kingdom of God.[80] Not all commentators agree.

The entire verse should be considered. Literally it is a type of progressive parallalism, not an adversative. The first line speaks of the fruit of righteousness, understood to mean that those who live righteously are productive in the kingdom of the Lord. This is referred to as a life-producing activity (the tree of life). The next line spells out more clearly what is meant. The righteous person who is the wise one "wins' "takes," and "leads" souls (persons) to this life. Various commentaries agree with the gist of this interpretation.[81]

One commentator, however, wrote that the phrase should not be taken to suggest personal evangelism. He offers the reading, "the wise take righteousness."[82] Still other commentators take 11:30 as an adversative parallel, reading "Right conduct is a tree of life, but crime takes lives away,"[83] Still another interprets 11:31a to mean that "the lives of the lawless are taken away entirely."[84]

It should not be doubted that the authors of Proverbs spoke readily of the bitter end of those who in folly, spurned the wise people and rejected wisdom. They wrote very positively of the blessed life of those who were wise and of their influence. The wise inherit honor (3:35); the wise will receive a reward (9:12). The tongue of the wise brings healing (12:18). The teaching of the wise is a fountain of life; it turns a man from the snares of death (13:14). The lips of the wise brings protection (from the foolish) (14:3). Additional passages could be quoted, referred to or explained. The main point to be emphasized is that a wise person's speaking, teaching, and living as a faithful covenant person has influence in life. They are covenantal mediatorial agents who serve their Lord as spokesmen for true wisdom and are doers of righteousness that have consequences for eternal life.

Personified. Wisdom is personified. It is given a clear and persistent voice. And it is a feminine voice. This may be because the Hebrew term for wisdom is a feminine noun. It has been said that wisdom is feminized to give mothers their due.[85] In this context one cannot avoid remembering that there is another persistent feminine voice in the book of Proverbs. It is that of the adulteress whose lips drip honey (5:3). "She preys upon your life my son," says the father (6:26). Avoid her lest you be captivated by her breasts (5:19, 20). The mouth of an adulteress is a deep pit in which the Lord's wrath only is present. The voice of the adulteress is the very antithesis of the voice of the "wisdom woman."[86]

K. L. Jensen, when discussing the "Cry of Wisdom," suggests that it is a reference to a speaker who could well be a prophet such as Jeremiah, forerunner of Paul or Christ.[87] In the passages that refer to wisdom calling aloud (1:20) "she" is either in the public square, at the head of the noisy street, or in the gateways of the city that had platforms and or chambers.[88] Dame wisdom is more precious than rubies; she has long life and has riches. All her ways are pleasant and all her paths are peace; she is a tree (source) of life to those who embrace her (3:15–18).

Wisdom personified is a home builder who prepares her meat and mixes wines. She invites the simple to come and eat her food and drink her wine so that they may live and walk in the way of understanding (8:5–6). Dame wisdom is properly compared with the virtuous woman/wife/mother described in 31:10–31. This female person not only demonstrates what wisdom is like in action but she also speaks wisdom and gives faithful instruction (31:26).

Wisdom is a God-given virtue. People who have the virtue of wisdom listen to the voice of wisdom that is portrayed as coming from an impersonation of wisdom—a woman, wife, and mother. Her voice and activities are heard and seen in homes, in streets, in the business areas, and in the gates of the city. This wisdom, an attribute, personified is personalized. Yes, wisdom is set forth as a very special and unique person.

Personalized[89]. Commentators have indicated that, whether they are of a conservative, critical, or liberal mind, they have a challenge confronting them when interpreting chapters 8 and 9. Some do not go beyond personification.[90]

This person wisdom has much to say concerning himself/herself. He/she calls to the simple, the foolish, to heed the call to gain prudence and understanding (8:1–5). This person has right, just, true information to communicate (8:6–11). He/she dwells with prudence and possesses knowledge and discretion; counsel and sound judgment belong with him/her (8:12–14). Kings, rulers, and princes govern by them. Tremendous blessings and gifts are imparted (8:15–21). Does this unique, powerful, rich, enabling one know itself and its origin?

Using the pronoun I, the answer is given. Appointed from eternity, before the world began this "I" was brought forth that is, revealed. Before oceans and mountains, the fields and heavens with clouds were in existence. The "I" was there—full of delight. The "I" was *'āmîn* at the side "his side" (8:30). "I" served as craftsman and director.

Who is this that refers to him/her self with pronouns *I, my*? Who was with the Creator, God himself, before creation happened and took place and form? It was wisdom in person.[91] The Psalmist referred to this One as the Word by whom creation came forth (Ps. 33:6). In the New Testament it is the Logos, who is the Son, the second person of the Trinity that brought creation into existence (John 1:11) and Paul refers to Christ as this wisdom in 1 Corinthians. 1:24, 30).

In Proverbs the Mediator is revealed. It is by him that life is present and given (8:35). This is a definite intimation that the second person of the Trinity, the Son, is the redemptive Mediator. When he is present and active, dame folly is rendered ineffective and eliminated (9:13–18). More specifically, the One who is the wisdom of Yahweh God is revealed as the Mediator in creation. In the New Testament the truths are amplified and explicated. Wisdom, the Word, the second Person of the Trinity, Jesus Christ, is the Mediator through whom creation and redemption have been accomplished. This Christ Jesus is both Lord of creation and redemption (Col. 1:15–20)

Summary

Is the Golden Cable present in the book of Proverbs? Does it function as a uniting integral reality? Yes!

Kingdom

Casual reading may not lead one to realize this but in the context of the entire Scriptures the book of Proverbs presents its own view of the kingdom.

Covenant

It has much to reveal and teach concerning the divinely prescribed way covenant life is to be manifested. And in the world in which mankind lives, saturated with folly and wickedness, confidence is not only possible, it is available.

Mediator

The Mediator, in creation and as source of redemption, is the giver of life, joy, and peace eternally. He and his Spirit enable one to fulfill the basic purposes of the book of Proverbs.

Live with God.
Live in creation.
Live with fellowmen.

Notes

1. Books and articles have been reviewed and some carefully studied. The following bibliography was composed with the assistance of a fellow Old Testament Professor, Mr. Vander Hart, and the librarians of Calvin Theological Seminary, Mid America Seminary, and Trinity Christian College. A helpful survey of the modern study of Proverbs has been produced by Whybray, *Survey.*

Robert L. Alden, *Proverbs: A Commentary on an Ancient Book of Timeless Advice* (Grand Rapids: Baker, 1983); William Arnot, *Laws From Heaven for Life on Earth: Illustrations of the Book of Proverbs* (London and New York: Nelson, 1883); David Jo Atkinson, *The Message of Proverbs: Wisdom for Life (*Downers Grove, Ill. InterVarsity, 1997); Michael P. V. Barrett, "The Gospel According to Wisdom: Proverbs 1:20–33" *Biblical Viewpoint* 33 no.2, (November 1999): 13–20; Evode Beaucamp, *Man's Destiny in the Book of Wisdom, (*Staten Island, Alba House,1970); Robert D.Bell, "Theology of Proverbs," *Biblical Viewpoint,* 33 no.2 (November 1999): 1–5; Lennart Bostrom, *The God of the Sages: The Portrayal of God in the Book of Proverbs* (Almqvist: Wiksell International, 1990); Charles Bridges, *An Exposition of Proverbs* (Grand Rapids: Zondervan [distributor], 1959); Jill Briscoe, *Queen of Hearts: The Role of Today's Woman Based on Proverbs 31* (Old Tappan:

Revell, 1984); Walter Brueggemann, *In Man We Trust* (Richmond: John Knox, 1972); Glendon E. Bryce, *A Legacy of Wisdom: The Egyptian Contribution to the Wisdom of Israel* (Lewisburg, Pa. Bucknell University Press, 1979); Claudia V. Camp, *Wisdom and the Feminine in the Book of Proverbs* (Decatur: Almond, Press, 1985); Richard J. Clifford., *The Book of Proverbs and Our Search for Wisdom (*Milwaukee: Marquette University Press, 1995); Johann Cook, "The Law of Moses in Septuagint Proverbs" *VT* 49 no.4 (October, 1999): 448–61; Franz Delitzsch, *Proverbs of Solomon* (Grand Rapids: Eerdmans, 1950); James T. Draper, *Proverbs: The Secret of Beautiful Living (*Wheaton, Ill.: Tyndale, 1977); Robina Drakeford, *In Praise of Women: A Christian Approach to Love, Marriage, and Equality* (San Francisco: Harper & Row, 1980); James M. Efird, *Biblical Books of Wisdom, A Study of Proverbs, Job, Ecclesiastes and other Wisdom Literature in the Bible* (Valley Forge: Judson, 1983); Daniel J. Estes, *Hear My Son: Teaching and Learning in Proverbs* 1–9, (Grand Rapids: Eerdmans, 1997); Jerry Falwell, *Wisdom for Living* (Wheaton: Victor, 1984); T. Forti, "Animal Images in the Didactic Rhetoric of the Book of Proverbs" *Biblica* 77 no.1 (1996): 48–63; Michael V. Fox, "Ideas of Wisdom in Proverbs 1–9" *JBL* 116 no.4 (Winter 1997): 613–33; Friedemann W. Golka, *The Leopard's Spots: Biblical and African Wisdom in Proverbs (*Edinburgh: T & T Clark, 1993); Ignatius G. P. Gous, "Proverbs 31:10–31—the A to Z of Woman Wisdom," *Old Time Essays* 9 no.1 (1996): 35–51; Patricia Gundry, *The Complete Woman* (Garden City, N.Y.: Doubleday, 1981); Joseph Hall, *Solomon's Divine Acts*, ed. G. T. Shepherd (Cleveland: Pilgram, 1991); Scott L. Harris, *Proverbs 1–9: A Study of Inner-biblical Interpretation* (Atlanta: Scholars, 1996); Wesley Haystead, *The 3,000–year-old Guide to Parenting: Wisdom From Proverbs for Today's Parents* (Ventura, Calif., Regal, 1991); Knut Martin Heim, *Like Grapes of Gold Set in Silver: An Interpretation of Proverbial Clusters in Proverbs 10:1–22:16* (Berlin and New York: Walter de Gruyter, 2001); Kenneth Jensen, *Studies in the Book of Proverbs* (Seattle: Pacific Meridian, 1971) and *Wisdom, the Principal Thing: Studies in Proverbs* (Seattle: Pacific Meridian, 1971); James B. Jordan, *Through New Eyes: Developing a Biblical View of the World* (Brentwood: Wolgemuth & Hyatt, 1988); Walter C. Kaiser, "Wisdom Theology and the Centre of Old Testament Theology," *Evangelical Quarterly* 50 no.3, (July-Aug.,1978): 132–46; Riad A. Kassis, *The Book of Proverbs and Arabic Proverbial Works* (Leiden: Brill, 1999); Balmer H. Kelly, "Studia Biblica: The Book of Proverbs" *Interpretation* 2 no.3 (July 1948): 342–55; Derek Kidner, *The Proverbs* (London: Tyndale, 1964); Paul E. Larsen, *Wise Up & Live! Wisdom from Proverbs* (Glendale, Calif.: Regal, 1974); James Loader, "Wisdom by (the) People for (the) People" *Zeitschrift fur die Alttestamentische, Wissenschaft* 111 no. 2 (1969): 211–33; Tremper Longman, *How to Read Proverbs* (Downers Grove: InterVarsity, 2002); Alex Luc, "The Titles and Structure of Proverbs," *ZAW* 112 no. 2 (2000): 252–55; Alex Luc and Elizabeth I. Huwiler, *Proverbs, Ecclesiastes, Song of Songs* (Peabody, Mass.: Hendrickson, 1999); William E. Mouser, *Walking in Wisdom: Studying the Proverbs of Solomon* (Downers Grove: InterVarsity, 1983); Ronald E. Murphy, *Seven Books of Wisdom* (Milwaukee: Bruce, 1960); and "The Kerygma of the Book of Proverbs" *Interpretation*, 20, 3–14; Roland E Murphy and Elizabeth I Huwiler, *Proverbs, Ecclesiastes, Song of Songs,* (Peabody, Mass.: Hendrickson, 1999); Paul Overland, "Did the Sage Draw from the Shema? A Study of Proverbs 3:1–12" *CBQ* 6 nos. 2 and 3 (July 2000): 424–40; Leo G. Perdue, *Proverbs (*Louisville: John Knox, 2000); Terry Rude, "Wisdom in Proverbs," *Biblical Viewpoint* 33 no.2 (November, 1999): 6–12; E. H. Scheffler," Archaeology and Wisdom." *Old Testament Essays* vol. 3 no.10, (1997): 459–73; Robert Balg Scott, *Proverbs and Ecclesiastes* (Garden City: Doubleday, 1974); Daniel C. Snell, *Twice-told*

Proverbs and the Composition of the Book of Proverbs (Winona Lake: Eisenbrauns, 1993); Andrew E. Steinmann, "Proverbs 1–9 as a Solomonic Composition" *JETS* 43 no.4 (December 2000): 659–74; Pete Steveson, "The Role of Parents," *Biblical Viewpoint* 33 no. 2 (November 1999): 28–40; C. H., Toy, *Proverbs* (Edinburgh: T & T Clark, 1970 [last printing]); S. W. Van Heerden, "A Bright Spark is Not Necessarily a Wise Person," *Old Testament Essays* 9, no.3, (1996): 512–526; and "Proverbial Wisdom, Metaphor and Inculturation," *Old Testament Essays* 3 no.10, (1997): 512–2: 7. Raymond C. Van Leeuwen, *Context and Meaning in Proverbs 25–27* (Atlanta: Scholars, 1948); Stephen Voorwinde, *Wisdom for Today's Issues* (Phillipsburg: Presbyterian and Reformed, 1981); Bruce Waltke, "The Book of Proverbs, an Old Testament Theology" *Biblia*, 302–17; Claus Westermann, *Roots of Wisdom: The Oldest Proverbs of Israel and Other People,* trans. J. Daryl Charles (Westminster: John Knox, 1995); Roger Norman Whybray, *The Book of Proverbs: A Survey of Modern Study* (Leiden: Brill, 1995); *The Composition of the Book of Proverbs* (Sheffield: JSOT, 1994); and *Wealth and Poverty in the Book of Proverbs* (Sheffield: JSOT, 1990); Ben Witherington, III, *Jesus the Sage: The Pilgrimage of Wisdom* (Minneapolis: Fortress, 1994); Christine ElizabethYoder, *Wisdom as a Woman of Substance: A Socioeconomic Reading of Proverbs 1–9 and 31:10–31*, (Berlin and New York, W. de Gruyter, 2001).

2. It should be noted that each book contains theological material. Alden, *Proverbs*, 12. Waltke has developed the thesis that the book of Proverbs is an Old Testament theology book. It reveals the same Lord, the same religious system, the same inspiration, the same authority, the same anthropology, and the same epistomology, the same spiritual demand, the same ethical demand, the same faith (*Proverbs and Old Testament Theology*). Various authors have referred to this. Consider for example, Bostrom's book, *God . . . Sages* that include chapter titles such as Theology of Creation and Order, God; Retribution and Order . . . God's Relationship to the World, and The Lord as Personal God. Eichrodt, who structured his two-volume *Theology Old Testament* around the theme of covenant referred to Psalm passages more than two hundred times particularly when he discussed "Wisdom of God" (vol. II, 81–91) and applied it when discussing cosmology, creation, man's place in it, and the relationship between God and man. Jacob, in his *Theology Old Testament* included fifty-three references to the Psalms. He pointed out that Yahweh God gave wisdom to men and it was expressed fully in the Messiah.

3. W. Kaiser was concerned to discern such a central theological core. He attempted to demonstrate that "Promise" is such a uniting core in wisdom literature. "Wisdom . . . Centre." In this essay he demonstrated the "Promise" was not really the answer. He also referred to "The Fear of God," 32–46. Gerald Sheppard referred to the effort of Protestant scholars providing an alternative to Roman Catholic rules of meditation. At the core of the issue was the exact nature of wisdom and its proper relation to theology. Both were considered essential aspects of Proverbs. Hall, "Role of the Canonical Context in the Interpretation of the Solomonic Book."

4. Some authors have attempted to give specific positive replies to this question. Cf. Arnot, *Laws. . .Heaven;* Witherington, *Jesus the Sage*. D. Kidner in the introduction to *The Proverbs* referred to the wisdom presented in Proverbs as "God-centered" "because God is self consistent." Wisdom is "a thread running through the whole fabric of the Old Testament," 13, 15. L. Perdue concludes his discussion of each specific section by a paragraph he entitled "Theology," *Proverbs*, 67, 76, 80, 84, 96, 100–101, 110, 114, etc. He included these sections on theology because in his introduction he wrote, "The God of the Sages of

Proverbs is Yahweh, whom they believed to be the One Universal God who created the world and providentially sustained all life" 36. Purdue added, "The Revelation of God in Proverbs is like a winding river with various tributaries," 37.

If one suggests that reference to God, Yahweh the covenant Lord, does not necessarily refer to the gospel, a read of M. Barrett's essay "The Gospel According to Wisdom: Proverbs 1:30–33" should be helpful. Cf. also Murphy's essay "Kerygma-Proverbs." Although he posits a critical view regarding authorship, he is positive that even if chapter 8 may not be properly Christological it surely is kerygmatic, as are parts of various other chapters. He considered that the kerygma of wisdom, as in Proverbs, can be summed up in one word "Life," 9.

5. Solomon is also the author of Proverbs 1–9. Cf. the essay, "Proverbs 1–9 . . . Solomonic."

6. *Proverbs*, 22.

7. Bridges, *Proverbs*, has 3 parts;. Toy, *Proverbs*, has five; Delitzsch did not include a concise, formal outline but referred to the Older Book, chapters 1–24, and Later Book, chapters 25–29. But he did not accept Ewald's view that Proverbs reveals a progressive development, *Proverbs X–XII,* 22. Scott, *Proverbs and Ecclesiastes,* developed five sections, based on his presupposition of the development of Proverbs (twice sayings) in Israel. Luc, "Titles," rejects common view of seven titles (parts). He discerned five because 22:17ff. and 24:23ff., do not have indications of being separate but he did concede that the LXX supports 22:17ff. as a distinct part, 253.

8. Cf. Kidner, *Proverbs*, 24. Cf. also Bryce, *A Legacy of Wisdom, the Egyptian Contribution*, and Kassis, *Proverbs. . . Arabic Proverbial Works.* McCane, *Proverbs*, wrote that the present work "a re-interpretation of the vocabulary of old wisdom and two sources are evident," Yahwistic and international Egyptian, Sumerian, and Assyrian. Scott implies that Egyptian and Turian influences are readily explained, *Proverbs,* 12.

9. One must keep in mind that other "Works of Wisdom" are attributed to Jewish sources, e.g., *The Book of Wisdom.* These wisdom writings are not to be considered as divinely inspired revelation. Murphy in *Seven Books* does not indicate he accepts this distinction. Cf. chapter 8. Clifford in his " . . . *Search For Wisdom*" does not either, 4, 5; but he also wrote the Bible books are "lifted up" to a "new" dialectical context, 8. T. Longman indicated he was fully aware of Mesopotamian, Egyptian, and Northwest Semitic proverbs and found that the similarity is so close between what wise men of other cultures had written and the biblical proverbs that it "is possible that" the Bible directly borrowed, *How to Read*, 62. Finally Loader's comment should be kept in mind. He wrote "I have no quarrel with the idea that many of Israel's sayings now found in the Book of Proverbs could have originated among people in villages and barns." "Wisdom for People . . . by People," 232. We, however, must add that this real familial time does not negate the inspiration of the writer of the Proverbs.

10. *Proverbs I*, 6.

11. Kelley, "The Book of Proverbs," 345–46.

12. Alden, *Proverbs*, 13, 14.

13. Kidner, *Proverbs*, 28, 112.

14. Scott, *Proverbs* 3. He added that instruction profited from this combination.

15. Toy, *Proverbs*, ix.

16. Longman, *How . . . Read*, 117.

17. Voorwinde, *Wisdom . . . Issues*; 55 themes are listed.

18. Johnson, *Proverbs to . . . Ethics*, 2. This phrase was taken from a writing by Craigie.

19. Ibid., 312. Johnson decided, however, that there are three "classes of proverbs": universally true in a temporal sense, universally true from an eternal perspective, and temporal and eternal, 309, 310.

20. Cf. Murphy-Huwiler, *Proverbs*, 10–12. An example the author gives is about seeing wine sparkling as it is poured out giving it an eye, Prov. 23:31. The NIV could have translated it better than to write "Do not gaze at wine."

21. Witherington, *Jesus the Sage*, 3.

22. The Hebrew term *mišĕl* has been translated and interpreted in various ways. The root term *mōsal* is translated "to be like." The generally accepted translation is proverb but it has been referred to as similitude, riddle, fable, satire, and maxim.

23. Ross, "Proverbs," 8: 8 and 9.

24. Barrett "The Gospel . . . Wisdom" correctly wrote that one cannot isolate precepts (Proverbs) from the rest of biblical theology. The proper use of Proverbs requires a belief in the essential truths of the gospel, 13, 18.

25. Cf. the concordance of NIV; there are seven references to God. Cf. 307, 309–10, in this chapter for further discussion of God in Proverbs.

26. Jordan, *New Eyes*, 262–64.

27. Cf. Voorwinde, *Wisdom*, who has listed 30 separate passages in Proverbs that refer to some aspect of wickedness, 160–69.

28. Ibid., 165–78.

29. Ibid., 83–86. The authors spoke of God's love as well as human love and also of the false love of the adulteress.

30. Students of Proverbs have presented various approaches to the purpose of Proverbs. Clifford, *Proverbs—Search* wrote that Proverbs was written in the framework of belief in "God of Israel" and as such is a visionary writing and a practical manual, 47. Jensen, *Wisdom Principal*, detected three purposes of Proverbs which were to present three thrusts: mental attitude, divine norms, and standards and overt activity, 1–9.

31. Bostrom, in *God—Sages,* having the sub-theme of Portrayal of God in the Proverbs, stated that there are forty-nine (49) references to God in the Book of Proverbs, 33.

32. See Richard J. Clifford, *Book of Proverbs*, 33.

33. Perdue, *Proverbs*, 47.

34. Ibid. Perdue added "through households, royal courts and law courts," 190.

35. Cf. his *God-Sages*. Chapter 2 is a study of creation theology.

36. Ibid., 43.

37. Ibid., 8, 112, 142, 146, 169, 193.

38. Forti, "Animal Images," 48.

39. Ibid.

40. Ibid., 50.

41. Forti discussed animals and birds employing stylistic and thematic aspects of "Dynamic Hermeneutics," ibid., 63.

42. There is further discussion concerning the cosmic kingdom under the heading of covenant: cultural dimensions.

43. Cf. Alden, *Proverbs*, 13.

44. See discussion of my study on the formation of the theocracy at Mount Sinai. *From Creation.* vol. I, 323–27, and the role of the theocracy in the entire world, 328.

45. Cf. comments by Alden, *Proverbs*, on this text, 34. The term *'allûp*, a derivative of the verb *'ālup* (to learn or cleave to, be intimate with), can be translated as friend, intimate one, or husband.

46. Cf. my study on covenant in *From Creation to Consummation*, 324–330, 373–74. Main aspects are Yahweh the covenant maker, the bonded people, promises, prescriptions, curses, and continuity.

47. The selection is not intended to be exhaustive but gives solid evidence that the covenant functioned as the redemptive administrative means in Yahweh God's dealing at all times with his people in the cosmic kingdom and particularly with those in the theocratic kingdom.

48. The verb *bārâ'* (create) does not appear in the book of Proverbs.

49. The text does not intimate at all that the Maker makes people poor.

50. Scott opined that 22:2 may mean (1) they share a common humanity; (2) God has willed their station in life; and (3) personal worth is more important than wealth. *Proverbs Ecclesiastes*, 127, 28. Kidner posited that this verse emphasizes that a significant bond has come from one hand (Yahweh God's), *Proverbs,* 196, 197.

51. It is interesting to note that the legislative aspect of the Torah is absent from Proverbs, e.g., decrees, ordinances, statutes. Nor does the term *'ēd,* usually translated testimony, appear in Proverbs. Cook, "The Law of Moses," was correct when he wrote that the Torah in Proverbs does not refer directly to Law but to instruction—that is to serve as a wall around the righteous, 460.

52. The authors of Proverbs were very interested in life. It is referred to in various contexts and situations of life forty-five times.

53. Voorwinde has listed 24 passages that refer to the fear of Yahweh, *Wisdom*, 32–34.

54. One should be hesitant to accept Scott's understanding of Prov. 1:7. He translated the verse as the first principle of knowledge is to hold the Lord in awe, *Proverbs*, 33. It is true that awe is an element of fear but more problematic is his use of the phrase "first principle."

55. Kidner, *Proverbs*, says the fear of Yahweh refers to a relation and worshiping submission to the God of the covenant, 59.

56. Alden, *Proverbs*, referred to synonomous passages such as Ps. 111:10 and Job 28:28 and used the term *reverence* to explain the phrase, 22.

57. There is no direct reference to family, e.g., the term does not appear but various aspects of family life do. Under the heading of Family, only that aspect of the covenantal social mandate will be discussed. Under the heading of Social Relationships other aspects of the Social Mandate will be discussed.

58. Social and cultural issues will be discussed in following sections.

59. In doing research for this study, various written works were consulted that present doubts concerning much of what is recorded about Solomon. Kenneth A. Kitchen wrote an instructive essay "How We Know When Solomon Ruled?" *Biblical Archaeology Review* vol. 27, no. 4 (2001): 32–37, 58.

60. The phrase "my son" appears twelve times in the first seven chapters which are from Solomon's pen. The wise men repeat it.

61. The term *mûsâr* appears over thirty times. Translators have rendered it in English as instruction, chastening, correction.

62. Cf. Delitzsch, *Proverbs II,* 86; and Kidner, *Proverbs,*147.

63. Toy, *Proverbs,* 419; Scott, *Proverbs,* the teachers came, implying corporal punishment, 128.

64. Bridges, *Proverbs*, 413.

65. Jensen has summarized the results of a committed heart. It has mastery of the details of life; it has spiritual peace; it has inner peace; it has capacity for love, and it has a grace orientation. *Studies—Proverbs*, 160.

66. The social and cultural dimensions of covenantal kingdom life are discussed in the following two sections of this study.

67. The broader dimensions of instructing/training and guiding each succeeding generation in academic education has been addressed from various perspectives in *Pro Rege*, a Quarterly Faculty Publication of Dordt College, Sioux Center, Iowa, 51250.

68. Voorwinde, *Wisdom—Today*, has listed these alphabetically. A select number of these topics are discussed.

39. Chapters 6, 7, 9, 22, 23, 30 continue to speak of adultery, of how tempting it is, and the tragically sad consequences of it.

70. Love functions at different levels, e.g, the highest is love for the Lord, the love in marriage is higher than the real love of parents for children. This parental love functions at a higher and more intense level than love for a friend. Love for cultural aspects should function at a comparative low level, but love for purity, righteousness, and justice should be exercised in the higher level of love.

71. The term *šākār* (strong drink) appears three times. The noun is derived from the verb *šākar* (to be drunk). Kings and rulers were not to use *šekar* lest they forget the law and deprive the oppressed of their rights (31:4, 5).

72. This is a quotation from the essay "Animal Images" . . . by Forti, 48.

73. Grass was watered by dew (19:12) as were vineyards in the Hebron area.

74. Forti, "Animal Images . ." 49.

75. Ibid., 57.

76. Ibid., 60.

77. The term *mediator* that appears in the NIV Old Testament in Job 33:23 is the translation of *mēlîs,* derived from the verb *mālaṡ,* to be smooth or slippery.

78. In the first chapter of this book 33, Part II, wisdom and wisdom literature were discussed.

79. Overland in "Sage . . . Shema" wrote that he who considers himself wise has "a psychological quest for personal worth," but that is a limited view. It has to include a reverence for the awe inspiring greatness of God., 431. Van Heerden in "Bright Spark-Wise Person" has a problem with the view that wisdom is a human attribute defined as superior intelligence, 512, 513.

80. Bridges, *Proverbs*, wrote "wise . . . to win souls." A soul is a kingdom and as many as we can bring back to God are so many kingdoms re-conquered; 130. Ross "Proverbs" wrote that "winning souls" means to capture i.e., to lay hold of or seize people with ideas or influence, 966.

81. Delitzsch, *Proverbs*, 249; Allen, "Proverbs," 966; and Kidner, *Proverbs*, 94. The latter two include reference to the LXX text that the passage can be understood to say that he who takes away life is violent, reading *ḥākām* as *ḥāmās* (violent).

82. Alden, *Proverbs*, 98.

83. Scott, *Proverbs*, 87.

84. Toy, *Proverbs*, 233.

85. Perdue, *Proverbs*, 49. It should not be denied that mothers are given their due but it is to be questioned if that was the intent of feminizing wisdom. Could it be that the modern prevalence of feminization makes its appearance. Take note that various writers have appealed to passages that refer to the woman. Gous, "Proverbs 31:10–31, Briscoe, *Queen of Hearts*, and Camp, *Wisdom and the Feminine.*

86. Perdue, ibid., stressed that the antithesis is present between the righteous wise and the wicked fool, the wise woman and the adulteress, 174. Cf. also Allen, *Proverbs*; he wrote that Dame Wisdom and Lady Folly each seek followers, 27.

87. Jensen, *Wisdom . . . Principal*, 111, 112.

88. Scheffler, in his essay "Archaeology and Wisdom," wrote that the idea of gate must not be thought of in terms of modern life but of the ancient city gate that had four to six chambers in which elders sat and taught, 464.

89. The term *personalize* is distinct from *personify*. The latter conveys the thought of a thing as having life or personality or to represent as a person. Personalize is to make personal and/or to endow with a personality.

90. E.g., Toy, *Proverbs,* continues to refer to the woman or sage as speaking when the pronoun "I" appears (8:4, 6 [2x], 13, 14, 17, 19, 20, 23, 25, 27, 30 [2x]; 9:5) and me or my (8:7 [2x], 8, 10, 15, 16, 17]2x], 18, 19, 21, 122, 33, 34 [2x], 35, 36; 9:11). Wisdom, objectively as a person, is referred to by the third person plural "she" or "her" nine times in (9:1–4).

91. Delitzsch, *Proverbs I—Wisdom*, (she) "transferred the creative thoughts originally existing in the creative will of God, and set in motion by his creative order, from their ideal into their real effectiveness, 121. Balmer Kelly, wrote that in the last part of chap. 8 the conception given as wisdom, a person, a separate identity is who is "co-eternal with Yahweh himself." "The Book of Proverbs," 351.

47

The Golden Cable in Ecclesiastes

I. Introductory Comments

II. The Kingdom

III. The Covenant

IV. The Mediator

V. Summary and Conclusion

47

The Golden Cable in Ecclesiastes

Introductory Comments

Large Bibliographies

Ecclesiastes is a relatively short Old Testament book. It is a unique work; it has challenged many biblical scholars to study it and to comment on it.[1] Evidence of extensive serious work on Ecclesiastes is verified by the bibliographies of authors who have commented on Ecclesiastes authors.[2] And if one should inquire concerning why there is so much writing on Ecclesiastes the answer may be in statements by the writers themselves. One wrote: "Qoheleth is one of the most difficult books in the Bible, it has long been an enigma and a source of fascination for its readers and students."[3] Another wrote: "The Book of Ecclesiastes has exercised the church of God to no common degree . . . it (is) among the most difficult books in the Sacred Canon."[4] Another commentator referred to Ecclesiastes as one of the most puzzling books of the Bible.[5] These comments lead one to ask, what are the specific difficulties in the interpretation of the book of Ecclesiastes?

Interpretation Difficulties

The difficulties are considered numerous and one gets the impression that an attempt to interpret the book of Ecclesiastes is not realistically possible. C. Bartholomew wrote that as in "the first century A.D., there was vigorous debate among Jewish scholars, now at the end of the second millennium there is still vigorous debate."[6] Sharp differences can be seen. One writer came to see Ecclesiastes as affirming joy while another scholar described Ecclesiastes as "vigorously hopeless" when attempting to "promote a theological hermeneutic for Scripture."[7]

A perusal of various books and essays leads one to understand that the purpose of the book is most difficult for students and scholars to discern and explain. There seems to be no unity in what is recorded. One could describe what some students would conclude, namely, that the book presents a hodgepodge of ideas and comments. Those who have attempted to outline the content of Ecclesiastes have presented a wide variety of efforts.[8] In the following three sections, additional reasons can be given for the difficulty in interpreting the book of Ecclesiastes.

How is the Book to be Considered?

Philosophically

D. Wilson wrote that "The Great Hebrew Philosopher" wrote the book of Ecclesiastes.[9] As a philosophical scholar he stressed four points. (1) Satisfaction does not come from anything in the power of man. (2) God is sovereign over everything. (3) This sovereignty gives power to enjoy the parade of variety. (4) Obstacles are removed and various practical answers are given to overcome discouragement. C. Shank emphasized what is generally considered to be a theme discussed in philosophical circles, namely, "Qoheleth's World and Life View." In the article, the main subject is ethics as the term *hebel* (vanity) is discussed.[10] Is the term to be considered negative or is it to be considered in conjunction with the injunction to fear God? And does Ecclesiastes distinguish between faith and sight, rather than between faith and reason? One would be drawn to conclude, after an evaluation of Shank's essay, that the book of Ecclesiastes is a joint work in philosophy and theology.

Harrison offers another approach to the interpretation of Ecclesiastes. He chose to consider the social location of the author(s) of Ecclesiastes. He joined scholars who have attempted to disown interesting relationships between biblical thought and the social world that is represented. Harrison proceeded to select what he considered to be realities in Qoheleth's changing circumstances. As for example, there was an important economic reorientation in an increasing Hellenization process. This included an important reorganization of social class with political repercussions. Within this Hellinization process cultural life was redefined.[11] It is obvious that Harrison's basic presupposition—not proven—was that strong influences of Greek, Eyptian, and Persian culture permeated Judean life and that Qoheleth reacted pessimistically to these.

Miller suggested a possible literary approach to understanding Ecclesiastes.[12] He thinks that his approach reflects the recent surge of optimism regarding the proper understanding of Ecclesiastes. He admitted that the inherent complexities have not been resolved but that there is a consistency to its thought and purpose. The key is to properly understand the term *hebel* (vanity), used forty times. This term serves as a symbol of all human experiences characterized by insubstantiality, transience, and/or foulness. Once people understand this, there is the possibility of experiencing hope and joy in life.

Among these and other attempts to understand Ecclesiastes is the feminist one.[13] Rudman referred to two passages, 7:26, 28 and 9:9. He wrote that in the context of the unattainableness of wisdom, woman can be considered a snare and net. Some say woman can be a menace. She is the agent of a deterministic force. She does not encourage people to sin but does represent punishment for her consort. Woman thus is God's agent in his execution of judgment. According to Rudman, terms used suggest a Persian context because terms in Ecclesiastes reflect Persian legal situations.

Summary Statement

Scholars have exhibited and/or demonstrated their specific preferences as ideologies when they sought to interpret Ecclesiastes. One must be careful when evaluating the different approaches and methods. One must not forget that Ecclesiastes includes references to social and cultural realities in life. One or more of these, however, should not be considered the main and basic issues. They are indeed aspects or parts of life. These aspects should not be considered to represent the entire message. That they can be included and referred to is because of the manifold riches and variations that characterize life in its entirety.

The chief point to be recognized is that the book of Ecclesiastes is not merely a humanly originated document. Indeed, it reveals that there was thought, consideration of aspects of life, reflection, and evaluation. These must be seen and accepted as responses to what had been revealed in the spiritual, social, and cultural dimensions of life. The point to be stressed is that the book of Ecclesiastes presents additional revelation given by God through the work of the Holy Spirit who inspired the writing of Ecclesiastes. Indeed, Ecclesiastes presents a divinely inspired message given within the *Sitz im Leben* of people at a specific period of time.

Textual References

Theological. A listing of texts that can be understood to highlight the theological aspect or character of Ecclesiastes are as follows: 2:24–26; 3:19–22; 5:13, 14, 20; 6:1–6; 7:13, 14, 19, 27–29; 8:12, 13; 9:1, 2; 11:5, 9; 12:1–7, 13, 14. These passages include reference to *'ĕlōhîm* (God). Passages that refer to specific works and deeds of God could also be added.

Philosophical. The passages listed refer to Qoheleth observing, reflecting, and thinking on life, the world, and the like: 1:2–11; 3:1–8; 6:7–12; 7:9; 9:2–8; 10:14; 11:1–5; 12:8–11.

Theologically

The question to be considered is: since the book of Ecclesiastes is not a philosophical, sociological, economic, or feminine treatise, is it correct in view of it being a divinely inspired book included in the canon,[14] to consider it a theological treatise? Careful consideration is necessary.

First, Ecclesiastes is not a prophetic book. It does not include phrases such as "The Lord said" or "The Lord appeared to" nor does it include historic accounts of Yahweh God making promises to his people, dealing with them providentially, and bringing judgment upon their enemies.

Second, Ecclesiastes acknowledges *'ĕlōhîm* (God) and refers to him forty times. But to think that Ecclesiastes is basically and only about God is not correct. Human life, with its exigencies, experiences, and blessings under God, is in a real sense a central theme. But note—*under God.*

Third, various commentators have pointed out that certain theological themes are to be considered as essential for men to know. Examples are creation, providence, and judgment, but there is no reference to God's love, man's need to trust God, or the possibility of intimate fellowship with him.[15]

Fourth, there is no direct reference to Yahweh God's covenant, from either the creation or redemptive covenantal[16] perspective. Ecclesiastes, however, refers to mankind's relationship with God when exhorting men to fear God and keep his commandments (12:13). Hearers and readers were reminded that men who differentiated from criminals "fear God" and the reverent before him will have it better (8:11–13).

Fifth, it is necessary to be aware of how the term *theology* is used and specifically what is to be understood by it. Three distinctions must be kept in focus. (1) Ecclesiastes is not a *theological book* as the book of Romans is. The doctrines of God, Christ, the Holy Spirit, the ecclesia, and eschatology are not main themes. Other theological Bible books require reading and study to learn what the theological context of Ecclesiastes is. (2) Ecclesiastes does not present much material to develop a theological system.[17] To state it in another way: Ecclesiastes is not a source for the development of a system of doctrines. It does not serve the scholar much, if at all, who wishes to carefully define and inter-relate the biblical dogmas. It is not a helpful source for dogmatic theology. (3) We might understand it properly as the term *biblical theology* does. The most helpful explanation of this title is that it is a branch of exegetical, not dogmatic or systematic theology. Biblical theology deals with the "process of the self revelation of God deposited in the Bible. This process of God's revelatory activity is revealed progressively in history. This revelation is embodied in history organically and is practically adaptable."[18] To be particularly acknowledged in this definition and explanations is that God revealed himself in word and deed progressively throughout history—from the time of creation to the establishment of the church. As God revealed himself he added to, explained, and fulfilled what was done as promised previously. There was a unity, cohesiveness, and integration in his revelatory words and deeds in the course of ongoing time. A metaphor has been taken from the natural world. From a seed a plant develops that produces branches, flowers, and fruit and thus becomes a mature plant that grows organically.

The question to be answered is: is a biblical theological study of the book of Ecclesiastes feasible? Are the major aspects of a proper biblical theological study present? A review of what has been attempted, or not, can be enlightening. A recent book entitled *Biblical Theology* refers twice to Ecclesiastes.[19] A doctoral candidate entitled his thesis *A Biblical Theology of Ecclesiastes.* In his conclusion he stated he found that a unity was exhibited but no logical structure could be detected. That can only mean that he did not discover an organic, progressive development of divine revelation in the book of Ecclesiastes. He also concluded that the theology of Ecclesiastes is extremely contrary for the contemporary Christian. If this is true, Ecclesiastes lacks the fourth characteristic of biblical theology: adaptability.[20] Attempts to discover some aspects of what was outlined as essential aspects of "biblical theology" could be referred to in this context. One possible attempt is by Keddie. He presented a progress in thought. The author of Ecclesiastes questioned the status quo of life in his day and sought for a meaningful life here and now that ended at the threshold of heaven.[21] Another author suggested that Ecclesiastes reflected on the inequalities in divine providence. These are presented in a poorly connected manner and thus there is no progression in thought.[22] There is, however, a message that is consistent with human experience and that is compatible with truth revealed in Scripture.[23]

I have studied thirty-six of the Old Testament books in a biblical theological context. Is it realistic in view of what various authors have concluded concerning the non-biblical theological character of Ecclesiastes to nevertheless develop a study of the book in that context? Specifically, the problem is: does the book of Ecclesiastes offer material on the three strands of the Golden Cable—the kingdom, the covenant, the Mediator? This study will proceed to determine the answers.

Inter-related Factors

Four important subjects have to be considered. These should provide a context and basis for the effort to consider the biblical theological character and contribution to the entire message of the Old Testament.

Author(s)

Who wrote the book of Ecclesiastes? Reading 1:1, one could get the impression that the author was David's son who was king *bĕrûšālāim* (in Jerusalem). Solomon is not named; he, however, was David's son and he reigned in Jerusalem. But a question arises: who was Qohelet? Was he the son of David? Commentators have pointed out that, not David, but Qohelet was king in Jerusalem. Was Solomon also known as Qohelet? The Hebrew term is the feminine participial form of the verb *qāhal,* but is used with masculine verbs. Hence it is not necessary to consider Qohelet as a feminine person.[25] To add to the problem is that the term refers to one who converses in the *qāhal* (a noun that the LXX translates as *ekklesiastes*). Qohelet is a convener, not a preacher,[26] in the assembly. This explanation has not satisfied all commentators. Many consider Solomon to be the author because he referred to himself (Eccl. 2:4–9), as described in 1 Kings 4:20–33. Others have insisted that Qohelet took up the personification of Solomon when he wrote in 300–250 *B.C.* These commentators refer to the Grecian terms used and to the environment alluded to in Ecclesiastes. But commentators who insist that Solomon was the author, when confronted by the references to the sad state of spiritual and social affairs, have an answer. They concede that the *Sitz im Leben* that Ecclesiastes refers to was not a description of the times when Solomon first reigned. Solomon wrote after he repented of his many sins when there was a gross situation in all aspects of life. Thus, even though the historical record does not refer to such a return to the Lord (1 Kings 11:41–43; 2 Chron. 9:29–31) it is assumed.[27]

The Time of Writing

All commentators consulted agree that there is a strong pessimism communicated in the book. The ever-recurring theme *hebel* unmistakably conveys this attitude and frame of mind. *Hebel* is the thematic word; it is one of the book's lead motifs. The term appears thirty seven times. According to one commentator, *hebel* is identical to the name of Cain's ill-fated brother. In Genesis 4 the term denotes a vivid image of vapor or breath, connoting something empty and worthless. In Ecclesiastes the term *hebel* is translated vanity, conveying futility, emptiness, ephemerality, meaningless, absurdity.[28]

When in Old Testament times were conditions such that an inspired writer would use the term to describe the *Sitz im Leben* of the population of which he was a member? The conditions were not only caused by human failings. The temporal and social conditions with its afflictions were under God's ordainment.[29] Those who would hold that Solomon wrote Ecclesiastes suggest that Solomon's sins during his apostacy were the setting for such a time of vanity, meaningless, and absurdity. The problem is that, as mentioned before, there is no reference to such a period of time. True, the kingdom divided after Solomon's death; there is no reference, however, in Scripture that Solomon's apostacy led to this rupture.

The social and religious conditions during the later Persian and earlier Greek eras are more compatible with what the author of Ecclesiastes described as the *Sitz im Leben* in Jerusalem and surrounding environs. Scholars continue to discuss the various options. Was it in Solomon's time? Was it in the later Persian era?[30] Or was it in the early part of the Grecian era? There is no agreement to which one can turn.

Place of Writing

There is no appreciable difference among students, scholars, and commentators on where Ecclesiastes was written. Whybray called attention to the reference to the temple (5:1–7) and concluded the book was written in Jerusalem.[31] He also referred to the thought as fundamentally Hebrew, written by a Jew living in Jerusalem.[32] This view is very acceptable. It is difficult to dispute that the book of Ecclesiastes exhibits a cultural and social *Sitz im Leben* that had been affected by foreign influences. It is also to be agreed that in Solomon's time, there was interaction with foreign entities. He had a wife from Egypt. Solomon had business transactions with Tyrians; he ruled over neighboring kingdoms (1 Kings. 4:24). Men from nations came to him (1 Kings. 4:34). The queen of Sheba visited him (1

Kings 10:1–9). The biblical testimony is that people from the many areas came to Solomon to listen to his wisdom. There is no direct evidence that these visitors influenced Solomon. But it cannot be substantiated either that Solomon, as author of Ecclesiastes, was not in some way affected by foreign influences.

What must be considered is that after an Israelite remnant returned from Babylonian/Persian exile to Jerusalem, various foreign influences did come into it. There were military occupational forces. There were increasing interactions among people living in various areas. Cultural and social influences impinged on Jewish society during the last centuries before Christ. And there were few, if any, charismatic and powerful political, social, and religious leaders who were able to influence Jewish life for any lengthy period of time to address the cultural malaise "that gripped much of the ancient world, including Israel, beginning with the Persian period."[33] The consensus is that the book was written in Jerusalem, either during Solomon's time or years after the exile.

Literary Characteristics

There is much agreement as well as disagreement among biblical scholars on how to deal with the literary characteristics of the book of Ecclesiastes. There is general agreement that Jewish influences and literary qualities are present. The thoughts expressed, while not in a consistent unified, progressive manner,[34] are fundamentally Hebrew.[35] Another scholar wrote that there is no single genre that "governs everything spoken." He added that the dominant literary type of reflection arises from personal observation. This personal aspect has raised questions about the writer's authority because of his daring observation.[36] At this point it is important to stress again that biblical writers who reflect on and respond to aspects of life were Spirit-inspired. The Holy Spirit was not limited in his inspiring activities to those who quoted Yahweh God directly, or indirectly. Human capabilities, such as observing, reflecting, thinking, responding, were employed by the Holy Spirit in order to assure that there was the reception by human beings of what was revealed in word and deeds in life and in realities in nature. Qohelet, the author of Ecclesiastes, exhibited his ability under the inspiration of the Holy Spirit to write what he had observed, evaluated, and concluded. And he did this employing literary techniques common to Hebrew writing. Three of these will be briefly referred to as follows.

Poetry. Within the body of material presented in prose, some sections reflect and exhibit a poetic character that is not foreign to Hebrew literature. Translators have not always agreed on what exhibited a poetic form. Some poetic features are clearly evident, such as parallelisms of various types. Of the many examples that could be listed, the following suffice to substantiate the presence of parallelism. A progressive parallel appears in 10:1: "As dead flies give perfume a bad smell, so a little folly outweighs wisdom and honor." Proverbs 10:20 presents a balanced parallel: "Do not revile the king even in your thoughts or curse the rich in your bedroom." An adversative parallel is employed in 9:11—the race, battle, food, wealth, favor come to various classes of men *but* time and chance come to all.

Didactic. In the book of Proverbs children were addressed as parents instructed them. There is no direct address by parents, counselors, teachers, or rulers in Ecclesiastes. Yet there is the unavoidable tone of the teacher or preacher who has his personal style. The book exhibits subtle argumentation and prescriptive power in its "rambling and circuitous manner of presentation."[37] There should be no doubt in any reader's or student's mind that Qohelet's desire was to present all of life under the sun as a God-given reality. He, as it were, had a bright and sharp spotlight that he moved up and down, forward and back, concentrating on scenes and situations. There is very little evidence of progression but many aspects of life, from birth to death, were covered. In this manner of presentation, no specific classes of people were addressed. Many, however, could locate themselves in one or more context or situation and receive insight and instruction.

Hortatory. The author of the book of Ecclesiastes, referred to as Qohelet, is translated "Preacher" in some books.[38] It could be reasonably said that one of the reasons the name Qohelet was translated Preacher is because of the hortatory character of the book. There is, however, the problem of identifying the reference to being "king in Jerusalem" and the position of "The Preacher." Commentators have sought to explain this by suggesting that "Qohelet put on the mantle of a Solomon."[39]

The point to stress here is, whoever he was or whatever position or office the author (Qohelet) held, the hortatory character of the book cannot be doubted. The presentation may be unlike a well-organized sermon or theological treatise. There are, however, clear hortatory evidences.[40] (1) The theme is stated *hăbēl hăbōlîm* (meaningless, meaningless, NIV, vanity of vanities, KJV and RSV). The statement, spoken-written pointedly, draws attention. (2) This is followed by questions, "What does a man gain . . .?" (1:3). "Is there anything . . . new?" (1:10). "What does pleasure accomplish?" (2:2b). "What more can the king's successor do? (2:12b). "What does the worker gain?" (3:9). "Where does the spirit of man go?" (3:21, 22). (3). There is skillful recitation of time for, seasons for, the varieties in life (3:1–8).

There are the personal addresses, "Guard *your* steps when you go to the house of God" (5:1); "Do not be quick with *your* mouth" (5:2); "You are on earth" (5:2b); "When *you* make a vow to God" (5:4); "If *you* see the poor oppressed . . ." (5:8); "Consider what God has done" (7: 13); "Why die before *your* time?" (7:17). Chapters 11 and 12 especially exhibit the hortatory voice–pen of the Preacher. "Cast *your* bread upon the water" (11:1); "As *you* do not know the path of the wind" (11:5a); "Sow *your* seed in the morning" (11:6); "Be happy, young man, while you are young" (11:9). "Remember *your* creator" (12:1); "Fear God and keep his commandments" (12:13a).

The purpose of Qohelet has been widely discussed. There should be no doubt that the "Preacher's" strong desire was to address his audience-readers with an appeal that they consider themselves and their lives in a troubled environment and to draw their attention to their Creator, Provider, and Judge.

The Strands of the Golden Cable?

After the above consideration of the various introductory issues confronting a biblical theological effort, the question arises: does the book of Ecclesiastes bear a basic resemblance to any of the other books of the Old Testament? This question should be confronted openly. All the other Old Testament books considered and studied gave clear evidence that the three strands of the Golden Cable were present not only but served to unite the Old Testament books' messages into an integrated whole. Is this the case with Ecclesiastes also? A study of the three strands follows.

The Kingdom

The Concepts

The term *melek* (king) occurs fourteen times in the book of Ecclesiastes: once in the plural (2:8), five times with the possessive (2:12; 4:15; 8:2, 3, 4), eight 8 times in reference to the "king" (1:1, 12; 4:13; 5:9; 9:14; 10:16, 17, 20); and once to the generic term *kingship* (4:14) David was acknowledged as having been king. Thus reference is to the united kingdom of Israel.

The Theocratic (Human) Kingdom

Qohelet, the teacher, referred to himself as king over Israel in Jerusalem (1:1). The reference is again to the united kingdom of Israel.[41] So also it can be construed that the reference is to the theocratic king in Jerusalem (2:12). Kingship, however, is basically the theme in 4:13, 14, 15; 5:9; 8:2, 3, 4; 9:14; 10:16, 17, 20. There is no other specific reference (except in 1:1 and 1:12) in these passages to the theocratic kingdom of Israel (Judah). It could be argued that the time of Ecclesiastes' author was 350–300 *B.C.* He was reflecting on the early time of the theocratic kingdom, employing it as an instance of kingship and kingdom. It is striking that Qohelet does not express a longing for an upright kingdom, whether in the past or present. The point to stress, however, is that the concepts of king, kingship, and kingdom were certainly not foreign to Qohelet. He could have experienced living within the kingdom of Persia and Greece, as well as in the kingdom of Israel/Judah.

A consideration of what specifically Qohelet wrote about the concept of royalty could be helpful. As king he devoted himself to study and to explore, by wisdom, all that is done by men under heaven or under the sun (1:12–14). He discovered that having knowledge and wisdom was not the way or key to grasping the true essence, purpose of, and meaning "all worldly phenomena, both human and natural."[42] In his search after worldly knowledge he found no satisfaction.[43] Even after the survey of all that *yāday* (my hands) had done and what he had toiled to achieve, he saw that everything was *hebel* (vanity or emptiness) (2:11). He had gained nothing.

There is a problem here that requires attention. If the author is Solomon, how is his testimony that he had accomplished nothing to be understood in the light of what is written of Solomon's life, work, wisdom, and accomplishments in 1 Kings 3:7; 10: 23–29 and 2 Chronicles 1:1–9:3. The Chronicler, understood to be Ezra, wrote circa 440, approximately 100 to 150 years before Qohelet is said (by many) to have written Ecclesiastes. The solution to this problem has been offered by those who consider Solomon to have written Ecclesiastes after his repentance shortly before he died. He then realized that his wisdom and knowledge had not kept him from worldly sin and evil living. If this is the solution, as was queried before, why is there no historical record of this turn-about in Solomon's old age?[44] Qohelet wrote objectively about the king and kingship. He referred to how a poor youth could become king (was he referring to David?) or one coming from prison becoming a king's successor (referring to Joseph or Jereboam?) (4:13–15). There is reference to a servant becoming king but his subjects squander good things (10:16, 17). He spoke of a king gaining profit from the increase of the land (5:9). He called for obedience to one's king (no names or reference given) and thus avoid harm (8:2–4). He referred to an incident (not specified) of a powerful king who beseiged a city but was defeated by a poor wise man (9:14, 15).[45] A king's power is less to be desired than wisdom. The implication is that a combination of wisdom and power enables a king to bring victory and well-being to his kingdom. In another passage Qohelet says wisdom makes one wise man more powerful than ten rulers in a city (7:21).

The Cosmic Kingdom

The theocratic kingdom of Israel/Judah did not exist in a vacuum nor did other kingdoms. These all had their existence, place, and role in the cosmic kingdom. This cosmic kingdom is referred to indirectly.[46]

A survey of certain terms gives evidence of a kingdom that is greater and more inclusive than human kingdoms.

Youth are exhorted *zĕkōr 'et bôrĕ' eykâ* (remember your Creator). This concept of Creator (create) is explained (11:5). God does incomprehensible work. Qohelet used the phrase *ma'ăśēh hā'ĕlōhîm* (God the Maker). Some translators (e.g., of the NIV) understand 11:5 to refer to God's creative activities but others to "what God is doing in the earth."[47] A commentator has referred to Ecclesiastes 3:11; 8:17; 9:12.[48] These passages speak of what God has done from the beginning. And no one but God comprehends what goes on under the sun. Nor does any man know his final hour as God does. God is presented not only as the Creator of all things (the cosmic kingdom), but as the omniscient and omnipotent King who knows all and can and does perform wonderfully and majestically within his created universe.[49]

Wisdom's Role in the Kingdom

The terms *ḥokmâh* (wisdom) and *hâkam* (wise) appear over fifty times in the book of Ecclesiastes. God gives wisdom. Not every man receives it; the one who pleases God does (2:26). But does it benefit him? He may work with wisdom but when he dies he has no benefit from it. Someone who has not worked for it may benefit from it (2:21). Wisdom, accepted and applied, does not prevent sorrow in this life (1:18). Wisdom, however, assures advantages. It is like an inheritance. It is good and brings benefits. It is a shelter and preserves life (7:11, 12). Wisdom motivated Qohelet to seek to be wise but he still was not sure what wisdom was (7:24). He realized he needed to search it out and thus understand "the scheme of things" and the stupidity or madness of folly and wickedness (7:23–25). Wisdom was a source of joy and enabled him to see all that God had done, but it did not enable him to comprehend all that he saw (9:14–17). And he learned that a little folly can outweigh wisdom and honor.

In these passages, though a challenge to understand, it nevertheless becomes evident that a definite antithesis exists in one's life and in the entire cosmos. Evil (4:3; 5:13, 16; 6:1; 9:3; 10:5), sin (5:6); and wickedness (8:13; 10:13) challenge the wise and their wisdom can be negated by these. But uprightness and righteousness complement wisdom. Wisdom thus is and serves as a great good in the cosmic kingdom in general and in the hearts, minds, and lives of obedient local kingdoms and cosmic kingdom members.

For past and present times, for local and distant governments, Qohelet has an exhortation that should be heard and followed. "The quiet words of the wise are more to be heeded than the shouts of a ruler of fools. Wisdom is better than weapons of war but one sinner destroys much good" (9:17, 18).[50]

The Covenant

Terms and Concept of Covenant

The term *bĕrît* (covenant) does not appear in the Hebrew text of Ecclesiastes; nor does the term *covenant* appear in various translations of it. Synonomous terms do not appear. Some commentators have referred to the absence of God's covenant name Yahweh in the Hebrew text. Longman suggested a possible reason for this is that covenant love was not compatible with Qohelet's thought and language.[51] Wright opined that Qohelet did not use the term *covenant* because he was writing about God in relation to the whole of mankind. Or, he added, writing in the closing period of the Old Testament times there was a growing "reluctance to use the sacred covenant name in daily speech.[52]

The concept of *bĕrît* (covenant) refers basically to a bond, a firm and re-established relationship. It has been described as a life-love bond.[53] The question to be answered is: does Ecclesiastes exhibit, refer to, or even explain and develop the concept of covenant as presented in all other Old Testament books? If it does not, is it a single exception? Does it stand isolated from the basic message of all other Bible books? The answer is that Ecclesiastes must be considered in the context of the whole Bible.[54] And it should be remembered that the Old Testament is also referred to as the Old Covenant in distinction from the New Covenant, the New Testament. The challenge before us is to demonstrate that Ecclesiastes is a covenantal book.

Administrative and/or Redemptive?

The term *administrative* could be, and is often, replaced by *creation covenant.*[55] The creation covenant, established at the time of creation, embodied all of creation. Yahweh God brought the created cosmos into existence and bonded it to himself. As Creator he continued to be the sovereign ruler over it and the all-sufficient provider for it. Doing this he, in effect, established a means to administer all of creation. Hence the term *administrative*. As will be developed in succeeding sections, the administrative covenant is the context of much of Ecclesiastes.

Within the context of the administrative covenant Yahweh God established the redemptive covenant when Adam and Eve fell into sin and were in dire need of redemption. Thus the sovereign reigning and providing covenant Lord initiated a means of salvation and restoration—the covenant referred to as redemptive, of salvation, and of grace.

The question before the reader/student of Ecclesiastes is: does Qohelet refer to the covenant of grace? salvation? redemption? The Hebrew term *yāšâ* (to save, and derivations of it, e.g., salvation) does not appear in the Hebrew text. Nor does the verb *pādâh* (to redeem) appear. When aspects of the covenant of grace and of the creation covenant are considered, it becomes plain that parts represent the whole.

Constitutive Aspects of the Covenant

There is agreement among commentators and theological writers that the Scriptures refer to elements that constitute a covenant.[56]

God is the sovereign Creator, Maker, and Maintainer of the covenant. God is not referred to in Ecclesiastes by his covenant name Yahweh. He is referred to by his name *'ĕlōhîm* forty times. He is to be revered (3:14; 8:12). Vows are to be made to and before him (5:4). He is to be pleased (2:24–26; 3:15, 17). God tests men (3:18) whom he has created for eternity (3:11). He placed man in a beautiful context and gave him gifts, food, drink, work, and time. Qohelet referred to more such aspects of covenant life God has included as the covenant Maker, Keeper, and Provider.

Mankind was referred to in ancient times as the vassal. Man and woman created in God's image are set forth by Qohelet as subservient to him but not in a slave context. They are portrayed as responsible agents but are limited in knowledge of all that their God has placed them in, before them, and around them.

Essential parts of all covenants were the prescriptions and mandates These are discussed under the succeeding heading of Mandates.

Twofold consequences were included in all covenants. These were determined by the covenant Maker and Keeper according to whatever response mankind made. Blessings of life are for the submissive and obedient one. Curse and death are for the disobedient and covenant breakers. In Ecclesiastes there are references particularly to the latter, the end, to death.

Continuity of covenantal relationships was a major aspect of historic covenants. Continuity was assured particularly through offspring or through family. This aspect of the covenant is not too apparent in the book of Ecclesiastes.

The Covenant Mandates

The Social Mandate

Its Divine Source. The covenantal social mandate covered all relationships between human beings. The central aspect of these relationships was that of husband and wife, parents and children.[57] God had commanded the male (Adam) and the female (Eve) whom he had created and placed in paradise to be fruitful and increase in number. They were to be united and be one flesh. This social mandate was an integral aspect of the Creation/Administrative covenant. This mandate had been repeated to Noah after the flood. God blessed Noah and his sons, commanding them to be fruitful, increase in number, and fill the earth (Gen. 9:1). This creational social mandate was an essential element in the covenant Yahweh God made with Abraham (Gen. 17:2, 16, 19).

Two Groups of People. There are two groups of social entities referred to in the book of Ecclesiastes.

The Family. In the introductory verse (1:1) the parent-offspring reltionship is stated: Qohelet (Solomon), son of David. God had covenanted with David and assured him that offspring from him would be raised up to succeed him (2 Sam. 7:12). David was assured that his house (progeny) would endure forever (7:16). The introduction to the book of Ecclesiastes, by referring to a central aspect of the social mandate, places the entire book in a general social context. It is the son of the covenant man who is introduced as the speaker, teacher, preacher, and counselor.

Family relationships are referred to in various contexts. To illustrate *hebel* (vanity, emptiness), Qohelet referred to an ever toiling man who had neither son nor brother to whom his wealth would go when he died. The implication is that a man who is a father works and provides for his children. The man who has no offspring "toils along to no purpose."[58] Such a man deprives himself of enjoyment (4:8). In another context, a father has nothing for his son because he hoarded it and lost it. Thus, in a world in which misfortune occurs, a father and son will be naked as a newborn child. The implication is that a father provides for his son. Misfortune can bring loss but it does not remove a father's responsibility for his family (5:3–15).

Qohelet also spoke as a father. He said *bĕnî hizzāhēr* (niph. imper. of *zākar*) (my son be warned) (12:12).[59] He had referred to various situations that involved the male, a son, before (4:8; 5:14). At the conclusion of his book Qohelet addressed the son concerning a specific issue. The Teacher[60] (NIV 12:9) had pondered, searched out, and organized extant wisdom sayings considered to be firmly established (12:11). The son was warned not to add to these. To do so would be wearying to the body and fruitless in the end.[61]

Qohelet had a word for the married man. So doing he reflected on the creation ordinance that the man and woman were to be one flesh. This union was to be united by love (9:9). This husband/wife love relationship, existing in what is described as meaningless days under the sun, should be a source of joy (9:9). The husband is encouraged to create the setting for the flourishing of this marital love/life. He is to eat and drink with pleasure at the table his wife has prepared with food and wine. He is to present himself properly dressed, in white clothes, and having groomed himself with oil on his head (9:8).

The family, with its various integral parts, was not considered to exist in isolation. It was a member of society.

The Social Context. It must be acknowledged that the social context cannot be isolated from the spiritual and cultural dimensions of life. These impinge on and influence the lives of people in their social context. Qohelet, however, sees a sharp distinction or division within the social context. The wicked and righteous live side by side. There is the good and evil.[62]

Of the righteous it is said God will bring them to judgment (3:17). Qohelet has seen righteous people perishing in their righteousness—this is meaningless (7:15). The righteous person can at times receive what the wicked deserve (8:14) but Qohelet went on to observe that the righteous and wise are in God's hands (9:1). Yet the righteous share a common destiny with all people, all die, the clean and unclean, those who sacrifice (worship) and those who do not (9:1, 2). As one considers what is written above, one can begin to understand, at least to a degree, why Qohelet referred to *hebel* (vanity, meaningless, emptiness) over forty times. From a strictly human social view, what advantage does the righteous person have in a divided society when in the end of earthly life all die?

Qohelet, however, did recognize the good. He referred to it fourteen times. He stood in line with the past. When God created the cosmos the creating work of each day was declared good. Indeed, all, including the male and female image bearers were, declared very good (Gen. 1:31). Sin had brought evil but Yahweh God preserved his image bearers and supplied them with good. When his covenant people were delivered from Egypt God provided two very good means for them to live and serve their Lord. He provided a good land (Deut. 6:18; 8:7, 10). And he gave them commands and decrees for their own good (Deut. 10:13). The Psalmist had sung "Surely God is good to Israel" (73:1), and he told his soul to "be at rest for the Lord has been good to you" (16:9). The authors of the book of Proverbs repeatedly referred to the good: good path, ways of good men, good name, to seek good brings goodwill, good understanding, good news gives health to bones, and a cheerful heart is good medicine.

Qolehet, in various contexts, challenged himself to find good in pleasure but it was to no avail (2:1). But he knew that being happy and doing good in life was to be in tune with God (3:12). When Qohelet stood in awe of God, he realized it was good to eat, drink, and find satisfaction in his daily work and receive God's gifts in life (5:18–20). When he, however, considered inequality and unfairness in life, then he questioned whether he knew the good or not (6:1, 12). Yet, he knew a good name is better than perfume. Then one can ask: does he contradict himself? He wrote a sad face was good for the heart (7:3) but to have wisdom, like an inheritance, is good (7:11). He called for happiness when times are good (7:14) but it was nevertheless good in this life to avoid extremes (7:16–18).[63] And he added one sinner destroys much good (9:18). Qohelet concluded with a positive reality: God will judge the good! (12:14), that is, judge it to be in keeping with his will.

Qohelet was aware that for a person to be and live righteously, to be and achieve the good that God had embedded in all of creation, an absolute necessary virtue had to be present and exercised. He needed wisdom and to be wise. God gave wisdom and knowledge (2:26). He had what he needed to explore all that was done (1:13) and he increased in wisdom in so doing (1:16). He learned that much wisdom, however, was accompanied by sorrow (1:18). But his mind guided him with wisdom (2:3). By considering wisdom he saw it was better than folly (2:13). Yet he asked what did he gain by being wise (2:15), since he as well as the fool must die (2:16). But in this life, the heart of the wise inclined to the right (10:2).

In Qohelet's social context, the righteous, the good and wise (having wisdom) were acknowledged by God. Within the cosmos, the antithesis was very prevalent and strong. Each God-given virtue had its antithetical counterpart. There is no reference to Satan as the archenemy of God and his people nor to evil spirits. He knew very well, however, that wickedness, evil, and folly were strong and influential forces in the everyday life of the covenant people who sought to exercise their God-given virtues. While this antithesis existed and impacted the lives of God's people, Qohelet knew that, in spite of the antithesis, there was a common bond between all human beings.

This commonness within humanity was expressed in various ways. All have a time to be born and to die (2:16; 3:2). All have life and all are faced with the challenge to work, to be useful, and to enjoy life (3:22; 5:19:11:8). To be remembered, however, there will be many days of darkness[64] that joy will have to contend with—namely, the frustrations of this world and the facing of death.[65]

Sources of frustrations are the antonyms of the virtues God gives that enable a covenant person to enjoy and to live a life pleasing to God.[66]

The antonym of righteous is wicked and the wickedness of men. Both will be judged (3:16, 17). A wicked man may live long in his wickedness (7:15). This wickedness with its stupidity is difficult to understand (7:25). Wickedness has a power to hold the wicked (8: 8d). Yet, Qohelet knew that a wicked man, committing many crimes and living a long time, will not enjoy the better life of the God-fearing man who is reverent before God (8:12). In the end wickedness and the wicked will be brought into judgment.

The antonym of good is evil. Evil resides in men's hearts (8:11:9:3). Evil in life leads to the oppression of people (who have no comforter) (4:1). It leads to hoarding of wealth that can lead to misfortune and miserly living (5:13, 14). A man with God-given wealth may not be able to enjoy it but a stranger does. This is an evil that weighs heavily on men (6:1). Evil times can unexpectedly trap men (9:12) but while life goes on eat your food with gladness and drink your wine with a cheerful heart. Do these as favors God gives (9:7). In the meantime, be aware of another evil brought on by a ruler who does not assign the right people to important positions (10:5–7).

The antonym of the wise and wisdom are the fool and folly. Qohelet learned when seeking to understand madness and folly, it was like meaningless chasing after wind (2:11). But he did realize that wisdom was better than folly and to be wise better than to be a fool (2:13; 8:25). He did conclude a fool folds his hands and ruins himself (4:5); it is better to have one hand and tranquility than toil with two hands (4:6). The fool gives God no pleasure when he does not fulfill his vow immediately. His speech with many words demonstrates his folly (5:3–5; 10:12–14). Quickly provoked anger is the trait of the fool (7:9) as are extortion and bribery (7:7). Hence, Qohelet admonishes the fool not to be over-wicked and die before his time (7:17). A fool is known by his little folly that outweighs wisdom and honor and his lack of sense (10:1–9).

Another set of opposites that are referred to in the social context are love and hate. There is time for each (3:8). Both are recognized as human emotions but conditions for each are not given. A man who reflects on the righteous and the wise, who are in God's hand, is not able to foresee if love or hate awaits him. He knows that after death these are no longer issues of concern (6:1, 6). It is to be observed that Qohelet, if he is aware of the command to love one's neighbor (Lev. 19:18), made no reference to it directly. It could be intimated that he did not deny this injunction when he called for the fear of God and the keeping of his commandments (12:13).

Finally, another case of opposites in the social context is the reference to life and death. Life begins at birth and ends when it is time to die (3:2a). All living people know they will die (9:3). Like the fool, the wise man too must die (2:16). The living person should take this to heart (7:12). Qohelet made some startling statements. The ones who died, that is, the dead, are happier than the ones not yet born and those that are still alive. They have not or will not continue to see the evil done under the sun (4:2). Man's fate in life is like the animal's. Both had the same breath and both die (3:19). A third such statement is: "Don't be overworked, don't be like a fool dying before your time" (7:17). Death can be bitter (7:26). To read Qohelet's words regarding dying and death can be confusing. Yet the basic truth is that man was made to live. Man brought death into the world. He must face its reality, its uncertain time, and its bitterness. It is to be noted that only by implication can it be said that human beings have continuous, that is, eternal life. Qohelet referred to the judging of both the wise and the fool but did not make definite statements concerning the ultimate future of both. He stressed social life and its relationships and that these would end.

The Cultural Mandate

The Historical Setting

When God created the cosmos and placed Adam and Eve in it as vicegerents, they were commanded to rule over all the creatures that move along the ground (Gen. 1:26). They were to fill and subdue the earth (Gen. 1:28), and to receive their sustenance from it (Gen. 1:28–30). After their fall, God pronounced a mitigated curse[67] upon them and the ground they had to cultivate with pain and sweat (Gen. 4:17–19).[68] A careful reading and rereading of the book of Ecclesiastes enables one to increasingly realize that Qohelet is an observer of society (cf. above) and of mankind, especially the remnant of the covenant people, living in the context of a troubled world. The continuing relevance of the cultural mandate, the fall, the mitigated curse, and mankind's continued existence must be clearly seen in order to understand Qohelet's observations and reflections.

Qohelet's Cosmic Perspective

Qohelet states that as he seeks to observe and evaluate life he does this while in Jerusalem. He insisted he was king over Israel and as such he devoted himself to the study and exploration of wisdom.[69] It was thus from a "palace setting in a royal city" that the book of Ecclesiastes was originated (1:12, 16; 2:7, 8). He, however, did not limit his horizon to only Jerusalem or the land of Israel. He indicated that he had a broad and inclusive cosmic view.

His phrase *taḥat haššāmeš* (under the sun) appears thirty times. The phrase *taḥat haššâmâyîm* (under heaven) appears three times. These indicate that "the writer's interaction was universal and not limited to his own people and lands."[70] Yet within the entire realm of living he finds vexation because he is not able to find the heart of human activity and identity.[71] So he introduces his book with *hebel habalem* (vanity, vapor-like, emptiness) and repeats these words with emphasis (1:2)—the inefficiency of all aspects of life.[72] He has given serious attention to these. He wrote of clouds and rain (11:3; 12:2), of animals (3:19, 21), of flies (10:1), of snakes (10:11), and of almond trees (12:5). These are part of creation that God has made beautiful in its time (3:11). He used metaphors drawn from nature, such as thorns crackling in a fire under a pot (7:6). He was confident that though generations of men come and go the earth remains (1:4). The sun, wind, and seas will also; there is nothing really new (1:4–10). In this cosmic setting man lives, thinks, works, and dies.

Human Aspects Considered

Qohelet stood in the midst of the cosmos. He knew that God was/is the "Maker of all things" (11:5). But he confessed that he did not understand or know the path of the wind or how a body is formed in a mother's womb (11:5). He reflected on what David the Psalmist had sung (139:13), and he referred to other aspects of human life.

He recognized the presence and role of a king who represented authority. The oath made to obey him had to be kept (8:2). Qohelet was aware that no king was perfect (10:16). An old king could be foolish, not knowing how to take warnings (4:13). A powerful king could be helped by a man (9:13–15). The king, in spite of human failures, in the context of oppression and of rights and justice denied to the poor, could hardly profit from the field (5:9). The king is not to be reviled, even in thought (10:20). The king of noble birth can be a blessing to the land (as well as the princes, 10:17). It is for the king to see that justice is carried out in situations of judgment. The sentence for a crime should be quickly carried out (8:11). All are to know that judgment on wickedness will, in the end, be carried out by God (3:16, 17).

Qohelet had much to say about work, what was achieved through it and the joy one could experience in the cultural context of cosmic kingdom life. The cultural mandate given at the time of the creation of the image bearers (male and female) of God demanded cultivation of the cosmos. Mankind was commanded to work. Qohelet's first question is: what does man gain from all his labors? (1:3). His initial answer is that by working nothing new comes under the sun (1:9). But that did not prevent him from seeing what worthwhile results could be achieved. He worked: built houses, planted vineyards, and made gardens and parks. He planted all kinds of fruit trees. He developed an irrigation system. He owned herds of cattle and flocks of sheep. He amassed gold and silver. He acquired a choir of men and women and a harem. He confessed he had all the delights of a man's heart 2:3–9). It is quite obvious that Qohelet was describing Solomon, especially in the initial part of his reign (1 Kings. 10:14–21). Yet he, when surveying and evaluating all he had done and achieved, concluded "everything is *hebel*" (emptiness, meaningless, a vapor). In reality he had gained nothing, (2:11). His wisdom was better than folly yet he, the wise man had the same fate as *haksîl* (the fool) who walked in darkness (2:14).

Work was grievous to Qohelet (it was vanity) (2:11). It gave him pain, grief, and restlessness (2:23). He toiled, knowing that what he gained in life would go after death to another –who might be a fool (2:17–23). Yet he knew if his successor was a man of wisdom, God would give him knowledge and happiness. Thus a sinner's work could become a blessing to his inheritor (2:25). Qohelet knew that there was nothing better than to be happy and do good. He may not, as a worker, gain (wealth?). He, however, would accept the satisfaction that to keep what he received from his toil, was a gift of God (3:9, 12–14).

Qohelet decided to have another look (4:1). Envy motivated his neighbor, a fool who folded his hands and ruined himself (4:4). Without the help of a friend, a lone man realized there was no end to this toil. Why am I doing this? he asked (4:7–12).

The question has been asked: does Qohelet consider that work and toil are cursed? He implies, if not suggests it openly, that work is a bane.[73] The question to be answered is: do Qohelet's "negative" comments concerning work reflect the curse, on the ground and on men's work, that God pronounced to Adam and Eve (Gen. 3:17–19)? Anderson wrote that he saw this curse in Qohelet's writing. Four such evidences of the curse are present: (1) curse on general work (1:3) in creation; (2) on intellectual work (1:12–18); Anderson wrote "all his hard work-intellectual work, was for nought,." it was cursed (108); (3) on business and achievements (2:4–28); Anderson wrote that Qohelet hated life because of the grievous work he had to do for these areas (1:11, 4:4); (4) on political work (8:1–10:20) because of corruption. The response to Anderson's presentation should, on the whole, be positive. All of life in the cosmic world was placed under the covenantal curse. All areas of cosmic existence, the natural, the national, the personal, were placed under the curse. But the curse was mitigated. The cosmos continued, all aspects continued. All these cursed aspects or areas of the cosmos could be restored through redemption. This reality gives the basis for the positive result of work in the cosmos. The curse will not be completely removed. Much of its effects can be alleviated and even obliterated to an extent. The evidence for this is included in what Qohelet wrote.

He referred to the beneficial and good results of work in the cosmos. Houses were built and vineyards were planted (2:4–8). Prosperity was evident and demonstrated (6:3–6). Money was at hand; it served as a shelter (7:12). The covenant cultural mandate, in spite of the mitigated curse, was obeyed and life was blessed. And that was cause for joy. The verb (*śām̄âh, 'śāmiâh*) is usually translated rejoice, be glad; joy, gladness, mirth, and derivations appear often in Ecclesiastes in various contexts.[74] Some scholars have argued that "the essential nature of Qohelet is one of joy not pessimism."[75]

A review of the passages in which joy, enjoy, rejoice appears may prove helpful in a decision if joy in the basic *leitmotif* of Ecclesiastes. The repeated use of *hebel* (vanity, empty, meaningless) has led the majority of scholars to consider Qohelet to have been a master of pessimism.

Qohelet's first use of *śimĕhâh* is in 2:1.[76] Crenshaw understood 1:18 as referring to sorrow and grief, that is, a statement about the futility of joy.[77] But Qohelet was prepared to test his "pessimism" with joy or pleasure and did so (2:10). He took delight in his work. His conclusion was *hebel* (vanity) (2:11). Yet he went on to say that he could find and receive enjoyment, wisdom, and knowledge from the hand of God (2:25, 26). He concluded his "investigation on a modestly upbeat note."[78] Qohelet continued to observe and reflect on life. He saw that in life there was continued tension—a time to be born and a time to die (3:2). He covered many aspects of life pointing out the opposites—antithetical realities (3:2–8)—and asked, what does a worker gain? (3:9). God has made him an eternal being and sovereignly placed him in time within the cosmos where men must work. God will test him, in preparation for judgment (3:16–21). He concludes with a positive statement. The better things to do *wes yismâh* (qal impf. of *śāmâh*), is to rejoice—really he *should* enjoy, yes, rejoice in his own work. He again concluded with the concept of "joy" in the natural areas of life (3:22).

Qohelet wrote: again I looked (4:1). He saw oppression (4:1–3) and envy (4:1–7). He saw workers who needed help (4:8–12) and dissatisfaction in advancement. Again his evaluation was *hebel* (vanity) (4:13–16). He saw poor people oppressed and denied justice and he saw a greedy love for wealth (5:8–12) and the seeming uselessness of wealth (5:13–17). And again Qohelet reflects on the positive aspects of cultural life. It was good to eat, to drink, to be satisfied, to enjoy wealth and possessions that God gives. The conclusion again includes joy because God enables man to have it (5:18–20).

Qohelet, however, also saw that a man might not enjoy his cultural advantages, even if he has a hundred children and lives a long life. The end of a wise or poor man is the same. There has been no gain (6:1–12). In reality, the heart of the wise lives in mourning and that of a fool in *śimhâh* (pleasure) (7:1–4). But living in obedience to the king and submitting to justice (8:1–14) is the context for the enjoyment of life (8:15). But don't try to comprehend all that God has done (8:16). Meanwhile as man lives, he is urged to "go, eat your food *běśimhâh* (with joy) and drink your wine with *śimhâh* (joy in your heart) (9:7; 10:19).

As Qohelet expressed his concluding thoughts he gave advice to men who may live many years to enjoy them all (11:8). He then addressed the young man who has a full life before him *śimâh!* (rejoice). It is an imperative. "Rejoice," and he added, "cause your heart to give you joy as you follow your heart and what your eyes may see" (11:9).[79]

In conclusion to this discussion of joy in Qohelet's inspired writings, the question to be answered, as asked before, is "joy" the leitmotif and not *hebel* (vanity, emptiness, confusion, contradictions, foolishness, meaningless)? The term *hebel* (vanity) occurs more often than *śimhâh* (joy). That does not mean, however, that Qohelet emphasized vanity more than joy. He certainly was a realist. He viewed life in the cosmos in a very honest manner. The cultural mandate had to be recognized and obeyed. If it was, was it done so correctly? Was there a purpose in doing so? Was there gain in doing so? Many readers and commentators have concluded that Qohelet's thinking was on the whole negative. A consideration of the spiritual mandate should be helpful to find a positive place in Christian theology for Qohelet's wisdom and challenge.[80]

The Spiritual Mandate

The Creator/Image Bearer Relationship

Qohelet acknowledged God the Creator in various ways. He wrote of God as the Maker of all things (11:5). His many references to God[81] indicate that God was not only aware of mankind but that an intimate relationship between God and mankind continued from the time of creation. He knew God is in heaven and man is on earth (5:2). That spatial separation did not cut off the relationship between them. Qohelet knew God was present and active in people's lives. God tests mankind (3:18) as he upholds and blesses them (3:19).

Qohelet revealed that he knew how the spiritual relationship had been established by God and that man had to acknowledge it, respond to it, and cultivate it. Man and woman are to go to the house of God to listen (worship) and to make vows to God (5:1). And doing so, "stand in awe of God" (5:7). Concepts such as faith or belief in God and love for God do not appear in Qohelet's writing.[82] He did write concerning the fear of God and fearing God and being reverent before him (8:12; 12:13). This concept of fear[83] is a correlate to awe. In Scripture the term *fear* can refer to being afraid or having terror. In many contexts it refers to the intimate relationship between God the Creator and Redeemer and mankind. It can and often includes the concepts of acceptance, love, and humble submission.

In addition to fearing God, Qohelet has three more specific exhortations that pertain to acknowledging the spiritual mandate and the cultivation of the spiritual relationship between God the Creator and his covenant people.

First, Qohelet addressed the youth *śĕmah* (to enjoy or rejoice). Youth is the time for the formation, development, and strengthening of the spiritual relationship between God and a person. This applies to both male and female. They are not to be worried, concerned, or overwhelmed by the *hebel* (vanity) in the cosmos, in its social relationship, and in the confusing broad views of cultural life and its many aspects. The youth are to have an open heart so that they can receive and experience joy (11:9). They are to banish anxieties from the heart and banish physically oriented troubles. These are basically meaningless and give no satisfaction or security.

Second, youth cannot, and will not, have joy if they attempt to do so on their own and with their own weak and inefficient abilities. The exhortation is clear, the intent unavoidable. In the text, the *waw* (and) informs the reader that the command relates to the previous imperative "to rejoice." *Zĕkôr bôrĕ'eykâ* (remember your Creator).[84] The Creator has brought you into this world. He has a way of life for you, a purpose and goal. Remember, think, place firmly in your mind that you are not autonomous and independent of your Creator who is your sustaining guide and provider in all of life. And get educated in your youth before your vitality decreases as you become older and social and cultural life becomes more confusing and challenging.[85]

Third, to fear God, to rejoice and to remember one's Creator it is necessary, absolutely so, to *miswôtâyu śĕmôr* (his commandments keep). The commandments refer to the Decalogue but in this context also to the entire revelation God has given to mankind. This statement by Qohelet emphasizes man's need more than God's demands.[86] To be spiritually alive, vibrant, and joyful in life, with all of its contradictions, passing fancies, confusion, and unreliability, requires the help and guidance that God' s will provides. At the heart of this will are his commandments which are an absolute necessity for life.

The term *śāmar* translated keep is also translated obey (8:2). The keeping of God's commandments is nothing other than to obey God (Deut. 6:24). Although it was noted above that man's need was stressed more in this context, it must not be interpreted that God's demands are secondary. God has demands that he holds before us. These are summed up in the Decalogue (Exod. 20:1–17). The summary of it demands love for God (Deut. 6:4) and one's neighbor (Lev. 19:18). This, Qohelet informs us, can be exhibited by *śalah laḥmĕkā* (cast your bread) upon the waters (11:1). If done, it will be found again and it will have increased so that seven or eight portions of it can be given to others (11:2). Generosity is a fruit of one's adhering to the covenantal spiritual mandate.

Theological Assertions

In various contexts[87] Qohelet indicated that the spiritual mandate was to be known and kept. Basic truths—theological concepts—had to be recognized and believed. The truths revealed in the past were very important for a God-fearing life.

The knowledge of God is indispensable. He, the Creator, is the author of the day and prosperity (7:14). Every good gift comes from his hand (2:24; 3:12–15;

5:19; 6:2).[88] He is the judge (3:14). He imparts wrath and grace (2:24), and inspires fear (3:14; 5:7). He is absolutely sovereign in his being, works, and gifts.

The knowledge of self is a corollary to the knowledge of God. Mankind is a creature, and must remember and obey his Maker. He must remember that his Creator has established a living relationship with him. Mankind has been given privileges, duties, and responsibilities. Covenant people must be filled with joy, and exhibit it. They must realize that work and worship have been decreed for them.[89]

The knowledge of human existence in a world of contradictions and confusion is necessary. In this context in which mankind is inextricably placed, he must know and remember God has ordained that "suffering is an adornment of divine law." God's righteousness "cannot leave even the sin of its own children unpunished."[90]

The knowledge of the passing of time (6:12) should spur the covenant person to be faithful to do his duties as he accepts the privileges and responsibilities God gives (11:6). Every person should be aware that in the time God gives, there are many activities to be assumed: to plant and uproot, to kill and to heal, to tear down and to build, to love and to hate, to be at war and at peace (3:1–8).

The knowledge and value of true wisdom is basic. Wisdom enables mankind to face this world as it is with its suffering and its many seeming discrepancies.[91] Wisdom is a gift. To have and exercise wisdom, that is, to be wise and to reject folly, is a very important reality in fulfilling the covenantal spiritual mandate.

The Cosmic Scope. Qohelet was very mindful of the cosmic scope. He referred to God's creating activity when he wrote of God's doings from the beginning to the end (3:11). He viewed all of time, existence, and activities that mankind was involved in within this entire span. His phrase, under the sun, expresses this continuity of time from its beginning to its end. God has been, is, and will be the constant sovereign Lord over time and all that transpires within it. Hence the exhortation to the youth: remember your Creator (12:1). Uphold, develop, and increase in the blessed knowledge that one is the object of his Maker's care and provision.

Mankind's Life. Qohelet spoke concerning a person's life span of time. His reference to birth and death indicate his awareness and belief that under the sun God has set a time for each person's beginning of life and for its end (3:2). He wrote concerning death as the destiny of every man (7:2), and that the day of death had its advantage.[92] In the world of vanities, it is better to have sorrow than laughter (7:3, 4). Death brings an end to the involvement in the vexations and contradictions in life yet Qohelet referred to death as bitter (7:26), and no one has power over the day of his death (8:8). God alone does.

Qohelet, when reflecting on God's creation, wrote that light is sweet and it is pleasant to see the sun. Thus one can enjoy many years of life—but in most of these, he must remember the many days of darkness (12:2). In preparation for the end of one's life one must therefore remember the Creator. Then when the sun grows dark (12:2), work ceases (12:13), bird songs grow faint, and desire (to live?) is stirred no longer, one is prepared to go to his eternal home (12:1–5).

The covenant man's destiny is to go to *bet 'olamo* (house of his eternity or eternal home). His body, consisting of the dust of the earth, will return to the ground (dust) (Gen. 3:19; Eccles.12:7), but the spirit of man returns to God who gave it (12:7). And man's spirit is able for this return and to enter his eternal home because God *natan ha'olam belibam* (gave) eternity in his heart (3:11). How is eternity in the heart to be understood?[93] Or did Qohelet mean that eternity was set in man's mind?[94] Or does it refer to man's deep-seated sense of eternity?[95] The proper answer is in the passage. Man was created physical and spiritual, a psychosomatic being. He was made a spiritual being when God breathed in him the breath of life at the time of his creation. Man and woman are therefore capable of knowing and obeying the spiritual mandate, that is, to live in intimate spiritual fellowship with their Creator.

Preparation for the Eschaton. Man and woman, as spiritual beings, face a great challenge while they as spiritual-physical beings live on the earth. They have the spiritual mandate; they are called to know it, obey it, and live according to it. Qohelet makes it clear that the people, when returning to dust and the eternal home, will be judged. There, at the end of time, in the eschaton, judgment day is awaiting them (3:15, 17; 11:9; 12:14). Both wickedness and righteousness will be criteria for the judgment of the righteous person and the wicked one (3:15–17). Qohelet exhorted the youth to enjoy life but to know that God will bring them into judgment. It was not a call to be anxious or troubled about life. Youths, as they lived, were to continue in happy and blessed fellowship with their Creator Judge (11:9, 10).

Qohelet referred to life from creation to judgment day. His references to and description of life in that span of time was *hebel* (vanity). To consider life throughout all of time, and all of a person's life could be and was empty, meaningless, without purpose or goals if considered only under the sun. Indeed, if human life was the same as and completely equal to an animal's, life was *hebel* (vanity). As both are earthly creatures, man has no advantage (3:19, 22).

Man, however, being an eternal spirit, must prepare in this life for judgment by God of every exposed or hidden good or evil thing (12:14). In the day of judgment, sure to come, every person will face the sovereign Judge. Whether he recognizes that this was to happen or not and did not prepare for it, he will be judged. The covenant person obeying the spiritual mandate will be judged also and all three mandates, the social, the cultural, and the spiritual will be standards by which every deed, good or bad, will be judged.

The revelation of God in word and deed had progressed from the time of creation to the time Qohelet observed life and pondered on what he saw and experienced. He did not include certain specifics such as who would be the judge. The New Testament later reveals that the Son would be. Qohelet did not refer to the outcome or results of the judgment. There is no reference to perdition or hell. His reference to the eternal home undoubtedly referred to heaven. Nor did he refer to the fellowship forgiven and cleansed saints would have with their Lord for eternity.

One could consider that Qohelet should have added to what Moses, the Prophets, and the Poets had said. Then his time would not be too difficult to determine. In a real sense, he did not indicate an awareness of the progress of revelation. He did, however, refer to the entire period of time between creation and judgment day. And, observing life and evaluating it when he lived and wrote, he did not contradict or deny any aspect of previous revelation. His concern was to speak to his and all following generations concerning life under the sun in which the antithesis was present, real, and affecting all existence. Thus a direct intention can be discerned: life under the sun, that is, here on earth and viewed only from an earthly perspective, is *hebel* (vanity). Face it! Admit it! But don't despair. There is a future for those who prepare for it by submitting to God and keeping his threefold covenantal mandates.

The Mediator

His Biblical Presence

The Mediator, the Messiah, had been promised after the fall of Adam and Eve (Gen. 3:15). His preincarnate presence and ministry had been progressively revealed by word, by deed, and by various types. David and Solomon were recognized as types of the royal person and office of Jesus Christ. These two persons were referred to (1:1), but not specifically as forerunners of the Messiah nor as foreshadowing Christ's presence and work on earth.

Since all prophets who had been faithful and true to God were types and forerunners of Jesus, the Messiah, they all foreshadowed Christ's prophetic office and work. Qohelet could be considered such a forerunner also. He did not refer to himself as a prophet or in any way as a spokesman and representative of God. The phrase "thus says the Lord" does not appear in his writings. What he wrote, however, did not contradict what others had proclaimed and written. In reality, his message concerning the condition of his time coincided with the message of other prophets, who, as most did, addressed the conditions of their times. Qohelet not only added to this message but he supplied aspects and details of how many covenant people failed to live according to the covenant mandates. He also, in somewhat indirect terms, referred to the destiny of covenant people after death (12:5).

The Stage for His Coming

Various Old Testament prophets had prophesied concerning what the Messiah would do when he came. The prophet Malachi spoke concerning the corruption prevalent in the worship of the covenant people (1:10–14; 2:10–13; 3:8–12), and in their social arena (2:14–17). He had spoken plainly: the coming Messiah would be as a refiner's fire or as a launderer's soap; a refiner and purifier. He would testify against socerers, adulterers, perjurers, defrauders, oppressors, and deprivers of justice (3:1–5, 14, 15). Qohelet's message regarding his time certainly adds to

Malachi's description of the spiritual, cultural, and spiritual conditions. A commentator has written, and that correctly, that the problems raised by Qohelet could only be solved by the coming of Christ.[96] Qohelet added urgency to the need for the promised Messiah.

A re-reading of this chapter and editing it has increased my readiness to accept Qohelet as a sage who wrote during the third century B.C. As he viewed life during this post-Old Testament prophetic era, he was deeply aware of the situation in the religious, social, and cultural aspects of life. And he was also fully aware of Yahweh God's abiding revealed Word with its promises and warnings. As a contemporary of people living in the third century B.C., he was inspired by the Holy Spirit to describe what life was like. Even more, he was inspired to reveal the joy that God had for his obedient people who lived in troubled, confusing, and often threatening circumstances. And to draw the attention of his fellow Israelites, he put on the royal robe of Solomon, who had lived, reigned, and spoken centuries earlier.

Notes

1. This is a select bibliography that I, the author of this chapter, have consulted. Some works may not be directly referred to in the notes.

G. CH. Aalders, *Het Boek De Prediker* (Kampen: Kok, 1948); William H. U. Anderson, "The Curse of Work in Qoheleth: An Expose of Genesis 3:17–19 in Ecclesiastes," *Evangelical Quarterly* 70 no.2 (April 1998): 99–113; and "The Problematics of the Sitz im Leben of Qoheleth," *Old Testament Essays* 12 no. 2, (1999): 233–48; L. Gleason Archer, "Ecclesiastes" in *The Zondervan Pictorial Encyclopedia of the Bible*, vol. II (Grand Rapids: Zondervan, 1975); Craig Bartholomew, "Qoheleth in Canon? Current Trends in the Interpretation of Ecclesiastes," *Themelios* 24, no. 3 (1999): 4–20 and *Reading Ecclesiastes* (Rome: Editrice Pontificio Instituto Biblico, 1998); Charles Bridges, *An Exposition of the Book of Ecclesiastes* (Edinburgh: Banner of Truth Trust, 1960); William P. Brown, *Ecclesiastes* (Louisville: John Knox, 2000); Walter Brueggemann, *In Man We Trust* (Richmond: John Knox, 1972); Brevard S. Childs, *Biblical Theology of the Old and New Testaments* (Minneapolis: Fortress, 1993); James L. Crenshaw, *Ecclesiastes* (Philadelphia: Westminster, 1987); Mitchell Dahood, "Canaanite-Phoenician Influence in Qoheleth," *Biblica,* 33, (March 1952): 33–52; 191–221; S. De Jong, "God in the Book of Qohelet: A Reappraisal of Qohelet's Place in Old Testament Theology," *VT* 47, no. 2 (April 1997): 154–67; Franz Delitzsch, *Commentary on The Song of Songs and Ecclesiastes* (Grand Rapids: Eerdmans Pub. 1950); Michael V. Fox, *A Time to Tear Down and A Time to Build Up* (Grand Rapids, Eerdmans, 1999); Robert Gordis, *Koheleth—The Man and His World* (New York: Schocken, 1973); Robert C. Harrison, Jr., "Qoheleth Among the Sociologists," *Biblical Interpretation,* no 2, (1997): Gerhard F. Hasel, *The Remnant* (Berrien Springs: University Press, 1972); Ernest Hengstenberg, *A Commentary on Ecclesiastes* (Evansville: Sovereign Grace 1960); Svend Holm-Nielsen, "On the Interpretation of Qoheleth in Early Christianity," *Vetus Testmentum*, 24, (April, 1974):168–177; Ernest Horton, "Qoheleth's Concept of Opposites,"

Numen, 19:1–21; Gordon J. Keddie, *Looking for the Good Life* (Phillipsburg: Presbyteritan and Reformed, 1991); Derek Kidner, *The Message of Ecclesiastes* (Downers Grove: Inter-Varsity, 1976); H. C. Leupold, *Exposition of Ecclesiastes* (Columbus: Wartburg, 1958); Tremper Longman, III, *The Book of Ecclesiastes* (Grand Rapids: Eerdmans, 1998); Douglas B. Miller, *Symbol and Rhetoric in Ecclesiastes* (Atlanta: Society of Biblical Literature, 2002); Roland Edmund Murphy and Elizabeth I. Huwiler, *Proverbs, Ecclesiastes, Song of Songs* (Peabody: Hendrickson, 1999); James S. Rietman, "The Structure and Unity of Ecclesiastes," *Bib Sac* 154 no.615, (July-September 1997): 297–319; Dominic Rudman, "A Note on the Dating of Ecclesiastes," *CBQ* 61 no.1, (January 1999): 47–52 and "Woman as Divine Agent in Ecclesiastes," *JBL* 116 no.3 (Fall 1997): 411–27; H. Carl Shank, "Qoheleth's World and Life View as Seen in His Recurring Phrases," *Westminster Theological Journal,* 37, 57–73; Andrew G. Shead, "Reading Ecclesiastes 'Epilogically,'" *Tyndale Bulletin* 48 no.1 (May 1997): 67–91; Martin A. Shields, "Ecclesiastes and the End of Wisdom," *Tyndale Bulletin* 50 no.1 (1999): 117–39; Gerard Van Groningen, *From Creation to Consummation*, vol. 1 (Sioux Center: Dordt Press, 1996) and *Messianic Revelation in the Old Testament* (Grand Rapids: Baker, 1990); Gerhardus Vos, *Biblical Theology—Old and New Testament* (Grand Rapids: Eerdmans, 1980); Roger N. Whybray, *Ecclesiastes* (Grand Rapids: Eerdmans, 1989); Neal David Williams, *A Biblical Theology of Ecclesiastes* (Ann Arbor: University Microfilms International, 1985) D. Wilson, *Joy at the End of the Tether* (Moscow: Canon, 1999); Addison G. Wright, "The Riddle of the Sphinx: The Structure of the Book of Qoheleth," *CBQ* 30 no.3, (1968): 313–34; J. Stafford Wright, "Ecclesiastes," *The Expositor's Bible Commentary,* vol. 5 (Grand Rapids: Zondervan, 1991); Marten Wyngaarden, *The Future of the Kingdom in Prophecy and Fulfillment* (Grand Rapids: Baker, 1955); Roy B. Zuck, ed. *Reflecting with Solomon: Selected Studies on the Book of Ecclesiastes* (Grand Rapids: Baker, 1994).

2. Cf. G. CH. Aalders, *Boek—Prediker*. He includes Dutch, German, and English authors, 26–28. C. Bartholomew in *Reading Ecclesiastes* included 28 pages of vocabulary; it includes wisdom literature titles, 275–301. The most extensive bibliography is included in Williams' essay "Interpretation-Qoholeth": "no other book in the Old Testament has been interpreted in so radically different ways than the book of Ecclesiastes," 168.

3. Wright, "Riddle of Spring," 313.

4. Bridges, "Ecclesiastes," 1137.

5. Wright, *Ecclesiastes, III*, 1137.

6. Bartholomew, "Qoheleth . . . Canon," 5.

7. Ibid. S. Holm-Nielsen began his essay "Interpretation-Qoholeth" stating "that no other book in the Old Testament has been interpreted in so radically different ways as the book of Ecclesiastes," 168.

8. Brown, *Ecclesiastes,* produced a 21–theme outline. He wrote:" a clear structure proves elusive," 16. Crenshaw produced an altogether different outline in an acrostic form with 98 themes, *Ecclesiastes*. He added that his "scheme lacks perfection" 39. Longman concluded that his analysis yielded a 4–point general outline, *Ecclesiastes*, 22. Meanwhile Williams in his doctoral dissertation, having reviewed the history of the problem of the unity of the book, evaluated arguments against unity and concluded that the unity of the message of Ecclesiastes could be adopted as a working hypothesis, 23–33.

9. Wilson, *Joy at End*, 12. Hengstenberg wrote that the human side of the book of Ecclesiastes belongs in the sphere of sacred philosophy. The writer does not profess to be an organ of direct revelation, 24.

10. Miller, "Symbol and Rhetoric," 1–15.

11. Harrison, "Qoheleth . . . Sociologists," 160–180. Harrison wrote in the abstract that Qoheleth's thought was set in the socological mileu of third-century Judaism, 180.

12. Miller, "Symbol and Rhetoric," 1–15.

13. Rudman, "Woman . . . Divine Agent," 412–21. In comments on 9:9 Rudman wrote that life with a woman one loves is typical of or reflective of the overall vanity (emptiness?) of existence, 421.

14. Various authors of books on Ecclesiastes referred to the hesitancy of rabbis to include Ecclesiastes in the canon during deliberations at the Council of Jamnia, held circa A.D. 100.

15. Whybray, *Ecclesiastes*, 29. The thought is fundamentally Hebrew and the book could only have been written by a Jew who did give his people a new perspective, 28, 29.

16. Cf. section in this chapter entitled "The Covenant."

17. S. De Jong, "God . . .Qoheleth," presented six "classifications of the forty statements" about God. (1) God is Creator and provides all things. (2) He is to be respected. (3) God's works are unfathomable. (4) They cannot be changed. (5) God acts deterministically. (6) God judges the just and wicked, 155–59. De Jong concluded that Qoheleth's main theme is human limitation in relation to God, 166. Another author wrote that Ecclesiastes is not an inferior piece of theology. As for example, "the teacher's faith in the justice and the goodness of God's comments run far deeper" than the analysis of most commentators on the book. Garrett, "The Theology and Purpose of Ecclesiastes," in *Reflecting—Solomon,* 156.

18. Vos, *Biblical Theology*, 58.

19. Childs, *Biblical Theology*. He made two references to Ecclesiastes: 3:1ff. and 3:11, 566, 569 in the section entitled "Humanity: Old and New." Bartholomew, *Reading Ecclesiastes,* discussed Childs' views on Ecclesiastes as these were recorded in his (Childs') *Introduction to the Old Testament as Scripture*. He commented on Childs' statements that Childs "has little to say about the main body of Ecclesiastes"; it contains collections of sayings. There "is no attempt to present" a unified reflection on life, 105. Vos made no reference to Ecclesiastes in his *Biblical Theology* and a consultation of some specific theological studies revealed no reference to Ecclesiastes, e.g., Hasel, *Remnant*, and Wyngaarden, *Future Kingdom*.

20. Williams, *A Biblical Theology*, cf. esp. 300–304.

21. Keddie, in *Looking—Life*, wrote that Ecclesiastes is not a work of full-orbed evangelism but it presents three facts of life: (1) Life is short. (2) There is no lasting satisfaction. (3) There is nothing new. He did offer an outline of contents that could be considered progressive: Basics (1–3), Problems (4–6), Answers (7–10), Decisions (11, 12), 1–11.

22. Rudman, "Structure—Unity," 297–319.

23. Ibid. 315. Rudman's 7–point outline stresses the futility and despair of man's search that moves him to seek the true path to wisdom in which there is moral authority, 317–19.

24. Cf., e.g., Delitzsch, *Song of Songs/Ecclesiastes*, 218.

25. Whybray, *Ecclesiastes*, 21, 22.

26. Ibid. 2.

27. The discussion concerning the authorship of Ecclesiastes has been widely and in many cases carefully discussed. A brief summary of what commentators and essayists have written suffices for this study.

28. Brown, *Ecclesiastes*, 21, 22.

29. Hengstenberg, *Ecclesiastes,* reflected on passages such as Eccl. 3:16, 17, referring to the "divine righteousness which cannot leave even the sin of its own children unpunished," 21.

30. Rudman "Note . . . Dating," wrote that terms used indicate a Persian setting, and rejected a Grecian setting, 48.

31. Whybray, *Ecclesiastes*, expressed the view that the social conditions referred to in Ecclesiastes point to the Ptolemaic era. He added, the book was written in Jerusalem, 13.

32. Ibid., 28.

33. Cf. Brown, *Ecclesiastes*, 7 ff.

34. Rudman, "Structure—Unity," wrote that Ecclesiastes is poorly constructed and that there is no progression of thought, nor is there evidence of what is unique to how Hebrew thought is expressed, 297–98.

35. Whybray, *Ecclesiastes*, 23.

36. Crenshaw, *Ecclesiastes*, 28.

37. Brown, *Ecclesiastes*, 17.

38. See 337–38.

39. Kidner, *Ecclesiastes*, 17. He was joined by others who suggested "impersonation of Solomon" and of a series of editors. Cf. also Longman, *Ecclesiastes*, 8, 9.

40. Cf. reference to these on 340.

41. Recall in a preceding discussion reference was to the teacher impersonating the king or putting on the mantle of the king.

42. Braun, *Ecclesiastes*, 29.

43. Delitzsch, *Song—Ecclesiastes*, 226. Longman, *Ecclesiastes*, wrote that the scope of Qohelet's enterprise is incredibly extensive, 78; it was "comprehensive," 80.

44. Cf. 338.

45. Crenshaw, *Ecclesiastes* entitled the paragraph (9:13–18) "Wasted Wisdom." He wrote that an example is offered, "perhaps hypothetical" of skill that did not bring success. A poor wise man could have saved a village besieged by a powerful king, but the residents forgot him, 165. Crenshaw recognized the alternative reading in brackets that the poor wise man did save the town but villagers forgot him afterward.

46. Various books, commentaries, and theological studies that were consulted paid little if any attention to the cosmic kingdom of the Creator, the reigning Lord.

47. Longman, *Ecclesiastes*, 257–58.

48. Crenshaw, *Ecclesiastes,* 180.

49. More evidence of the cosmic kingdom and of mankind's involvement will be discussed on 354.

50. G. Ogden, in his essay "Variations on the Theme of Wisdom's Strength and Vulnerability, Eccl. 9:17—10:20." Zuck, *Reflecting . . . Solomon*, 331–340, wrote of the notorious difficulty in delimiting units of thought in Qohelet (331) and discerning the relationship between the units of thought (335, 336, 338) The passage under consideration places before the reader the antithesis between wisdom and folly—and though wisdom is vulnerable it can overcome *hata'im gedolim* (offenses great) (10:4), 336.

51. Longman, *Ecclesiastes*, 35.

52. Wright, "Ecclesiastes," 1148. Wright's implication that the covenant name Yahweh was only for Israel is difficult to accept. Job was not an Israelite; the name *Yahweh* appears when the Lord spoke to him (Job 33:1).

53. See Van Groningen, *Messianic Old Testament*, 60, 62, 103. Ezek. 20:37 refers to the bond of the covenant.

54. One definite consideration is that it was included in the canon as an integral part of the whole biblical message. Cf. what I wrote in *Messianic Revelation in the Old Testament* under the heading of the unified Message of the Bible, 62.

55. Cf. my discussion of the creation covenant in *From Creation to Consummation*, 65–70.

56. These elements are present, in various references, in the creation/administrative, redemptive covenants and also in legal, political, business covenants. These can also be referred to as compacts, pacts, or leagues.

57. The social mandate was pronounced at the time of the creation of male and female (Gen. 1:27–28a; 2:22, 24).

58. Castellino, "Qohelet and His Wisdom" in Zuck, *Reflecting . . . Solomon*, 37.

59. Some commentators translate *bĕnî,* root term *ben,* other than referring to a male child. The term in the Old Testament is employed to refer to servants, students. In Ecclesiastes the term refers predominately to son, or children; cf. e.g., 1:1, 13; 2:3, 8; 3:10, 18, 19, 21; 4:8; 5:14 [MT 13]; 8:11; 9:3, 12; 10:17.

60. According to the Hebrew text, the term is Qohelet, but translated as Teacher in NIV. Longman considers a "frame narrator" to be summarizing Qohelet's teaching. *Ecclesiastes*, 276, 277.

61. Commentators vary in their understanding of what Qohelet wrote in the Epilogue. Essayists have also. Cf. Shead, "Reading . . . Epilogically" and Shields, "Ecclesiastes . . . Wisdom."

62. The wicked are referred to nine times, wickedness four times, the good, fourteen times, and wise is referred to twenty-four times. These "opposite" terms are sure indicators of the antithesis in the lives of covenant people.

63. This passage has given rise to much discussion. Is Qohelet teaching to *hold* on to a compromise—not too righteous and not too wicked? Does Delitzsch help by describing the terms as overly righteous and overly wicked? *Songs—Ecclesiastes*, 326. Longman, *Ecclesiastes*, in parenthesis wrote "Qohelet is not always consistent. He pleads against overweening righteousness and wickedness," 192–97.

64. Commentators differ in understanding the phrase *yĕmēy hahōsek* (days of darkness). Bartholomew, *Reading Ecclesiastes*, wrote "old age leading to death," 250. Aalders in *Prediker*, referred to *den tijd des doods* (the time of death) 239. Longman understood the phrase to say "old age and death," *Ecclesiastes*, 259.

65. Kidner, *Ecclesiastes,* 99.

66. Horton in "Koheleth's . . . Opposites" published in 1972, a digest of it in 1975 in *Theology Digest*, 265–67. The opposites referred to are loving-hating; prosperity-adversity; life-death; growth-decay. A concluding comment refers to Qohelet's conviction that existence is inconsistent and ambiguous. Horton considers Qohelet to be reflecting on problems raised in different parts of the world. Also, he considers Qohelet to be consistent with philosophically oriented Taoists in Asia and Plato and Heroditus in the Greek world, 20 (72 essay).

67. See author's *From Creation to Consummation* for a discussion of the phrase "mitigated curse," 125–26.

68. Shank in "Qohelet's World and Life" wrote that "the historical-redemptive *antecedents* of Qohelet's sight-perspective find their point of reference in the fall and curse of Gen. 3," 62, 63.

69. Cf. what was written on 337–38.

70. Wright, "Ecclesiastes," 1152.

71. Brown, *Ecclesiastes*, 23.

72. Ibid., 2.

73. See Anderson, *Curse of Work.* Anderson also sees implications of the curse on work in Genesis 4—Cain and Abel episode, 107–12.

74. Cf. e.g., 2:1, 2, 10, 26; 3:22; 4:16; 5:20; 7:4, 8, 15; 9:7; 10:19; 11:19.

75. Anderson, "Curse of Work," referred to Whybray's essay, "Preacher of Joy," note 1, 99, but he went on to write that Qohelet's "message of joy has not been accepted" by some scholars but the view is gaining momentum.

76. *Śimĕhâh* in this context has been translated as mirth, pleasure, enjoyment, sensual pleasure.

77. Crenshaw, *Ecclesiastes,* 77.

78. Brown, *Ecclesiastes*, 37.

79. Commentators have translated the hiphal form of the verb as "let," Aalders, *Predeker*, 240; "make," Delitzsch, *Ecclesiastes*, 400; "let," Kidner, *Ecclesiastes,* 98.

80. Cf. Brown, *Ecclesiastes*. Brown considered Longman's *Ecclesiastes* short on seeking a positive place for Qohelet in his interpretation of Ecclesiastes, 121.

81. It has been noted previously that Qohelet referred to God over forty times.

82. Qohelet did use the term *love* in various contexts (e.g., 9:1, 6:1).

83. Cf. passages such as Job 1:1; Pss. 76:11; 59:7; Prov. 14:2; 1 Chron. 10:25; Josh. 24:14.

84. The imperative form of *zākar* is translated to think. Aalders, *Prediker*, 141, wrote *gedenk* (think), remember, Crenshaw, *Ecclesiastes*, 181.

85. Cf. Wright, "Ecclesiastes," "The thrill of youth fades into a lack of zest for life," 1192.

86. Kidner, *Ecclesiastes*, 107.

87. Some of the following material has been referred to in previous contexts.

88. Cf. Brown, *Ecclesiastes*, 132.

89. Brown, ibid., 135, wrote that to instruct his readers, Qohelet reveals that he is sage and commoner, student and teacher, skeptic and servant, victor and failure. He covers the gamut of human experience.

90. Hengstenberg, *Ecclesiastes*, 22.

91. Leupold, *Ecclesiastes*, 29.

92. Kidner referred to 7:1b as a "body blow." *Ecclesiastes*, 64. In the New Testament one can read that to be with Christ is better. Qohelet, however, does not have that vision. Could he be expressing the idea that the day of death has more to teach us than the day of birth? 65. Crenshaw opined that the tone of 7:1b "typifies Qohelet's' attitude toward life," *Ecclesiastes,* 133, 134. Delitzsch wrote that 7:1b expresses a thought that is not "in the spirit of O.T. revelation of religion" but he adds, it was possible within the N.T. revelation. *Ecclesiastes*, 314.

93. For a review of what scholars have posited as the intent of the phrase "eternity in heart" see Aalders, *Prediker*, 76, 77. He translated *'olam* as *"tysverloop,"* course of time.

94. Kidner, *Ecclesiastes*, 37, 39, 40.

95. Leupold, *Ecclesiastes,* 91.

96. "In a negative way it may be claimed that this book gives prominence to the Messianic element in revelation." Leupold, *Ecclesiastes*, 31.

48

The Golden Cable in the Song of Songs

I. Questions Concerning Song of Songs

II. The Kingdom

III. The Covenant

IV. The Mediator

48

The Golden Cable in the Song of Songs

Questions Concerning Song of Songs[1]

What is the Correct Title?

What is the correct title of this biblical book usually classified with the wisdom literature of the Old Testament? The Hebrew text has two titles: *šîr haššîrîm* (song of songs). *šîr* as a verb means to sing, as a noun it refers to what is sung. The phrase "Song of Songs" indicates that this song was considered the best and most beautiful and exquisite of all songs. It was read or sung when the Passover feast was celebrated. The second title is "Canticum Canticorum." It is not clear why this Latin title appears in the Hebrew text. It is a direct translation of *šîr haššîrîm* and this Latin title was translated Canticles. It appears in various versions of the English Bible.

A third title is Song of Solomon. One commentator reminded the readers of the song that this title could mean that the Song was about Solomon, not necessarily by Solomon.[2]

Who is the Author?

There are scholars, who for various reasons, do not believe Solomon is the author. Murphy wrote that there is no support in the book itself for Solomon's authorship. There are third-person references to him (1:5; 3:7, 9, 11, 12). He believes that different authors produced the material, but he offered no positive conclusion.[3]

The question, however, is: should the objections raised against Solomonic authorship be taken seriously? Is there a unity? Scholars have referred to three parts,[4] but one writer suggested it was a collection of thirty-one poems.[5] Should Syrian influence be considered a valid criticism? The reply is: these suggested problems, when considered, have not proven to be weighty objections. Various scholars have produced valid negative evaluations of these suggested problems concerning the unity and single authorship of Song of Songs.

Those who accept Solomon as the author do so for various reasons. The title that attributes it to Solomon has been recognized for over two thousand years. The book reflects the time of the united kingdom of Israel. Its many references to plants, animals, and places reflect a Palestinian context. The Song places itself in Solomon's palace.[6] Solomon is recorded by Scripture to have written 1,005 songs (1 Kings. 4:32). A review of the evidence referred to above tends to lead one to accept Solomonic authorship.[7] However, in my study I came to the conclusion the book is about Solomon, not by Solomon.

Does Song of Songs Contribute to the Theology of the Scriptures?

Various scholars have referred to the lack of theological references. The name of God is not mentioned. There is no reference to any person of the Trinity or to the attributes or works of God. There are no references to or quotations from other parts of the Old Testament and it is not quoted in the New Testament.[8] The book does not include a specific reference to its place and role in the revelation given in the Scriptures. Christian scholars in the past and present have resorted to various methods of interpretation to discover the theological message of the book.[9]

How Has It Been Interpreted?

The introduction to various articles/essays written by scholars could tend to make one hesitate to enter into a discussion on the "Interpretation of the Song of Songs."[10] Pope challenges the determined scholar to seek an answer to the question, how to interpret? He has written a long detailed introduction to his commentary on Song of Songs. In his outline, he listed twelve interpretations and discussed and evaluated these including the historical setting on which each one was developed.[11]

R. Gordis, a Jewish commentator on the Song of Songs, also reviewed the interpretations of the book. He wrote that the allegorical interpretation of the book and references in it to Solomon led to its inclusion in the biblical canon.[12] In modern times, according to Gordis, the cult theory developed from the allegorical.[13] However, the literal theory was already held by rabbis in earlier centuries.[14] Later the dramatic theory was developed.[15] Gordis concluded that Song of Songs, a compilation of twenty-eight songs and fragments, was basically a love poem, rich with symbolism, that celebrated human love in courtship and marriage.[16]

A quick review of what contemporary evangelical Christians have written does not fully satisfy one who would read and understand the Song of Songs. There is the literal interpretation of it as a love song that in emotional and tender ways gives expression to the love the lover has for his bride (to be?) and her love for her country man.[17] There is what one could refer to as the historical interpretation. It is a song that includes various quotations but is integrated into one production. It was composed in Solomon's court depicting true love in a setting of Solomon's disgraceful conduct exhibited by his taking many foreign wives and developing a large harem of women from many cultures and religious practices.[18]

Consultations of studies presented in books, essays, and articles have confirmed what many have written. There is no complete agreement on precisely how to interpret Song of Songs. Students of Scripture feel compelled to address the problem of how to interpret a book that has human love and the relationship between male and female lovers as the central themes.

Are There Evidences of the Three Strands of the Golden Cable?[19]

The three strands that form the Golden Cable that unites the entire message of the Scriptures are kingdom, covenant, and Mediator. Each of these have integral parts that become very evident, in some books more than in others. The question before us is: does Song of Songs include direct or indirect references to the three strands and parts of each?

Parts of the kingdom strand are kingship, theocratic, and cosmic kingdom. What is the relationship of these three to each other? All are interrelated. The covenant is inseparable from kingdom and Mediator. The covenantal prescriptions include the three mandates—the spiritual, the social, and the cultural. These mandates can only function properly in the context of relationships—God and man, man and fellowmen, man and the created world.

The basic question is: does Song of Songs contribute to the unified message of Scripture? Does it indicate a role in progressive revelation of the Triune God as set out in the Scriptures? If it does, what and how does it make a contribution?

What follows is basically a biblical theological study. As mentioned in the preceding, there are few references to theological concepts in the entire book.[20] There have not been many studies published that could be considered as an effort to produce a biblical theological study of Song of Songs.[21] Hence there are very few sources to study or refer to. This chapter presents an effort to satisfy, to an extent, the need for such an approach.

The Kingdom

Terms Indicating Aspects of Royalty

The term *malkût* (kingdom) does not appear, nor does the term *malkâh* (queen). The term *melek* (king) appears a number of times (1:4, 12; 3:9, 11; 7:5 [MT 6]). Twice Solomon is referred to directly as king and indirectly in three other passages. There is no indication at all that God was considered the King, sovereign, everpresent, omniscient Lord over all.

The Cosmic Kingdom

Nations

The book refers to nations that, in the wider biblical context, are considered integral aspects of the cosmic kingdom over which Yahweh God reigns omnipotently and sovereignly. Hence there is a universal scope set out. Damascus, capital of Syria, is mentioned (7:4) but this reference should not lead one to think the Syrian influence can be detected in the book. Tirzeh, a Canaanite city in northern Ephraim, was described as lovely (6:4). Kedar (1:5) was an Arabian city described by Isaiah as a city of pomp and military prowess. Lebanon (7:4) was known for some of its prominent features and assets. Heshbon (7:4) was an original Moabite city on the east side of the Jordan. The author of Song of Songs was very evidently well acquainted with geographical and historical features of his broader environment. His interests were far beyond Jerusalem and the palace.

Natural Aspects

The sun and moon are referred to. The sun darkens exposed human skin (1:6). It is described as bright and the moon as fair (6:10). In this context the stars are said to be majestic in their procession (6:10). These references indicate a reverent acknowledgment of astronomical dimensions of the universe, the cosmic kingdom.

Other natural aspects of the cosmic kingdom are referred to as evidences of life's environment. Fir and cedar trees (1:17, 5:15); palm (7:7, 8); flowers (2:12), lily and rose (2:14; 5:13; 6:3; 7:2); henna blossoms (1:14; 4:13); mountains and hills (2:8, 17; 4:6; 8:14); rocks (2:4); foxes (2:15); gazelle (2:17; 3:5; 4:5; 7:3; 8:14); desert (3:6; 8:5); wood, posts (3:9, 10); gold, silver (3:10; 5:11, 14, 15; 8:9, 11); birds (4:1; 5:2, 10, 12; lions, leopards (4:8); spice (3:6; 4:10, 14, 5:1, 13; 6:2); spring (4:12); wind (4:16); honeycomb (5:1); dew (5:2); streams (5:12); ivory (5:14); marble (5:15). Truly, a reading of the book will impress one of the beauties and wonders of the natural aspects of the cosmic kingdom. Song of Songs surely includes an appreciation of and love for God's great out-of-doors."

Man's Productions

In the setting of a rich natural environment mankind had been able to grow, make, and produce many products, gifts, and assets. Cultivating the fields, having to deal with thorns (2:2), men planted and kept vineyards (1:6; 8:11, 12). They raised productive vines (2:13; 6:11; 7:12). Wine (5:1; 7:2, 9; 8:2) was appreciated very much but human love was much preferred (1:2, 4; 4:10). Apple orchards were planted, tended, and enjoyed (2:3; 7:8). Fig trees formed their fruit (2:13). In tended pastures sheep and goats rested, fed (1:7, 8), and were shorn (4:2) by shepherds. Milk[22] was used in various ways (4:11; 5:1). Honey, sweet and pleasing, was taken from honeycombs (4:11; 5:1). Perfumes were produced and used to compare the wonder of love (1:3, 12; 4:10; 5:13). Jewelry was produced, enjoyed, and used to compare the girls' (brides?) features (1:10; 4:9; 5:14; 7:1).

Craftsmen were active. They built houses and these were useful in various ways (1:17; 3:4; 8:2, 7). Rooms and furniture were included (1:4, 16; 3:1, 4; 5:13; 6:2). Tents were present and used by shepherds (1:5, 8). Walls having been built were referred to in various ways (2:9; 5:7; 8:9, 10). Wells, not identified, flowed with water (4:15).

Relationship of Mankind to the Cosmic Kingdom

A reading of the Song of Songs, paying particular attention to the rich variety of blessings available to man, one can get a sense of the advantages God placed before his vicegerents. God, the Creator, had placed his image bearers in a setting of beauty, peace, and goodness (Gen. 1:24–31). This was the general *Sitz im Leben* in which the characters in the Song lived. The many aspects of creation were apprehended by them and were employed by the author of the Song to describe and compare particularly the personal characteristics of the Shulamite young lady. And the suitor and friends took full advantage of these to adoringly describe her. Doing that they demonstrated that they were intimate parts of and participants in the wonderfully created cosmos. Thus they were cosmic royal representatives of their Creator Lord in a "setting of almost Edenic quality.[23]

The Theocratic Kingdom

The theocratic kingdom, that is, the kingdom of Israel, is not referred to directly. Various references, however, indicate that it was the immediate context in which the Song was composed. There are no references, however, to its origins, neither to the patriarchs, Abraham, Isaac, Jacob, nor to men of historic importance such as Moses and Joshua who were divinely chosen agents in the origin and initial formation of the theocratic kingdom. Nor are there references to the priests, nor to the prescribed religious cult or to the temple. And there is no specific reference to the palace that the biblical testimony places in the very heart of the theocracy.[24]

There is evidence in the text, however, that the theocratic kingdom was the very context in which the Song of Songs was composed. There are eight references to Jerusalem. It is described as *nāwâh* (an adj. derived from the verb *nā'âh,* to be comely, desirable, or beautiful (6:4). The term is used in Scripture in reference to women or to songs. Jerusalem is referred to the home of the daughters who as palace attendants are repeatedly charged not to arouse love or lovers (2:7; 3:5; 5:8; 8:4). This strongest evidence for the theocratic setting for the Song of Songs is the five references to Solomon (1:5; 3:9, 11; 8:11, 12).[25] It was none other than Solomon as king who had enabled Jerusalem the capital of the theocratic kingdom to become a pre-eminent city in the world known at that time. This theocratic kingdom, with Solomon as the king, possessed and enjoyed most of the richest assets that were inherent aspects or realities present in the wider context of the cosmic kingdom. The descriptions of Solomon's kingdom (1 Kings. 4:1—10:29) are confirmed by the detailed references to the wealth in the Song of Songs.

The Covenant

Terms

The term *bĕrît* does not appear in Song of Songs. Nor do translations of the term or references such as league, pact, compact, appear in translations. But some writers have discussed the covenant as they considered it reflected in the Song. One entitled his essay "Interpreting the Song of Solomon in the Light of the Davidic Covenant."[26] He particularly refers to the bond between David and Israel as a political covenant.[27]

Biblical References

Aspects of the Covenant

The *bĕrît* (covenant) is a major and central theme in the entire Old Testament. And, according to the New Testament, Jesus is the Mediator of the covenant (Heb. 8:6; 9:15; 12:24). Since Song of Songs is in the canon, the question is: does the Song of Songs indicate or reflect the role of the covenant in it? If so, how does it?

The constitutive elements of the covenant were reviewed in the previous chapter.[28] A reading and study of Song of Songs convinces one that the concept of the life/love bond, set forth in the Scriptures, is a major reality in it. Indeed *love* is the major theme. Love is a present and functioning relationship. This relationship throughout Scripture must be present and functioning according to Yahweh God, the covenant Lord's prescriptions. The three biblically functioning relationships are between God and mankind, between fellow human beings, and between human beings and the created natural world. And each of these relationships are to be developed in obedience and controlled by the love relationship that God established when he created the cosmos and particularly the human race. Thus, one can readily regard these relationships as spiritual (God-man), social (between people), and cultural (people and natural world). Yahweh God has given definite instructions concerning each of these relationships that can most properly be referred to as mandates.[29]

The Mandates of the Covenant

The Spiritual Mandate. There are no specific theological statements or references in Song of Songs.[30] Authors of commentaries and essays on the book are almost unanimously agreed that *love* is the over-riding theme of the book.[31] The question has been asked, "Is the Song of Songs primarily about the love of a man and a woman, or about the love of God and his people, or a combination of the two?"[32] There is no doubt that love between a man and a woman is emphasized. This love, God-given and implanted at the time of creation, referred to in various ways throughout Scripture, is recognized as a bonding relationship. No specific instructions or command concerning the love for God or the love between a man and a woman is included in the entire Song of Songs. What is said and implied should be understood according to the biblical concept of God's love and of human courting and married love. This means that the Song of Songs should not be separated from or treated in isolation from the whole of Scripture.[33]

A study of the other two relationships and the mandates regarding each, the cultural and especially the social, will illuminate the presence and reliance on the spiritual relationship between God and his male and female imagebearers.

The Cultural Mandate. The cultural mandate was originally given to Adam and Eve when they were created and given the Garden of Eden as their home (Gen. 2:8, 15). Yahweh God established a good life bond between them and the natural world. Thus they were blessed, that is, given the privilege and ability to be God's vicegerents. They were mandated to rule, be fruitful, subdue, and receive food from plants (Gen. 1:28–30). And God added that his vicegerents were to work and take care of the garden (Gen. 2:15). When Yahweh God had created the cosmos he included the potentials and possibilities for mankind to obey this cultural mandate and to enjoy the benefits of their rule and cultivation.[34] Sin became a tragic reality but it in no wise lessened the full import of the cultural mandate. In reality sin would cause more effort and cause pain and sorrow as the mandate was obeyed (Gen. 3:16–19).

There is no reference to God having given the cultural mandate nor to humans receiving and obeying it in Song of Songs. There is reference to the craftsmen plying their trade (7:1). The vineyardists knew their duty in regard to helping others and caring for their own (1:6). The king hired tenants to cultivate his vineyard (8:11, 12). The shepherds had their tent near their flocks of sheep and goats (1:8). The king prepared military equipment (3:7–10).

One can conclude from reading the Song of Songs that covenant life flourished. The spiritual dimensions of it are implied. The cultural aspects were worked on, developed, and results of obedience to it were enjoyed. These realities supply a rich and meaningful *Sitz im Leben* for the social relationships and mandate to be recognized, developed, and seen as serving the motifs and overall theme of Song of Songs.

The Social Relationship and Mandate in Song of Songs

Characters Referred to as Participants

There is no unanimity among students of Song of Songs on how many characters are included in the scenes that are presented. Were there only two? Or three? Or more? B. Webb has summarized the cast of characters correctly. He asked, "How are we to understand the voices that we hear in the Song?"[35] Are there two voices,[36] a pair of lovers who spoke typical expressions of love as in modern love lyrics?[37] Or are there the voices of the Shulamite maiden, Solomon, and a shepherd who loves the maiden? And what about the references to mother, brothers, watchmen, women of Jerusalem, and other friends? What was their role? Considering the reality that there are those various references, should the Song of Songs be considered a drama?

Evidences of Drama

The drama proposal could be defended on the basis of the various characters mentioned. But writers have pointed out that to refer to it as a cultic drama is hardly acceptable for there are no clear cultic (worship rites) present.[38] Nor is there progression of thought throughout the Song. There is no consistent movement; there is no story line.[39] So there is no real basis to consider the Song a "drama pastoral" or "drama wedding."[40] Yet, it can be asked what precisely is said of or what is the role of the main characters?

Roles of the Main Characters

The Maiden. The young woman is introduced as a member of a family. The mother and brothers are referred to as country folk who cultivate a vineyard. She has joined in outdoor activities but it has not dimmed her beauty even though she received a dark complexion (1:5, 6). She was noticed by Solomon as he traveled about the land and he brought her into Jerusalem and gave her a place among his harem. She was deeply unhappy there. She loved a man who also was from the country. She repeatedly, while surrounded by the advantages of the royal court, spoke longingly of the country man she deeply loved. In the course of time, she is able to leave the court and rejoin her country man.

The Country Man. The country man, whom the maiden loved deeply, was in the fields with his sheep (1:7, 8). He knew sheep very well; when he thought of the maiden that he loved he described her with terms he derived from his shepherding work (4:2; 6:3). He longed for her and reflected on her with descriptions that indicated he knew she had been taken to the royal court in Jerusalem. He considered her wearing jewels (1:10, 11). With her in the harem of the palace, he thought of her as a lily among thorns (2:1). When he went to the grove of nut trees or to the valley where new grass grew or to the vineyard to see if new buds had sprouted or to the pomegranate trees to see their blooms, he dreamed of being in the royal chariot of the people (6:11, 12). (Was he daydreaming about riding in a wedding chariot?)

Friends. It is a real challenge to decide precisely who the friends are. There did not seem to be friends of the shepherd-orchardist-vineyardist. The general consensus is that when the maiden was brought into the palace, she wanted to go to the "chambers" where other women lived. Whether these were veiled singers, the harem choir, or attendants for the queen and other women existing in a royal environment is not clear.[41] A reading of the text leads one to accept that these women presented themselves as friends and welcomed the maiden into the palace courts and chambers. When in there, the maiden spoke of the man she loved. To which these "friends" replied, asking if he was better than others (5:9), to which she had a ready reply. She described him to them in lavishly charming words (5:10–16). If one should ask what precisely was the role of the various groups of women, the answer is twofold: first, they contributed to the attraction of the palace scene into which the maiden was brought. Second, they were supportive of the king and palace life, thus they added to the maiden's anguish because her heart was out in the country with the man she loved. It could be interpreted that the "friends" contributed to the effort to make the maiden turn from the man she loved.

The King. The king is Solomon (3:7, 9, 11). He was described coming from the desert in his chariot[42] escorted by sixty warriors. He was wearing his crown with which his mother had crowned him on his wedding day. The bride is not referred to by name or any other designation.[43] There should be no doubt that Solomon had an important role in the Song of Songs. He is not quoted, but his desire and influence are very discernable. He had a harem; he had seen a beautiful country girl whom he took from her family. He brought her to his harem. It is very difficult to determine from the text itself whether Solomon loved her or not. The text in 1 Kings 11:1 reads *wĕhemmelek šĕlōmâh 'āhab nāsîm* (and Solomon loved women); many of them had been taken from various foreign countries. Thus, if the maiden was loved, it was certainly a shared love at best. She knew that she was loved fully and passionately by one man. And that love she did not want to ignore or reject. She basked in that love. Solomon, providing the setting for what Song of Songs records, did not reveal or demonstrate a love that negated love for her country man.

Courtship and Marriage. The first question to be answered is, "does the first chapter present a courting scene or does it indicate that marriage has been consummated? The maiden is said to refer to their verdant bed—marriage bed? Or did she speak longingly for marriage that has not been consummated (1:1–4)? The second question is: what does she long for? to go into the king's chambers, or to be with the shepherd who is grazing his flocks out in the pastures (1:4–7)? Commentators do not present definite answers.[44] There is no specific or direct reference to a married relationship. Love, longing for love to be more fully experienced and expressed, is recorded. But a basic issue is: in which of the two suitors in the courtship scene does the maiden love? The answer seems clear. Taken from the family farm setting, the maiden, when brought to the palace, asked to be brought into the king's chambers where the members of the developing harem resided. She did not say "bring me to the king himself." The maiden's deepest desire was to be courted by her farmer/shepherd lover.

The language used to express the love between the shepherd and the maiden reveals a deep admiration for each other. The shepherd employed language that was filled with images and reminders of the glories of nature. His deep appreciation for the cultural environment in which he lived and worked enabled him to give unique descriptions and explanations of his love for the bride to be and when married, his bride. She is his dove with a sweet voice (2:14). She is beautiful (4:1); her temples are like halves of a pomegranate (4:3); her breasts are like twin fawns of a gazelle (4:5). Her lips drop sweetness (4:11). She is a garden fountain (4:15) and he referred to her as "my bride" (4:8).

Her language was that of one who loved and was loved, whether as a betrothed woman or as a bride. She spoke of him as radiant and ruddy (5:10), with cheeks like beds of spice, his lips like lilies dripping myrrh (5:13). She said she belonged to her lover and that his desire was for her (7:11). She invited him to go to the countryside to spend the night in villages and in the morning go to the vineyards to see if the vines have budded (7:11, 12).

The answers to the questions mentioned in the first part of this section (4) is that Song of Songs presents both a courting and a marriage setting interchangeably. As stated before, there is no consistently developed, progressive line of thought.[45] The author took, as it were, a series of snapshots, not in the order they were taken, and looking at them, told what was seen and said in each one. Courtship and married life are both described as settings in which lasting conjugal love is developed and fully realized.

Conclusion

First, the covenantal social relationship is a basic and unifying theme in Song of Songs.[46] This relationship comes to expression in various realistic settings: the king's palace and life in it; the rural areas, where flocks are tended and vineyards cultivated and life is rewarded. This social relationship exists between royal persons, court attendants, and lovers. Second, married love is the basic and unifying theme of this Song. This love in its premarriage stage was cultivated and developed in a setting of rural and urban life. Strong attractions arose in the urban setting. It was finally developed and fully realized in the rural (country and village) life. The lover (male) and the beloved (female) were united as man and woman. They were married and became one flesh. Love was and is key to this fulfillment of Yahweh God's covenant social mandate (Gen. 2:24).

Third, Webb has written correctly and effectively that God had established this love in beautiful Eden. It was there, and throughout the canon that "this love is set out as a reflection of the love of God himself."[47] Since the fall in Eden this love of God and its human reflection and expression has not been perfectly realized among the human males and females. Distractions and powerful influences have affected it. But in spite of these, conjugal love can and does prevail. This reality is a basis for joy and song.[48]

Fourth, a concluding statement is apropos. The covenant strand of the Golden Cable is present and is a unifying reality in the Song of Songs. Hence it is very correct to refer to the Song of Songs as a covenantal book. It contributes to the central covenantal theme of love that is inherent and integral to the entire Scriptures. It adds to the covenantal theme of love between a man and a woman that the covenant Lord gave to the human race. The Song reveals that various potential distracting factors can and do have strong influences that could thwart and prevent this covenantal love/life bond between a man (groom) and woman (bride) to be fully realized. The staying and invincible strength of love, however, is victorious and glorious. It is rooted in Yahweh God's innate character. Yahweh God's image bearers, the male and female, however, were ordained by him to experience and demonstrate this divine implanted virtue—love—predominately by and within the marriage bond.[49]

The Mediator

The Third Strand

The Messiah is declared in Scripture to be the Mediator of the covenant (1 Tim. 2:5; Heb. 8:6; 9:15; 12:24). In the Old Testament the Mediator is referred to by the term *māšîah* (Messiah or the Anointed One). Kings (e.g., David) were anointed as Yahweh's vicegerent over the covenant people. In preceding studies of the books of the Old Testament,[50] the Mediator was seen to be present or referred to in each book. In Song of Songs the terms that refer to the Mediator as a person, or the mediatorial agency, or his purpose or task are not present. The question to be considered now is this: is Song of Songs one of the exceptions that does not refer to the Mediator directly? But is there an indirect reference or intimation of his role as Mediator? The question is pertinent in view of the reality that the Messiah was the Mediator of the covenant and it was shown that the covenant is a basic concept for the interpretation and understanding of the message of Song of Songs.[51] Is then, the Mediator, the Messiah, also to be understood as present without direct reference to him? Efforts to discern him have been made.

Efforts to Discern the Mediator

Allegorically

Much has been written concerning the allegorical character of the Song of Songs.[52] Elliott has presented a lengthy study of the use of allegory in the early centuries of New Testament Christianity.[53] Pope has written an extensive review of allegorical interpretations of Song of Songs in the first centuries of New Testament Christianity. He pointed out that Origen had followed Hippolytus who wrote circa A.D. 200.[54] Theodore of Mopsuestia at the end of the fourth century rejected the allegorical interpretation of Song of Songs.[55] Throughout the following centuries it remained a dominant interpretation.[56] Various scholars have opined that because of the allegorical interpretations in early centuries, Song of Songs was included in the canon. There is no specific corroboration for that view. One cannot deny, however, that Origen's use of the allegorical interpretation of Song of Songs abetted the development of the Christological debates and even some conclusions concerning the contribution of Song of Songs to the formulation of the doctrine of Christ.

The allegorical interpretation employed by the church fathers followed the Jewish interpretation that saw the Song depicting the relationship of Yahweh and Israel his bride.[57] In Christian circles the Song was related to mutual love of Christ and the church as his bride. Additional allegories were developed with great imagination and ingenuity.[58]

The basic problem with the allegory is that it is not rooted in history or the real world. Rather it is drawn from the mind and imagination of authors.[59]

The critical scholars' view is that the allegorical interpretation is merely arbitrary, amusing, and devious. Some have added that the content of Songs is overly amorous and much of the physical language is an embarrassment.[60] Such views of allegory have not dissuaded certain biblical writers to reject allegory as a correct interpretive method to understand Song of Songs and its messianic role in the canon.

Typologically

The typological approach to Song of Songs could be in some aspects compared quite well with the allegorical. There is, however, a fundamental difference. The basic issue concerns how a type is understood.[61] In the course of redemptive history, before Christ was born, ministered, died, and rose, Yahweh God revealed aspects of his redemptive work, purposes, and goals by having men serve as kings, prophets, priests, and leaders who had roles that pointed forward to and served as representatives of the preincarnate Son of God, the Christ to come. In addition such types were ancestors also (e.g., Abraham, David, and Solomon).

The Song of Songs does not reveal any direct aspect of redemptive history unfolding as types and anti-types of the Mediator. Furthermore the characters in the Song do not serve as types of Christ. If Solomon is to be so considered he should be presented as a king who performs redemptive activities such as he did building the temple and ruling wisely before his moral downfall.[62] Nor does the New Testament refer to any aspect of its recording of history as having been somehow presented by the Song of Songs.

Literal Historical

The literal historical view had various emphases. Calvin, the Genevan reformer, held that the Song dealt with human love[63] as it was expressed and experienced in the course of human life. He accepted the Song as inspired; hence it revealed an accurate and trustworthy account of love in courtship and marriage in Old Testament biblical times. Longman wrote that the literal/natural (historical) reading of the Song "resists the idea that the Song is a code." His view is that the Song does not imply anything different than what the words say.[64] Webb has written that the song is a rhapsody of love, an "outpouring of the feelings of people who are in love."[65] The Song reveals flesh experiencing love with attendant paens and pleasures. Olyott wrote that as the book of Ecclesiastes focuses on the intellect, the Song does on emotion.[66] Most writers such as these do not discuss whether Christ is typified or not.

The view taken in this study is that Song of Songs is not a mystical dream of marriage, a melodrama, a wedding week description, a cultic expression of love, an historical allegory, or a melodramatic manifesto for the emancipation of women.[67] The reading and evaluation of these and other approaches to the Song of Songs should lead one back to the biblical text. The book is canonical. It is authoritative due to the Holy Spirit's inspiration of it.

In spite of what various writers of articles and books have written claiming Solomon as the author, the correct approach is to insist that in a very definite way, the Song is not by him but basically about him. Solomon had become a polygamist. He employed human courting and married love as a means to advance himself as a political and social lord. The author of the Song of Songs, very much aware of Solomon's abuses of love and marriage, wrote the Song of Songs to present the correct God-given virtue of love and its coming into full bloom through courtship and marriage. The Song has an historical setting but it is written in a poetic style. It was written in such a manner that different scenes would fill out and enrich the experiences of a budding and developing love relationship that flowered into a fully mature reality. In this process, various distracting influences were encountered. The main obstacle to the fulfillment of the love between the shepherd/vineyardist and beautiful rural maiden was the ruthless action of the polygamous king who wished and tried to disrupt that God-given and blessed love relationship. He failed and the maiden and the rural man maintained their love for and faithfulness to each other.

Summary: Love between a man and woman is the main theme. This love was an historical reality. Solomon attempted to disrupt and negate that love. The rural man and beautiful maiden were persistent in demonstrating how God-given and honored love in courtship and marriage endured. The Song of Songs thus portrays a fulfillment of the divinely instituted marriage bond (Gen. 2:23, 24). It also presents a solid basis of the marriage, family, and home that the Psalmists sang about (127, 128). It is in this context that the relevant and important question to be answered is, does the Song dealing with love and marriage present additional revelation concerning the Mediator who was promised and expected in Old Testament times?

His Presence in Song of Songs

Negatively

It bears repeating: the Mediator of the covenant is not directly referred to nor by clear inference. Solomon, a type of Christ as Son of David, anointed king of Israel, is not presented as such in the Song of Songs. Solomon did the very opposite of fulfilling the role of a faithful agent of the covenant and maintaining the marriage bond. Solomon did not cleave to his first wife; he broke the covenant bond between him and her by taking many more women as wives.

Positively

Various writers have attempted to present a positive view. One has referred to the book as the most Christological in the whole Old Testament. It reveals the constancy of the eternal romance of true love.[68] Another wrote that the Song presents a human love that is expressive of the believer's love for Christ—a love that cannot remain static.[69] Still another wrote that human love as revealed in the Song is a microcosm of the larger divine love. The purity and beauty of this human love as a divine gift is the theme of the book.[70] How does this theme of the divine gift give a positive presentation of the Mediator?

One must keep in mind that biblical scholars have distinguished between the narrower and wider conceptions of the biblical concept of the Messiah.[71] The narrower, as a rule, refers to a person, an anointed king, priest, or a prophet called by

God. The wider concept is used, as a rule, to refer to additional aspects involved in the concept of the Messiah, the Mediator. These aspects include promises of salvation, the work to be executed to fulfill the promises, the qualifications, the means employed, goals, the realm over which the Messiah reigns, and the results of it. One will immediately realize that the narrower view, the anointed king, is not revealed in Song of Songs.[72] The wider conception, however, is included in several ways.

First of all, true, pure, and beautiful married love binds a man and woman in the covenant marriage bond. This love flows from and exhibits the sovereign and all-inclusive love of Yahweh God for his covenant people.

Second, the love of Yahweh God was demonstrated in the giving of his Son, who redeemed and redeems the elect people of God. They are saved from evil and sin and are sanctified by his blood through the work of the Holy Spirit.

Third, the redeemed covenant saints are united as a body, the ecclesia or the church. Christ lives with and reigns as Lord over this body of redeemed saints who are referred to as the bride of Christ (Rev. 18:23; 19:7; 21:2; 22:17). Christ loves his bride and provides for all her needs. Consider the many references the apostle John makes concerning this love of God (John 3:16; 1 John 3:1, 17; 4:7, etc.).

Fourth, this love of God for his chosen covenant people was revealed after mankind's fall into sin. In love he rescued them. This love was progressively revealed and demonstrated to his redeemed saints, the ecclesia in Old Testament times. Moses wrote about it (Exod. 34:6, 7; Num. 14:18, 19; Deut. 7:12, 13). The Psalmists knew this love and sang about it (23:6; 25:6; 32:10; 33:22; 69:13, 16; 100:5).

Fifth, this great love of Yahweh for his people is the source of the love that he gave to and installed by the covenant marriage bond between a lover and his beloved. This enduring love is reflective and exhibitive of Yahweh God's love for his people and Christ's love for the redeemed sanctified saints, the body, the bride.

Sixth, Song of Songs is to be seen as a stage in the progressive revelation and application of the love of God, made real in the person and presence of Jesus Christ. Thus by the revelation of the love of the Father and the Son in the courtship and marriage of the shepherd and maiden, the love of the Mediator was exhibited. Where love was and is, the source of it is Jesus Christ. Thus Jesus Christ, in his pre-incarnate state, was revealed in the Song of Songs.

Notes

1. In the NIV the title of the book is Song of Songs; in the KJV and RSV it is Song of Solomon. The title and many other issues raised by or about the book have given rise to much discussion, many essays, and books. Bibliographies appended to various books list anywhere from five to fifteen pages. Here follows a small, but representative selection:

G. CH. Aalders, *Het Hooglied* (Kampen: Kok, 1952); Fiona C. Black, "Beauty or the Beast? The Grotesque Body in the Song of Songs," *Biblical Interpretation* 8 no.3 (2000):

302–23; Roland Boer, "The Second Coming: Repetition and Insatiable Desire in the Song of Songs," *Biblical Interpretation* 8 no.3, (2000): 276–301; George Burrowes, *A Commentary on the Song of Solomon* (London: Banner of Truth Trust, 1958); Ian D. Campbell, "The Song of David's Son: interpreting the Song of Solomon in the Light of the Davidic Covenant." *WTJ* 62 no.1 (Spring 2000): 17–32; Franz Delitzsch, *Commentary on Song of Songs and Ecclesiastes* (Grand Rapids: Eerdmans, 1950); Mark W. Elliott, *The Song of Songs and Christology in the Early Church*, 381–451 (Tubingen: Mohr Selbeck, 2000); Marcia Falk, *Love Lyrics From the Bible* (Sheffield: Almond, 1982); Michael V. Fox, *The Song of Songs and Ancient Egyptian Love Songs* (Madison: University of Wisconsin Press, 1985); S. Craig Glickman, *A Song for Lovers* (Downers Grove: InterVarsity, 1976); Robert Gordis, *The Song of Songs and Lamentations* (New York: Ktav, 1974) William E. Griffis, *The Lily Among the Thorns* (New York: Revised Press, 1989); R. K. Harrison, "Song of Songs," in The *Zondervan Pictorial Encyclopedia of the Bible,* vol. 10, ed. M. Tenney, (Grand Rapids: Zondervan 1975); Othmar Keel, *The Song of Songs* in Continental Commentaries Series (Minneapolis: Fortress, 2000); Dennis E. Kinlaw, "Song of Songs," *The Expositor's Bible Commentary* (Grand Rapids: Zondervan, 1991); George A. E. Knight, *The Songs of Song* (Grand Rapids: Eerdmans, 1988); Andre Lacocque, *Romance She Wrote* (Harrisburg: Trinity Press International, 1999); Tremper Longman, III, *Song of Songs* (Grand Rapids: Eerdmans, 2001); Roland Murphy, *The Song of Songs* (Minneapolis: Augsburg, 1990); Stuart Olyott, *A Life Worth Living and a Lord Worth Loving: Ecclesiastes and Song of Solomon* (Darlington: Evangelical,1990); Greg W. Parsons,"Guidelines for Understanding and Utilizing the Song of Songs," *Bibliotheca Sacra* 156 no.624 (October-December 1999): 399–422; Marvin H. Pope, *Song of Songs* The Anchor Bible, vol. 75, (Garden City: Doubleday, 1977); Iain Provan, *Ecclesiastes/Song of Songs,* The NIV Application Commentary (Grand Rapids: Zondervan, 2001); Calvin Seerveld, *The Greatest Song* in *Critique of Solomon* (Amsterdam: W. Ten Have, 1967); Raymund J. Tourney, *Word of Love, Song of Love*, Commentary on the Song of Songs (New York: Paulist, 1982); Jan Van Andel, *Solomon's Hoogleid* (Kampen: Kok, 1909); Gerard Van Groningen, *Messianic Revelation in the Old Testament* (Grand Rapids: Baker, 1990); H. Viviers, "Clothed and Unclothed in the Song of Songs," *Old Testament Essays* 12 no. 3 (1999) 609–622; Carey Ellen Walsh, *Exquisite Desire: Religion, the Erotic, and the Song of Songs* (Minneapolis: Fortress, 2000); Barry Webb, "The Song of Songs: a Love Poem and as Holy Scripture" *Reformed Theological Review* 49/3 (September-December 1990), 91–99; Connie J. Whitesell "Behold, Thou Art Fair, My Beloved" (sexuality in Song of Songs and Hymn to Inanna)" *Parabola,* 20 (November,1995) 92–99.

2. Aalders, *Hoogheid*, 27.

3. Murphy, *The Song* 3. Murphy asked if it was possible that the Song reflected popular culture in a concrete social setting, e.g., a wedding? Or was it a refined literary creation produced by the educated? Elite? Or is it a sample of love poetry found in all levels of society?

4. Aalders, *Hooglied*, 9–15.

5. Falk, *Love Lyrics,* employed a higher critical method in "an effort to combine scholarship with a conscious poetic craft and sensibility," 5.

6. Van Andel, *Solomon's Hooglied*, 12.

7. Cf. Olyott, *A Life*, 74.

8. Cf., e.g., what Griffis wrote, *The Lily*, 14.

9. Gordis, writing from his Judaism perspective, concluded that "over and beyond its eternal youthfulness and inherent charm, the Song of Songs . . . serves to broaden the horizon of religion." *The Song*, 44.

10. Parsons, "Guidelines," quotes Lacoque: "the Song of Songs presents the interpreter with the 'greatest hermeneutical challenge' in the Old Testament, if not the whole Bible." 399. His quotation from Lacoque was taken from "Romance, She Wrote." J. Hunter wrote, "The Song of Songs has been the subject of controversy since the time of Rabbi Akiba." "The Song Protest " 109. Hunter did not give clear evidence that this book contains a "Song of Protest." B. Webb introduced his essay "Song of Songs" referring to two problems—its meaning and its place in the canon, 99. Campbell wrote that the evangelical preacher joins the ranks of generations of Christians who have not known quite what to do with this enigmatic book. "The Song . . . David's Son."

11. Pope's bibliography in his commentary on *Song of Songs* is detailed, 233–88. His section entitled "Translation and notes" covers pages 292–99. Twelve interpretations by Jewish Christian writers are listed. They are: (1) Dream Theories, Melodrama; (2) The Wedding Week Theory; (3) Cultic Interpretation; (4) Jewish Mysticism; (5) The Shekinah; (6) Shekinah—Matronet in Qabbalah; (7) Historical Allegory; (8) Mystical Marriage; (9) Mariology and the Lady of the Church; (10) Catholic Views of Canticle as Songs of Human Love; (11) French Protestant View: Sacred and Sexual; (12) The Song of Songs and Women's Liberation. Pope added Love and Death because "it has been recognized by many commentators that the setting of Love and Passion in opposition to the power of Death and Hell in 8:6, c, d, is the climax of the Canticle and the burden of its message: that love is the only power that can cope with death," 210.

12. Gordis, *Song of Songs*, 2, 43.

13. Ibid., 4.

14. Ibid., 8, 9.

15. Ibid. Delitzsch and Ewald are quoted as espousing the dramatic theory, the Song is believed to be a drama with either two or three characters, 10.

16. Ibid., 16, 35–46. Cf. also Longman's review, *Song,* 20–47.

17. Glickman, *A Song*, 12ff. The real love that is expressed is not the king's love and the girl's love for him, but the love between the shepherd and the girl.

18. Seerveld, *Greatest Song*. This is a true story. The Greatest Song tells of "vowed" love between a maid and her shepherd love being tested by Solomon's royal glitter, 68, 69.

19. Cf. chap. 47 for reference to aspects of the Golden Cable.

20. Cf. 366.

21. There are some studies that included a very brief section entitled Theology. There are some studies that discuss "covenant." These will be referred on 370.

22. The text does not indicate the source of milk, e.g., cows or goats.

23. Kinlaw, "Song of Songs," 1207.

24. The Psalmists referred to it, singing that they would dwell in the house of the Lord (Ps. 23:6), flourishing in it (52:8), loving that house (Ps. 20:8).

25. Campbell, in *Song . . . David's Son* wrote that Solomon is "in the Song by default . . . the role he plays is superficial and minimal," 19. He, however, later added that the role of Solomon cannot possibly be ignored by evangelicals, 21. And he added that Solomon received wisdom from God and wrote in Song of Songs the opposite of what he wrote in Ecclesiastes—life not despair, love not friendliness, fulfillment not meaningless, 23. Finally he wrote that Solomon is the primary actor, 29, a conclusion that is difficult to accept.

26. Ibid., 17.

27. Stadelman, *Love—Politics*. Cf. his table of contents, III, V, and 53, 54, 190, 191, 211.

28. Chap. 47, 343–56.

29. Consider what was written in more detail about God establishing the covenant and its mandates in the preceding first volume of *From Creation to Consummation,* 60–72.

30. Cf. 366, above.

31. Webb, "Song of Songs, a Love Poem," 97.

32. Parsons, "Guidelines," 400.

33. Song of Songs must be first of all and primarily interpreted and understood in its biblical context and not primarily as a "love song" like those found in other nations.

34. Cf. 73.

35. Webb, "A Love Poem," 92.

36. Gordis, *Song of Songs*, 10, referred to Delitzsch, who held that there were two main characters.

37. Webb, "A Love Poem," referred to M. Falk.

38. Ibid., 92, explaining it as an expurgated liturgy of a fertility cult.

39. Parsons, "Guidelines," 411. Gordis, *Song of Songs* wrote that a drama presupposes it to be a literary unit and on the basis of linguistic considerations he has ruled it out, 13. Other writers have not considered linguistic considerations as important criteria.

40. It is difficult to accept C. Seerveld's studied effort to present a dramatic presentation of the *Greatest Song*, 23–65.

41. Seerveld seems to imply that many women were in the royal court for various purposes, *Greatest Song*, 22ff. It is not clear either why J. Stek, in his translation, NIV, has the "friends" speak concerning sheep, goats, and shepherds (1:8).

42. An example of the difficulty of precisely translating and interpreting Song of Songs is the term *miṭṭātô*. Commentators have translated it as palaquin, bed, couch, carriage, chariot. Was Solomon on a portable platform carried by men on which was his throne, or couch, bed? (Pope, *Song of Songs*, translated: Behold Solomon's bed, sixty heroes around it, 412.) Or was he in a horsedrawn means of transportation? Whatever translation is preferred, Solomon's royal status and assets are described.

43. Aalders, *Hooglied*, points out that the bride is not mentioned, 71. Delitzsch, however, referred to the maiden as the bride and that the queen mother was present with joyful consent, *The Song*, 69. Longman, *Song* devoted a section, 133–39, to the interpretation of the section (3:6–10). He referred to various linguistic and literary problems that scholars have discussed without supplying definitive solutions. Nor did he.

44. Cf. the brief review of Kinlaw, "Songs. . .", 6. It would seem that there is some textual evidence for whatever conclusion is reached, e.g., Kinlaw. The simplest solution is that we are really dealing with a royal romance, 1216.

45. Cf. 372.

46. The social relationship is of the warp and woof of the covenant. This relationship, at the heart of which is love, is clearly expressed in the Song of Songs. Hence, one may ask if it really is helpful to attempt to declare a covenantal message in the Song by an appeal to the Davidic covenant. Cf. Campbell, *Song, David's Son*, esp. 21, 26–30.

47. Webb, "Love Poem," 98.

48. Psalm 45 can be considered such an expression.

49. It bears repeating that efforts to demonstrate that Song of Songs can be considered covenantal by appealing to political agreements do not prove conclusive to the highlighting of the love-marriage central theme and message. Cf. notes 25–27.

50. Cf. *Messianic Revelation* and *From Creation*, vols. I, II, III.

51. Cf. 370–71.

52. The bibliography selected for this chapter contains only a small portion of the extensive bibliographies some have included in their books, see notes.

53. Elliott, *Song of Songs*, 1–15.

54. Pope, *Song of Songs*, 115.

55. Ibid., 119.

56. Elliott wrote that Marcia Falk, a contemporary author, considered the Song to be composed of a string of metaphors. But, there is a prima facie case for reading it as an allegory—an extended metaphor. *Song of Songs,* 83. Cf. also what Kinlaw wrote, "An allegory is an extended metaphor." "Kings," 1203.

57. Pope, *Song,* 89.

58. Ibid.

59. Kinlaw, *Song*, 1203.

60. Murphy, *Canticle*, 15. Cf. also Longman's discussion concerning the rejection of the allegorical approach. *Song,* 35–38.

61. Cf. my study of typology in *Messianic Revelation*, 153–167.

62. Even if Solomon is considered to be the main character as Glickman, *A Song*, held throughout his 198-page book, he is not serving in a pre-redemptive role. Nor is the maiden portrayed as a representative of God's people. Griffis wrote of Solomon as a polygamous old king; the book is an explicit condemnation of him and his relationship with women. *The Lily*, 22.

63. Pope, *Song*, 127. Hendriks wrote in the foreword that Glickman in *A Song,* accepted a literal interpretation of love in Solomon's time as a part of normal life, 9.

64. Longman, *Song*, 38. It would seem that Longman did not correctly read Pope on Calvin's view of the Song, 38.

65. Webb, "The Song," 91, 92.

66. Olyott, *A Life*, 73.

67. These approaches, interpretations, are reviewed at length in Pope's *Song*, 112–205. Other writers, some referred to in preceding notes, have also reviewed and evaluated various views.

68. Griffis, *The Lily*, 20, 21.

69. Olyott, *A Life*, 112–17.

70. Harrison, "Song," 493.

71. Van Groningen, *Messianic Revelation*, 15–23.

72. Evidence in preceding paragraphs has been given why Solomon cannot be considered as a type of Christ.

49

The Golden Cable in Lamentations

I. Introductory Comments

II. The Kingdom

III. The Covenant

IV. The Mediator

49

The Golden Cable in Lamentations

Introductory Comments

Sources for Study

The book of Lamentations is an intriguing source for studying human reactions to misfortune and tragedy. In the initial stages of my study of this book I was disappointed when I began to discover that secondary sources for the study of Lamentations are comparatively few.[1] Some of these are brief. Enough material, however, is available for acquiring helpful insight into Lamentations.

Lament Defined

To understand the concept of "lament" one must realize that it is to be understood in a context. Laments do not occur in a vacuum. An author has pointed out that tragedy of some sort is the scene or source of lament.[2] Disappointment also can be a context, a *Sitz im Leben* for laments. Personal experiences that result in emotional reactions such as overwhelming sorrow and grief can produce laments. Tribulations experienced by communities are often a source of laments.[3]

The term *lament* is derived from the Latin words *lamentari*, to mourn, and *lamintum*, a mourning, wailing, grieving, weeping. To lament is to give an outward expression of extreme sorrow or grief. The Old Testament records many instances of grief and sorrow and the reasons for these. This should not surprise one. The Bible has a definite human aspect. Human experiences of disappointment and tragedy are recorded.[4] The emotional responses to these are included. The Spirit, who inspired the Scriptures, led and guided writers to refer to and describe these expressions of deep sorrow and grief. David is recorded as lamenting over Saul's death (2 Sam. 1:17, 18) and over Abner's (2 Sam. 3:33). Isaiah prophesied concerning the Moabites lamenting the downfall and destruction of their nation (Isa. 15:1–16).

Lament Psalms

Attention is drawn in this study of Lamentations to the lament Psalms for the following reasons.

First, laments, included in a number of Psalms, reveal that Yahweh God's covenant people lamented certain definite realities in life. Their sin, their disappointments, their failures, and their tragedies were recognized as aspects of life under Yahweh God's sovereign reign. Laments included self-incrimination and accusations. These led to confession of failure and sin.

Second, laments included a deep concern for truth, righteousness, and justice to prevail. The violations of these were involved in reasons for laments. But the lamenting persons gave expression to their helplessness. Their laments became calls on their sovereign almighty helper and sustainer.

Third, scholars have been correct to stress that lamenting provided people with an emotional catharsis that could lead to submission and prospects for hope. The reality is that in the context of lament, praise was expressed. Indeed, Psalms of lament invariably led to and included expressions of praise to Yahweh God.[5]

A reading of the book of Lamentations will enable any reader to realize that the reason for lamenting did not result in absolute pessimism and hopelessness. As will be discussed later Lamentations includes expressions of faith, trust, and hope.

Specific Issues Regarding the Book

Authorship

The Hebrew text of Lamentations does not indicate who wrote it. The book has been placed after the book of Jeremiah in many Old Testament Bibles. In the Hebrew text it follows Ecclesiastes and precedes the book of Esther.[6] Ancient Jewish and Christian traditions ascribe it to Jeremiah. The Chronicler, when he recorded the death of Josiah, added that Jeremiah composed laments for Josiah (2 Chron. 35:26). Commentators correctly point out that the Chronicler made no reference to Jeremiah composing laments over Jerusalem when it fell.[7] Keil has written, after reviewing various characteristics of the five laments composing the book, "one must not consider the authorship of Jeremiah as improbable."[8] A compromise has been offered. Reference was made to moderate scholars, who have not presented a strong case for Jeremiah as the author, that "we do well to respect the seal of anonymity impressed on the book by the Holy Spirit."[9]

It is this writer's position that one does not offend the Holy Spirit when, in spite of various problems raised, such as literary characteristics, Jeremiah continues to be considered the author of Lamentations. He is also the author of the prophecy of Jeremiah in which one can read of Jeremiah's pain and grief. He wrote " I am crushed, I mourn, horror grips me, I would weep day and night" (8:20–9:3). Immediately following Jeremiah's heart-wrenching lament he quotes the Lord, "See, I will refine and test them" (9:7). Lament was followed by hope.

Setting

The first word in the book is *'êkâh* (1:1). It is repeated (2:1; 4:1). It is an emphatic exclamation that introduced reference to the city, once full of people but now deserted. The daughter of Zion (2:1) is a reference to Jerusalem and its gold that had lost its luster (4:1). There can be no doubt about the setting: Jerusalem was in ruins, it was depopulated. It was the setting in which Lamentations was composed. Foes had become the master of Jerusalem; Yahweh had brought grief; the people had gone as captives into exile. The time was 586 B.C., when God handed Jerusalem, the temple, and the inhabitants over to Nebuchadnezzar and the Babylonian army (2 Chron. 36:17–19). Jeremiah, the prophet, was there at the time. He witnessed the coming of the Babylonians, the devastation they wrought, and the deportation of many inhabitants that had not died at the hands of the Babylonians.[10]

Literary Aspects

Critical scholars are quick to point out that the five parts, poetic in structure, do not form a well-composed literary unit. But, there is no doubt that the themes of devastation and hope unite the five sections. They are similar, being built on the basis of an alphabetic acrostic, except for chapter 5. It has twenty-two verses as do 1, 2, 4, which are acrostic. It has been said it is a literary convention that controls the expression of profound grief and symbolizes completeness.[11] That some literary differences can be detected by critical eyes does not indicate that one author cannot reveal some dissimilarities. The five parts were undoubtedly not written in one setting. Over a period of time after the Babylonians had done their devastating destructive deeds, Jeremiah composed his book, undoubtedly affected and influenced by different scenes and experiences.

Questions have been raised about influences from other countries on the composer of Lamentations. References have been to Syrian influences especially.[12]

Comparisons can be highlighted, some scholars agree. But that some similarities may be observed in the broader Semitic world should not be surprising. Nor do they give solid reason for positing influences. Gordis wrote that similar circumstances lead to similar descriptions of conditions and similar expressions of mood.[13] It should be kept in mind that many countries suffered from devastating attacks in those times when the Babylonians scoured the then known civilized world.[14]

Purpose

One commentator has written that Lamentations really has no specific theological purpose for modern Christians. It could have historical and antiquarian interest. That the Bible has room for every element of human experience does not present a specific purpose for Lamentations to be included in the canon. Lamentations was written in the context of Jerusalem's and the Temple's destruction—an historical reality in 586 B.C. Other passages in Scripture, especially in the

Psalms and some prophetic laments are more universally acceptable.[15] Another writer, however, stated his understanding of the purpose of Lamentations. He wrote that even with the rootedness in Palestinian soil, some 2,500 years ago, Lamentations transcends these local boundaries of Palestine. It speaks to successive generations in a remarkable manner of sin, suffering, and evil. These are included in the very stuff of human existence.[16]

When one reads and studies the works of feminist writers one could conclude that Lamentations was written to belittle women.[17] The Old Testament Scriptures are considered to be very patriarchal. Women are often denigrated. Lamentations is said to be a specifically extreme case. Patriarchs are considered to be hiding behind "the naked woman." Guest described how, as she saw woman in Lamentations, she was a loose woman, a fit symbol to describe Israel's sin.[18] Guest decided to challenge the text and refused to accept it as conventional exegetes did and do.[19] Her view is that Lamentations is a male text with an unacceptable thesis. It is regrettable that reference to and recognition of Jerusalem as a beautiful and resourceful woman is omitted. Repeatedly Jerusalem is referred to in various contexts by the pronouns *she* and *her*.[20]

Various biblical theological writers have discussed or referred to the book of Lamentations. Childs has stated that over against Israel's election there is also the warning of rejection; the terms *election* and *rejection* form an essential polarity.[21] As will be discussed in following sections, this polarity demonstrated the antithesis in Yahweh God's dealing with humanity.

Another biblical theological author has reminded students that Lamentations records that Yahweh God's warning of wrath to come on those who rejected God was carried out. Yahweh's day of wrath became a tragic reality for Jerusalem. The guilt of fathers and contemporary inhabitants of Jerusalem were the immediate reasons for and causes of Jerusalem's devastation.[22] But the ultimate purpose for the experiences of punishment was salvation.[23]

The Golden Cable

In this biblical theological study of Lamentations the challenge is: are the three strands of the Golden Cable that unite the entire revealed message recorded in Scripture present and functioning in Lamentations? And does Lamentations contribute to the progressive revelation set forth in the Scriptures? The answer to both questions is positive. It contributes to what is recorded in other books concerning the fall and destruction of Jerusalem. The kingdom and covenant strands are more dominant than the mediatorial strand.

Kingdom

The terms referring directly to the king, kingdom, and kingdoms are few.[24] Jeremiah, however, in various ways and settings indicated that he was definitely "kingdom conscious." This becomes clear as one considers how the concept of kingdom comes to expression.

Yahweh **'Adon** *the King*

Names

Jeremiah was very God-conscious as he expressed his laments, hopes, and assurances. He addressed or called on Yahweh twenty-six times.[25] This covenant name was on his heart and lips. Jeremiah was obviously fully aware that his covenant Lord, in spite of tragic circumstances and conditions, was present and a hearer of his people's prayers. He spoke of Yahweh's *ḥesed, ḥasdê, yĕhwâh* (and his great love and mercy, 3:22).

It is of interest to note that Jeremiah did not refer to God by the full name *'ĕlōhîm* (God). He did refer to his Lord once as *'ēl*, the most high (3:41) to whom hands should be lifted up. He also addressed him as *'elyôn* also translated "most high" (3:35). Reference in this passage could be construed to be to God as judge.

Jeremiah used the name *'adon* nine (9) times.[26] This name revealed that God was recognized as the "Master," the Sovereign One who saps strength and hands one over to invincible opponents (1:14), because as Sovereign Master he rejects his people with a cloud of anger (2:1) and his wrath destroys Israel his people. He swallowed them up without pity in his wrath and anger (2:2, 3). As *'Adon*, he, in his sovereignty and power destroyed Judah, the land, and Zion his city. The temple, along with feasts and sabbaths, were made to be forgotten (2:5–8). Jeremiah referred to his God both by the names Yahweh and *Adon* in this context.

Character

It is important to note that Jeremiah remembered to declare that he knew the character of his covenant Lord and master. He declared that Yahweh is *śaddîq* (righteous) (1:18). Yahweh, the sovereign master, performs all his deeds according to his perfect will revealed in his law. Jeremiah, speaking for himself and his people, confessed rebellion against his commandments.

As referred to in the preceding, Jeremiah spoke of Yahweh the Master the Most High. He is the exalted one over all and yet this exalted Lord revealed his *hesed* (great love) (3:22), by not consuming all his rebellious people. The prophet added that his God revealed his *rāḥām* (compassions); "they were new every morning." His 'ĕmûnnâh (faithfulness) was *rabbâh* (great) (3:21, 22). His covenant goodness *tôbh* is there for those who hope in him and for his *tĕšû'âh* (salvation). It is always there for those who wait on him (3:26). Yahweh, as the exalted, loving, compassionate, faithful and good Master can be and do as such for his people who confessed their sin (3:42) because, as Jeremiah confessed *'attâh yĕhwâh lĕ 'ôlām tēšeb kis'ăka* (you yahweh forever sit on your throne) (5:19). Translations seek to clarify this phrase by translating "You, O Lord, reign forever, your throne endures from generation to generation" (NIV 5:19).

Yahweh *Adon*, the ever faithful God, sits on his throne eternally from which he demonstrates and pours out his love and mercy and reveals his righteousness as he reigns over his cosmic kingdom.[27]

Cosmic Kingdom

The term *cosmic kingdom* refers to the entire cosmos with all of the inherent aspects in it. Thus reference is to the natural world. It includes heaven and earth (2:1; 3: 41, 50); clouds (3:44); darkness and light (3:2); the seas (1:19); fire (1:13; 2:3, 4; 4:11) and soot (4:13). In the earth are rocks (3:9, 53); dust (2:10, 21 ; 3:16, 20); paths (3:9); calamities (3:38); and pits (3:53, 55). References to the military are numerous; swords (1:20; 2:21; 4:9); strongholds (2:2); chains (3:7); prisoners (3:34); bows and arrows (3:12, 13), sticks (4:8); towers (4:17). Ash heaps (4:5) were well known to Jeremiah. He spoke of personal aspects of life such as garments (4:14), filthiness (1:9, 17), bones (4:8), and gall (3:19). He referred to treasures (1:10); gold (4:1);[28] gardens (2:6); and food and bread (4: 4). In the animal and bird world he was of aware of deer (1:6), jackels (4:3; 5:18); lions (3:10); eagles (4:14); and ostriches (4:3). In regard to man's working world he referred to the yoke (1:14); the winepress (1:15); nets (1:13); millstones and loads of wood under which boys staggered (5:13) and for which a price had to be paid as well as for the water to drink.

Jeremiah also indicated that he knew that under Yahweh the Master's reign other nations became involved in the lives of the covenant people (4:12; 5:2, 4). They were made slaves ruled over by foreigners. He referred to Egypt and Assyria (5:6), to Edom (4:21, 22), and to nations among whom Judah was once known as great but had become a slave to them (1:1, 3, 5, 7; 5:2).

A study of Lamentations certainly can make a student aware of Jeremiah's knowledge of the cosmic kingdom in which he lived and did his duty as a prophet.

Theocratic Kingdom

Judah

In a study of Lamentations one can become impressed with the fall and degradation of Judah. Israel, the northern kingdom, had fallen and suffered exile in 722 B.C. Judah, under the reign of Davidic descendants, continued to exist longer, until 586 B.C. It had become increasingly rebellious and sinful. Jeremiah, at times, referred to himself as a representative of his land, confessing sin and wickedness, and iniquity (1:14, 18, 20, 22; 3:39, 43; 4:13; 5:7, 16). The nation of Judah, the once cherished theocratic kingdom, had become a nonexistent nation. The country was no longer a homeland for the remnant of the covenant people.

Zion

The heart of the land of Judah was the city of Jerusalem. It had been captured and established as the royal city by David. It was loved; it was the golden city with treasures (1:7; 4:1, 2). This heart was often referred to as Zion.[29] It was on a low hill in the southeast part of the modern city. David had captured it and made it the legal, cultural, and religious center of the entire nation of Israel. Solomon had expanded the city, building the Temple on an adjacent hill, Moriah. As the original city, Zion, expanded, it became known as Jerusalem, but the expanded city continued also to be called Zion.

Jeremiah referred to the city as Jerusalem seven times. He referred to its treasures (1:7); its gates (4:12); its women (2:10, 13, 15); its sin (1:8); and its filthiness (1:9). He used the name Zion to refer to it fifteen times. The women of Zion are spoken of as representatives. Their hands are stretched out (1:17), but a cloud of the Lord's anger covers it (2:1) and a fire was kindled in Zion (4:11). Roads to Zion mourned (1:4); walls and ramparts of Zion were torn down (2:8, 18) and had become desolate (5:16). Tragedy overcame the elders who sat on the ground with dust on their heads, clothed in sackcloth (2:10). Sons of Zion referred to as *hayĕqārîm* (the precious), worth their weight in gold,[30] are considered as *ḥereś* (earthen vessels) made by human potters (4:2). The point is that young men who became the future theocratic kingdom agents had no future role as such. As earthen vessels they were smashed as Zion was captured and destroyed.

Agents of Zion

In Israel, Judah, Jerusalem, and Zion there were three recognized categories of leaders who in one way or another were appointed, possibly anointed, or assumed leadership roles.

King. Jeremiah referred to "kings" and "princes" who were no longer present and functioning; they were spurned and exiled (2:6, 8). Elders, who often had political power to exercise local authority and to judge, sat on the ground in silence (2:10) and not in the city gates (5:14). Many perished (1:19). Those who lived were showed no favor (4:16) or respect (5:12). The law was no more (2:9). Anarchy would have reigned had not aliens and foreigners taken control (5:2).

Priests. Priests were not referred to often by Jeremiah. When he did, he had only tragic words. The meeting place—the Temple where they had served, had been laid waste (2:6).[31] Appointed feasts and Sabbaths were no longer kept and celebrated (2:6). Priests were spurned by the Lord (2:6). Jeremiah asked Yahweh if priests should be killed in the sanctuary (2:20). To be understood is that if priests did function in the last days of the sanctuary existence they would be killed.

Prophets. Prophets were kingdom agents.[32] Jeremiah knew he was. As mentioned before, Jeremiah would speak as a direct representative or identify himself as Judah, Jerusalem, or Zion.[33] He referred to the "prophet" when he inquired if they should be killed (2:20) and that at the Lord's will. In his prophecies he had accused the prophets of speaking by Baal (Jer. 2:8). He had said prophets were but wind (5:12) and they prophesied lies (5:31). The Lord had said he had sent them (25:21) but they were diviners (27:9; 29:8). The sword that would be against the Babylonians, its officials and wise men, would be against Judah's prophets (50:36).

Jeremiah, having prophesied against false prophets, included words in his laments against the prophets who had sinned. He accused them of causing enemies to enter the gates of Jerusalem and abetting the shedding of the blood of the righteous (Lam.4:13). The prophets no longer received visions from Yahweh (2:9) but the visions they included in their messages were false and worthless, and did not ward off captivity. Jeremiah added, addressing these false prophets, "the oracles the visions gave you were false and misleading" (2:14).

Kingdom Summary

The kingdom was an abiding reality. Yahweh God established it when he created the cosmos. He reigned over it. His virtues were revealed in his rule and providential care. The cosmic kingdom was rich with many assets that were available to its inhabitants.

The theocratic kingdom was established as an integral part of the cosmic kingdom. It came into full existence under David and Solomon. It had divided and Judah, the southern part, was ruled over by Davidic kings. Some were loyal vicegerents, others were not. Increasingly the kingdom of Judah, with its capital city Zion/Jerusalem, the Temple, and the cultic activities within, became corrupted. Yahweh *Adon's* kingdom agents, kings, priests, and prophets, became increasingly unfaithful and rebellious. Jeremiah became a lone prophetic voice for a doomed theocratic kingdom and its people. The covenant was upheld by Yahweh *Adon* but violated and broken by the people. The life-love bond was strained and suffered severely from the human perspective. Yahweh *Adon* upheld it.

The antithesis, as stated above, was in the context of the polarity between Yahweh's election and Judah's rejection. Within the kingdom of Judah the antithesis came to an extreme expression. It was not first of all between the kingdom of Judah, the covenant people, and neighboring kingdoms. The antithesis had become a tragic reality within the kingdom of Judah.

The kingdom of Judah continued to be Yahweh God's elect people. The election stood! But Judah's rejection of Yahweh God and his prescribed will (2:9) became a tragic alternative.

Two irreconciable stances became a positive reality. Kings, priests, and prophets were leading opponents of Yahweh God. Jeremiah was a solitary agent for Yahweh God. He thus stood as the opponent of all those who rejected Yahweh and his revealed will for all aspects of covenantal kingdom life. But Jeremiah, in spite of his proclamations and protests, came to see and realize that the opposition to Yahweh was too entrenched to be overcome.

The message Jeremiah proclaimed was that Yahweh *Adon* the righteous (1:18) Lord reigned (5:19). His plan would not fail, his purposes would be achieved. Sinful people, covenant breakers, were removed. Yahweh spurned the king and priest in his anger (2:6). The antithesis led to a complete destruction of Judah. But Yahweh *Adon* continued to reign. His covenant, not heeded by the people, was upheld by the covenant Maker and Keeper.

The Covenant

The Basic Concept for Understanding Lamentations

The Historic Relationship

God had called Abraham from Ur of the Chaldees to move to Canaan, where the covenant would be confirmed. Yahweh God assured Abraham that his descendants would be many and that they would become a great blessed nation (Gen. 12:1). Centuries later Moses organized Abraham's descendants into a national entity. Joshua led them as a nation into the land Yahweh had promised Abraham, Isaac, and Jacob. In time David and Solomon finalized the establishment of the theocratic kingdom. The laws and instructions for life and worship given through Moses were instituted as covenantal prescriptions for kingdom life under Yahweh *Adon*'s reign. When Jeremiah was called about three centuries after David's reign, he proclaimed the calamity that was to come upon the land, the city, and the temple (Jer. 1:10)

Implied Throughout the Book

The term *bĕrît* (covenant) does not appear in the book of Lamentations. When one consults the prophecies of Jeremiah, most of these were proclaimed before he wrote Lamentations; he referred to the covenant repeatedly. Hence, it is important to realize that Jeremiah's laments have a definite covenant context. Aspects of the covenant are directly referred to as he lamented.

The Covenant Lord. Jeremiah, when referring to God, used his covenant name predominantly.[34] He expressed his relationship to his covenant Lord when he cried out "I am despised." The people despised him in his prophetic role when they groaned, searching for food, using their treasures as barter (1:11). Yahweh had given his people Zion, appointed feasts and Sabbaths, their king and priests, covenant blessings, all of them. He destroyed these and made them to be forgotten. As he, their covenant Lord, had given, so now as covenant Lord he took them away. Jeremiah, however, assured the people that their covenant Lord loved them because in that love he kept them from being consumed (3:22). Jeremiah knew that the covenant Lord of Israel could and would be fiercely angered and give vent to his wrath (4:11). Moses had spoken clearly: when Yahweh covenanted with Israel he would punish those who hated him (Exod. 20:5). Moses had repeated that Yahweh was a jealous God, a consuming fire (Deut. 4: 24). Jeremiah, in his concluding laments, addressed his covenant Lord when he referred to how covenant blessings had been turned over to aliens (5:1, 2).

The Covenant People. Yahweh God had chosen his people to be bonded to him in life with love. Jeremiah gave evidence that he and the people of Jerusalem and Judah were privileged people. They knew they had been given a covenantal heritage (5:2). They had been a crowned people but the crown had fallen from their head. A crown meant honor, prestige, glory, authority, and privileges.[35]

Jeremiah, speaking personally yet as representative of the people, called for an examination of their ways and to test them. So doing they are called to return *našîbâh 'ad yĕhwâh* (let us return to Yahweh). This counsel, "let us return," indicates that there had been a prior relationship of submission to and peace with their covenant Lord (3:40).

Promises. The promises included in the covenant were not explicitly stated. The promise of "I will be their God and they my people" was not explicitly stated by Jeremiah. The mutual admonition to return to Yahweh and to lift up hearts and hands to God in heaven (3:41) reflected the promises that had been given that Yahweh God would hear and forgive. Such prayers had been offered before (1 Kings. 8:30), taking Yahweh God at his word (Exod. 22:23, 27; Ps. 28:2–6).

Yahweh God had promised to love his people and to keep his covenant of love (Deut. 7:9, 12). He promised that he would love and bless his people (Deut. 7:13; 33:3). This promise of love was acknowledged and claimed when the prophet spoke on behalf of the covenant people that it was because of the promised great love of Yahweh that some were alive (Lam. 3:22). Because of the promised love, compassion would not fail nor would Yahweh's faithfulness (3:22). In love, goodness would be given to those hoping in him and seeking him and his salvation (3:25, 26).

Stipulations. The Law, decrees, statutes, commandments, and precepts given to Israel from the time Israel stood at the foot of Mount. Sinai were subsumed under the general theme or part of the covenant referred to as stipulations. Jeremiah, in his prophecies, referred to law, and aspects of it in various contexts. He had called his fellow citizens of Judah to hear him prophesy about disaster because they had not listened to Yahweh's words and had rejected God's Law (Jer. 6:19). The people were quoted as saying they had the Law but they were reminded that their scribes had handled it falsely (8:9). People conspired against Jeremiah for teaching the Law (18:18).

Once Zion/Jerusalem had fallen to the Babylonians Jeremiah lamented that with the destruction of the city, the Law had also been removed. He declared that when the king and princes were sent into exile, the Law was no more (Lam. 2:9). The Law no longer served in Jerusalem as the divinely appointed constitution of Israel. It had been abolished and destroyed, not by Yahweh the covenant Lord, but by his people living in Zion/Jerusalem/Judah.

The Covenantal Mandates

In the preceding studies of the Old Testament the three covenantal mandates were seen and developed as major elements of the covenant Yahweh God made with his people. The question is: are these mandates and their integrally related relationships also present in the book of Lamentations?

The Spiritual Mandate. Jeremiah the prophet was not only aware of this mandate, but it was a major factor in his laments. The spiritual mandate served in the context of the divinely established spiritual relationship. This involved an intimate fellowship with the covenant Lord. Jeremiah repeatedly called on Yahweh, saying *rĕ'êh yĕhwâh* (look Yahwah) (1:9, 11, 20; 2:20; 3:63; 5:1). He thus freely revealed his intimate relationship with Yahweh. He added "remember what happened to us" (5:1) and he pled with Yahweh to reply (3:56, 58, 61, 64; 5:21). He spoke intimately: "Yahweh is my help" (portion). The prophet meant that although he may not have many earthly possessions, his riches were the spiritual relationship he had with Yahweh, his covenant Lord.

This relationship reflected and exhibited the spiritual mandates that demanded that Yahweh *Adon* be recognized as the sovereign, supreme Lord. And Jeremiah alluded to the spiritual mandate's requirement that Yahweh God be worshiped. He referred to priests who groaned (1:4). Priests were to have led people in sacrifices and worship, as prescribed, thus keeping appointed feasts and Sabbaths at the place of meeting (2:6).[36] He went on to ask: should they be killed in the sanctuary as some were, in the very place they were mandated to serve?

In the midst of destruction, banishment, and death, Jeremiah proved he was a true prophet of Yahweh[37]who knew the great love of his Lord. He recognized the goodness of the Lord (3:22–25a). But he also proclaimed what was required of him to obey the covenantal mandate and maintain the spiritual relationship. Covenant members were to wait for, hope in, and seek for the Lord (3:24b–26). They were to do so humbly, burying their faces in the dust and offering their cheeks to whomever would strike them (3:29, 30).

The Social Mandate. At the heart of the social mandate was the marriage bond. A man was to leave his parents and be united with his wife (Gen. 2:24) until death parted them. In the extremely strenuous situation that existed at the time that Jeremiah lamented he did not make reference to husbands and wives. Children, seed of the covenant, and their mothers were spoken of as suffering tragically (2:19, 20; 5:3). The maternal bond was violated by women. The social mandate to be fruitful and multiply (Gen. 1:28) was violated. The promise concerning covenant seed (Gen. 17:7) was rejected. Jeremiah boldly stated that Yahweh in his anger slaughtered young men and women with hands and weapons wielded by enemies (2:21, 22). Then Jeremiah added that Yahweh does not willingly bring affliction or grief to the children of men (3:33). He does, however, when covenant people sin and turn away from their Lord. Then in anger Yahweh demonstrates that the spiritual mandate has a defining effect upon social relationships and mandates.

The renewing of the social relationship was addressed directly by Jeremiah. It can be inferred, however, that with an eventual restoration of a remnant the social mandate would continue to be upheld and obeyed with Yahweh's help.

The Cultural Mandate. In Jeremiah's time the covenant people had very little opportunity to obey the mandate to cultivate, till, and subdue the cosmos. Jerusalem was attacked. (1:4). The people of Judah had gone into exile (1:3; 2:22). The roads to Zion had no traffic (1:4). Her treasures were gone, enemies had taken them (1:10), gold had lost its luster (4:1). The markets had no food (1:19; 4:4; 5:9).

An army had invaded, Judah's warriors were gone (1:15; 2:16; 3:46, 47), defenses were overthrown (2:2, 5, 8, 9).

Reading the book of Lamentations one realizes how totally cultural life and activities had ceased. The covenant people did not obey the cultural mandate because in the cultural dimension of their lives they no longer were in charge. The crown had fallen from their head (5:16). They had no ability or authority to serve as any kind of royal representative of their Creator and covenant Lord. If alive, they were made homeless exiles or slaves to their enemies.

The disobeying of the covenant mandates and the devastating effects this had on the relationships between Yahweh and his people, his people with other people, and the people and their everyday cultural environment gave occasion for many sins. Repeatedly Jeremiah spoke of sin and its results.

The Rupture of the Covenant Life-Love Bond[38]

Causes

Prophets preceding Jeremiah had referred to various causes for the rupture of the covenant between Yahweh the covenant Lord and Israel/Judah, the covenant people. These causes have been summed up as follows: (1) individualism of profligates; (2) oppression by the rich; (3) voluptuous lifestyles; (4) corruption of justice; and (5) corruption of ritual worship.[39] Jeremiah had prophesied against these (Jer.7:21).

In the book of Lamentations Jeremiah referred to Judah, Yahweh's covenant bride, having lovers (1:2) and becoming unclean (5:17). The appointed feasts were ignored (1:4). The prophets referred to false visions (2:14) and priests shed innocent blood (4:14, 15). The people had become heartless (4:3). Jeremiah used the term such as sin to refer to all the evil deeds (1:8, 14; 2:14). He spoke of rebellion (1:18, 20; 3:42) and of wickedness (1:22; 4:22).

Yahweh God's Response

Throughout Israel and Judah's history, Yahweh God instructed his covenant people to be faithful in obeying him and keeping all the prescriptions of the Law he had or given at Mount Sinai (Exod.19:1–24:18). He had warned if any aspect of his covenant was not heeded his anger would be aroused (Exod. 22:24; Deut. 11:17). Jeremiah, in his prophecies, referred to Yahweh God's anger repeatedly.[40] In his laments Jeremiah used the term *'aph* (anger) ten times. The adjective *hărôn* (fierce) described the heat and intensity of his anger (Lam. 2:3, 6; 4:11). The term *'abrâh* (wrath) appears twice. Reference is to Yahweh's wrath (2:2) and to his rod of wrath (3:2). The idea of wrath expresses a great degree of Yahweh's negative reaction to sin. The metaphor of a fire with smoke billowing forth from nostrils is used to refer to the most intense negative reaction. God's wrath utterly consumes. Without pity Yahweh wrought his anger and wrath upon his rebellious covenant people (2:2, 17, 21; 3:43). The execution of Yahweh God's anger and wrath without pity (2:21) was not done capriciously, as if on the spur of the moment. Jeremiah understood that very well. He referred to what Yahweh had done. The verb *zāmam*

(2:17) refers to Yahweh's consideration. Yahweh had a purpose he had made known and decreed long ago (2:17). He had spoken of and warned his people of the covenant curse that would be executed upon a rebellious and wicked people.[41]

The Curse

Jeremiah did not use the term *'ārar* (curse) in Lamentations as he had done repeatedly in his prophecies. He used the term *ta'ălātêka*, a form of the noun *'ălâh* (oath) and understood as an oath of curse (3.65).[42] He, however, knew what Moses had spoken of as Yahweh God's curse and its effects and results. The passive participial term *'ārîen* (be cursed, from the verb *'ārar*, to curse) appeared often in Deuteronomy.[43] He did speak of the object of Yahweh's curses and its tragic results. A review of this leads one to realize the overwhelming extent of the application of Yahweh God's anger and wrath—the covenant curse. Keil has written, "The curse of God is followed by destruction."[44] As will be shown, the curse Yahweh God executed upon Judah was mitigated as the curse on Adam and Eve was.

Jeremiah lamented that the curse came on all aspects of life for the people of Judah. Family life suffered severe atrocities. Women and virgins were ravished (5:11); children were taken into captivity (1:5) or became orphans and their mothers widows (5:3). Homes were taken and occupied by aliens (5:2). Sons were demeaned (4:1, 2) and princes hung by their hands (5:12). There was no bread to be gotten or found (2:12; 4:4, 9, 59); children fainted from hunger in the streets (2:19). Women ate their children (2:20). Life in the city became atrocious. People were stalked (4:18); enemy killers soaked their clothes with the blood of their victims (4:13, 14). Plots and insults were devised against the people (3:60) and the people were made the scum among the nations (3:45). As people passed by they clapped their hands, shook their heads, and scoffed at the victims (2:15). They were made slaves to their foes (1:5, 14) and were betrayed by aliens (1:19). Judah as a people, their land and city, were pressed into hard labor (1:3) as grapes pressed in the winepress (1:15). Judah's nakedness was exposed (1:8) and her treasures were stolen (1:10). The beautiful city was made desolate (1:1, 3); her splendor was destroyed (2:6). Zion was laid waste (2:6) and her gates and walls were broken and destroyed (2:9). Every horn[45] was cut off (2:3) and the king and princes were exiled (2:9). The Lord's house was invaded by pagans (1:10) and the Lord rejected his altar (2:7). The king was exiled (2:9), vengeance was demonstrated (3:60) as Mount. Zion became desolate (5:1). Zion's punishment was greater than Sodom's had been (4:6).[46] Yahweh God, carrying out the curse, brought affliction; Jeremiah referred to it again and again (1:3, 7, 9; 3:1, 19, 33).

Covenantal Assurances

Mitigated Curse. Yahweh God had pronounced a mitigated curse on Adam, Eve, and the cosmos after they had sinned (Gen. 3:14–19).[47] It had been a full curse on Satan but on mankind and his habitat, provision of grace was included. Jeremiah, in his prophecies and lamentations, spoke of grace to be revealed and executed during and after the curse was executed over Judah the people, the temple, the city, and the "promised land." The covenant was upheld when the threatened curse was executed. It was in a real sense, carried out more positively and wonderfully by the assurances of grace and well-being that are included in the book of Lamentations. There are no direct statements concerning the continuity of the covenant and the succeding new covenant as Jeremiah had prophesied would surely be initiated (Jer. 31:31–34) Thus, if there was to be a continuation, the curse that Jeremiah saw executed was not full and final.

Proclamation of Grace. When Jeremiah had prophesied that the people of Judah, whom he represented, had suffered the fierce anger of Yahweh (1:12, 15), he spoke clearly: *'seddîq hû' ỹehwâh* (righteous [is] he Yahweh). The covenant Lord remained true to his character and revealed will. He punished because of sin, but in his righteousness he would also carry out his promises of grace—the covenant would be upheld in every aspect. Recall Jeremiah's prophecy concerning the covenant.

Before a study is made of what has been referred to as the apex of the theology of Lamentations,[48] consideration should be given to a few other passages that reflect hope. Jeremiah spoke of *tôḥaltî* (3:18). This term is derived from the verb *yāḥal.* It usually means to wait. The one who waits, he expects, hopes for that not yet acquired. Jeremiah knew that Yahweh *Adon* was the only source from which he would receive what he waited and hoped for. The prophet was realistic. He knew *nishî* (splendor or glory) was gone (3:18). He had referred to his misery and wondering, his bitterness and gall;[49] yet he could say that as he called these to mind, he continued to *'ôhîl,* to hope. Then follows his theological affirmation.

Jeremiah had not given up hope completely. He knew that Yahweh would look down from heaven and see him grieving (3:49, 50). He knew that Yahweh *gā'altâ* (redeemed) his life (3:58). He was also assured that the Daughter of Zion's punishment would end when the time of the exile was fulfilled (4:22).[50] As Jeremiah concluded his laments he spoke positively. You Yahweh reign *lĕ'ôlām* (forever). *kis'ăkâh* (Your throne) endures from generation to generation. Hence Jeremiah pled *hăšibênu* (restore us).

Jeremiah could include these passages of hope and expectations because he knew Yahweh *Adon* was a faithful covenant Lord. He would always be the same; a righteous God who would punish sin and execute the threatened curse. But his character and virtues would never change. Jeremiah knew that what Yahweh God would declare through Malachi was absolute truth (Mal. 3:6) *'ănî yĕhwâh lo' šānîtî* (I, Yahweh do not change).

A consideration of Lamentations 3:22–32 brings to mind that Yahweh had revealed his covenantal characteristics repeatedly. When Israel, camped at the base of Mount. Sinai, worshiped the golden calf Yahweh God forgave them after Moses had interceded for them. It was then that Yahweh God's covenantal virtues were summed up (Exod. 34:6). The Psalmists had gloried in the reality that Yahweh and his virtues remained unchanged (Ps. 86:15, 16; 103:8–13; 145:8, 9). The prophet Joel referred to Yahweh's virtues when he called Israel to repentance (2:13) as did Nehemiah when he sought to spur the returnees from exile to be faithful in rebuilding Jerusalem (Neh. 9:17).

When Jeremiah considered the tragic realities that surrounded him: the Temple destroyed, Jerusalem in ruins, most of the people exiled, and the tragic situation of the few that remained in Jerusalem and Judah, he proclaimed that not all had been *tămēnû* (from the verb *tāmam,* to be completely finished). Jeremiah knew that in spite of his people's many sins, Yahweh God had not completely ended the existence of the covenant people. It was because of Yahweh's *ḥasde* (mercy, often translated great love). Ellison stated correctly "the covenant had called Israel into existence and the Lord's loving mercy to what he had created would not end."[51] What had come forth from Yahweh, as a babe from a mother's womb, would never fail to experience *raḥămaywe* (his compassion). And this was because of Yahweh's *rabbēh 'ĕmûnêh* (great faithfulness). The root term *'āman* (to confirm) has various derivatives such as *'āmen* (faithfulness) said by Isaiah to be perfect (25:1); *'ammen* (translated as verily); *'āmun* (trusting, faithfulness).[52] Note should be taken of the phrase *habdāšîm lăbĕqārîm* (new every morning). With Yahweh *Adon* no aspect of his covenant ever becomes stale, old, or worn out. Yahweh God would be his portion forever.[53] Jeremiah also added *tōb yehwāh* (good is Yahweh) (3:25). In his person Yahweh is completely whole; his actions and virtues combine to be an integral expression of perfection—particularly in his relationship with his covenant people.

Jeremiah summed up his proclamation concerning Yahweh *Adon's* relationship with his people. Covenant mankind was not cast off by Yahweh forever. Though he brought grief, he would show compassion *kirōb hăsādâw* because so great was his covenant loving kindness and his mercy (3:31, 32). Jeremiah then made a statement that, taken in isolation from the text, could be appealed to, to say Yahweh God is not free in all his actions toward his people: *kî lo' 'innâh millibbô.* This phrase has been translated as "For he does not afflict out of his own will"[54] or "For he does not willingly bring affliction."[55] Commentaries explain that the thought is that Yahweh's affliction of his people is never arbitrary.[56] Keil wrote that God does not send affliction willingly, as if it brought him joy but because chastisement is necessary to sinful man for the increase of his spiritual prosperity.[57] Adeney reminded his readers that God himself grieves to inflict distress and brings it only to an extent that is absolutely necessary.[58]

Summing up, Jeremiah proclaimed a blessed assurance for those covenant people, afflicted and grieved, that Yahweh *Adon* has not forgotten to love his people. His covenant with them stood. His love and faithfulness never ended. Yahweh remained the Lord of hope, love, faithfulness, and salvation. A confessing penitent child of Yahweh had to wait patiently for full salvation (3:26).

The Mediator

No Direct Prophecy: The Narrower View

Jeremiah prophesied concerning the Mediator in his prophecies.[59] There are no specific prophecies of the messianic Mediator in the book of Lamentations. So while we can conclude from the prophecies that Jeremiah spoke concerning the Mediator and there is an absence of any direct reference to him in Lamentations, we should not conclude that there are no inferences to him. Though the narrower view is not included the broader view of the promised Mediator can be discerned.[60]

Messianic Types

King

Throughout the Old Testament books there are references to messianic types, including Abraham, Joseph, Moses, Joshua, David, and Solomon. Kings were particularly singled out as types. The references to kings in Lamentations (2:6, 9; 4:12) indicates that Jeremiah was aware that kings no longer had a role. There is no messianic significance included in these passages. Elders who had had an authoritative role likewise were no longer functioning. They had perished (1:19). Those that still lived were shown no honor (4:16; 5:12). Princes who had not fled as deer (1:6) or been exiled (2:9) were executed (5:12) for they had become blacker than soot (4:7).

Priest

Priests served in a typical role during Israel's existence as a nation. Their role in worship, especially in regard to sacrifices and maintaining standards of purity and holiness, was typical of the promised Messiah. References to priests indicate that they no longer functioned as they had been instructed and ordained to service. They were iniquitous, shedding the blood of the righteous (4:13), and they exhibited no honor (4:16). They joined the remaining people in Jerusalem in their groaning (1:4) if they were still alive (1:19).

Prophet

Prophets no longer were spokesmen for the Lord. They neither received nor found visions from the Lord (2:9) and the ones they spoke were false (2:14). Jeremiah asked, "should prophets with priests be killed?" (2:20), because their sins were a reason for the invasion of Jerusalem by enemies and foes (4:12, 13). Jeremiah stood and served Yahweh *Adon* alone in the midst of sinning and failing servants. None foreshadowed the Messiah or served as his forerunner. There was an exception—Jeremiah, who was typical of the promised Messiah.

First, as referred to before, Jeremiah at times took the role as personal representative of the covenant people. He personally identified with them. He used the pronoun *I*, not *they* (1:16). I am despised representing the people who groan for bread. Referring to his covenant people's situation he asked if any suffering was like "my suffering?" (1:12). He referred to himself as a representative of the people receiving fire in his bones, heavy as a net spread before him and made faint all the day (1:13). Jeremiah spoke of his rejection by those who burdened (yoked) him with the sins of others and had his strength sapped by Yahweh (1:14). He spoke of his suffering (vicariously) (1:18) and of his betrayal by allies (1:19). He referred to his enemies rejoicing because of what they had done to him (the covenant people, 1:21). The prophet spoke of Yahweh dealing with him because of all "my sins," that is, the sins of the people I represent (1:22). Jeremiah spoke objectively also when he proclaimed that Yahweh, as planned, had "overthrown *you* with pity, letting the enemy gloat over *you*"(2:17).

Jeremiah spoke vicariously when he spoke of being afflicted by the rod of Yahweh's anger (3:1). He spoke of having his heart pierced and being made a laughing stock of his people (3:46, 61–63) (reading Jeremiah's word, one's mind is immediately drawn to Christ on the cross).

The New Testament testifies concerning Jesus weeping over Jerusalem (Matt. 23:37; Luke 13:34, 36). Jeremiah was a weeping forerunner of the weeping Messiah. Jeremiah has been referred to as "the weeping prophet" and rightly so. He referred to his grief and tears because of Jerusalem's—the covenant people's—sins and punishment (Lam.1:16). Jeremiah poignantly referred to his grief, saying streams of tears flow from my eyes because my people are destroyed. My eyes flow increasingly. What I see brings grief to my soul (3:48, 49, 50).

Salvation

Jeremiah wept and grieved over Jerusalem and its people. But he also spoke of salvation for his covenant brothers and sisters. True, he did not speak directly of the Messiah as the immediate source and agent of salvation as he did in his prophecies. He did speak of salvation in various ways; salvation brought by God.

The prophet spoke of Yahweh who "redeemed my life" when he was surrounded by opponents and enemies (3:58). He personally knew and believed that redemption in life and death was a reality for those who called on Yahweh *Adon*. Thus he concluded his laments with words of hope for salvation. "Restore us to yourself, O Yahweh, that we may return and be renewed" (5:21).[61]

Notes

1. Walter F. Adeney, "The Lamentations of Jeremiah," in *The Expositor's Bible*, ed. W. R. Nicoll (Grand Rapids: Eerdmans, 1940), 527–610; Richard Brooks, *Great is Your Faithfulness: Lamentations* (Darlington: Evangelical, 1987); Brevard S. Childs, *Biblical Theology of the Old and New Testament*, (Minneapolis Augsburg Fortress, 1993); and *Introduction to the Old Testament as Scripture* (London: SCM, 1979); F. W. Dobbs, "Tragedy, Tradition, and Theology in the Book of Lamentations," *JSOT* 74, (1997); W. Eichrodt, *The Theology of the Old Testament,* 2 vols., trans. J. Baker (Philadelphia: Westminster, 1967; H. L. Ellison, in "Lamentations," *The Expositor's Bible Commentary*, ed. F. E. Gabelen, vol. 6, (Grand Rapids: Zondervan, 1986); J. C. Exum, *Fragmented Women: Feminist Subversions of Biblical Narrative (*ValleyForge: Trinity Press International, 1993); Robert Gordis, *The Song of Songs and Lamentations* (New York: New York, 1974); N. K. Gottwolk, *Studies on the Book of Lamentations* (London: SCM, 1954); Deryn Guest, "Hiding Behind the Naked Woman in Lamentations: A Recriminative Response," *Biblical Interpretation* (October

1999): 413–48; R. K. Harrison, *Jeremiah and Lamentations: An Introduction and Commentary* (London: Tyndale, 1973); C. F. Keil, "The Lamentations of Jeremiah," in *Jeremiah, Lamentations*, vol. 8 (Grand Rapids: Eerdmans, no date); M. McClintock, *Changing the Subject: Women's Discourse and Feminist Theology* (Philadelphia: Fortress, 1994); T. Meek, "Lamentations: Introduction and Exegesis," in *The Interpreter's Bible*, vol. 6 (Nashville: Abingdon, 1956); I. Provan, *Lamentations* (London: Marshall Pickering, 1991); J. Renkema, "The Meaning of the Parallel Acrostics in Lamentation," *VT* 45 (1995): 379–83; T. H. Robertson, *The Poetry of the Old Testament* (London: Duckworth, 1946); L. E. H. Stephens-Hodge, "Lamentations," in *The New Bible Commentary*, ed. F. Davidson (Grand Rapids: Eerdmans, reprint 1958), 640–44; L. E. Walker, *The Battered Woman* (San Francisco: Harper & Row, 1979); Willem Van Gemeren, "Psalms," in the *Expositor's Bible Commentary*, vol. 5 (Grand Rapids: Zondervan, 1991); G. Van Groningen, *From Creation to Consummation*, vol. 1 (Sioux Center: Dordt, 1996); and *Messianic Revelation in the Old Testament* (Grand Rapids: Baker, 1990); Gerhardus Vos, *Biblical Theology* (Grand Rapids: Eerdmans, 1980, 11th ed.); C. Westermann, *Lamentations: Issues and Interpretation* (Edinburgh: T & T Clark, 1994).

2. Dobbs, "Allsopp Tragedy, Tradition," 30.

3. Gordis, *Song of Songs and Lamentations*, 126.

4. Ellison "Lamentations." The Bible finds room for every element of human experience, including overwhelming human sorrow, 697.

5. Van Gemeren's "Lament and Praise" section in his commentary on the "Psalms," 30, 31.

6. Adeney, "The Lamentations of Jeremiah," 541.

7. Ellison, "Lamentations," 696.

8. Keil, "Lamentations . . ." 341.

9. Ellison "Lamentations," 606.

10. R. Youngblood, in his introduction to Lamentations in the NIV Study Bible, 1985, wrote "Since the prophet Jeremiah was an eyewitness to the divine judgment on Jerusalem, it is reasonable to assume that he was the author of the book that so vividly portrays the event," 1215.

11. Ellison, "Lamentations," 698.

12. Gordis, *Lamentations*, 127–28.

13. Ibid., 127.

14. Adeney, *Lamentations*, 1246–47.

15. Ellison, "Lamentations," 597.

16. Dobbs-Allsopp, "Tragedy, Tradition," 54.

17. Cf. the writings of such as Exum, "The Fragment Woman"; Guest, "Hiding Behind . . ." Mc Clintock, "Changing the Subject"; Walker, *The Battered Woman*. These offered various approaches to the feminist view of the literary character of Lamentations.

18. Guest's detailed description includes the following: woman is solitary, isolated, denuded, and publicly displayed, raped, ignored, abandoned, physically and mentally abused, betrayed, bereaved, and articulating her own guilt. "Hiding Behind," 412–20.

19. Ibid., 422.

20. Cf., e.g., Ps. 46:5, "Yahweh is in the midst of her." Psalm 48 describes the beauty of the city; God is in *her* citadels, he is *her* fortress; God makes *her* secure.

21. Childs, *Biblical Theology*, 427.

22. Eichrodt, *Theology*, vol. 1, 421.

23. Ibid., vol. II, 257, 267.

24. The term *melek* appears in 2:6, 9; 4:2; *mamlĕkâh* in 2:2.

25. 1:11, 12, 17 , 18, 20; 2:6, 8, 9, 17, 20, 22; 3:22, 25, 26, 50, 55, 59, 61, 64, 66; 4:11, 16, 20; 5:1, 19, 21.

26. 1:14, 15; 2:1, 2, 5, 7, 18; 3;36, 58.

27. Keil, *Lamentations,* commented that "Yahweh is the God of salvation. Since his throne endures eternally in heaven, he cannot let his kingdom perish on earth," 451.

28. Gordis indicates that the term *yū'am* should be replaced by *yū'abh* (abominated) as *yizza'em* should be (hated) because gold does not tarnish or lose luster, *Lamentations*, 189.

29. The origin of the name Zion and meaning of the term is unknown in spite of efforts to find its root. Conjectures include a structure erected, a dry place to be protected, and a stronghold.

30. Gordis, discussing 4:1, 2 suggested that gems refers to sons with the connotation that they are "God's special property," *Lamentations*, 187.

31. Jeremiah did not refer to the Temple directly but did speak of the sanctuary (1:10; 2:7, 20).

32. When discussing the Mediator, references will be made to king, priest, and prophet.

33. Cf. 386–87.

34. See 389.

35. Commentators are divided on how to explain the crown. Keil considers "crown" to be a figurative expression for the honorable position of the people in its entirety, *Lamentations*, 453. Keil referred to other views such as crown meant Zion or that reference is to Jerusalem as the mistress or princes among the nations.

36. The phrase, "law is no more," according to some commentators meant there were no priests to interpret the Law for the people. Ellison, "Lamentations," 712.

37. Keil, "Lamentations," 391.

38. Vos, *Biblical Theology*, entitled a section "The Rupture of the Bond," 263. The idea of rupture means that the covenant bond was not entirely broken and no longer in existence.

39. Ibid., 264–76.

40. Jeremiah used the term *'aph* (anger) twenty-four times when he prophesied to Judah.

41. He did ask that the curse of God be upon the enemies of the covenant people (3:65). Keil "Lamentations," "Thy curse to them," 429.

42. Jeremiah called for Yahweh to pronounce by an oath a curse on the enemies of God's people. He knew God had pronounced curses on Israel. He called on God to execute an absolute, irrevocable curse on Israel's enemies.

43. See e.g., Deut. 27:15–26; 28:15–65.

44. Keil, "Lamentations," 429.

45. The horn was the emblem of strength and ability to keep and defend the city.

46. Jeremiah could have alluded to Sodom's sudden and complete destruction in a short period of time while Zion's punishment extended over a long period of time.

47. See my *Messianic Revelation*, 110–12, and *From Creation to Consummation*, vol. I, 116.

48. Youngblood "Introduction to Lamentations" NIV, 146.

49. Ellison, "Lamentations," 719.

50. The daughter of Edom, living peacefully would be stripped and punished. No hope for the future was proclaimed in the context of hope for Judah (4:22).

51. Ellison, "Lamentations," 720.

52. The much appreciated hymn by Thomas O. Chisholm "Great is Thy Faithfulness" is based on this passage from Lamentations.

53. Cf. Ellison, "Lamentations," 720. Keil, "Lamentations," 414, wrote that this was said to Aaron the priest who had no possessions but the high priest was to have "his possessions and enjoyment in *Jahveh*."

54. Gordis, *Lamentations*, 181.

55. Ellison, "Lamentations," 720.

56. Ibid., 721.

57. Keil, "Lamentations," 416.

58. Adeney, *Lamentations*, 578.

59. Cf., e.g., *Messianic Revelation*, 697ff., 714ff.

60. Ibid., 19, 20.

61. It is disappointing that Dobbs did not address a fourth Theme—Triumph—in addition to the three he did, Tragedy, Translation, and Theology. Under the heading of theology he referred to the themes—evil, 55, resistance to evil, 55, compassion 56–58, and healing 58, 59, ethical faith, 59—a concept that falls short of redemption and full salvation.

Epilogue

I. Introductory Comments

II. Comments on the Introduction in Volume I

III. The Role of History

IV. The Role of Mankind

V. The Role of the Messiah

Epilogue

Introductory Comments

From Creation to Consummation is the title of the forty-nine chapters published in these three volumes. The subject of creation was studied at length.[1] There is no specific study of the subject of consummation. There are references to eschatology throughout the forty-nine chapters. Eschatology is a term employed to refer to the future, in time and/or at the end of time. Consummation refers specifically to the very end. The term brings to mind the concept of completion. That what was set out as the final goal would be reached. All things would have been carried out to the utmost point. Perfection had been achieved.

Comments in the Introduction to Volume I

At the very beginning it was pointed out that this study was limited to the Old Testament. The presupposition was, and is, that Yahweh God gave the message of the thirty-nine books of the Old Testament. God, the Holy Spirit, inspired the human authors. Thus the Old Testament was, and is, authoritative, infallible, and absolutely trustworthy.[2]

In the Introduction it was also stated that there are links that render a unity to the entire message of the Old Testament. Among those mentioned are creation, history, and consummation. Creation was and is considered to have been completed during the time that Scripture relates it was. History was considered as begun at creation. It refers to the ongoing process under the direction and guidance of the sovereign Lord of the universe. Consummation is explained as follows. "Consummation expresses the idea that after the sudden beginning of creation, there is a process that eventuates in a completion." This process would have an end. The heading under which these statements were made is "The Eschaton in Creation."[3] Yahweh God had a specific determined end in mind when he created the cosmos. History records what transpired between the beginning and the end. But history is not complete. It records what has been done and will record in the future what transpires until the end has come, that is, when consummation is a reality.

The Role of History

History Records the Past

As stated above, history records what has transpired. Yahweh God established the cosmic kingdom when he carried out his creation activities. The cosmic kingdom was and is the setting and context in which all historical activities occur. History records Yahweh God's activities as time progressed.

The Antithesis Established

God established the antithesis when Satan challenged his lordship and mankind succumbed to his diabolical schemes. Yahweh God maintained the good embedded in all of creation as evil penetrated all aspects of life. History records the battle between "Good" and "Evil" and the final outcome. It is not yet here but it is nevertheless assured. Yahweh God triumphs. The good, always severely and repeatedly challenged by evil, is fully and perfectly realized in the consummation.

The Role of Mankind

The Covenant Agents

Mankind appeared in the cosmic kingdom when Yahweh God created Adam and Eve in his own image. In creating them he established a bond of life and love between himself, the Creator and his created imagebearers. They were declared to be Yahweh God's covenantal agents. He mandated them to increase and to subdue and rule over the created natural kingdom, an integral aspect of the cosmic kingdom.

The infallible and trustworthy historical account of mankind, under divine sovereign rule, records the role of the specific covenantal agents. They were prepared and called to serve in the progressive unfolding of Yahweh God's plan to realize the perfect end—the consummation.

The Role Maintained after Sin Entered

Adam and Eve, the first parents, had a role even after they fell into sin and were banished from the Garden of Eden. Their mandate to subdue, cultivate, and rule was never rescinded. They had their divinely given role in the initiation of cosmic kingdom life.

Other Old Testament Covenantal Agents

Noah had his appointed task to preserve a very small portion of humanity amid the destruction of the natural world by means of the flood. Abraham was called to produce a specific seed that would represent and assure that the good would triumph. Moses was appointed to bring freedom to the seed so that they could serve as a theocratic kingdom on earth. Thus a context was provided for the seed of Abraham to serve among the nations from whom men and women would be chosen to participate in Yahweh God's eternal kingdom. Joshua's role was to establish the people as a nation in the promised land. David's role was to establish the theocratic kingdom and serve as a type of the promised Messiah. Solomon's role was to establish the theocratic kingdom among the nations as a type of the consummated kingdom of God on earth. Subsequent kings were called to serve in this ever-developing work of God. Prophets, poets, and wise men were called to carry out Yahweh's intent to prepare a faithful people. From this people the Christ would come to greatly advance Yahweh God's plan to usher in the consummation.

The Role of the Messiah

The Old Testament message did not, nor does it, include a record of the Messiah's actual coming and work. It did prepare for these. And the many references in the Old Testament to the consummation that Christ came to usher in are included in the often- repeated words, translated as eternal, eternity, everlasting, and forever. No faithful servant of Yahweh God, be he a king, judge, priest, prophet, poet, counselor, general, scribe, builder, or watchman considered himself as the final eschatological agent of Yahweh. Rather, they served as types and forerunners in their own time that was a moment in the constant outworking of God's plan to bring all things to perfection in the all-inclusive consummation.

Notes

1. G. Van Groningen, *From Creation to Consummation*, vol. I (Sioux Center: Dordt, 1996); 5–92.
2. Ibid., p. 5.
3. Ibid., 12.

General Index

Scripture Index

Ecclesiastes

Song of Songs

www.ingramcontent.com/pod-product-compliance
Lightning Source LLC
Chambersburg PA
CBHW020945310726
48980CB00001B/62

* 9 7 8 0 9 3 2 9 1 4 5 9 0 *